D1393788

Jewish and Christian Self-Definition
Volume Two

JEWISH AND CHRISTIAN SELF-DEFINITION

Volume Two
Aspects of Judaism in the
Graeco-Roman Period

EDITED BY E. P. SANDERS
WITH A. I. BAUMGARTEN
AND ALAN MENDELSON

SCM PRESS LTD

334 00819 0

First published 1981
by SCM Press Ltd
58 Bloomsbury Street, London

Phototypeset by Input Typesetting Ltd
and printed in Great Britain by
Richard Clay (The Chaucer Press) Ltd,
Bungay, Suffolk

Contents

pp
17-48
are
missing!!

Contents

Contributors

Albert I. Baumgarten
Associate Professor of Religious Studies, McMaster University

Joseph Blenkinsopp
Professor of Old Testament, University of Notre Dame

James H. Charlesworth
Director, International Center on Christian Origins, Duke University

Ferdinand Dexinger
Dozent, Institute for Jewish Studies, University of Vienna

Jonathan A. Goldstein
Professor of History and Classics, University of Iowa

David Weiss Halivni
Morris Adler Professor of Rabbinics, Jewish Theological Seminary of America

Bernard S. Jackson
Professor of Law and Head of the Department of Law, Liverpool Polytechnic

Reuven Kimelman
Assistant Professor of Talmud and Midrash, Department of Near Eastern and Judaic Studies, Brandeis University

Sid Z. Leiman
Professor of Jewish History and Literature, Dean of the Bernard Revel Graduate School, Yeshiva University

Lawrence H. Schiffman
Associate Professor of Hebrew and Judaic Studies, New York University

Contributors

Alan F. Segal
Associate Professor, The Department of Religious Studies and Centre for Religious Studies, University of Toronto

Ephraim E. Urbach
Professor, The Israel Academy of Sciences and Humanities

Preface

There is a sense in which one can say that the entire history of the people of Israel has been marked by a series of challenges to their existence as a separate and identifiable entity. The present collection of essays focuses on a part of that long history and on a particular aspect of it. Chronologically, the essays treat aspects of the period from the Maccabean assertion of Jewish identity in the face of the challenge of Hellenism to the solidification of Rabbinism after the wars with Rome. Thematically, they treat the question of efforts towards achieving normative identity within Judaism – the establishment not just of its physical existence, but of a certain way of being Jewish.

These essays constitute the second collection of papers published in connection with a continuing research project at McMaster University on Jewish and Christian Self-Definition. They are revisions of papers originally presented at a symposium held at McMaster in the spring of 1979. The research project is funded by a generous grant from the Social Sciences and Humanities Research Council of Canada.

The research project takes as its starting point the observation that in the first century both Jews and Christians had numerous options before them, including that of retaining a great deal of diversity. By the early part of the third century, however, both Judaism and Christianity had decisively narrowed their options. In different ways, but during approximately the same period, both religions moved towards excluding some views of what it meant to be either Jewish or Christian and took measures to assure that the favoured options became normative.

We call this development 'the process of achieving normative self-definition'. We intend by this phrase to indicate that we are aiming for more than a description of the triumph of the winning options – rabbinic Judaism and orthodox Christianity. We are hopeful that we can probe behind the conventional accounts

ix

to the question of why Judaism and Christianity developed in the way they did. What were the driving forces? In what social setting did Judaism and Christianity insist with increasing effectiveness not only that it was important to be Jewish or Christian, but to be so in a certain way? These become tantalizing questions when one realizes how pervasive this insistence is; for it characterized not only the victorious parties, but also many who made a bid for dominance, but lost. We shall further see, in a third volume of essays, the degree to which, in the same Greco-Roman world, the thrust towards normativeness characterized Judaism and Christianity, but not their pagan competitors.

I have already mentioned the series of challenges which faced the people of Israel, referring primarily to those which repeatedly came from the outside. From the essays in the present volume, however, it would seem that the push towards normative self-definition within Judaism was more the result of internal momentum than the response to external challenge. The nation might rally against the decrees of the Greek overlord, but, far from settling what Judaism should be, this only signalled a new phase in the internal struggle for the right kind of Judaism. Again, the competition with an already distinct Christianity seems to have affected Judaism's self-definition less than one might have expected. It is premature to generalize, and the external pressures should indeed be borne in mind, but it may be that the call to be the people of God was itself the overwhelming factor in making it important to decide what God desired his chosen people to be.

As co-ordinator of the research project and principal editor of the present volume, I wish first of all to acknowledge the great assistance of the co-editors, Drs A. I. Baumgarten and Alan Mendelson, without whose help a technically difficult collection of essays could not have been prepared for the press. Miss Jean Cunningham of SCM Press has done her customarily admirable job in editing the typescript, and she has also saved the editors from some embarrassing mistakes. I am indebted to Ms Phyllis DeRosa Koetting for typing and retyping, for numbering and renumbering footnotes which kept changing, and for preparing the bibliography and the indices. Dr Benno Przybylski meticulously proofread both the final typescript and the page proof. A word of thanks goes to Mrs Gesine Wisse and Dr Frederik Wisse for preparing a translation of Dr Dexinger's paper. Most of all, thanks go to the contributors, who not only responded promptly and effectively to numerous queries and proposals from the editor, but who also generously wrote to one another as the revisions to the various papers were being made.

McMaster University   *E.P.S.*
Hamilton, Canada

Abbreviations

AB	Anchor Bible, Garden City, New York
AGAJU	Arbeiten zur Geschichte des antiken Judentums und des Urchristentums, Leiden
ANF	Ante-Nicene Fathers, New York (= Ante-Nicene Christian Library, Edinburgh)
ANRW	*Aufstieg und Niedergang der römischen Welt*, ed. H. Temporini and W. Haase, Berlin and New York
ASTI	*Annual of the Swedish Theological Institute* (in Jerusalem), Leiden
BA	*Biblical Archaeologist*, New Haven, Conn., Ann Arbor, Mich.
BDB	*Hebrew and English Lexicon of the Old Testament*, ed. F. Brown, S. R. Driver and C. A. Briggs, Oxford 1907, repr. 1957
Bibl	*Biblica*, Rome
BJRL	*Bulletin of the John Rylands Library*, Manchester
BZAW	Beihefte zur *Zeitschrift für die alttestamentliche Wissenschaft*, Giessen, Berlin
CBQ	*Catholic Biblical Quarterly*, Washington, D.C.
CCSL	Corpus Christianorum. Series Latina, Turnholt
CIS	*Corpus Inscriptionum Semiticarum*, Paris 1881ff.
CPJ	*Corpus Papyrorum Judaicarum*, ed. V. Tcherikover and A. Fuks, 3 vols., Cambridge, Mass., 1957–64
CSEL	Corpus Scriptorum Ecclesiasticorum Latinorum, Vienna 1866ff.
DBS	*Dictionnaire de la Bible. Supplément*, Paris 1928ff.
EB	*Encyclopaedia Biblica*, ed. T. K. Cheyne and J. S. Black, 4 vols., London and New York 1898–1904

EJ	*Encyclopedia Judaica*, 16 vols., Jerusalem 1971–72
ET	English translation
EvTh	*Evangelische Theologie*, Munich
FG	Fourth Gospel
GCS	Die griechischen christlichen Schriftsteller der ersten drei Jahrhunderte, Leipzig, Berlin 1897ff.
HDB	*Dictionary of the Bible*, ed. James Hastings, Edinburgh and New York 1898–1904
HR	*History of Religions*, Chicago
HTR	*Harvard Theological Review*, Cambridge, Mass.
HUCA	*Hebrew Union College Annual*, Cincinnati
IDB	*Interpreter's Dictionary of the Bible*, 4 vols, New York and Nashville 1962
IDBSuppl	*IDB, Supplementary Volume*, New York and Nashville 1976
IEJ	*Israel Exploration Journal*, Jerusalem
ILR	*Israel Law Review*, Jerusalem
Interp	*Interpretation*, Richmond, Va.
IURA	*IURA. Revista internazionale di diritto romano e antico*, Naples
JAAR	*Journal of the American Academy of Religion*, Boston, Mass.
JANES	*Journal of the Ancient Near Eastern Society of Columbia University*, New York
JBL	*Journal of Biblical Literature*, Philadelphia, Missoula, Mont., et al.
JE	*Jewish Encyclopedia*, 12 vols., New York 1901–06
JJS	*Journal of Jewish Studies*, London
JLA	*Jewish Law Annual*, Leiden
JLASuppl	*JLA Supplementary Series*, Leiden
JNES	*Journal of Near Eastern Studies*, Chicago
JQR	*Jewish Quarterly Review*, os London, ns Philadephia
JR	*Journal of Religion*, Chicago
JRS	*Journal of Roman Studies*, London
JSJ	*Journal for the Study of Judaism in the Persian, Hellenistic and Roman Periods*, Leiden
JSS	*Journal of Semitic Studies*, Manchester
LQR	*Law Quarterly Review*, London

*LTK*²	*Lexikon für Theologie und Kirche*, Freiburg im Breisgau ²1957–65
MGWJ	*Monatsschrift für Geschichte und Wissenschaft des Judentums*, Breslau
NEB	New English Bible, Oxford and Cambridge 1970
nF	neue Folge
NovT	*NovumTestamentum*, Leiden
ns	new series
NTApoc	*New Testament Apocrypha*, ed. E. Hennecke and W. Schneemelcher, ET, 2 vols., London and Philadelphia 1963–65, repr. 1973–74
NTS	*New Testament Studies*, Cambridge, England
os	old series
OTL	Old Testament Library, London and Philadelphia
PAAJR	*Proceedings of the American Academy for Jewish Research*, New York
PEQ	*Palestine Exploration Quarterly*, London
PG	Patrologia Graeca, ed. J.-P. Migne, Paris 1857ff.
PGM	*Papyri Graecae Magicae*, ed. K. Preisendanz, 3 vols., Dresden 1928–42
PL	Patrologia Latina, ed. J.-P. Migne, Paris 1844ff.
PW	*Realencyclopädie der classischen Altertumswissenschaft*, ed. A. Pauly and G. Wissowa, Stuttgart 1894ff.
RB	*Revue biblique*, Paris
REJ	*Revue des études juives*, Paris
*RGG*³	*Religion in Geschichte und Gegenwart*, Tübingen ³1956–63
RHR	*Revue de l'histoire des religions*, Paris
RIDA	*Revue internationale des droits de l'antiquité*, Brussels
RQ	*Revue de Qumran*, Paris
SBL	Society of Biblical Literature, Philadelphia, Missoula, Mont., et al.
SBLDS	SBL Dissertation Series
SBLMS	SBL Monograph Series
SC	Sources chrétiennes, Paris
SCS	Septuagint and Cognate Studies, Missoula, Mont.

SH	*Scripta Hierosolymitana*, Jerusalem
SJ	Studia Judaica, Berlin
SJLA	Studies in Judaism in Late Antiquity, Leiden
SNTS	Society for New Testament Studies
SPB	Studia Post-Biblica, Leiden
STEI	Z. W. Rabinovitz, *Shaarei Torat Erets Israel*, Jerusalem 1940
Suppl*NovT*	Supplements to *Novum Testamentum*, Leiden
Suppl*VT*	Supplements to *Vetus Testamentum*, Leiden
TDNT	*Theological Dictionary of the New Testament*, ed. G. Kittel and G. Friedrich, ET, Grand Rapids, Mich. 1964–76
ThLZ	*Theologische Literaturzeitung*, Leipzig
TK	*Tosefta ki-Fshutah*, ed. S. Lieberman, 9 vols., New York 1955–73
TU	Texte und Untersuchungen zur Geschichte der altchristlichen Literatur, Leipzig, Berlin
VC	*Vigiliae Christianae*, Amsterdam
VT	*Vetus Testamentum*, Leiden
ZAW	*Zeitschrift für die alttestamentliche Wissenschaft*, Giessen, Berlin
ZNW	*Zeitschrift für die neutestamentliche Wissenschaft*, Giessen, Berlin
ZTK	*Zeitschrift für Theologie und Kirche*, Tübingen

1

Interpretation and the Tendency to Sectarianism: An Aspect of Second Temple History

JOSEPH BLENKINSOPP

My purpose in this paper is to explore some of the ways in which the interpretation of texts bears on the formation of movements of dissent and sects in the Second Temple period down to the Hasmonaean principate. I do not propose to engage in a study of biblical interpretation in Pharisaism, Essenism (including Qumran) or early Christianity, though I hope to lay some groundwork for such studies. What I shall be trying to do is state how the interpretation or reinterpretation of tradition expressed in texts determined the self-understanding and self-definition of Judaism in Palestine, and the different groups which arose within it, during the period indicated; or, to put it somewhat differently, how interpretation served as a factor in shaping alternative versions of an ideal envisioned in or pre-supposed by the texts.

Sociologists of religion – Weber, Troeltsch, Wach, for example – have found it extraordinarily difficult to come up with a satisfactory definition of 'sect', and the difficulty has been compounded by the rather pejorative associations which the term has sometimes borne. At one stage of development a dissident group can simply exhibit separatist tendencies and therefore be more aptly designated a party, school or something of the sort. Without offering a definition, we would suggest that a sect is not only a minority, and not only characterized by opposition to norms accepted by the parent-body, but also claims in a more or less exclusive way to be what the parent-body claims to be. Whether such a group formally severs itself, or is excommunicated, will depend largely on the degree of self-definition attained by the parent-body and the level of tolerance obtaining within it. We shall also have to bear in mind that once they have begun to go their own way sects can change their character very quickly, especially when they are successful. The Pharisees, for example, do not look much like a sect in the period immediately prior to the great revolt against Rome.

It will be unnecessary to labour the point that many factors, including economic, social and political ones, are at work in the emergence of sects and that these can combine in a variety of ways. Admonished by Max Weber, we shall also give due importance to the role of the charismatic individual who appears on the scene at the opportune moment. It will also be generally agreed that such phenomena tend to emerge at times of political, social or cultural disorientation and *anomie*. While trying to unravel one strand in a complex skein, therefore, we shall bear in mind that interpretation is carried out by specific individuals and groups, some disposing of power and others deprived of it, but all engaged in this activity in and, to a certain extent, as a function of the specific situation in which they find themselves.

The history of the Second Commonwealth confirms the assumption that what we have agreed to call 'normative self-definition' is worked out in situations of inter-group conflict, and especially in the situation in which one group within the larger community proposes, in effect, an alternative version of how the community ought to understand itself and to embody that understanding in certain prescriptive institutional forms. Theravada Buddhism, for example, had to consolidate when faced with the challenge of a more liberal interpretation of sacred texts by the Mahayana schools. The Counter-Reformation was instigated by the Reformation in the sixteenth-century church with its claim to repristinate the tradition. In much the same way, the rationalistic reinterpretation of the laws by the Hellenistic reform party in Jerusalem during the Seleucid period provoked conservative elements to an even firmer insistence on the entire corpus of laws, strictly interpreted, as of the essence of Judaism and as establishing qualification for membership.

Before turning to our historical survey a word of caution is in order. Some recent studies give the impression of a gradual but unbroken process going on from the end of the Babylonian exile to the Antiochean persecution, the book of Daniel and the sects as described by Josephus. Different stages in this process can

2

be identified and described as proto-apocalyptic, early apocalyptic and full-blown apocalyptic. Sometimes a progressive evolution is traced from the first indications of movements of dissent to sects properly so called. Such theories of development call for careful scrutiny. Throughout the period in question, which covers about six centuries, we can identify what may be called 'apocalyptic situations', situations, that is, which are apt to instigate reactions and solutions such as are found in the apocalyptic literature. The political troubles following the death of Cambyses when it seemed to many that the Persian Empire might fall apart, the disturbances attendant on the change from Persian to Macedonian rule, the troubled reign of Antiochus IV are the obvious examples, though there were no doubt others. Reactions to such events on the part of those who suffer from their effects or whose hopes are kindled by them are apt to exhibit common features. There are also groups within the parent-body, especially among those deprived of power, which are more or less predisposed to go their own way. We shall meet some of them in the course of our survey. Connections of some kind can no doubt be established between separatist movements during the two centuries of Persian rule and those at the end of our period, as also between the visions of Zechariah and those of Daniel. But it is quite another thing to posit an unbroken development or trajectory from one end to the other of a period which is after all very long and for the most part poorly documented.

My initial assumption in this paper will be that the common element is provided by a shared tradition which had already, at the beginning of the period, reached a mature stage of cohesion and articulation in writing. This written material, however, did not constitute a canon, dissent from which could be viewed as heresy or sectarianism. On the contrary, the emergence of a canon was one aspect of a struggle for self-definition which continued throughout the entire period. If, for example, the familiar tripartite arrangement is attested in the Prologue to Ecclesiasticus (Ben Sira), the Greek version (LXX) and Ben Sira itself (39.1) presuppose a different order. Throughout most of the period, moreover, none of these parts was immune to expansions and modifications, the prophetic books in particular undergoing considerable amplifications down into the Graeco-Syrian period. Our intent will be to argue that continuity and discontinuity in Palestinian Judaism were primarily a matter of the interpretation of these texts, serving the goal of either affirming existing conceptual and societal structures or authorizing new departures. It will be clear, then, how much was at stake in the claim, advanced from different directions, to provide an authoritative interpretation of these texts.

From the first return to Ben Sira

According to the meagre sources at our disposal the history of Palestinian Judaism during the early Persian period focuses on the relatively small group[1] which returned from Babylon during the quarter-century following on the edict of Cyrus (538 BCE). The Chronicler, whose presentation of the past at this point as at others is somewhat idealistic, describes it as a fairly well-defined group known as the *golah* or 'holy race'.[2] From the outset it stood apart from the 'natives'. In one respect at least this was hardly unexpected since the latter took the view that the deportees had in effect been expelled from the Yahwistic cult-community, a position which had the advantage of allowing them to expropriate their real estate.[3] The explicitly stated grounds for separatism, however, were laws of ritual purity which in some cases had only recently been codified.[4] Thus, still according to the Chronicler, only those were permitted to celebrate Passover with the *bene haggolah* who had 'separated themselves from the uncleanness of the peoples of the land'.[5] Given this situation, marriage outside the group was bound to emerge as a major issue throughout the first century of Persian rule (e.g. Mal. 2.11–16). On his arrival as official representative of the Persian government, probably in the year 458 BCE,[6] Ezra found to his dismay that the members of the 'holy race', including the priesthood, had widely disregarded the prohibition of intermarriage with foreigners. He therefore obliged the entire community to take a solemn oath and enter into a covenant to put aside foreign wives on penalty of excommunication from the community and forfeiture of title to their property.[7] At another plenary session, which the Chronicler places shortly thereafter at Sukkoth, and which reminds us of the Qumran covenant ceremony (1QS 1–2), separation from the peoples of the land (*'amme ha'areṣ*) remained the major issue.[8] Nehemiah also took measures to purge the community of all Jews of mixed descent, this time on the basis of disqualifications listed in the Deuteronomic law (Deut. 23.3–5).[9]

4

While it would be inappropriate, especially in view of the *Tendenz* of our principal source, to speak of the *bene haggolah* as sectarian, its marked separatism may be said to have set the pattern for later developments already under way at the time of the Chronicler. It formed a minority; it represented itself as the 'true Israel' or, in other words, the genuine successor of the old pre-exilic Israel; and it developed specific norms for membership which included the prohibition of exogamy, strict observance of Sabbath and support of the temple and its personnel.[10] A the time of Ezra and Nehemiah the members entered into a covenant, took an oath, and could be excluded by a form of excommunication.[11] It therefore thought of itself as a group apart, qualification for membership depending on the observance of certain laws which provided a pragmatic rather than a theoretical basis for self-definition. It seems that the final stages in the formation of the law-codes in the Pentateuch cannot be understood apart from the need of the postexilic community to affirm its identity and embody it in appropriate institutional and organizational forms.

The traditional view has it that Torah was 'canonized' by Ezra and the men of the Great Assembly. Despite widespread scepticism about the existence of such a body, the view that it was the Pentateuch which Ezra brought with him to Jerusalem and subsequently promulgated there is still frequently advanced.[12] In point of fact, however, the letter commissioning Ezra which purports to be from the hand of Artaxerxes (Ezra 7.11–26) provides few and uncertain clues as to the identity of this 'law of the God of heaven' (vv. 12, 21). It is also by no means certain that he brought it with him,[13] and it is in any case clearly implied that it should be familiar to Jews in the Trans-Euphrates province (v. 25). Since we are therefore forced to conjecture, we may note that the injunction to appoint magistrates and judges is reminiscent of Deut. 16.18 and the allusion to 'the wisdom of your God with which you are entrusted' (v. 25), synonymous with 'the law of your God with which you are entrusted' (v. 14), recalls the kind of language which Deut. uses in speaking of the laws.[14] The prohibition of exogamy, which seems to have been Ezra's main concern, is urged on the basis of Deut.,[15] and most of the stipulations of the great covenant assembly held at Sukkoth (Neh. 8–10) can be traced to the same source.[16] There are, however, significant exceptions. The laws governing Sukkoth itself presuppose the Holiness Code (H) rather than Deut.[17]

and those governing the septennial *shemiṭṭah* (10.31b) represent a conflation of both;[18] further, there are stipulations which occur nowhere in the Pentateuch, namely, the payment of one-third of a shekel as temple tax (10.32–33) and the wood offering (10.34; cf. 13.31).[19]

The impression which remains after an examination of the legal material in Ezra-Nehemiah, and indeed in the Chronicler's work as a whole,[20] is that the Deuteronomic law-code – though perhaps not exactly as we have it[21] – was still basic. The so-called Holiness Code (Lev. 17–26) and much of the priestly legislation scattered throughout Ex., Lev. and Num., however, were also known. It is tempting to think of a fusion of legal material of Palestinian (D) and Babylonian (P) origin occurring in connection with the missions of Ezra and Nehemiah, but such solutions are certainly oversimplified. The common assumption that Ezra's law was our Pentateuch *tout court* is, at any rate, mistaken. There is, for example, no celebration of *Yom Kippur* at the point where we would expect it,[22] and the half-shekel temple tax stipulated in the Priestly Code (Ex. 30.11–16) must surely postdate the one-third shekel tax referred to above, given the inexorable tendency for taxation to increase.

The conclusion seems to be warranted that progress towards a definitive legal corpus correlates with the struggle for self-definition in the post-exilic community. We are clearly not yet at a point where we can speak of a canon, if by this term we wish to imply a fixed and unchangeable text to which all new enactments, dictated by the changing conditions of the times, must in some way be referred.[23] Of new legal enactments which came into force during this period some certainly found their way into the law-codes in the Pentateuch. Others, which are introduced without any suggestion that they require justification *via-à-vis* a canonical corpus, did not: rituals of fasting (Zech. 7.3–7; 8.19),[24] the prohibition of divorce under certain circumstances (Mal. 2.16),[25] the requirement of sending away foreign wives (Ezra 10.3), the temple tax and wood offering already mentioned, the *maʿamadot* or orders of clergy (I Chron. 24.19; II Chron. 8.12–14), the Maccabean decree permitting fighting on Sabbath (I Macc. 2.41), and the decrees establishing new festivals, 'Sukkoth in Kislev' and 'the Day of Nicanor'.[26] Even in the Roman period prior to the revolt there was no one clearly established practice with respect to a canonical law-code, as can be seen from the different positions of Pharisees, Sadducees, the Qumran community, early Jewish Christians and others. Despite their sectarian origin, both the Qumran Psalms Scroll (11QPs[a]) and the Temple Scroll confirm the impression that the entire issue of canonical scriptures in the Second Temple period must be reappraised.[27]

The purpose of the last few paragraphs was less to contribute to this issue, however, than to suggest that the formation of the law-codes is inseparable from the ongoing attempt to define what is or is not compatible with or necessary for membership in the community. Needless to say, the adoption and interpretation of such laws provided numerous occasions for dispute and division. There were those who favoured the admission of foreigners and eunuchs, though the former category was partially excluded by the Deuteronomic law and was totally excluded by the cultic programme of Ezek. 40–48, and the latter by the Deuteronomic law alone.[28] Such an open admissions policy had no place in the reforms of Ezra and Nehemiah though it continued to find proponents throughout the Second Temple period and proved to be a source of dispute in early Christian churches.[29] Other matters regulated by law, some of quite basic importance, were subject to dispute right from the beginning. There were some who deemed it inopportune to restore the temple cult, perhaps on the basis of their own interpretation of the seventy years of Jeremiah's prophecy.[30] It seems that others, however, had more radical objections to the resumption of animal sacrifice.[31] In this instance too a minority view, one not without precedent in Israel's history, re-emerged later and was also represented in early Christian circles.[32]

The point is, then, that the emergence of divisions within Palestinian Judaism, divisions which had the potential for hardening into sects, cannot be understood apart from the adoption and interpretation of such legal stipulations as we have been discussing. The situation is much clearer for the later period when such issues as the adoption of a certain calendar or the legitimacy of the high priest played a decisive role in movements of dissent.[33] Given the critical lack of source material for the long period prior to the Maccabean revolt, the situation is bound to be much less clear. But from the period between the Restoration and Ezra there are, for example, allusions in Isa. 56–66 to opposition between the righteous (*saddiqim*), the devout or God's chosen ones (*'anshe-ḥesed*), his servants (*'abadim*) on the one hand and the wicked (*resha'im*), the rebellious people

(*ʿam sorer*) etc., on the other, and such passages reflect divisions in the community over the observance or non-observance of laws.[34] If, however, we take account of the partiality of our source – for the anonymous seer is writing from the perspective of the elect, to which category he himself belongs – it would be reasonable to conclude that the issue is also that of differing interpretations of laws, including the questions which were more or less important, which more or less binding and the like. The same issue will confront us when we come to consider the programme of the 'reform party' opposed by the *ḥasidim* during the Seleucid period.

Reference to the elect in Third Isaiah points to the existence within the *golah*-community of an élite corps which at some stage was rejected and persecuted by the majority. In his attempt to purify the community of foreign influences Ezra was supported by people referred to as 'those who trembled at his (God's) word' (Ezra 9.4; 10.3). Under the leadership of a certain Shecaniah they seem to have taken the initiative in persuading the group to set aside their foreign wives, a measure which exceeds in severity anything prescribed in the Pentateuch. We meet these 'Quakers' also in a passage in Third Isaiah from the early Persian period where they are identified with the poor and contrite in spirit and, what is more, are being persecuted and cast out by their brethren.[35] We shall naturally be reminded of references in certain psalms to the poor and humble who pray for relief from oppression.[36] Granted the obliqueness of the reference, the regularity in the way the verbal adjective occurs in these four instances in Isa. and Ezra suggests that these *ḥaredim* constituted a well-defined minority which was prepared, given the occasion, to enforce a rigorous interpretation of the laws and therefore also of the legal definition of the community as a whole.[37]

This may be the best point at which to introduce a further aspect of division within the post-exilic community. In the passage just referred to (Isa. 66.5) the opponents of the *ḥaredim* are quoted as saying, 'Let Yahweh be glorified that we may see your joy!' – a taunt which makes it clear that opposition to this group had something to do with their prophetic-eschatological beliefs. The series of poems which, it is generally agreed, form the original nucleus of Third Isaiah (chs. 60–62) speaks precisely of these themes: the final manifestation of the glory of Yahweh and the rejoicing and exaltation of the elect. It would therefore be natural to conclude that the taunt represents one reaction to the publication of these poems.[38] Since the *haredim* are also exponents of a strict interpretation of the laws, we may conclude that for this particular group, and no doubt others of similar persuasion, the eschatological hope nourished by reading and study of prophetic books provided the essential motivation for the observance of the laws. Hence it is no surprise that the Latter Prophets ends with an admonition to observe the laws followed by an announcement of the last days which will be inaugurated through the ministry of a prophetic figure (Mal. 3.22–24).[39]

That opposition to the *haredim* was occasioned by their prophetic-eschatological beliefs suggests that the reinterpretation of prophecy also played a role in the divisions already in evidence in the early post-exilic period, as also in the emergence of sects at a later time. The basic issue here is the self-understanding of the community elaborated either by its official representatives or by dissident groups which in the course of time came to be alienated from the official leadership. In either case it could be worked out only on the basis of the tradition; and given the decisive remoulding of the tradition by the prophets, collections of whose sayings were now available, the interpretation of prophecy was bound to play an important role. It is not surprising, therefore, that designations for the community taken from the old prophetic tradition occur frequently in our sources: the remnant of the people, the escaped remnant, the Lord's servants, the Lord's planting, and the like.[40] Also significant in this respect are the frequent reinterpretations of pre-exilic prophetic sayings. A study of these would, of course, be a major undertaking, but the point may be made clearly enough by taking one example: Jeremiah's prophecy of seventy years' exile (Jer. 25.12; 29.10). Whatever the reason for the choice of this particular number, it came to provide a starting point for speculations which moved in different directions. While the Chronicler understood it in a purely cultic way, with reference to the sabbatical rest of the land (II Chron. 36.21; Ezra 1.1; cf. Lev. 26.41–3), the restoration prophets, and no doubt many of their fellow Jews who were stirred by the political unrest at the beginning of the reign of Darius, took it to indicate a great turning-point in their fortunes (Zech. 1.12; 7.5; cf. Hag. 1.2; 2.6). At a much later time a Hasidic sage came across the same text when engaged in prayerful study of 'the books' and, on that basis, calculated the end of the persecution and the advent of God's kingdom (Dan. 9.2). Despite the eventual disappointment of these hopes, the prophecy continued to fuel messianic and millenarian expectations throughout the Roman period inclusive of early Christianity.[41]

Other Jeremianic motifs, the Branch (*ṣemah*) and the Signet Ring (*ḥotam*), for example, helped to give body to the hopes which focused on Zerubbabel during the early Persian period.[42] Indeed, throughout the entire period Jer. seems to have played an important role, one rather neglected in modern scholarship, in the development from prophetic eschatology to apocalyptic.[43]

It may be objected that this ongoing reinterpretation of prophecy is already amply attested in the pre-exilic period. Isaiah, for example, applied the message of Amos to the kingdom of Judah in the eighth century and Jeremiah that of Hosea in the seventh. This is of course true, but it is not the whole story. It is not just that Haggai, Zechariah, the Third Isaiah and Malachi, while continuing some of the conventions of their pre-exilic forbears, are in many respects very different from them. Allusions to 'his servants the prophets' and 'the former prophets' give the impression of an epoch in the history of prophecy which has now come to an end.[44] A revealing pointer to a decisive shift can be detected in the visions of Zechariah (1.7–6.8). In each instance an angel or heavenly messenger is present to explain the visionary scenario to the seer, often with explicit or implicit reference to older prophetic material.[45] Since *mal'ak* occurs in writings of the period as a synonym for prophet[46] it is significant that the heavenly intermediary also fulfils the prophetic function of intercession and the giving of oracles.[47] What, then, this first appearance of the *angelus interpres* seems to indicate is a shift from direct prophetic discourse ('thus says Yahweh') to the inspired interpretation of prophecy. This new situation will appear even more clearly in Dan., where prophecy has been displaced by apocalyptic revelation mediated by a heavenly emissary, and the same will also be attested in early Christianity.[48] We can hardly exaggerate the importance of this shift whereby the prophetic claim to authority is taken over by the interpreter of prophecy.

From this point on, one of the major issues in the religious and social history of the period is the correlation between different hermeneutics of prophecy and competing views on the nature, function and form of the community. The interpretation specifically of prophecy was of major importance since it was in prophetic circles that the destiny of the people, the possibility of a future and the conditions under which it might be realized were fought out. The crucial issue of God's purpose for the nations also depended on the interpretation of prophecy and of the prophetic office, as is apparent in Jonah.[49] The promulgation and interpretation of the laws also came to depend on claims comparable to those staked by the prophets. The Deuteronomic law itself was recommended by virtue of the prophetic authority of Moses, and both the ritual legislation of P and the programme of Ezek. 40–48 were presented as the outcome of visionary experiences. Other laws, customs and practices introduced during the Second Commonwealth, not excluding the Pharisaic oral law, were deemed to require prophetic warrant, at least to the extent that their authors could claim to be heirs of the prophets.[50]

Much of the history of the interpretation of prophecy in the Second Temple period has to be reconstructed from the prophetic books themselves; a difficult task, given the severe problem of dating editorial additions and expansions.[51] A few studies have addressed themselves to this task, usually with reference to the origins of apocalyptic and the development of sects, but much work remains to be done.[52] Working back from Dan. and the *asidaioi* mentioned at I Macc. 2.42; 7.13 and II Macc. 14.6, Otto Plöger has attempted to trace a trajectory linking pre-exilic and restoration prophetic eschatology with apocalyptic of the kind found in Dan.[53] Since his work is well known and has been much discussed[54] only a brief summary will be necessary. Throughout the entire Second Temple period, he argues, tension was developing between the theocratic leadership, whose point of view is represented by P and Chron., and pietistic groups whose faith was nourished by devotion to the laws and by prophetic eschatology. The decisive period for the consolidation of the apocalyptic world-view was the poorly known age from Ezra and Nehemiah to the Maccabean uprising. It was then that the prophetic collection reached its final form, and a study of the latest additions to it suggests that it was edited within eschatological conventicles which must be seen as the ancestors of the *hasidim*. Plöger examines only three deuteroprophetic passages (Joel 3, Zech. 12–14 and Isa. 24–27) but these, he believes, suffice to show how a progressive widening and deepening of divisions within the community went in tandem with a gradual transformation of the prophet into a spokes-man for the apocalyptic world-view. To avoid any possible misunderstanding it should be added that Plöger does not set prophecy and Torah over against each other, as if the former were represented by the eschatological conventicles and the latter by the theocratic leadership. The dissident groups were, on the contrary, particularly zealous in the observance of the laws, but they observed them in light of the eschatological hope. Their message, in other words, was to maintain Torah without surrendering the millennium.[55]

More controversial and somewhat less nuanced exegetically is Morton Smith's contribution to this aspect of Second Temple history.[56] The Old Testament, he maintains, is a collection of partisan documents which record or reflect religious conflicts, alliances and compromises. What he calls the 'Yahweh alone party' was in perpetual conflict with the syncretist majority throughout the pre-exilic period, consolidated its position dur-ing the Babylonian exile when the writings of the prophets, considered as apologists for the party, were edited, and emerged under the leadership of Zerubbabel after the return. During the early Persian period the lines were drawn between the *bene-haggolah* in Jerusalem who now controlled the cult and the syncretists in the province of Judah who are referred to in our (partisan) sources as the *'am ha'areṣ*. A new divisive issue coming to the fore at this time was that of ritual purity which, in effect, determined qualification for membership.[57] After the disappearance of Zerubbabel from the scene the syncretists were in the ascendancy – as may be seen from Mal. – until Ezra's arrival in 458. Ezra and Nehemiah were, of course, the great champions of the 'Yahweh alone party'. As the Chronicler tells it, the latter laid the basis for non-sacrificial cult and the emergence of private cult groups which emphasized the purity laws and table-fellowship.[58] From then on the interpretation of these laws will provide the most important occasions for divi-sion and sectarianism.

Since Smith goes on to say that only in the fourth century CE did the 'Yahweh alone party' finally win out with the ascend-ancy of rabbinic Judaism and the triumph of Christianity, early Jewish Christianity is presumably to be seen as one branch of the party. On this issue, however, he does not enlarge.

Parties and Politics that Shaped the Old Testament has, inevitably, been criticized as reductionist, and reviewers have taken issue with it on many points of detail. For our present purpose it will be enough to acknowledge the point about conflict of traditions and interpretations, the grounding of that conflict in parties, conventicles or sects, and its bearing on the formation of the Old Testament canon.

A somewhat new perspective on this cluster of issues was opened up by Frank Moore Cross Jr, who argued that the seedbed of apocalyptic was the exilic community as it strove to come to terms with the radically new situation created by the loss of monarchy.[59] Following a pattern firmly established in the 'Albright school',[60] he assigned considerably higher dates than the majority of scholars in the modern period to Isa. 24–27, Zech. 9–14 and Isa. 56–66, all of which fit into a stage of development to which he gives the name 'proto-apocalyptic'. Paul D. Hanson has developed this position further in a detailed study of Isa. 56–66 and a rather more cursory examination of Zech. 9–14 and Isa. 24–27.[61] His conclusion is that apocalyptic can be traced back to the Second Isaiah (proto-apocalyptic) and the work of his disciples represented by the three texts alluded to, none of which postdates the fifth century (early apocalyptic). More to our present purpose, he believes it possible to trace with some accuracy in these texts, but especially in Isa. 56–66, an increasingly bitter struggle in the early Persian period between a pragmatic, realistic, anti-eschatological Zadokite group which controlled the temple and a prophetic-visionary group which included disenfranchised Levites. It was among these latter, spiritual heirs of the Second Isaiah, that apocalyptic developed. Hanson makes some interesting observations about the restoration period, even though his view of party struggle at that time is greatly oversimplified.[62] But what he calls the 'contextual-typological method',[63] which draws heavily on 'syllable-counting' as a guide to dating, raises serious doubts about the validity of the reconstruction in general. And even if the high dates for the passages in question were correct – and they are simply assumed rather than argued – we still have a large and unexplained gap between the fifth and the second century: a passage from dawn to high noon with nothing in between. One also suspects that the results would look rather different if it were assumed, as it should be, that apocalyptic is not an exclusively Jewish phenomenon.[64]

From Ben Sira to the Roman period

I have argued that the interpretation or reinterpretation of both the laws and prophecy was carried on as a function of the self-understanding of the post-exilic Palestinian Jewish community and the conflicts and divisions which it occasioned. This was not taken to imply that the Law and the Prophets were already there as sacred scripture waiting to be interpreted. On the contrary, the history of these conflicts of interpretation and their eventual resolution is an aspect of the formation of the biblical canon which was going on throughout the entire period.[65] Conflicts of interpretation, moreover, presuppose conflicts among real people, among different interest-groups and parties within the community on a wide variety of issues: organizations and leadership, qualification for membership, relation to outsiders, role in history, etc. The point of view represented by the eschatological and apocalyptic additions to prophetic books, for example, was not shared by the majority at any point during this period. The few sources at our disposal allow no more than a glimpse here and there of the actual situations in which this process unfolded. They do not permit us to draw an unbroken line from mild dissent and prophetic eschatology at the beginning to open sectarianism and full-blown apocalyptic at the end of our time-span.

Given the fact that interpretation is a specialized and learned activity involving scribal expertise, the preceding point may be illustrated with reference to the work of Ben Sira from the early years of Seleucid rule. The author, a devout scribe, might be considered a typical representative of the theocratic point of view. He urges his readers to honour and support the priesthood and sacrificial system and has high praise for the priestly line from Aaron to Simon son of Onias (Onias II), his contemporary.[66] Yet he also prays for an end to foreign domination, for God to 'hasten the day' when Israel will be reunited and her enemies punished (36.1–17); he is familiar with the tradition of Elijah as precursor of the messianic age, whose ministry will replicate that of the Isaian Servant (48.10);[67] he knows of an Isaiah who predicts the last things (48.24–25) and prays for the revival of the bones of the Twelve Prophets (49.10). While, therefore, his view of the last things may be materially different from those found in the deuteroprophetic material, the prophetic-eschatological tradition is by no means foreign to him.

14

He also speaks out strongly against those members of the aristocracy, including the priesthood, who were no longer concerned with the faithful implementation of the laws (e.g. 41.8–9).

In listing the activities of the ideal scribe, Ben Sira gives pride of place to the study of the Law, the investigation of ancient wisdom and the elucidation of prophecy – in other words, what we today would call biblical studies (39.1). The first of these is what the author elsewhere calls 'seeking the Law' or, in other words, exposition of the laws (32.14–15),[68] a responsibility which scribes, and especially temple scribes, shared with the priesthood.[69] Wisdom, identified with the Law at one point (24.1–29), is of course the special preserve of the scribe. The same is not so obviously true of prophecy, and yet, as we have just seen, Ben Sira is very interested in the prophetic tradition. It originates with Moses and is passed on to Joshua (46.1), and thence through the history to the *Dodekapropheton* (49.10) without distinguishing between Former and Latter. We are reminded of the opening verse of *Aboth* and the prophetic *diadochē* of which Josephus speaks.[70] It seems to presuppose the idea, also stated in Josephus and rabbinic texts,[71] of a definite epoch of prophetic inspiration during which the biblical books were written. This supposition notwithstanding, the author attests that the work of interpretation which is the scribe's primary responsibility requires an inspiration comparable to that of the prophet. As a result of study and prayer he is 'filled with the spirit of understanding' (39.6) and 'pours out teaching like prophecy' (24.33).[72] It appears then that by the time of Ben Sira scribalism has taken over from prophecy and that inspired interpretation, including the interpretation of prophecy, has taken the place of prophecy itself. The claims of both the theocratic leadership and of apocalyptic seers like the author of Dan. are implicitly contained in this transition.

We would have to suppose that the interpretative activity of which the author speaks was carried out in a definite institutional setting, and in fact Ben Sira refers at one point to a *bet hammidrash* (51.23).[73] Unfortunately, however, we know remarkably little of the scholastic *Sitz im Leben* of Israelite wisdom in this or any other period.

Ben Sira stands at a mature point in the evolution of Israelite-Jewish scribalism. The scribes of whom we hear under the monarchy were for the most part state officials, perhaps based originally on the Egyptian model of statecraft.[74] That they are often associated with priests, and appear to have had some responsibility for the upkeep of the temple,[75] is not surprising since the temple and its personnel were part of the state establishment. They seem to have first assumed responsibility for the laws in connection with Deut., which makes use of vocabulary and themes common among the sages, requires wisdom of rulers and judges and speaks of the observance of the laws as Israel's wisdom.[76] Moreover if Jeremiah, contemporary with Deut., speaks of the false pen of the scribes turning the law into a lie (Jer. 8.8–9), he is presumably referring not just to the writing but also to the interpreting of laws.[77] The conflicting claims of law-scribes and prophets did not, at any rate, have the opportunity to develop into open conflict. The changes brought about by the exile made the function of the former more than ever necessary and bound them more closely, after the return, to the temple and its personnel. The Chronicler is certainly reflecting the situation of his own day in referring to levitical scribes active at various points of the history.[78] Ezra is described as both priest and scribe and is assisted by Levites in promulgating, teaching and interpreting the laws.[79] The scribal class must have consolidated its power and prestige during the long period between Ezra and Ben Sira, by which time the *soperim* were, as suggested above, attributing to themselves the authority and inspiration of prophecy.[80]

Not more than a quarter-century after Ben Sira wrote his book, a life-and-death struggle had broken out in Palestinian Judaism with the very existence of the Jewish religion as previously understood, and especially as reconstituted by Ezra and Nehemiah, at stake. Our principal source, I Macc., represents it simply as the attempt of 'lawless men' (1.11), supported by Antiochus IV, to extirpate the traditional Jewish way of life. I Macc., however, speaks for the party which eventually prevailed. Many would now agree with Bickerman's thesis that the situation can be more accurately described as a conflict of interpretations between what might be called the reform party and the conservatives.[81] The former turned the conservative position upside down by arguing that the laws and practices which were most distinctive – circumcision and certain food taboos in particular – were superstitious additions to the original Mosaic Law. The more radical may have gone further and maintained that the Law of Moses was a human institution entirely

The Christian Additions to the Apocryphal Writings

the best of the Hebrews, who will one day cause the sun to stand, speaking with fair speech and holy lips.

The Christian insertion, 5.257 (indicated by italics),[44] while it certainly defines the 'one exceptional man' as Jesus who was crucified, also attributes inadvertently to Jesus a phenomenon unrecorded in Christian traditions; according to them he did not 'one day cause the sun to stand'. In contrast to the interpolations discussed above – especially those in the Testaments of the Twelve Patriarchs – these are forced and unsophisticated.

The Christian passages in Books 1 and 2 are considerably more sophisticated; these were composed by CE 150.[45] Book 1 is originally a Jewish oracle, a recital of *Heilsgeschichte*, with emphasis upon man's evil character, from creation to Noah and the Titans. It received extensive Christian redactions, so that beginning with line 324 until the end it is Christian. All of Book 2 is Christian, although Jewish traditions may be incorporated in it.

The Christian redactor is interested in eschatology and places considerable emphasis upon punishment of the impious. In 2.282–312, he describes the punishment of the wicked. This is a climax to the description of the coming of Elijah, 'driving a heavenly chariot' (2.187) after which there is violent destruction and the final judgment. The function of Christ is of particular importance; he is the one seated at the tribunal judging both the pious and the impious ($\beta\dot{\eta}\mu\alpha\tau\iota$ $\varkappa\varrho\dot{\iota}\nu\omega\nu$ $\varepsilon\dot{\upsilon}\sigma\varepsilon\beta\dot{\varepsilon}\omega\nu$ $\beta\dot{\iota}o\tau o\nu$ $\varkappa\alpha\dot{\iota}$ $\delta\upsilon\sigma\sigma\varepsilon\beta\dot{\varepsilon}\omega\nu$ $\tau\varrho\dot{o}\pi o\nu$ $\dot{\alpha}\nu\delta\varrho\tilde{\omega}\nu$, 2.241–44). These images are of considerable importance for helping us to understand the redactor's self-definition; he would have identified himself, of course, with the pious whom Christ would judge worthy of rewards and eschatological joys. The redactor has considerably reworked the Jewish eschatology so that it is specifically Christian and, hence, a powerful tool for propaganda and self-identification. It is difficult to overestimate the potential power of these eschatological pictures.

As the redactor lists the virtues and vices of men, he includes some concepts that help us to understand how he has distinguished himself both from earlier Jewish traditions and from contemporaneous or earlier Greek ideas. He gives special attention to concern for martyrs (2.46), virgins (2.49), usury (2.267–70), widows and orphans (2.70f.), and sexual offences (2.279–82). The special attention he gives to these matters, especially in contrast to the traditional Jewish and Greek ethical tractates, suggests that they were major concerns for him and his own community. We catch a glimpse of his self-identification with those who have suffered martyrdom, leaving (perhaps) widows and orphans, and with those who are repelled by usury or by sexual abuse of virgins and other sexual offences.

The redactor clearly distinguishes himself from Israel; he holds a vile hatred of Israel and writes a stunning polemic in Book 1, lines 365–75 (cf. 1.387–96). His description of the crucifixion and the events that immediately preceded it is directed less to their importance for salvation than to a description of Israel's impiety; attributed to 'Israel' are 'abominable lips and poisonous spittings' and 'eyes more blind than blind rats, more terrible than poisonous creeping beasts, shackled with heavy sleep'. These lines are best understood – it seems to me – not in terms of inherited traditions, but in light of the scribe's self-consciousness of being appreciably different from his Jewish contemporaries. The ideas under examination now are noticeably distinct from the earlier Jewish-Christian concepts and the strongly Jewish tone of the Christianity reflected, for example, in the Hellenistic Synagogal Prayers and in the Testaments of the Twelve Patriarchs.

The scribe conceives of his community as 'a new shoot' from the nations (βλαστὸς νέος, 1.383). In contrast to the Christian redactor who added the portions to the Martyrdom and Ascension of Isaiah, he emphasizes that there will be wise leaders who will be followed by only a few prophets (1.385f.). The description of the new shoot as sprouting from 'the nations' reveals that he sees himself primarily in terms of the Gentiles and not as a sect of, or development from, Israel; but his self-consciousness – in contrast to Book 8, as we shall see – has evolved out of dialogues with post-Yavnean Jews.

The climax of these first two books is the confession of the sibyl and her prayer to the Saviour to be rescued (2.339–47). She laments her former 'lawless deeds' and confesses that she is 'a brazen one' who has done 'shameless deeds'. Her lament ends with her request for 'a little rest from the song, holy giver of manna, king of a great kingdom' (2.345–47). By adding these lines, the Christian redactor has 'baptized' the sibyl through the Christian tradition and so is able to couch his ideas in this formerly pagan genre.

The sixth book in the Sibylline Oracles is not a sibylline oracle but a hymn to Christ that is difficult to date, although it may derive from the latter part of the second century.[46] All we can learn about the author's self-identification is that once again he reveals a polemical tension with the Jews, describing the land of Israel as the 'land of Sodom' (Σοδομῖτι γαίη, 6.21). His hatred of Israel is again connected with the crucifixion; he can promise for the Jews only 'evil afflictions'. Joined with this polemic is an emphasis upon the cross, which receives considerable elevation: it was upon it that 'God was stretched out' (ὦ ξύλον ὦ μακαριστόν, ἐφ' οὗ θεὸς ἐξετανύσθη, 6.26); hence the 'wood' will leave the earth and 'see heaven as home' (6.25–28). This twofold emphasis reveals how he perceives himself in distinction from Israel and in identification with the cross; he is thereby distinguished from the other redactors and Christian interpolators we have examined. The redactor here identifies himself with a type of Christianity that has moved far away from Judaism and is perhaps dangerously on the verge of many tendencies and ideas associated with Marcion.

The seventh book of the Sibylline Oracles is difficult to date, although it may be as early as the end of the second century CE.[47] Only three features of this book seem to pertain to the search for the author's self-understanding. The most notable feature is the lengthy and frequent references to impending destruction (7.1–28, 40–63, 96–131). The author describes the destructions to come upon the major cities and countries in the world and depicts the evil and fate that will befall them. Not only people will be destroyed but the entire earth will be consumed by fire (7.120f.). Another world will replace the evil and corrupt one (7.140). By this means, the author clearly distinguishes himself from existing nations, powers, and peoples and identifies himself with the world to come. He claims, furthermore, that these events are related to the fulfilment of promises: 'all will be fulfilled through the house of David' (7.31). As with Book 2, so Book 7 climaxes with the confession of the sibyl (7.150–62). But there are considerable differences: she again confesses that she has been 'utterly faithless' (7.154); rather than pleading for rescue, however, she now urges that she be stoned, 'May you stone me! Stone me all of you! For thus will I live and fix my eyes on heaven' (7.161f.).

In many of the interpolations and expansions discussed above, we have found ample evidence that early Christianity as it moved towards normative self-definition did so in distinction from Judaism; in Book 7 we find evidence that the Christian author reveals that his own community has been developing in some relationship with Gnosticism. Geffcken[48] and Kurfess[49] drew attention to the gnostic parallels in Book 7; but Gager[50] and Collins[51] are certainly correct to point out that they exaggerated the gnostic character of the book. Book 7 is not a gnostic book. There are, though, two self-contained sections in which we find terms and concepts usually associated with Gnosticism, as reflected, for example, in the Pistis Sophia, in the gnostic codices among the Nag Hammadi Library, and in the description of the Gnostics found in Irenaeus' work (cf. esp. *Adv. haer.* 1.5). The first section is found in Book 7, lines 71–73; 'Great Heaven established three towers for him in which the noble mothers of God now live: hope and piety and desirable holiness.' It is significant that the Christian scribe by the prepositional phrase 'for him' has made the 'Great Heaven' and 'the noble mothers of God' subservient to and obedient to the 'Word' (*logos*, which is Christ, 7.69). Similarly their functions are redefined (or, like the sibyl, baptized), as can be seen by lines 74 and 75: 'They do not rejoice in gold or silver but in reverential acts of men, sacrifices and most righteous thoughts.' On the basis of this passage, it seems that the author has defined his own Christianity in distinction from a kind of gnostic Christianity; but he has by no means composed a polemic against Gnosticism, as did Epiphanius and Irenaeus.

The second self-contained section in which so-called gnostic terminology is employed is in lines 139 and 140: 'In the third lot of circling years, of the first ogdoad, another world is seen again.' Here the author unabashedly, without explanation, employs terminology horrifying to some early Christian Fathers to explain how the world will be restored after the cosmic destruction. It is practically impossible to understand these lines in terms of the traditional paradigms for perceiving the developing self-consciousness of early Christianity; they warn us that many early christologies and Christian theologies were very complex and diverse from the so-called evolving mainstream that flowed on to 'orthodox' Christianity.

Book 8 is not easy to understand. It is wise to follow Collins's lead and divide the book into distinct sections (1–216 and 217–500) and to assign to the first section only lines 194–216 as clearly Christian. The date of this Christian section is difficult to discern. It certainly predates Lactantius because he quotes from it; it post-dates 180 because lines 65–74 portray the return of Nero during the reign of Marcus Aurelius, who died in 180 CE.

Lines 194–216 do not adequately mirror the Christian's self-definition. About all that can be said with some assurance is that he prays, 'May I not be alive when the abominable woman reigns' (194), but 'when heavenly grace comes to rule' (195). He thereby associates and identifies himself with a future rule that will be inaugurated by 'the sacred child, the destroyer of all [who] destroys the malignant abyss with bonds, opening it up' (196f.). The near future will be one characterized by cosmic confusion, destruction, resurrection of the dead, and judgment by God. He clearly identifies himself with God and God's final actions which had been foretold ('then all the oracles are fulfilled', 215).

The second portion of Book 8, lines 217–500, is clearly Christian. The author who composed these lines conceives of himself as one of the 'faithful' or 'holy ones' who were living in tension with the 'faithless' ones (8.220, 287; cf. 416), and who recognize that there is only one God (8.377). He, therefore, realizes the absurdity of idols (8.378–411) and frequents none of the temples (8.487–95), but rather offers to God his psalms and songs (8.496–500). He identifies himself with the believers who are promised eternal life (8.225), who are those who can confess, 'This is our God, now proclaimed in acrostics, the king, the immortal Saviour who suffered for us':

(οὗτος ὁ νῦν προγραφεὶς ἐν ἀκροστιχίοις θεὸς ἡμῶν
Σωτὴρ ἀθάνατος βασιλεύς, ὁ παθὼν ἔνεχ᾽ ἡμῶν 8.249f.).

In light of the Christian additions discussed above, it is significant that the Christian who added these lines did not blame the Jews for the crucifixion. He describes the crucifixion in some detail but uses a generic imagery so that 'God' comes 'into the hands of lawless and faithless men' (εἰς ἀνόμων χεῖρας καὶ ἀπίστων ὕστατον ἥξει, 8.287). Likewise, it is worthy of note that when he describes the Jews as 'a disobedient people' it is in terms of the giving of the Law during the time of Moses (who, however, is not mentioned by name; 8.300f.). It appears obvious, therefore, that in contrast to the redactor of Books 1 and 2 he (and his community) have been evolving a normative self-definition more in dialogue with Greeks and Romans than with rabbinic or post-Yavnean Jews.

The author would have identified himself with those who

have repented (8.357f.); hence he will be able to endure the impending collapse of the world and subsequent death of all living things (8.337–58). It is significant for a better understanding of his self-identity that the author intermittently refers to the impending destruction of the world (cf. also 8.225f.), the judgment (8.217), and punishment (8.227). Although these concepts are arranged frequently in confusing chronological order it seems that he affirms the traditional sequence of destruction followed by resurrection and culminating in judgment (cf. 8.412–28).

Conclusion

We have seen some of the ways that the early Christians both in their liturgy – especially as reflected in the Hellenistic Synagogal Prayers – and in their teaching – especially as reflected in the Testaments of the Twelve Patriarchs, the Martyrdom and Ascension of Isaiah, IV Ezra and the Sibylline Oracles – felt it necessary considerably to alter or expand received traditions. In these alterations, we have found reflected the movement of the early Christians (and their communities) towards normative self-definition. Only infrequently have these alterations been prompted because of divergent ideas within Christianity, such as docetism, or with competing Graeco-Roman ideas, such as Gnosticism. The major tension, when it was evident, was almost always with Judaism. Not only ancient Judaism but apparently also Judaism contemporaneous with the authors influenced the Christians' perception of their own religion.[52] Most prominent, especially in the interpolations in the Hellenistic Synagogal Prayers and the Testaments of the Twelve Patriarchs, are additions that can be classified as an example of teleological determinism; their interest was not primarily doctrinal or historical, but to specify the only proper means of interpreting the fulfilment of prophecy. It is clear that early Christians read ancient prayers and narratives in light of the life of Jesus of Nazareth, whom they claimed to be Christ. The Christ event tended to become the singular teleological force behind many steps towards normative self-definition.[53]

The interpolations and expansions of ancient traditions help us also perceive the movement towards canonization in the early Christian communities. In the paradigmatic movement of textual traditions from being open to being closed, interpolations or expansions may denote that canonization has been achieved. But an accepted text, even with interpolation or expansion, is not a fixed canon or a definition of what should be included in and excluded from sacred scripture.

As the canon took shape and became normative in the Christian communities, the Christians who depended upon the 'apocryphal' books were eventually moved to the fringes of triumphant Christianity. Their own interpolations and expansions provide us with a rare glimpse into their ideas. We receive a significant reminder of the existence of non-normative Christianity. The 'shepherds' and 'elders' labelled as faithless by the author of the Martyrdom and Ascension of Isaiah could very well have denoted some of the leaders now regarded as saints by the church.

The Christian expansions to the Jewish apocryphal works warn us that the early roads to normative self-definition were confused and buffeted by many forces.[54] The most forceful of these was probably not a search for dogma. To assume a developmentalist approach, according to which all the 'superior' insights and ideas eventually triumphed, is to recast earliest Christianity not only confessionally but retrospectively from Nicaea. While the foregoing research must be seen in light of the studies directed to other documents, it does warn us that a normative self-definition in Christianity does not move in a line from Jesus through Paul, John, Ignatius and Irenaeus to Athanasius. The foregoing study helps to clarify the insight that if there is a normative self-definition for Christianity it is one that has come from the 'triumphant' church; but only finally, not historically, does it flow from creeds and doctrines. The complexity of traditions, both within the Christian additions to Jewish apocryphal writings and within the 'canonical' New Testament, indicates that for hundreds of years (at least) there were numerous normative self-definitions within Christianity.

3

Inspiration and Canonicity: Reflections on the Formation of the Biblical Canon

SID Z. LEIMAN

Determination of the inspired status of biblical books

In a previous study,[1] I had occasion to raise the following questions regarding the biblical canon of the rabbis:

> Assuming that only inspired books could qualify for inclusion in the biblical canon, on what grounds was it decided that the book of Enoch and the Testaments of the Twelve Patriarchs were to be excluded from the biblical canon? To be more precise, how did the talmudic rabbis, or their predecessors, determine the inspired status of any given book?

I did not have the answers to the questions then, nor do I claim to have them now. Nevertheless, I welcome the opportunity afforded by the Symposium on Normative Self-Definition in Judaism from the Maccabees to the Mid-Third Century to explore some answers proffered by ancient and modern scholarship, as well as to offer some suggestions which may stimulate others to productive scholarship as they demolish my argument.

Literary history was not a major concern of the rabbis. One searches in vain through the talmudic and midrashic literatures for a systematic account of the formation and closing of the biblical canon. There are, however, scattered throughout talmudic literature numerous bits of evidence which, when combined and evaluated, may serve the historian in reconstructing the history of the formation and closing of the biblical canon. It is evident from a careful reading of rabbinic texts that it was the perception of the rabbis that only inspired books qualified for inclusion in scripture.[2] Moreover, not every inspired utterance of the biblical authors was included in scripture. Only those inspired utterances whose message was necessary for all generations were included in the biblical canon.[3] Nowhere do the rabbis clearly delineate how they determined whether or not a book was inspired, or how it was determined that a particular book carried an inspired message for all generations. Indeed, one suspects that to all intents and purposes the major decisions had already been made before the tannaitic period. That is, the rabbis inherited a more or less fixed biblical canon from their rabbinic predecessors. They introduced some modifications as late as the third century CE, but such modification amounted to no more than cosmetic surgery.[4] Since the canonization process occurred in large part prior to the formulation of our earliest rabbinic texts, the speculative nature of our investigation becomes apparent. We are attempting to reconstruct the history of events that took root no later than in the Persian period, and blossomed in the early Hellenistic period, two periods about which we have almost no contemporary Jewish evidence.[5] Nothing definitive can be said about criteria for the inclusion of books in, or their exclusion from, the biblical canon as it developed in the late Persian and early Hellenistic periods. Nevertheless, speculate we must; for that is the nature of the scholarly enterprise; and often enough, one scholar's speculation leads to another scholar's establishing the facts והיה שכרי.

I shall begin with a representative survey of suggestions proffered by classical and modern scholars. After listing these suggestions, I shall explain why I find them unpersuasive, and shall then proceed to offer other, I hope more palatable suggestions in their stead.

Solutions proffered by classical and modern scholarship

1. The earliest[6] Jewish justification for the rejection of a specific book from the biblical canon is preserved by Jerome at his commentary to Jer. 29.21–23.[7] Jerome repeats a Jewish tradition first publicized by Origen in his *Letter to Africanus*.[8] It identifies the two elders who incriminated Susanna as Ahab and Zedekiah, the two false prophets who were roasted in fire by Nebuchadnezzar, king of Babylon (cf. Jer. 29.21–23).[9] Jerome's text reads:[10]

The Hebrews say that these are the elders who wrought folly in Israel and committed adultery with the wives of their fellow-citizens, and to one of whom Daniel said: 'O you who are grown old in evil days' (Susanna 52) and to the other of whom he said: 'You seed of Canaan and not of Judah, beauty has deceived you and lust has perverted your heart! Thus you did with the daughters of Israel and they, in fear, spoke with you; but a daughter of Judah did not abide your iniquity' (Susanna 56–57). And that which the prophet now says, 'And they have spoken a word in my name falsely which I did not command them' (Jer. 29.23) they (the Jews) think that this is indicated by the fact that they (Ahab and Zedekiah) thus deceived wretched little women who are carried about by every wind of doctrine by saying to them, because they were of the tribe of Judah, that the Messiah must be born from their seed, who, having been enticed by desire, furnished their bodies, as if they were future mothers of the Messiah. But that which is said at present 'whom the king of Babylon roasted in fire' (Jer. 29.22), seems to contradict the history of Daniel (i.e., Susanna); for he asserts that they were stoned by the people according to the opinion of Daniel (Susanna 61–62). This indeed has been written (Jer. 29.22) that the king of Babylon roasted them in the fire. Whence this fable (i.e., the book of Susanna) itself, as it were, is not accepted by very many, including almost all the Hebrews, nor is it read in their synagogues. 'For,' they say, 'how could it be that the captives had the power of stoning their leaders and prophets?' And more than this, they affirm to be true that which Jeremiah writes, that the elders indeed were refuted by Daniel, but that sentence was brought against them by the king of Babylon who had power against the captives as victor and lord.

According to Jerome, the Jews rejected the book of Susanna because of two fatal objections: (1) A captive nation was in no position to administer capital punishment, and (2) Jeremiah's account contradicts the account set forth in the book of Susanna with regard to who administered the capital punishment (as well as with regard to the mode of punishment – S.Z.L.). In the light of these objections, the historicity of the Susanna account is impugned and, together with it, its canonicity.

2. Zvi Hirsch Chajes (d. 1855) suggested that various books of the Apocrypha were rejected by the rabbis because of halakic discrepancies between the accounts in the Apocrypha and normative Judaism.[11] Regarding the book of Susanna, for example, he noted that according to talmudic teaching capital punishment was administered in the Diaspora only when the Sanhedrin was in session at the temple in Jerusalem.[12] Since the Sanhedrin was not in session during the captivity, capital punishment could not have been administered by Daniel. Moreover, according to talmudic teaching, conflict of testimony between witnesses suf-

fices only to invalidate their testimony; it is hardly a capital offence.[13] For these reasons, the rabbis denied the book of Susanna a place in the biblical canon.

3. Solomon Zeitlin postulated that the third and final section of the biblical canon (with the exception of Ecclesiastes and Esther) was canonized in 65 CE.[14] Well aware that at that late date virtually all of the apocryphal and pseudepigraphical books were in circulation, Zeitlin felt constrained to explain away the deliberate rejection of those books by the rabbis. He adopted Chajes' approach and applied it to a wide variety of non-canonical books. Thus, e.g., according to Tobit 7.14, Raguel gave his daughter away in marriage by means of a legal document which he wrote. But according to normative Jewish practice, the groom writes the legal document and hands it over to the bride. Zeitlin concluded that the rabbis 'would never canonize a book which was in direct contradiction with their Halakah'.[15]

4. Alluding to the rabbinic rejection of some of the pseudepigrapha, Rudolf Meyer wrote:[16]

> There was also differentiation against the pre-Mosaic period. Since the Torah was the source of all knowledge, there could be no work of greater antiquity if the system was to stand. This implied the rejection of any religious claim which the literature of the patriarchal period might have.

Thus, according to Meyer, such pseudepigraphical works as the Life of Adam and Eve, the books of Enoch, and the Testaments of the Twelve Patriarchs were rejected by the rabbis simply because the Torah faithful would not tolerate a work claiming greater antiquity than the Torah itself.

Critique of the solutions proffered

Solutions 1–3 are of a kind. In common they postulate that discrepancies between candidates for scripture and rabbinic teaching sufficed to bring about the exclusion of the various apocryphal and pseudepigraphical works from the biblical canon. When, however, one allows for the range of discrepancy tolerated by the received scriptures, as well as the range of discrepancy tolerated in mishnaic and talmudic teaching, the specious character of solutions 1–3 becomes evident. Thus, for example, Gen. 26.34 and 36.2 (similarly Gen. 28.9 and 36.3), passages generally ascribed by source analysis to the same document (P), are contradictory. Nevertheless, the editors of P – if one accepts the documentary hypothesis – as well as the redactor(s) of the Torah saw no problem in incorporating and canonizing a contradiction for all generations. Nor can it be argued that such picayune discrepancies are hardly analogous to the more substantive discrepancies raised by Jerome's Jewish informants, by Chajes, and by Zeitlin. More fundamental discrepancies, whether apparent or real, were incorporated into scripture. Two different versions of the Ten Commandments, each claiming to be the *ipsissima verba* of the Lord, are embedded in scripture. Deut. 24.16 proscribes vicarious punishment; Ex. 34.7 presupposes it.[17] Num. 18.18 flatly contradicts Deut. 15.20. Deut. 17.15 either requires or tolerates the appointment of an Israelite monarch; the clear implication of I Sam. 8.5 ff. is that no such verse was known in Samuel's day. The list could go on and on, but enough samples have been adduced to prove the point. Whether we assume that all of scripture was canonized simultaneously, or that it was canonized in stages, the authorities responsible for its canonization were not troubled by apparent or real inconsistencies – at least with regard to according books biblical status.[18] Inconsistency was not equated with heresy. (A modern Yiddish proverb sums it up well: פון א קשיא שטארבט מען נישט – one doesn't die from a question.) It would appear that the authorities were more concerned with 'Who said it?' than with what was said. And as will be suggested below, they were more concerned with identifying the circles from which a particular book emanated than with the details of its message.[19]

In the light of the discoveries at Qumran, solution 4 is no longer tenable. The central significance of the Torah was no less the case at Qumran than it was at Jerusalem or Jamnia. Nevertheless, Jubilees, Enoch, the Testaments of Levi and Naphtali, *and the Torah* co-existed at Qumran. Moreover, not a few rabbis (see bBB 15b; pSot 20d; and GenR. 57.4, pp. 614–15) assigned Job and his book to the patriarchal period; obviously they did not feel that the authority of the Torah was jeopardized by the existence of books of greater antiquity. That the book of Job – and not only Job himself – was assigned by some rabbis to the patriarchal period is implied by the talmudic text at bBB 15a. It is perhaps not superfluous to add that in 1980 hundreds of pious and learned Jews include in their library of 'sacred texts'[20] a mystical treatise entitled The Book of the Angel Raziel, which they are persuaded was authored by the angel Raziel, who then presented it to Adam (for so it is stated on the title page). Its alleged antiquity and authority have never been viewed as a threat to the Torah.

Some suggestions

In the light of an examination of the evidence bearing on the formation and closing of the biblical canon of the rabbis,[21] the following suggestions may provide a more adequate response to the questions raised at the start of this essay.

1. Books believed to have been authored after the cessation of prophecy did not qualify for inclusion in the biblical canon of the rabbis. Since the cessation of prophecy was thought to have occurred in the late Persian period or in the early Hellenistic period (but certainly before the Maccabean revolt), much of the extant apocryphal, pseudepigraphical, and Qumran literature probably was never considered for inclusion in the biblical canon. This for one of two reasons:

(*a*) If the books were known to have been authored in the third century BCE or later, they could not qualify for inclusion in the biblical canon because they were not inspired.

(*b*) The effective date for the closing of the biblical canon was not 65 CE, as suggested by Zeitlin, but somewhere in the early Maccabean period, perhaps circa 150 BCE. Nowhere in rabbinic literature (or, for that matter, in the books of the Apocrypha or in Josephus) is it suggested that a book was *added* to the biblical canon that obtained in the second century BCE. Some rabbis attempted to constrict the corpus of canonical books by removing Ecclesiastes, Song of Songs, or Esther from the biblical canon.[22] They did not suggest *new* candidates for inclusion in the biblical canon. Thus, books published for the first time in the first centuries BCE and CE, even if ascribed to the biblical period, were not candidates for biblical canonicity because their candidacy was declared after the fact, i.e. after the biblical canon of the rabbis, or their immediate predecessors, was closed.

2. Books composed in Greek were automatically disqualified from inclusion in the biblical canon.[23] Only Hebrew was viewed as an appropriate vehicle for recording inspired literature. Thus, on linguistic grounds alone books such as the Wisdom of Solomon and II Maccabees were automatically disqualified from attaining biblical status.

3. Books written in Hebrew and ascribed to the biblical period which challenged *central* halakic teachings of the rabbis were *ipso facto* excluded from the biblical canon. Thus, the book of Jubilees, which is predicated upon a calendar at variance with the rabbinic calendar, could not be considered a serious candidate for inclusion in the biblical canon. A call to celebrate all the festivals on the 'wrong' days of the year (with the consequence that all the festal offerings were invalid; the High Priest's entry into the Holy of Holies was on the 'wrong' day – a capital offence; etc.) could only be viewed as rank heresy. I stress 'books which challenged central halakic teachings of the rabbis', for books which challenged central theological teachings of the rabbis, while problematic, were not necessarily excluded from the biblical canon. Ecclesiastes is a case in point. Its seemingly antinomian, pessimistic, and often contradictory sentiments left the rabbis nonplussed. Despite the theological problems it created for the rabbis, Ecclesiastes retained its position in the biblical canon precisely because it did not challenge central halakic practices in any substantive way. Halakic Judaism has managed to survive for over 2000 years despite its retention of Ecclesiastes in the biblical canon. Indeed, in the medieval period halakic Judaism instituted the public reading of Ecclesiastes in the synagogue service.

4. Books whose biblical status was uncertain, such as the book of Ben Sira,[24] were sometimes excluded from the biblical canon precisely because they were venerated as biblical by sectarian groups. In Judaeo-Christian circles, the apocryphal and pseudepigraphical literature formed an inspired literary continuum between the Old and New Testaments. Rabbinic Judaism, however, recognized that prophecy had ceased prior to the Maccabean period. The rabbis could not accept the apocryphal books as inspired literature, nor did they have any ulterior motive for doing so. The book of Ben Sira was in all likelihood excluded from the biblical canon as part of a general rabbinic polemic against literature with biblical pretensions. Its content, *per se*, presented no problem to the rabbis. Indeed, in a later period when the biblical canon was irrevocably fixed and when Jewish sectarian canons no longer posed a threat to rabbinic Judaism, the book of Ben Sira was read and expounded in rabbinic circles much like any other biblical book. It was considered an uninspired canonical book. It was thought to be uninspired because it was authored in the post-prophetic

period; nevertheless, it was canonical for the rabbis in that they accepted it as an authoritative guide for religious doctrine and practice.[25]

It is noteworthy that for the rabbis the notions of inspiration and canonicity were separate and distinct. An inspired book was a book believed to have been composed under divine inspiration. A canonical book was a book considered authoritative for religious doctrine and practice. The biblical canon of the rabbis consisted of those books they considered at once inspired and canonical. Other books, such as Ben Sira, retained their canonical status while being excluded from the biblical canon.

The biblical canon and normative self-definition

The biblical canon was shaped by a community; it would then contribute to the shaping of that community.[26] What scripture did for the Jews was more than what the Jews did for scripture. If Jews have survived to this very day as Jews, it is precisely because scripture provided a framework for Jewish survival. Throughout Jewish history, normative self-definition was very much bound up with scripture and how it was perceived. It is not simply the phenomenon of being a people of the book, however, that is distinctive. Jewish sectarians, and the various Christian and Islamic religious communities through the ages, would make the same claim. Ultimately, the critical differences go back to a more fundamental question: sources of authority. Who determines whether or not prophecy has ceased? Who determines whether or not a prophet or a messiah will be viewed as true or false? Who decides whether or not a book will be accorded biblical status? Who decides whether or not a given biblical verse is to be taken literally or figuratively? What criteria will be used in making these determinations? The most potent factor in normative self-definition rests in the answers to these questions.

4

Jewish Acceptance and Rejection of Hellenism

JONATHAN GOLDSTEIN

Introduction

'The Greek confronted the Hebrew. Judaism confronted Hellenism.' Thus runs the conventional wisdom of our time. Surely that confrontation has been a major theme in the modern study of the cultural history of the period extending from the fourth century BCE to the fifth century CE and even later. Still more fruitful in modern research has been the extended concept of a Hellenistic culture which confronted all other ancient Mediterranean and near eastern civilizations from the fourth century BCE on. The concepts of Hellenistic culture and of confrontation themselves have a history, which began no later than the sixteenth century. The early investigators took as their point of departure the text of the Acts of the Apostles 6.1, which opposes Hebrews to Hellenists: 'Now, in those days, when the disciples were increasing in number, the Hellenists murmured against the Hebrews because their widows were neglected in the daily distribution.' Whatever the text may mean, clearly it opposes Hebrews to Hellenists, and it was Johann Gustav Droysen[1] in the nineteenth century who continued the misinterpretation of Acts 6.1 and produced the fruitful extended concept of Hellenism as the great confronting culture which arose in the fourth century BCE.[2]

Though the concepts of Hellenism and of the confrontation had their origin in the interpretation and misinterpretation of Acts 6.1, they fit well the usage of Paul and the church fathers, who oppose 'Jew' to 'Greek'.[3] Better yet, there would seem to be strong confirmation of the validity of the concept of Hellenism as opposed to Judaism, in the fact that II Maccabees tells of the war to defend *Ioudaismos*[4] and condemns *Hellēnismos*.[5]

Great works have been written on the broad phenomenon of Hellenism and on the narrower problem of how the Jews reacted to it. The latest important study is that of Martin Hengel,[6] who has assembled a mass of evidence in the attempt to show that the Judaism even of believers in the Torah, down to the reign of Antiochus IV, was heavily Hellenized, though there was some Jewish opposition to Hellenism as evidenced in the book of Ben Sira. Hengel goes on to argue that as a result of the persecution under Antiochus IV, those devoted to the Torah closed ranks against full assimilation of Hellenism. Though Hengel himself insists that even the later Palestinian Judaism of the Pharisees and the Essenes must be regarded as Hellenistic Judaism,[7] still he gives his Part III the title, 'The Encounter and *Conflict* between Palestinian Judaism and the Spirit of the Hellenistic Age', and he labels his summary of Part III as 'Palestinian Judaism between the Reception and the *Repudiation* of Hellenism'. The feat of fully assimilating Hellenism into a monotheistic religion, Hengel implies, was left for Christianity.

If a historical concept was discovered through the misinterpretation of a text, one must test its validity very carefully. With all due respect to the industry and intelligence of my predecessors, including Hengel, I believe it is necessary to make a fresh beginning: one must define terms more carefully, and one must examine the sources on each period for what they themselves say. I believe that Hengel, too, stands in the tradition of the misinterpreters of Acts 6.1. In some respects he has far overstated the opposition between Judaism and Hellenism.

It goes without saying that the present paper cannot deal with the subject on the scale of Hengel's work, but nevertheless the proposed fresh beginning can be made. As a first limitation in scope, I intend to look only at Jews who believed in the validity of the Torah: what was *their* reaction to Hellenistic culture? The restriction is not very great, since such Jews wrote most of our sources, and they, if anyone, felt the supposed confrontations with Hellenism. Pagan writers hardly mention Jews who rejected the authority of the Torah.[8]

'Culture' is a modern concept. There was no word for it in ancient Latin or Hebrew or Aramaic, and even the Greek *paideia* has different connotations.[9] Nevertheless, we can validly distinguish, even in the ancient world, resistance to foreign rulers from resistance to the foreign culture of those rulers. Hindus and Muslims of British India could adopt the culture of English gentlemen and still work for the independence of India and Pakistan. The pious Daniel of the biblical stories bore a Babylonian name, was adept in Babylonian wisdom, spoke and wrote Babylonian Aramaic, and still prayed for an end to foreign domination. Fighters in the army of Judas Maccabaeus bore Greek names,[10] and the martyr mother and her seven sons are presented as speaking Greek.[11] Thus, in looking for evidence of resistance to Hellenistic culture, we must be careful to exclude the abundant evidence which points only to hostility towards Greek-speaking rulers.[12]

We must take account of the religious impediments to Jewish adoption of Hellenistic culture, but we must not overestimate them. The members of the Muslim Aligarh movement in British-ruled India on no account would adopt Christianity, but otherwise the members of the movement aimed at becoming gentlemen in the English mould.[13] Just as Islam left the way open for many forms for Anglicizing, so the Torah left the way open for many forms for Hellenizing. Jews who accepted the authority of the Torah could not worship Greek gods[14] or practise or tolerate (as did many Greeks) male homosexual intercourse. Some Jews were rigorous in interpreting the sacred texts which put restrictions on Jewish contacts with Gentiles, and some were more lenient.[15] But for most Jews, some Greek practices and some polite intercourse with Greeks remained compatible with obedience to the Torah. In the *Letter of Aristeas to Philocrates*, the high priest Eleazar and the Jewish elders who translated the Torah into Greek will not violate Jewish law but manage otherwise to behave like perfect Greek *kaloi kai agathoi*. Condemnations of Gentile idolatry and immorality are commonplaces of Jewish biblical and post-biblical literature. Even if a Jewish source should specify that it is condemning *Greek* idols or *Greek* homosexuals, we should hesitate to take the passage as evidence that *Hellenism* rather than mere idolatry or homosexuality was an issue for pious ancient Jews. In each period we must try to ascertain which aspects of Hellenism were permitted and which were forbidden by the Torah as then interpreted. In every period we must expect to find pious Jews differing on how the Torah should be interpreted.

The characteristics of Hellenism and biblical law

We cannot proceed further without defining Hellenism itself, a highly controversial task. I shall not attempt a complete definition. Rather, I shall list a number of traits or distinguishing characteristics on which all observers, ancient and modern, should agree:

1. 'Hellenism', even in a non-Greek environment, implies that some Greeks are present, and that the non-Greeks have some contacts with them.

2. In a Hellenized culture, there must be some knowledge and use of the Greek language.

3. For intellectuals, the Hellenistic age was characterized by the development and spread of rational philosophies which often were sceptical of traditional religion.

4. In literature, Hellenistic culture typically produced high emotional epic, dramatic, and lyric poetry.

5. Very important in Hellenistic culture were the athletic and educational pursuits of the Greek gymnasium.[16]

6. In architectural remains, these cultural traits of Hellenism left an enduring legacy, in the surviving traces of ancient gymnasiums, stadiums and theatres. Greek stone theatres are especially durable and conspicuous among archaeological remains.

Our six traits are peculiarly Greek. Modern investigators such as M. I. Rostovtzeff have suggested that Hellenistic civilization was marked also by rational organization of human enterprises, by vigorous and often unscrupulous business methods, and by daring experiments in technology and social organization.[17] Jews may on occasion have disapproved of the business acumen shown by wealthy Israelites in the Hellenistic age. But acumen and rationality are *human* traits, conspicuous in but not limited to Hellenistic Greeks. Amos, long before the Hellenistic age, condemned Israelite business acumen (8.4–5; cf. Hosea 12.8–9). If an ancient Jewish moralist attacks Jews for exhibiting the traits which so interested Rostovtzeff, one cannot assume that moralist is attacking Hellenism unless he stigmatizes the traits as Greek.

What do the Torah and the rest of the Hebrew Bible have to say concerning our six traits? Not one is specifically forbidden. Some Jews could hold that all were permitted, while rigorists could infer from sacred texts that all were forbidden.

Thus, according to the Torah, the nations which inhabited the Promised Land before Joshua conquered it were to be driven out or killed. They were not to reside in it with the Jews, nor were Jews to make any covenant for peaceful relations with them.[18] Nothing in the Torah directly bars tolerating the residence of other Gentiles or making covenants with them. Indeed, covenants with 'distant nations' are specifically permitted.[19] Surely Greeks came from a distant country!

Rigorists, however, could point out that the texts give a reason for removing the former inhabitants of the Promised Land: otherwise Israelites would copy their idolatry and their abominations. Greeks, too, worshipped idols and might practise abominations. Should they not, therefore, be excluded from Judaea?[20] On the other hand, some Jews who accepted the rigorist interpretation could believe that God would allow residence on Jewish soil by Greeks who abstained while there from acts forbidden by the Torah, and that God permitted association even with idolatrous Greeks at times when those Greeks were not engaged in prohibited acts.

Nehemiah[21] found it dreadful that Jewish children spoke the language of Ashdod and did not speak or understand the Jewish tongue. Though the use of Aramaic had already invaded scripture itself, rigorists could have objected to Jewish use of Greek as Nehemiah objected to Ashdodite.[22]

The biblical texts forbidding Jews to practise Gentile customs also lend themselves to various interpretations. The passages in the Torah specify that the practices not to be imitated are those of Egypt and Canaan and involve idolatry, human sacrifice, and forbidden sexual acts.[23] Greeks were neither from Egypt nor from Canaan. Could not Jews imitate those Greek practices which involved neither idolatry nor human sacrifice nor forbidden sexual acts? On the other hand, almost all Greeks were idolaters, and some practised forbidden sexual acts. Rigorists could claim that the Torah forbade imitating the practices of any nation, the members of which were widely guilty of idolatry and forbidden sexual acts. Then should not Greek literature and Greek-style theatres be banned?[24] Those who would ban them would have to explain away the implications of Dan. 1–6, chapters accepted as true by many, if not most, Jews before the middle of the fourth century BCE. Babylonians certainly practised both idolatry and forbidden sexual acts, yet those chapters

attest that the pious Daniel and his friends could adopt Babylonian names and study and use Babylonian wisdom.[25]

The rejection of Hellenism by conservative Romans

Rejection of Hellenistic culture by ancient peoples is not a figment of the imagination of modern scholars. Members of at
least one ancient nation other than the Jews confronted Hellenistic culture in hostile fashion, and the writers and especially
the moralists of that nation condemned the six traits listed above
as well as those singled out by Rostovtzeff. The Romans so
confronted Hellenism and labelled the traits they condemned
as Greek.[26]

Latin vocabulary shows that Romans viewed many types of
immorality as peculiarly Greek. Plautus and Titinius, Roman
writers of comedy, were contemporaries of Ben Sira in the early
second century BCE. In their plays, 'to Greek it thoroughly'
(*pergraecari, congraecare*) means to pursue pleasure or gluttony
without any sense of shame.[27] Cicero and his contemporaries
used the contemptuous Latin diminutive *Graeculus* ('Greekling')
to express their low opinion of Greeks and to stigmatize any
feature of Hellenistic civilization which they did not like.[28] If a
Roman political figure exhibited any of the despised Hellenistic
traits, his enemies were quick to twit him with being an imitator
of Greeks.[29]

We may study the Roman reactions to Hellenism under the
headings of our six traits:

1. Archaeological and literary evidence shows that Greeks
were present in Campania, just to the south-east of Rome's own
district of Latium, from the middle of the eighth century BCE,
the traditional date of her foundation. The Greeks' settlements
in Italy were numerous and deep-rooted.[30] Nevertheless, in the
second century BCE the outspoken conservative Marcus Porcius
Cato, a contemporary of Jesus ben Sira, repeatedly called for
the expulsion of the Greeks, not merely from Rome but from
all of Italy.[31]

2. Romans could condemn the very use of the Greek
language, even when employed to address Greeks.[32]

3. Conservative Romans tried to exclude all kinds of Greek
philosophy, especially Epicureanism,[33] and even Cicero could
echo Roman contempt for Greek philosophy in general.[34]

4. Cato disapproved of any Greek poetry on the lips of a Roman.[35] His general assessment of Greeks and Greek literature is worth quoting in full:

> Concerning those contemptible Greeks, Marcus my son, I shall speak to you in the proper place. I shall show you what I learned from my own experience at Athens: that it may be good to dip into their literature, but not to learn it thoroughly. I shall convince you that they are a most wicked and intractable nation. You may take my word as the word of a prophet: whenever that contemptible nation bestows its literature upon us, it will ruin everything. . . .[36]

5. Cato and other Roman conservatives had the same contempt for the Greek gymnasium.[37] There were no public gymnasia at Rome under the republic, and even private gymnasia are not attested until the time of Cicero.[38]

6. The typical structures of Greek culture – the gymnasia, stadia and theatres – are strikingly absent from republican Rome before the first century BCE, and we hear that Roman conservatives brought about the demolition of such structures when they were erected.[39]

We may add that Romans could disapprove of Greek business methods and found strange the Greek insistence on doing business for cash and their refusal to grant credit.[40] Cicero believed Greeks were bent only on making money and would do anything for money.[41] Thus, conservative Romans and even Cicero felt themselves to be in hostile confrontation with Hellenistic culture.[42]

One would think that Jews devoted to the Torah felt a similar confrontation. But did they? Let us search the many and varied remains of Jewish literature, whether written originally in Hebrew, Aramaic or Greek.

Jewish attitudes towards Hellenism

Scholars hitherto have not taken note of the stark contrast between ancient Jewish literature and the Roman texts we have just examined. Although ancient Jewish literature is full of ethnic, moral and religious polemics against non-Jews, Jewish texts, whatever their language, contain no verb comparable to the Latin *pergraecari* and no contemptuous noun or adjective comparable to the Latin *Graeculus*. Jews could have created a verb *hityavven* ('become, or act, Greek') on the model of *hityahed* ('become, or act Jewish'; Esth. 8.17), as has been done in modern Hebrew. Ancient Jews could so have used the Greek *hellē-nizein*, as the church Fathers did,[43] Jews could have used *yavan* ('Greece') and *yevani* ('Greek') as terms of reproach. Yet there is no trace that Jews so used such expressions. The word 'Greek' is somewhat infrequent in the Jewish Apocrypha and Pseudepigrapha, in Qumran texts, and in rabbinic literature. Philo and Josephus employ it as a linguistic and ethnic term, usually without suggesting any opposition between 'Jewish' and 'Greek'.[44]

One who nevertheless believes in the sharp confrontation between the Jews and Hellenism might insist that in the Jewish vocabulary of the Hellenistic age, the word 'Gentile', so frequently opposed to 'Jew', really means 'Greek'. Indeed, in Paul's epistles and in patristic literature, 'Greek' often means simply 'non-Jew' or 'pagan'.[45] Modern scholars have argued, however, that the word 'Greek' in *Jewish* texts cannot be taken to mean 'Gentile'.[46] Thus, one may expect that the word 'Gentile' in Jewish texts ought not automatically to be taken to mean 'Greek'. Nevertheless, we shall leave open the possibility that 'Gentile' (*goy, ethnos*) in Jewish texts may on occasion mean 'Greek'.

For the purposes of this paper we shall divide the history of the Jews in the times when Hellenism was a factor into four periods. First, there is the time before the priest Jason usurped the high priesthood at the beginning of the reign of Antiochus IV (in late 175 or early 174 BCE). Second, there is the period which began with Jason's high priesthood and extended down to the time when the Jews received from Antiochus V the letter restoring to them their laws and their temple (II Macc. 11.23–26; early 163 BCE).[47] So important was this period that it deserves a special name; let us call the time from 175 to 163 BCE the 'critical period'. Third, there are the years between the critical period and the death of the Hasmonaean prince Simon in 134 BCE. Fourth, there is the time between the death of Simon and the completion of the Babylonian Talmud in the fifth century CE.

From all these periods we have evidence on our topic. In particular, we have Jewish literature either written in or reflecting each period. In this study we cannot possibly give a thorough survey of the literature of all four periods. I believe, however, that the essential truths can be demonstrated by a proper study of the first two.

Jewish reactions to Hellenism: The early period

Let us proceed to consider the evidence for the earliest period, the one before Jason usurped the high priesthood. Hengel[48] tried to prove that it was a period of high Hellenization, obstructed or opposed only by a few Jewish conservatives such as Ben Sira. If we examine the evidence under the headings of our aspects of Hellenism, we shall find that Hengel, surprisingly, has overestimated the opposition to Hellenism and has read into the words of Ben Sira an opposition which does not exist there. For this period we have the testimony not only of Jews but of pagans, especially of Hecataeus of Abdera. Since the Jews were under Graeco-Macedonian rule, they could not cut themselves off from all contact with Greeks. Contacts are attested both in the literary remains and in the papyri, to say nothing of the Greek pottery and artifacts found in the archaeological strata.[49] The period shows no opposition to the use of the Greek language. Indeed, the Torah itself was translated into Greek.[50] Far from sealing themselves off from Greek literature, pious Jews drew even upon its myths[51] and took to writing Greek poetry themselves.[52]

Greek tourists with philosophic training at first found the Jews so interesting that Jews for a while may have been as much pestered by visiting 'philosophers'[53] as modern primitives are by anthropologists. There is no sign that Jews tried to exclude the teachings of the philosophers. Indeed, they soon claimed that the philosophers, when correct, had borrowed from the Torah.[54] Modern scholars have found traces of Greek philosophy in the thought of Qohelet and Ben Sira,[55] and even in the Greek translation of the Torah.[56] It is not beyond question that those scholars are correct. For example, Qohelet did not need the help of Greek thinkers in order to question the general biblical belief in providence. The mere amoral facts of history could lead him to do so. Nevertheless, Greek influence on those writings is possible and even likely.

Strange, however, is Hengel's insistence that Ben Sira wrote in opposition to Hellenism.[57] Hengel himself may have been aware of the insecure basis of his theory here, for his argument is full of words like 'probably' and 'presumably'. Nevertheless, his conclusions on Ben Sira have gained unjustifiably wide acceptance. Simple considerations suffice to refute them. The words 'Greek' and 'Greece' nowhere appear in Ben Sira's work. And should one suggest that he abstained from hostile mention of Greeks for fear of his Graeco-Macedonian overlords, Ben Sira certainly could have directed his hostility at unnamed 'Gentiles', as does so much of Jewish literature. Yet in the entire book of Ben Sira there is no preaching against the Gentiles. Ben Sira does not tell his fellow Jews that they must not imitate foreigners, nor does he tell Jews to shun pagans. He may deplore the oppression of the poor by the rich or the questioning of divine providence, but nowhere does he say that the oppressors or the questioners imitate Greeks or Gentiles.[58] For Ben Sira, Hellenism was simply not an issue.

Surely Hellenistic culture must have challenged the Jews; even the mighty Romans felt the challenge. How are we to explain the strange fact that Ben Sira shows no trace of such a challenge? To answer this question, we must consider evidence ignored by most modern writers. In this earliest period, the Jews in fact could not be completely open to Hellenism and were not. So great was the interest of philosophers in Jews that one might have expected Jews to have taken advantage of it to propagate their own religion among philosophers. One would then expect that the Greek translation of Genesis would have been full of the technical cosmological terminology of the Greek philosophers, yet that terminology is strikingly absent.[59] At least from the time when Aristophanes wrote his *Clouds*, ordinary Greeks knew enough of that terminology to make fun of it, even when they could not understand it. Thus, I believe the Jewish translators, too, knew something of the cosmological vocabulary of Greek philosophy.[60] They knew enough of it to avoid it completely in rendering Genesis.

This avoidance of philosophical vocabulary was not necessarily hostile. Very likely the purpose was to prevent Greeks from making the charge that Jews had plagiarized from the philosophers. Hence, this fact is but a feeble example of Jewish rejection of Hellenism.

More significant is the evidence of Hecataeus of Abdera,[61] that the Jewish way of life, even in his time, was 'misanthropic' (ἀπάνθρωπον) and 'hostile to strangers' (μισόξενον). How much contact did Jews of Judaea have with Greeks? Rigorist interpretations of the Torah in fact shaped much of life in Judaea. Hecataeus also lets us know that Jews did not tolerate the existence of pagan altars and shrines in Judaea: sometimes by paying fines for insubordination, sometimes by obtaining pardon from the provincial governors, the Jews of Judaea, by the late fourth century BCE, secured the privilege of not having to tolerate pagan worship on their own soil. It was a privilege they needed, for they believed their God would inflict ruinous punishment upon them if they tolerated idol-worship in the Holy Land, even if only pagans practised it.[62]

Scholars have not considered the implications of this privilege. Few if any non-Jews would reside on Jewish soil if they could not practise their own religion there. There were numerous Greek cities and villages in Palestine, but until Antiochus IV established the Akra, in Judaea proper there was not even a Greek village, much less a Greek city. In mentioning how Jews destroy pagan altars and shrines, Hecataeus does not speak of foreign settlers but of foreign 'arrivals' or 'visitors' (τῶν εἰς τὴν χώραν πρὸς αὐτοὺς ἀφικνουμένων). There must have been many Greek visitors, even pilgrims to the famous temple in Jerusalem, such as were said to have been contemplated already by King Solomon.[63] Even Graeco-Macedonian kings brought or sent sumptuous gifts.[64]

The Zenon papyri from our period attest estates held by Greek landlords in Palestine, but none in Judaea proper.[65] They also attest that Greeks did business at Jerusalem and Jericho, but not that they resided there. Finds of Greek pottery and other artifacts give more evidence of business contacts.[66] Even resident pagan *soldiers* were few. In Judaea proper, we hear only of a small garrison of pagan soldiers in the citadel of Jerusalem,[67] and they may have been selected for their willingness to conform to the Jews' laws barring pagan worship. The Gentiles whom Judas Maccabaeus drove out of Judaea may have been settled there only a few years before as part of the punishment of the Jews by Antiochus IV.[68]

A royal decree directly excluding Gentiles from settling in Judaea would have been so great a privilege for the Jews that our sources could not have passed over it in silence. Hence, the absence of Greeks from Judaea probably was a consequence of the ban on pagan worship there. This absence of resident Greeks goes far to explain the slow progress of the Greek language in Judaea,[69] whereas Jews in the Diaspora quickly adopted Greek as their sole vernacular. It also explains why in

Ben Sira's Judaea Hellenism was still no issue. There were few if any Greeks in the country to imitate. Cato could well have envied Judaea's freedom from Greeks.

The exclusion of resident Greeks removed from Judaea one important ingredient of Hellenism, but the exclusion in itself was certainly not directed at others of our traits of Hellenism. Not only Greeks but all idolaters were excluded from residence, and pagan Syrians seeking to enter Judaea may have been far more numerous than Greeks.

Against this background one can also easily understand how demand for the institutions of the gymnasium might have been slow to develop, and why no traces from this period have been found in Judaea of the typical Hellenistic structures, gymnasia and stadia and theatres.[70] How much was their absence owing to lack of demand, and how much to interpretations of the Torah which blocked their introduction? Whatever the answer, there is only one of our ingredients of Hellenism against which we can be sure that the expounders of the Torah in the earliest Hellenistic age put strong restrictions: contacts with Greeks were reduced by the absence of permanent Greek settlers. Nothing forbade Jews in the Diaspora to live among pagans; indeed, though some Jews of the Diaspora tried to avoid contact with pagans,[71] they could hardly achieve complete success. We can thus account for most of the contrasts between the Jews of Judaea and those of the Diaspora.

Concerning the other ingredients of Hellenism, there probably was controversy, and many believers, both in Judaea and in the Diaspora, may have been inclined to view them as having been permitted by the Torah. The significance of the second 'critical' period is that within it the course of history seemed to demonstrate that God himself viewed some of our distinguishing characteristics of Hellenism as abominations.

The critical period

Only a few years after Ben Sira wrote, fateful innovative movements brought on the critical period. Among some Jews of Judaea grew a desire for closer associations with Greeks and for the establishment of a gymnasium at Jerusalem. The leader of this group was Jason, brother of the incumbent high priest, Onias III.[72] The strange policies of the new Seleucid king, Antiochus IV, gave Jason his opportunity. I have argued that Antiochus IV sought to make his realm a fit match for the Roman empire by establishing republican institutions on the Roman model, an Antiochene republic with an Antiochene citizenship. I have presented evidence to show that among the civic institutions of the Antiochene republic were the gymnasium and the associated athletic and educational pursuits. Just as Roman citizens were able to mingle freely with one another, so should Antiochene citizens be. Near the beginning of his reign the king invited his subjects as communities or as individuals to accept Antiochene citizenship. Jason was quick to exploit the opportunity, in 175 or early in 174 BCE.[73] The king might have been sufficiently pleased by the acceptance of citizenship. When Jason added to the acceptance strong financial inducements, the extravagant king, perennially in need of money, not only issued decrees permitting the goals desired by Jason and his followers; he also deposed Jason's brother Onias and made Jason high priest in his place.[74]

The mere fact that Jason had to approach the king for permission shows that the hitherto prevailing interpretations of the Torah forbade important aspects of what he desired. We are told, indeed, that the king's decrees for Jason set aside the earlier 'humane concessions' which the ambassador John had won for the Jews, surely from Antiochus III.[75]

Unfortunately, we do not know the exact manner in which the dominant rigorists interpreted the Torah before Jason's reform. Theirs were the interpretations ratified by Antiochus III. Nor do we know the exact content of the decrees of Antiochus IV which enabled Jason to proceed. We must try to make sense of the somewhat incoherent clues in the sources.

Our earliest explicit information on Antiochus's decrees in response to Jason's petitions is in I and II Maccabees. Both texts were written over half a century after the events, so that in interpreting them, we would do well to look at any evidence contemporary with the events. Jason of Cyrene, the author of the work of which II Maccabees is an abridgement, quoted verbatim, near-contemporary evidence in the letter of Antiochus V to Lysias, which is datable in very late 164 or early 163 BCE.[76] That document refers to the decrees of Antiochus IV as 'the changeover to Greek practices' (τῇ ἐπὶ τὰ Ἑλληνικὰ μεταθέσει) (II Macc. 11.24).[77]

A document of Antiochus IV himself, dated in 166 BCE, can be used to confirm that he viewed his grants to Jason as in-

volving the introduction of Greek practices. In the document
the king states that the Samaritans are not to be punished along
with the Jews because they have proved that 'they are not
implicated in the charges against the Jews but rather live according to Greek ways'.[78]

What was permitted to Jason and his followers that had not
been permitted before? In the seemingly detailed account at II
Macc. 4.7–9, Jason applies for the power to establish a gymnasium and an ephebic organization and to draw up the list of
the Antiochenes in Jerusalem. Gymnasia and ephebic organizations were purely Greek, and to be an Antiochene citizen was
to be a citizen of a Greek commonwealth. Nevertheless, the
writer in II Maccabees does not let the word 'Greek' appear
either in his account of Jason's petition or in his report of the
king's decrees. *We* can draw the inference that the Jewish Antiochenes must have associated at Jerusalem quite freely with
Gentile Greek Antiochenes, but the writer in II Maccabees says
nothing of the kind. He presents the facts as if only Jason, not
Antiochus IV, perceived the Hellenizing implications of the
petition. Only after Jason has received from the king the coveted
powers does 'Hellenism' come on the scene,[79] purely through
Jason's perverse initiative.

The writer says that Jason 'overthrew the civic institutions of
the Torah' and 'brought in new usages which were contrary to
the law'. What new usages? Jason founded the gymnasium
'beneath the very citadel of Jerusalem', and he 'made the education of the noblest adolescent boys consist of submission to
the broad-brimmed Greek hat'.[80] The very peak of 'aping Greek
manners' (*Hellēnismos*) lay in the fact that priests were interested more in the activities of the gymnasium than in their tasks
as professional butchers in the offering of sacrifices![81] For anyone aware of how far Hellenism could go, with idolatry, sin
and truly complete abandonment of the Torah, the assertions
of Jason of Cyrene have a touch of the ridiculous. Nothing
explicit in the Torah forbade the existence of a gymnasium
down the slope from the temple itself; much less did anything
forbid a gymnasium beneath a secular citadel, manned at least
in part by Gentile soldiers.[82] Had the Hellenizers dared to ape
the Greeks completely by having the participants at the gymnasium of Jerusalem exercise naked, surely our indignant writer
would have trumpeted the fact! All he can say is that the boys

wore the broad-brimmed hats. Hence, at least they covered their loins (cf. Thucydides 1.6).

Some Jewish priests may have preferred the activities of the gymnasium to their duties in the temple, but the number of priests far exceeded the number required for temple functions.[83] We know that the offering of sacrifices at the temple remained uninterrupted until the fateful days in Kislev, 167 BCE, which saw the desecration of the temple and the full implementation of the punitive decrees of Antiochus IV.[84] So loyal to the Torah were the Hellenized Jewish participants in the pagan gymnastic games at Tyre, that they would not even go through the perfunctory form of paying their admission-fee until they received the assurance that the money would be employed for building ships rather than for the usual purpose of paying for a sacrifice to Tyrian Herakles.[85]

Thus the account in II Maccabees is strange indeed. We can readily find the reason why the writer did not use the word 'Greek' in summarizing the decrees of Antiochus IV and ascribed all the Hellenization to the wicked usurping high priest. At this stage of his narrative, the writer wished to portray Antiochus IV as an ordinary, reasonably benevolent Seleucid king. He believed that the sins of Jason and his followers brought God to turn Antiochus IV into the 'rod of his anger'.[86] But the evidence of II Macc. 11.24 shows that the royal government must have been aware of Hellenizing aspects in the decrees of Antiochus IV on behalf of Jason. Surely the word 'Greek' must have appeared somewhere in the decrees. The account in II Macc. 4 must therefore be tendentious and distorted. Probably the writer of II Maccabees could write as he did because he took II Macc. 11.24 to refer to the persecution rather than to Jason's 'reform'.[87]

The author of I Maccabees does not deign to mention the names of the wicked,[88] nor does he specify that their goal was Hellenization. He views the events from the perspective of a rigorous interpreter of the commandments in the Torah, in which Gentiles, not Greeks, are mentioned. He does not pretend to quote either the exact words of the Hellenizers' petition or those of the king's decrees. Rather, he describes their content and effects in terms taken from the Torah. For the author of I Maccabees, the goal of the new deviant group among the Jews was closer association with the neighbouring Gentiles. They presented a petition to the king, who granted them liberty to

follow the practices of the Gentiles.[89] 'Thereupon, they built a
gymnasium in Jerusalem according to the customs of the Gentiles . . . They joined themselves to the Gentiles and became
willing slaves to evil-doing.'[90]

Our author, unlike the writer of II Maccabees, openly condemns civic association with Gentiles. On the other hand, just
as the writer of II Maccabees identified the 'new usages contrary
to the law' only as the gymnasium and its activities, so the
author of I Maccabees identifies the 'practices of the Gentiles'
at first only as the gymnasium. He does go on to assert that the
deviants 'underwent operations to disguise their circumcision,
rebelling against the sacred covenant'.[91] Isolated cases of such
acts may have occurred then, as in many other periods, but
there is good evidence in the sources contemporary with the
events that our author's sweeping generalization here is false.[92]

Further removed from the time of the events, Josephus found
the basically accurate account in I Maccabees vague and unsatisfactory. In paraphrasing it,[93] he added what he thought was
precision: the Jewish deviants wished to *desert* the ancestral
laws and to follow the *Greek* way of life. He infers that the Jews
in the gymnasium exercised naked. The added precision probably reflects Josephus' preconceptions. Using another source,
Josephus identified the deviants as Menelaus and the Tobiads.
I show elsewhere that Josephus' other source contains untrust-
worthy material.[94] Hence, we need give no further consideration
tion here to Josephus's account.

In the absence of good evidence, we can only guess at how
the content of Antiochus' decrees made it possible for the royal
government to refer to them as 'the changeover to Greek practices'. We may assume that the decrees provided that Greek
law rather than the Torah was to be followed in at least some
aspects, which surely included those touching the civic pursuits
of the Jews who became Antiochenes.

The authors of both I and II Maccabees are indignant over the
wicked acts of the deviants, but neither reports that pious Jews
resisted the deviants in any way until much later. Indeed, both
authors imply that the wickedness of the deviants and the
acquiescence of the pious roused the wrath of God, who turned
Antiochus IV into the rod of his anger.[95] Hecataeus of Abdera
reported how in his times pious Jews took to violence and faced
martyrdom rather than tolerate on their soil the things known
to provoke the wrath of God.[96] We can explain the acquiescence

of the pious to the programme of the high priest Jason only if the vast majority of Jews at the time saw nothing contrary to the Torah in it. The assertions in I and II Maccabees, that Jason's programme constituted heinous sin, would then be conclusions after the fact. If God himself suddenly allowed the sacking of Jerusalem and of the temple and thereafter the desecration of the temple and the persecution of the Jews, he must have been suddenly and grievously provoked by sin. Only one set of great innovations came in the years which just preceded those disasters: the 'reforms' of the high priest Jason. How could they not be the cause of God's wrath?

Fortunately, we have Jewish sources contemporary with the events to let us know that the authors of I and II Maccabees are indeed giving us judgments after the fact, and we also have sources after the time of the events which disagree with the judgments in I and II Maccabees.

For our purposes, the book of Jubilees is the most important of the contemporary sources. It was written between autumn, 169, and spring 167 BCE,[97] almost in the immediate aftermath of Jason's reforms. The book shows that the author and his sect[98] regarded some aspects of Jason's policies as violations of the will of God. Running through the entire book is the theme that God requires Israel to shun *all* Gentiles, including Greeks.[99] I Macc. 1.11 thus could reflect misgivings of contemporaries of the events. On the other hand, nothing in Jubilees attacks the institution of a gymnasium at Jerusalem. Since the participants there did not exercise naked, at most Jub. 3.31 is a warning against the possibility that they might do so.

Already in his own time, the author of Jubilees had to explain how God, beginning in 169 BCE, could permit 'the sinners, the Gentiles', to perpetrate cruel attacks upon the Jews and sack their city and their temple. In cataloguing the sins which brought God to do so,[100] the author says not a word about a gymnasium or about imitating the Gentiles or about idolatry. His chief concern seems to be with violations of Jewish laws peculiar to his own sect, especially those requiring a calendar with a 364-day year and a 49-year jubilee, as well as rules of ritual purity. The author's 'prediction' to Moses reflects how the sect came violently to resist the wicked,[101] who, however, are described not as Hellenizers but as embezzlers, robbers, and violators of the laws of ritual purity. On recalling the detailed narrative of II Maccabees,[102] we recognize here the sins of the high priest Menelaus[103] rather than the Hellenizing reforms of Jason.

Written even earlier than Jubilees was the earliest stratum of Enoch 85–90.[104] Somewhat later is Dan. 7–12, written at various times between spring 167 and summer 163 BCE.[105] In Enoch 90.1–19 and Dan. 11.5–39 there are surveys of the important events or trends in the history of the Jews and their region under the rule of the Ptolemies and the Seleucids. If Jason's acts had been of pivotal importance, they would have been singled out for mention in both surveys. Far from ascribing the sack or the persecution to the effects of Jason's programme, Enoch and Daniel do not even allude to Jason's Hellenizing reform as an event. Jason's reform occurred at the beginning of the reign of Antiochus IV, in 175 or 174 BCE. Acts of violence against the Jews in the reign of Antiochus IV did not begin until after Menelaus became high priest in 172 BCE. At most, Jason and the Hellenizers are included among the 'blind sheep' of Enoch 90.7f. (a passage which refers to the acts of violence against the Jews perpetrated in the reign of Antiochus IV) and among the 'deserters of the Holy Covenant' of Dan. 11.30 (a verse which describes only events of 168 BCE).[106]

The Testament of Moses was written in 166 or early in 165 BCE,[107] and it places part of the blame of the disasters on the contemporary sins of Israel. But the sins are listed as sectarian division over interpretation of the Torah, perversion of justice, and ritual defilement of the temple, especially by unfit priests.[108] The words suggesting that idolatry was involved contradict our other sources and are probably an interpolation.[109]

Thus, of the contemporary sources, only Jubilees expresses concern over closer contacts with Gentiles. Not even one contemporary source speaks out against the gymnasium or against any of the reforms of Jason or regards them as the cause of God's subsequent wrath. We may conclude that the authors of I and II Maccabees were truthful in implying that there was no resistance to the introduction of Jason's programme: most pious Jews then believed that his Hellenizing innovations were not serious violations of the Torah.

The third and fourth periods

I Maccabees is propaganda for the Hasmonaean kings and may well reflect the opinions of early members of the dynasty.[110]

Already Mattathias and Judas Maccabaeus may have held that the 'covenant with the Gentiles' and the gymnasium were what roused the wrath of God. The writer of II Maccabees, who so often disagrees with I Maccabees, here agrees on the gymnasium as the cause which provoked God's wrath. We must take note of another striking feature in I and II Maccabees. In neither book is there a report of the closing or destruction of the gymnasium. One can only guess at the reason for such silence. Could it be that the Hellenizers themselves were appalled at the effects of the divine wrath and closed the gymnasium? Could Menelaus himself have been the one who put an end to the gymnasium? In any case, most pious Jews eventually came to agree that the gymnasium brought dire punishment upon Israel.

Nevertheless, from Hasmonaean-ruled Jerusalem two strange documents survive. We have them preserved, one quoted within the other, at II Macc. 1.1–10.[111] In a letter of 143 BCE, the Jews of Judaea and Jerusalem called upon the Jews of Egypt to observe the 'Days of Tabernacles in the month of Kislev', i.e., the festival of Hanukkah. The writers describe the persecution as punishment for sins of the high priest Jason but say *nothing* of his Hellenizing policies. One might explain this peculiar silence by suggesting that the writers were being tactful with their audience, the Greek-speaking Jews of Egypt. It is likely, however, that the senders, like the authors of Jubilees, Enoch, Daniel, and the Testament of Moses, still did not regard Jason's Hellenizing policies as heinous sin. Late in 124 BCE, a second letter from the Jews of Judaea and Jerusalem went out to the Jews of Egypt, to the same effect.

Despite this surprising evidence, we can infer from the points of agreement between I and II Maccabees that after the critical period most Jews believed God's wrath would be roused if they tolerated either permanent Gentile residents or a gymnasium in any part of the Holy Land held by Jews.[112] Pious Jews seem to have inferred from God's disapproval of a gymnasium in Judaea that he would also be displeased there by the other large structures characteristic of Greek culture: theatres, stadia and hippodromes.[113]

Before the critical period theatres and the other structures may have been absent from Judaea proper only because there was no demand for them. Archaeology and the explicit testimony of Josephus show that Herod was the first to dare to erect theatres and amphitheatres in Judaea proper.[114] Though Herod built gymnasia for pagan cities outside Judaea,[115] apparently even he did not dare to build one in Judaea proper.[116]

Jews thus inferred from the harsh facts of history that God hated the residence of pagans in the Holy Land and the presence there of the characteristic Greek structures. Most Jews seem to have refrained from further generalizing to conclude that God hated the introduction there of the other distinguishing characteristics of Hellenism. Nevertheless, we have seen how biblical texts could be interpreted as excluding all the characteristics which we listed above, and it is conceivable that in the third of our periods (the time between the end of the critical period and the death of the Hasmonaean prince Simon) some Jews drew the broad inference that all our traits of Hellenism were forbidden. We have one important piece of evidence on this topic: the *Letter of Aristeas to Philocrates* which was written c. 138 BCE.[117] In my view *Aristeas* is a reply to claims that now Jews must not live in the Diaspora, must not submit to pagan rulers, must not use Greek, must not associate with Greeks, must not read Greek literature, and must not dabble in Greek philosophy.[118] The work demonstrates that pious Jews did all those things and prospered and produced an authoritative Greek translation of the Torah. Even the author of *Aristeas* does not venture to suggest that Jews can participate in gymnasia, and though he gives a favourable opinion of watching serious plays in the theatre, he recommends them only to the pagan king, not to Jews.[119] Association with Gentiles can be compatible with the Torah, he suggests, but only if the laws of diet, ritual purity, and abstinence from idolatry are strictly observed.[120]

The probable opponents against whom *Aristeas* was written may have been the last considerable group of Jews to take the extreme position, the one regarding all our traits of Hellenism as forbidden. At least, I have found no further traces of such a group. The author of *Aristeas* is more cautious about association with Greeks and approval of the theatre than were later writers from the Jewish Diaspora.

Indeed, God had manifested his wrath against association with Gentiles and against the building of a gymnasium only in the case of the Holy Land, never in the case of the Diaspora. From the last of our four periods of ancient Jewish history we have good evidence that Jews believed all our traits of Hellenism to be permitted by God to Israelites living on Gentile soil.[121]

The synagogue of Delos, first built in the second or early first century BCE, was situated near the gymnasium and the stadium, and after the gymnasium was abandoned, stones from it were used to build a partition-wall inside the synagogue.[122] Unfortunately, nothing informs us whether the Jews at Delos who used the synagogue also participated in the gymnasium. However, the great synagogue of Sardis, begun in the second half of the second century CE, was an integral part of the gymnasium complex.[123] Jews of Antioch who were too pious to use the oil of pagans nevertheless seem to have participated in the gymnasium there.[124]

Philo admits he has seen plays in the theatre[125] and has watched the fights of pancratiasts in the stadium.[126] He takes it for granted that cities contain gymnasia[127] and that parents see to it that their children receive training in one.[128] He freely uses metaphors taken from the gymnasium.[129] From the Emperor Claudius we learn that Jews infuriated the pagans of Alexandria by intruding themselves into the games presided over by the gymnasiarchs and ephebic officials of the city.[130] Rabbinic authorities disapproved of the close and friendly social contacts between Jews of the Diaspora and their pagan neighbours, but even the rabbis felt compelled to be lenient.[131] On the other hand, there is no sign that the pious in Judaea ever believed that God might accept a Jewish gymnasium or theatre in the Holy Land.

Conclusion

We have now considered throughout our four periods of Jewish history those of our aspects of Hellenism which Jews came to reject most, as a result of the experiences of the critical period. I do not propose to examine in detail the voluminous literary sources reflecting the Jews' acceptance and rejection of our traits of Hellenism from the death of the Hasmonaean prince Simon down to the completion of the Babylonian Talmud. The general picture is that the Jews regarded each one – with the exception of participation in the gymnasium and unlimited association with Greeks – as permissible and sometimes even desirable.

In Judaea itself, pious Jews and Hasmonaean princes bore Greek names and spoke Greek. King Aristobulus I was called *Philhellēn*.[132] Hasmonaean rulers put Greek legends on their coins. Although the Hasmonaeans were bitterly opposed by some of the pious Jewish sects, in no ancient source do we find them condemned for Hellenizing. The Qumran texts never mention the sin of imitating the Greeks. Josephus, writing for a Greek audience, could well abstain from adverse judgments upon Herod as a Hellenizer in summarizing the king's character.[133] But *no* ancient Jewish or Christian writer attacks Herod for being a Hellenizer.[134]

A pious Jew not only translated the Hebrew book of Esther into Greek; he also altered it to fit the patterns of Greek romances.[135] Rabbis in Jewish Palestine used Greek widely and praised the Greek language.[136] Only in a period of grave stress did they decree that Greek not be taught to Jewish children.[137]

Aristobulus' comments on the Torah,[138] the books of Wisdom and of IV Maccabees, and Philo's writings give eloquent testimony to how pious Jews in the Diaspora could adopt and study Greek philosophy. Jason of Cyrene himself took pains to have the martyred sage Eleazar resemble Socrates in character.[139] The rabbis believed in devoting almost all their waking hours to Torah. Nevertheless, they did not forbid the *study* of philosophy. Whatever the supposed rabbinic ban on teaching *ḥokmat yevanit* ('Greek wisdom'?) was, it is unlikely to have been a ban on philosophy, and we hear how the patriarch Gamaliel II himself kept five hundred Jewish youths studying *ḥokmat yevanit!*[140]

Plato banned the reading of Homer from his projected ideal state.[141] In the Diaspora, the Jewish sibyl calls Homer a liar and a plagiarizer, but praises his art and certainly does not suggest that his poems must not be read.[142] The rabbis specifically forbid Jews to read the book of Ben Sira and permit them to read the books of Homer and later Greek authors.[143] Only once in the whole Babylonian Talmud is there any suggestion that Greek literature can lead to ruin. The question is asked concerning the heretical Rabbi Elisha b. Abuyah: why did not his knowledge of Torah protect him from error? The answer is given: because he was continually singing Greek songs.[144] The isolation of this instance speaks for itself.

Jewish rejection of the gymnasium in the Holy Land continued. In principle, Jews also continued to believe that God wanted to exclude Gentile residents and idolatry from Judaea, but they had to yield to the pressure of events. When the Romans put an end to the independence of Hasmonaean Judaea, they restored the Greek cities of Palestine,[145] and Jews could hardly prevent the residence of pagans and the practice of pagan religion on what they still regarded as their own soil.[146] The situation became much worse with the influx of Gentiles and the removal of Jews after the failure of the revolts against Rome. Jews had to acquiesce. Even so, Jews did what they could to exclude idolatry and keep to a minimum the number of Gentiles residing in the Holy Land.[147]

How, then, can we explain the contrast between the Jews and the conservative Romans? The factor of the long absence of Greeks from Judaea proper goes far to explain the phenomena in Judaea, but the Jews of the Diaspora lived surrounded by Greeks. Perhaps we can suggest an answer along the lines of the McMaster project: Romans, long before the moral crisis of the time of Cato, had been exposed to Greek influences. Roman religion had come in large measure to be identified with Greek religion. Greek Bacchus was worshipped at Rome on the Aventine hill. Roman Jupiter was held to be Zeus, etc. Conservative Romans felt it urgent to distinguish themselves from immoral Greeks. It was a problem of self-definition. The Jews, in contrast, found their self-definition in the Torah, which sufficed to distinguish them from any pagan, Greek or non-Greek. The 'immoral' traits which so shocked Cato drew the opposition of Greek moralists as well. Jews knew that some Greeks lived upright lives. As for the other Greeks, Jews saw them as no more wicked than the rest of the pagans and viewed them on a par with Syrians, Phoenicians and Babylonians.

To summarize: initially the Jews were open to all our traits of Hellenism, except that Greeks were excluded from residence in Judaea proper. This exclusion slowed the growth of a demand for the introduction of non-idolatrous Hellenistic patterns into Judaea. When that demand finally developed, in the 170s BCE, Hellenistic patterns, of the gymnasium and of civic organization, came to Jerusalem, and there was no resistance by pious Jews. A complex and unforeseeable series of events brought it about that Antiochus IV punished the Jews severely and imposed upon them a cult which they viewed as pagan. In accordance with hints in scripture, pious Jews inferred that God in wrath had used Antiochus as the rod of his anger, but that Antiochus had arrogantly exceeded his mandate.[148] The inference allowed the Jews to resist Antiochus. Surprisingly, they won. They still had to ponder the question: what was the cause of God's wrath? Though not all Jews agreed, the ruling Hasmonaeans and many of their opponents came to believe that it was the existence, on the holy soil, of the gymnasium and of close associations with Gentiles. Thereafter, the Jews of Judaea never again built a gymnasium. Many Jews also held that God forbade the other characteristic Greek structures: theatres, stadia, and hippodromes. As long as Jews had the power, they barred Gentiles from permanent residence in Judaea proper. In the Diaspora, God had never demonstrated his opposition to Jewish participation even in these aspects of Hellenism. As for Jewish participation in the other aspects, God had shown no opposition either in Judaea or in the Diaspora, and we find Jews throughout regarding them as permitted.

5

Limits of Tolerance in Judaism: The Samaritan Example

FERDINAND DEXINGER

Preliminary remarks

The purpose of this paper in the context of the symposium is to try to provide a description of the limits of tolerance in Judaism in terms of the example of the Samaritans. At first glance the procedure would seem to be very straightforward. First one would determine how the Samaritans evolved. Then the causes which led to the schism would be brought forward. This process should indicate the limits which were transgressed at the point of the break with Judaism.

It is impossible, however, to proceed in this way. The origin of the Samaritans is not so unambiguous that such a simple procedure can be followed. The sources provide only some clues with which one can try to reconstruct the origin of the movement. It goes without saying that such a reconstruction will not be free from subjective elements. This applies to the Jewish attitude of that time, and also to the self-understanding of the Samaritans and the scholarly attempt to describe the origin of the Samaritans.

It is not the purpose of this paper to propose a new theory about the origin of the Samaritans; what is required, rather, is to form a unified picture from the many separate observations made in Samaritan studies over the last number of years. Thus, besides its stated purpose in the context of the symposium, this paper will also clarify the origin of the Samaritans; and this is a task which also needs to be done. For in spite of the advances in Samaritan studies, the outdated theories which connect the Samaritans with the Cuthians are still held and propagated.

One more basic observation needs to be made. In discussing

the Samaritans in the symposium it should not be argued *a priori* that they moved away from the root of Judaism at some time or other and thus transgressed the limits of tolerance. A further aspect is that the Samaritans would not be relevant as a topic for the symposium if they were nothing more than partially converted Gentiles who never came within the limits of tolerance of Judaism, but always stood outside. This already raises the question whether there existed at some time or other a normative Judaism to which the Samaritans either had to be converted or from which viewpoint they appeared as violators of the limits of tolerance.

The problem as formulated here is, of course, one-sided. For it is also quite possible to speak of the limits of tolerance in Samaritanism and to view rabbinic Judaism as the violator of the limits of tolerance. As a matter of fact this is done in Samaritan sources.

In the following pages the relevant sources will be analysed. The evidence of the history of the tradition in these texts will also gradually outline the limits of tolerance.

The origin of the Samaritans and II Kings 17

II Kings 17 reports the situation after the fall of the northern kingdom. The rabbinic literature[1] as well as earlier scholarship[2] regarded the events related there as a description of the origin of the Samaritans. More recently scholars have questioned whether the text supports this interpretation. From the outset one must distinguish carefully between the original meaning of II Kings 17.24–41 and the effects it had at a later point. These effects become apparent exactly in the era with which the symposium is concerned. The theological intent behind the incorporation into the book of Kings after the exile[3] of the portion of text in question is proven by the formula 'until this day' (*'ad hayyom hazzeh*). The critical question is against whom the polemic of this text portion is directed. On the basis of II Kings 17.29 this should be clear; the '*somronim*' are mentioned here. But are these the Samaritans in the present sense of the word?

Recently Coggins[4] and Talmon[5] have dealt with II Kings 17 in connection with the problem of the Samaritans. Talmon undertook a more precise literary delimitation of II Kings 17.5–41 in relation to the context. There can be no doubt that the pericope in question was inserted in its present context at a later point.[6] Coggins considers the passage a deuteronomic element. But in contrast to Talmon he isolates two sources in II Kings 17.24–41. The first runs from II Kings 17.25–28 while the second includes II Kings 17.29–31 and 34b–40. Thus he sets the formula *'ad hayyom hazzeh* in II Kings 17.34a and 41 apart as a later *relecture*.

One could put forward the thesis that the layers of tradition which can be distinguished indicate three successive stages of reinterpretation.

II Kings 17.25–28 directs its negative emphasis against Bethel.[7]

II Kings 17.29–31 and 34b–40 explain the syncretism in the north.[8]

II Kings 17.34a and 41 re-use the preceding negative aspects for a contemporary polemic.

The question should be raised when this polemic was relevant. The formula *'ad hayyom hazzeh* points towards the origin of the final *relecture* in the work of the Chronicler. The contemporary polemic of the Chronicler reinterprets the two earlier layers, namely the deuteronomic (II Kings 17.25–28) and the somewhat later one (II Kings 17.29–31, 34b–40), in a sense which becomes clear in Ezra 4.1–5. Ezra 4.2b establishes the relationship to II Kings 17. The preceding layers of tradition are interpreted by means of II Kings 17.34a, 41 in such a way that they can function as the basis for the rejection of the inhabitants of the north found in Ezra 4.1–5. It is conceivable that II Kings 17.29–31, 34b–40 belong to the Hebrew source which is also the foundation of Ezra 1.1–4.5.[9] The additions of the Chronicler which encompass II Kings 17.32–34a, 41[10] must have originated in about the fourth century BCE.

II Kings 17.25–41 and Ezra 4.1–5 must be seen as a unit. From whom the Chronicler wants to differentiate himself and what the limits of tolerance are in this case must be discussed in connection with the analysis of the passage in Ezra. A few observations in connection with II Kings 17 must still be added.

An important starting-point for all later interpretations of II Kings 17.25–41 is the circumstance that reading it leaves the impression that the *whole* populace of the northern kingdom was deported after 722 BCE. Stiehl pointed out[11] correctly that II Kings 23.19 actually contradicts II Kings 17.24, since the former contains the historically more plausible picture in which not all subjects of the former northern kingdom were deported.[12] Accordingly, it is clear that after the destruction of the northern kingdom two distinct groups of people were living side by side in Samaria. These were the Israelites of the northern kingdom and the newly arrived Gentile settlers.[13] In this context it must now be clarified who the *somronim*, mentioned in II Kings 17.29, are. The intent of this whole post-deuteronomic pericope is to explain the syncretistic religion of the populace of the north as a consequence of the apostasy of the northern Israelites after the division of the kingdom. Since the passage presupposes the complete deportation of all the subjects of the former northern kingdom, no other interpretation is possible than that the *somronim* refer to the northern Israelites and not, as Coggins assumes,[14] to the pagan settlers.

Traditional Jewish commentators had already clearly recognized this situation. Rashi comments on the passage: '. . . which the *somronim* had made, i.e. Israel, when it was still there.' In a similar vein Radak (David Kimhi) explains: ' "The *Somronim* made" refers to the Israelites when they were still in Samaria and (it happened) on the high places which they had made.' No reference is made to a Samaritan temple on Mount Gerizim,[15] but to a continued use of the holy places.

A sober analysis of the text in view of the actual historical circumstances after the fall of the northern kingdom allows for the following reconstruction. The report in II Kings 17 is not a description of historical facts but a post-exilic polemic with the purpose of justifying the rejection of the Gentile worshippers of the God of Israel, who were living in the former northern kingdom.[16] Because of this interpretation in the last phase of the history of the tradition of II Kings 17, the passage must be seen in close connection with Ezra 4.1–5.

Therefore, since II Kings 17 originally had nothing to do with the origin of the Samaritans, but only referred to the syncretistic population of the north, a longer process must be assumed before the condemnation of the syncretistic settlers of the north was finally applied to the orthodox part of the population. A first step in this direction was the Chronicler's description of the events during the reconstruction of the temple in Jerusalem.

The reconstruction of the temple in Jerusalem and the preventive measures of Ezra

The central text which should concern us here is Ezra 4.1–5. Time and again this account was taken to refer to the relationship between the Jews and the Samaritans. In this passage two kinds of opponents of the returned exiles are mentioned. They are the 'enemies of Judah and Benjamin' (Ezra 4.1) on the one hand and the 'people of the land' (*'am ha 'ares*) on the other. But nowhere is there a term which could unequivocally be taken to refer to the Samaritans. The opponents mentioned are located outside the province of Judah. The relationship of Judah to Samaria at this time was largely determined by the political realities. Regardless of whether one assumes an early or a late dating,[17] in Ezra's time Judah was governed politically by Samaria.[18] An interesting testimony to this is Papyrus 30 (Cowley's numbering) from Elephantine. The Jewish community there takes its request to Samaria first and only later to Jerusalem. This letter, which dates from the year 408 BCE, also shows that there was not yet a religious break between Jerusalem and Samaria.[19] This does not mean that there were no tensions, religious as well as political.

In order to understand these tensions better, it is necessary to define the population structure in Samaria more exactly. To do this, it is of primary importance to make a terminological distinction and to apply it consistently. The Jewish population of the north, from which the Samaritans later developed, should be called 'proto-Samaritans' from Ezra's time on. The Gentile inhabitants of Samaria, on the other hand, should be called 'Samarians'.[20]

Although the sources do not say so specifically, it can be inferred from II Kings 23.19 that the proto-Samaritans had a cultic place, but probably not yet a temple, on Mount Gerizim.[21] For these proto-Samaritans Jerusalem was a generally recognized holy place (cf. II Chron. 35.18). They could not, however, accept its exclusive claims. After all, not until shortly before the exile (II Kings 23.15–19) had Josiah tried to enforce these claims. This attitude of the proto-Samaritans must have looked suspicious to those returning from exile. The difference between them and the Samarians could only too easily be overlooked.

It is against this background that the two antagonistic parties mentioned in Ezra 4.1–5 need to be identified. Although the proto-Samaritans were certainly not ill-disposed towards the holy place in Jerusalem, the Samarians had a certain interest in it for political reasons. If the political interests of the Samarians were not to conflict with the building of the temple, it would, of course, be necessary that it remain under their control. The Gentile population of Samaria, however, had also no religious qualms about participating in the Yahweh cult. In whatever way one views the role of Ezra, it certainly was not compatible with the ideas of the Samarians.[22] This becomes clear, for example, in the arguments of Koch which so aptly describe the functions of Ezra: (*a*) 'Ezra's march from Babylonia to Jerusalem was a cultic procession which Ezra understood as a second Exodus and a partial fulfilment of prophetic expectations.'[23] (*b*) 'Ezra came to Jerusalem as the real high priest of the family of Aaron. His purpose was to change his people into a "holy seed" around the holy place, which God had given as a tent-peg and source of life during the times of political servitude.'[24] Smith is justified in asking whether the fulfilment of these tasks would not, as already in the time of Josiah, include the removal of all possible cultic places in the north.[25] But the Samarians would effectively have thwarted such a measure.

Ezra 4.1–5 should be seen in this light. The 'enemies of Judah and Benjamin' mentioned there are the Samarians on the basis of the unambiguous allusion to II Kings 17.24–41. In the eyes of the Chronicler, they are only half converted.[26] If one does not want to go so far as to label the whole story 'a figment of the imagination of the Chronicler',[27] then one can see in the references to the second group of opponents, the *ʿam haʾareṣ*, an allusion to the Jewish part of the population which, in contrast to the exiles, had remained in the land.[28] Thus one must agree with Bickerman that in Ezra 4.3 it is not the proto-Samaritans who are rejected,[29] but rather the Samaritans, who had a syncretistic cult and wanted to exert their influence also in Jerusalem. That the book of Ezra refers here to the non-Jewish settlers follows from the connection between Ezra 4.2 and Ezra 4.10.[30]

At this point one must guard oneself against too hastily identifying the people from the north with the Samaritans. This was Coggins' original opinion which he later revised. He now correctly sees it as a caricature of the purpose of the Chronicler to assume that Ezra 4.1–4 in its present context refers to the Samaritans.[31] Unfortunately, Talmon again overlooks the possibility that neither place in Ezra 4 refers to the really Jewish Yahweh worshippers, but to the ethnically and religiously mixed Samarian population.[32] Ezra 4.4 shows the ʿam haʾareṣ to be the real, active opponents of the building of the temple, which makes them appear as collaborators of their Gentile, political leaders. There can be no doubt that this constitutes a first step in the disqualification of that part of the population which had not been exiled, a step which reaches its culmination later in the writings of Flavius Josephus. The fact that II Chron. 30.6–10 does not deny the existence of pious Jews in the north, even after the deportation to Assyria, proves that the total disqualification of a later time did not yet exist at the time of the Chronicler.[33] Thus no anti-Samaritan tendency can be attributed to Ezra 4.1–5, and it is not possible to speak of Samaritans in the time of Ezra.

The question remains what really was the concern of the Chronicler. But before considering this, the third of Koch's theses about the tasks of Ezra should be discussed. This third thesis can be accepted here on the condition that the term 'Samaritans' be replaced by the more exact name 'proto-Samaritans'. Koch himself recognizes, albeit indirectly, that there were no Samaritans then, in the actual sense of the word, when he points out that in Ezra 9.1 the Samaritans have not even been mentioned yet.[34] As far as Ezra is concerned, there are only members of the northern tribes. From this point of view the third of Koch's theses is also acceptable: (c) Ezra was sent 'to all his people beyond the river', including the Samaritans. His aim was to establish one Israel out of all twelve tribes, which explains the later acceptance of the Pentateuch by the Samaritans.[35] Against this background the actual intention of the Chronicler becomes clear. He wants to emphasize (cf. II Chron. 30.6–10) the uniqueness of Jerusalem without, however, explicitly polemicizing against other holy places.[36] Ezra 4.4 shows the seam where the historically correct tradition of the rejection of the Gentile Samarian upper class from participating in the building of the temple is joined to the depreciation,[37] started by the Chronicler, of the ʿam haʾareṣ as a group not respecting the temple monopoly of Jerusalem. In II Chron. 13.4–12 the main concern of the Chronicler becomes clear inasmuch as the topic there is the exclusive legitimacy of Jerusalem.[38] Another characteristic of the Chronicler is that, although he is opposed to other holy places, he does not have the same negative attitude towards the peoples who worship there. Proof of this is provided by the fact that there is no parallel to II Kings 17 in the books of Chronicles.[39]

In analysing Ezra 4.1–5, therefore, we must distinguish the historical core from the trimmings supplied by the Chronicler, especially the efforts to establish a centralized cult in Jerusalem. When the Chronicles were written, this concern received a literary elaboration which gave it more prominence than it in fact had at the time of Ezra. Looking at it this way, we may easily recognize the original purpose behind the rejection.[40] The new community in Jerusalem did not want to have anything to do with syncretistic Gentiles. Already the people of Jerusalem on the whole were sceptical of the proto-Samaritans. What was true for the immediate post-exilic era, was even more appropriate at the time the Chronicles were written. The same may also be true for another aspect of this problem. It is obvious that priestly interests joined to purely political motives were competing here. II Chron. 13.4–12 contains a plea for the exclusive legitimacy of the priesthood of Jerusalem.[41] The Chronicler's view is the product of a spiritual controversy about the rebuilding of the temple in Jerusalem and its significance which lasted more than a hundred years[42] (cf. Ezra 4.5).

Both at the time of Ezra[43] and when the Chronicler was writing his history, the limits of tolerance were not considered to have been violated either in the eyes of the Judaeans or from the viewpoint of the proto-Samaritans. Nevertheless, there were two sources of considerable tension: first the existence of the cult on Mount Gerizim and then the fact that the proto-Samaritans had not been part of the development of self-awareness of the religion of Yahweh during the exile – especially the emphasis on the uniqueness of Jerusalem. This tension, together with the political realities, started a process which later led to the actual schism.[44] Thus we see that the limits of tolerance are defined over the course of a long history and cannot be regarded as springing from an isolated fact. In every case – and here Judaism is not an exception – schisms are the result of a gradual drifting apart.

About 300 BCE the controversy about the centralization of worship provides one such potential cause for separation. Interwoven with this are questions about the legitimacy of the priesthood and the self-esteem of each of the two groups which are associated with specific holy places. Concretely this means that the claim of uniqueness by the exiles who had returned to Judaea grew stronger. But this claim did not constitute a limit of tolerance until, under another pretext, it was also made binding upon the north.

The building of the temple on Mount Gerizim

Only Flavius Josephus reports the building of a temple on Mount Gerizim. This could lead to the opinion that one is dealing here with a late tradition from the first century CE. But an analysis of the Josephus text (*Ant.* XI. 302–47) shows that it deals with material which is much older. The history of tradition of this section is very complex.[45] Yet a careful analysis not only provides information about the building of the temple on Mount Gerizim, but also highlights other aspects of the increasing tension between Jerusalem and Shechem. It is not possible in the present context to discuss all the particulars of the source differentiation in the report of Josephus. The important findings of Büchler[46] on this matter should be supplemented primarily by the observations of Shmueli[47] and Segal.[48] In this way five units can be distinguished; these will be named for their main theme or their origin.

(a) The Macedonian source: *Ant.* XI.304f., 313–314, 317 up to and including ἐπολιόρκει Τύρον; XI.320 starting with λαμβάνει τὴν Τύρον.

(b) The proto-Samaritan Sanballat source (end of third century BCE): *Ant.* XI. 321, 324: συγχωρήσαντος δὲ ᾿Αλεξάνδρου, πᾶσαν εἰσενεγκάμενος σπουδὴν ᾠκοδόμησεν ὁ Σανβαλλέτης τὸν ναόν. Inserted into this Samaritan source is another tradition connected with Sanballat, in which the holy place on Mount Gerizim is connected with apostate priests from Jerusalem. Whereas the Samaritan Sanballat source shows a clearly positive attitude towards the cult on Mount Gerizim, the tradition which centres on Manasseh is opposed to the Mount Gerizim cult. Thus it must be a Jewish tradition which emphasizes the illegitimate character of this cult and its adherents.[49] This Jewish source is:

(c) The Manasseh source (approx. 170 BCE): *Ant.* XI.315f., 322f. By means of his own editorial parenthesis [comprised of *Ant.* XI.324, except the words quoted under section (b), and *Ant.* XI.325] Josephus connected this Jewish source to another Jewish tradition.[50] This second Jewish tradition is:

(*d*) The Jaddua source (at the time of Caesar): *Ant.* XI.317–20, 326–39. Joined to this is yet a further Jewish tradition which is an explicit reaction to the Samaritan Sanballat source.

(*e*) The anti-Sanballat source (probably later than [*d*]): *Ant.* XI.340–45.

If one succeeds in ordering these traditions connected by Josephus in a relative chronology, and then in establishing an absolute chronology, the report of Josephus offers an excellent source for determining the relationship between Jerusalem and Shechem from the fourth century BCE until the time of Josephus. But as far as method goes the situation is that, although the description by Josephus has been treated time and again in the literature, the rich contours of the history of tradition which it contains were hardly used to shed light upon the events between the fourth and second centuries BCE.

With the Macedonian source, Josephus laid down the absolute chronological framework. Whether this actually holds true for all the inserted elements remains to be tested by the following literary-critical examination. The Jewish Manasseh source is evidently a reaction to the Samaritan Sanballat source, making the latter appear to be the oldest of the five sources mentioned. Behind the Jewish reaction are events which are reported in Neh. 13.28. Another Jewish reaction to the Sanballat source is the Jaddua source. Its aim is to weaken or even refute the Samaritans' claim that the legitimacy of their temple was acknowledged by Alexander the Great. The relation between Jaddua and Alexander the Great is the mirror image of that between Sanballat and Alexander the Great. The anti-Sanballat source follows the same lines as the Jaddua source, and since it presupposes the latter, it originated at a later time. For the visit of Alexander the Great to Jerusalem is the starting point of its anti-Samaritan polemic. Thus a relative chronology puts the traditions in the order (*b*), (*c*), (*d*), (*e*).

In the context of the question about the origin of the Samaritan 'schism' the building of the temple on Mount Gerizim has been posed frequently as the decisive factor.[51] That Josephus does not use his sources at all for the purpose of establishing the origin of the Samaritans was usually overlooked.[52] He had done that already in the interpretation of II Kings 17 which appears in *Ant.* IX.288–91. Here Josephus is concerned only with establishing the illegitimacy of the Mount Gerizim cult over against competing claims from the side of the Samaritans.

Nor is he interested in describing the *first* construction of a shrine on Mount Gerizim,[53] but only in the construction of a temple.

When the individual traditions are tested for their historicity, it becomes clear from their respective literary genres that only the proto-Samaritan Sanballat source and the Jewish Manasseh source can have a historical background.

First, however, there is the problem of dating. From Neh. 13.28 we know of a Sanballat, but he lived one hundred years before the Sanballat of Josephus.[54] The Samaria papyri from Wadi Daliyen, however, have now opened the possibility of identifying the Sanballat mentioned by Josephus as a contemporary of Alexander the Great and of distinguishing him from the one in Neh. 13.28.[55] This Sanballat could be called Sanballat III. One no longer needs to assume, as was customary in the past,[56] a historical error on the part of Josephus or, to be more exact, of the proto-Samaritan Sanballat source. It is remarkable that in this source Sanballat is called neither Samaritan nor Cuthian.[57] Since this is the only report from antiquity about the building of the Samaritan temple on Mount Gerizim it is impossible to compare it with other descriptions. Since Sanballat seems to be linked to Darius III, it follows that the building of the proto-Samaritan temple on Mount Gerizim took place in the last third of the fourth century BCE.[58] The emphasis on special permission from Alexander the Great should be viewed as an aetiology meant for a Hellenistic audience.[59] The report by Sanballat III[60] on the building of the temple would thus remain as the historical core. Then the reference to Alexander the Great could be ascribed to faulty dating rather than an overstatement.[61]

Can Josephus, or his proto-Samaritan Sanballat source, possibly be correct in placing the start of the building of the temple in the fourth century? The Elephantine papyri, which make no mention of a temple on Mount Gerizim, fix a *terminus a quo* for the building. The fact that the brief period at the end of the Persian rule and the beginning of the reign of Alexander the Great was propitious for such a venture[62] favours the date of the building of the temple suggested by Josephus. The fact that the Bible does not mention the building of the temple is not surprising since the ignoring of issues is a standard weapon in religious quarrels of all times.

The date proposed by Josephus receives further positive support from the excavations which took place on Mount Gerizim until 1967.[63] The excavators concerned themselves with the history of the city of Shechem as well as with Mount Gerizim. Under the remains of the temple of Hadrian they came upon foundations from the fourth century BCE which can be explained as remnants of the Samaritan temple, and indeed were explained as such by the archaeologists.[64] It is necessary to clarify the relevance of this Samaritan tradition for our problem. First of all, there is the question whether the building of the temple on Mount Gerizim as such indicated the final break between Shechem and Jerusalem. Second, it should be asked in what kind of situation the Samaritans felt the need to link the building of their temple to Alexander the Great.

Josephus' description of the building of the temple on Mount Gerizim includes a factor of decisive importance at this period in the Jewish religion, namely the priesthood. Now if we see Sanballat as a member of the Samarian – to use the more precise terminology – upper class, then the building of the temple had some important consequences for the further development. If one relies on the testimony of the proto-Samaritan Sanballat source it becomes quite clear that the Samarian ruling class was really the active element. Undoubtedly, political factors were decisive for them.[65] A temple of their own on Mount Gerizim would enable them to tie the proto-Samaritan population more strongly to the secular centre of government; for Judah had seceded from the province of Samaria in the fifth century BCE.[66] The interest of the Samarian ruling class in a temple on Mount Gerizim is a counterpart of similar efforts in Jerusalem. In this they certainly met the wishes of the proto-Samaritans. The problems which were raised from Jerusalem's point of view against such a holy place did not exist for them at all. The events pictured in Ezra 4.1–5 are in no way a basis for saying that they made Mount Gerizim as it were *ex abrupto* into a holy mountain. Talmon almost goes that far when he takes the proto-Samaritans to be the rejected ones of Ezra 4.1–5, who in their disappointment chose Mount Gerizim as their new cultic place.[67]

It is necessary to examine the reasons behind this building more closely in order to be able to say something about the effects it had on the relations between the proto-Samaritans and the Jews of Jerusalem. It would indicate totally unhistorical thinking to want to see the building of the temple as just an arbitrary, though clever, move by the leaders of Samaria. This site presented itself for various reasons. In Deuteronomy the location of the central holy place had not been clearly determined. Along with Shechem,[68] however, Mount Gerizim has a fixed place in the Pentateuch. Moreover it is very likely, as was explained earlier, that Mount Gerizim was a cultic place for the proto-Samaritans before the temple was there. Indeed it has remained so to this day although the temple has long been destroyed.[69] It goes without saying that a site so full of historical significance is open to every kind of ideology in later years. Thus it also is not surprising that the controversy about the only legitimate site for the holy place became the point where minds parted. There can be no doubt that as early as the fourth century BCE, the religious relationship between Shechem and Jerusalem was severely strained by the building of this temple, since it was diametrically opposed to the efforts of Jerusalem to centralize the cult. So the question arises here whether the building of the temple on Mount Gerizim brought about the final break with Jerusalem. One runs into this assumption time and again.[70] It is based on the presupposition that the centralization of the cult was so strictly observed that a holy place outside Jerusalem would irrevocably have led to the exclusion of those oriented to this holy place. An indirect indication that this was not so is evident from the fact that, as late as 160 BCE, during the reign of Ptolemy VI, priests from Jerusalem founded a temple in Leontopolis which was not closed until 72 CE by the prefect Lupus.[71]

Now the source not only reports the building of the temple but also adds proof of legitimacy. This indicates that the *Sitz im Leben* of the description was such that the proto-Samaritans had to justify their cult on Mount Gerizim. Josephus describes such a situation in *Ant.* XII.10[72] and *Ant.* XIII.78. These events take place in the reigns of Ptolemy I Soter (305–283 BCE) and Ptolemy Philometor (180–145 BCE). Thus the aetiology with reference to Alexander must have been for the benefit of the proto-Samaritan Diaspora in Hellenistic Egypt at the close of the third century BCE.

The Jewish Manasseh source represents a Jewish, rather than Hellenistic, polemic against the cult in Mount Gerizim. In this polemic we must differentiate again between two aspects: the historical background and the literary genre of the polemic.

It is now possible to answer the question whether the building of the temple itself caused the break. One can completely agree with the opinion of Rowley 'that the erection of the Samaritan Temple and the Samaritan schism are two quite separate questions, and the one may not have synchronized with the other'.[73] This Jewish source of Josephus obviously ties in with events as they are pictured in Neh. 13.28.[74] It differs in that it is not concerned about the problem of mixed marriages, but about the willingness of many a group of Jerusalem priests to take care of a holy place outside Jerusalem. From Jerusalem's point of view, as stated by Josephus, *Ant.* XI. 346, the building of the temple on Mount Gerizim was only a new peak in the course of an alienation that had been going on for a long time. Of course the question of historical accuracy must be asked before any conclusions for determining the limits of tolerance can be drawn. The problem of mixed marriages and the role of the priests lie within the realm of historical reality. Much less probable are the visits of Alexander the Great to Jerusalem and Shechem, which obviously have an aetiological purpose.[75] About the limits of tolerance Neh. 13.28 indicates that it was possible at that time for the daughter of a high priest in Jerusalem to marry a leading Samarian. If that was possible, how much more the marriage to a proto-Samaritan![76] In this respect the limits of tolerance of the Jerusalem community must have been very broad indeed.[77] If the tradition assimilated by Josephus has a historical core, then this openness to mixed marriages still existed at the time of Alexander the Great. Even at the time the Manasseh source originated it did not yet constitute a basis for the split into Jews and Samaritans.[78] This fits the scope of the Manasseh source, since it treats the attitude of the highest priestly circles in Jerusalem towards the Mount Gerizim cult. In Schalit's opinion the Jerusalem priesthood was split into an Ezra-Nehemiah party and a pro-Samaritan faction.[79] The latter group was responsible for the building of the temple.[80] So initially the temple on Mount Gerizim received priests from the line of the Zadokites, which also supplied the high priests in Jerusalem.[81] At first this was not an issue which would have completely separated the proto-Samaritans from Jerusalem. It did not exclude the fact, however, that there were problems with mixed marriages and internal rivalries.[82] In this way the Zadokites again achieved a sphere of influence outside Jerusalem, something they had been denied since Josiah closed the shrines throughout the country.[83] These measures of Josiah had applied to the northern kingdom. During the exile the priesthood retained the spiritual leadership. Yet after the return Nehemiah imposed a limitation in that he recognized as real Zadokites only those who supplied the high priest.[84] The establishment of a priesthood on Mount Gerizim also stems from this time. If there still was an old priestly class associated with it, their authorization as Zadokites would have been undertaken at this time. The leaders of Samaria were also interested in this for the aforesaid political reasons. It is nevertheless remarkable that to this very day the role of the priest is an inextricable part of the Samaritan self-understanding.[85] In this context it is not possible to determine what these priests contributed to the theological teaching.[86] Likewise it is not possible to test here the correctness of the contention of Bowman, who says of the Samaritans: 'They are our only link with the old Zadokite priesthood of Jerusalem.'[87] The controversy in Jerusalem about the office of high priest, as reported in II Macc. 4, and finally the assumption of this title by Jonathan in the year 152 BCE (I Macc. 10.21), led to the ousting of the Zadokites and confirmed the priesthood on Mount Gerizim as well as the priests who had moved to Qumran[88] in their opposition to Jerusalem. These events in themselves brought matters to the verge of a definitive break. On top of this, the Pharisaic movement was in the ascendant in Jerusalem from about 180 BCE on.

In view of what we have seen, it is possible to conclude that the limits of tolerance follow a different course for a Judaism with a functioning priesthood from the one followed when the priesthood no longer has a practical role. This aspect should always be kept in mind when the separation of Jews and Samaritans is discussed. At this time installation of dissident priests on Mount Gerizim did not yet mean a complete break. Nevertheless, the development of such differing groups of priests had a delayed effect. Once such rival groups exist they tend to establish criteria for legitimacy and for mutual excommunication.[89] Besides the report about the role played by the priests in the building of the Samaritan temple, the Manasseh source also contains an evaluation of this role which culminates in these words: 'It was also an advantage to the king (i.e. Alexander), he (i.e. Sanballat) said, that the powers of the Jews should be divided in two, in order that the nation might not, in the event of revolution, be of one mind and stand together and so give trouble to the kings as it had formerly given to the Assyrian rulers' (*Ant.* XI.323).

Herewith this process which began with the rivalry of groups of priests clearly seems to have come to an end. The Jewish people are split in two. But evidently the stage has not been reached in which the origin of the Samaritans is linked to II Kings 17. The transgression of Manasseh is not the mixed marriage, but the founding of a separate holy place.[90] But this also means that the Samaritans still can be regarded as *homoethnoi* (fellow countrymen) (*Ant.* XI.322). This term contradicts the explanation Josephus himself gave of the origin of the Cuthians and so shows that it is older. This terminology agrees with that of Sirach 50.25, which will be discussed presently. All in all, the Manasseh source is proof that around 170 BCE Jerusalem's view was that some sort of break had already occurred. But the ethnic disqualification of the northern Yahweh worshippers is still missing. In many respects the limits of tolerance seem already to have been crossed.

For the period from the fourth to the second century BCE there are no direct testimonies to the relation between the proto-Samaritans and the Jews. Such witnesses from the second century BCE as are available, besides the Manasseh source, indicate that the split between the two groups was not final. The dating of the Manasseh source is not possible until we have discussed Sirach 50.25–26. This passage occupies an important place in dating the Manasseh source as well as the Jaddua source. After the erection of the temple on Mount Gerizim further steps were needed in the process of alienation before it came to a final break between Shechem and Jerusalem. As has been demonstrated, even before the rule of the Maccabees the relationship between Shechem and Jerusalem was very strained. This becomes even more clear from two texts which refer to the pre-Maccabean period, Sirach 50.25–26 and II Macc. 6.1–3. In Sirach 50.25–26 we read:

> With two nations (*goyim*) my soul is vexed,
>   and the third is no nation (*'am*):
> Those who live on Mount Seir, and the Philistines
>   and the foolish people (*goy*) that dwell in Shechem.

First we should ask who 'the foolish people' are and what this negative designation implies. For our problem two aspects are important, both of which were already pointed out by Kippenberg.[91] The general interpretation today is that the Samaritans are meant here.[92] Keeping our terminology in mind, we might well ask whether the people of Shechem mentioned in this passage are not still regarded as proto-Samaritans and if the final break with Jerusalem still has not occurred, even from the Jerusalemite viewpoint.[93] In spite of some doubt[94] the text can be dated about 180 BCE. Whether it refers to Samaritans or proto-Samaritans can best be determined from the terminology used. First we must note the description, 'people that dwell in Shechem'. There is no mention here of either 'Samaritans' or 'Cuthians'. So around 180 BCE the proto-Samaritans are still named for the place where they lived and the terminology employed by Josephus is not yet used. A second terminological indication that the people of Shechem at this time were not yet separated from Jerusalem can possibly be found in the Hebrew terms *goy* and *'am* (people). Even if Coggins is right in observing that not too much significance should be attached to these two expressions, since they are not yet used in the later exact sense,[95] nevertheless it becomes apparent here that the proto-Samaritans still are not called Cuthian and thus are not put on a level with the Philistines. This also establishes a *terminus a quo* for the Samaritan interpretation of II Kings 17 presented by Josephus. How long after 180 BCE this tradition arose depends on how long after 180 BCE the Manasseh source can be dated. An answer to one question could be helpful in this respect: why is there a negative view of the proto-Samaritans in Sirach 50.25f.? The context of these two verses is an ode to the high priest Simon II the Just. That in itself is interesting, since the scholium of the Megillat Taanit mentions that at the beginning of the reign of Alexander the Great, and with his permission, the Samaritans had tried to destroy the temple in Jerusalem.[96] Purvis wants to dismiss the reference to Alexander the Great as an anachronism and to accept Antiochus III as historically possible. Thus the legendary narrative would get a historical tint.[97] But Purvis does not deny that we have little more here than a secondary development of themes found in the Jaddua source. Tcherikover[98] and Coggins[99] also have advocated this interpretation. So it is not possible to connect Sirach 50.25f. to a specific historical event. No point of contention other than those already mentioned can be brought up to explain the derogatory reference in this place.

The further development can be found in two texts which

will be discussed presently. II Macc. 6.1–3 describes an event from the time of Antiochus IV Epiphanes. The tradition was taken from the writings of Jason of Cyrene and thus was put in written form at the end of the second century BCE.[100] The transformation of the temple on Mount Gerizim into a shrine of Zeus Xenios appears in the context of anti-Israelite activity. At the same time, however, the local population is supposed to have made a request for such a transformation. This agrees with what is contained in the correspondence transmitted by Josephus in *Ant.* XII.257–64. The analysis of these documents[101] led to the conclusion that in principle they are historically reliable. So we can agree with Kippenberg's general conclusion:

> The memorandum was written by a colony of Sidonians who were very superficially linked, through Sabbath observance and offerings, to the worship on Mount Gerizim. When the persecution of the orthodox oriented Israelites began, this colony distanced itself and, without consulting the Samaritan priests, asked Antiochus for permission to call the god of the Mount Gerizim temple Zeus.[102]

There were, of course, also Hellenistic proto-Samaritans as Kippenberg has shown.[103] But mainly the proto-Samaritans, like their brothers in Jerusalem, were devout Jews, whose cult centre had been desecrated, just like the temple in Jerusalem, as part of the religious policies of Antiochus IV Epiphanes. Because of the forced merger with a pagan cult, the special claim of the cult on Mount Gerizim succumbed, in view of Jerusalem, to pagan influence. From the beginning of Maccabean rule this special claim may have been considered illegitimate and the Jewish people as split. This also determines the historical *Sitz im Leben* of the Manasseh source. It is a reflection of this era. Of course the Samaritans were still regarded as Jews and even as 'fellow countrymen'. On this assumption, however, it is not possible to explain adequately the actions of John Hyrcanus with respect to the temple on Mount Gerizim.

It could very well be that I Macc. 3.10 (ἀπὸ Σαμαρείας δύναμιν) refers to proto-Samaritans who believed in Yahweh.[104] But even if this proof is discounted, one has to assume that the people of Jerusalem, where fewer and fewer distinctions were made between the pagan cult and the legitimate Yahweh worship of the proto-Samaritans, felt politically abandoned by them.[105] If the Manasseh source is a polemic against the claims to legitimacy of the cult on Mount Gerizim, then the political dimensions may have led to the denial of the Jewish character of the Samaritan people. We can only guess how the relation developed in the last fifty years before the destruction of the temple on Mount Gerizim. It is in this period that the interpretation of II Kings 17 as referring to the Samaritans must have originated. In any case, this may have been the pretext which gave John Hyrcanus the moral authority to destroy the temple on Mount Gerizim in 128 BCE as well as the Samaritan settlement at Shechem in 109 BCE.[106]

The interpretation of II Kings 17 as referring to the Samaritans

There can be no doubt that, no later than Josephus, this text was turned against the Israelite Yahweh worshippers in the northern kingdom, as *Ant.* IX. 277–91 shows. Josephus, in the first century CE, is the first to transmit this tradition.[107] Every exegete who tries to use our pericope against the Samaritans finds himself in difficulty. This is illustrated by the fact that on the one hand Josephus has to prove the inadequacy of their religious worship, while on the other he can make the averting of the 'lion plague' intelligible only by admitting that 'they worshipped him in a respectful manner'. Of course, in that way the ethnic aspect as a 'limit of tolerance' takes on extra significance for Josephus. He completely ignores the difficulty which arises from the statement in II Kings 17.34 ('To this day they do according to the former manner'). Precisely at this point it is shown to be impossible to apply this text to the Samaritans of the time of Josephus. The Samaritans of his time were definitely not syncretists.[108] So, in order to justify the view expressed by Josephus, traditional research [109] made the assertion that once upon a time the Samaritans had been idolaters. The internal discrepancies in interpreting II Kings 17 as referring to the Samaritans clearly show its intention: the cult of the Samaritans should look illegitimate in a variety of ways. Their religion is syncretistic since they are only half-converted.[110] The reason for this evil is their ethnic origin which puts them on a level with the Hellenistic opponents of the Maccabees.[111] Here there is a basic difference with the Manasseh source regarding the role of the priests. In the interpretation of II Kings 17 as referring to the Samaritans, the priest conducts himself correctly, but the ethnic-religious prerequisites of his 'congregation' are absent.[112] The Manasseh source, on the contrary, contains a strong anti-priestly bias. The tensions between the two traditions cannot be resolved, and thus they confirm through their respective tendentious characters the reconstruction of the actual historical events as offered in this study. It is simply a historical fact that the area of the former northern kingdom was inhabited not only by a population of Gentile colonists, but also by an indigenous Jewish group, whose religion was essentially the same as that of Jerusalem, and who were, ethnically speaking, descendants of the northern tribes.

But when was the anti-Gentile barb of II Kings 17 turned into an anti-Samaritan one, or, more specifically, how long before Josephus did the identification of the Samaritans with the Cuthians take place? If one takes II Macc. 6.1–3 and its opinion of the Samaritans into account, then the *Sitz im Leben* of the interpretation of II Kings 17 as referring to the Samaritans falls at the beginning of the Maccabean period.[113] This also agrees with the relative chronology derived from the Manasseh source.[114] Both of the arguments against the Samaritans were formulated from Jerusalem's point of view. This viewpoint led to further widening of the differences.

The most important event which followed the verbal polemics was the destruction of the temple on Mount Gerizim mentioned above, and later the destruction of Shechem by John Hyrcanus. Through this action, if not before, it became clear to the inhabitants of Shechem, who by this time can be called Samaritans, that no distinction was any longer made between them and the Gentiles. They were not, however, willing to submit to the Judaean demand.[115] The actions taken by Jerusalem only served to harden their position. As a consequence all the objections of the Samaritans against Jerusalem could now come to fruition. Jonathan's assumption of the high priestly office in 152 BCE and the resultant removal of the Zadokite priesthood in Jerusalem could not help but make the latter look illegitimate to Shechem.[116] But this was aimed directly against the Maccabees. The destruction of Shechem, which at least in part must have been motivated by the anti-Maccabean attitude, prepared the Samaritans emotionally for a complete break with Jerusalem. From that time on, one can no longer speak of proto-Samaritans but only of Samaritans.[117] The obvious thing to do was to thematize the question about the legitimacy of the temple on Mount Gerizim and to make it a fundamental controversy. Thus begins that phase of the process in which differences which had slowly developed and were originally unobjectionable were transformed through theological arguments into fundamental, distinctive characteristics. All further controversies, as they are found in the later rabbinic literature and the Samaritan sources, are just an elaboration on these basic positions after the breach was complete. This is probably true for the Jaddua source, which may have originated as late as the time of Caesar.[118]

The chronological order of the events mentioned is decisive for establishing the legitimacy of this topic as a part of the symposium. The actual separation of proto-Samaritans and Jews did not take place until the late second or early first century BCE; it thus falls within the period covered by the symposium.

The Samaritan reaction: the Gerizim commandment

The Gerizim commandment in the Samaritan Decalogue is, with regard to the 'limits of tolerance', an important dividing point. In an earlier study I have tried to show what will be repeated here in a summarized form.[119] The text of the Samaritan inter-polation or expansion after Ex. 20.17a (MT) belongs to the proto-Samaritan text-type, as it developed from about the fourth century BCE on. Several indications can be cited for dating this text expansion. The age of the text-type points to the period after the exile, from which time the various text-types developed. The anti-Samaritan variant in the MT (Ebal instead of Gerizim), which is also found in the mainstream of the Septu-agint manuscripts, indicates that rabbinic circles had already created this variant at the time of the establishment of the consonantal text of the MT from the first century BCE to the first century CE. For interpolation from the Samaritan side one would therefore have to pose an earlier date.

The 'expanded' texts known from Qumran (although the first and really Samaritan interpolation after Ex. 20.17a, of course, cannot be found in Qumran) indicate when such recensions took place, namely in the Hasmonaean period in the second and first centuries BCE. If one looks for a specific historical *Sitz im Leben* for this interpolation, then the destruction of the temple on Mount Gerizim by John Hyrcanus would be the most likely candidate. Actually the interpolation could also have been made earlier in order to have as it were scriptural proof for the legit-imacy of the worship on Mount Gerizim.[120] In proto-Samaritan groups they may have used – perhaps in the worship service – a conflation of texts which contained our interpolation, with the result that the interpolation was gradually incorporated into the biblical text itself.[121]

So here was a religious group which sought to furnish a central article of its creed with revelational authority. In any case, the choice of Mount Gerizim had a biblical basis.[122] This foundation was worked out in rich detail and the origin of the holy place was dated as far back as possible.[123] Here one can quote the pertinent words of Bickerman: 'The whole controversy between Jews and Samaritans was now subordinated to the question: Which place was chosen by God for His habitation, Zion or Gerizim?'[124] The circle closes at this point. While the Samaritans are trying to prove that their temple is the only legitimate one, they appear from the Jerusalemite viewpoint as nothing more than half-pagan Cuthians. The break is now evidently complete. The Gentile Samarians provided Jerusalem with the foil according to which the proto-Samaritans became Samaritans. The latter in turn established their special traditions as normative and thus tried to disqualify Jerusalem. This process then continued in rabbinic and Samaritan casuistry. This shows, however, that the two groups had more in common than the respective polemic expressions would indicate.

In view of these developments one now could ask whether the break between Jews and Samaritans occurred, in the final analysis, on the basis of a so-called normative Judaism. It seems appropriate to raise this question since from a Christian perspective there is very often reference to a 'Samaritan schism' and the like, although it is certainly inappropriate to take such terms from Christian ecclesiology and apply them to Judaism and the groups on its margin.

The question of normative Judaism

If one inquires about the reason behind the formation of a sect in the Christian sphere, then doctrinal deviation will certainly play an important part. The question is whether, in the Judaism of the first century BCE and the first century CE, doctrinal content played such a central role that accepting or not accepting it could be the basis for exclusion from Judaism. This question is discussed here in order to show its possible relevance for the separation of Samaritans and Jews. McEleney proposed the thesis that there were three points which served as criteria for orthodoxy in the first century BCE and that proselytes were converted to them: (*a*) the God of Israel, (*b*) his people, (*c*) keeping the law of Moses.[125] He believes that there was an orthodoxy of minimal content which was binding on a Jew, even if it was not explicitly incorporated into a creed.[126] Essenes, Pharisees and Sadducees all could ascribe to this common minimal formula. The question is whether this formula would not also include the Samaritans. The validity of this formula would have to stand the test of the objections against the Samaritans in the time of Josephus. His interpretation of the name 'Samaritans' would still mark the limits of tolerance in his time. At any rate, what is said about the Cuthians is intended to characterize them as not belonging to Israel. What exactly are the objections against the Cuthians? 'They feared the Lord, and also served their graven images' (II Kings 17.41). 'They do not fear the Lord, and they do not follow the statutes or the ordinances, or the law or the commandment. . .' (II Kings 17.34). The ethnic origin ascribed to them, combined with this behaviour in the religious sphere, formed an insurmountable barrier to full membership in the Jewish people. The criteria set up by McEleney actually agree with this. It must be kept in mind, of course, that the viewpoints advanced by Josephus do not name the actual reasons for the schism; they only rationalize it. McEleney himself knew that he presented only part of the problem. He was severely criticized, however,[127] which should be seen in part as an unjustified over-reaction. David Aune sees 'McEleney's central thesis, together with each of the supportive arguments adduced, as both fallacious and a serious distortion of the religious integrity and structure of first century Judaism'.[128] So severe a verdict gives one pause, since Aune recognizes the root of the problem himself when he says, 'The crux of the problem lies in the necessity of making a balanced assessment of the relative structural significance and function of the belief system *vis-à-vis* ritual practice and ethical behaviour within Judaism of the Graeco-Roman period.'[129] It is obvious that such questions could also be relevant for setting the limits of tolerance with regard to the Samaritans. Thus far, the presentation of the development of the Samaritan 'schism' has shown that the criteria mentioned here do not appear to be applicable without qualification. To be sure, McEleney does not deny that this minimum of religious beliefs constitutes the common denominator which an outsider can recognize, rather than an ecumenical creed, to which each Jewish group would feel committed.

Any such attempt to fit Judaism into a dogmatic frame is basically problematic. To do justice to Judaism one must maintain that there were no set formulae of authoritative credal statements which had a dogmatic binding force. Besides, there was no authority which could issue such 'dogmas'. Leo Baeck formulated this very succinctly: 'Whereas in the area of halakah a set of concepts was worked out in a penetrating way and down to the minutest detail, it is conspicuously absent in the area of haggadah.'[130]

According to the Jewish concept, however, religious doctrines belong to the second category. That the situation is exactly the opposite in Christianity is due to the different social structure of each religion. Since Judaism is in the first place a people, the religious law and its observance fulfil a constitutive function. One could therefore advance the thesis, which could then explain the origin of Samaritanism in terms of its essence: the main difference between Jewish and Christian sects lies in the fact that in Christianity sects originate from deviating teaching while in Judaism they arise from deviating actions. Thus it is not surprising that in Samaritan studies, though usually only on the fringes, the terminological question is asked whether the Samaritans were a sect at all,[131] or whether one should speak of a 'heresy'[132] or whether we are dealing with a 'schism'.[133] It is very questionable whether it is appropriate to apply any of these concepts, which were formed against the background of Christian ecclesiology, to Judaism and more concretely to the Samaritans.[134]

In the case of the Samaritans it must also be noted that it is not at all the case that they moved away from a fixed point. Rather the origin of the Samaritans is the result of a process that took place in the same way in pre-rabbinic Judaism as it did in proto-Samaritan circles. Since the existence of Samaritanism as a religion distinct from that of the Jews cannot be denied, the question about 'normative' Judaism is no longer *a priori* answerable, but must be guided by the concrete historical events. If the facts of the case are presented in this way, then the problem of normative Judaism itself is different from the way in which it appears in the discussion referred to above.

Lester Grabbe poses the following, rather revealing, question, 'Is Rabbinic Judaism "orthodox" and Karaism "heterodox"?

Shall we label modern Orthodox Judaism good while denouncing Reform Judaism as bad?. . .The terms themselves belong within confessional belief rather than historical investigations.'[135] This, however, confuses several things which should be carefully separated. 'Orthodox' and 'heterodox' are value judgments only when used by adherents of a religion considered orthodox. In themselves the terms express nothing more than the presence of agreement or disagreement with a teaching considered binding for a particular group.

Abstractly *doxa* implies in the first place that which in Christian circles belongs to the articles of faith, the *dogmata credenda*. But if one also uses the term *dogmata agenda*, which is not uncommon in Roman Catholicism where it refers to binding moral norms which were interpreted quite specifically by the church, then this approximates what in Judaism is called halakah. Behaviour conforming to halakah could be called orthopraxy. One should never forget, however, that behind such orthopraxy there is always a significant amount of orthodoxy.

In the period of history under discussion no structure can be found which could have transformed a conflict with what one could call 'orthodoxy' into a concrete, social schism. At no time did Judaism have a dogmatics established by properly designated authorities. Whatever religious convictions there were, were considered *self-evident*. Belief in God could serve as an example of this, or the conviction that God should be worshipped in Jerusalem and not on Mount Gerizim.

In Judaism there is more tolerance for non-fulfilment and yet belonging than in a religion where the rational denial of religious truths leads to exclusion. Put in Christian theological terms, this would mean that Judaism can have not only a church of sinners as in Christianity, but also a 'church' of heretics.

The fact that there are Samaritans shows that there are limits to the flexibility of Judaism. The breaking point comes when the divergent views of the two parties in question are equally furnished with exclusive claims.[136] The issues at stake in such controversies vary and are time-bound. Thus the existence of functioning holy places is the special circumstance which influenced the early relation between Samaritans and Jews.

The limits of tolerance with respect to Samaritanism

The limits of tolerance with respect to Samaritanism came about in Judaism as the result of a rather long development. The concrete polemic (II Kings 17) has obscured this process, and the objections brought against the Samaritans are even misleading.

On the religious plane the following factors can be recognized in the process:

(*a*) the changed self-awareness of the returning exiles;

(*b*) the problem of mixed marriages combined with the ethnic factor;

(*c*) problems concerning the cult centralization in Jerusalem;

(*d*) questions about the legitimacy of the priesthoods.

The following elements from the political sphere had a bearing on the process:

(*e*) political and economic rivalry between Samaria and Jerusalem;

(*f*) the fact of a Gentile ruling class in Samaria;

(*g*) the blending of political and religious interests in the building of the temple on Mount Gerizim;

(*h*) the blending of political and religious interests in the destruction of the temple on Mount Gerizim and of Shechem.

The factors enumerated here in abbreviated form are those which clearly emerged in the preceding presentation of the events. If the question arises why these and not other viewpoints shaped the limits of tolerance, the answer is relatively simple. The political and economic situation of the post-exilic era in Samaria and Judaea brought the factors listed in (*a*) to (*d*) to the foreground. Other external circumstances would have given rise to other factors.

These basic factors which actually were decisive for the separation should be differentiated from the later theologizing of the differences. This theologizing tells us nothing about the original limits of tolerance but indicates what kind of limits were operative at a later time. This is well illustrated by the fact that in the rabbinic polemic against the Samaritans the question of the priesthood no longer occupies a central place. The Samaritans on the contrary emphasize it strongly, precisely because the priesthood continued among them.

Samaria's claims to political leadership were diametrically opposed to the theological claims of Jerusalem. The proto-Samaritan population of the north, which had not shared in this development during the exile, could not help but fall into a strained relationship with Jerusalem. From the point of view of Jerusalem, the proto-Samaritans were bound to appear politically unreliable and religiously underdeveloped. This difficult situation intensified, reaching its definitive peak with John Hyrcanus and the destruction of the cultic and civil centres. This action of Hyrcanus accurately reflects the two levels of the conflict which were apparent time and again during the lengthy course of the controversy. This resulted in a gradual drifting apart, and only then the theologizing started which completed the break. The Samaritans then became Cuthians. In the MT Mount Gerizim was replaced by Ebal. In the Samaritan Pentateuch, on the other hand, Mount Gerizim was even incorporated into the Decalogue. The Jerusalem priesthood was declared illegitimate. This theological antagonism finally came to a head, with each side declaring to the other that only they were the true Israel. As the development of events has shown, however, this theological controversy is secondary. It is preceded by a process of alienation which finally becomes an intrinsic aspect of the 'secular and spiritual' spheres.

It must not be overlooked that any use of the Samaritan example in determining the limits of tolerance in rabbinic Judaism is legitimate only in so far as it keeps in mind that the development towards Samaritanism took place *before* the destruction of the second temple. The entire development must be viewed against the background of the specific structure of Judaism of that time,[137] and cannot simply be considered a model for possible developments in the rabbinic Judaism of a later period.

6

At the Crossroads:
Tannaitic Perspectives on the Jewish-
Christian Schism*

LAWRENCE H. SCHIFFMAN

Introduction

The purpose of this study is to determine why it is that Judaism,
after tolerating sectarianism and schism for the entire length of
the Second Temple period,[1] elected to regard Christianity as
another religion entirely. This study will concentrate on the
attitude of Judaism in the pre-Christian and early Christian
periods to Jewish identity and the nascent Christian Church. It
will seek to understand why Christianity was not simply regarded as one of the sects, and why, when, and how Judaism
sought to dissociate itself fully from Christianity.

The research presented here will be largely based on tannaitic
evidence for two reasons. First, by the time Judaism and Christianity made their final break, it was the tannaitic tradition which
was almost completely representative of the Jewish community
in Palestine and that segment of the Diaspora which remained
loyal to its ancestral faith. Second, the evidence available does
not indicate any differences of opinion regarding Jewish status
between the various sects of the Second Commonwealth and
later tannaitic traditions.[2] This is not to be dismissed as an
argument from silence. In almost all aspects of halakah known
from both Second Commonwealth and tannaitic sources, variations and differences of opinion do exist.

It can be argued that it is purely by coincidence that disagreements regarding the subject of Jewish identity did not come
down to us. It is most likely, however, that there were none.
Indeed, contention regarding the very notions of who was a

Jew and who a Gentile would have been of such great import- ance as to figure prominently in the sources. Further, nothing could have served as a more forceful polemic than to accuse opposing sects of not being Jewish. Yet despite all the sectarian animus found in various texts from or about the Second Com- monwealth period,[3] even the most virulent never accuse the members of other groups of having left the Jewish community. Sinners they were, but Jews all the same.[4]

What then caused the Jews of the tannaitic period to reject the Christians? Let us examine how the Jews viewed their own identity and how they evaluated Christianity and the Christians within this framework. (Beyond our concern will be the attitude of the Christians to Judaism and the self-definition of the early Christian communities.)

The causes of the Jewish-Christian schism may be classified in two categories – doctrinal and socio-historical. In Judaism the doctrinal factors are expressed through the halakah, the Jewish legal system. Therefore, it will be necessary to understand the halakic definitions of the born Jew and the convert. Some know- ledge of the tannaitic legal view of heresy will also be important. The traditions to be examined must also be dated as precisely as possible to be certain that they do, in fact, form part of the background for the parting of Judaism and Christianity.

The socio-historical factors are the result of the evolution of Judaism and Christianity in this period. Specifically, the Jewish attitude towards Christianity was influenced greatly by the changes that took place in the emerging church during the first two centuries of this era. Only by considering these changes will it be possible to understand why Jewish self-definition led the Jews to regard Christians first as heretics and later as mem- bers of a separate and distinct religious community.

It is in the nature of all societies and groups that certain formal or informal regulations exist regarding membership in the group and the behaviour of the members. Religious groups, in addition to adherence to their codes of behaviour and belief, also make additional requirements for membership or rites of initiation. These procedures may differ depending on whether the member stands in hereditary relationship to other members or whether he is an entirely new member, usually termed a convert. The requirements for membership or entry into reli- gious groups would have no significance if they were only arbitrary or accidental. But we know them to reflect the perceptions of the group about its own identity and nature. We can, therefore, learn a great deal about a religious group from the study of its regulations for membership or conversion. We can understand how the group characterizes itself and its relationship to the society within which it functions. Conversely, we can compare the perceptions of the society at large to the group's requirements and regulations. Is the group's image of itself consistent or inconsistent with that of outsiders, and what do outsiders consider the basic character of the religious group?

Within this framework the following study will seek to determine what the requirements were for hereditary membership in the tannaitic Jewish community, and how one could enter the Jewish people as a convert. From these regulations we shall see what the rabbis regarded as the essence of Judaism and Jewish identity. The history of the legal practices we encounter will be examined to see how far back the tannaitic approach can be traced.

Most important is the establishment of the halakic definitions of a Jew which existed in the period in which Christianity developed. After we consider how one may enter the Jewish people, we shall ask whether it is possible to leave or to be expelled from the polity of Israel. We shall see that a Jew continued to be regarded as a Jew by the Tannaim even if he espoused Christianity. The Tannaim, however, did impose legal sanctions upon the early Jewish Christians whom they regarded as trangressors, but Jews nevertheless. Eventually, as the Christians turned further and further away from the halakic definition of a Jew, the tannaitic sources portray a progressive exclusion of the Christians. It is, therefore, the halakah which ultimately determined the expulsion of the Christians from the Jewish community.[5]

The Jew by birth

The starting point for an understanding of the tannaitic definition of the Jew must be mKidd 3.12 and the complementary tKidd 4.16. MKidd 3.12 states:[6]

(If) any (woman) is disqualified from marrying not only[7] this (man) but also any other (Jew), (then her) child is equal in status to her. And to what (case) does this (refer)? This (refers to) the child of a bondwoman[8] or a non-Jewess.[9]

117

The Mishnah is here discussing the question of the personal status of the offspring of various unions. It first deals with the offspring of a legitimate marriage in which the status of the child (priest, Levite, Israelite) is determined by the lineage of the father. It then discusses cases in which the marriage involves a transgression of marriage law, but in which the marriage is nevertheless considered valid. These are cases in which a person married someone of lower status, and the law fixes the status of the child as that of the inferior partner (whether the mother or the father). Then the Mishnah discusses the *mamzer*, the offspring of a prohibited marriage[10] in which the woman would have been permitted (by virtue of her Jewish status) to marry another man. Finally the Mishnah comes to the case quoted above and indicates that in a marriage between a Jewish man and a bondwoman or non-Jewess, the status of the child is the same as that of the mother.

Can this text be dated? J. N. Epstein[11] has noted that mKidd 3.12–4.14 constitutes a literary unit which he refers to as a 'tractate of forbidden marriages and pedigrees'.[12] He sees the anonymous material, constituting almost the entire text, as coming from the period before the destruction of the temple. While there is no way of confirming Epstein's dating, it is certain that the named material in this section has been interpolated into a previously existing 'text'. In view of the identity of the named authorities, all of whom flourished in the Yavnean period, we would have to say that our mishnah would date, if not from the time the temple stood, at the latest from the Yavnean period. We can therefore set a *terminus ad quem* for this mishnah of 125 CE. It should be noted that this ruling is not contested in any tannaitic sources.[13]

What if a child were born to a Jewish woman and a non-Jewish man? TKidd 4.16 supplies the answer:[14]

> If a non-Jew or a slave had intercourse with a Jewish woman, and she gave birth[15] to a child, the offspring is a *mamzer*. Rabbi Simeon ben Judah[16] says in the name of Rabbi Simeon.[17] The child is not a *mamzer* unless it is (the offspring of a Jewish man) from a woman who is forbidden to him by the laws of prohibited consanguineous marriages (*'erwah*)[18] and on account of (having intercourse with) whom he is liable to the punishment of excision (*karet*).[19]

This passage presents a debate as to whether or not a child born from the union of a non-Jew or slave and Jewish woman is considered a *mamzer*. We can loosely translate *mamzer*[20] as one whose ancestry disqualifies him from marriage with free, hereditary Jews of the classes priest, Levite or Israelite.[21] The often-used translation 'bastard' or 'illegitimate offspring' is misleading since it conjures up the Western legal systems in which one born out of wedlock is so stigmatized. Here we refer to one born of a union which is itself illegal. There is, however, some controversy as to whether all forbidden unions confer the state of *mamzerut* or only some. The anonymous teacher of the first part of our Tosefta statement believes that the offspring of a Jewish mother and non-Jewish father is a *mamzer*,[22] while Rabbi Simeon disagrees.[23]

To grasp the full significance of this dispute for our study, we must remember that *mamzerim* are considered full-fledged Jews from all points of view except that of marriage law. They are obligated to observe the commandments and may bear witness. In short, they are Jews, albeit of low estate.[24] It is generally assumed that the purpose of the stigmatization of the offspring of illegal marriages was to serve as a deterrent to such unions. On the other hand, the law of *mamzerut* may be the result of the tendency of all societies to look down on children whose parents' union represented a violation of the norms of the society which, in turn, was viewed as an infringement on the cosmic order.

Our dispute, then, makes it clear that the offspring of the union of a Jewish woman and a non-Jewish man was certainly considered a Jew. Can we arrive at any dating of the Tosefta passage? Here again we are dealing with a unit of anonymous statements into which occasional named glosses representing variant views have been interpolated. R. Simeon ben Judah is a fourth generation Tanna, and it might have been expected that the tradition he handed down was that of Simeon bar Yohai, a third generation Tanna who lived during and after the Bar Kokhba rebellion. On the other hand, mYeb 4.13 cites a similar view in the name of Simeon the Temanite. It seems, then, that he is the Simeon of our Tosefta. The anonymous view expressed in the first clause of our Tosefta passage is most probably identical to that of Rabbi Akiba in mYeb 4.13[25] and assumed by mYeb 7.5.[26]

MYeb 4.13 fixes the law according to Simeon the Temanite who lived in the period of the Yavneh Sanhedrin (c. 80–125 CE). By his time there was certainly no question of the Jewishness of the offspring of a Jewish mother and a non-Jewish father,

119

while the child of a non-Jewish mother and a Jewish father was not considered to be a Jew.[27] How early can these rulings be documented?

Several biblical passages prohibit the marriage of Israelites with the previous inhabitants of the land of Canaan. Ex. 34.15 indicates that covenants with the inhabitants of the land (*yosheb ha-'arets*) are forbidden lest they lead to participation in pagan worship, and, as a result, to the marriage of pagans to Israelite girls. Deut. 7.1–4 specifically refers to the Hittites, Girgashites, Amorites, Canaanites, Perizzites, Hivites, and Jebusites, the seven nations who are elsewhere said to have been the original inhabitants of the land. After commanding the utter destruction of these nations, the passage again repeats the prohibition of entering into a covenant with them and specifies that intermarriage with them, either on the male or female side, is prohibited. For intermarriage will result in the turning away of the sons[28] who will worship idols (cf. Josh. 23.7, 12f.).[29]

In addition, Deut. 23.4–7 imposes further restrictions on nations which may not 'enter the congregation'. These passages as well are usually understood to proscribe intermarriage. The Ammonites and Moabites are prohibited for ever, for they refused to supply food and water to Israel after the exodus and hired Balaam to curse Israel. Deut. 23.8f. indicates that the Egyptians and Edomites may 'enter the congregation' only in the third generation. I Kings 11.1f. says that intermarriage was forbidden with Moabite, Ammonite, Edomite, Sidonian, and Hittite women according to the Torah. The editor of Kings simply updated the names of those very same seven nations of pre-Israelite Canaan in accord with the realities of his day.

One of the first problems Ezra faced upon his arrival from Babylonia was the existence of mixed marriages (Ezra 9–10). Returning exiles had married non-Israelite women, and children had been born to them. These women were from the *'amme ha-'aratsot*, 'the peoples of the land'. The suggestion was made by one of the leaders that the people enter into a covenant to expel these wives and their children, the proper procedure according to 'the commandment of our God and according to the Torah' (Ezra 10.3). Ezra accepted this suggestion, and the people swore to put it into effect.

Kaufmann[30] is probably correct in assuming that there could not have been an institution for religious conversion at this time. According to him, conversion originally was accomplished by attachment to the land and to the collective fate of the people of Israel. The early Second Commonwealth, however, was a period of transition. The old process, followed for example by Ruth,[31] had gone out of use, yet the later methods of conversion, based upon a conception of Judaism as a religion rather than Israel as a national entity, had not yet developed. It is only in this light that one can understand why conversion was not used to avoid the separation of families and the hardships it must have brought about.

It is not necessary to concern ourselves here with the halakic midrash which served Ezra as the basis of his conclusion that all these marriages were illegal.[32] What must be noted is a peculiar contrast between the narrative material in Ezra and the legal statements of Ezra and Nehemiah. The legal texts (Ezra 10.11; Neh. 10.31; cf. 13.23) specifically state that intermarriage is forbidden regardless of which partner, the male or female, is Jewish. Yet the story (Ezra 9.2; 10.2, 10; cf. Neh. 13.23) relates only to the non-Jewish wives and their offspring. Further, we are told that marriage with a non-Jewish wife leads to the diluting of the 'holy seed among the peoples of the land' (Ezra 9.2).

The most likely explanation is that already at this time there was a definite distinction between males and females regarding intermarriage. Whereas all intermarriages were prohibited, the offspring of Jewish mothers were considered Jewish. The offspring of non-Jewish mothers were not. Hence, the non-Jewish wives and their children were the primary area of concern. It was they who represented the loss of Jewish descent (*zera' ha-qodesh*, Ezra 9.2). Further, Neh. 13.23 once again emphasizes that these children were regarded as not Jewish.[33]

It would seem, then, that the laws expressed in our Mishnah and Tosefta passages regarding the qualifications of the born or hereditary Jew go back as far as the mid-fifth century BCE. There is no evidence for such regulations in First Temple times. In fact, it seems that, apart from Ammon and Moab, with whom intermarriage was eternally prohibited, Israelites might marry those who sought to become part of the people of Israel.[34] No formal conversion was necessary. Because Israel was conceived of as a land-related national entity, an informal system was sufficient. When the exile caused Judaism to adapt to its new, extra-territorial existence, the importance of genealogy and descent increased. This is clearly seen in the views of the editor

121

of Kings, Ezra and Nehemiah. Hence, it seems that the regulations regarding the determination of Jewish descent enshrined in our tannaitic texts must have originated in the Babylonian exile.

Conversion to Judaism

Besides being a Jew by birth, one might also become a Jew by conversion, also termed proselytism. The halakah regarding conversion was much more complex than that regarding hereditary Jews, as it was important to ensure that converts were seriously committed to their new faith and that they would be absorbed fully into the Jewish people. We shall see that in legislating the laws of proselytism, Judaism expressed its concept of what Jewish identity meant within the historical context of the Graeco-Roman world.[35]

Since Second Temple times, there have been four basic requirements for conversion to Judaism:
1. Acceptance of the Torah
2. Circumcision for males
3. Immersion
4. Sacrifice (no longer required after the destruction).

These requisites are explained in a statement attributed to Rabbi Judah the Prince in Sifre Num 108 (p. 112):[36]

> Rabbi says: Just as Israel did not enter the covenant except through three things, through circumcision, through immersion, and through the acceptance of a sacrifice, so it is the same with the proselytes.

This statement is based on a series of haggadot to the effect that Israel was circumcised shortly before the eating of the first paschal lamb, was immersed, and offered sacrifices in preparation for the giving of the Torah at Mount Sinai.[37] Rabbi Judah the Prince understands the entire conversion procedure as an opportunity for the proselyte to celebrate his own reception of the Torah as Israel did at Mount Sinai, for only through sharing in this historic religious experience could the convert become a Jew.

The conversion procedure and ceremony is described in a long baraita in bYeb 47a–b:[38]

> Our rabbis taught: A proselyte who comes to convert at this time,[39] we say to him: Why did you decide[40] to convert? Do you not know that Israel at this time[41] is afflicted, oppressed, downtrodden,[42] and

rejected, and that tribulations are visited upon them? If he says, 'I am aware, but I am unworthy', we accept him immediately, and we make known to him[43] a few of the lighter commandments and a few of the weightier commandments,[44] and we make known to him the penalty for transgression[45] of gleaning (the poor man's share),[46] the forgotten (sheaves),[47] the corner,[48] and the poor man's tithe.[49] And we make known to him the punishment for violating the commandments. . . And just as we make known to him the punishment for violating the commandments, so we also make known to him their reward[50]. . .We are not too lengthy with him nor are we too detailed. If he accepts (this),[51] we circumcise him immediately. . .Once he has recovered, we immerse him immediately. And two scholars[52] stand over him[53] and make known to him some of the lighter and some of the weightier commandments. If he immersed validly, he is like[54] an Israelite in all matters. (In the case of) a woman, women[55] position her in the water up to her neck, and two scholars stand outside[56] and make known to her some of the lighter commandments and some of the weightier commandments. . .[57]

From the language of our baraita with its stress on the persecution and downtrodden nature of Israel it is most likely to have been composed in its present form in the aftermath of either the Great Revolt of 66–74 CE or the Bar Kokhba revolt (132–5 CE). Regardless of which of these two dates is correct, the baraita reflects the legal rulings prevalent among the Tannaim by the Yavnean period, as will be seen below. That the baraita does not represent the procedure as followed before 70 CE is certain from the absence of mention of the sacrifice which would have been included had the temple cult still been in operation.

Much attention has been paid by scholars to the question of the attitude of the Jews to proselytism. While extended discussion of this question is beyond the scope of this study, one point should be made. The discouragement of would-be proselytes as envisaged in our text is designed to avoid leading them into a spur-of-the-moment decision. Nevertheless, talmudic sources make clear that the true convert is to be accepted.

It is true that for much of Jewish history converts were by and large strongly discouraged. This was for the most part a result of the precarious position of the Jew among his non-Jewish neighbours and of various legal disabilities under which Judaism and conversion to it were placed, factors beyond the control of the Jewish community.

Acceptance of the Torah

The Torah which the convert had to accept is to be understood in its widest sense. The proselyte must identify fully with the past, present, and future of the Jewish people and live in accord with halakah, the Jewish way of life. The Tannaim expected the convert to become part of the nation of Israel and to suffer its collective destiny. It was not, in their view, possible to convert and at the same time to avoid the lot of the Jewish people. Only a convert who understood and was willing to accept the mission of the people of Israel could be accepted for proselytism.

It would have been too much to expect the new convert to master the entirety of the halakah before converting. After all, so much of the practical side of Judaism is learned through experience. For this reason, it was decided that the proselyte would be informed in advance of a sampling of the commandments of the Torah. Of these, some had to be easier to fulfil and some more difficult. Only in this way could the prospective proselyte properly evaluate the lot he was choosing. He had to understand as well the reward and punishment dimension of the laws for which he would now assume responsibility.

Laws regarding charity for the poor are specifically singled out as the only essential subject of discussion. To the rabbis one who did not identify with the Jewish value of *tsedaqah*, loosely translated as charity, was not ready to become part of the Jewish people. It would not verge on the homiletical to indicate what this shows about the tannaitic view of the importance of sustaining the poor.

That the proselyte's acceptance of the Torah must be total is emphasized in tDem 2.5:[58]

> We do not accept a convert who has accepted upon himself all the laws of the Torah except one.[59] R. Jose son of R. Judah says: Even a minor[60] law of the subtleties of the scribes (rabbinic ordinances).[61]

According to the baraita in bYeb 47a–b, the prospective convert must be told some of the commandments and laws of Judaism. If the candidate refuses to accept a law of the Torah (of which he knows), he is to be rejected. The anonymous first clause is taken much further by R. Jose b. R. Judah who says that even if he rejects only one of the minor rabbinic ordinances, he is to be disqualified.

R. Jose b. R. Judah's words, if they are in the original form, constitute a gloss to the already formulated first clause. If so, we can assume that the anonymous words of the baraita are to be dated at least as early as the words of R. Jose b. Judah. Unfortunately, this conclusion does not aid us in establishing an early date for the anonymous part of this tosefta. R. Jose b. Judah, son of Judah b. Ilai, was a contemporary of Rabbi Judah the Prince, compiler of the Mishnah.

Comparison should be made here with the famous tannaitic narrative regarding Shammai, Hillel, and the proselyte.[62] The story relates that a non-Jew wanted to convert to Judaism on the condition that he accept only the written and not the oral Law. Shammai rejected him. Hillel convinced him to accept the oral Torah as well. Regardless of the exact dating of this haggadah,[63] or of the dating of the dual-Torah concept as it appears in tannaitic times,[64] it is clear that the haggadah is in agreement with R. Jose b. Judah in that it requires the acceptance of both the oral and written Torah for conversion.

We should note that in the conversion of Helena of Adiabene and her son, Izates (c. 30 CE), as described by Josephus (*Ant.* XX. 34–38), instruction in and acceptance of the Torah were part of the conversion process.[65] While we cannot document the requirement of acceptance of the Torah for conversion before 30 CE, this requirement must have existed from the very beginnings of proselytism in Second Temple times. After all, the institution was specifically created to allow those who had come to accept Judaism and its scriptures to enter the Jewish people formally.

Circumcision

From the pentateuchal references to circumcision (Gen. 17.23–27; Lev. 12.3) it is clear that already in the biblical period circumcision was viewed as a *sine qua non* for Israelite males and for male slaves. The only evidence we have for its not being practised is during the slavery in Egypt and the period of desert wandering (Josh. 5.2–9). At this time it was probably dispensed with because of the risk it involved.

Circumcision has been customary in many areas in the world. Specifically, Herodotus[66] cites this practice among Egyptians, Syrians, and various people in Asia Minor. He attempts to prove that its origin is in Egypt. Evidence points as well to familiarity with circumcision in Canaan, although it is not known in ancient Mesopotamia. The Arabs were circumcised

already in the pre-Islamic period. It appears from Jer. 9.24f. that
the peoples of Transjordan (Edom, Ammon, and Moab) were
also circumcised. On the other hand, the Philistines are deni-
grated as uncircumcised. Eventually, 'uncircumcised' became a
term of derision so that it could be applied even to nations in
which it was the usual custom.

The observance of circumcision by non-Jews waned in the
Second Temple period, perhaps as a result of Hellenistic influence, and circumcision became the sign of the Jew. Thus Judith 14.10 tells us of the requirement of circumcision for
conversion, and I Macc. 1.15 tells us that those wishing to as-
similate and Hellenize attempted to reverse the sign of their
circumcision. Jub. 15.33f. accents the importance of this rite as
well. When the Seleucids imposed their restrictions on Judaism,
they chose, among other things, to prohibit circumcision (I
Macc. 1.60–64).[67]

Graeco-Roman sources regarding the Jews uniformly characterize them as circumcised. In fact, the manifold references to
this aspect of Judaism show that it was seen by the non-Jew as
the distinguishing feature of the Jew. References to it continue
unabated throughout the Hellenistic and Roman periods and
relate both to Palestinian and Diaspora Jews of both Hebrew
and Greek speech and manners.[68]

It was not only under the Seleucids that circumcision became
so prominent in the international affairs of the Jews. Circumcision was also outlawed by Hadrian, most probably before the
Bar Kokhba rebellion.[69] Indeed, tShab 15.9 informs us that many
practised epispasm during this period in order to hide their
circumcision. This tosefta seems to indicate that during the
rebellion, when beyond Roman control, many of these Jews
were circumcised again.[70]

Several instances of intermarriage between members of the
Herodian household and various aristocratic non-Jews also
show the centrality of circumcision. It was the practice of the
Herodians, despite their willingness otherwise to disregard the
halakah and its sages, to require circumcision of these 'converts'.[71] The Herodians knew full well that their only claim to
rule over the Jews and their land was their claim of Jewish
descent. Therefore, they could not dare to intermarry with those
not circumcised.

The requirement of circumcision in the conversion process
may be clarified by an understanding of its various meanings.

Among Jews and Moslems the popular conception is that circumcision renders the boy a member of the religious community. From the biblical point of view circumcision was a sign of the covenant between God and the descendants of Abraham.[72] In the case of a convert, it served as a test of sincerity and dedication. Therefore, it seems most natural that once a conversion procedure developed it would be incumbent upon the candidate to be circumcised. After all, without circumcision one could not be considered a member of the Jewish people.

Some scholars have claimed that while Palestinian Judaism in the Graeco-Roman period required circumcision for proselytism, the Hellenistic Jews did not.[73] Evidence for this is extremely weak, especially in light of the widespread understanding among the non-Jews at this time that circumcision was the characteristic sign of the Jew.[74]

The story of Ananias and Izates of Adiabene in *Ant.* XX.38–42, often cited as proof that Hellenistic Judaism did not require circumcision for conversion, actually proves the reverse. Ananias never stated that circumcision was not necessary for a proselyte, but rather suggested that the king observe Jewish law without formal conversion lest his undertaking circumcision and entering the Jewish fold result in a rebellion.

It is logical to assume that circumcision was required from the earliest beginnings of the conversion procedure in Second Temple times. Before the Maccabean revolt such a requirement cannot be documented, however, for the Second Temple sources are very scanty.

Immersion

The requirement of immersion in a ritual bath takes on its greatest importance when we remember that the obligation of circumcision of proselytes only applied to males, and that the sacrifice was eliminated with the destruction of the temple. Therefore, for women, from the Yavnean period on, the only requirement besides acceptance of Judaism and the Torah was immersion.[75]

There is considerable debate about the purpose of the immersion of converts. One point of view is that the immersion is to purify the proselyte from the impurity of Gentiles. This concept of post-biblical origin was considered a rabbinical ordinance by the sages.[76] The convert would purify himself in preparation for his new Jewish status. Others have seen the immersion as initiatory, much like Christian baptism which, we shall see, derives from Jewish proselyte immersion.[77]

If the purification view is accepted, then the Hebrew Bible provides ample background for understanding the requirement. Indeed, immersion as a purification ritual is a central part of the Israelite cult. On the other hand, the Hebrew Bible gives no basis for understanding this procedure as symbolic of the creation of a new or reborn person, and no reference to it is to be found in the Hebrew Bible, the Apocrypha, Philo, or Josephus. It should be noted that there is no evidence of the use of water lustrations for *initiatory* purposes in the Dead Sea Scrolls.[78] Thus, some have maintained that this Jewish practice was a result of Christian influence. Nevertheless, prevalent opinion now sees Jewish immersion of proselytes as antedating the Christian usage.

It is probable that the debate as to whether the ritual bath is initiatory or purificatory is best resolved by understanding proselyte immersion as combining both elements.[79] The immersion should be seen as an initiatory rite in which the convert is cleansed of his transgressions and impurities and emerges from the bath as a new person, starting a new life.

An important feature of the conversion (as discussed in the baraita in bYeb 47a–b) is the presence of the scholars who serve as witnesses to the action.[80] It is only with such witnesses that conversion is valid, specifically because the convert is joining the Jewish people, not simply expressing his willingness to believe in the Torah of God. He makes a covenant with both God *and* the nation of Israel. The scholars serve as the representatives of the Jewish people in admitting the proselyte.

Jewish proselyte immersion is increasingly being seen as the basis for Christian baptism. The Christians must have been using this ceremony as part of their initiation rites at the very least by the time the early New Testament documents were being redacted. We can then state with certainty that this practice existed amongst the Jews already by the mid-first century CE. Earlier evidence has been adduced from rabbinic passages to which we shall turn presently.

MPes 8.8 has been cited as evidence that immersion of proselytes was practised already before the destruction and in the later first century BCE:[81]

If a proselyte converted on the day before Passover, the House of Shammai says: He immerses and eats his paschal offering in the evening. But the House of Hillel says: One who departs from (his) foreskin is (as impure) as one who departs from a grave.

This mishnah concerns a convert who was circumcised on the fourteenth of Nisan, the day on which the paschal sacrifice is slaughtered. The House of Shammai says that he is to immerse that day and to eat the paschal sacrifice in the evening. The House of Hillel says that this proselyte should be considered at least as impure as one who had been at a grave and who therefore had contracted the impurity of the dead (cf. Num. 19.18f.). This would mean that following the completion of the conversion (including the immersion), the proselyte would still have to wait seven days and undergo the required ablutions to be cleansed of the impurity of the dead.[82] BPes 92a explains this as a rabbinic ordinance designed to ensure that the new Jew would not err in future years by thinking that he could purify himself from impurity of the dead in the morning before coming to the temple and partake of the paschal sacrifice that same evening. A passage in tPes 7.14 supports this interpretation:[83]

Said R. Eleazar son of R. Zadok:[84] The House of Shammai and the House of Hillel (both) agree[85] that an uncircumcised male[86] (Jew) receives sprinkling and then eats. About what do they disagree? Regarding an uncircumcised non-Jew. For the House of Shammai says: He immerses and then eats his paschal offering in the evening. But the House of Hillel says: One who departs from (his) foreskin is (as impure) as one who departs from a grave. The law is the same for the non-Jew who was circumcised and the female slave who immersed. R. Eliezer b. Jacob[87] says: There were soldiers[88] and gatekeepers[89] in Jerusalem who immersed and ate their paschal offerings in the evening.

R. Eleazar b. Zadok explains that all agree that in a case wherein a Jew is circumcised on the day before Passover, he may be sprinkled in advance to remove the impurity of the dead. After circumcision, it is known from parallels, he immerses and then may eat of the paschal offering. The disagreement in our mishnah, the Tosefta tells us, concerns only a non-Jew who was circumcised on the day before Passover. The House of Shammai, because a non-Jew does not contract impurity of the dead, allows him to eat of the paschal offering immediately after his immersion. The House of Hillel regards him as being impure as if he had visited a grave. He must, therefore, wait the seven-day purification period to be cleansed of impurity of the dead. This is in order to be certain that he will not err in future years and partake of the paschal offering or visit the temple while in a state of impurity. So the House of Hillel actually required two immersions, one for conversion and one for impurity of the dead, while the House of Shammai only required one.

Our tosefta then notes that the House of Hillel takes the same view regarding a handmaiden who has immersed.[90] In order for her to partake of the paschal offering, she must be purified of impurity of the dead.

Finally, to illustrate the view of the Shammaites, R. Eliezer b. Jacob relates that there were Roman soldiers and gatekeepers in Jerusalem who converted and were allowed to eat of the paschal offering after immersion without purification from impurity of the dead. There is no further evidence as to why these Roman soldiers would have decided to convert at the last minute. One may speculate, however, that the pageantry and beauty of the preparations for the paschal sacrifice and the Passover festival enticed them to enter into the Jewish people so as to be able to participate.

This material has been treated at length here in order to clarify a passage which has been treated facilely in some discussions of conversion. It is certain that when the mishnah and tosefta under discussion refer to immersion[91] it is to the immersion which was part of the conversion ceremony. When the Tannaim wanted to designate the purification from the impurity of the dead which is also required by the Hillelites, it is referred to as sprinkling.[92] It can be stated with certainty, then, that our passages assume the requirement of immersion for conversion.

How precisely can we date this material? First, the mishnah and tosefta concern a dispute of the Houses of Hillel and Shammai which must have taken place either while the temple still stood or in the early Yavnean period. By this time, there is no disagreement at all about the requirement of immersion. Different versions of the baraita[93] place the explanations in the name of R. Eleazar b. Zadok, R. Jose b. Judah, and R. Simeon b. Eleazar. There were two Tannaim named Eleazar b. Zadok. It is probable that we are dealing here with the latter. Nevertheless, it should be remembered that he lived during the temple period and related things about the temple in his teachings. Jose b. Judah is a contemporary of Rabbi Judah the Prince, redactor of the Mishnah. The statement also appears in bPes 92a in the name of R. Simeon b. Eleazar, a pupil of R. Meir and contemporary of Judah the Prince.

On the one hand, we have failed to establish a definite attestation of our tradition at an early date. On the other hand, the transmission of this statement in the names of three separate Tannaim may indicate that it was widespread, and we may therefore take it as reliable evidence that the dispute of the Hillelites and Shammaites circulated from the Yavnean period on in the schools of the Tannaim.

R. Eliezer b. Jacob supports the Shammaite view. Lieberman sees him as the second rabbi of this name, the contemporary of R. Meir. In any case, we have further evidence for this discussion in the tannaitic period when there is no question that immersion is required.

What can now be said about the evidence for the dating of immersion as a requirement for conversion? First, it seems that it is necessary to date it before the time of John the Baptist and the rise of Christianity in order to understand the background against which baptism comes to the fore. Second, tannaitic evidence, although admittedly lacking early attestation, lends support also to the claim that immersion was already a necessary requirement for conversion in late Second Temple times. Nevertheless, we cannot prove that immersion was a *sine qua non* for conversion before the early first century CE.[94]

Sacrifice

Regarding the sacrificial offering which a convert must bring, mKer 2.1 states:[95]

> Four are lacking in atonement . . . the gonorrheac,[96] the woman with extra-menstrual bleeding,[97] the woman who gave birth, and the *metsora'*.[98] R. Eliezer b. Jacob says: The proselyte is lacking in atonement until the blood is sprinkled on his behalf, and the Nazirite (is also lacking in atonement). . . .

'Lacking in atonement' is a technical term for those who have completed the prescribed purification ritual, including immersion, but are still not permitted to partake of sacrifices until they have brought an offering and its blood has been sprinkled on the altar. The use of the word *kippurim*, 'atonement', in this way does not imply sin or the need for any form of forgiveness.[99] Rather, the term is used here in a technical sense devoid of its usual connotation.[100]

The Mishnah presents a list of those falling into this category. R. Eliezer b. Jacob modifies the anonymous list of the first clause by adding two more cases, one of which is the proselyte.

There is no question that a proselyte must bring an offering before he may eat of other sacrifices. The debate concerns the reason for this offering. The anonymous mishnah takes the view that the sacrifice is a part of the initiatory conversion rites and, therefore, until it is offered the convert is not a Jew and may not eat of the sacrifices. Hence, the convert does not fit the classification of the 'one lacking in atonement'.

To R. Eliezer b. Jacob the main purpose of the sacrifice is one of purification (or atonement) and, hence, he sees the convert as fully Jewish without the sacrifice. The offering, in his view, is necessary only to purify him so that he may now eat of the sacrifices. For this reason he adds the proselyte to the list of those lacking atonement.

In the view of bKer 2b, reference to 'four' who lack atonement specifically excludes the case of the proselyte. If this interpretation is correct, the practice of the convert's sacrifice can be dated as early as the anonymous mishnah. On the other hand, it is possible that it was only discussed in the days of R. Eliezer b. Jacob, whose view regarding the proselyte was rejected by the sages of his time. Nevertheless, we can deduce from this mishnah that by the time of R. Eliezer b. Jacob there was no disagreement about the necessity for the convert to bring a sacrifice, only about the specific reason for this requirement.

It appears from the attribution to R. Eliezer b. Jacob that the tradition dates to Second Temple times. Scholars have concluded, however, that there were two rabbis named Eliezer b. Jacob, the earlier of whom lived before the destruction of the Second Temple.[101] Since many of his teachings (including the tractate Middot) dealt with the temple and its cult, it is most logical that he is the author of our tradition.[102]

The requirement of a sacrifice must have been in force while the temple stood. But how far back can it be established? From mKer 2.1 we can date the practice to the last years of the Second Temple. It seems from Josephus (*Ant.* XX.49) that after Helena of Adiabene converted to Judaism (her immersion is not mentioned), she went to Jerusalem to offer a sacrifice. If this sacrifice was a conversion offering, it would date our practice to as early as c. 30 CE.

The problem of what would be done about the sacrifice after the destruction of the temple in 70 was dealt with immediately. A baraita in bKer 9a reads:[103]

> Our rabbis taught: A proselyte at this time[104] must set aside a fourth (dinar)[105] for his pair (of sacrificial birds). Said R. Simeon:[106] Rabban Johanan ben Zakkai already resolved to eliminate it[107] (the setting aside of money) because of the danger of error.

The first clause of the baraita is anonymous and clearly reflects the view taken in the immediate aftermath of the destruction. It states that it is obligatory for the proselyte, even in the absence of a temple, to set aside the money to pay for his sacrificial offering; for, as Rashi explains, the temple may be rebuilt and then he would be able to offer his sacrifice. Nevertheless, we are told that Rabban Johanan b. Zakkai at Yavneh, soon after the destruction, negated this practice to avoid the possibility that by accident the money would be used for some other purpose and the proselyte be guilty of misappropriation of funds dedicated for temple sacrifices.

The abolition of this practice by Rabban Johanan b. Zakkai is mentioned in a statement attributed to R. Simeon. Normally, we would assume that this is R. Simeon b. Yoḥai, who lived at the time of the Bar Kokhba revolt. However, a parallel text in bRSh 31b states it in the name of R. Simeon b. Eleazar,[108] a slightly later Tanna who was a contemporary of R. Judah the Prince. It is unfortunate that we do not have an earlier attribution for the elimination of this practice by Johanan b. Zakkai. Therefore, we cannot be entirely certain if he did eliminate it, or if, in an effort to justify its elimination in the second century, the Tannaim appealed to his authority to strengthen their argument.

Thus far, the principal sources relating to the requirements of conversion have been investigated. Careful attention has been paid to the dating of the sources as well as of the practices they describe. We have concluded that circumcision and the acceptance of the Torah must have been part of the ceremony from its earliest date in Second Temple times. For immersion, we cannot prove that it was practised for proselytes before the early first century CE. In regard to the sacrifice, it was certainly offered in the early first century CE.

Several baraitot attributed to sages in the late first or second century might seem at first glance to contradict the dating proposed here for the various requirements of the conversion ceremony. It is therefore necessary to analyse these passages. Specifically, we shall examine a baraita appearing in two versions (with significant variation) in the Palestinian and Babylonian Talmuds, and a baraita taught by a Palestinian Amora[109] which appears in connection with the first baraita.

The baraita as it appears in bYeb 46a is as follows:[110]

> Our rabbis taught: A proselyte who was circumcised, but did not immerse, R. Eliezer says that indeed this is a (valid) proselyte, for thus we have found regarding our fathers,[111] that they were circumcised but did not immerse. If he (the proselyte) immersed but was not circumcised, Rabbi Joshua says that indeed this is a (valid) proselyte, for thus have we found regarding our mothers, that they immersed but were not circumcised. But the sages say: If he (the proselyte) immersed but was not circumcised, (or) was circumcised but did not immerse, he is not a (valid) proselyte until he is circumcised and immerses.

The version of the baraita found in pKidd 3.12 (3.14, 64d) is considerably different:[112]

> (A Tanna) taught: A proselyte who was circumcised but did not immerse, or immersed and was not circumcised, the entire matter is dependent upon the circumcision; the words of R. Eliezer. R. Joshua[113] says: Even the (lack of) immersion renders it (the conversion) invalid.

In contradistinction to this baraita the Palestinian gemara then quotes a second baraita taught by an Amora:[114]

> Bar Kappara taught: A proselyte who was circumcised but did not immerse[115] is indeed a fit (proselyte), for there is no proselyte who has not immersed[116] because of his seminal emissions.[117]

R. Eliezer of our controversy is R. Eliezer b. Hyrcanus,[118] and R. Joshua is Joshua b. Hananiah. Both men were leading scholars of the period between the Great Revolt and the Bar Kokhba revolution. The controversy recorded here is ascribed, therefore, to the late first or early second century CE.

In other words, the debates recorded here occurred some time after we have maintained that the essential requirements were already fixed beyond dispute. Some have sought to use these sources to show that, in fact, the dispute over the essential requirements of conversion was not settled as early as proposed here.[119] Yet a correct understanding of the dispute will show that there was by this time no question of the requirements.

Comparison of the Palestinian and Babylonian versions shows some confusion about the views of the various Tannaim. In the Babylonian version, R. Eliezer makes circumcision the *sine qua non*, accepting as valid the proselyte who has not undergone immersion. R. Joshua takes the reverse view and sees immersion as the *sine qua non*. In his view, the convert can be considered a Jew even without circumcision.[120] It is the view of the sages that both immersion and circumcision are essential for male converts.[121] The Palestinian version ascribes to R. Eliezer the view that the *sine qua non* is circumcision and that immersion is not essential. Here, however, R. Joshua is seen as taking the view that *both* circumcision and immersion are absolute requirements, this view having been ascribed to the sages in the Babylonian version.

The difference between the Babylonian and Palestinian versions may be explained, as suggested by D. Halivni,[122] as having arisen in the following manner. Originally, there was the view of R. Eliezer to the effect that circumcision was decisive. To this was added R. Joshua's view that 'the (lack of) immersion renders it (the conversion) invalid'.[123] R. Joshua meant to state that the only *sine qua non* is the immersion. The redactor of the baraita in the Palestinian version understood R. Joshua to say that *both* circumcision and immersion are required. Accordingly, the redactor added 'even'[124] in order to clarify matters. In so doing, he misconstrued the words of R. Joshua and brought about the contradiction between the Palestinian and Babylonian versions.

It must be noted that the view of Bar Kappara in the Palestinian amoraic baraita is almost identical with that of the sages in the Babylonian version. The sages require both circumcision and immersion, and Bar Kappara agrees that both are absolutely essential. Bar Kappara, however, thinks that the requirement of immersion, if omitted, can be considered fulfilled, since all proselytes would begin immersing regularly after assuming the obligations of a Jew.[125]

One other major difference exists between the Babylonian and Palestinian versions. The Babylonian version contains an explanation of the reasons for the views of R. Eliezer and R. Joshua. Indeed, it is these explanations which the gemara immediately comments on in analysing this baraita.[126] The absence of these explanations in the Palestinian version would lead us to believe that it is probably an earlier recension.[127]

The Babylonian version of the baraita states the reasoning behind the views of R. Eliezer and R. Joshua. The opinion of the sages is not followed by an explanation. Therefore, it is most likely that the sages' view was added later to a previously existing baraita.

Now let us return to the basic issue posed by these baraitot. Is it possible, despite all the evidence we have marshalled so far, that as late as the end of the first century CE the sages would consider the possibility that one could enter the Jewish people with the omission of either circumcision or immersion? Indeed, one might be tempted to see here the source of the Christian rejection of circumcision and acceptance of baptism as a sufficient rite for entry into the church.

Nevertheless, the correct view is undoubtedly that of B. Bamberger.[128] He explains the argument as a technical dispute regarding when in the process of conversion the proselyte may be considered a Jew. Is the act of circumcision or that of immersion the decisive factor? Can a proselyte who has only undergone one of these rites be considered a full Jew before completing the ceremonies?

Behind this dispute is a larger question. Which rite is the actual conversion rite? Should it be understood that circumcision is the final step with immersion only a halakic requirement which the new Jew must fulfil to purify himself of the impurity of the Gentiles? Or, on the other hand, is immersion the actual conversion rite and the proselyte now obligated, like any other Jew, to be circumcised? Finally, the third view is simply that both are essential parts of the conversion process.

The disputes under discussion, then, are best understood as being technical, rabbinic debates regarding the exact point at which the proselyte becomes a full-fledged Jew. They cannot be seen as evidence for essential disagreements regarding the conversion procedure or its requirements.

The converts spoken about thus far have been free people who have decided of their own free will to join the Jewish people and to accept Judaism. There was, however, another type of convert, the *'eved kena'ani*, literally the 'Canaanite slave', but designating all non-Jewish slaves.[129]

When non-Jewish slaves were bought, they were circumcised

in accordance with the law of Gen. 17.12f. (cf. Ex. 12.44).[130] Slaves refusing to be circumcised were resold to Gentiles, although prevalent tannaitic opinion allowed a twelve-month period for convincing the slave that he should undergo circumcision. In addition, the new slave was immersed. These rites qualified him fully as a Jew in all matters, and his status regarding observance of the commandments was the same as that of minors and women. The common denominator was that women, slaves, and children below the age of religious majority were exempted from commandments with specific time requirements because they were not in control of their own use of time.

If the master wanted to free his slave, a practice encouraged by the Tannaim, he was again immersed and given a writ of manumission. He was now a free Jew with a status similar to that of a convert.

Later authorities assume, rightly so, that the procedures followed in regard to proselytes were also followed for 'Canaanite' slaves.[131] Thus, before immersion, the slave had to be familiarized with the commandments and had to indicate his assent. Further, although the sources are silent here, it is possible that a newly-freed slave after his immersion (for the purpose of initiation as a free man) would bring the same sacrifice as the convert.

While undoubtedly the origins of these laws lie in forced conversion of captives and slaves, by tannaitic times only those who freely accepted Judaism and circumcision could go through the rituals. On the other hand, there is no question that the Hasmonaean kings still practised forced conversions,[132] and it is possible that private individuals in the Hasmonaean period also forced their slaves to accept Judaism and to be circumcised.

The proselytes described above have been those who joined the Jewish people by following the procedures prescribed by the halakah and became full members of the Jewish community. Hellenistic and rabbinic sources, regarding both Palestine and the Diaspora during the Graeco-Roman period, tell us of semi-proselytes or God-fearers who attached themselves to the Jewish people.[133] Apparently, as a result of the general interest in oriental religions and of the waning of the old Graeco-Roman cults, many people in the Hellenistic world were attracted to various Jewish customs including the Sabbath, synagogue attendance, and abstention from pork, among other things. Some went so far as to adopt almost all Jewish practices as well as the ethics and theology of Judaism. On the other hand, these people never underwent actual conversion. We know that in some cases this was because of the requirement of circumcision. In other cases, family members or fear of public embarrassment prevented actual proselytism. Such God-fearers or semi-proselytes were found throughout the Hellenistic world in substantial numbers, and it may be that the Jewish community actually encouraged this behaviour, especially in the Diaspora.

Nevertheless, these people had no legal status in the Jewish community, whether in Palestine or outside. They were not converts, regardless of the extent of their loyalty. Only the fulfilment of the requirements of conversion which, as far as we know, were agreed upon by all Jews, would allow entrance to the Jewish people. These semi-proselytes apparently did not desire legal status within the Jewish community. Their practices differed, and they were in no way organized. While the Jewish people approved of such individuals, they could never conceive of them as Jews since they had not undergone formal conversion.

Since the tannaitic sources regarding the hereditary or born Jew and the means of entering the Jewish people by conversion have been thoroughly investigated, it ought to be possible to extract from them some significant findings regarding the self-image and self-definition of the tannaitic Jewish community.[134] Such conclusions ought to serve us well when we consider early Christianity in the context of tannaitic thought as expressed in the halakah.

To begin with, Judaism is centred on the Jewish people, a group whose membership is fundamentally determined by heredity. If one is not born a Jew, how can one become a Jew? Here the halakah demands the maximum of commitment, for the convert is literally changing his heredity. He will pass on to his children descent which he did not inherit but rather acquired. For this reason, he must go through an extensive process to acquire fully the main characteristics of what Jewishness is.

He must be committed to the acceptance of the Torah. He himself must stand at Sinai, for Sinai was the formative event in the Jewish historical experience. There he, like the people of ancient Israel, must accept not only the laws of the Torah, but also the rabbinic interpretation or oral Law which, according to the Tannaim, was given at Sinai as well.

He must also identify with the entire historic experience of the Jews. He must understand that his fate is now linked with his new co-religionists, for he has literally switched his heredity to become a part of the Jewish people. He must at the same time acquire the characteristic of charity and kindness which Jews have been proud to maintain.

The male convert must be circumcised, for this is considered the ultimate sign of Jewish identity and of the covenant in which he is now enrolling. Even more important, he is to become a descendant of Abraham, and the Torah has commanded that Abraham's descendants be circumcised.

He must purify himself in a ritual bath, for the Jewish people saw itself, from its earliest origins, as striving to live a life of purity and holiness.

Finally, he must bring a sacrifice, an act which receives the assent of God, for without God's favour and acceptance, no Jew could sustain himself. In bringing the sacrifice, he shows that he is ready to draw near to the divine presence and to come under its wings as a full member of the people of Israel.

Heretics and apostates

Thus far the definitions of the born Jew and the convert have been established for the period immediately preceding and contemporaneous with the rise of Christianity. What must be asked now is whether anyone can be excluded from the Jewish people and lose his Jewish status as a result of any beliefs or actions. Indeed, it will be shown conclusively that this cannot occur and that only the criteria described above could serve to indicate who was or was not a Jew in the early centuries of this era.

A word of definition is in order. A heretic is one whose *beliefs* do not accord with those of the established religion to which he claims adherence. An apostate is one whose *actions* are not consonant with the standards of behaviour set by his religious group. We shall have to treat these separately as they involve different halakic categories.

In this context, it would be wise to remember that tannaitic Judaism and, indeed, biblical Judaism is primarily a religion of action rather than belief. Only a small number of beliefs have ever been seen as mandatory in Jewish life, and when compared with the requirements of action and behaviour, it is easy to see that the primary emphasis of Judaism is on the fulfilment of commandments and not on faith.

The starting point for any discussion of heresy in tannaitic Judaism must be the *locus classicus* of mSanh 10.1:[135]

> The following[136] are those who do not have a portion[137] in the world to come:[138] the one who says there is no resurrection of the dead,[139] (the one who says) the Torah is not from Heaven, and the *'apiqoros.*[140]

It is this passage which has served as the basis of most claims that Judaism has a creed.[141] This mishnah effectively suggests that those who hold certain beliefs are excluded from the world to come, and that opposite beliefs are normative and required.[142] We shall investigate the specific offences mentioned and show that exclusion from a portion in the world to come does not imply expulsion from the Jewish people.

The case of one who does not believe in the world to come is explained in a baraita in bSanh 90a:[143]

> (A Tanna) taught: He denied resurrection of the dead. Therefore, he will not have a portion in the resurrection of the dead.[144] For all the retributions of the Holy One, blessed be He, are measure for measure. . . .[145]

This baraita is noteworthy in that it indicates that the Tannaim understood the phrase 'world to come' as it appears in our mishnah to refer to the period after the resurrection of the dead. For this reason, the baraita substituted the term 'resurrection of the dead' for 'world to come' in recapitulating the content of the mishnah. From mSanh 10.3 we learn that after resurrection there will be divine judgment followed by the world to come. The baraita explains that since the person in question denied the existence of the resurrection of the dead, he will be denied the right to be resurrected. Accordingly, he will not attain a portion in the world to come.

The mishnah is most probably directed against the Sadducees, who, Josephus tells us, did not accept either the immortality of the soul or the idea of reward and punishment after death.[146] Indeed, both of these doctrines are inextricably connected with the doctrine of resurrection as mentioned in our mishnah, and the Pharisees saw resurrection as a prelude to the world to come. Our mishnah states that those Sadducees, who deny resurrection of the dead, would therefore have no share in the world to come.[147]

The second class of non-believers are those who deny the heavenly or divine origin of the Torah. It might be tempting to view the Torah here as a reference to *torah she-be-'al peh*, the oral Law, which the Tannaim believed was given to Moses on Sinai along with the written Torah. (Indeed, this meaning might perhaps be attributed as well to the statement of mAbot 1.1 that 'Moses received the Torah from Sinai'.) Unfortunately, we cannot date the use of the term 'oral Law' any earlier than the Yavnean period.[148] Since, as will be shown below, it is likely that this mishnah predates the destruction of the temple, the term 'torah' here is probably limited in meaning to the written law.[149] The person described by our mishnah, therefore, denies the prophetic character of Moses and, in effect, asserts that Moses himself was the author of the Pentateuch.

It is known from Graeco-Roman sources that some classical authors attacked the Torah, claiming that Moses had made it up and formulated divine authorship only in order to assure observance of its laws. Indeed, from Philo of Alexandria and from some much later midrashic sources it seems that some Jews came to believe the same thing.[150] In fact, it is probable that those who wished to substitute the constitution of the Greek *polis* for that of the Torah in Hellenistic Jerusalem did so out of belief that both were man-made, whereas the *polis* offered greater possibilities for advancement, both economic and political.[151] It is most likely that our mishnah is directed against those who, perhaps under Hellenistic influence, have come to deny the divine origin of the Torah. They, therefore, are a class who will not share in the world to come.

How did the rabbis arrive at such a conclusion? The case of the denial of resurrection was understood by the Tannaim as based on the doctrine of equivalent recompense ('measure for measure'). The same doctrine must have motivated the rabbis here. The promise of ultimate bliss in the world to come after resurrection and divine judgment is meant as a reward for observance of the commandments. For Jews this means observance of all the commandments of the Torah. For non-Jews it is sufficient to observe the Noachian laws. Only one who accepts the premise on which the entire system of the commandments is based, the divine origin of the Law, can be worthy of receiving the reward which the life of Torah is meant to assure. Hence, he who denies the divine character of the Law cannot reap its rewards.

The third class excluded for reasons of belief from the world to come is the *'apiqoros*. There can be no question but that this word is derived from Greek *Epikouros*,[152] the name of the famous Greek philosopher (342/1-270 BCE). The only question is whether this term signifies a follower of this philosopher or if it has somehow become a more general term for a heretic. The talmudic definitions of this word,[153] which are based on a Semitic derivation,[154] are amoraic and clearly do not reflect the actual tannaitic usage.

Josephus mentions Epicureans in his discussion of the book of Daniel.[155] There he says that Daniel's correct prophecies show that the Epicureans who deny providence and assert that the world is without a 'ruler and provider'[156] are in error. In other words, to Josephus the Epicurean is one who denies God and his role in the world. It can be assumed that Josephus is using the term 'Epicurean' in the way it was understood by the people of his day. The chronological proximity of the mishnah under discussion to the works of Josephus would lead us to the conclusion that the meaning of *'apiqoros* in our mishnah is this: one who denies God's involvement in the affairs of men and the world.

Why did the *'apiqoros* lose his portion? Indeed, he denied the very basis of the resurrection, divine judgment, and the world to come. For he denied the role of God, even the concern of God, for the affairs of mankind. Hence, he was unworthy to share in the blessings which God had stored up for mankind in the end of days. Again we find the principle of 'measure for measure'.

Against whom were the rabbis polemicizing when they excluded the *'apiqoros* from the world to come? According to Josephus[157] the very same beliefs ascribed to the *'apiqoros* were held by the Sadducees. Now it must again be remembered that Josephus wrote at a time not so far from the composition of this mishnaic statement, and so his descriptions of the Sadducees may be taken as accurate for the last days of the temple. Of course, one must never forget the tendency of Josephus to picture the sects as if they were Greek philosophic schools.[158] Nevertheless, Josephus does testify to an affinity between the views of the Sadducees and the Epicureanism of the very same period. If so, it is safe to conclude that the *'apiqoros* of our mishnah was often a member of the Sadducean group.

If so, we have found that this mishnah describes three forms of heresy, two of which are attributed by Josephus to the Sadducees. Indeed, we must conclude that this mishnah is Pharisaic in origin and polemicized against the Sadducees and certain Hellenized Jews. At the same time, anyone holding these views, regardless of his affiliation with one of the prevalent groups of the Second Temple period, was considered to have lost his portion in the world to come.

Can the statement under discussion be dated?[159] We have omitted from discussion so far the second part of this mishnah in which R. Akiba and Abba Saul add to the list several heterodox *practices* (as opposed to beliefs dealt with in the anonymous first half of the mishnah) which also exclude the transgressor from the world to come.

The qualitative difference between the offences of creed listed in the first anonymous part of the mishnah and the offences of practice listed in the sections attributed to R. Akiba and Abba Saul would tend to support the idea that the original teaching was composed at a time when issues of belief were central, whereas the Yavnean period (the time of R. Akiba and Abba Saul) was one in which there was an attempt to strengthen and standardize practice in order to close ranks and to ensure the survival of Judaism in the aftermath of the destruction of the nation and its temple.[160]

Further, we have seen that the heresies catalogued by this mishnah can all be attributed to or connected with the Sadducees or the Hellenized Jews. It is therefore most probable that the anonymous first clause of the mishnah was composed before the destruction of the temple while Sadduceeism and Hellenism were still issues for the Pharisaic leaders. After all, the Sadducees were to disappear soon after the destruction with the removal of their power base, the central sanctuary in Jerusalem.

Can it be determined from the material presented thus far whether loss of one's portion in the world to come implies also loss of one's status in the Jewish people, or whether the status of a Jew is inviolable regardless of his beliefs? One thing is certain. No intrinsic link can be claimed between Jewish status and the possession of a portion in the world to come. MSanh 10.3, for example, indicates that the men of Sodom have no portion in the world to come. If a portion in the world to come went hand in hand with Jewish status, why even mention the men of Sodom? Indeed, tSanh 13.2 contains a tannaitic debate about whether the righteous of the nations of the world can have a portion in the world to come. Again, the question of Jewish status and that of a portion in the world to come are separate issues. The fact that certain heretics or non-believers are excluded from the world to come in no way implies expulsion from the Jewish people.

Thus far the offences which disqualified a person from a portion in the world to come were doctrinal. The Tosefta, however, adds several offences of commission. The context is a statement attributed to the House of Shammai in which three classes are delineated: those righteous receiving immediate reward, the average people who will be punished and then receive their reward, and the worst offenders who will be consigned permanently to purgatory. TSanh 12.5 concerns this last group:[161]

> But as to the heretics (*minim*),[162] the apostates (*meshummadim*), the informers, the *'apiqorsin*, those who denied the Torah, those who separated from the ways of the community,[163] those who denied the resurrection of the dead, and everyone who transgressed and caused the public to transgress . . .,[164] Gehenna[165] is shut in their faces (or 'before them'), and they are punished in it (Gehenna) for ever and ever.

It is easy to see that this passage represents an expansion of the list found in the Mishnah, adding certain offenders whose transgressions had such major consequences as to cause the loss of their portion in the world to come and to bring upon them eternal punishment.

Minim in this context means early Christians. This term as well as the halakic status of this group will be treated in detail below (pp. 149–55.)

While the role of informers in talmudic literature is in need of a thorough study, at least it can be observed that these were people who denounced Jews who practised rituals forbidden during the Hadrianic persecutions and perhaps at other times as well.[166] Such denunciations were extremely dangerous to the Jewish community. For this reason, potential informers were threatened with loss of their share in the world to come in order to deter them from committing this offence.

The term *meshummad*[167] is usually translated as 'apostate'.

While this English word denotes one who forsakes his religion, the Hebrew term *meshummad* is more complex. Literally, it means one who has been destroyed. We shall see that it refers to one who ignores the commands of the Torah and the demands of Jewish law. According to Lieberman,[168] the term originally referred to those forced to worship idols and only later came to refer to those who committed offences of their own free will. In any case, this wider meaning is already represented in the tannaitic sources before us.

The distinction between the *meshummad le-te'avon*, one who apostasizes for desire of forbidden pleasures, and the *meshummad le-hak'is*, one who does so out of spite, is an amoraic distinction which will not be relevant to this study. This distinction was developed as a response to the ambivalent attitude of tannaitic halakah towards the apostate. This ambivalence was resolved in amoraic times by the assumption that there were two different types of *meshummad*.

Only two tannaitic passages can be presented in an attempt to reach a more exact definition of the *meshummad*. An anonymous baraita in bHor 11a attempts to define which commandments are such that their violation labels the offender a *meshummad*:[169]

> Our rabbis taught: If one ate forbidden fat, he is a *meshummad*. And who is a *meshummad*? one who ate[170] animals not ritually slaughtered or afflicted with fatal diseases,[171] forbidden animals and reptiles,[172] or who drank the wine of (idolatrous) libation. R. Jose son of R. Judah[173] says: even one who wears a garment of wool and linen.[174]

This baraita represents the conflation of two sections. The first was an anonymous baraita indicating that one who ate forbidden fat was a *meshummad*. The second asked the question of who was a *meshummad* and answered that one who ate certain forbidden foods fell into this category.[175] To this anonymous definition was added a dictum in the name of R. Jose b. R. Judah to the effect that the wearing of *sha'atnez*, a garment of mixed wool and linen, also qualified the offender as a *meshummad*.

R. Jose b. Judah was a late Tanna, a contemporary of R. Judah the Prince. We have no way of asserting that even the anonymous parts of the baraita are earlier than the last days of the tannaitic period, although no evidence against an early date can be marshalled either.

This definition of a *meshummad* is clearly halakic in character and presents the *meshummad* as one who violated certain dietary restrictions. Indeed, even one who wears mixed linen and wool, in the view of one late Tanna, is a member of this class.

A more general definition is found in a *midrash halakah* based on Lev. 1.2. The version in the Sifra is as follows:[176]

> (Speak to the children of Israel and say to them: When any of you presents an offering of cattle to the Lord. . . .) Any: To include the proselytes. Of you: to exclude the *meshummadim*. The text (of the Torah) says children of Israel: Just as Israel are those who have accepted the covenant, so also the proselytes are those who have accepted the covenant. But the *meshummadim* are excluded since they do not accept the covenant.[177] For indeed, they have declared the covenant void. . . .

This statement sees the *meshummad* as the opposite of the proselyte. While the proselyte has undergone acceptance of the Torah as part of the conversion process, the *meshummad* has denied that very covenant, as is evidenced by his actions.

BHull 5a contains a version of this halakic exegesis which is more expansive:[178]

> Of you:[179] Not all of you, excluding the *meshummad*. Of you: Among you (Israel) have I made a distinction, but not among the nations. Of cattle: to include people who are likened[180] to cattle. From this they said,[181] it is permitted to receive sacrifices from the transgressors of Israel in order that through them they may come to repent, except from the *meshummad* or one who pours (idolatrous) libations, or violates the Sabbath in public.

Now this midrash halakah is germane to the central issue: Is the *meshummad* considered part of the people of Israel? The midrash answers in the affirmative. Whereas all non-Jews (including idolaters) may send voluntary offerings to be sacrificed in the Jerusalem temple, this right is denied to certain Jews, namely to those who have apostasized to the extent of performing idolatrous worship or violating the Sabbath in public. These *meshummadim* are, therefore, still Jews, for if they were excluded from the Jewish people, their offerings *would* be acceptable. Indeed, this principle is seen by the Tannaim as derived from the Torah itself. There can be no question, therefore, that the *meshummad*, like the heretic and the *'apiqoros*, is never deprived of his Jewish status.[182] Nevertheless, there is a legal disability under which he lives as a consequence of his actions.

Tannaitic Judaism and the early Christians

It is time to pause to consider the implication for the Jewish-Christian schism of the tannaitic sources studied thus far. The halakic definitions of a Jew in the pre-Christian era have been established: ancestry through the mother or conversion including circumcision for males, immersion, acceptance of the Torah, and sacrifice. These continued to be the only possible ways to enter the Jewish people in the period in which Christianity came to the fore. Further, it was determined that the Tannaim did not view heresy or apostasy in and of itself as negating the offender's status as a Jew. Indeed, Jewish status could never be cancelled, even for the most heinous offences against Jewish law and doctrine. It is against this background that the tannaitic reaction to the rise of Christianity must be viewed.

As far as the Tannaim were concerned, when Christianity began, it must have appeared simply as a group of Jews, otherwise generally conforming to the norms of the Jewish populace of Judaea, who had come to believe that the Messiah had come in the person of Jesus. As long as the new group preached its gospel primarily among Jews, this view continued to be held by the Tannaim.

While our sources point to general adherence to Jewish law by the earliest Christians in Judaea, we must also remember that some deviation from the norms of the Tannaim must have occurred already at the earliest period. Indeed, the sayings attributed by the gospels to Jesus would lead us to believe that he may have taken a view of the halakah different from that of the Pharisees. Nevertheless, taking into account the halakic material discussed thus far, the Tannaim did not see the earliest Christians as constituting a separate religious community. After all, there was no sin in making the error (as it was to the Tannaim) of believing someone to be the Messiah.[183] In regard to the other deviations that must have occurred, Judaism had long been accustomed to tolerating both differences of opinion and deviation from the norms of observance by its members.

The Pharisees presumably regarded Jesus as yet another false Messiah of a type which was not so unusual in the last days of the Second Temple. Indeed the existence of all kinds of sects and religious leaders was the norm of the day in the Second Temple period as we know from so many sources. Judaism was in what we might call an experimental stage. The biblical tradition was being adapted in many different ways in an unconscious effort to see which approach would best ensure the future of Judaism and of the Jewish people. For this reason, little opposition to the very concept of sectarian divergence existed. Each group argued for its own primacy and superiority, yet no voice called for the unity of the people as a virtue in and of itself. It was in such a context that Christianity arose. It was seen by the Tannaim in its earliest stages as no greater a threat than any other sect, and the halakic regulations discussed above determined the identity of the early Christians as Jews.

This situation changed with the destruction of the temple. Divisions within the people, after all, had made the orderly prosecution of the war against the Romans and the defence of the Holy City impossible.[184] The temple had fallen as a result. Only in unity could the people and the land be rebuilt. It was only a question of which of these sects would unify the populace.

For all intents and purposes the Pharisees were the only sect to survive the destruction. The smaller sects were either scattered or destroyed. The Sadducees had been deprived of the temple, their base of power and authority. Disturbance of the social and economic order wrought by the war deprived the Sadducees of their previous status. This was clearly the time for the entire nation to unite behind the Tannaim, the inheritors of the Pharisaic approach to Judaism. For Pharisaism, with its flexibility in adapting the halakah to new circumstances, would be best fit to deal with the new realities after the unsuccessful revolt and the destruction of the temple.

But where would the Christians fit into this newly constituted Jewish community? The evidence indicates that the Christians, although still Jewish, had only moderate success in winning converts among the Jews of Palestine.[185] At the same time, the nascent church turned more and more to Gentiles as prospective converts.[186] Undoubtedly, some of the new converts were Hellenistic Jews for whom the new religion seemed but a variety of Judaism. On the other hand, the vast majority of the new Christians consisted of Gentiles and the former semi-proselytes.

Of the vast numbers of Graeco-Roman non-Jews who were attracted to Christianity, only a small number ever became Jewish Christians. The new Christianity was primarily Gentile, for it did not require its adherents to become circumcised and convert to Judaism or to observe the Law. Yet at the same time, Christianity in the Holy Land was still strongly Jewish.[187]

While the destruction of the temple was drawing near, the differences between Judaism and Christianity were widening. By the time the temple was destroyed, the Jewish Christians were a minority among the total number of Christians, and it was becoming clear that the future of the new religion would be dominated by Gentile Christians. Nevertheless, the Tannaim came into contact primarily with Jewish Christians, and so continued to regard the Christians as Jews who had gone astray by believing in Jesus.

A new set of circumstances confronted the tannaitic leadership when it reassembled at Yavneh after the war was lost. By this time, the need to close ranks and to face the future as a united community was greater than ever. We shall see, though, that the rabbis still did not elect to see the Jewish Christians as a separate religion. After all, they still met the halakic criteria of Judaism. Instead action would be taken to bar them from officiating as precentors in the synagogue in order to make them feel unwanted there and to exclude their books from sanctified status. Tannaitic law would eventually have to face the Gentile Christians, but the rabbis as yet had little opportunity for contact with them.

Jewish Christians in tannaitic halakah

While our sources show no attempt on the part of the Tannaim to read anyone out of the Jewish people on account of heretical beliefs, the rabbis did impose certain restrictions on those whom they regarded as standing outside the accepted system of Jewish belief. Such heretics who were subjected to legal restrictions are termed *minim*.

While this term itself has been a major scholarly problem, it is now agreed that it was a general term for heretics, applied at various times in the rabbinic period to different groups which presented doctrinal challenges to rabbinic Judaism while remaining from an halakic point of view within the fold.[188] A number of tannaitic restrictions directed against *minim* clearly refer to the early Jewish Christians, as can be shown from their content and date.[189] These regulations show how the rabbis attempted to combat those beliefs they regarded as outside the

Jewish pale while never rejecting the Jewishness of those who held them.

The primary area in which the Tannaim imposed restrictions on the Jewish Christians was in regard to the synagogue. The *birkat ha-minim*, the benediction against the heretics, was directed at excluding such people from serving as precentor in the synagogue.[190] Indeed, this restriction probably went a long way toward making the Jewish Christians feel unwelcome in the synagogues and causing them to worship separately.

A baraita in bBer 28bf. states:[191]

> Our rabbis taught: Simeon Ha-Faqoli ordered[192] the Eighteen Benedictions[193] before Rabban Gamaliel in Yavneh.[194] Rabban Gamaliel said to the sages: Is there no one who knows how to compose a benediction against the *minim*?[195] Samuel Ha-Qatan stood up[196] and composed it. Another year (while serving as precentor), he (Samuel Ha-Qatan) forgot it[197] and tried to recall it[198] for two[199] or three hours, yet they did not remove him.[200]

Despite some ingenious claims to the contrary,[201] the Gamaliel of our baraita is Rabban Gamaliel II of Yavneh in the post-destruction period. Simeon Ha-Faqoli set the Eighteen Benedictions in order before Rabban Gamaliel as part of the general effort at Yavneh to fix halakah. Rabban Gamaliel asked for a volunteer to compose the benediction against the *minim*. Samuel Ha-Qatan stood up and adapted a previously existing benediction to include the *minim*.[202] In another year, he was called upon to serve as precentor. In the course of the service, he was unable to recite the benediction against *minim*. Nevertheless, even after he spent several hours trying to recall it, the rabbis did not remove him as precentor.

BBer 29a asks why he was not removed. After all, it was the purpose of this blessing to ensure that the precentor was not one of those heretics cursed in the benediction.[203] The Talmud answers that since Samuel Ha-Qatan had himself composed it, it could be assumed that he was not a *min*.

For many years there has been debate about the identity of the *minim*. Most recent opinion sees the term *min* as referring at different times to various forms of heresy that threatened rabbinic Judaism in talmudic times. It is therefore essential to clarify who the *minim* of this benediction are. Palestinian texts of the Eighteen Benedictions from the Cairo Genizah present us with a text of the benediction which elucidates the identification of the *minim*:[204]

For the apostates may there be no hope unless they return to your Torah. As for the Christians and the *minim*, may they perish immediately. Speedily may they be erased from the Book of Life and may they not be registered among the righteous. Blessed are You, O Lord, Who subdue the wicked.

While other specimens of the Palestinian liturgy show slight variation, the Christians and *minim* are always included in this benediction. Some may wish to debate whether the Christians and *minim* here mentioned are to be taken as one group or two. Yet the fact remains that the Christians were included with other apostates and heretics in the Genizah documents.

May we assume that this version of the benediction represents the text as it was recited before the sages of Yavneh? On the one hand, the Palestinian liturgical material found in the Cairo Genizah generally preserves the traditions of Palestinian Jewry in the amoraic period. On the other hand, there is external evidence that this benediction was recited during the tannaitic period and that it included explicit reference to Christians.

Three passages in the gospel of John (9.22; 12.42; 16.2) mention the expulsion of Christians from the synagogue. This expulsion may have been the result of the institution of the benediction against *minim*. Justin Martyr, writing in the middle of the second century CE, says in his *Dialogue with Trypho*, 'You, the Jews, curse the Christians in your synagogues. . . .' Similar testimony comes from Origen (c. 185–c. 254). Epiphanius (c. 315–403) says of the Jews that they curse the Christians three times daily in their prayers. Further evidence is preserved by Jerome (c. 340–420).[205]

This curse could only be found in the Eighteen Benedictions since it would be the only thrice-daily recitation in the synagogue services. If Justin Martyr was referring to this benediction, then we would have confirmation from the mid-second century that the Christians were specifically mentioned in this prayer. Further, while the version before us differentiates *minim* and Christians, it should be remembered that many rabbinic texts speak of the *minim* and clearly designate believers in Jesus. It is most likely, however, that our benediction meant to distinguish Jewish Christians from Gentile Christians, and that the *minim* were Jewish Christians while the *noṣerim* ('Christians') were Gentile Christians.

If this last interpretation is correct, it is possible to trace the development of this benediction. The original threat to Judaism was from Jewish Christianity, and so a benediction against the *minim* (a general term here referring to Jewish Christians) was instituted. At some later date, perhaps by 150 CE but definitely by 350 CE, as the fate of Christianity as a Gentile religion was sealed, the mention of Gentile Christians was added as well to the prayer.

The specific function of the benediction was to ensure that those who were *minim* would not serve as precentors in the synagogue. After all, no one would be willing to pray for his own destruction. It was assumed that the institution of such a benediction would lead ultimately to the exclusion of the *minim* from the synagogue. Such a benediction in its original form can only have been directed against Jews who despite their heretical beliefs were likely to be found in the synagogue. Gentile Christians would not have been in the synagogue or called upon to serve as precentor.

When the separation of the Jewish Christians from the synagogue was accomplished, the prayer was retained as a general malediction and prayer for the destruction of the enemies of Israel. Therefore, the *noṣerim* were also added.

That such a development actually took place in the benediction is clear from the church Fathers.[206] Only in Epiphanius (c. 315–403) and Jerome (c. 340–420) do we find explicit mention of the *noṣerim* in the Graecized form *Nazōraioi* and the Latinized *Nazaraei*. This is because the *noṣerim* were added to the benediction after the time of Justin and Origen, whose accounts of the benediction make no mention of this specific term. By this time, the Roman empire (now Christian) had imposed various anti-Jewish measures. It was only natural to add explicit mention of the Gentile Christians to this prayer.

It cannot be overemphasized that while the benediction against the *minim* sought to exclude Jewish Christians from active participation in the synagogue service, it in no way implied expulsion from the Jewish people. In fact, heresy, no matter how great, was never seen as cutting the heretic's tie to Judaism. Not even outright apostasy could overpower the halakic criteria for Jewish identification which were outlined above.[207] When the method of excommunication was used to separate heretics from the Jewish community in the Middle Ages,[208] even this measure, which was to a great extent a medieval halakic development, did not in any way cancel the Jewish status of the excommunicant. Indeed, regardless of the transgression of a Jew, he was a Jew under any and all circumstances, even though his rights within the halakah might be limited as a result of his actions.

While the benediction against the *minim* was certainly the most important step taken by the Tannaim to combat Jewish Christianity, they also took steps to emphasize that the Christian scriptures were not holy.[209] First, the Jewish Christians themselves wrote scrolls of the Bible (*sifre minim*). The question here was the sanctity of the entire text.

Second, beginning in the second half of the first century, early recensions of the gospels and epistles began to circulate. The sanctity of those sections of these Christian texts which quoted the Hebrew scriptures directly had also to be determined. In view of the role of the gospels and epistles as a vehicle for spreading Christianity, it is easy to understand why the rabbis went out of their way to divest them of sanctity and halakic status.

TShab 13 (14).5 deals with these texts:[210]

> We do not save from a fire[211] (on the Sabbath) the gospels[212] and the books of the *minim* (heretics). Rather, they are burned in their place, they and their Tetragrammata. R. Jose Ha-Gelili says: During the week, one should cut out their Tetragrammata and hide them away and burn the remainder. Said R. Tarfon: May I bury my sons![213] If (these books) would come into my hand, I would burn them[214] along with their Tetragrammata. For even if a pursuer[215] were running after me, I would enter a house[216] of idolatry rather than enter their (the Jewish Christians') houses. For the idolaters do not know Him and deny Him,[217] but these (Jewish Christians) know Him and deny Him. . . . Said R. Ishmael: If in order to bring[218] peace between a husband and his wife, the Ever-present has commanded[219] that a book[220] which has been written in holiness be erased by means of water, how much more so should the books of the *minim* which bring enmity[221] between Israel and their Father Who is in Heaven be erased,[222] they and their Tetragrammata. . . . Just as we do not save them from a fire, so we do not save them from a cave-in,[223] nor from[224] water nor from anything which would destroy them.

The passage contains no disagreement regarding what to do if the gospels or other books of the *minim* (texts of the Hebrew scriptures) are caught in a fire on the Sabbath. These books are not to be saved, since they have no sanctity. There is, however, debate regarding what to do with such texts during the week. R. Jose Ha-Gelili suggests removing the Tetragrammata and burning the rest. Apparently, he feels that regardless of who wrote it, the Tetragrammaton retains its sanctity. R. Tarfon permits the burning of the texts with their divine names. R. Ishmael agrees with R. Tarfon and supports his view with an analogy to the bitter waters of the suspected adulteress. Further, R. Tarfon regards these Jewish Christians as worse than idolaters; for while a pagan might embrace the new faith, it was a great source of frustration that Jews, raised in the traditions of Judaism, would have done so as well.[225]

In regard to dating, the named authorities in the debate are all Yavneans who flourished in the period leading up to the Bar Kokhba revolt. We see that the Jewish Christians were using Hebrew texts of the Bible and that already there were early recensions of the gospels in circulation. A decision, therefore, had to be rendered regarding their halakic status.

This Tosefta passage is indicative of the emerging view of the Tannaim. By this time, more and more Gentiles had joined the church, and the scriptures of the Christians had begun to be read in Palestine. The rabbis had to take a stand indicating the heretical nature of these texts in the early years of the first century.

Further reference to the very same texts appears in tYad 2.13:[226]

> The gospels and the books of the *minim* ('heretics') do not defile the hands. . . .

The 'defilement of the hands' was a sign of canonicity in tannaitic texts.[227] Books of the Bible which defiled the hands were holy scriptures. In spite of the appearance of verses from the Hebrew Bible in the gospels, this text indicates that they and even texts of the Hebrew Bible written by *minim* have absolutely no sanctity.

While there is no indication of date in this passage, it seems that it would emerge from the same period as the passage before. Indeed, in the years before the Bar Kokhba revolt, there was a need to accent the illegitimacy of Jewish Christianity. The two passages we have studied here indicate clearly that the transgressions of the *minim* were sufficient to render their texts of the Hebrew Bible unholy. The Tannaim sought in this way clearly to differentiate Christianity from Judaism, but they did not attempt to disavow the Jewishness of the *minim* at any time.

Apparently, then, the Tannaim still regarded the Jewish Christians they knew as Jews even as late as the end of the first century CE. Although by this time Gentile Christians constituted a majority of the believers in the new religion, the impact of this situation had not yet been felt in Palestine, where Jewish Christianity still predominated until the Bar Kokhba revolt.

The final break

The years between 80 and 130 CE were for the Jewish community of Palestine years of reconstruction of the country and preparation for the Bar Kokhba revolt. Throughout this period Christianity kept growing, and simultaneously its Jewish element was being reduced. While in actual fact the juridical basis for the Gentile domination of Christianity was laid in the time of Paul,[228] the effect of these actions was not actually felt by the Tannaim until the early years of the second century.

By the time of the Bar Kokhba war (132–135 CE), Gentile Christianity had most probably still not taken over the Jerusalem church. As such, the Tannaim would still have seen Christianity as a form of Judaism. When Bar Kokhba began his revolution, in which he was definitely seen by some in a messianic role, the Jewish Christians refused to participate in the rebellion. After all, Jesus was their saviour, and so they could not unite to fight on behalf of another Messiah. Furthermore, they probably shared the view of the church Fathers that the destruction of Jerusalem and Judaea in the Great Revolt of 66–74 CE was a just punishment for the Jewish rejection of the messiahship of Jesus. As a result of this refusal to join in the revolt, Bar Kokhba attacked Jewish Christians and executed many.[229] Subsequently, the attacks of Bar Kokhba, the dislocation of the war, and other factors – some of which are still not clear – led to a large decrease in the number of Jewish Christians in Palestine,[230] and this at a time when the number of Gentile Christians in the Roman world was increasing rapidly.

But the Romans indirectly brought about the final break. When the city of Jerusalem was turned into Aelia Capitolina in the aftermath of the war, Jews, including Jewish Christians, were prohibited from entering the city.[231] Therefore, the newly re-established Jerusalem church was to be an essentially Gentile one. The Roman prohibition of circumcision, probably promulgated before the war but enforced immediately after it, must have discouraged conversion to Jewish Christianity even further. The Jewish Christians, then, dissipated into small sectarian groups, so that after the Bar Kokhba war Christianity was no longer Jewish but Gentile.[232] The rabbis ceased to be dealing with Jews who had gone astray but who fulfilled the halakic requirements of Jewish identity. They now confronted Gentiles who had converted to a religion which had rejected circumcision, Jewish proselytism and the requirements of life under the halakah. Only in this way had Christianity become a separate religion. It was now that the rabbis dealt with Christians as members of a different and hostile religious community.[233]

The ultimate parting of the ways for Judaism and Christianity took place when the adherents of Christianity no longer conformed to the halakic definitions of a Jew. From then on, Christians and Jews began a long history of inter-religious strife which played so tragic a part in medieval and modern history.

7

On the Problem of Roman Influence on the Halakah and Normative Self-Definition in Judaism*

BERNARD S. JACKSON

1. Introduction

The comparison of Jewish with Roman law, and speculation regarding their historical relationship, have exercised scholars for centuries.[1] Overall, the results may be thought to be inconclusive. In the space of a single article, it is hardly possible to review the whole problem, much less come to new and definitive conclusions. My object, instead, is to consider the principal obstacles in the way of a clear solution, in the course of which some directions for further investigation may emerge.

The relationship between two past legal systems involves study of the historical background as well as of substantive parallels. This paper commences, therefore, with the institutional relationship between the two systems (2. Problems of Jurisdiction) and problems of access (3. Literary Transmission) before proceeding to consider substantive questions (4. Influence on Form; 5. Influence on Content). In conclusion, an attempt is made to relate these issues to the overall theme of the McMaster Project (6. Normative Self-Definition).

In one respect, this treatment is wider than my title suggests. Although my brief was stated in terms of the possible connection with Roman law, it is hardly possible, as regards the development of the halakah, to exclude (or sometimes even to separate) Greek and Hellenistic data, which some may think represent the more significant influence. Nevertheless, the primary focus remains Roman.

Jewish and Christian Self-Definition

Some Theoretical Preliminaries

Over the past century, attitudes towards foreign influence among legal historians have gone through cyclical changes, often in the wake of fashions in anthropology:[2] the late nineteenth century was dominated by Maine and his followers, whose orientation was evolutionary;[3] thereafter, spurred by the discovery of the Laws of Hammurabi and the consequent 'Bibel und Babel' flurry, there was a strong diffusionist movement;[4] a reaction, in turn, stressed the importance of functional considerations;[5] and this too is now coming under neo-diffusionist attack.[6] Some scholars have attempted to break out of these currents by setting up methodological criteria for the objective establishment of foreign influence,[7] but in reality such strategies serve only to conceal the real problems. For these lie at the level of the theory of history.

The underlying theoretical problems include the following: (1) What do we regard as an historical fact? In particular, do we limit ourselves to that which is stated in the historical sources, and at the conceptual level so stated? (2) How does causation work within history? Can we identify a single factor to which to attribute primary influence in any particular event? (3) What is the acceptable range of causative elements which is to be considered in constructing hypotheses? Do some of them, perhaps social or economic pressures, deserve a primacy of consideration? Are there grounds for suspecting that some deserve primacy in some contexts, others in others? (4) How do we conceive social change to occur? Do we look first to the effect of stimuli on the general populace, or do we look instead to élites of various kinds? If there is no single answer of general application, how do we distinguish the contexts in which we should expect the differences to occur? (5) To what extent do we allow our positions on these questions to aid in the reconstruction of the historical account, where the sources of the period are deficient?[8]

These questions will assume more concrete form in the course of this study, and may provide, if nothing else, an explanation of the source of many of our uncertainties. Elsewhere, I have sketched my own position on some of the central issues.[9] I suggest, *inter alia*, that consideration of the underlying theoretical problems leads us to pose one further question, all too rarely addressed by students of the inter-relationship of legal systems: once 'influence' has been established, how do we assess its *significance*?

2. Problems of Jurisdiction

The history of civil jurisdiction[10] up to the end of the tannaitic period is relevant to our problem for a number of reasons. First, the very existence in Judaea/Palestine of a functioning Roman legal system makes it reasonable to suppose a certain degree of knowledge of Roman law among the Jewish inhabitants. The extent of that knowledge depends in part on the nature of the jurisdiction and the degree to which it impinged upon Jewish life. The impact of Roman law will thus have been greatest where Roman jurisdiction was compulsory and exclusive, as in the case of capital jurisdiction after 70 CE.[11] But we should not overlook the importance of voluntary and concurrent jurisdiction, *a fortiori* where we find indications that Jews not only invoked it but also were involved in its administration. A second and distinct reason for looking at Roman jurisdiction is for the 'pressure'[12] it may have exerted on those responsible for the development of Jewish law, as a result of both its actual attraction of litigation from Jewish parties and its capacity to override the Jewish courts when the Roman administration thought fit. Whereas the first of these considerations may be thought relevant to the problem of Roman influence on the *content* of Jewish law, the second is likely to prove significant primarily as one of the factors influencing its *form*.

Historical Survey

The history of civil jurisdiction was not necessarily smooth even before the Romans began to intervene in Jewish affairs. A late tradition, preserved in the Yerushalmi, suggests that *dine mamonot*[13] were 'taken away' in the days of Simeon b. Shetah,[14] a leading Pharisee of the period of Alexander Jannaeus. While there is good reason to suspect here a confusion with Simeon b. Yohai,[15] the possibility that the tradition is correct should not be completely dismissed. The period concerned was one of some turbulence, and it is far from inconceivable that some form of civil jurisdiction then being exercised by the Pharisees was lost or suspended as a result of the conflict with the king.[16]

With the advent of Pompey, Judaea became in effect a vassal state. In formal terms, autonomy was preserved. But this deceived no one. The juridical status of such treaty-linked states appears to have been uncertain,[17] and the practical possibility of Roman intervention was ever-present. Of course, the Romans would not, at this period, have intervened purely in order to interfere in mundane civil disputes, but once involved in the affairs of the state they were not inhibited from acting as if the territory were already a *provincia*. Thus when Caesar restored Hyrcanus in 47 BCE, he took it upon himself specifically to grant him – and perhaps thereby the Sanhedrin under his Presidency – powers of internal jurisdiction in matters of Jewish law.[18] There could be no better illustration of the realities of the situation: the autonomy of the subject is incompatible with the sovereignty of the ruler.

The establishment of the *provincia* in 6 CE may not have made much practical difference. In 1914 Juster noted that there was no evidence during the period 6–70 CE of any actual exercise of Roman civil jurisdiction (i.e. even as a concurrent jurisdiction) over Jews or pagans.[19] Nevertheless, the threat was there, now clothed with juridical status, as may be inferred from statements of Cicero.[20] Moreover, it may be noted that Judaea was at this time an equestrian province, a regimen imposed where local conditions were such that the strict implementation of the ordinary regulations might require to be varied.[21] It is hardly likely that, in these circumstances, the powers of the Roman governor were reduced, despite his military dependence upon the governor of Syria;[22] but whatever the precise relationship between the two, the threat of Roman interference in the working of the courts was not thereby removed.

The effect of the first revolt

The juridical effect of the defeat in 70 CE has been disputed. Roman law had a special status for surrendered enemy aliens: they became *peregrini dediticii* (a low but free status; see nn. 23 and 31), to the extent that they were not reduced to actual slavery, as *captivi*. This status, the precise effects of which are not well attested in the sources, may have involved some loss of personal law,[23] though whether it can have precluded any resort to native tribunals may be doubted.[24] Whether the Jews fell into this category after 70 has been disputed.[25] In all probability, there is no uniform answer. As Momigliano has pointed out,[26] there were grounds for differentiating between different sections of the Jewish population according to their involvement in the revolt; there would have been no reason to penalize the inhabitants of a city such as Sepphoris, which remained loyal to the Romans.[27] On the other hand, the inhabitants of some cities which did participate in the revolt were either killed or reduced to slavery.[28] Some groups, it seems, were accorded the status of *dediticii*,[29] but on the whole this appears to have been exceptional.[30] In any event, the status adhered only temporarily.[31] That there was an interruption in the normal functioning of the organs of internal self-government may be conceded on general grounds, but such an hiatus did not result from the indiscriminate acquisition of the status of *dediticius*. Nevertheless, the very fact that the status was applied to some but not to others – including, so it seems, a section of the population of Jerusalem[32] – could only serve to enlarge the areas of uncertainty regarding the legal status of the civil courts which already resulted from the wide discretion to interfere possessed by the governor and from the likelihood that successive governors would approach this discretion differently.[33]

Revival of autonomy between the revolts

By the end of the century, under R. Gamaliel II, and perhaps from the beginnings of the Yavnean period, from c. 75 CE under R. Johanan b. Zakkai,[34] concurrent jurisdiction in civil cases was resumed.[35] Whether this came about with the formal *imprimatur* of the Roman authorities is unclear[36]. That there were official contacts directed to this end has been suggested, on the basis of three rabbinic traditions describing contacts between the two sides, the first involving Johanan b. Zakkai, the latter two concerning R. Gamaliel II.[37] It is possible that there is no historical basis whatsoever for these traditions; they could be understood simply as rabbinic attempts to claim legitimacy for a resumption of jurisdiction which in fact had no formal basis. But this is unlikely.[38] Nevertheless, the historicity of the details of the incidents may be doubted, and their relevance to the resumption of jurisdiction may, in varying degrees, be questioned.

The first tradition, preserved in a number of versions,[39] records certain questions[40] about Jewish law put to R. Johanan b. Zakkai by a *hēgemōn* (ruler) whose name is variously recorded.[41] Herr accepts an identification of the *hēgemōn* with Marcus Antonius Julianus, procurator of Judaea at the time of the destruction and (perhaps) the author of a work on the Jews, and he dates the encounter to between June 69 and the end of 70 CE.[42] If this reconstruction is correct, the incident hardly assists us in tracing the history of Jewish jurisdiction: the date is too early to concern the revival at Yavneh, and the nature of the governor's interest would appear to have been scholastic. However, there is good reason to doubt this reconstruction, on the grounds of both the uncertainty of the identification of the Roman governor, and the implausibility of such a meeting at that particular time. More likely, the tradition reflects a contact of some kind after the end of the war; indeed, in terms of content it resembles[43] a tradition concerning R. Gamaliel II,[44] and it is not impossible that it has a shared literary history with the latter.[45] Whether the questions recorded in the versions are historical is unclear. At any rate, we need not conclude that a great deal turned on R. Johanan's ability to give satisfactory answers. The tradition may best be viewed in the context of others concerning R. Johanan's contacts with the Roman authorities with a view to their sanctioning the foundation of the school at Yavneh,[46] as indicating that R. Johanan's concerns included matters of civil law.

The second tradition is that of mEduy 7.7, which records a journey of R. Gamaliel II to the governor of Syria 'to get permission'. The text is used by Safrai to argue (along with other indications) that the governor of Judaea was still subservient to the governor of Syria at this time.[47] Even if this is so, it seems unlikely that such a journey to Syria would have been required for the purpose of securing permission to operate a concurrent jurisdiction in matters of civil law,[48] and certainly this highly uninformative text is capable of other interpretations. Urbach may well be right in suggesting that the significance of this source lies rather in the status it implies was conferred on R. Gamaliel by virtue of the fact that the Romans had contact with him at all, rather than as evidence of any specific power conferred upon him.[49]

The third text further illustrates the difficulties involved in attempts to give precise historical significance to these traditions.

Our Rabbis taught: The Government of Rome had long ago sent two commissioners to the Sages of Israel with a request to teach them the Torah. It was accordingly read to them[50] once, twice and thrice. Before taking leave they made the following remark: We have gone carefully through your Torah, and found it correct [*ve'emet hu'*] with the exception of this point, viz. your saying that if an ox of an Israelite gores an ox of a Canaanite there is no liability, whereas if the ox of a Canaanite gores the ox of an Israelite, whether *Tam* or *Mu'ad*, compensation has to be paid in full. . . .We will, however, not report [*modi'im*] this matter to our Government.[51]

The other two versions of the tradition both specify the Sage involved as R. Gamaliel (II), who in the Palestinian Talmud is said to have responded by abolishing by *gezerah* a comparable discriminatory rule regarding property stolen from a Gentile.[52] Although the purpose of the Roman mission is not stated,[53] it has been suggested that the enquiry was mounted in connection with Roman recognition of the Jewish courts.[54] But this is unlikely, for a variety of reasons. First, the whole setting sounds decidedly apocryphal.[55] Second, the baraita commences by stressing that it is not a contemporary account. Third, there was every reason to concoct a tale such as this: the passage appears in the Gemara which comments on the discriminatory rule of the Mishnah, BK 4.3, for which some *apologia* or explanation clearly seemed required. And finally, the climax of the story is not a considered judgment of the Romans not to report back their one prejudicial finding;[56] it is, in fact, a rather good joke. Jewish law was not to be held *mu'ad* [*eyn anu modi'im*[57]] in respect of its attested vice in discriminating against Gentile animal owners.

The evidence for an official act on the part of the Roman administration, authorizing the revival of the jurisdiction of Jewish courts in civil matters, is thus not strong. That there was such a revival seems clear enough. In all likelihood, it was simply assumed, once the dust had settled, that the civil courts could continue as before subject to the major institutional changes which had occurred in Jerusalem as a result of the destruction of the temple and the undermining of the position of the priesthood. Since the status of *dediticii* did not adhere to the Jewish population as a whole, those who had not been enslaved or reduced to that status could proceed more or less as normal. There must, however, have been an increase in the uncertainties attending the exercise of jurisdiction, resulting from the fact that in Jerusalem a section of the population had become *dediticii* as well as from the possibility that the Romans would decide on more radical measures.

In one respect, there was a change. Whereas before 70, the concurrent Roman jurisdiction appears to have been no more than a theoretical possibility, after 70 it was actually invoked. For this conclusion we are not dependent upon enigmatic texts in rabbinic literature, with all their problems of dating and historical reliability. We now have the evidence of the archive of Babatha, discovered in the Cave of Letters at Ein Gedi.[58] Before moving to Ein Gedi, Babatha had lived in Maoza (probably on the south-east shore of the Dead Sea)[59] in the recently established[60] province of Arabia (Petraea). Not only do her family documents display a sensitivity to Roman as well as Jewish law;[61] she has direct recourse to the court of the Roman governor at Petra, where she sues one of the guardians of her fatherless son. There is little doubt that Babatha and her family were Jewish,[62] and no suggestion that they enjoyed Roman citizenship;[63] indeed, one of the documents mentions a hearing before *xenokritai* – which some have interpreted as meaning 'judges for *peregrini*'.[64] It should be noted that the archive dates from the years *before* the second revolt;[65] the situation is thus not explicable in terms of the suspension of Jewish jurisdiction after the defeat of Bar Kochba.

The discovery is revealing as regards the attitudes of both Jews and Romans. Whether Babatha had any real choice as to where to sue is not clear. Quite likely, there was no *rabbinic* court in Maoza, but that does not necessarily mean there was no *Jewish* court.[66] Alon has rightly directed attention to the variety of judicial institutions existing within the Jewish community,[67] some of them enjoying Roman authorization. Even so, Babatha – whose practical instincts and sense of organization are manifest throughout the archive – may well have calculated that at the end of the day she would have to resort to the Romans for enforcement, so that she might as well go to them in the first place. Whether the situation would have been the same in a major centre of population is uncertain.[68] Nevertheless, Babatha's strategy reminds us that litigants do look to the practicalities of the local situation in making their choice of forum, a fact to which the rabbis were sensitive.[69] Even more surprising is the willingness of the Roman administration at Petra[70] to entertain such actions, and that within twenty years of the establishment of the province. Indeed, Babatha has provided Romanists with significant evidence of Romanization in the provinces nearly a century before Roman law was made available *de iure* by the *constitutio Antoniniana's* grant of citizenship to most provincial *peregrini*.[71] Of course, the willingness of the administration at Petra to entertain Babatha's suit may reflect its appreciation of those same practical considerations which led her to bring it; it does not follow that the administration in Judaea would have taken the same view in cases which could equally have been brought before local Jewish tribunals. Nevertheless, the practice once established was capable of extension, and the matter lay fully in the discretion of the governor. To what extent such concurrent Roman jurisdiction was exercised in Judaea is unclear. But the rabbinic sources which oppose it may certainly be taken as serious evidence of its existence.[72] And here, as elsewhere, the uncertainty of the situation was itself a major factor which could not be overlooked by the Jewish leadership.

The second revolt and subsequent reconstruction

A second cycle of interruption and reconstruction appears to have occurred after the second revolt (132–135 CE), the effects of which are thought to have been more severe than those after 70.[73] The tradition of the removal of *dine mamonot* in the time of R. Simeon b. Yohai[74] may well signify a suspension of Jewish civil jurisdiction pending a further political settlement. Once again, the status of *dediticius* may have been more or less selectively bestowed, although the indications (for which, on this occasion, we have no Josephus) are that the Romans adopted more severe measures.[75]

Nevertheless, reconstruction and a revival of Jewish civil jurisdiction was to follow. By the end of the second century, under the Patriarchate of Judah I, we find a revival even of Jewish capital jurisdiction – probably exercised without *de iure* authority but nevertheless without Roman interference.[76]

In 212 CE[77] Roman citizenship was conferred on most inhabitants of the Empire by the famous *constitutio Antoniniana*.[78] One effect was that the personal law of those who fell within its terms became Roman law, instead of their native local law.[79] In Palestine this may have involved the termination of the recognition of Jewish jurisdiction in civil matters,[80] and the reduction of the status of rabbinical courts to that of arbitral tribunals. Yet there are strong indications that this did not occur. Indeed, a further imperial constitution, to much the same effect, was directed specifically to the Jews in 398 CE.[81] Perhaps the Jews fell within one of the two apparent exceptions to the range of the *constitutio Antoniniana* (*dediticii*[82] and those subject to the poll tax[83]), or – more likely in view of the evidence that they did in fact acquire citizenship[84] – were the subject of some concession (whether *de facto*[85] or *de iure*[86]) which allowed for the continuation of recognized jurisdiction in matters of private law.

The difficulties which beset modern scholarship on the problem may well mirror comparable complexities at the time. Daube argues from a rescript of 213 CE that the decree can be observed in immediate operation.[87] The emperor was asked to decide the validity of a bequest in a will, apparently by a Jewess, 'to the body of Jews who are settled in the city of Antioch'. By Roman law a benquest could not be left to an 'uncertain person', – a limitation not observed by Jewish law. The emperor held the bequest invalid.[88] Unless the testatrix had acquired Roman citizenship by some other title, or all parties to the dispute had consented to the settlement of the dispute by recourse to Roman law,[89] the rescript shows that Roman private law would henceforth exclude Jewish private law.[90] As observed above, this does not appear to have happened. But the very fact that Jewish jurisdiction came so close to final termination in 212 CE may be a factor to be taken into account in interpreting developments in the halakah in the first half of the third century.

Further jurisdictional complexities

The uncertainties sketched above, which flowed from the peculiar political history of Judaea under Roman rule, were increased by the many problems of conflict of laws which could arise in a province which boasted not only a multiplicity of personal laws, but also a variety of local government institutions reflecting different municipal citizenships. Indeed, one object of the *constitutio Antoniniana* may have been to reduce these very problems.[91]

(i) Multiple citizenship

Despite the strong view of Mommsen to the contrary, it is now generally accepted that Roman citizenship did not necessarily exclude local citizenship,[92] so that Jews who acquired Roman citizenship possessed a choice of law. Baron has noted the theoretical possibility that Jews in Alexandria could have enjoyed Roman, Macedonian, Persian and Alexandrian citizenships.[93] As for Judaea, the number of Jews possessing Roman citizenship is unknown, but there must have been at least sizable pockets. Roman law had the strange rule that a formally manumitted slave acquired not only freedom but also Roman citizenship, irrespective of his status before enslavement. Thus the reduction of sections of the population to slavery after the two revolts created the potential (especially where the slaves were sold to private owners locally) of a considerable increase in the roll of Jews who were Roman citizens, and already in the first century we hear of the 'Synagogue of the Freedmen'.[94] According to one view, the *constitutio Antoniniana* itself provided that even the new citizens should be allowed to retain the use of their local city law, and it has also been suggested that the decree required all new citizens to be enrolled as a *municeps* of a local city.[95] And in all this, we should not neglect the phenomenon of Jews living in autonomous Greek cities – for whom the choice of law will have been equally important. The position will have been further complicated by the presence of converts to Judaism, from among both the Greek and the Roman populations, who will have retained, in some measure, their original law.[96]

(ii) Romans applying Roman law to Jews

Where a Jew had a dispute with a Roman, the latter could unilaterally insist that the matter be resolved by the application of Roman law in a Roman court. From the evidence of Cicero, it appears that one important function of the *edictum provinciale* was to make the Roman *ius honorarium* available in the province for this and other purposes.[97] The Roman governor possessed the *imperium* of the *praetor peregrinus* in respect of the province. Further, Jews might find themselves in a Roman court by agreement between the parties. We have seen that this is probably what occurred in the litigation of Babatha. On one view of the meaning of *xenokritai* in the 'formulae'[98] in that archive, the judges themselves might have been Romans – the term designating not 'foreign judges' but 'judges for foreigners'.[99]

(iii) *Jews applying Roman law to Jews*

The alternative view of *xenokritai* in the Babatha archive is that the judges were indeed 'foreign'[100] – *iudices peregrini*, in the terms of Cicero – even though the law they were called upon to apply[101] was certainly Roman. In the circumstances, it may perhaps be unlikely that such 'foreign judges' (at Petra) were Jews. Nevertheless, the possibility that Jews were delegated by the Romans to judge cases involving other Jews according to Roman law has been raised by Alon,[102] and the case brought by Babatha may, on this understanding of *xenokritai*, indicate that there was, in principle, no objection to the use of non-Roman judges. There are a number of reasons why the Romans might encourage such a jurisdiction, and why litigants might wish to avail themselves of it: the governor's own court might have a backlog; the parties, while wanting the benefits of Roman jurisdiction, might feel less disloyal to the community if the judges were in fact Jews.

(iv) *Jews applying Roman law to non-Jews*

A remarkable rule, preserved in the Tosefta and Yerushalmi, states:[103]

> If the ox of a Gentile injured the ox of another Gentile even though (the parties) have agreed to be judged by the laws of Israel, he must pay full damages, since there is no (distinction between) *tam* and *mu'ad* in the (law) of damages of Gentiles.

If the Roman administration was inclined to use *xenokritai* (in the sense of 'foreign judges'), there would appear little reason to restrict their activities to cases involving Jews. The remarkable feature of the rule is that Gentile law must be applied even though the parties 'have agreed to be judged by the laws of Israel'. It is unlikely that the Roman administration would be appointing Jewish judges for this purpose. One could understand a desire on the part of the rabbis to make clear the distinction between rabbinically appointed *dayanim* and Roman appointed Jewish judges. If the text has in mind the latter, the effect of the rule would be to prevent the application of Jewish law by such judges even where the parties (perhaps Jewish manumitted slaves?) requested it. But the text is a difficult one to explain. An alternative, simpler approach might be to say that *some* rabbis did not wish a Gentile litigant to receive less damages than he would receive in a Roman court, lest the name be profaned, *mipne ḥillul ha-shem.*[104] But this, too, is a difficult conjecture.

(v) Romans applying Jewish law to Jews

It is believed, on the basis of rabbinic sources, that Roman courts might decide disputes between Jews on the basis of Jewish law.[105] *Prima facie*, this seems unlikely. Nevertheless, there does now appear to be evidence from Egypt of Romans judging according to Egyptian law.[106] But the differences between the provinces are considerable, and one should regard this comparative evidence with some circumspection. In fact, the rabbinic evidence for the practice appears less than solid. The baraita in bGitt 88b has R. Tarfon prohibit recourse to Gentile courts even though the law applied is *kedine yisra'el*; in the Mekilta, Lauterbach's text speaks of Gentiles who judge *bedine yisra'el*,[107] but there are variants, perhaps preferable in the light of Gittin, which have *kedine yisra'el*.[108] The difference is that *kedine yisra'el* implies no more than that the law applied is *like* Jewish law, not that Jewish law is itself being applied. Thus the texts might be understood as condemning not an actual jurisdictional practice, but rather an argument, put forward by those in the position of Babatha and others, that really there is no objection to recourse to Gentile courts, since the law there applied is very much the same as Jewish law.

Jurisdiction and foreign influence

We may now revert to the problems raised at the beginning of this section. To what extent does the presence within the province of a functioning Roman legal system, to which Jews – both Roman citizens and non-citizens – on occasion had resort, imply knowledge of Roman law such as might have influenced the content of the halakah, and to what extent does it imply 'pressure' such as might have affected the halakah's formal development ? Quantification, of course, is impossible, and account must also be taken of non-jurisdictional considerations (such as literary access – the subject of the next section) which may also be relevant to the overall question of Roman influence. Nevertheless, our survey suggests a number of preliminary conclusions, as well as raising further – often unanswerable – questions.

First, as to the *content* of the halakah. Our data suggest the following further questions: (i) *Who* would have knowledge of Roman law? (ii) *How deep* a knowledge would they possess ? (iii) *Of what kind* of Roman law would such knowledge consist? As to (i), it is evident that knowledge was not confined to (to the extent that it was possessed by) rabbinic circles. A property-possessing individual, such as Babatha, living outside the major population centres, could still get access to the knowledge necessary to make decisions regarding litigation and family arrangements.[109] Clearly, there were scribe/notaries (whether themselves Jewish or not) with sufficient knowledge to write private legal instruments based on Roman law. To what extent knowledge of Roman law permeated through other sections of the community may only be guessed. It would seem reasonable to suppose that some very basic knowledge of Roman criminal practice was widespread.[110] And we may expect that Jews involved in local administration – both judicial and non-judicial – will have been familiar with some aspects of Roman public law, especially in matters of citizenship.

As to the depth of such knowledge (ii), we should be sceptical. The problems of everyday life do not require any substantial academic knowledge of the law, such as would entail access to literary sources; at the most, the scribe/notary requires a 'form-book' for his guidance. Even today, we find a host of 'para-legal' workers engaged in matters of practice and procedure without personal recourse to the primary sources. We also find a popular, and often inaccurate, general knowledge of such legal institutions as commonly impinge on life's arrangements, and everyday language itself frequently carries implications as to the content of legal norms. It follows that we should not assume that influence may flow only from deep, scholarly knowledge.

The areas of Roman law (iii) which the jurisdictional situation will have brought to the attention of the public have already been indicated in (i). Surprisingly, perhaps, we find Babatha having recourse to the Roman legal system in family law matters – guardianship and family property – which one might have thought would have claimed the greatest loyalty to Jewish law. It may be that these were areas of family law where Jewish law was out of touch with changing social and economic conditions. If so, jurisdictional practice may be directly relevant to foreign influence, in that Jews choosing to have recourse to foreign law in certain areas may thereby have exerted special pressure in the direction of change in those particular areas of Jewish law. Guardianship may well be a good example of this.[111] But we are not sufficiently informed as to Babatha's reasoning to be able to claim that her case exemplifies such as a process. It has, in fact, been remarked that in cases of double citizenship (where *a fortiori* there would be a choice of forum), there was a tendency to use local law in commercial matters but Roman models in wills and family relations.[112]

Our data permit one further observation regarding the kind of Roman law which the jurisdictional situation will have made public knowledge. It was (already) a mildly Graecized version of Roman law. We need not inquire who spoke or read Latin. The relevant documents in the Babatha archive, including the two blank formulae, are in Greek – as, of course, is the mass of documents from Egypt related to Roman law. In fact, we may expect some difficulties on the part of the Jewish population in distinguishing between Hellenistic law (as in the autonomous Greek cities) and Roman law as administered in the Greek language. The rabbinic sources, at least, fail to make the distinction. In the Tosefta/Yerushalmi text discussed above, the [law] 'of damages of Gentiles' could be Greek or Roman.[113] In terms of the situation facing Jews resident in the autonomous Greek cities, much the same conclusions may be drawn as regards their knowledge of Greek law as have been argued from the effects of Roman jurisdiction. Indeed, Jewish knowledge of Greek public law, in the form of local government and municipal institutions, will have been that much greater, and the influence of Greek models has rightly been noted in the presence in Jewish cities of such officials as the *agoranomos*.[114]

Knowledge, of course, is a necessary but not a sufficient condition of foreign influence. Its relationship to other conditions is taken up elsewhere in this paper. But we may note that in assessing the likely impact of a foreign, concurrent jurisdiction upon the content of the halakah, it may be relevant to look to comparable situations elsewhere – not only within the Roman Empire (notably, in terms of the available sources, in Egypt) but also in later imperial situations where the conquering power has encountered strong indigenous legal traditions (as did the British in India).

The presence of Roman jurisdiction in the province is likely to have affected also the *form* of the halakah, and particularly its scope and internal coherence – at least if we accept the view of Mary Douglas[115] on the 'pressure' needed to explain the increasing scope and coherence which the halakah undoubtedly attained in this period. Our survey has revealed two important features of this pressure. First, there are discernible high points, the results of specific political events (the two revolts and the *constitutio Antoniniana*). Second, the pressure appears to have taken the form, predominantly, of uncertainty: the lack of definition of vassal status from 63 BCE to 6 CE; the wide discretion of the provincial governor from 6 CE, perhaps compounded up to 70 by his equestrian status; the acquisition after the revolt(s) of the status of *dediticii* by sections of the population, and the uncertainty of identifying them made the greater as time went on by both mobility and descent; and the ambiguities of the effects of the *constitutio Antoniniana*. Add to all this the pressure from the multiplicity of personal laws and citizenships and the variability of the willingness of Roman administrators to entertain suits under their concurrent jurisdiction (as in the case of Babatha).

The relationship between data such as those surveyed above and general theories of development is, at this stage at least, a reciprocal one. General theory may assist in the interpretation of doubtful data; historical data (to the extent that they can be viewed independently of other, unarticulated theories) may assist in the falsification of general theory. Applied to the present context, it is possible to argue that Mary Douglas's theory of 'pressure' would lead us to expect especially significant development in the scope and coherence of the halakah after 70, 135 and 212, and this may assist in the forming of hypotheses regarding the history of the tannaitic period. Conversely, those who see a steady and progressive development throughout the tannaitic period, and *a fortiori* those who see the formal features of tannaitic literature as descending complete from the period before 70, are likely to argue that this is so much the worse for the theory of pressure. It would lead us too far afield to attempt here any full consideration of these alternatives. For myself, I am content to suggest that our knowledge of the formal development of the halakah during the tannaitic period is not yet sufficient to eschew the stimulus of general theory.

3. Literary transmission

We turn now to the second major possibility as regards the transmission of knowledge of Roman law – literary transmission. Roman law early became, for most practical purposes, a system of *ius scriptum*, and it becomes important to determine the extent to which the rabbis had access to its written sources. Moreover, the dating of individual elements within the written tradition of Roman law is easier than in the halakah, since the statutes and edicts are dated by reference to the magistrates concerned, and the juristic fragments, although edited in the sixth century by the compilers of Justinian's Digest, were preserved each below a rubric identifying the jurist, the title of the work extracted, and the number of the *liber* in that work. Thus it is possible, with the help of Lenel's *Palingenesia Iuris Civilis*, to study the law of a particular date within the classical period, the task being complicated only by the existence of some post-classical interpolation (which the current generation of Romanists considers less extensive than did scholars in the first half of the century). It should, therefore, be possible to adopt a proper historical perspective in considering problems of Roman influence, rather than invoke Roman sources regardless of their date.

The history of Roman law is reasonably well documented from at least the last half century of the Republic, the period in Judaea from the very end of independence under the Hasmonaean dynasty into the first decade of Herod. The last century of the Second Jewish Commonwealth corresponds to the first century of the Roman Principate. The tannaitic age in Judaea corresponds to what Romanists call the Classical Period of Roman law – a period of fairly settled political conditions at Rome (until the early third century), during which the principal form of creativity in Roman law was the writings of the classical jurists. Of these, it may be noted, some came from the provinces, including Ulpian, who stands pre-eminent in Justinian's Digest (compiled in the sixth century) for the proportion of the work extracted from his writings, and who came from Tyre.

The written sources of Roman law were listed by the jurist Gaius in his elementary textbook, *The Institutes* (written c. 160 CE), as statutes (*leges*: enactments of the *comitia*), resolutions of the *concilium plebis* (*plebiscita*), recommendations of the senate (*senatusconsulta*), imperial constitutions (*constitutiones principum*), magistrates' edicts (*edicta*), and juristic responses to questions posed (*responsa prudentium*). The distinction between the first four became, from early in the Principate, largely of formal and historical interest. The emperor *de facto* controlled all legislation and merely used the old Republican forms at his convenience. Moreover, legislation in all these four forms was of a piecemeal character comparable to individual Acts or Laws of a modern legislature, in contradistinction to Codes or even legislation consolidating specific areas in their entirety.[116] Thus these statutes, whose primary concern, certainly as regards private law, was with the law relating to Roman citizens, are unlikely to have been of great interest to the rabbis (with one possible exception, to be considered shortly); moreover, their effect, as regards life in the provinces, will have been mediated through the Roman governor[117] and his legal staff. On the other hand, the *edicta* of the magistrates and the *responsa prudentium* will have been of more direct concern.

Statute law

Roman statutory law, in its various forms, was not likely to have been directly accessible to the rabbis. Indeed, one may wonder what exactly was the content of the libraries available even to the Roman legal officials working in such provinces as Judaea. From an early date, the administration of the imperial civil service was highly centralized, with officials rotating between postings and having frequent periods in Rome. It seems not unlikely that such officials came equipped with the Roman edicts (to be considered below) and little else.[118] Of course, the civil service came to include many trained jurists, including some of the foremost academic writers in the classical period. No doubt they took with them their personal collections of juristic writings. But the more advanced the juristic writings, the less accessible they will have been to the rabbis.

There is one likely exception to the characterization of Roman statutory law as piecemeal and inherently of little real interest to the intelligentsia of the provinces. The Roman Twelve Tables, written in the early Republic, around 450 BCE, were sufficiently wide-ranging (though far from comprehensive) to be regarded by the Romans as the 'source of all law, public and private'[119] and to be described by Sir Henry Maine (though much criticized on this score) as a 'code'. Cicero notes that in his childhood it was learned by heart at school. No doubt this famous document

174

was known to the intelligentsia of the provinces, and Boaz Cohen has listed a number of parallels between its contents and Jewish law (though reserving his position on the question of influence).[120] In fact, the only arguments in favour of the influence of the Twelve Tables on rabbinic law are those of chronological priority and probable accessibility. When one looks at the content of the parallels, one sees that there is such a difference between the technical level of the Twelve Tables and rabbinic law that influence becomes more unlikely.[121] In at least one of the examples, the likely historical contact between the systems is that rabbinic law formed part of the oriental milieu which later was to shape the *post-classical* development of the Roman institution. Cohen compares the Twelve Tables institution of *usucapio* (prescriptive title attained after one year for land, two for movables) with the rabbinic *hazakah* of immovable property after three years. In fact, three years was one of the periods chosen by Justinian in his reform of the law of prescription in 531 CE – though here the three-year period was applicable only to movables.

Edicts

A more significant source of Roman law as regards the rabbis will have been the magistrates' edicts. From early in the Republic it had been normal for the magistrates with major judicial functions (from the fourth century BCE the praetor, and to a much lesser degree the quaestor) to issue an *edictum* on assuming office, stating the principles on which they intended to administer the law. (Only from 67 BCE, following the scandal of Verres's governorship of Sicily, were magistrates legally bound to follow these principles.) The edict came to cover the whole private law, whether its sources were statutory or (at first) procedural innovations made by the magistrates themselves. The magistracies were elected annually, and candidates did not seek successive terms. Thus each year there would be a new praetor issuing a fresh edict. It is generally assumed that the praetor would not use this institution as an opportunity for major law reform; he was first and foremost a politician seeking to rise right up the *cursus honorum,* and would normally readopt the edict of his predecessor, with perhaps occasional changes in some area or another; the regularly readopted material was called *edictum tralatitium,* in contrast to the *edictum novum* (and perhaps *edictum praelatum*: that which was in fact carried forward in a particular year, but which had not become 'traditional'). This process of readoption became more marked in the Empire, and eventually the Emperor Hadrian commissioned the jurist Julian to put the edict into a final and authoritative form (c. 125 CE). Thereafter, the edict continued to be reissued each year, but changes in its terms were no longer permitted. The edict, like some of the *leges*, attracted the jurists into writing commentaries – and this well before its final consolidation by Julian.[122] This is good evidence that from the beginning of the Empire the text of the edict was already more or less stabilized.

This brief description of the role and history of the edict refers, of course, to the situation in Rome itself. But it is also applicable to the provinces with some significant caveats. We know that the Roman provincial governor had the *imperium* of both the *praetor urbanus* (who dealt with disputes involving only citizens) and the *praetor peregrinus* (who dealt with disputes involving one or more non-citizens) at Rome. He too was expected to issue an edict, the *edictum provinciale*, on assumption of his office. In principle, therefore, the *edictum provinciale* could have proved a vital channel of transmission for one of the most important literary sources of Roman law. Whether it did so, however, is uncertain, in the light of doubts as to both its content and the manner of its publication in the province.

Our information regarding the content of the *edictum provinciale* comes from Cicero's account of his own practice as governor of Cilicia[123] and from papyrological and inscriptional evidence from Egypt.[124] Neither may be taken as typical of practice in other provinces at other times. Cicero implies that in some respects, at least, he was innovating, and the main conclusion to be drawn from his account is the breadth of the governor's discretion in the matter. His description of his own edict as 'short' may, however, support the view that in the late Republic it was not uncommon to reproduce the text of the Roman edict(s)[125] – since one of his innovations appears to have been the use of an incorporation of the latter by reference. At the same time, Cicero still considered it proper to include explicitly 'such matters as cannot conveniently be handled without an edict, as possession of inheritances, possession of property, appointment of receivers, sale of property, things which are usually litigated and otherwise transacted in accordance with the edict'.[126] Further evidence that the *edictum provinciale* contained (apart from fiscal and administrative matters) a not in-considerable private law content may be thought to reside in the commentary of Gaius *ad edictum provinciale*,[127] although argu-ments to the contrary have been advanced.[128] On the other hand, the Egyptian edicts appear to represent a different genre,[129] reflecting in part the fact that Egypt continued to be an equestrian province.[130] For Judaea, there is no direct evidence in one direction or the other. It is, however, likely that the position there was more like Egypt than Cilicia until at least 70 CE (the earliest date when Judaea may have ceased to be an equestrian province). By this date it is likely that the content of the *edictum provinciale* was becoming stable, and by c. 125 CE further development was excluded by the Julianic consolidation of the edicts ordered by Hadrian. Henceforth, if not before, we can speak of one *edictum provinciale*, rather than separate edicts for each province,[131] and this may have made publication of the private law content more practical,[132] if less necessary. At the very least, we may expect that in the period before the Julianic consolidation, the *edictum provinciale* was used to bring new legislation to the attention of Roman citizens in the province.[133]

As for publication of the edict, the precise manner will have depended upon the nature and availability of the public build-ings in the provincial centres concerned. In Rome itself, it was inscribed on wooden tables in black letters on a white back-ground, sectionalized under red captions, and posted in the forum.[134] In Egypt, the largest surviving example of a provincial edict[135] has been found in an inscription in the temple of Hibis in the oasis of Thebaid (Khargeh), preceded by a covering mes-sage from the local *strategos* and extending to 66 lines. No doubt this falls far short of the size of the edict at Rome, but it signifies nevertheless a willingness to surmount the logistical problems of making official acts accessible to the local population. But as regards Judaea we have no evidence of the manner of publication.[136]

No such uncertainties beset the Jewish population of Rome, for whom both the private law content and the manner of publication of the edict is clearly established. Thus the Palesti-nian rabbis will have had at least this indirect source of know-ledge, as well as such information as they may personally have acquired on visiting the capital. There was, however, one major difference between the edict in Rome and that in Judaea (even assuming the latter to have included private law material); in

Rome it was published in Latin, while in Judaea it is likely (at least if we follow the model of Egypt) to have been in Greek.[137]

Juristic writings

To what extent had the juristic contribution to Roman law developed in our period, and how far was it accessible to the rabbis? *Responsa prudentium*, replies by jurists to questions posed by both litigants and judges, were given from at least the late Republic, and were not dissimilar in nature to the later Jewish *she'elot uteshuvot* which modern scholarship describes by the same Roman term. These *responsa* were not binding on the judge in the Republican period, and perhaps never achieved this status *de iure*; nevertheless, their *de facto* authority was great and increased in the Empire when leading jurists could receive an imperial endorsement, the *ius publice respondendi*.[138]

The *responsa* of the jurists frequently became available to the general public in the form of collections which the jurist might himself subsequently publish. Whether this was a genre of literature which was likely to commend itself to foreign legal experts may perhaps be doubted; certainly it was not the most accessible form of juristic writing. But there were other genres of Roman juristic writing which might well have attracted the attention of the rabbis – for their form perhaps as much as their content. The history and characteristics of this literature have been considered by Fritz Schulz in his *History of Roman Legal Science*,[139] a book (along with the *Palingenesia Iuris Civilis*) which no one who wishes to consider the possible influence of Roman juristic writing on the halakah can afford to neglect. In this context it must suffice to extract just a few of the facts which may be regarded as relevant to any such investigation.

(i) Despite the modern commonplace regarding the Roman separation of *ius* and *fas* (civil and religious law), we find that in the late Republic lay jurists (the successors of the earlier class of legal experts, who were *pontifices*) did concern themselves with religious law. For example, the same Servius Sulpicius Rufus who wrote on dowry, published collected *responsa*, and wrote probably the first rudimentary commentary on the Edict, also wrote *De sacris detestandis libri*. Indeed, Cicero tells us that he also lectured on *ius pontificium 'qua ex parte cum iure civile coniunctum esset'* (*Brut.* 42.156).

Roman juristic writing on civil law may well be regarded as

having developed naturally from juristic treatment of Roman religious law. This phenomenon is largely obscured by the fact that later legal disinterest in such matters, allied with the change in the state religion, resulted in the failure to preserve works of this kind. Its existence is none the less quite certain, from the titles of books that are preserved, and from various references. It presents a possible parallel of some importance given recent work in early rabbinics, in so far as it now seems likely that the ritual law enjoyed some priority over the civil law in terms of juristic elaboration.[140] For comparative dating purposes it may be noted that there was a revival of juristic writing on the sacral law under Augustus and Tiberius, but nothing thereafter.[141]

(ii) Commentaries, rare in the Republican period, burgeon under the Empire. Their form is lemmatic, and indistinguishable from that of the widespread non-juristic commentary of the period. In formal terms the parallel to the rabbinic genre of halakic midrash is close, but whether the impetus came from the juristic commentaries and is to be designated Roman in origin may well be doubted. On the other hand, the Roman juristic commentaries produce a phenomenon from the second century which may be relevant to the literary forms adopted by the halakah: from commentary on primary legal sources (*leges*, the edict, etc.) we find a progression to commentary on other juristic writing. In particular, the *Ius Civile* of Q. Mucius Scaevola, the outstanding example of Republican systematic jurisprudence, attracted commentary after commentary.

(iii) Introductory works – which would have been the most intelligible to foreign intelligentsia – were lacking in the Republic and began to flourish only after Hadrian. To this, there is one significant exception, the first-century treatise of Sabinus, *Libri tres iuris civilis*. The second century also saw the development of a genre of literature regarded by Schulz as akin to that of the introductory manual: books variously called *regulae, definitiones, differentiae* and *sententiae*, where the emphasis was non-casuistic, but rather stressed principles and maxims. Though having little in common with the form of rabbinic works, they may be relevant as affording a genre particularly accessible to the outsider.

(iv) The systematic treatise was known from the Republic (the *Ius Civile* of Scaevola, referred to above), though it was not, in the nature of things, attempted particularly often. But despite the persistence of interest in sacral law into the early Empire,

179

there is no evidence of the existence of systematic treatises which combined civil and ritual law.

(v) Although the genre of *responsa* originated out of consultation in actual cases, the published collections came to include hypothetical cases put to the jurist. Schulz suggests that this may be true as early as the collection of Servius.

Whether any of these genres was available to the rabbis early enough to influence that aspect of the development of the halakah which the particular genre may have suggested depends, of course, on the view one takes of the dating of such aspects of the halakic development – problems which lie beyond the scope of this paper. It should, however, be noted that positive evidence for channels of transmission of this juristic literature is lacking. For Egypt, where one might assume the market for such works to have been larger, Taubenschlag noted that the works of classical jurisprudence began to penetrate (only) in the second half of the third century.[142] Nor may we place much reliance upon suggestions of a Roman law school in Caesarea since the third century (in any event too late for the purposes of this inquiry)[143] although the school at Beirut is thought to have been in existence by 200 CE.[144] That there was eventually a Roman law school in Caesarea is established. Tribonian, Justinian's chief Law Commissioner, refers to it in scathing terms.[145] On the other hand, we must not take too narrow a view of the matter. Law was taught, at a lower level, also in the schools of rhetoric. Moreover, the rabbis could certainly have gained access to these works via the community at Rome, – though to suggest that they sought access is a very different proposition from the proposal that they could not avoid it at home. In the absence of positive evidence of the ready availability of Roman juristic texts to the rabbis, the question becomes one of necessary inference from actual parallels. In this context, parallels found in juristic commentaries *ad edictum provinciale* may deserve special attention,[146] since such commentaries may be regarded as one of the likeliest forms of juristic writing to have been available in the provinces. Thus it would be useful to compare the number of parallels with Jewish law in Gaius's commentary *ad edictum provinciale* with the number found in another type of juristic work of the same period. If the number in the former were significantly greater, that would constitute indirect evidence of the availability of the commentary *ad edictum provinciale* within the province.

4. Influence on form

In this and the following sections, consideration is given to some parallels between Roman and Jewish law. Whether such parallels betoken 'influence' is a question involving more than mere matching of the parallels against our knowledge of the historical background. The availability of channels of transmission is not a sufficient condition of 'influence'.[147] Something more is needed, namely a general theory of influence. For 'influence' is an inferential theory derived from the data; the data do not speak for themselves.[148] In seeking here to construct a typology of the problematics of Roman influence on the halakah in the light of such a theory,[149] I stress again the reciprocal nature of the relationships between parallels, historical background, and general theory. We must be prepared to approach any one in the light of the combined strength of the other two: an extremely close parallel combined with a clearly attested[150] channel of transmission might require modification of a preconceived general theory of influence; a parallel supported by a general theory leading one to expect influence in such a situation might indicate the existence of an otherwise unattested channel of transmission; and an attested channel of transmission combined with a theory leading to the expectation of influence might guide one's interpretation of a parallel. In addition, a general theory of influence may assist in determining the relative significance to be attached to a parallel once identified.

Scope

In post-biblical times, there was an enormous increase in the scope of the halakah. Whole topics not treated in the Bible are extensively considered. Are we to attribute this development to foreign influence?[151] Parallels are certainly available, in the form of the range of both Roman law[152] and Hellenistic law[153] achieved at least within the last century BCE,[154] and channels of communication for this feature of the foreign legal systems were certainly available.[155] It is, however, possible to view such developments as 'natural', in the sense that intellectual systems, like the capacity of the human individual, have a tendency towards greater range and complexity.[156] According to this view, foreign influence cannot be a sufficient explanation of the fact of development in this direction, although foreign influence is one type of environmental factor required to explain why the development took place at that particular time and with such speed. Such, then, would be the significance of foreign influence in this model: in one sense it is not a necessary (much less a sufficient) cause of the development, in that a comparable development is likely to have occurred within the system at some time; in another sense, it was a necessary condition – to the extent that a comparable development is thought unlikely at that time and with such speed in its absence. It is, in short, a contributory cause in a natural process. We shall find that there is reason to adopt this model of development in considering foreign influence in some (but not all) other types of legal phenomena, both formal and substantive. For convenience, we may refer to it as the N + E (Nature + Environment) model.

In speaking of the increased scope of the halakah, it is important to distinguish the literary presentation of the norms from the process of their generation. The N + E model may certainly be applied to the latter, and in this context we should look to jurisdictional pressures, and the knowledge resulting therefrom, as the particular form of Roman stimulus that may have contributed to the process. But this in itself would not entail the presentation of those norms in a consolidated literary form – a 'code'. Quite different factors, and a different model of development, may be thought appropriate to that question.[157]

Coherence

The N + E model may also be applied to the increasing coherence of the halakah, i.e. its increasing feeling for consistency in language and principles, a development linked to increasing conceptualization, where problems are treated less as isolated concrete occurrences and more as contexts for the application of accepted ideas. Arguments from consistency are prominent in Greek forensic rhetoric, and the same feeling underlies Roman juristic attempts to classify the whole law under a series of major and minor headings, each *genus* and *species* possessing internal common elements which differentiate it from others.[158] It is unlikely that such Roman juristic writings were available to the rabbis, but in this respect both Roman law and Jewish law may be regarded as recipients of Greek learning and technique.[159] Such an explanation, however, is hardly available in respect of the use by the rabbis, in contrast to the biblical sources, of a settled and consistent terminology. This, too, is a feature of Roman Republican jurisprudence, but it is not likely to have been accessible to the rabbis. In this respect we must look to different environmental factors to fulfill the role of spurs to the actualization of the natural tendency of the system.

Content of classificatory divisions

When one turns to the content of some of the major classificatory divisions of the halakah one enters a sphere where the N + E model is inappropriate; with a few possible exceptions,[160] there is no reason to suppose the existence of any natural tendency to articulate particular classificatory divisions. Thus when we find Graeco-Roman parallels to such halakic classifications as *dine qenasot*,[161] *torah shebiktab/torah shebe'al peh*,[162] and the division, implicit in the arrangement of Neziḳin, between public and private law,[163] combined with the fact that all three are likely to have been known to the rabbis, through either jurisdictional practice[164] or general education,[165] we may be tempted not only to suspect foreign influence but also to attach a higher significance to that influence than in the N + E model.

But caution is required in respect of both temptations. It takes a brave man[166] to embrace a single-factor explanation such as is represented by a theory of foreign influence irrespective of the needs and pressures working within the recipient society. Most theorists would still prefer to find some special function for the foreign element, as an explanation of *why* it was received. Views often differ as to whether such a role should be sought only in response to socio-economic pressures, or whether it may be found equally in fulfilment of some intellectual or ideological need,[167] but such differences[168] are secondary to the common search for further explanation. The problem is well illustrated by asking the further question: if some foreign elements were received, but others were not, what criteria guided or determined the choice?[169] That latter criterion, whether intellectual (deriving from the properties of a particular cultural system) or socio-economic, will itself be a product of the particular environment. Thus we may label this model, in contrast to N + E, E + E. As for the significance of any foreign influence found to have been at work within this model, much may turn on whether one is inclined to attach more importance to an N factor because it is N (a value-judgment as to which conventional historical method has nothing to say). If N is regarded as qualitatively different from E, then a different type of significance will attach to foreign influence in the two models. But whether or not this view is taken, it seems possible to conclude, as regards E + E, that some sort of evaluation of the relative strengths of the two E factors may in principle be possible. The significance of foreign influence within the E + E model may thus be more variable than in N + E. In some cases, pure intellectual attraction[170] may greatly outweigh any particular function within the recipient system.

Legal argument

Both models may be involved in assessment of parallels relating to the form of legal argument. A distinction must here be made. As regards the capacity of the system to utilize arguments of a particular level of abstraction and complexity, the N + E model is appropriate. There is a natural tendency towards sequential development in this sphere, but this tendency requires actualization by the stimulus of environmental factors, one of which may be foreign influence.[171] But as regards the choice of particular forms of argument (within that cognitive level – the achievement of which is, of course, a necessary condition of the capacity to make the choice) we may prefer E + E.

In terms of the question of the indebtedness of some of the rabbinic *middot* (exegetical principles) to Hellenistic rhetoric,[172] this distinction suggests the following problem. Did Hellenistic rhetoric provide the spur (E) to the actualization of the *capacity* of the system, or did it merely influence the choice of particular *forms* of argument[173] of a particular conceptual level, once the capacity for that level had been achieved as a result of the interaction of other factors? Important evidence of the dating of this advance may be found in the Dead Sea Scrolls, but I refrain from substantive judgment on the matter. Whatever answer is given to this problem, the further question remains as to the significance to be attached to any foreign influence that may be thought to have played a role. Here as elsewhere the issue will turn on the philosophical problem of assessing the relative roles of E in the two models. In this case, however, the assessment of the significance of E in the E + E model must take account of the fact that N + E is a necessary condition of the operation of E + E at all.

Roman influence is unlikely to have been a major factor in these developments. Apart from the general problem of access,[174] it may be worthwhile investigating whether the features of rabbinic argument which have been associated with foreign models reflect forensic or scholastic *Sitze im Leben*.[175] The answer may assist us in determining both the source of the influence and the location of its reception within Judaism. Roman legal argument is represented by the scholastic texts of the jurists – their arguments influenced no doubt by rhetoric but not synonymous with it – and will have been received, if at all, by the scholarly élite; Hellenistic rhetoric is predominantly forensic, and this may have been received in the first instance by those involved in litigation in Greek cities.

Legal drafting

The grammatical form and complexity of individual legal sentences, and their relationship one to another, also reflect the conceptual level of the system. There is a need here for comparative form-critical analysis such as has been undertaken in relation to biblical and ancient Near Eastern laws.[176] Here too we may have to invoke both the N + E and the E + E models, according to the particular question posed.[177] For it appears that while Near Eastern law displays technical superiority over Roman law at the time of the initiation of the tradition of written law in the latter (the Twelve Tables – fifth century BCE), the Roman jurists and legislators had taken the lead by the end of the Republic.

Reduction to writing

Neither Roman nor Hellenistic systems of law suffered any inhibition against the reduction of their law to writing, such as appears to have occurred among at least some sections of Jewish opinion after the canonization of the Pentateuch. However, the use of written law has been a feature of a probable minority of the world's legal systems, and it may be instructive to inquire, in respect of each occasion when a body of law is committed to writing (even within a system which had developed a tradition of written law), what were the historical factors, here within an E + E model bearing upon that particular decision. We may suspect that the outside events that are most likely to have been influential are the peaks of jurisdictional threat,[178] in the wake of the two revolts and the enactment of the *constitutio Antoniniana*. But our knowledge of the history of codification of Jewish law in the tannaitic period – and even the precise dating of the Mishnah of R. Judah (whether before or after the *c.Ant.*[179]) – is too uncertain to allow for conclusions at this stage. It is possible that Roman influence came to bear also through the consolidation of the *edictum provinciale* around 125 CE,[180] but it is doubtful that this event will have had any significant impact in the province.

Arrangement

Our approach to foreign influence as regards the arrangement of material within literary statements of the law should be similar to that regarding the content of classificatory subdivisions; frequently, the arrangement of material constitutes an implied statement of such classifications. Thus we have noted the implied distinction between public and private law reflected in the arrangement of Seder Nezikin.[181] Daube suggests that the collection of private (or civil) law in the Mishnah may reflect the influence of the Roman edict:[182] while the Roman scheme is not followed in detail,[183] and the idea of civil law already attains some rudimentary recognition early within the biblical period,[184] the attraction of succession from its biblical context (which might well have suggested a location in the Mishnah Seder Nashim) into Baba Kamma-Baba Batra is a notable movement in the Roman direction.

We should not, however, be disposed to accept that this is the whole story. Even within the E + E model, we should be alert to internal needs which the foreign influence serves to meet. These are more or less likely to be purely scholastic needs according to the philosophical predisposition of the observer. At the same time the N + E model may also prove to have some relevance to the problem of arrangement – if, that is, one accepts the legitimacy of recent attempts to apply structuralist analysis to literature (including, notably, biblical narrative[185]) and the natural status of the deep structures which such analysis seeks to reveal.[186]

Literary form

If one uses the term 'literary form' to designate the major patterns of literary organization (rather than patterns of argument, drafting or arrangement), there appears no reason to qualify the judgment that the appropriate model is E + E. The data here to be explained consist of such forms as 'mishnah' and 'midrash'. As for the latter, there is a clear antecedent in the lemmatic commentary of the early scholiasts to the Greek classics, which Schulz notes in connection with the development of lemmatic commentary in Roman law.[187] As for mishnah, it is possible that the Roman edict[188] prompted renewed awareness of the possibilities of restatement independent of the original or primary source: the Roman magistrates were, in theory, merely giving effect to Roman statutory law, just as the Mishnah, in theory, merely restated the antecedent traditions (written and unwritten) of the Sinaitic legislation. Such a judgment is not affected by the fact that there already existed within Judaism earlier examples of post-biblical reformulation, in the manuals of the Qumran community.[189] For the E + E model alerts us to the need to decide why a particular development occurred at a particular time; greater emphasis may thus be placed upon the more proximate factors.

Conclusion

To many of the questions raised in this section, it is not possible even to attempt to give answers. We have been reviewing the elements of legal science, which it is virtually impossible to do in the absence of written sources of law. For the rabbinic development, at least, such sources begin in the early third century. If we ask what was the state of legal drafting, legal argument, conceptual classification and patterns of arrangement in, e.g., 50, 100 and 150 CE, we can hardly begin to provide answers.[190] It is here that the lack of a Jewish *Palingenesia Iuris Civilis* most impedes our progress. If we had, or were able to construct, such a document, it is unlikely that it would reveal Jewish temporal priority to Hellenistic developments in legal science – to do which would entail a reading back of the technical level of 200 CE by as much as 300 years. But it would allow us to gauge the temporal proximity of developments in Jewish legal science to events in the Graeco-Roman environment in a manner which is essential if we are to achieve any satisfactory level of understanding.

5. *Influence on content*

In considering influence upon the content of the halakah we must continue to reckon with the interaction of three types of question: the closeness of the parallel, the availability of channels of transmission, and the contribution of general theory.

As to the last, it may be useful to invoke a different model of explanation,[191] one which like N + E and E + E takes account of the multiplicity of operative factors but which assumes a scalar form and assigns a different role to N. For convenience, it may be termed I + E, where I represents both considerations internal to the logic of the system and a predominantly implicit mode of expression, and E represents considerations (whether foreign or domestic) external to the logic of the system and a predominantly explicit mode of expression. The theory, in short, is this. The (surface) phenomena of the law reflect an interaction between internal and external factors (in the senses used above), the phenomena tending to be more concrete and explicit than the internal logic of the system. The role of external factors is thus to influence the choice of possible surface solutions, more or less within a range determined or guided by the internal features of the system. External factors include, but are not limited to, environmental pressures as conventionally understood, but may extend also to ideas external to the system. The internal logic of the system is itself the product of interaction between natural and culturally-contingent factors – the innate disposition of the human mind and the unarticulated belief-value system of the culture concerned. In this sense, N plays a parameter-setting role even in the I + E model. The model is scalar in this sense. The closer our surface phenomenon comes to the conceptual level of the internal system, the lesser the role we should be inclined to attribute to E factors in its generation.[192]

It will again be convenient to review the problematics of foreign influence in terms of different types of legal phenomena. For the types differ in terms of both their locations on the I – E scale and their inherent visibility, the latter being relevant to our assessment of the available channels of transmission.

Rules

According to a useful distinction much discussed in contemporary jurisprudence,[193] a 'rule' means a single, concrete norm which is binding, whereas a 'principle' denotes a more general and abstract normative proposition which guides the judge in arguing for the choice of rule in difficult cases. This in itself suggests that some rules at least cannot be viewed in isolation; they form part of a system with logical properties of some kind. The I + E model presupposes a theory that goes somewhat further. It claims that every rule must be viewed in the context of the internal logic of the system; indeed, some would assert that central to the identity of any rule is its relationship to others.[194] The adoption of this viewpoint entails an important conclusion as regards foreign influence: such influence, viewed in terms of the individual rule, cannot provide any sufficient explanation.

One might incline to the view that the more technical the rule, the less visible it is likely to have been, and thus the less the chance that a parallel signifies foreign influence. Many technical rules are known only to the legal élite, so that access on the part of the rabbis would require the availability of Roman juristic texts (or persons intimately familiar with them). An example is the ruling of R. Simeon that sacrilege does not extend to the misappropriation of sacred property in the charge of one (such as a carrier) who bears the risk of its loss,[195] adopted also by the Roman jurist Labeo a century earlier in defining *peculatus* as *pecuniae publicae aut sacrae furtum non ab eo factum, cuius periculo fuit*.[196] But some technical rules will have been visible, because of their practical importance. For example, Cohen points to R. Hoshaya's knowledge that *traditio* is not necessarily required in Roman law (while *kinyan* is required in Jewish).[197]

A further example illustrates the interaction of general theory with problems of access.[198] Jewish law developed a remedy for non-fatal injuries occasioned to a free man by an animal which was *tam*[199] no earlier than the mid-second century.[200] To do so, it had to overcome a serious inhibition: biblical law dealt only with *fatal* injuries caused by a *tam*, and there declared the owner of the animal 'free'.[201] Roman law faced a similar problem. The *actio de pauperie*, which originated in the Twelve Tables, appears to have applied at first only to land and livestock, being extended only later to slaves, and later still to free men. Assuming,

189

as seems likely, temporal priority for the extension in Roman law, is there a case to be made for Roman influence? The contrary argument could be based upon both general theory and channels of transmission. It could be said that the Jewish development merely constituted a 'natural' extension of the existing remedies,[202] and that the Roman extension appears not in the edict but in a juristic commentary thereon. But the case for influence should not be thus lightly dismissed. First, we should be wary of applying our own value judgments to the historical material, in the form of categorizing a development as 'natural'. In the light of the biblical background itself, the development was clearly controversial. Second, even if we may perceive an alternative underlying logic emerging in the tannaitic law of damages (to which the extension would conform), we still have to ask why the development occurred at that particular time (and in that particular form).[203] Third, there are indeed possible channels of transmission:[204] we might expect the rule to be visible for practical reasons (such injuries are hardly unusual in an agrarian society); and its earliest occurrence in a Roman juristic work is found in none other than the commentary of Gaius *ad edictum provinciale*,[205] the juristic work which is the likeliest to have circulated in the provinces.

Finally, we should note that 'Roman influence' should not be conceived solely in terms of the influence of Roman law. Roman-inspired environmental factors which played a role in the development of the law should also be considered, as in Sperber's studies of the effects of economic conditions.[206] But we should resist any tendency to regard such factors as providing complete explanation. While they may stimulate transformation in the underlying logical system, they do not necessarily indicate the form which change must take.

Principles

Whereas students of biblical law have interested themselves in the underlying principles of the law, and their comparison with those of neighbouring legal systems,[207] there appears to have been little concern with such problems in the tannaitic period. Perhaps the reason lies in the greater range and extent of other types of legal phenomena at this period. At any rate, the question cannot be neglected. It is, however, significantly different from that facing the biblical scholar. For whereas the principles of biblical law largely[208] have to be inferred from concrete data – which poses a methodological problem as yet unsolved[209] – tannaitic literature not only is more replete with such statements but often explicitly presents them as having the status of a general principle, by designating them a *kelal*. There is little doubt that this development reflects the Hellenistic cultural milieu, with its penchant for the *kanōn* and the *regula*.[210] A systematic comparative study of the corpus of rabbinic *kelalot* and the Roman collections of *regulae*, etc.[211] would be worthwhile; one suspects that this is a genre of literature inherently more likely to cross cultural boundaries than many of the other forms of juristic writing, so that influence in the content of the *kelalot* may be more prominent than in other types of legal phenomena.

This last observation does not conflict with the theoretical stance which expects a lesser role for foreign influence (or other environmental factors) the closer one gets to the inner logic of the system.[212] In dealing with rabbinic literature, the principles of the system may take any one of three forms: they may be stated *and* presented as *kelalot*; they may be stated *without* being presented as *kelalot*; and they may be left unstated. The foreign literary model may well influence the choice, but this is not the same as saying that it has influenced the content of the principle concerned (although the latter is by no means excluded). Moreover, there is no necessary identification of the stated principles with the inner logic of the system; indeed, there is reason to expect that the true inner logic will remain unstated.

Institutions

Legal institutions are sets of principles and rules applicable in a discrete life situation, directed to particular social ends, and accompanied by defined procedures whereby they are constituted and terminated.[213] Examples are slavery, marriage and mortgages. Their social importance may dispose us to think that they are located well on the 'I' side of the I – E scale, so that foreign influence is less likely. But it is possible to view them rather as contexts for the application of the principles, rules and procedures of the system, rather than as discrete phenomena. Thus new social conditions or a new cultural environment may produce wholly new contexts for the interaction of internal and external forces. To the extent that foreign influence may operate with this effect, its significance may be rated high. But we must note that foreign influence which produces the reception of a new institution does not necessarily entail the adoption of particular rules or principles for the working of that institution. In this sense, once again, foreign influence is incapable of providing any complete explanation.

Thus our theory creates no predisposition against foreign influence in legal institutions. Moreover, institutions are, of their nature, among the most visible aspects of a legal system. We may therefore expect this to be one of the most productive areas for the student of influence. Examples include the Roman institution of *peculium*,[214] the Greek institution of the will[215] and Hellenistic influence in various institutions of property[216] (including family property[217]) law. Greek terminology is particularly prominent in the institutions of the civil law,[218] and although terminology does not entail the reception of the foreign institution in all its detailed rules and principles, we should be wary of arguments that the influence was confined to terminology.[219]

The bias in favour of Greek and Hellenistic rather than Roman institutions should come as no surprise; institutions, unlike some of the other phenomena here considered, are transmitted through social contact rather than via scholastic channels, and the Jews had longer experience of living cheek by jowl with Greeks than with Romans. There is, moreover, a technical reason which may support this tendency. The Roman law most prominent in the provinces will have been the *'ius gentium'*[220] since *peregrini* were very often involved. But the Roman *ius gentium*, in contrast to the older, often more technical and archaic *ius civile*, was itself the more Hellenized section of Roman law.[221]

Concepts

Concepts differ from institutions in their distance from the life situation, and they resemble principles in their range of application. They differ from principles in that they are not directly prescriptive: their normative force is attained only when they are incorporated within a normative proposition such as a rule or a principle. Essentially, they belong to the sphere of reflection upon or argument within the legal system, and this scholastic milieu requires literary channels of transmission if a concept is to be transferred with any accuracy. On the other hand, there may be considerable transmission of hazier versions of technical concepts through the medium of ordinary language, and this too may provide a channel for the influence of non-juristic concepts.

Examples include *dolus* and *peshi'ah*,[222] *physis/natura* and *derek*,[223] *obligatio* and *hiyyub*[224] (and particularly the modalities of *obligatio*: *naturalis/civilis*[225] and the functionally cognate classification of *lex* as *perfecta, minus quam perfecta* and *imperfecta*,[226] to be compared with *dine 'adam/dine shamayim*[227]). Here, too, it is frequently difficult to isolate the Roman elements from the Greek. The Romans commonly gave more precise juristic expression and application to Greek philosophical concepts. In so far as the sources of such concepts in rabbinic law are concerned, it is necessary to decide in each case between a Roman juristic source and a more popular (albeit sometimes rhetorical) form of Greek mediation.

Notarial Practice

Deeds and notarial practice represent a type of legal phenomenon particularly open to foreign influence. They are especially visible; they present both a challenge and an opportunity to the scribe to devise a form having the desired effects according to both the legal systems whose jurisdictions may conflict;[228] and they belong close to the 'E' end of the I – E scale.[229] In fact, considerable foreign influence upon Jewish law does appear to have been established in this area.[230] Not only particular formulae but whole genres of document, such as the *get shihrur*,[231] reflect foreign practice. Here too it may be difficult to distinguish Roman from other sources of inspiration.[232] Although Romans, particularly in the provinces, made use of such deeds, the genre is particularly associated with Greek and Hellenistic law, and itself influenced Roman law particularly in the post-classical period, with the shift of power to the East.[233]

Notarial practice is particularly important in that it provides us with evidence of the reception of foreign practice which is independent of rabbinic views. The Elephantine papyri[234] and the Murabba'at documents[235] are especially significant in this respect.[236] It is instructive to attempt a comparison, albeit impressionistic, of the relative extent of foreign influence in (1) these corpora taken from the actual practice of the people; (2)

the rabbinic texts (which, according to the genre,[237] involve varying types of combination between descriptive and prescriptive material); and (3) the norms of such a 'sectarian' group as the Qumran community. Such a comparison may perhaps support the view that receptivity to foreign influence is in inverse proportion to religious introspection.

Court Procedures

Our approach to influence in court procedures will resemble that to deeds and notarial practice. Here too we have an essentially visible type of legal phenomenon, and one, moreover, which has captured the imagination since the beginnings of recorded Western culture. However, court procedures are likely to involve values internal to the system more directly than notarial practice, so that influence, where established, may be counted as less significant.

Nor surprisingly, the Graeco-Roman sources of inspiration appear to divide in accordance with the jurisdictional situation. Knowledge of Roman procedures has been perceived chiefly in criminal, particularly capital,[238] cases; as regards civil procedure, where Roman practice involved Jews to a lesser extent, the Greek sources appear more prominent.[239]

6. Normative self-definition

To what extent do the data here surveyed assist in our understanding of how and why Judaism moved towards normative self-definition in the first three centuries?[240] Such a movement is here understood as meaning the process by which Judaism 'moved towards excluding some views of what it meant to be . . . Jewish . . . and took measures to assure that the favoured options became normative'.[241]

Roman influence on such a process can be considered only once two prior questions are answered: (1) Where does one look for 'normative self-definition'? Should one confine oneself to the conscious thought of the period, or must one probe, in addition, below the surface, into those subconscious levels of thought which pose such acute methodological problems for the historian? (2) On either of these tests, what aspects of the halakah contributed to the process of normative self-definition?

The answer to the first of these questions is, to my mind, clear in principle. The subconscious level cannot be excluded from our calculations, however difficult the task that such a view may set us. But not everything that exists at the subconscious level will be relevant. In so far as normative self-definition implies the search for a group identity distinct from others, it excludes those realms of the subconscious which belong to the common nature of mankind – except, perhaps, to the extent that a cultural tradition may chose to regard such traits as peculiar to itself. The search for normative self-definition thus raises, in an acute form, the need to distinguish the natural from the culturally-contingent levels of the subconscious mind. The perspectives, *inter alia*, of social psychology would appear to be an appropriate and necessary element in any comprehensive search for normative self-definition. This may appear unacceptably hazy and imprecise a discipline to suit the tastes of historians and lawyers. But times are changing. One leading American law teacher – a Californian, but that should not be held against him – has begun to deal in 'shared images'.[242]

The answer to the second question is less easy to state, even in highly general and formal terms. It is far from self-evident that the halakah can be regarded as a single undifferentiated block for the purposes of an enquiry into normative self-definition. We may need to distinguish between all the types of legal phenomena identified in sections 4 and 5 of this paper. For each, it will be appropriate to ask (a) whether there is any evidence that the thought of the period itself articulated the view that this type of legal phenomenon was part of what makes Judaism different; and (b) whether there are grounds for inferring the existence of such a view, in the absence of its explicit articulation by the sources. (There is a third and equally legitimate inquiry (c), namely whether there exist (analytical) grounds on which we, the modern generation of scholars, might conclude that Judaism became different in this period, even in the absence of either (a) or (b). Some would deny that this last inquiry is any part of 'history' – even though in practice it is all too frequently confused with (b).) I am not in a position to marshal the evidence on questions of either type (a) or (b), and for the purposes of the rest of the discussion – designed, as before, merely to clarify the kinds of question which must be asked in assessing the significance of Roman law – I shall pose the issues in terms of what are no more than personal hunches.

While I suspect that the whole range of phenomena here surveyed – whether existing at the conscious or unconscious levels
and whether articulated explicitly or not[243] – may be relevant to
normative self-definition, I do not exclude the likelihood that
they may be relevant in different ways, according to their location and manner of articulation. Thus, it is important that
someone should undertake a study of the extent to which claims
are made in the sources for the uniqueness to Judaism of legal
phenomena of each of the types considered above.

Normative self-definition in the form of the halakah

(i) Scope

The scope of the halakah is a phenomenon which, as Judaism
is likely to have realized, distinguished it increasingly from
Christianity in the course of the first three centuries. Indeed, it
may be possible to use Christian views of Jewish identity, as
found in the New Testament and the early Fathers, as part of
the historical evidence for Jewish self-definition,[244] along with
such internal questions as the extent of the oral law considered
as Sinaitic.[245] Roman law may well have provided both a model
and a jurisdictional pressure for this increasing scope, its significance in this regard to be assessed in the light of the N + E
model of development outlined above.

A particular facet of this question is the scope of the ritual
law and the civil law respectively. Neusner's work on the agenda of the Pharisees before 70 CE[246] suggests that the increasing
scope of the halakah may have manifested itself in the ritual
law before the civil law. This should incline us towards the
view that different explanations are to be sought for the increasing scope of the two areas. But the obvious hypothesis, that the
ritual law developed naturally from the religious ideas peculiar
to Judaism (if not to the Hebrew Bible[247]) while the civil law
increased in scope under the influence of foreign secular laws,
is not the only one. We have noted the early development of
Roman juristic literature on the sacral law (itself a reflection of
the descent of the jurists from a sacerdotal legal authority), and
it is not impossible to understand the developing scope of the
civil law as in part a reaction against Christian criticism of the
hypocrisy of those who devoted what was seen as dispropor-
tionate energy to the study and practice of ritual.[248] Such an
explanation, it may be noted, goes some way towards implying

that the Christian view was not one which rejected the concretization of morality in specific rules, as do some modern Christian existentialists and situationists.[249]

(ii) Coherence

By contrast, it is unlikely that the rabbis were in a position to judge the relative coherence of the halakah in comparison with other normative systems. Nevertheless, there is one sense in which the rabbinic sources make an implied claim regarding relative coherence, such as may entitle us to take it into account in the search for normative self-definition. The rabbinic methods of argument – of which the rabbis were especially conscious[250] – imply a (literally) superhuman degree of consistency in the draftsmanship of the biblical law.[251] Interestingly, this does not lead to the conclusion that there can be no differences in opinion as regards the content of the oral law; indeed, the 'dispute form' has been identified as a particularly significant component of the tannaitic literature, including that part of it which was to become the most normative – the Mishnah.[252]

(iii) Content of the classificatory divisions

Some of the classificatory divisions of the halakah are directly relevant to the achievement of normative self-definition, in that they imply a difference between the law applicable to Jews and that applicable to others. The major step in this regard had, of course, been taken before our period, in the biblical claim of a covenant peculiar to Israel. But further classifications dating from rabbinic times added significant glosses to the biblical teaching, and here the relevance of Graeco-Roman models may have played a role. The notion of *torah shebe'al peh*, for example, served to deny commonality between any part of Jewish law and Gentile law: it was no longer possible to argue that, biblical law apart, Jewish law and Gentile law were of comparable status. Similarly, the notion of Noachian law emphasized that even where there was common moral content, Gentile law lacked the status that attached to superior technical development. The parallel with the Roman *ius gentium* goes beyond the fact that both Jews and Romans had the idea of two legal systems, one restricted to citizens and one common to all mankind. The Roman *ius gentium*,[253] like the Jewish idea of Noachian law, implied a set of rules stripped of the technicalities of the citizens' system, and constituting a rather pale reflection of it.

(iv) Legal argument

There is reason to believe that the rabbinic *middot* were regarded as a distinguishing feature of the halakah. Not only do they imply, by the manner of their employment, a superhuman level of biblical drafting;[254] rabbinic awareness of their importance (if not their distinctiveness) is indicated by the collection and classification of *middot* found in the famous baraita of R. Ishmael.[255] As it happens, the Roman jurists did not undertake any comparable classification, though they did collect and classify both the sources and some of the substantive principles of law. Thus legal argument may be one aspect of the development of Jewish law particularly relevant to the achievement of normative self-definition; and foreign (in this case Greek) influence may well be a factor in it.

(v) Other aspects of formal development

Rabbinic consciousness of the distinctiveness of biblical drafting has already been mentioned. Reduction of the oral law to writing may be viewed as a means towards the achievement of normative status for the developed oral law,[256] even though the notion of written law was not peculiar to Jewish law, and can hardly have been so regarded by the rabbis. In this sense, the role of foreign influence in providing either the model or part of the impetus for reduction to writing may be relevant to normative self-definition.

With arrangement and literary form we come to phenomena where rabbinic consciousness of the distinctiveness of what they were doing is a matter of inference. Neusner's studies of both the arrangement and form of the mishnaic material at the very least suggest rabbinic awareness of the importance of form and of its use as a medium of communication.[257] As to comparability with foreign materials, one suspects that this question was not addressed. Unfortunately, we are not in a position to assess the historical process by which mishnaic arrangement and the literary forms of tannaitic legal literature become normative within the tannaitic period. The question of when such features became standard is relevant to normative self-definition. One speculation may perhaps be permitted. In so far as the process of canonization of the biblical material involved consideration of arrangement, and in so far as the rabbis may have been involved in such decisions from the time of Yavneh, the notion of a standardized arrangement also of the *oral* law would not appear incongruous for at least a century before R. Judah I.

Normative self-definition in the content of the halakah

In seeking to identify areas where the content of the halakah may be relevant to normative self-definition, it is less easy to follow the divisions adopted in putting the problem of foreign influence. Whereas the rabbis were clearly conscious of the separate existence of such phenomena as scope, legal argument and arrangement, we may not so readily impute to them our modern understanding of the distinctions between rules, principles,[258] institutions, concepts, notarial practice, and procedures.[259] Rather, they show themselves aware of divisions according to subject-matter, as exemplified by the sedarim of the Mishnah. It may thus be appropriate to ask whether any such divisions were regarded as particularly relevant to Jewish distinctiveness, and if so, to address our questions regarding foreign influence most particularly to those areas.[260] We may perhaps expect that particular distinctiveness would be thought to reside in the ritual law. That, at least, was a view implicitly held in the middle ages,[261] and one modern orthodox thinker has strongly denied any distinctiveness to the content of the civil law.[262] Personally, I would prefer to enter a *non liquet*.[263]

In one important respect, our modern analysis of the phenomena of the content of legal systems does have an important bearing on the question of normative self-definition. If we accept the view that concrete and explicit rules are interrelated by more abstract and implicit principles or thought structures, we must then ask ourselves whether normative self-definition must be restricted to the plane of the concrete and the explicit. The (anticipated) denial of this suggestion may take either a weak or a strong form: the weak form would accept an extension of normative self-definition into the non-concrete, non-explicit, provided there were grounds for believing that this latter level of meaning was consciously intended; the strong form would accept the extension even without such conscious intendment. In both cases, normative self-definition is sought at some level of inner logic. According to the theoretical stance which informs this paper, the subconscious level of inner logic is likely to be more abstract and approach more closely to the innate and universal features common to the human mind, than the conscious (but implied) level of inner logic. Thus the quest for normative self-definition requires the researcher to take a position on two fundamental questions: (*a*) is he prepared, along with the structuralist, to enter the realm of the subconscious at all?; (*b*) if so, where will he draw the line between the culturally contingent and the universal levels of the subconscious?

We are not in a position to answer these theoretical questions with any certainty, however desirable a preliminary to further study that may be. Our approach has to be, for the moment, more inclusive: we should look at all the forms of inner logic, and assess their potential importance for normative self-definition, while reserving our right to take a more defined and thereby categorical position when eventually it becomes possible to do so.

I conclude, therefore, with a glance at three different kinds of inner logic, all of which have been the subject of recent discussion. One observation common to all of them must be made. Since they represent systems of relationships between concrete rules, and not the concrete rules themselves, any foreign influence that may be demonstrated in respect of an individual rule does not affect the inner logic itself. Foreign influence, to be significant in this respect, must relate to the system of relationships itself.[264] Thus if one were to hold that normative self-definition is to be located exclusively at the level of inner logic, and at the same time adhere to a theory of foreign influence which restricted its potential to the level of concrete rules, one would have a logical reason for denying any relevance of foreign influence to normative self-definition. Few perhaps would subscribe to such a combination of extremities, at least in their conscious moments.[265] The argument may serve, however, to illustrate the role which our stances on the underlying theoretical issues may play in our assessment of particular historical questions. In what follows, I shall adopt less restrictive views of the proper spheres of both normative self-definition and foreign influence: I shall assume that normative self-definition may extend into the inner logic of the system, but is not necessarily restricted to it; equally, that foreign influence may affect at least the culturally-contingent levels of inner logic, as well as the surface, concrete phenomena.

(i) The 'moral logic' of the civil law

Following a long-standing Jewish tradition of speculation upon the reducibility of the *mitsvot*, Shalom Albeck seeks to base most of the civil law upon two basic principles, *gemirat da'at* (the formation of a firm decision) and *shimush binekhasim* (the use of property).[266] These, in his view, are the static elements in the halakah; the detailed rules are changeable concretizations reflecting the particular social conditions of the time. According to such a view,[267] foreign influence may well be one of the operative social conditions which determine the choice, at any particular time, of the concrete rules which reflect the basic principles; equally, the static nature of the basic principles leaves little if any role for foreign influence. A writer like Albeck would therefore be likely to deny or at least minimize the relevance of foreign influence to the question of normative self-definition, since the latter, in his view, would be equated with the static elements of the system.

I have some sympathy for this model, but with two important qualifications.[268] First, I do not think that Albeck has located the underlying principles at the right level: *gemirat da'at* and *shimush binekhasim* appear to me to be concepts[269] frequently found at the explicit level, rather than underlying principles. Second, I am unhappy with the simple opposition between the static and the changeable. Anything truly static would belong to the sphere of the natural and the universal: any peculiarly Jewish inner logic should be expected to reside at some intermediate level, where change (and foreign influence) – though no doubt slower and less likely than with respect to surface phenomena – would not be completely excluded. This is certainly a level which should be considered in the search for normative self-definition, but the significance of foreign influence is not likely to be great.

(ii) The 'metaphysical order' of the ritual law

Jacob Neusner's interpretative work on the law of purities[270] alerts us to the underlying system of metaphysical belief, such basic notions as time and space not excluded, which the ritual law was designed to express. Here, it is suggested, the signification of such metaphysical conceptions by means of the concrete rules of the ritual law was a conscious purpose of the draftsmen. This may be seen from the manner of articulation of the message, which proceeds not from the mere logical relation (not, of course, that of necessary implication) between the rules and the inner logic, but from the form and particularly the arrangement of the material.

Such a form of inner logic may well be relevant to normative self-definition. Foreign influence (perhaps that of the jurists of Republican Rome on the form and scholarly elaboration, rather than the content, of ritual law) may have played a role, but here too one suspects that its significance is unlikely to have been great.

(iii) The 'theological order' of the halakah

In a recently published article, I have suggested that many rules of the halakah may be viewed as reflections upon the dividing line between the respective natures of God and man.[271] The basic proposition that there is a difference between the two remains static, but the dividing line is subject to change. This model differs from that of Neusner in that it proceeds merely from logical inference rather than from the formal properties of the material, and it does not suggest that the signification of this message was a conscious purpose of the writers. Of course, there is no incompatibility between the 'metaphysical' and the 'theological' orders here described; the same material may simultaneously bear different levels of meaning. But whereas the student of normative self-definition may address himself to Neusner's metaphysical order on the 'weak' view of the extension of normative self-definition into the realm of the inexplicitly articulated, he will be entitled to inquire into the kind of theological order here suggested only if he is prepared to embrace the 'strong' view.[272] That such a difference should exist is perhaps not surprising: the theological order is not confined to any particular sphere of Jewish law (such as the ritual), but represents a more all-embracing, and therefore deeper, level.

Conclusion

The possibility that normative self-definition may extend beyond explicit rules and beliefs[273] into the realms of the implied and the implicit not only enlarges the range, difficulty and importance of such enquiries; it also raises further questions as to the meaning of normative self-definition itself. For whereas we may readily understand what it means to ask whether an explicit rule or belief was related to the distinctiveness of Jewish identity, or whether it became normative (in the sense that it was expected that every Jew[274] would hold such a view of Jewish distinctiveness), it is far less easy to pose the same form of questions in respect of the implied and implicit levels, certainly as far as matters of content are concerned. Nevertheless, inter-disciplinary research may assist in devising tests whereby even collective images and subconscious logical systems may reveal themselves as normative.

8

The Reception Accorded to Rabbi Judah's Mishnah

DAVID WEISS HALIVNI

Nowadays when one inquires about the reception of a book, one wants to know whether it was noticed by the critics. If it was, did they deem it to be of lasting value? Did they go so far as to declare it a classic, constituting seminal work, or supplanting what was said before on an old topic?

Judged by these criteria the Mishnah of R. Judah ha-Nasi was, of course, accorded a good reception. It was noted by the critics of its time, deemed by them to be of enormous value and declared a classic. It supplanted earlier mishnayot to the extent that most of them did not even survive, while those that did survive were called baraitot, outsiders, outside the standard Mishnah collection. Rabbi Judah's Mishnah became second in importance to the Bible. One has to accept that even if one does not punctuate – as some erroneously do – the letter Nun in the word משנה with a סגל, משנה,[1] and read it as a construct with Torah, Mishneh Torah, second (vice) to the Bible. The Mishnah is second to the Bible *de facto* though not in nomenclature.

If we nevertheless persist in inquiring about the reception accorded R. Judah's Mishnah we are obviously asking different questions and employing different criteria. Our questions concern R. Judah's intentions and the extent to which these intentions were realized.

Our criteria are the degree of authority and margin of acceptability granted to R. Judah's Mishnah. The assertion that R. Judah's Mishnah is second to the Bible does not tell us whether, like the Bible, nothing contained therein may be rejected. Or is it the most authoritative book after the Bible, but falls short of the Bible in that some of its decisions are reversible?

Also, whatever it was, was it so from the very beginning?

Was it accepted by all the people? In other words, was there opposition to R. Judah's Mishnah at the time of its appearance and, if so, from whom, and for what reason? It is to these questions that we address ourselves in this paper.

The conventional view of the reception accorded to R. Judah's Mishnah at the time of its appearance, I suppose, is that of the oldest historian of the Mishnah, Rav Sherira Gaon (966–1006) who, in his famous Epistle[2], writes:

וכד חזו כולי עלמא צורתא (או שופרא) דתרצתא דמתניתין ואמתת
הדברים (או טעמיה) ודוקא דמלות, שבקו הנך תניני דהוה תני ופשטין
אלין הלכתא בכל ארץ ישראל והוויין שאר הלכתא כלהו אשתביקו
והוויין כגון ברייתא. ומאן דמעיין בהו כמאן דמעיין בפירושי או בלישני
רויחי. אבל סמכא דישראל על אלין הלכתא הוה. וקבלינהו ישראל
כד חזינין באמונה וליכא איניש דאפליג בהון.

> When the people saw the beauty of the structure (the smoothness) of the Mishnah (R. Judah's Mishnah), its true reasoning and exact expression, they forsook all the other mishnayot they were learning. These laws (of R. Judah's Mishnah) spread all over the land of Israel. While the other laws were forsaken and became like baraita (outside), consulting them was like consulting a commentary or a (more) lavish version. But the authoritative source was only these laws (the laws of R. Judah's Mishnah). Israel accepted (the laws of R. Judah's Mishnah) as soon as they saw them, confidently (without hesitation). There is no person who disagrees with them on this.

The impression one gets from this passage of R. Sherira Gaon is that R. Judah's Mishnah was an instantaneous success. As soon as it appeared, people realized its beautiful harmony, its true reasoning, its neat and exact expression. They committed themselves immediately to its binding authority, relegating the many older competing collections of mishnayot to mere auxiliary functions. All this was done באמונה, confidently, full of assurance. As with the Bible, nobody opposed it then and nobody has opposed it since.

The conclusion which one reaches after having critically examined the relevant sources in the Talmud, however, is quite different. There was opposition to R. Judah's Mishnah at the time of its appearance, and what is even more startling, the later Amoraim politely sidetracked many a decision made by R. Judah in his Mishnah,so much so that one may genuinely doubt whether R. Judah's Mishnah ever exercised binding authority.

To be sure, the evidence for the opposition to R. Judah's

Mishnah is indirect. Openly the Amoraim had nothing but praise for R. Judah and for his Mishnah. No direct criticism of him or of his Mishnah was allowed to come to the surface. Nevertheless, hints to the contrary are too numerous to be ignored. Many stories can be explained only in light of such an opposition; many expressions make sense only in the context of friction between R. Judah and his contemporaries.

On the other hand, the deviations from R. Judah's Mishnah are quite open and direct. No apologies and no justification. A later Amora felt free to override a codificatory decision made by R. Judah in his Mishnah if he had the support of another Tanna. The codificatory decisions made by R. Judah in his Mishnah were apparently treated on a par with his private opinions, which do not necessarily prevail. Even when R. Judah codified a law anonymously, signifying that there was no worthy opposition to it, a later Amora could revive the old controversy and override R. Judah's decision. Without entering into the debate as to whether or not R. Judah intended his Mishnah to be a code for practical behaviour, it is almost certain that he preferred some opinions over others and expressed his preference through a hierarchy of classifications. Those that he preferred most he quoted anonymously without a dissenting view; while those that he preferred less he quoted anonymously with a dissenting view, and those that he preferred still less he quoted as the majority view along with a minority view.[3] A later Amora often reverted back to the original controversies of the early Tannaim, ignoring R. Judah's hierarchical classifications. A later Amora often acted as if R. Judah's classificatory system did not exist.

The very existence of the Tosefta is testimony to the opposition to R. Judah's Mishnah. There would have been no need for the Tosefta had the Mishnah of R. Judah been fully satisfying to the different representative schools. We know precious little about the relationship between R. Judah's Mishnah and the Tosefta.[4] Both adopted the mishnaic genre (arranged according to content) as against the midrashic genre (arranged according to scripture). Both stem, more or less, from the same school as against the Sifre Zuta, for example, which stems from a totally different school. The major differences between them are in the codificatory classifications. What is anonymous in R. Judah's Mishnah is often a minority view in the Tosefta. Tradition attributes our Tosefta to R. Hiyya and R. Hoshaia. Nevertheless, an analysis of (*a*) the baraitot quoted in the Palestinian and Babylonian Talmuds in the name of R. Ḥiyya and R. Hoshaia that are not found in our Tosefta and (*b*) the baraitot quoted in the Talmuds in the name of other Amoraim that are found in the Tosefta does not support this contention.[5] Despite these reservations, there seems to be little doubt that R. Ḥiyya and R. Hoshaia were among the earliest authors (more exactly, anthologizers) of a Tosefta (not necessarily our Tosefta). There are too many references in both Talmuds to the baraitot of R. Ḥiyya and R. Hoshaia to deny their involvement with a Tosefta. Their Tosefta may not have survived (or may have survived poorly) but it certainly existed.

What prompted them to add so extensively to R. Judah's Mishnah, and often to reverse its codificatory decisions? I can think of only one answer: they were dissatisfied with R. Judah's codificatory decisions and with his selections (they deemed them to be too abridged), and dissatisfaction breeds opposition.

Proponents of the conventional view of the reception accorded R. Judah's Mishnah have to minimize drastically the contributions of R. Ḥiyya and R. Hoshaia and reduce them to mere follow-ups of R. Judah's Mishnah. Indeed, in three instances[6] where R. Ḥiyya seems to have challenged R. Judah's codificatory decision, the Babylonian Talmud[7] expresses amazement: וכי רבי לא שנאה, ר' חייא מניין לו?, 'If R. Judah did not teach it, from where does R. Ḥiyya know it?' According to this view, R. Ḥiyya included in his baraitot only those laws that R. Judah taught him after he completed the Mishnah. They complement and do not contradict R. Judah's Mishnah. R. Ḥiyya, on his own, cannot gainsay R. Judah's Mishnah. This harmonization, however, runs counter to the many differences and disagreements that exist between R. Judah's Mishnah and the baraitot, some of which are undoubtedly by R. Ḥiyya and R. Hoshaia. They certainly were not always complementing R. Judah's Mishnah.

These discords strained the relationship between R. Judah and his student-colleagues (תלמיד חבר) R. Ḥiyya and R. Hoshaia and made it less cordial than we are given to believe in some rabbinic sources. An echo of this strain may still be heard in the statement of Rava – a fourth-century Babylonian scholar – in bBK 111b and BM 63a. He prefaces his explanation that the Mishnah there is in agreement with R. Hoshaia's baraita by saying: 'When I die, R. Hoshaia will come out to meet me (in heaven) because I am explaining a mishnah according to his teaching.' Mindful of the many disagreements that existed between R. Judah's Mishnah and the baraitot of R. Judah's younger contemporaries, R. Ḥiyya and R. Hoshaia, and mindful of the probable strains and attendant pain that these disagreements must have caused, particularly to the latter, Rava felt that R. Hoshaia would be delighted to hear that at least in those two instances there is harmony between R. Judah's Mishnah and R. Hoshaia's baraita. In appreciation, R. Hoshaia will welcome Rava in heaven.

It is worth mentioning that according to pTaan 4.3 (68b) and parallels,[8] R. Ḥiyya's pedigree was superior to that of R. Judah. R. Ḥiyya was a descendant of King David from a son and R. Judah was a descendant of King David from a daughter, while according to bKet 62b it is the reverse. R. Judah is a descendant of King David from a son and R. Ḥiyya from a daughter. This is in consonance with the general tendency of the Babylonian Talmud to assign a more exalted role to R. Judah. In either case it probably added strain to an already strained relationship.

Besides disagreements over R. Judah's codification of some laws, criticism was also voiced that R. Judah had overly condensed his Mishnah, leaving out many a decision. The response on the part of R. Judah's followers was that R. Judah's Mishnah contains all the important decisions explicitly while the less important decisions are included implicitly. We deduce this from a story of Ilfa, a disciple of R. Judah, recorded in both Talmuds.[9] He was once standing on a deck of a ship and said: 'Whoever quotes to me something from (a baraita of) R. Ḥiyya or R. Hoshaia for which I cannot find a parallel in the Mishnah of R. Judah, let him throw me off the ship.' A sage (סבא) came forward quoting to him something from a baraita (which is also found in our Tosefta and is presumably either by R. Ḥiyya or by R. Hoshaia) and asked him for a parallel in R. Judah's Mishnah. Ilfa gave him a parallel (albeit a very tenuous one) and was saved from being thrown overboard.

To the defenders of R. Judah's Mishnah, it, like the Bible, ought to be studied exegetically; when so studied, many of the baraitot become superfluous. The other side did not think so. To them, R. Judah's Mishnah just did not contain all the relevant material necessary to become an all-inclusive code.[10]

Unlike his younger contemporaries who voiced their criticism of R. Judah's Mishnah, later Amoraim voiced no criticism yet

dealt him a more serious blow by simply ignoring his codificatory decisions. A law which R. Judah codified as anonymous,
signifying the highest degree of acceptance, later Amoraim
often declared as the opinion of an individual, with no binding
authority. (They did so by reverting back to the pre-codificatory
state.) When the Babylonian Talmud asks: 'Who is the author
of this anonymous law?' and proceeds to identify him, it does
so not merely out of historical curiosity, to know who exactly
said what, but also out of a desire to provide a possible opening
for rejecting R. Judah's codificatory decision. This is tantamount
to saying: Once we know who was the original author of this
law and who were his adversaries, we can make our own codificatory decision.[11] The most faithful follower of R. Judah's
Mishnah in this regard was R. Johanan. He is reported as having
said (bShab 46a and parallels), 'The law is according to the
anonymous mishnah.' Even he sometimes did not follow the
anonymous mishnah, the inconsistency of which prompted the
Babylonian Talmud (Yeb 16b and parallels) to say:

אמוראי נינהו ואליבא דר' יוחנן.

There is a difference of opinion among R. Johanan's disciples
whether or not he actually said that the law is like the anonymous Mishnah, while the Palestinian Talmud (Taan 2.13; 66a
and parallels) limits this saying of R. Johanan to instances when
the original controversy was between two individual scholars.
When, however, the original controversy was between a minority and a majority and R. Judah codified anonymously
according to the minority view, the law does not follow the
anonymous mishnah.[12]

Characteristic is the dispute between R. Zrachiah Halevy
(d. 1168), the author of the book *Hamaor*, and R. Moses Ben
Nachman (1194–1270) in connection with what the Babylonian
Talmud says in BK 96b. The Talmud there expresses surprise
that Rav (one of the earliest pupils of R. Judah) would follow
a minority view. R. Zrachiah was constrained to add:

אע"פ שיש הרבה בתלמוד שמניחין דברי רבים ופוסקים כדברי יחיד ולא
מקשה, הכא שאני משום דרב תלמידיה דרבי הוה דסידר סדרן של משניות
וסתמן ואיהו הוה במניניה דרבי. וא"כ היכי שביק מאן דסתם במתניתין
כוותיה ועביד כר' מאיר.

> Even though there are many instances in the Talmud where the
> majority view is 'put aside' and the minority opinion is followed
> without the Talmud expressing surprise, here it is different because
> Rav was a disciple of R. Judah, who arranged the order of the

mishnayot and codified some laws anonymously. Rav was also a member of R. Judah's court (which made the decisions). [See bGitt 59a.] How then does he 'abandon' the one whose opinion is codified anonymously in the Mishnah and follow the view of R. Meir?

To which R. Moses Ben Nachman (Ramban) objects:

אמר הכותב אין זה נכון שלא מצינו מי שחושש אפילו לסתם משנה בלא
מחלוקת אלא ר' יוחנן ורב לא סבר לה כוותיה.

Only R. Johanan holds the view that one follows an anonymous mishnah. Rav doesn't share this view.

To the Ramban, even Rav, a participating member of R. Judah's court when the codificatory decisions were made, did not accept R. Judah's decisions.

Let me also add that these medieval authorities are talking about following an anonymous mishnah when there is an explicit controversy in the baraita. When there is no explicit controversy in the baraita, no Amora can take issue with the Mishnah. This is in accordance with the tacit assumption of the Babylonian Talmud that no Amora can disagree with a Tanna, certainly not with a mishnah without the support of another Tanna. The Palestinian Talmud, however, does occasionally say that the mishnah or the baraita disagrees with the Amora, and leaves it at that. Apparently, the Palestinian Talmud does not feel constrained always to harmonize the words of the Amora with that of the mishnah or baraita. A possible explanation for this divergence between the two Talmuds – which is also an indication that the spread of R. Judah's Mishnah was slower in Palestine than it was in Babylonia – is that R. Judah's Mishnah, which is so heavily tilted in favour of the school of R. Akiba,[13] must have provoked discontent among students of other schools. In Palestine, where most of these students resided, the resistance was greater; and it took longer for R. Judah's Mishnah to prevail. In Babylonia, where there were very few of these students, R. Judah's Mishnah prevailed almost immediately after Rav (the veteran student of R. Judah) established his Academy in Sura.

We called R. Sherira Gaon's idealized conception of the reception accorded to R. Judah's Mishnah the conventional one, for that view persisted through the ages even among those who had no access to his famous Epistle. I know of only two scholars who stated an explicit contrary view, and even theirs was brief and undocumented. I am referring to R. Yair Bachrach (1638–

1701) and R. Aaron Azriel (1819–1879). The former, in his famous book *Ḥavot Yair* (a book, by the way, which contains a lot of unorthodox questions and answers), in ch. 94 (s.v. ומ"ש) says:

ומ"ש בש"ס בכמה דוכתי לדחות המשנה ולומר יחידאה היא או לומר
מאן חכמים ר"מ, ל"ק כי אפ"ה שרבי ראה דברי אותו יחיד ושנה סתם
או בלשון חכמים, מ"מ באיסוף הגדול בימי רב אשי לא ראו דבריו כמו
שלא פסקו הלכה במה שאמר בפירוש במשנה הלכה כדבריו ודעת רבי
גופיה.

Here R. Yair Bachrach explains that even where R. Judah decided in favour of a minority view and had it codified in his Mishnah as anonymous (with or without a dissenting view) or as the 'word of the sages', the Amoraim, during the great collection of the time of R. Ashi (R. Y. Bachrach means at the time when the Talmud was edited by R. Ashi) did not agree with R. Judah (and did not follow his decision), just as they did not follow him when he explicitly stated that the law follows the opinion of a particular Tanna[14] or when he expressed his own private opinion. R. Y. Bachrach does not say whether the realization that later Amoraim often overrode R. Judah's codificatory decisions is new with him or was known already before him.[15]

On the other hand. R. A. Azriel, in his book called *Kapei 'Aharon* (Jerusalem 1914) claims it to be his own discovery. He says in ch. 7:

והנלע"ד שהנה האמוראים ז"ל חידשו לנו כללים הרבה בדרכי הוראה
אף שהם הפך רבינו הקדוש ז"ל, שהרי הם אמרו ר"מ ור"י הלכה כר"י
וכן הלכה כר"ע מחבירו ודומיהם. ואין ספק שרבנו הקדוש כשחיבר
המשניות לא דרך בכללים אלה. שא"כ היה לו להזכיר דברי ר"י כסתם
משנה ולא להזכיר דברי ר"מ כלל... וגדולה מזה מצינו דבכמה משניות
השנויות סתם, שקיל וטרי הש"ס ואמר מני מתניתין ואשכח דהך מתניתין
אתייא אליבא דחד תנא דלא כהלכתא. אלמא האמוראים אינן חוששין
להכרעתו דרבי ופוסקים שלא כמותו.

The first part of this passage can be easily dismissed. R. Azriel sees, in the rules adopted by the Amoraim to guide them in how to decide a case which is codified as a controversy between minority opinions, a refutation of R. Judah's codificatory decisions. If the law follows R. Akiba whenever he disagrees with another single Tanna (one of the rules), why, argues R. Azriel, did not R. Judah codify R. Akiba's view anonymously, or as the 'words of the sages'? Undoubtedly because R. Judah did not accept this rule of the Amoraim. Here R. Azriel is mistaken. R. Judah did not codify R. Akiba's view anonymously or as the 'words of the sages' because the degree of authority of an anonymous mishnah (or of that which has the phrase 'the words of the sages') is greater than the degree of authority of a favoured opinion which is recorded in the Mishnah as a minority view. The former is accepted because of its intrinsic value. The latter is favoured because of the stature of the scholar who propounded it. Most of the time there is no practical difference between the two. Should a new situation occur, the chances of changing the favoured opinion are better than the chances of changing the anonymous mishnah.

The second part of R. Azriel's passage is correct and significant. By not following R. Judah's codificatory decisions and declaring a law which he codified as anonymous or as the 'words of the sages' to be the opinion of a minority, with no binding power, later Amoraim disregarded R. Judah's intentions and plan for the Mishnah.

R. Judah was not the author of the Mishnah; he anthologized it. Most of the material in the Mishnah pre-dated him. The structure and form of the Mishnah, to a large extent, existed before him.[16] His original contribution consisted primarily in making a manageable selection out of what must have been a bewildering array of Mishnah collections and in providing a codificatory classification. His selection was criticized by his younger contemporaries, and his codificatory decisions were ignored by the later Amoraim.[17] R. Judah's ambitions were not realized. The Mishnah did not become second to the Bible in binding authority.[18]

The adulation of R. Judah ha-Nasi has no parallel in rabbinic literature. He bears the epithet of 'our holy teacher' and miraculous deeds are attributed to him. It is not unprecedented in the annals of human history to have someone's teaching ignored while he remains highly adulated. The situation with R. Judah is not different. He was revered no end yet his ambition was not granted. To me, at least, this sounds tragic.[19]

9

The Politics of Reconciliation:
The Education of R. Judah the Prince

ALBERT I. BAUMGARTEN

Introduction

'Yet, even then, when they are in the land of their enemies, I will not reject them or spurn them so as to destroy them, annulling My covenant with them: for I the LORD am their God (Lev. 26.44).' . . . We learn in a baraita. 'I will not reject them,' in the days of the Chaldeans when I provided [leaders] for them – Daniel, Hananiah, Mishael and Azariah.[1] 'Or spurn them,' in the days of the Greeks, when I provided [leaders] for them – Simon the Righteous, and Mattathias son of Yohanan the High Priest, Hasmonaean and his sons.[2] 'So as to destroy them,' in the days of Haman, when I provided [leaders] for them – Mordechai and Esther. 'Annulling My covenant with them,' in the days of the Romans when I provided [leaders] for them – the dynasty of Rabbi and the sages of his generation.[3] 'For I the LORD am their God,' in the future no nation or tongue will again be able to rule over them.[4]

In this review of God's merciful care during the long exile, the Hillelite dynasty occupies a prominent place.[5] Leaders and saviours of the Jews during the Roman period, they are placed on a par with some of the greatest men of Jewish history. The laudatory evaluation of the Hillelites is not unique to this text, and similar sentiments can be found in a number of other sources.[6] This high praise was well merited; the Hillelites reigned for more than three hundred years, many of these years filled with difficulty, crisis and threat both internal and external.

The success of the Hillelites is notable, but such success is rarely, if ever, achieved without great effort and skill. Inquiry

213

into the means employed by the Hillelites is thus natural and obvious. The history of other dynasties can be a useful guide. An important part of founding or maintaining a dynasty is the process by which loyalties are built: the bonds uniting the ruling group must be firmly tied. A hierarchy of officials and agents is usually needed: great deeds, as Velleius observed, require great associates and subordinates.[7] Opponents must be engaged and dealt with.[8] Evidence for all these processes in the case of the Hillelites is therefore to be sought, and this search has had a prominent place in recent scholarship, especially in the work of Alon and Urbach.[9]

It is in this context that I have recently suggested that Akibans formed an important group of opponents to Patriarchal rule in the years after the Bar Kokhba revolt.[10] If this suggestion is correct, we should find evidence that R. Simeon b. Gamaliel II tried to deal with his Akiban opponents in re-establishing Patriarchal authority; such evidence is not hard to find. Thus the appointment of R. Meir as חכם of the academy-court (bHor 14a and pBikk 3.3;65c), and the decision at Usha not to punish elders with the ban (pMKat 3.1;81d) can both be seen as indications of the attempt to conciliate opponents, Akibans in particular.[11] Additional evidence exists. There are many stories about relations between individual Akibans and the Patriarch. I suggest that these contain much valuable information concerning the techniques employed by the Hillelites in coping with their Akiban challenge.[12] This article will concentrate on one group of stories, those concerning R. Eleazar b. Shammua.

R. Eleazar b. Shammua's place among Akiba's students is established by the list of GenR 61.3, p. 660.[13] He appears to have been on particularly close terms with his fellow student R. Meir.[14] Thus R. Eleazar b. Shammua and R. Meir discussed interpretations offered by another Akiban, R. Eliezer b. Jacob.[15] R. Eleazar b. Shammua reports a conversation he had with R. Meir.[16] Finally, R. Judah the Prince based his decision to exclude areas around Bet Shean from the theoretical limits of the Holy Land on testimony concerning the practice of R. Meir. This seems to have embarrassed some of R. Meir's later admirers, who rushed to his defence (pDem 2.1;22c).[17] It is noteworthy that in the Babylonian Talmud's version of these events, bHull 7a, the defence of R. Meir is begun by R. Eleazar b. Shammua. R. Eleazar b. Shammua is thus firmly placed in anti-Patriarchal circles.[18] It is therefore surprising to note that five sources report that R. Judah was his student. It is to these passages that we must now turn.

R. Judah and R. Eleazar

> Rabbi said: I sought but did not find (i.e. I did not succeed in understanding)[19] the words of Ben Shammua concerning the *androgynos* because the group [of his students] combined against him (pYeb 8.6;9d).

An ambiguity in the text must first be resolved: against whom did the students combine, R. Eleazar b. Shammua or R. Judah? Since R. Judah says that the students combined against *him* (עליו), it would seem that R. Eleazar b. Shammua was the target. This, however, makes little sense; R. Judah would make a more appropriate target, as confirmed by the manuscripts of the Babylonian version of our story, some of which read עלי (see below n. 24). It is also confirmed by the discussion which follows our passage in pYeb, in which it is clear that R. Eleazar b. Shammua was seen as free to decide whether or not to explain his opinion to R. Judah; the choice was his, not made for him by students. I therefore suggest that R. Judah was the victim of the student attack.[20] Should one then emend עליו in pYeb to עלי, as proposed by Rabinovitz?[21] In view of the manuscript evidence in both pYeb and the Babylonian parallel (discussed below), emendation would not seem appropriate; an interpretation which retains both the sense of the passage and the MS reading is to be sought. Such an interpretation is suggested by the aphorism attributed to R. Eleazar b. R. Simeon in Sifre Zutta: 'If a person has to mention [anything unpleasant with reference to] himself, he should word it as if it referred to someone else.'[22] R. Judah's experience at the academy of R. Eleazar was not a pleasant one. Hence the slight change, making it seem as if R. Eleazar was the one attacked. Patriarchal honour has been salvaged.[23]

A similar story is told in the parallel baraita in the Babylonian Talmud:

> Rabbi said: When I went to study Torah with R. Eleazar b. Shammua his students combined against him[24] like the cocks of Bet Buqia and they only allowed me to learn one thing in our mishnah:[25] R. Eleazar[26] says one is liable to stoning for [sexual relations with an] *androgynos* as [if he were] a male (bYeb 84a).

215

Note that the Babylonian version too has R. Judah minimizing the insult done him by making it seem as if the students combined against R. Eleazar. Both versions agree, nevertheless, that R. Judah's reception was not pleasant.

In narrating this story a phrase of crucial significance is used: 'I only learned one thing in our mishnah from . . .' Understanding this phrase permits a fuller comprehension of the meaning of this baraita. This phrase appears at least one more time in Babylonian rabbinic sources, bErub 53a:

> R. Johanan said: I spent eighteen days (i.e. years) with R. Oshaya *Beribi* and I only learned one thing in our mishnah from him: [One is to read] How is a piece added to a town (מאברין) with an *aleph* [in mErub 5.1].[27]

The Babylonian version must be compared with the Palestinian parallel:

> R. Johanan in the name of[28] R. Hoshaya: one adds a piece to it. [R. Hoshaya] looked at him and stared.[29] [R. Johanan] said to him: Why are you staring at me? When he needs you he smiles at you, when he does not need you he opposes you.[30] [Nevertheless, R. Johanan] spent thirteen years unnecessarily going in and out before his teacher.[31]

R. Johanan and his teacher exchanged unpleasant words.[32] This is explicit in the Palestinian version; in the Babylonian it is indicated by the phrase, 'I only learned one thing in our mishnah from him.' This phrase, as we would already suspect from our texts in Yebamot, is not friendly, but a way of expressing hostility and anger.

At first sight, the meaning of this hostile phrase seems arrogant, but obvious: my teacher was an old fool, who had little to teach a competent student (like me). Careful examination of the sources, however, reveals that the phrase 'I only learned one mishnah from X' has an almost technical meaning. There are several discussions of the question: Who must one regard as one's teacher? Among the answers cited is that of R. Jose, which itself exists in two versions. According to one version, R. Jose ruled that a person must regard as a teacher anyone who enlightened him with respect to his mishnah.[33] According to the other version, R. Jose taught that even if one has only learned one mishnah from someone that person must be treated as one's teacher.[34] Similarly, we are told that one must respect a person from whom one has learned one chapter, one law, one verse, one saying or even one letter.[35] The idiom under discussion is now clear: when someone asserts that he only learned one mishnah from X he is admitting that he did study with that person. The idiom, however, has turned the admission into an attack: 'I only learned one mishnah from him', and I am thus his student in only a purely formal and minimal sense. In effect, the idiom disassociates a scholar from his teacher, and is thus evidence of bad feelings.

Returning to the Yebamot stories about R. Judah and R. Eleazar b. Shammua, both stories record that R. Judah studied with R. Eleazar; both stories report the action of R. Eleazar's students. R. Eleazar neither hindered nor overruled his students. Perhaps he even instigated their action. Whatever the case, relations between R. Judah and R. Eleazar were not good. This interpretation is confirmed by the Babylonian version in which R. Judah disassociates himself from R. Eleazar, declaring that he only learned one mishnah from him.

The third source introduces a different view of relations between the two men. Since there are a few textual difficulties, I quote it in the original:

והתניא אמר רבי כשהלכתי למצות מדותי אצל רבי אלעזר ברבי שמוע
ואמרי לה למצות מדותיו של רבי אלע' בן שמו' מצאתי...[36]

This baraita contains a double tradition, giving two alternative explanations of why R. Judah went to study with R. Eleazar b. Shammua.[37] The second of the alternatives is clearer. מצוי המדות is an idiom attested in mBetz 3.8 and parallels. Two righteous grocers in Jerusalem, we are told, went to great lengths not to rob their customers. Accordingly, they prepared liquids for sale at night, so that every drop could drain out of the measures by morning, and the customer would receive every drop for which he had paid.[38] Applying this idiom to our text, R. Judah went to study with R. Eleazar b. Shammua in order to 'drain his measures', i.e. to learn everything he could from R. Eleazar.[39]

In the light of this analysis the first alternative as preserved in the manuscripts and first edition is somewhat difficult. According to their reading, למצות מדותי, R. Judah went to R. Eleazar to drain himself out. The phrase could mean that R. Judah went to test his capacities to the utmost, and was so understood by Rashi. This meaning, however, is a bit forced and also lacks the clarity of למצות מדותיו in the second alternative. I suggest that למצות מדותי in the first alternative is an error caused by the proximity of the similar phrase in the second alternative. The reading cited by Nathan of Rome, להרצות מדותי is preferable.[40] The root רצה in the *hiphil* means to 'fill up' or 'pay back'.[41] Accordingly, the first alternative states that R. Judah went to have his measures filled up. The first and second internal versions both mean virtually the same thing,[42] and the passage as a whole should be rendered as follows:

> Rabbi said: When I went to have my measures filled up at [the Academy] of R. Eleazar b. Shammua, others say to drain the measures of R. Eleazar b. Shammua, I found . . .[43]

According to both alternatives, R. Judah went as a student seeking the instruction of a master. We are not told of any hostility, and R. Judah was received well. Coming as an empty vessel in need of filling, he was accepted by his superior in learning.

The fourth and fifth passages are relatively straightforward:

> Rabbi said: When we were studying Torah with R. Eleazar b. Shammua they brought him[44] dates and grapes, and we ate them [as an] incidental meal not in the sukkah (bYom 79b).[45]

> Rabbi[46] said: When we were studying Torah with R. Eleazar b. Shammua we used to sit . . . (bErub 53a).

As a former student of R. Eleazar, R. Judah reports various incidents that occurred during his student days. No mention is made of unusual tension or conflict between student and master. R. Judah acts with the apparent approval of his teacher in eating fruit outside the sukkah. Their relations, as must have been usual for students and teachers, were presumably cordial.

Modern interpretations

The passages analysed above pose an important problem. Two of the passages tell us about the hostile reception R. Judah received when he went to the academy of R. Eleazar (pYeb and bYeb); R. Judah was not welcome as a student and had harsh things to say about R. Eleazar (bYeb, 'I only learned one mishnah from him'), suggesting that relations between R. Eleazar and R. Judah were not good. One passage presents R. Judah as an eager student, anxious to learn all he could from R. Eleazar (bMen). R. Judah must have had great respect for the man from whom he hoped to 'fill up his measures'; relations between the two men, according to this source, were apparently very good. Consistent with this picture are the final two passages (bYom and bErub), which portray R. Judah and R. Eleazar as typical student and master. In summary, two contradictory views of relations between R. Eleazar and R. Judah are contained in these sources: their relations were either bad and hostile, or good. Some explanation of this contradiction is needed.

This question is an old one, already asked and answered by *Tosafot*. They proposed a solution in two parts. First, both the hostile and friendly receptions occurred, but they occurred at different times. Second, R. Judah's intentions were different each time, hence his reception differed. When he came to study Torah the students attacked him (pYeb and bYeb); when he came as an admirer, intending to fill himself up from R. Eleazar's learning, he was well received (bMen).[47]

This solution is not acceptable. There is not a word in the sources indicating that R. Judah made two visits to the academy of R. Eleazar. More significantly, the idea that the reception was appropriate to the intention is contrived and forced. Thus if it were not for the bMen story and the problem it creates, no one would argue that coming to study Torah in pYeb and bYeb was an intention which merited the treatment R. Judah received. Why else would a student come, if not to study Torah?

Another tack was taken by I. H. Weiss. The picture of R. Judah visiting the academy of R. Eleazar b. Shammua and being poorly received fitted one of Weiss's crucial notions about how the Mishnah was compiled: Weiss believed that R. Judah went from academy to academy collecting materials which would be ultimately shaped into the Mishnah.[48] Weiss accordingly accepted the version of pYeb and bYeb as historically accurate; these sources recorded one of R. Judah's failures. Rabbi Judah's project of collecting and compiling materials did not find favour in the eyes of R. Eleazar's students, hence they prevented him from learning the mishnah of R. Eleazar. Turning to bMen, Weiss believed the terms there to be unclear. Building on this basis, he also noted the divergent manuscript readings and concluded that the meaning of the bMen story was not definite. The baraitot in Yebamot could therefore be accepted.[49]

Weiss's solution is also open to criticism. First, I have tried to show that the meaning of bMen is clear and internally consistent, but different from pYeb and bYeb. The alternative presented by bMen cannot be dismissed with the ease proposed by Weiss. Second, R. Judah studied in the academies of his several teachers as a young man, long before he conceived the idea of compiling the Mishnah.[50] Thus it is implausible to say that R. Judah went from academy to academy in order to collect materials for the Mishnah. Finally Epstein has shown that the mishnah of R. Eleazar occupied an important place in the Mishnah of R. Judah.[51] Weiss's entire conception of R. Judah's failure to learn the mishnah of R. Eleazar is thus disproven.

The discussion of Weiss's solution adds a further layer of complication to the underlying issue. Not only do we have to contend with the contradiction between the texts in the Talmuds, but there is additional evidence on the relations between R. Eleazar and R. Judah, the evidence of the use of R. Eleazar's mishnah by R. Judah. A proper solution of the contradiction between the texts will also have to explain the facts of literary and/or halakic dependence as shown by Epstein.

Patriarchs and Akibans

There are a number of instances in which a contradictory set of stories concerning R. Judah's relations with his contemporaries is preserved in our sources. These sets, as I have shown elsewhere,[52] usually have a fairly simple explanation. Underlying both versions is some (possibly factual) common foundation; each version retells or develops that foundation to conform to its point of view and political persuasion. Thus the divergent versions are really expressions of differing political affiliations. In the case of stories concerning R. Judah, one version usually comes from circles favourable to the Patriarch and his policies, the other from opponents.

R. Eleazar b. Shammua, we should remember, was an Akiban; as I have shown elsewhere, there was a good deal of tension and competition between Patriarchs and Akibans.[53] These feelings of ill-will continued into the third century, and groups of third-century scholars viewed themselves as heirs to the interests and outlook of patriarchs and Akibans of the second century. Several sets of stories in our sources are best understood as having been told and preserved as part of that ongoing conflict.[54] If the diverging sets of stories about R. Judah's student days with R. Eleazar can be assigned to Patriarchal and Akiban circles they would fit in a clear historical and polemical context.

Underlying both sets of our stories, I propose, is the common tradition that R. Judah studied with R. Eleazar. This common foundation, I would argue, is factual. The best evidence for this conclusion is the data of literary/halakic dependence of R. Judah's Mishnah on the mishnah of R. Eleazar, as shown by Epstein. R. Judah studied with R. Eleazar and thus learned the material he worked into the Mishnah. This common foundation has been expanded and interpreted in diverging ways in our two sets of sources. One set is Akiban, the other Patriarchal; but which is which? Which set is pro-Patriarchal and which is Akiban? This choice can only be made in the light of knowledge of the usual practice of dynasties. Like all matters relating to succession, the education of the heir apparent was regularly a matter of conscious policy, not left to accident.[55] Since R. Judah studied with R. Eleazar, this cannot have been by chance. That is, R. Judah is unlikely to have wandered into the academy of R. Eleazar and to have decided on a whim to remain and study. If the experience of dynasties indicates anything it is that R. Judah went to R. Eleazar as the result of a careful and calculated policy decision. If these considerations are correct, the pro-Patriarchal group was likely to be embarrassed by a story that R. Judah was attacked and not allowed to learn very much; the Yebamot stories show the failure of the policy pursued in sending R. Judah to R. Eleazar. The Menahot, Erubin and Yoma stories show its success. I would therefore suggest that the Yebamot stories belong in the Akiban column and were preserved among their intellectual and political heirs. The Menahot, Erubin and Yoma stories come from pro-Patriarchal circles.

What policy goals were pursued in sending R. Judah to study with R. Eleazar? This question deserves careful attention. Educating the heir apparent, important in any dynasty (as noted above), was especially important in the religious and intellectual élite of the sages:[56] in their world it would be the functional equivalent of dynastic marriage. R. Judah's education must have been a matter of highest concern to his father; future ability to rule successfully could be hindered or enhanced by education. If, as we have seen, R. Judah was sent to study with an Akiban opponent, R. Eleazar b. Shammua, decisively beneficial results must have been anticipated.

Other information concerning R. Judah and the Akibans suggests an answer. R. Judah disliked R. Meir intensely.[57] Nevertheless, he based the decision to exclude Bet Shean from the

221

theoretical limits of the Holy Land on testimony of R. Meir's practice. R. Judah, as I have proposed elsewhere, was deliberately trying to put on the mantle of Akibans and to protect himself from extreme critical reaction. This interpretation is confirmed by the response of R. Meir's successors, who try to protect their predecessor from what they see as misuse and usurpation.[58] Sending R. Judah to R. Eleazar had a similar purpose. It was another way in which the Patriarchate attempted to don the mantle of its opponents, a form of co-operation uniquely suited to the rabbinic élite. The goal was to reconcile opponents with leadership, to give the opponents a stake in the future of the Patriarchate by sending the heir to study with them. Furthermore, the future Patriarch would know their traditions from the inside and could use this knowledge to his advantage. While studying, he could build personal contacts and loyalties with members of the opposition. Future members of the same group of opponents might then find it harder to oppose his policies. These considerations are admittedly speculative, but are supported by our knowledge of the practice of dynasties.[59] I suggest that these were R. Simeon b. Gamaliel's objectives when he sent his son and heir to R. Eleazar b. Shammua.[60]

In the light of this analysis details of the two sets of stories become more significant. The Yebamot stories should now be classed with those in which R. Meir's later defenders protect their predecessor from what they saw as Patriarchal appropriation. That is, the Yebamot stories have an important polemical point to make through their account of R. Judah's poor reception. One must therefore ask whether the account of R. Judah's reception is historical or was manufactured to achieve polemical goals. On the possibility that the abusive reception actually occurred, I propose that it was the response of R. Eleazar's pupils to Patriarchal policy. R. Simeon b. Gamaliel II, as suggested above, had certain goals in mind. Opponents might view these goals harshly and cynically, and see the Patriarchal programme as intended to strengthen the Patriarchate at the expense of the opposition. Determining and evaluating these goals required little more than political sense and knowledge of techniques employed by dynasties, abilities surely not lacking among opponents of the Patriarchate. Hence R. Eleazar's students tried to frustrate Patriarchal intentions through their hostile reception.[61] On the other possibility – that the account of the reception was invented – one needs to restate the intentions attributed to R. Eleazar's students so as to be those of some group of Akibans (perhaps some time after R. Judah studied with R. Eleazar). Certainty is impossible, but it seems likely that R. Judah was poorly treated at some point during his studies with R. Eleazar b. Shammua. It would have been most unusual if only some other group of Akibans (not R. Eleazar's students at the time) had resented R. Simeon b. Gamaliel's policies and made up the stories in Yebamot. It would have been extraordinary had there been no negative Akiban response to Patriarchal intentions at the time R. Judah was attempting to realize them, and by the people among whom he was trying to realize them.[62] It is therefore likelier that R. Judah was abused in some way by R. Eleazar b. Shammua's students. Perhaps the extent of the hostile actions has been exaggerated by other (later) Akibans.

One detail in the bYeb story should definitely be considered an invention: R. Judah's alleged confession that he only learned one thing in his mishnah from R. Eleazar. The force of this idiom, as shown above, is to disassociate a scholar from his teacher. The idiom indicates bad feelings and turns the fact of the teacher-student relationship into an attack. Given Patriarchal motives, as discussed above, there would be little reason for R. Judah to want to increase the distance between himself and R. Eleazar. One would imagine that R. Judah would want to achieve the opposite result. On the other hand, putting statements calculated and created to damage an opponent's case into the mouth of that opponent was a favourite tactic of political polemicists.[63] This is what has happened here. R. Judah (or his supporters) would never have laid the charge that he only learned one mishnah from R. Eleazar. On the other hand, in the light of Patriarchal policy, those around R. Eleazar and their later successors had good reason for wanting to separate R. Judah from R. Eleazar. Hence they made R. Judah assert that he had learned little from R. Eleazar.

An aspect of the bMen story is also clarified. No reference is made there to the abusive reception R. Judah most likely received. The omission is easily explained: reflecting Patriarchal policy, the account in bMen would want to suppress references to difficulties or obstacles that policy encountered.

In summary, I suggest that R. Judah did in fact study with R. Eleazar. This seemingly absurd step was taken consciously by R. Simeon b. Gamaliel II as part of efforts to reconcile the Akiban opposition. R. Judah did manage to learn some of R.

Eleazar's teachings and incorporated these in the Mishnah. On the other hand there is the story (probably historical) that R. Judah was at one time effectively kicked out. Whatever the case, the Patriarchal party stressed its successes, as preserved in baraitot in Menahot, Erubin and Yoma;[64] the Akibans and/or their successors stressed the opposite point of view, as in Yebamot.[65]

Other Akibans

The case of R. Eleazar b. Shammua is not unique. Evidence for at least two other principal Akibans is remarkably similar (and can thus be presented in summary form). This evidence has additional significance: the interpretations offered concerning R. Eleazar b. Shammua have been admittedly speculative; the history and experience of other dynasties have been employed to help supply motives and objectives concerning which our sources are silent. The evidence for the other two Akibans fits extremely well into the framework of these interpretations, and thus increases the likelihood that these suggestions are accurate.

We are told that R. Judah studied with R. Simeon b. Yohai;[66] literary/halakic analysis indicates that R. Judah used the mishnah of R. Simeon in the Mishnah.[67] I suggest that the objectives pursued in sending R. Judah to the academy of R. Eleazar b. Shammua were the ones which motivated his being sent to R. Simeon. We thus have another example of the attempt of the Hillelites to don the mantle of the Akibans and thereby to reconcile that significant group of rivals. As discussed above, the Akibans did not appreciate R. Judah as a student; they viewed Patriarchal policy with a cynical eye, as an undesirable and unacceptable attempt to appropriate their teaching and to strengthen the Patriarchate at their expense. This interpretation is confirmed by the sources reporting friction between R. Eleazar b. R. Simeon and R. Judah. Especially revealing is R. Eleazar's rude remark to R. Judah when the latter quoted an opinion of R. Simeon: 'I learned more from my father standing than you did sitting';[68] in effect, how dare you misquote my father to me? Patriarchal intention to become legitimate bearers of accurate Akiban traditions is explicitly repudiated.

The case of R. Judah b. Ilai differs slightly from the pattern above. R. Judah studied with him and used his mishnah in the Mishnah.[69] R. Judah's reception on the part of this Akiban was apparently different; no sources report that he was unwelcome or rejected. On the contrary, our sources note that R. Judah b. Ilai occupied some sort of office at the Patriarchal court.[70] He also reported many of the traditions of R. Gamaliel II.[71] These are not mere coincidences. That is, we have no indications that R. Judah b. Ilai rejected (or was claimed to have rejected) R. Judah as a student because the former was more sympathetic to the Patriarchal position and welcomed R. Judah more warmly than his fellow Akibans. Furthermore, R. Judah b. Ilai's willingness to take a pro-Patriarchal stance is consistent with his occupying some sort of office. When and why R. Judah b. Ilai moved closer to the Patriarchate we do not know, as we have no information about when he received whatever office he filled.[72] His case does, however, provide confirmation of a different sort for the interpretations offered. Not only does another piece of the puzzle fit well in place, but in addition the proposal above that R. Judah was sent to the Akibans as the result of policy (not chance) receives indirect confirmation. If he was sent as part of a policy it is not surprising that those disposed to the Patriarchal position and willing to accept him should occupy a role in the Patriarchal court, loyalty is rewarded.

Conclusion

If the analysis proposed here is correct and the conclusions sound, R. Simeon b. Gamaliel II attempted a grand strategy designed to bring Akiban opponents and competitors into the circle of Patriarchal influence. As part of that policy he sent his son and heir to study with at least three Akiban masters.[73] That policy had at least some visible success, as in the case of R. Judah b. Ilai, and those willing to be closer to the Patriarchal camp were duly rewarded. As always in human affairs, success was far from universal and there were inevitable failures. The extent of success or failure is hard to determine,[74] but the policy was to have lasting consequences. The future Patriarch, R. Judah the Prince, received at least some of his training at the schools of these Akibans and – perhaps trying to complete what his father had begun – was to incorporate their teachings into the Mishnah.[75] The Mishnah was thus to acquire a decisively Akiban coloration,[76] and at least some of the teaching of Akiban opponents was to find a permanent home under the Patriarchal roof.

10

Birkat Ha-Minim *and the Lack of Evidence for an Anti-Christian Jewish Prayer in Late Antiquity**

REUVEN KIMELMAN

Introduction

A decisive stage in the process of communal self-definition is reached when a community sets criteria for exclusion. The exclusionary benediction, *birkat ha-minim*, played such a role in the process of achieving normative self-definition in rabbinic Judaism.

Since the talmudic period *birkat ha-minim* has constituted the twelfth benediction of the rabbinic statutory prayer, the so-called 'eighteen benedictions' or ʿ*amidah*. The ʿ*amidah* is recited thrice daily on weekdays. On the Sabbath or holidays an alternative form is employed which does not contain *birkat ha-minim*.

The publication of the Genizah version of *birkat ha-minim* over eighty years ago[1] has renewed interest in the benediction as a major document in the history of Jewish-Christian relationships in the first centuries of the Common Era. This version reads as follows:

1. For the apostates let there be no hope.
2. And let the arrogant government be speedily uprooted in our days.
3. Let the *noṣrim* and the *minim* be destroyed in a moment.
4. And let them be blotted out of the Book of Life and not be inscribed together with the righteous.
5. Blessed art thou, O Lord, who humblest the arrogant.

Recent studies of the benediction have argued cogently that not long after the destruction of the Second Temple (70 CE) the rabbis, under the aegis of Rabban Gamaliel, had an old blessing reformulated. The blessing had functioned as a denunciation against separatists who defected from the community in times of woe. In the light of the reference to the 'arrogant government' it is possible that the benediction had uppermost in mind Jews who collaborated with the Romans against the Jews. In any case, the benediction, as reformulated, included a denunciation of the *minim*.[2] This resulted in a single benediction denouncing both the heterodox and separatists. Apparently, post-temple Judaism perceived the threat from communal separatists and theological dissidents on a similar plane.[3] In actuality, it was probably difficult to distinguish between the two.

The reformulated benediction became known as *birkat ha-minim*. What was the purpose of *birkat ha-minim*? In general three positions have garnered scholarly support. The first position is based on the manner in which the benediction functioned, which was to exclude any *min* from acting as reader in the synagogue. This, of course, assumes that a *min* would not want to curse himself. If he erred or glossed over the benediction he would thereby expose himself to suspicion.[4] Since he also would not want to be cursed by others, the insertion in the statutory prayer would lead to the exclusion of Minim from the synagogue.[5]

The difficulty with this position is that it assumes that *min* has a denotation more limited than 'heretic'. A condemnation of heretics in general without a specific reference to which heresy was meant would have a limited effect, since it is unlikely that a theological dissident would see himself included in the term 'heretic'. This understanding is thus dependent on the assumption that *min* had a specific denotation.[6] Even if that were true initially, it is clear that *min* loses any specific denotation, as will be shown below. Thus, the benediction would lose its purpose.[7]

The second position holds that the term *minim* refers to Jewish Christians and that the benediction is a declaration that these are equivalent to apostates, thereby excluding them from the people of Israel. The result of such a declaration would lead to their exclusion from the life of the synagogue.[8] We shall allude to this position in our discussion of the terms *minim* and *noṣrim*. In the meanwhile, it is worth noting that some variation of this position is behind the oft-repeated assertion that about the year 100 the breach between Judaism and Christianity became irreparable.[9]

The third position is that the purpose of the curse is simply that of all curses, namely, a request to God that the *minim* be cursed and damned. This position has much to recommend it. It does not assume that *minim* had a specific connotation beyond heretics or, what may be closer etymologically, sectarians.[10] Second, it accounts for why *minim* are so easily classed in tannaitic literature with other nondescripts such as apostates and informers whose destruction is to be sought[11] and/or who are locked in hell.[12] Third, it corresponds with the rabbinic source that assumed that *birkat ha-minim* is an elliptical expression for *birkat qellelat ha-minim*, i.e., the benediction for the cursing of the *minim*.[13]

Whatever the case may be, the benediction would lead to the exclusion of the *minim* and whoever is associated with them from the synagogue. Who was actually excluded depends on the meaning of the terms *minim* and *nosrim*.

Minim

Much has been written on the meaning of the word *min* and its identification.[14] Suggestions range from viewing it as a catch-all term for heretics to viewing it as a specific denotation of some heretical group such as Jewish gnostics and/or Jewish Christians.[15] Some have even contended that *min* can denote Christian[16] and/or pagan Gentiles.[17]

The confusion results from poor formulation of the question. To ask about the meaning of *min* in rabbinic literature is to assume terminological consistency for over half a millennium over different bodies of literature. The question should be sub-divided as follows: what does *min* denote (*a*) in tannaitic literature? (*b*) in the amoraic literature of Palestine? and (*c*) in the amoraic literature of Babylonia?

(*a*) In tannaitic literature, there is unambiguous evidence that *min* can denote a deviant Jew. This can be shown by an example from each of the major compositions of tannaitic literature, the Mishnah and the Tosefta.[18] In the Mishnah (Meg 4.8) it says that if one places the phylacteries on the forehead or on the palm it is a way of *minut*. It is not our concern here to investigate whether this is based on a literal reading of scripture and/or on sectarian practice,[19] but rather to emphasize that a way of placing phylacteries was identifiable as a way of *minim*, clearly a non-rabbinic way of placing phylacteries. The Tosefta (tBM 2.33) also clearly understands *minim* as Jews when it categorizes the following two groups. On the one side are Gentiles,[20] shepherds and small cattle raisers; on the other side are *minim*, apostates and informers. Similarly, it distinguishes between meat in the hands of a Gentile and meat in the hands of a *min* (tHull 2.20). In both cases the distinction is significant since the law is more severe with regard to a *min*.

(*b*) In the amoraic literature of Palestine, there is also solid evidence that *minim* are Jews. Here, however, it is important to base the argument, as much as possible, on the earliest edited amoraic documents such as the Palestinian Talmud, Genesis Rabbah, and Leviticus Rabbah which in all probability were compiled in the first half of the fifth century. So, for example, a statement of the third-century Palestinian, R. Johanan, employs the term *minim* for Jewish schismatics: 'Israel did not go into exile until it had split into twenty-four sects of *minim*' (pSanh 10.6; 29c). On the other hand, when Palestinian amoraic literature refers to known positions of Gentile Christians it tends to place the argument in the mouth of 'the nations of the world' and not that of the *minim*. So, for example:

> Moses asked that the Mishnah also be in written form like the Torah. But the Holy One, blessed be He, foresaw that the nations would get to translate the Torah and reading it, say in Greek, would declare: We are Israel; we are the children of the Lord. The scales would appear to be balanced between both claims, but then the Holy One, blessed be He, will say to the nations: What are you claiming, that you are my children? I have no way of knowing other than that my child is he who possesses my secret lore. The nations will ask: And what is Thy secret lore? God will reply: It is the Mishnah. (Pesiqta Rabbati 5.1, ed. Friedman, 14b.)

This source clearly protests against that type of patristic exegesis which wrenched scripture from its Jewish moorings. The same protest apparently lies behind the declaration of a Palestinian amora that the Sinaitic revelation was 'an elixir of life to Israel, but a drug of death to the nations of the world' (CantR 2.3.5).

Sometimes, a known Christian argument is placed in the mouth of a 'philosopher': for example, the classical patristic argument against circumcision which holds that, if circumcision were necessary, God would not have created Adam uncircumcised,[21] or the contention that God rejected the Jewish people.[22]

Finally, two recent studies which have identified the opponent of some rabbinic polemics on the Song of Songs with Origen have emphasized that his arguments are placed in the mouth of 'the nations of the world'.[23] If there ever were a Gentile who would be referred to as a *min* it would be Origen. Origen was a Christian biblical scholar who resided in Palestine. He possessed a rudimentary knowledge of Hebrew. Moreover, he studied under 'Hebrew' teachers and maintained contact with some rabbinic authorities.[24] If, nevertheless, he is still referred to as one of 'the nations of the world', all the more so other Gentile Christians who had less in common with Judaism.

Thus in Palestinian literature, be it tannaitic or amoraic, it is reasonable to conclude that *minim* had a Jewish sectarian denotation and was not used to refer to Gentiles.

(c) The problem arises in the amoraic literature of Babylonia, namely the Babylonian Talmud. Those scholarly hypotheses based on it have wrecked havoc with the term *min*. Most prominent among those who have argued that *min* can denote a Gentile is S. Lieberman, who cites the following data:[25]

> The text of TB (Pes 87b) reads מינא, which very often means Gentile, especially in sources originating in Palestine (see Krauss [*Griechische und latienische Lehnwörter im Talmud* I, 1898], p. XV, n. 2). Seder Eliyyahu Rabba ibid. [p. 54] states clearly that the man who questioned R. Juda the Patriarch was הגמון, ἡγεμών, a general. Similarly, TB (Aboda Zara 6b) records that a מין presented the same Rabbi Juda the Patriarch with money, whereas the parallel story in TP (ibid. I. i, 39b) mentions a דוקינר (δουκηνάριος, *ducenarius*) instead of מין. In both cases the מין was a heathen Roman official.

These notices prove only that a host of Greek terms were rendered in the Babylonian Talmud as *min*. They prove nothing with regard to Palestinian usage of the term *min*. In Palestine the Greek terms would be understood, as reflected in the above parallels. And since *min* had an actual sectarian denotation it is not haphazardly used to indicate anyone of dubious identity. On the other hand, elsewhere (bBer 7a) a Palestinian *min* who badgered R. Johanan's older compatriot R. Joshua b. Levi with scriptural passages is identified by Lieberman as a Jewish Christian.[26]

This highlights the complexity of the problem. To resolve it, one must ask whether the language of a statement preserves the idiom of its original context, or whether it has been altered by the redaction of the document in which it is recorded. A Palestinian statement may reflect Babylonian terminology if it appears in the Babylonian Talmud. So, for example, the Palestinian amora R. Yohanan is alleged in the Babylonian Talmud to have used the expression מין שבאומות (= a *min* among the nations)[27] an expression which allows for a *min* to be a Gentile. The parallel discussion in the Palestinian Talmud,[28] however, has instead *goy* (= Gentile). There is therefore no evidence that the Palestinian, R. Johanan, employed *min* to refer to a Gentile. A Büchler's contention that *minim* are sometimes 'Bible-reading heathens'[29] is also based on Babylonian material and thus not pertinent to determining the denotation of *minim* in Palestine. The point is not that *min* in the Babylonian Talmud must refer to a Gentile, but that it might do so. In each case the argument must be made on the context, if possible, and not the term.

Why is there this difference in terminology between Babylonian and Palestinian sources? In Palestine, the term *min* had a sectarian connotation, indeed some have speculated that the word itself denotes a specific sect.[30] This prevented the indiscriminate use of the term. In Babylonia, owing to the lack of *minim* in the Palestinian sense (see bAZ 4a; bPes 56a) the word assimilated the meaning it had in the local vernacular as we know it from Syriac and Christian Palestinian Aramaic.[31] It would be a methodological mistake, indeed, to extrapolate from its usage in these languages its meaning in Palestinian texts.[32]

One of the sectarian meanings that *min* had in Palestine was Jewish Christian. This can be surmised from the mention of *min* and Jesus in the same episode in several Palestinian texts, tannaitic and amoraic. The first tannaitic source (tHull 2.24) reads as follows:

> It happened that R. Eliezer was arrested for words of *minut* and they brought him to the tribunal for judgment. . .When he was released from the tribunal he was troubled that he had been arrested for words of *minut*. His disciples came in to comfort him but he would not accept (it). R. Akiba entered and said to him:. . .Perhaps one of the *minim* said to you a word of *minut* and it pleased you. He replied: By Heaven, you reminded me. Once I was walking in a street of Sepphoris and chanced upon Jacob the man of Kefar Sichnin and he told me something of *minut* in the name of Yeshu (=Jesus) ben Pantiri.[33]

The second one (ibid. 2.22) records that Eleazar ben Dama was bitten by a snake and that Jacob the man of Kefar Sama came to cure him in the name of Yeshu ben Pantiri.[34] In the nick of time ben Dama was prevented from being subjected to the cure of Jacob by the intervention of R. Ishmael.

The *min*, Jacob, is in both cases associated with Jesus. In the Babylonian version of the first story Jesus is referred to as Yeshu the Nazarene.[35] The two different place names are not difficult since modern geographers hold that they correspond to two villages in Galilee, lying north of Nazareth, namely, Kefar Semai and Saknin. The same Jacob was associated with both. Indeed, as will be discussed below, Saknin was known as a place of Nazaraeans.[36]

From this it can be concluded that one of the prominent groups which could be included in the term minim was Jewish Christians. This fact is also reflected in the interpretation of R. Issi of Caesarea that Eccles. 7.26 refers to *minut*. Accordingly, he applies the last part of the verse, 'The good before God will escape from her: but the sinner will be ensnared by her', to different known cases including the aforementioned ones:

> The good – R. Eleazar, *But the sinner* – Jacob of Kefar Nibbuyara.
> The good – Eleazar b. Dama, *But the sinner* – Jacob of Kefar Sama.
> The good – Ḥananiah the nephew of R. Joshua, *But the sinner* – the inhabitants of Capernaum.
> The good – Judah b. Naqosa, *But the sinner* – the *minim*.
> The good – R. Nathan, *But the sinner* – his disciple.
> The good – R. Eliezer and R. Joshua, *But the sinner* – Elisha.[37]

From this it is clear that *minim* can include at least Jewish Christians. Hence it is safe to conclude that the Palestinian prayer against the *minim* was aimed at Jewish sectarians among whom Jewish Christians figured prominently.

Noṣrim

The term *noṣrim* is as problematic as the term *minim*. Since the discovery of the Genizah text some scholars have argued that it was part of the original prayer text of *birkat ha-minim*. Some have argued on the basis of stylistic considerations.[38] Others have argued that evidence from patristic sources, pointing to a Jewish practice of cursing the Christians 'while they read the prayers', indicates that *noṣrim* was part of the original text.[39] This, of course, assumes that *noṣrim* means 'Christians' by way of the cognate Nazarenes. Others have contended, albeit circularly, that *noṣrim* must be original, for if *minim* is ambiguous there is no explicit mention of Christians.[40]

A significant number of scholars have contended that *noṣrim* has been added. The major argument has been the difficulty of rendering smoothly both terms together.[41] Those who contend that *noṣrim* is original have had to render the phrase as 'Jewish Christians and other heretics'.[42] The fact that 'other' has to be supplied highlights the difficulty of rendering an apparently redundant text such as 'Jewish Christians and heretics'.

Informing the debate on the meaning of the text are also assumptions about the impact of Christianity (including Jewish Christianity) on rabbinic Judaism in the first century and a half or so. Generally, those who perceive a significant impact by Christianity argue for the inclusion of *noṣrim* in the original formulation.[43] Those who perceive a minimal impact tend to exclude *noṣrim* from the original formulation.[44] A careful review of the evidence for the Christian impact on rabbinic Judaism will show that most generalizations are based on ambiguous evidence, a conclusion I intend to discuss elsewhere. It would be safe therefore not to base positions unduly on the general situation, but to argue each case on its own merits. When evidence is lacking for the particular case, the prudent course is to withhold judgment rather than to assume a Christian impact on Judaism.

[One of the results of the McMaster Symposium which lies behind this volume was a highlighting of the lack of evidence for any formative impact of Christianity on any major element of tannaitic Judaism, including the development of rabbinic law, the formation of the Mishnah, the structuring of the liturgy, the closing of the canon, and the major propositions of rabbinic theology. This itself is sufficient to question the thesis that *birkat ha-minim* was primarily directed against Christianity. We must be careful of anachronistically overestimating the impact of Christianity on Judaism in the first two centuries.]

In addition, there are several major considerations for excluding *noṣrim* from the original formulation. First, in all six versions of *birkat ha-minim* published by A. Marmorstein, the opening word is *noṣrim*, not *minim*.[45] If *noṣrim* were present *ab initio* the talmudic nomenclature would likely have been *birkat ha-noṣrim*. Second, if the term were a part of the statutory liturgy from the first century onwards, the term *noṣrim* should have become a common term in rabbinic literature. In fact, *noṣrim* does not appear in tannaitic literature. Indeed, in that form, it appears unambiguously only once in amoraic literature in a passage by

R. Johanan (c. 200-279) which will be discussed below. Jesus is also referred to in the Babylonian Talmud as *ha-noṣri*[46] (as he is called in the gospel ὁ Ναζωραῖος, Matt. 2.23 and elsewhere),[47] and a day is called 'of the נוצרי/נוצרים' in the same document by the third-century Babylonian Samuel.[48]

Thus internal rabbinic evidence makes it highly unlikely that *noṣrim* was part of the original *birkat ha-minim*.

What about the alleged Christian evidence for Jews cursing Christians during prayer? Discussions of this evidence frequently commit the fallacy of filling in the lacunae of first- and second-century sources with fourth-century material, oblivious to the fact that differences may be due to developments in the meantime.[49] The fact that the thrust of contemporary scholarship has highlighted the major developments which took place within Judaism and Christianity from the second to the fourth century should be a warning against the hazards of such an approach.

Before dealing with the patristic evidence, some comments are in order on the supposed role of *birkat ha-minim* in the gospel of John, if only because such a role is assumed more and more by students of the gospel.[50] This is despite the fact that scholarship is becoming increasingly less sure about the setting of the gospel.[51]

The issue with regard to the gospel of John has two aspects which are not necessarily related. First, is there awareness of *birkat ha-minim*? Second, is there any evidence that it then contained a reference to *noṣrim*? John mentions three times that Jews who 'confess Christ' were excluded from the synagogue ἀποσυνάγωγος, 9.22; 12.42; 16.2). There is no evidence that this situation was prevalent anywhere else.[52] The context of the mention of 'Pharisees' (12.42) indicates that it is a derogatory reference to local leadership.[53] Indeed the absence of any mention of such exclusion by early Christian authors argues against its being a pervasive practice. It is hard to believe that a major rabbinic practice which is supposed to have originated in Yavneh about the turn of the first century is attested to in only one Christian document. If it were aimed against Christians it would have been widespread.[54] Thus it is of no surprise that the term for exclusion from the synagogue, ἀποσυνάγωγος, appears nowhere else in early Christian literature and has no precise parallel in rabbinic terminology.[55] It is even possible that the whole charge was concocted to persuade Christians to stay away from the synagogue[56] by making them believe that they would be received with hostility. Thus the Jews are generally represented in a negative fashion.[57] Alternatively, the gospel wanted to convince Jews who had 'confessed Christ' that there was no turning back, since such confession marks one as rejected by the synagogue. It is more likely that the final edition of the gospel is addressing Gentiles who are far removed from Judaism. This accounts for the gospel's having to explain so much of Judaism, even the well-known festivals.[58]

In any case, John makes no reference to the prayers of the Jews nor to any curse and thus is not helpful for establishing any part of the formulation of *birkat ha-minim*. This conclusion holds even if John were responding to a situation, that resulted from the adoption of *birkat ha-minim*.[59]

It is not uncommon to buttress the alleged evidence from John by references to patristic literature. The pertinent patristic evidence derives from Justin, Origen, Jerome and Epiphanius.

In his *Dialogue with Trypho* Justin Martyr mentions nine times that Jews cursed Christ and/or those who believe in him. Of these, five make no mention of the synagogue (93, 95, 108, 123, 133); of the remaining four, which mention the synagogue (16, 47, 96, 137), only one (137) mentions it in the context of prayers. It reads:

> Scoff not at the King of Israel, as the rulers of your synagogues teach you to do *after* your prayers (my italics).

Only this statement really pertains to our investigation. With regard to the others, there is no necessary connection between *birkat ha-minim* and the cursing of Christ or Christianity. There were undoubedly Jews in Rome in Justin's time who cursed Christ to avoid suspicion by the Roman authorities of any illegal connection with Christianity.[60] And Justin knows that the Jews regard as blasphemous at least five Christian assertions.[61]

The connection between the comment of Justin just cited and *birkat ha-minim* is, to say the least, problematic. First, there is no mention of Christians. Second, although elsewhere Justin employs καταράομαι (=curse) and καταναθηματίζω (=anathematize) or forms thereof, here he uses only 'ἐπισκώψητέ ποτε (=scoff), a term which would not be appropriate to *birkat ha-minim*. Third, whatever did take place occurred after the prayers (μετὰ τὴν προσευχήν), while *birkat ha-minim* is in the middle of the statutory prayers (the twelfth of the 'Eighteen Benedictions')! Justin clearly proves inadequate as evidence for positing the existence of a statutory Jewish prayer which cursed Christians.[62]

The next patristic witness is Origen. He offers less evidence than Justin. One comment merely says that the Jews curse Christ everywhere up to the present time.[63] Two other pertinent comments appear in his *Homilies on Jeremiah*. The first comment (10.8.2) accuses Jews of cursing and blaspheming Jesus and plotting against those who believe in him. The second source (19.12.31) says, 'Enter the synagogue of the Jews and see Jesus flagellated by those with the language of blasphemy.' One must be careful of Origen's hyperbole. For instance, in another of the same *Homilies* (12.13.20–23) he says that Jews are still responsible for the murder of Jesus since they understand the Law and the Prophets according to its plain sense! Thus for Origen the mere practice of Judaism is an affront to the coming of Christ and could be conceived as blasphemous.[64] Whatever the case may be, Origen makes no mention of Christians being cursed nor of any connection to the prayers. Thus, P. Nautin is misled when he writes in his annotated French translation of the *Homilies* as follows: 'Sans doute faut-il y voir une allusion à la malédiction portée dans les *Schemone Esre* contre les "minim", désignant les chrétiens.' Even he must have had some misgivings about this judgment, for he goes on to say, 'Origène, qui n'est pas parfaitement renseigné en parle ici comme d'un blasphème contre Jésus lui-même.'[65]

It is inadequate to contend that Origen was poorly informed on such a visible public practice. There probably was no church Father, of his time, as well informed about the Jews.[66] Besides his rabbinic contacts he was acquainted with Jewish converts to Christianity. These may have been the source of his information on the clandestine tribunals of the court of the Patriarch. The *Homilies on Jeremiah* themselves were composed during the 240s after Origen had spent over a decade in Palestine. Several years earlier, in fact, he had reflected his awareness of addressing on Sunday those who had just been to synagogue on the Sabbath.[67]

The only reason to contend that Origen was misinformed is to force his comment into a pattern which has been imposed on both the gospel of John and Justin. Once it is realized how weak the evidence is from John and Justin, the cogency for foisting on Origen an understanding which cannot be supported by what he says disappears and Origen's statement is left to stand as it is. Origen reports Jews blaspheming Jesus. [Even this may have to be taken *cum grano salis* in the light of his aforementioned *Tendenz*. It is likely, as de Lange suggests, that Origen's harping on the hostility of the Jews reflects a long-standing theological theme rather than reflecting current events.[68]] Origen does not report Jews cursing Christians in their prayers, and there are insufficient grounds to assume that he thought they did.

The nature of the references is quite different in the writings of Epiphanius and Jerome. They wrote, however, about a century and a half after Origen. Much has happened within and between Judaism and Christianity in the meanwhile.[69]

Only in Epiphanius and Jerome are there clear references to Jews, Nazoraeans, and cursing *during* the prayers thrice daily. At first glance, they appear to diverge on the denotation of the word *noṣrim* in the prayer. Jerome apparently sees in it a reference to Christians while Epiphanius sees it as a reference to the contemporary Jewish Christian group, the Nazoraeans. In four places Jerome makes the point that the Jews in the synagogues curse the Christians thrice daily under the name Nazoraeans (*sub nomine Nazarenorum*).[70] This alone constitutes evidence that *noṣrim*, in Jerome's time, appeared in *birkat ha-minim* and that Jerome would have the reader believe that it referred to Christians.

But did it? It is not clear. According to S. Krauss, Jerome is saying that 'the malediction in the liturgy is nominally directed against the Nazorenes but really against the Christians. From the turn of the phrase it is evident that Jerome thought he had made a discovery. "How artful the Jews are," he seems to say, "they curse the Nazarenes when they mean the Christians." '[71]

Two additional factors make it difficult to accept that Jerome himself believed that it referred explicitly to Christians. First is Jerome's tendency to present Judaism and Jews pejoratively.[72] Second is the existence of a second statement of Jerome which tends to undermine the first and coheres better with what Epiphanius wrote and with the results of our analysis of the rabbinic material below.

In one of his epistles to Augustine (112.13) Jerome wrote:

> Until now a heresy is to be found in all parts of the East where Jews have their synagogues; it is called 'of the Minaeans' and cursed by Pharisees up to now. Usually they are named Nazoraeans. They

believe in Christ . . . but since they want to be both Jews and Christians, they are neither Jews nor Christians.[73]

Jerome is pointing to a group of Jewish Christians who are called Nazoraeans. They are associated with Minaeans and are cursed by the Jews. This dovetails with what Epiphanius wrote in his *Panarion* about twenty years earlier. Both present evidence for the association of Jews, Nazoraeans, and cursing *during* prayers. Epiphanius's comments appear in his discussion of the Nazoraean heresy:

> . . . they are rather Jews and nothing else. However, they are very much hated by the Jews. For not only the Jewish children cherish hate against them but the people also stand up in the morning, at noon and in the evening, three times a day and they pronounce curses and maledictions over them when they say their prayers in the synagogues. Three times a day they say: 'May God curse the Nazoraeans.'[74]

Epiphanius clearly considers the Nazoraeans to be Jews. The reference to cursing the Nazoraeans thrice daily, while standing in the synagogue, with the words, 'May God curse the Nazoraeans', leaves no room for doubting that Epiphanius is referring to the formulation of *birkat ha-minim* as found in the Genizah. Epiphanius goes on to say that their proclaiming that Jesus is the Christ is what provoked the malediction.

It is of particular note that the first Christian source clearly to mention cursing thrice daily in the synagogues makes no mention of Christians. The same source is also the first patristic mention of the Jewish Christian sect of the Nazoraeans. Jerome, who next mentions the Nazoraeans, associates them with the Minaeans and infers that both are cursed by the Jews. This, along with the fact that the term *nosrim* first appears in rabbinic literature in the mouth of R. Johanan of the third century, warrants the conclusion that the Genizah formula which reads *ha-nosrim ve-ha-minim* (= the *nosrim* and [?, see below] the *minim*) was composed between the time of R. Johanan (d. c. 279) and the writing of the *Panarion* (377). The data also warrant the conclusion that *nosrim* does not denote Christians, but rather Nazoraeans, a Jewish Christian sect whose existence is vouched for by at least two fourth-century sources.[75]

What was the status of these Nazoraeans? The testimonies of Epiphanius and Jerome seem to conflict. According to Epiphanius, 'They are Jews and nothing else.' According to Jerome, 'They are neither Jews nor Christians.' It is possible that Jerome's harsher judgment on their Jewishness reflects the growing effect of an explicit reference to them in *birkat ha-minim*.[76]

Besides the chronological correlation of the insertion of *nosrim* in *birkat ha-minim* and the mention of the Jewish Christian Nazoraeans by Jerome and Epiphanius, there are several additional considerations for understanding *nosrim* as denoting Jews. The first is the internal evidence from the text of the benediction; the second is the patristic evidence that Christians were not excluded from the synagogue.

After mention of the *nosrim* and the *minim*, line 4 of the benediction goes on to say: 'Let them be blotted out of the Book of Life and not be inscribed together with the righteous.' This is a way of execrating Jews by removing them from the covenant (see Jub. 36.10) and consequently from the community of the saved. Exclusion from the covenant entails loss of salvation.[77] There is no reason explicitly to exclude Gentiles from the Jewish Book of Life. That this was a contemporary practice can be gathered from Jerome, who mentions that apostate Jews were 'expelled from the community'.[78]

What about the patristic evidence? Not only is evidence lacking from rabbinic sources that Gentile Christians were excluded from the synagogue, there is abundant evidence from patristic sources that Christians were frequenting the synagogues quite often. Indeed, there is far-flung evidence that it was the church leadership that strove to keep Christians away from the synagogue and not the Jews who were excluding them. Such protest from the church Fathers demonstrates the receptivity of the synagogue to Christians. This situation is highly unlikely if the synagogue liturgy contained a daily curse against Christians.[79]

It is of no small significance to note that Jewish receptivity to Christians is precisely where rabbinic Judaism had made its strongest impact, namely, Asia Minor, Palestine and Syria. So, for example, the *Martyrium Pionii*, which has been dated from the end of the third to the middle of the fourth century,[80] records Pionius (d. 250 – Smyrna) as saying: 'I hear that the Jews call some of you to the synagogues.' Indeed, the Jews seem to have mounted a missionary campaign among the Christians of Smyrna.[81]

Origen, as mentioned above, is also aware that he had congregants who attended synagogue on the Sabbath. Indeed, Origen also alludes to Jewish missionaries who induced Christians to practise Jewish rites.[82]

In the late fourth century, Jerome stressed that Christians imitated the rites of the synagogue, probably as a result of familiarity with synagogue practice.[83] Jerome also pointed out, to his chagrin, that Christians were often the beneficiaries of Jewish generosity. This reached such a level, that he urged that such charity be refused lest it attract them to Judaism.[84]

Finally, the evidence from John Chrysostom is overwhelming. In the *Homilies Against the Jews*, he harangues against the Judaizing activities of Christians, in general, and their frequenting of synagogues, in particular. The latter was so serious that he felt impelled to denounce it over fifteen times.[85] His vituperative attacks probably indicate that the Christian legislation against Christian attendance at Jewish religious meetings was ineffective.[86] Chrysostom, himself, reported that Christians who frequent synagogues urged their household, friends and neighbours not to report them to the priests.[87] Clearly, the synagogue was a very real attraction for Christians.

Significantly, in an effort to dissuade Christians from rushing off to the synagogue begging the Jews to help them, Chrysostom asserts that the Jews laugh and scoff at them. Then most revealingly he concedes: 'Even if they do not do it openly . . . they are doing this deep down in their hearts.'[88] Not only can Chrysostom not adduce evidence for Jews cursing Christians, he cannot even adduce evidence for Jews scoffing at them. The Jews must have been quite receptive to Christians seeking their assistance and the succour of the synagogue.[89]

If one of the most virulent antisemites of the church cannot produce evidence for official Jewish denigration of Christians, then its existence is seriously called into question. Not only is evidence lacking from Christian sources that *birkat ha-minim* was directed against Gentile Christians, but there is also evidence, direct and indirect, that it was not. Indeed, the preponderance of the evidence points to a fourth-century Jewish Christian sect, called by Epiphanius and Jerome the Nazoraeans, as the group to which the term *nosrim* refers.[90] Once it is clear that *nosrim* does not refer to Christians but to Nazoraeans, it is not at all surprising to discover that the Hebrew was originally *nasrim* and thus more assonant with Nazoraeans.[91]

Naṣrim in rabbinic literature

The identification of what now have to be called the *naṣrim* with Jewish Christian Nazoraeans is supported by the two talmudic references to *naṣrim*. Both derive from Palestine, although they are found in the Babylonian Talmud.[92] The first reference is generally unknown since the text is corrupt. The text reads 'Kefar Sekania of Egypt',[93] an otherwise unattested place. The word for Egypt is, however, מצרים (*MSRYM*), which is identical to *naṣrim* (נצרים), except for the first letter, which is a מ rather than the נ of *naṣrim*. J. N. Epstein has pointed out that these two liquid letters are sometimes transposed in names.[94] It thus becomes easy to read or understand the text as 'Kefar Sekania of *naṣrim*'.[95] Kefar Sekania is identical with the aforementioned Kefar Saknin, which was known as a place of *minut*.[96] Since one of the major sects behind the term *minim* is Jewish Christianity, it is of no surprise that a place of *minut* should also be known as a place of Nazoraeans.

The second mention of *naṣrim* is in the following source:

> Our rabbis taught: . . . the men of the stations [in temple times] assembled in their synagogues and observed four fasts, on Monday, Tuesday, Wednesday and Thursday of that week. . . . On Friday they did not fast out of respect for the Sabbath; and certainly not on the Sabbath. Why did they not fast on Sunday? – R. Johanan said: On account of the *naṣrim*.[97]

Whom did R. Johanan mean by the *naṣrim*? Since the source is dealing with the first century, did he mean first-century Christians who were called Nazarenes (Acts 24.5)? or was he reflecting on his own reality and pointing to the Jewish Christian Nazoraeans? J. Z. Lauterbach unequivocally concluded: 'It designates the Christians who observe Sunday.'[98] S. W. Baron also holds that it designates Christians.[99]

Conversely, R. T. Herford, after considering a similar passage in *Maseket Soferim*,[100] remarks, 'R. Johanan transferred to the time of the Temple a feature of the religious life of his own totally different time'.[101] H. J. Schoeps also ponders, albeit equivocally, the possibility that these 'are to be identified with these Jewish Christians'.[102] Finally, W. D. Davies is of the opinion that R. Johanan 'claimed that Jews did not fast on Sundays because of Jewish Christians'.[103]

There are two major considerations which militate against the probability that the explanation relates to first-century conditions. First there is no evidence that Sunday was the Christian 'Sabbath' in Palestine before the destruction of the Second Temple in the year 70.[104] And even if it were, it is difficult to believe that Christianity was sufficiently influential in Palestine before 70 to have affected official Jewish practice.[105]

Conversely, there are cogent considerations for understanding R. Johanan's statement as a reflex of his contemporary reality. First, it was R. Johanan's practice to comment on the contemporary situation using the backdrop of an alleged first-century reality.[106] Second, there was a contemporary Jewish Christian sect which observed both Saturday and Sunday in a special manner. Based on a combination of the testimonies of Eusebius and Epiphanius it seems that this sect was sometimes referred to as Nazoraeans.[107] Finally, Jewish Christian communities populated areas not far from R. Johanan's home-town of Tiberias.[108]

To return to the original question: Why did they not fast on Sunday? The traditional answer is: 'Lest they say: We rejoice on Sunday; they fast on it' (*Maseket Soferim*, 17, 4, ed. Higger, p. 301). Baron follows V. Aptowitzer: 'He may well have meant that the Christians should not be led to think that the Jews abstain from work on that day as an acknowledgment of the Christian claim to its sanctity.'[109]

The traditional answer can be supported by references in Christian literature which encourage rejoicing on Sunday.[110] The position adopted by Baron is somewhat difficult. It assumes that abstinence from work on a day is an acknowledgment of its sanctity. This is a Jewish assumption. It is not clear that Sunday in the third century was distinguished by Christian abstinence from work.[111] In addition, it assumes that abstinence from food requires abstinence from work. Those who fast regularly know that this is not necessarily so. Indeed, the rabbis remonstrated against those who worked on the national fast of the ninth of Ab (bTaan 30b).

The third possibility is that R. Johanan does not want Jews to fast on Sunday lest they be confused with those Jewish Christians who fast on Sunday.[112] The evidence for this assertion is meagre, but worth considering. The first is in the Greek version of the *Acts of Thomas* 29, which says concerning the Apostle Thomas:

And when he had blessed them he took bread and oil and herbs

242

and salt, and blessed and gave to them; but he himself continued in his fasting, for the Lord's day was about to dawn.[113]

Possibly, Thomas continued to fast through 'the Lord's day'. The second source is the Syriac *Didascalia Apostolorum* 21, which reports[114] that after the crucifixion, Jesus appeared

> in the morning of the first day of the week. . . . And He said to us, teaching us: Are ye fasting for Me these days? or have I any need that ye should afflict yourselves? . . . For it is not lawful to you to fast on the first of the week, because it is My resurrection. . . . Fast then from the second day of the week, six days wholly, until the night after the Sabbath; and it shall be reckoned to you as a week.

This seems to be a polemic against those who *are* fasting on Sunday. Both of the above documents are early third-century products of Syrian Christianity.[115] The first is considered a Gnostic-Christian or Encratite document. The second, according to A. Marmorstein, 'was written with the specific purpose of frightening away Jewish-Christians from Jewish practices and usages'.[116] G. Strecker also emphasizes that the *Didascalia* is not dealing with Judaizing Christians but with Jewish Christians.[117] Schoeps cites Marmorstein's judgment approvingly, adding that the work is specifically directed against Ebionitism.[118]

In light of the judgments of Marmorstein and Schoeps on the *Didascalia*, the opinions of Zahn and Kretschmar on its provenance take on added significance. T. Zahn, whose position was adopted by H. Achelis in his monograph in J. Flemming's German edition of the *Didascalia*, placed it among the Nazoraeans of Aleppo in Coele-Syria. A. Harnack, C. Schneider and G. Kretschmar placed it in south-eastern Syria, most likely Bostra,[119] a place which was not only a centre of Jewish Christianity, but also a place frequented by third-century rabbis.[120]

In the light of the Syrian Christian material which points to a group of Jewish Christians who fast on Sunday and the fact that *The Apostolic Constitutions*[121] also opposed Sunday fasting, it is not unlikely that R. Yohanan's comment about not fasting on Sunday was concerned with distinguishing between the Jews and the Nazoraeans,[122] who were known to be ascetically inclined.[123]

Once it is clear that *nasrim* refers to the Jewish Christian Nazoraeans, this should be of help in understanding the formulation *ha-nasrim ve-ha-minim* that posed such difficulty at the beginning.

If the formula were original it should read smoothly. The roughness indicates a composite text; that is, *naṣrim* was attached to a fixed text or replaced some other opening term which had combined smoothly with *minim*, such as 'apostates' or 'informers'. Originally there must have been two distinct categories such as 'heretics and defectors'. This seems to be the pattern behind the other versions.[124]

The version under discussion remains difficult, but understanding *naṣrim* as referring to contemporary Jewish Christians does help. Although it is possible to allow for the rendering 'the Nazaraeans and other Jewish heretics', it is unlikely once *naṣrim* is seen as a later interpolation. It is more likely that the *vav* of *ve-ha-minim* is explicative as it frequently is in Palestinian rabbinic literature.[125] The result would translate as 'the Nazoraeans *who* are the *minim* (i.e. heretics of our day)'. It is even possible to follow a comment of S. Lieberman on a similarly difficult expression,[126] and translate as 'the Nazoraeans *of the minim*'. This rendering receives striking support from Jerome's comment cited above on the relationship between the Nazoraeans and the *minim*, where he said that the Nazoraean heresy is called 'of the Minaeans' (= *Minaeorum*)!

Conclusions

The following are the salient results of our investigation of *birkat ha-minim*:

1. *Birkat ha-minim* was not directed against Gentile Christians, but against Jewish sectarians.

2. The Genizah version which reads *ha-noṣrim ve-ha-minim* was primarily directed against Jewish Christians.

3. There is no unambiguous evidence that Jews cursed Christians during the statutory prayers.

4. There is abundant evidence that Christians were welcome in the synagogue.

5. Thus *birkat ha-minim* does not reflect a watershed in the history of the relationship between Jews and Christians in the first centuries of our era.

6. Apparently, there never was a single edict which caused the so-called irreparable separation between Judaism and Christianity. The separation was rather the result of a long process dependent upon local situations and ultimately upon the political power of the church.

11

Ruler of This World: Attitudes about Mediator Figures and the Importance of Sociology for Self-Definition

A. F. SEGAL

The problem of normative group self-definition is nowhere more evident than in the discussions of the rise of Gnosticism. Although the question of the origins of Gnosticism has occupied scholarly attention for a century, there has been surprisingly little interest in the social situation in which the orthodox and heretical groups separated or in how the various sects and denominations came to the conclusion that they were different from their neighbours. All too often a simple answer to the problem of gnostic self-definition has been assumed: Gnosticism is the inevitable outcome of the combination of Hebrew and Greek thought – the spirit of late antiquity, the dominant form of late Hellenistic spirituality. Just before, during or after this encounter, Christian and Jewish orthodoxies arose to defend the faithful from such a radical synthesis.[1] Some form of this intellectual dialectic has been widely assumed by many recent scholars, perhaps to sidestep the overall problem of gnostic origins in order to address more specific exegetical problems within their own fields of competence. Of course, I do not mean to say that this enterprise has been profitless. Rather, it has been advantageous to set aside some of the larger questions, in order to concentrate on the specific textual problems inherent in the publication of the Nag Hammadi material.[2]

Though recent sociological studies on the rise of Gnosticism represent a different perspective they are nevertheless important and complementary.[3] By looking for the social forces which contributed to the rise of Gnosticism, their authors are attempting to get beyond the tacit assumption of an intellectual dialectic operating in history to face the social settings within which Gnosticism developed. The force of the new sociological perspective has been towards the general once again, but we should not feel prevented from trying to locate specific textual evidence about the issue of normative self-definition; for when it comes to this thorny problem, archaeology, the primary body of data available to the social historian of antiquity, is almost totally useless. Rather than solve the problem of the origins of Gnosticism, these general sociological analyses have so far had the function of giving us a new set of questions about the role of sociological encounter in the development of a group's normative self-definition. In this paper I shall try to show how a social scientific perspective can help clarify the meaning of an ambiguous history of tradition precisely because it helps shift our emphasis from the issue of the origins of the tradition to the issue of its use within two communities in conflict. I hope I can show how conflict determines each party's self-definition and, at the same time, reveals an important clue in the origin of Gnosticism.

The tradition I have in mind is that of 'the Ruler of the World'. Though, as we shall see, the tradition is quite broad, 'the Ruler of the World' remains one of the minor figures of the gospel of John. He is nevertheless closely connected to the issue of the Gnosticism within that document. He occurs three times in the Fourth Gospel (hereafter FG)[4] and is probably related to the 'God of this World' who appears in the Pauline corpus.[5] Obviously, he is not a major character in the drama. Like Rosencranz or Guildenstern in Shakespeare's *Hamlet*, he performs a small and necessary if dishonourable function. He is the leader of the supernatural forces who oppose Jesus but 'who already have been beaten'.[6]

Most of the occurrences in the New Testament evince the theme of supernatural opposition, but I shall confine myself to the gospel of John for the purpose of this paper.[7] Though the Ruler of the World is not explicitly identified with Satan in the FG there can be no question that his demonic role is primary. In John 12.31 Jesus states that the Ruler of this World is about to be driven out, while Jesus shall draw all men to himself. In John 14.31 Jesus comments that the Ruler of this World approaches, but that he has no rights over Jesus. In John 16.11 Jesus says that he is about to pass from sight and return to the Father, while the paraclete will convince the Jews that divine judgment will soon be upon them. The comment is occasioned as an answer to the synagogue, which has ostracized Johannine Christians from worship[8] and which is supposed to believe that persecuting Christians is a religious duty.[9] The paraclete provides an answer to this alleged hostility by revealing that divine judgment awaits the Jews from God because they are of this world. The sign of this coming judgment is that the Ruler of this World stands already condemned. Here the Ruler of this World is part of one of the strongest anti-Jewish polemics in the New Testament. For the moment I can only note that the supernatural figure and the anti-Jewish polemic are related; I want to return to the relationship later, to show that, ironically, where the gospel is being most anti-Jewish, it is relying heavily on Jewish traditions.[10] And it is precisely at this point that the problem of group definition will come clearly into focus.

In apocalyptic and Christian traditions, the demonic aspect of the Ruler of this World became more and more evident. Ignatius implies that the Ruler of this World is the captain of evil.[11] In the Ascension of Isaiah the figure is Beliar, evidently identified with Melchira, which is probably one name for the evil angel opposing Melchisedek at Qumran.[12] Thus it seems clear that Christianity is using traditions which it shares with apocalyptic Judaism.

While these statements about the Ruler of this World may impress us as a strange corner of the Johannine universe, the really striking aspect of the tradition does not become clear until one contrasts the Pauline, Johannine and apocalyptic portrayal of the Ruler of this World with the rabbinic one: the rabbinic view contains no trace of the negative characterization which seems absolutely essential to the other portraits.[13]

In rabbinic literature, the Prince of the World is regarded as the reciter of certain psalms in praise of God. For instance, in bYeb 16b, he is said to be the speaker of Ps. 37.25: 'I have been young, now I am old, yet I have not seen the righteous forsaken or his children begging bread.'[14] In bHull 60a, Ps. 104.31 is ascribed to the Prince of the World: 'May the glory of the Lord endure forever. Let the Lord rejoice in His world.' In bSanh 94a, he appears in a puzzling discussion about the identity of the Messiah. The Prince of the World becomes an advocate for the messiahship of Hezekiah by pointing out that during Hezekiah's time the earth fulfilled God's desire for a song of praise. The identity of the Messiah, however, remains hidden as one of the secrets of God. In each case the Prince of the World offers praise, not opposition, to God. In III Enoch, the Prince of the World is sometimes the leader of the princes of the kingdoms of the earth. In other places, he is the ruler or prince of the heavenly bodies. In the Enoch-Metatron traditions, Metatron often takes over the functions essential to the Prince of the World.[15]

All these passages are quite late. But both Gershom Scholem[16] and Hugo Odeberg[17] (whatever their other differences) have noted that the Prince of the World also has a role in merkabah mysticism which would allow us to push the date of these traditions much further back. In fact, Scholem suggests that the figure of the Prince of the World has the same titles and functions – hierophant and angelic guardian of Israel – as does the archangel Michael. Furthermore this makes him rather similar to Metatron or to the 'Angel of the Lord' or 'YHWH the Lesser' in mystical speculation, all of whom are said to 'carry the tetragrammaton'.[18] This means that the intermediaries are not just angels but come dangerously close to being anthropomorphic hypostases of God himself. A first-century date for traditions of this type is virtually assured by the appearance of Yahoel in the Apocalypse of Abraham. The details of the tradition need not concern us. I merely want to point out that there is evidence for a positive portrayal of the figure in mystical and rabbinical speculation while Christianity and apocalypticism share the negative image of the Prince of the World.

The question is why? Why should the traditions differ so completely in the two literatures? A history of religions study might yield convincing evidence for the priority of either a negative or positive portrayal of the character. There is a rich classical and Jewish background to the titles. Biblical usage is probably the basis for all the speculation, but the Bible itself appears to be adopting the ancient Near Eastern usage in polemical fashion.[19]

Equally or more important for the Hellenistic period is the use of the titles similar to 'Ruler of the World' in the cults of Syria and Palmyra. We know that Ba'al Shamin was called *mr' 'lm* or *Zeus megistos keraios* by the second century.[20] A similar history can be seen in the inscriptions of the Nabataeans. Ba'al Shamin and Bel are invoked as *mry 'lm* in Palmyrene.[21] Thus, the term is used both of earthly and heavenly rulers, in a normal corresponding fashion. As in the older material, there is confusion as to whether the title can be an independent divinity as well as an epithet.

Rabbinic literature directly parallels this usage.[22] Without reference to dating for the moment, we may note that the rabbis often called God *'dwn h'wlm*, 'Lord of the World', *'dwn h'wlmym*, 'Lord of the Worlds'.[23] In the Targumin (see Ex. 24.10) the term is *mry dy 'lm'*.[24] In probable polemic against the Christian 'Lord' the rabbis stress that God himself is to be called 'Lord'. Simeon b. Yohai is reported to have taught that Abraham first called God 'Lord' (Gen. 15.2),[25] while R. Aha, a later rabbi, apparently contradicted his predecessor.[26] R. Isaac speaks of God as *adwn kl h'wlm*.[27] Of great importance is the polemic against the arrogation of the term by Pharaoh and the impudence of a man calling himself God.[28] In the Mekilta of R. Simeon b. Yohai *b'l h'wlm* is reported as a title for God by 'the contemptible', which perhaps reflects gnostic or Christian usage. There are innumerable other references to God as the great one of goodness or the World (*'wlm*). Of course, the rabbis never call God merely the God of *this* world. Whenever the subject is broached, they explicitly point out that He is God of this World and the next.[29]

A good many of these references are late and, like *mlk mlky hmlkym* may reflect rabbinic reaction to an already existent title for earthly rulers and divinities. Nevertheless, some usage of the term 'Lord of the World' is certainly antique, for Gen. 21.33 calls God *'l 'wlm* and Ps. 10.16 has *mlk 'wlm*. Furthermore, by the first century, there is certain evidence that usage like the rabbinic one had already evolved in Judaism, as is shown by the plural ending in Gen. Apoc. 21.20, *mrh 'lmyh*.

There is some evidence that the title was used even outside the semitic language group. In one of the fragments of the Acts of Paul the title 'ruler of this world' is applied to 'woman'. The use, though late, may suggest some of the irony which must have figured in development of the polemic against the Jews in the FG:

> Woman, ruler of this world, mistress of much gold, citizen of great luxury, splendid in thy raiment, sit down on the floor and forget thy riches and thy beauty and thy finery. For these will profit thee nothing if thou pray not to God.[30]

A certain reference to Adonai as Lord of the World occurs in the Magical Papyri,[31] in which the Hebrew God is reduced to an angelic demon, though still a positive one.

The evidence then is not meagre but manifold. It gives us an enormous range of possibilities for deriving separate usages in Judaism and Christianity. In view of this extensive evidence it is unsatisfactory merely to claim that the Christian and apocalyptic evidence represents the entrance of a title for a pagan god into apocalyptic Judaism and Christianity as a demon while the rabbinic evidence represents an independent use of the tradition as an angelic figure. The title was a loose, not a close epithet. Though it was associated with pagan gods and with the Roman Emperor, it was also clearly a normal epithet for the Hebrew God as well. Thus we have to give up the idea of any simple development for the term. Whatever the origin and development of the term, the rabbinic and Christian uses represent opposing transformations of it.

The real question then is to discuss both the negative portrayal in Christianity and its contrast with the angelic figure in Judaism. We cannot be absolutely sure that a positive independent angelic *figure* existed in Judaism before the Christian usage, but it seems clear that the *term*[32] was at least used of God and was in the process of becoming a hypostasis in pagan usage and possibly even an angelic title in Judaism in the first century. My point is only that when the traditions differ so greatly one has to wonder if any information would be gained by attempting to clarify a multifaceted origin. Are we not falling prey to a kind of genetic fallacy in assuming that one single original usage could explain the development of the tradition? Since the bodies of material are so different we should be willing to posit many possible derivations and try to specify the conditions in each community which made the tradition evolve in unique ways. We have to ask the perplexing question: What are the different functions of these opposing portrayals of the Prince of the World?

It is already clear that we are dealing with communities in conflict and must seek a paradigm which will allow us to discuss friction and social change as well as a basic social charter. Mary Douglas, in *Natural Symbols*,[33] provides us with a summary statement of this kind of social paradigm, because she asks a key question in a very concise way: 'Do definable relationships exist between a group's social position and its symbol system?'[34] Since her answer is positive, she goes on to develop a model of

250

society which allows both for an analysis of social change and for cross-cultural comparisons.

In *Natural Symbols* Douglas designs a very elegant system which exposes the relationship between a society and its concept of divinity in a Durkheimian fashion. We do not need to discuss the merits of her entire scheme, whether or not she subscribes to Durkheimian social reductionism, or even whether Durkheim's social reductionism is desirable. Since Douglas's writing is being used here as an example of a general perspective we do not have to enter into the methodological issue of whether either variable – social structure or religion – is independent of the other. For our purposes we can assume that they are mutually dependent. Sometimes social structure affects theology; sometimes the opposite. All we have to note is the frequent parallel relationship between a given social structure and a society's ideas of divinity. In this case we can be very pragmatic. We almost always know the ideology of early Jewish groups, we sometimes know their structure. If the relationship between them could be defined more completely, we might be able to discover why the figure of the Lord of the World has such different colouring in different communities. Based on Douglas's inquiry, we should expect that societies undergoing deep social conflicts would seek to express those conflicts in their ideologies and divine economy, if the chance for expression were presented. Douglas's description of the phenomenon, though still very general, would help us locate more details. Dualism, she finds, is characteristic of small, competitive communities: 'Small competitive communities tend to believe themselves in a dangerous universe, threatened by sinister powers operated by fellow human beings.'[35] She tries to show that groups which have negative opinions of the world and who personify it as hostile often live in small, closed communities with a characteristically high degree of internal social pressure. They often perceive themselves as passing through a period of persecution, a situation which may be partially confirmed in fact but which is often magnified and projected into hostility on the part of cosmic powers. It often serves as the justification for fission and expulsion, as in some African witchcraft accusations.[36]

Obviously the 'Prince of the World' occurs as part of a larger and very complicated symbolic system which, under the name of Johannine theology, has been a subject of New Testament scholarship for generations. Modern scholarship has also noted that the social context of Johannine Christianity is discoverable, and most scholars would agree that Douglas's descriptions of dualistic communities are generally applicable to the Johannine group.[37]

We may now return to the relationship between the Ruler of this World and the anti-Jewish polemics in which he participates. The references to the Ruler of this World appear in highly charged contexts where the targets of the hostility are specifically mentioned as Jews. Scholars have noticed the symbolic character of the FG's usage of the term 'Jew'. Unlike the other gospels the FG uses the term 'Jew' frequently and often uses it in places where the other gospels would have distinguished between the various Jewish sects in Palestine. Having noticed this shift, Rudolf Bultmann maintained that the Jews of the FG serve as symbolic representatives of the world in its hostility to the Christian God.[38] Although it is true that the Jews are often used in a typological way, it is equally important to note the obvious fact that it is the Jews and not some other group who have been chosen for this onerous symbol. The Johannine group is not using symbols arbitrarily. Some social reality must be reflected in the symbolic statement. We should therefore expect that the 'Lord of the World' and 'the God of the Jews' should be linked somehow.

It would be very difficult to characterize the entire social reality from the FG account alone; for, like most historical and religious documents, it is highly tendentious. Nevertheless, one can start by characterizing the Jewish position in the FG. For instance, according to John 9.22, if anyone confessed Jesus as Messiah, the Jews excluded him from the synagogue. This implies that the Johannine community feels itself ostracized as heretical from the Jewish synagogue and that it is quite bothered by the fact.[39]

If the extent of the Jewish opposition is clear in the FG's portrayal, its nature and content come out only in polemic contradistinction to the Johannine position. The debates with the Jews concerning the identity of the Messiah in the FG, and even those about the Law and Sabbath observances,[40] are but occasions for the question of the authority of Jesus.[41] When the Jews reject Jesus as Messiah because he does not bring national redemption,[42] the evangelist does not directly argue against them. Instead he states that they understand Jesus in a this-worldly way;[43] for the Johannine Christ, though called Messiah explicitly (1.41; 4.25), is far more than an anointed one, the usual Jewish understanding of Messiah (18.33–7). He is the *Logos* and the Saviour of the world. It is particularly interesting that these claims give him the status of what might be described as a principal, angelic mediator in other kinds of Judaism, relating him to traditions about the figure of the 'Prince of the World' in other Jewish communities. One unusual aspect of the Johannine description of Jesus, however, is the claim that he is a divine hypostasis. The evangelist states this claim clearly and unambiguously at the very opening of the gospel. Obviously the link between the Messiah and a divine hypostasis is an exceedingly important aspect of the Johannine church's beliefs. Furthermore, according to a commonly accepted interpretation of John 8.58f., Jesus claims the divine name *Yhwh* translated as *ego eimi* (I am). If this is correct the FG makes an explicit identification of Jesus with the divine mediator who is the Name of God:

> The Jews then said to Him, 'You are not yet fifty years old and you claim to have seen Abraham?' Jesus said to them, 'Truly, truly I say unto you, before Abraham was, I am.' So they took up stones to throw at him . . .

True to form, it is the claim of the Messiah's divinity, not primarily the messianic claim itself, which accounts for Jewish opposition to Johannine Christianity, according to the gospel. This is demonstrable by appeal to several passages in the FG where the issue between Jesus and the Jews is precisely that he seeks to make himself equal with God. Each time the penalty is stoning:

> For this reason, the Jews sought all the more to kill him – not only was he breaking the sabbath; worse still he was speaking of God as his own father, thus making himself God's equal (John 5.18).

> We stone you for no good work but for blasphemy; because you, being a man, make yourself a God (10.33).

It is significant that the Jews oppose Jesus for claiming divinity and that the penalty is stoning, not crucifixion. These details suggest a setting in the life of the community and not from the life of Jesus. Though the social situation cannot be reconstructed in detail, it can be characterized. The Johannine community is obviously being criticized by a Jewish community (rabbinic or not) for the basic tenet of its faith. A considerable breach is perceived on both sides. The generalized Johannine use of the term 'Jew' (which does not distinguish between parties), therefore, appears to derive from a time when the rift between Jews and Christians had become irremediable. This must have occurred at the end of the first century or later, certainly not in the days of Jesus himself, though the FG explicitly says that the hostility started then (see e.g. 12.42).[44] The gospel expresses the breach between the Jewish and Christian communities and tries to come to terms with it in a number of ways. One of those ways, it seems to me, is through dualism. But it is a dualism of a specific type, a dualism which has helped the Johannine Christians understand how they can continue to consider themselves heirs to the prophecies of the Jewish Bible when the synagogue has rejected both them and their understanding of how biblical prophecy has been fulfilled.

The characterization of the Jews in the FG, though tendentious and exaggerated, must be based on a real Jewish charge against Christians, for the position attributed to them corresponds to the position rabbis take against unnamed heretics in rabbinic literature. The rabbis, as well as other Hellenistic Jews, objected to some concepts of divine mediators and to the redemptive role of angels.[45] Rabbinic Judaism was especially intolerant of angelologies when the unity of God was in question. A brief look at those heretics called 'those who believe in two powers in heaven' will illustrate the rabbinic position.[46] The rabbis objected to any biblical exegesis which implied a plurality in the divinity. The name of God in the Hebrew Bible represented a special problem. *Elohim* is an archaic plural and sometimes takes a plural complement. The tetragrammaton, *Yhwh*, might also be taken as a divinity separate from Elohim. The rabbis stated that the divine name *Yhwh* does not imply that there is either a creature separate from God or a plurality of deities.[47] Most of the time, the heresy implied in the rabbinic description involved a heavenly hierarchy with two corresponding powers in heaven. Occasionally the rabbinic description may imply an opposing configuration of divinities in heretical thought, but the emphasis in early rabbinic texts is almost completely on defeating the idea that a corresponding figure or angel is divine. The biblical passages at the heart of the heresy, however, are remarkably consistent throughout the many different reports. They include any place where a plural was used to describe God – such as Gen. 1.26 – together with any reports of the physical shape of God or his angels – such as Ex. 24.10; Ezek. 1; Dan. 7.13 etc. Since the Dan. 7 passage was crucial to Christian exegesis, many of these reports probably refer to Christians; but some aspects of the heretical traditions of the sort opposed by the rabbis are reported in the writings of Philo, who even describes the *Logos* as a second divine manifestation and as a *second God*.[48] The reference to 'two powers' in rabbinic sources occurs without any uniquely Christian polemic, so that Christianity was probably seen as but one of a number of different systems of thought which the rabbis wanted to brand heretical.

The rabbinic defence against the threat is remarkably simple. The rabbis merely invoke the places in the Old Testament where God claims to be unique – Deut. 6; Deut. 32; Isa. 44–47. They also note that claiming divine honours was the sin of the Prince of Tyre and the King of Babylon.[49]

The Johannine community itself objected to several doctrines of mediation. In arguing with Nicodemus, the Pharisee and ruler of the Jews, Jesus is made to say: 'No one has ever gone up to heaven except he who descended from heaven, the Son of Man' (3.13). The Johannine community seems to be limiting the class of mediators to a unique figure – Jesus, who was able to make a heavenly ascent because he is a heavenly creature. The FG claims that no simple man could ascend to heaven, a polemic against beliefs found in Enoch literature, mysticism and other pseudepigrapha, where similar claims are often made for specific mediators,[50] to say nothing of Roman emperors who claimed to ascend to heaven after death.[51] The FG claimed that no one could make a mystical ascent to see God unless he really was a divine creature himself – a polemic against *Yhwh* the Lesser, Yahoel, and other concepts for God's principal angel (by whatever names he was known) but whom the FG acknowledged only as *Logos*, Messiah or Son of Man. Evidence of this type has persuaded many New Testament scholars that the Johannine community was interested in clarifying the Christian message to a group of mystical Jewish-Christian sectarians whose beliefs may have included non-orthodox understandings of mediation and even loyalty to Jewish law (though probably not to the rabbinic canon of Torah).[52] Both rabbinic and Christian exegesis, then, oppose in differing degrees and in different ways the angelic mediator traditions of mystical and apocalyptic Judaism, such as those about *Yhwh* the Lesser, Metatron (or even possibly the Prince of the World), and particularly those agents who began as humans and later achieved a kind of divine status in some communities, like Jacob-Israel or Moses or Enoch-Metatron. Of course, the rabbis would object to the Christian confession as a variety of the latter.

Therefore we have an intriguing and complicated historical phenomenon. On one hand, the Johannine community restricted ideas of mediation to the Christ, outlawing any other concept of mediation. On the other hand, the rabbinic community outlawed any idea of divine mediation which implied that the Godhead is composed of two or more hypostases – a polemic which excluded Christianity among a wider variety of Jewish heresies. It therefore seems necessary to posit at least three rough groupings: the rabbinic community, the Johannine community, and other heterodox Jewish or Christian communities. The last grouping embraces a spectrum of belief about mediation from the divine to the human in ways outlawed in both the rabbinic and the Christian communities. Though there appear to us to have been at least three logical groups in this spectrum, neither the Johannine nor the rabbinic community felt the need to distinguish more than two – an in-group and an out-group. The rabbis saw the dividing line to have been between orthodoxy and ('two powers') heresy. The Johannine community distinguished between the Jews and the followers of Jesus, who were the real Israel.[53]

The Jewish penalty for such crimes may have been exclusion from the synagogue, as the Johannine community stated.[54] But it probably was not accomplished exactly as the FG has it, by a direct threat against the life of Christians. The rabbis, for instance, excluded from leadership in synagogue services any *min* or sectarian whose beliefs were questionable. Rabbinic literature ascribes to R. Gamaliel the order to add a curse against sectarians to the service, which would have been tantamount to an invitation to leave synagogue life.[55] Since the tradition has been ascribed to the rabbinic Sanhedrin at Yavneh in the late first century, it may correspond directly to the events described by the FG; but, at any rate, it provides a convincing background to the reports of Jewish opposition in the Johannine community.[56]

A fair consensus of the various views on the *birkat ha-minim* would make the following points: A pre-existent curse against informers and separatists appears to have been extended to sectarians and implicitly to Christians by R. Samuel's addition. The Christian community, in turn, appears to have correctly understood this as a criticism of their position. This action, as pointed out by Martyn, is more likely to have been the principal instrument of Jewish opposition than *herem* or *nidui* were. It would be unfair to say that this action was a watershed. It appears to have organized what was already the dominant Jewish reaction to Christianity. If the events in Acts have any historic validity, they appear to describe an instinctive reaction in synagogues to the preachings of Christianity without any necessary official sanction. The promulgation of the new text for the curse was but one natural step in the growing hostility.[57]

We should note that the rabbinic defence against Christianity, however strong it may be supposed, was not uniquely applied to Christians and probably predated the origin of Christianity. In other words, the rabbis used pre-existent categories and penalties to attack Christian heresy, only adapting them for the Christian heresy.

Not only may this development be supposed to be the case with the *birkat ha-minim*, but it can be shown to be relevant in other midrashic reports of Christianity. In a baraita introduced in bSanh 43a the charges adduced against Jesus are magic (*mkshf*), enticement (*msyt*) and leading astray (*mdyh*). The former is a charge made by Jews in the New Testament (see Mark 5 and parallels). The latter terms can easily be compared with the verb *planein*, which appears as a charge against Jesus in John 7.42 and Rev. 2.20, as Martyn shows.[58] No doubt bSanh 43a represents Jewish reaction to the gospel story of Jesus (and hence an implicit threat to Christians), but not a piece of historical evidence about Jesus. It too corresponds to the evidence in John. The application of charges of this nature reflect the growing antagonism of the Jewish community to the preaching of the church.

Again, it does not seem necessary to conclude that the opposition reported by the Johannine community is more formal than the kind of opposition reported by Paul or Luke/Acts. The passage of time since Paul might allow for a more organized or prepared reaction, and it is clear that the Johannine community is far more bothered about the actions of the Jews than Luke was. Given the Johannine admission that members of the Christian community had been excluded and the allegations that some Jewish leaders believed in Jesus but would not confess him lest they be excluded (12.42), it is probably better to describe the Jewish reaction as 'ostracism' rather than 'excommunication'. That action, together with threat of prosecution for capital offences in midrash and occasional illegal or mob actions reported in other places in the New Testament, would be more than enough to raise the apprehension among the Johannine followers to the level evinced in the gospel, since unlike other Christians they appear to have had a closer association with the Jewish community and may have continued to visit it.[59]

Here then are the theoretical possibilities for the history of tradition of the Lord of the World:

If one accepts the evidence of Scholem that many Jews speculated about a principal angelic mediator hypostasis of God, which was another understanding of the name *Yhwh*, then one sees that the existence of the principal angelic mediator *per se* was not debated in every community. Rather, it was the identity, role and rank of the mediator that was at issue. Some people identified the figure as Yahoel, some as Michael or Gabriel, some as Enoch and some as Melchizedek. Since the primary characteristic of this angel is that he manifests one of the names or titles of God, it is not inconceivable that the 'Prince of the World' had already evolved from merely a title into a divine hypostasis, as previously happened in other Near Eastern cults. It is impossible to say for sure when the evolution took place. Thus, it is possible that the 'Prince of this World', like *Yhwh* the Lesser, signified the name of God, the Master of the World, re-understood as a separate angelic hypostasis.[60] Through such 'mystical' speculation on the divine name a plausible (but not necessary) explanation can be found for the development of the positive term before the FG and the apocrypha. Of course, it is also possible that the negative figure developed from the rabbinic expression 'Master of the World' or from the Near Eastern gods without the emergence of a prior positive figure. Then, the rabbinic traditions later on can be seen as being independent – or, less likely, as resulting from a deliberate revaluing of an explicitly demonic figure or even from the transfer of a divine title from another divinity.

What is not speculation is that Christians believed their mediator to be the Jesus who died as a messianic pretender and who was justified in the title 'Messiah' ironically given to him by the Romans after he was believed by his followers to have been resurrected and ascended (or reascended) to divinity. As such he had a claim to the term *kyrios*, which is further inter-preted as the 'I am' tetragrammaton. Since Johannine Christ-ianity had its own candidate for mediator and could accept no other candidates, all other titles and functions for a divine me-diator, especially any title with reference to this world, could signify only the supernatural opposition to him. In the gospel, 'this world' could only contrast with the salvation of Jesus who was 'not of this world' and was therefore beyond the reach of the synagogue which had excluded Christians from worship. Furthermore, the Johannine church would know that a mediator figure like Michael or Metatron possibly with titles like 'Lord of the World' was viewed as Israel's guardian angel by many Jews. The negative reaction of the Jews towards Johannine Christ-ianity, which had compromised monotheism from the rabbinic perspective, could then be projected into the heavenly realm by the FG as a reflection of the negative reaction of the Lord of the World (which was at the very least a name of the Jewish God, but could have been a title for God's principal angel even at that time). Thus, the guardian angel of Jewish sectarians could become a fitting opponent of Jesus in the supernatural sphere. As Lord of the World he became a symbol of the world's rejec-tion of Jesus.

The later tradition of the Prince of the World in rabbinic Judaism is most anomalous since it reflects a positive view of the world, after the figure of the angel is unambiguously de-moted to a subsidiary role and thus is not an independent power, but only God's supervisor on earth. Though no honest theory of the origin of the epithet and figure can be convincing, we are not completely unable to analyse the term, since the portrayal of the Prince of the World is not just doctrine. It is an allegory about the world written into the heavenly hosts, so that its interpretation lies in each community's experience in the world. For the Johannine Christians (as for others), the Prince of the World became evil because the world (in this case in its opposition to the gospel) is evil; or, again for the Johannine community, the world is evil because the Jews, who symbolize the world, oppose the message of Christianity. The meaning of the allegory is parallel to the sociology of the Johannine church. The dualist theology is partly a symbolic portrayal of the socio-logical position of the church. Its function is to reassure and exhort the believer to remain uncompromisingly true to the uniqueness of the Christian message – even in the face of opposition from a variety of Jewish sects, indeed, from the whole world – because God's plan for the destruction of the opponents of his people would certainly soon be manifest. That social message is expressed by the FG's attitude towards a supernatural figure representing the heavenly opposition and at the same time is linked to the real earthly opposition Johannine Christians felt but could not explain as prophesied.

Now we can see why the FG constantly links Jesus' role as Saviour with the theme of retribution. In John 12, Jesus reveals that his fate is to glorify the Name of God, an occupation clearly suitable to angels as well as connoting martyrdom. In this context, the Lord of the World, Jesus' direct supernatural opponent, is said to be judged and defeated (John 12.31), though he still appears strong. In chs. 14 and 16, Jesus predicts that once he leaves, the church will have an angelic protector, called variously the Spirit of Truth or Paraclete. Other Jewish communities at this time were applying the same titles to principal angels.[61] In the FG it is clear that the Paraclete is supposed to function as the Holy Spirit, but this does not preclude or mask the angelic background of the concept.[62] Again, it is in the context of the prophecy of the Paraclete that the Ruler of the World is mentioned as Jesus' antagonist (John 14.31; 16.11). This usage is quite close to the theology of Qumran, where the angelic leader of the forces of the good was also called the Spirit of Truth.

Once the angelic battle is mentioned, the corresponding social significance of the allegory can be clarified. John 8.40f. shows us how this allegory works. The Jews say: 'We are not base born; God is our father, and God alone.' But Jesus says: 'If God were your father, you would love me, for God is the source of my being. . . . Your father is the Devil and you choose to carry out your father's desires.' The heavenly allegory explains why the earthly Jews oppose the Christian message. To be sure, the Prince of the World and the Devil are not overtly equated in the FG, but such a conclusion is not difficult to derive from it. Both the Prince of the World and the Jews are taken to be symbols of the opposition to God. The Jews are said to be the offspring of the Devil, while the Prince of the World is made into a demon. In that way the Prince of the World and Satan can be explicitly identified by later tradition. The difference between the Prince of the World traditions in each community can be understood as based on the antagonism and polemic between Christians and Jews.[63]

One of the ways in which this association is made can be seen in the Christian evidence. In the Ascension of Isaiah, an interesting combination of traditions about the Lord of this World, the Roman emperor and Satan come together:

> And now Hezekiah and Josiah my son, these are the days of the completion of the world. After it is consummated, Beliar the great ruler, the king of this world, will descend, who hath ruled it since it came into being; yea, he will descend from his firmament in the likeness of a man, a lawless king, the slayer of his mother: who himself (even) this king will persecute the plant which the twelve apostles of the Beloved have planted. Of the twelve, one will be delivered into his hands. This ruler in the form of that king will come and there will come with him all the powers of this world, and they will hearken unto him in all that he desireth. And at his word the sun will rise at night and he will make the moon appear at sixth hour. And all that he hath desired he will do in the world: he will do and speak like the beloved and he will say: 'I am God and before me there has been none'[64] (Ascens. Isa. 4.1–6).

The reference is apparently to Nero, who slew his mother Agrippina in 59 CE.[65]

But note that besides calling Nero king of this world, the redactor of this document has equated Nero with Beliar, a supernatural opponent – in short, Satan. Furthermore, he adds to this description an application of prophecies concerning the Prince of Tyre (Ezek. 28) and the King of Babylon (Isa. 14), in which a great ruler has become corrupt because he considers himself a god. Now this move in itself is not an innovation. Nebuchadnezzar (Judith 3.8; 6.12), Antiochus Epiphanes (Dan. 11.36f.), probably Pompey (Ps. Sol. 2.28), Caligula (Philo, *Legat.* 22; 74–80; 93–97), and Nero (Sib. Or.5.33–5, 137–54, 214–21) are all despised as those who tried to be gods. Nero is the first to be considered a supernatural evil-doer, in the estimate of the writers. Hence, there is a new sense of irony in accepting the claim of supernatural aid, only transforming it into demonic opposition. The same irony may be presupposed to lie behind the FG treatment of the Jews whose claim to supernatural mission is accepted but transformed into a demonic one. No doubt Paul's prophecy in II Thess. 2.3f. and Rev. 13.1, 5–6 are indicative of the Christian atmosphere causing this application. But it is the gospel of John which is crucial, because it is John's usage which turns the figure of the Lord of this World into a technical term for Satan. Thus, in the Ascension of Isaiah we have a supernatural evil-doer, identified with the earthly rulers of this world (no longer explicitly the Jews, though still in league with them). By the time of the Ascension of Isaiah, the Jews, the earthly powers and Satan are seen as the demonic opposition to Christianity. The only part of that equation which is yet ambiguous in the gospel of John is the relationship between the Jews and the political powers of this world, though a close alliance is certainly implied.

Thus, Douglas's typological hypothesis is useful in the study of sectarian Judaism. It has allowed us to form an idea of the function of the Prince of the World even when we cannot be sure of the genesis of the tradition. It has allowed us to see the value of the figure in explaining the Christian fissure from Judaism, a fissure which grew more puzzling to Johannine Christianity as it grew more evident. The Prince of the World must be evil because the Johannine community perceived itself as under persecution from the synagogue in this world, even as it felt justified in the coming age. It knew that Jewish opposition was wrong. Yet it needed to rely on Jewish prophecy to legitimate its truth-claims.[66]

Social science could not provide an awareness of the historical dimension, for its models are of a general nature and must be constantly tailored to fit new situations. We historians cannot totally reconstruct the historical situation either, but we can see how the debate actually developed and how the exaggerations grew into dualism, when we are helped by the experience of observers of other religions.

Now, one may ask, is not the Prince of the World a minor aspect of Johannine Christology? So it is. But it is still a very important aspect, for within the conception of the Lord of the World lies the clue to the negative portrayal of the demiurge in Gnosticism. There is a very important analogy between this Johannine evidence and the traditions we find in extreme Gnosticism. Here I can only offer suggestions for further research.

It would be easy just to say that the Prince of the World is seen as evil because the Johannine Christians were Gnostics. But there are important differences between the proto-Gnosticism in the Johannine community and the extreme Gnosticism witnessed by the church Fathers and evidenced in some of the Nag Hammadi writings. First, the Lord of the World is not yet the gnostic demiurge, for he is not the creator of the world.[67]

He is, at most, the Lord of the Demons, as he is in apocalyptic Jewish systems. Second, although the Johannine Christians maintain that the Jews are the offspring of Satan, they do not want to say that the God of the Old Testament is evil. Rather, they claim that Johannine Christians alone are loyal to the promises made to the prophets.[68] For instance, in a significant place (John 19) the Jews are made to say: 'We have no king but Caesar!' The FG is saying by means of irony that the Jews themselves, in rejecting Jesus, have rejected the reign of God and hence have given up the title of Israel.[69] The FG may even be implying that the Jews are the agents of Caesar, Caesar being the embodiment of Satan in this place. This might imply the same situation as that reflected by Luke in Acts, namely that the Jews are complaining to civil authorities that Christians are disturbing their worship. Yet the complete identification of the Lord of the World with the creator demiurge (who is at the same time God of the Jews and Prince of the Demons) must be from a later, more desperate time. In many respects, the gnostic configuration is more logical and more effective argumentation against the Jews in the polemic, since it avoids the ambiguities in the status of the Jews which are reflected in the FG. In the less radical gospel of John, some of the historical roots of the controversy are still evident and are being interpreted as part of the gospel narration. The radically gnostic solution, as I shall shortly outline, appears to be a later and neater way of dealing with the Jewish question; but it is a more polemical and mythologically antisemitic solution in the sense that even the historical roots for the polemical exaggeration have been obscured.

In the battle between these competing sects, the issue of normative group definition has been a strong undercurrent, but it has arisen in an unexpected way. We normally assume that basic theological differences lead to the formation of sects. This can be partially borne out here as well: the issue of the divinity of God's principal angel or mediator is a central defining issue in the split between the two communities. But significant social factors have also intervened, enforcing group self-definition and contributing to the fissure. One can summarize these factors by noting again the mythological loading around the term 'Jew' in this Johannine context.[70] The oddity of this use of 'Jew' in its new mythological context is that although it serves as a sanction or charter for the Johannine group definition (i.e., we are Israelites, not Jews) it functions equally well as polemic against

opposing parties who claim to know the authoritative interpretation. While it is not a commonly listed function of myth,[71]
clarification of one's world-view in the presence of opposition
is, logically, a necessary part of the whole mythological process.

It is, as well, the very role which mythology will play in
Gnosticism. In the gnostic documents from Nag Hammadi and
in the reports of the church Fathers, the gnostic demiurge
speaks all the lines of the Old Testament God. He claims to be
unique on the basis of Deut. 32 and Isa. 44–47. But, for the
Gnostics, this claim of the demiurge is ignorant. The Gnostics
know that there is a god of salvation above the god of the Jews
who claims to be unique.

Now it is extremely interesting to note that the claim of the
demiurge to be 'God' in some gnostic documents not only reflects Isa. 14 and Ezek. 28 but is a re-understanding of the scripture which the rabbis quote as a defence against the heresy of
'two powers in heaven' – precisely the scripture which was
used against church Fathers by docetists, monarchianists and
patripassianists.[72] It seems likely then that one ingredient of
radical Gnosticism was social alienation by means of these arguments against monotheism. The Gnostics accepted the scriptural proof that the Old Testament God claimed to be unique; they
defended their position by radically reinterpreting Old Testament passages so that the God who spoke was not the highest
God. More revealing still, according to recent studies by Pagels
and Koschorke,[73] the gnostic description of the demiurge, together with the mythological description of evil archons, directly parallels gnostic description of the orthodox bishops. In
other words, in radical gnostic interpretation, the same vague
sociological condition existed as we saw in the Johannine community, but the radicalization of the role of the Jewish demiurge
now signifies not primarily persecution of Christians by Jews
but persecution of Gnostics by Christians (and Jews?) who use
Jewish scriptures to bolster their point against the Gnostics.
Hence there is an analogy by opposition and polemical self-
definition between Jewish and Christian self-definition on the
one hand, and Christian and gnostic self-definition on the other.
Though it is too much to say that it was Johannine Christianity
that produced Gnosticism, it is not too much to say that the
social situation which produced Johannine Christianity was parallel to that situation which eventually produced Gnosticism.
One of the mythological contributions of John – clarifying that

the Messiah was a unique divine Mediator who preceded creation, effected it, was incarnated and then returned to the Father in a milieu of supernatural opposition to the saving knowledge – is an important and necessary (though not a sufficient) step towards the mythological scenes in many of the Nag Hammadi documents.

I do not mean to suggest that the gospel of John inevitably produced Gnosticism. Rather, I wish to point out only that similar social conflicts have a similar effect on theology and hence in normative group definition. In this case there is a sequence of perceived social conflicts between many competing groups of Jews and Christians, all of which tended to make each group's central definition stronger. The gospel of John was important to Christian Gnostics as it was to all varieties of Christians. Some of the themes in it were radicalized by extreme Gnostics under analogous circumstances of perceived opposition. One of the results of social conflict is almost always the sharpening of any sect's understanding of its central principles in contradistinction to its feared and hated enemies. Yet, seen from the perspective of the dominant group, a dangerous heresy which occasions conflict is not necessarily perceived immediately in clear-cut categories. Rather the conflict itself may be the impetus to closer self-definition in answer to the heresy. Thus conflict, though normally thought disfunctional, has one positive effect of aiding both the 'sect' and the 'orthodoxy' in defining themselves more closely.[74] One might even say that conflict is one of the strongest impetuses to group self-definition.

Because the social situation in the community that produced the FG can be deciphered, I would caution my colleagues in the search for the social background of Gnosticism: it is not always necessary to jump immediately to the social malaise infecting the Empire, when the reasons for gnostic propaganda may be more subtle and localized in nature. It may be granted that gnostic groups were alienated from the emperor's regime and that the gnostic division of mankind parallels the social distinctions in the Empire, but such statements do not always differentiate Gnostics from their neighbours and do not do justice to all the gnostic documents. When one looks into those documents, one discovers that although it is important that the gnostic demiurge resembles the Caesar, he also speaks the lines of the Old Testament God: 'I am the first and the last; besides me there is no other.' The Gnostics know that the statement is to be interpreted ironically, for the demiurge is ignorant of his own past. Similarly, the description of the archons parallels terminology used for the orthodox, non-gnostic bishops. It is clear that some of the Gnostics' real enemies lie closer to home, and they want to link any description of the power of their enemies with counterfeit kingship exercised by unjust Emperors and with demonic opposition to their message as well.

Now, from the evidence that we have reviewed, we can be sure that different ideas of divine mediation and agency were central to Johannine Christianity, as Bultmann said. It is undeniable that in the FG the Christ is portrayed as the mediator *par excellence*. This may, in part, distinguish Johannine from other varieties of dualism. Even so, we do not have a complete gnostic salvation myth. The obvious explanation for this is that the Johannine community is not an example of pre-Christian Gnosticism historicized but of what turns out to have been, with our historical perspective, an important Christian step towards the later and not inevitable creation of extreme Gnosticism. Although there is no direct or inevitable link, one way in which gnostic writing evolved was by means of this progressive, polemical mythologizing, so evident in the cases under consideration. From the material we have reviewed, it seems to me that the FG demonstrates traditions which were originally part of Jewish lore but which have become Christian and have thereby taken on a specific polemical form. From communities like the Johannine one (though not always Christian ones) will come full-fledged, extreme Gnosticism in the next century.[75] Therefore the steps towards radical Gnosticism were determined not just by the development of a 'spirit of late antiquity', not just by an intellectual dialectic, but by the social position of the various groups with traditions about a principal angelic mediator. Those groups (the Jewish Gnostics, mystics and hermetics) which did not overtly compromise monotheism from the rabbinic perspective did not encounter strong rabbinic opposition and had less need to polarize the world. Most of those who seemed to compromise monotheism were definitively evicted from the synagogue (as later some of them were evicted from the church). Among them were some who employed allegorical and mythological polemics to represent their position. We are beginning now to see some of the social dynamics which contributed towards the development of Gnosticism. But we must not assume facilely that the same social situation obtained all over the Empire. Rather each document needs to be analysed to yield its own specific data.

As in the witchcraft disputes discussed by Douglas,[76] we have seen how the Johannine community tried to enforce conformity within while meeting opposition from without. Its members were trying to understand contradiction and conflict in areas where none should have existed; for, according to the Christian perspective, all Jews should have accepted the message of their Messiah and certainly none should have opposed it. It may even be that they were trying to articulate the correct social role for a Jewish Christian party that was beset by the conflicting claims put on it by Judaism and Christianity.[77] But there is an important difference between the Johannine community and the typical society believing in witchcraft. In the normal witchcraft accusation, the offenders are expelled or recant so that the beliefs of the society are maintained without any further re-adjustment of ideology; i.e., the function of the witchcraft accusation is to promote fission, after which it ceases to be an issue. The Johannine community, however, lacked this easy safety valve because it both cared about the promises of the Old Testament and was sensitive to the rejection by other Jews. It therefore had to develop a new, more sophisticated ideology – the movement towards Gnosticism – to explain its social situation. In Douglas's terms, Johannine Christians were meeting the challenge by developing a higher grid.

From the perspective of social science we discover that we must go beyond the purely intellectualist interpretation of Gnosticism. Gnostic ideas do not inevitably emerge from the synthesis of Hebrew and Greek thought in some mysterious dialectic. Extreme Gnosticism, rather, is partly a social phenomenon. In the Johannine context it seems to have arisen among those groups interested in Judaism but excluded from the synagogue. The negative portrayal of the theology of the oppressor parallels opposition on the social level and enforces the pariah mentality of the sectarian group. It projects that opposition into the heavenly realm where the new revelation of the process of salvation, the *gnosis*, could indicate who would triumph. It is both a kind of oblique aggression and an attempt at consolation. Extreme Gnosticism was also partly a polemical attack against the ideology of a dominant group. The sectarian group which mounted such an attack, whether viewed as a Christian or

Jewish heresy, must share the dominant ideology to an extent but must also resent its own expulsion from the congregation of the faithful.[78]

12

Self-Isolation or Self-Affirmation in Judaism in the First Three Centuries: Theory and Practice

EPHRAIM E. URBACH

Introduction

The term 'self-isolation' in connection with rabbinic Judaism is often used as a description of a tendency in Judaism, beginning at least at the time of Yavneh, to become a self-enclosed movement which discouraged openness to outsiders. It is said that Judaism, which once had a strong missionary impulse, gave it up under rabbinic leadership in order to constitute itself as a self-enclosed entity.

It seems to me that the topic of self-isolation needs to be considered in a wider context and should not be limited only to the problem of missionary activities or the lack of them. Hence the rather lengthy title of my paper. The reason for not being content with the description 'self-isolation' in order to deal with the phenomenon we have in mind can be easily explained. In our context, self-isolation carries with it a heavy burden of deprecation and apologetics, the latter sometimes taking the form of a counter-offensive by scholars who thought they were representing Judaism against its critics. In studies of Jewish history and religion terms such as 'particularism and universalism', 'limitation and delimitation',[1] are frequently used. This terminology also serves ideological purposes, and accordingly acquires a different value weighting, depending on whether it is used by the opponents of Judaism or its defenders, while both fervently uphold the ideal of universalism.

To illustrate the above, let me quote a passage from Leo

Baeck's *The Essence of Judaism*, which was first published in 1905
as an answer to Adolf Harnack's *Wesen des Christentums*:

> A variety of factors have combined to make it possible for ignorance
> and easy for ill-will to misunderstand and to deny the universal
> character of Judaism. To begin with, the so-called national particu-
> larism has been a necessary foundation of its strength of
> existence. . . . All human ideals are conditioned by an actual histor-
> ical life. . . . This national particularism, which is always a favourite
> reproach against Judaism, is nothing but the intense and vivid in-
> dividuality, that solid selfhood, which alone safeguards perma-
> nence. . . . Even where the teaching was intended for the whole
> world, it had first to be addressed to Israel. . . . Universality and
> limitation in teaching and proclamation do not conflict one with the
> other. . . . It proves the power of the words of Jesus, and not the
> narrowness of his outlook, if he limits his teaching to Israel, and
> enjoins the same limitation upon his disciples. But it is a good thing
> that his exhortation is not contained in the Old Testament, and still
> less in the Talmud, for it would have found small grace in the eyes
> of these austere Protestants who investigate the Old Testament and
> the New, and who without compassion would have dubbed it as yet
> another manifestation of the narrow, national religion of the Jews.
> The Prophets speak of the world and its salvation, but they speak
> to Israel: it is only their later and colourless imitators who constantly
> summon all mankind to listen and admire.[2]

A similar conception has been expressed by the outstanding
philosopher and historian of Jewish philosophy, Julius Guttmann. In a less emotional but more precise formulation, Guttmann states in a paper on the idea of a religious society in
Judaism[3] that Judaism is recognized as a tribal religious society
which became the standard bearer of universal religious content. Opinions differ, however, in the evaluation of this development. According to the exponents of Christian theology, the
new religious content acquired by Judaism was not powerful
enough to break through the fence of the ancient religious
community, and Judaism therefore remained in an interim position, between a national and a universal religion. On the Jewish
side it is pointed out that the concept of universalism in Judaism
is accompanied by the idea of the universal mission of Israel as
the prophet of all the nations. According to Guttmann it is
important to prove that the idea of a religious society limited to
one nation does not imply an intermediate stage between a
universal and a particularistic religion but is a meaningful religious creation. The concept of election in Judaism, as it developed from the concept of the covenant, implies that Israel exists

to do the will of its God. Accordingly, the very existence of Israel has a religious meaning. Its fate depends upon the fulfilment of its religious mission. Thus, religion is not the basis of the national life, but the national society itself becomes a religious community without becoming a church. Instead it claims to be the people of God.

The dialectical antithesis between the two attitudes, the one of retrospective seclusion and the other of extroverted accessibility, between emphasis on the particularist and divisive in contrast to the universalistic (which stresses the common ground of the various religions) – 'this jumble of contradictions' as Franz Rosenzweig called it – continued to arouse controversial opinions and keep the discussion alive. In our own day, after the tragic events of the holocaust of European Jewry, and following the establishment of the State of Israel, the study of this issue has taken new and different trends and found various types of expression and solution.[4] All these investigations rely upon tannaitic and amoraic sources and upon liturgical texts of the period. I am not going into the different ideological propositions, but I think it well to keep in mind, while investigating the meaning of the rabbinic sources in their own times, that we are dealing with a problem that is still highly charged with emotional and practical implications, and we could easily run into the danger of confusing the past with the present.

Universalism and particularism

In his treatise *Contra Apionem* I.58–63, Josephus tries to explain the silence of Greek historians on the subject of the Jews and their history in the following way:

> Ours is not a maritime country, neither commerce, nor the intercourse which it promotes with the outside world has any attraction for us. Our cities are built inland, remote from the sea; and we devote ourselves to the cultivation of the productive country with which we are blessed. Above all we pride ourselves on the education of our children and regard as the most essential task in life the observance of our laws and of the pious practices based thereupon, which we have inherited. If to these reasons one adds the peculiarity of our mode of life, there was clearly nothing in ancient times to bring us into contact with the Greeks. . . .

In this explanation, Josephus adopts an apologetic line of argument to prove the antiquity of his nation notwithstanding the fact that it had remained isolated and unknown to the outside world. The objective reason for the isolation of the Jewish people is geographic, but the subjective cause is their adherence to their ancestral laws and practices. The words of Josephus already contain a hint of the distinction we have made between 'self-isolation' and 'self-affirmation'. The desire to give expression to one's faithfulness, and acts confirming the authenticity and inspirational quality of one's tradition, may lead to isolation; but they are not necessarily the outcome of self-isolation.

The guidelines set by Ezra and Nehemiah are often described as the beginning of Jewish exclusiveness. But, as George Foot Moore has pointed out, the prohibition of intermarriage had already been enjoined in the ancient law of Israel and such a restriction is not a feature peculiar to the Jewish heritage. It has its analogies in the Athens of Pericles and in Rome. The law proposed by Pericles, according to which only those born of parents who were both Athenians should be considered true citizens of Athens, brought about consequences which make the proceedings of Ezra seem tame in comparison. The motives for this type of legislation are usually explained as being measures for self-preservation, through the perpetuation of a pure-bred race. In the ancient laws of Judaism, in the account of the reform of Ezra, and in the subsequent development of legal principles, however, the main motive stressed for observing this prohibition is the preservation of the purity of the national religion. It is true that such a consideration is also implicit in the Athenian example and is stated explicitly in Roman law. Where then lies the difference? Moore[5] points to the fact that 'the Jews under Persian rule had no political existence; they had only a national religion and in its preservation lay their self-preservation'. But just as Moore recognizes that the ritual laws were not primarily invented in order to put hindrances in the way of intercourse with the heathen, so one may also argue that the main aim of these laws was the preservation of the religious inheritance for mankind, and that the self-preservation of the Jewish people was a condition for it. God had revealed the true religion to one people so that through them it should be proclaimed to all nations. Hence, however widely scattered, they still felt themselves members of one nation, and even after generations of exile they still looked upon the land of Israel as their native land and shared in hopes and dreams for the rebirth and recovery of their national power and glory there.

The prophetic concept of the world order had to demand the separation of Israel from the life of the neighbouring peoples. Exclusiveness is the outcome of commitment, of the longing to confess one's faith. It is the necessary consequence of the commandment: 'Thou shalt have no other gods besides me.' It denotes religious integrity which refuses to bow or submit to any strange god. Wherever separatism is lacking syncretism speedily intrudes. In the religion of Israel particularism has also acquired an ethical expression as a manifestation of divine judgment. Israel is chosen by God, therefore God acts as its judge: 'You only have I known of all the families of the earth, therefore I will visit upon you all your iniquities' (Amos 3.2). The election of Israel is conceived as a prophetic calling involving the whole people. Israel is chosen as a messenger, as a servant of God who is to guard religion for all peoples and to radiate its truth to all nations. The existence of monotheism is bound up with the continued existence of the community of Israel, and Israel's future is predicated on the future of religion. The stronger the stress placed by the prophets upon universalism, the greater is their emphasis upon the special position of Israel. Whenever the idea of Israel's role in the world is brought into prominence, the consciousness of Israel's personal possession of the truth and of its unique relationship to its religion is also emphatically stated.

The belief common to all Jews at the beginning of the first century was that their God was the only God and their religion the only true religion. It appeared self-evident to them that this God and this religion would one day be acknowledged by all mankind. In the meantime the Jewish people, to whom God had revealed himself and to whom he had entrusted his Torah, had been elected to practise its teachings, to fulfil its commandments and to propagate its ideas. Thus Judaism manifests a twofold character which has been described as both particularistic and universalistic. This dichotomy continued to exist even after certain changes in basic doctrines took place. The introduction of the idea of reward and punishment after death and the belief in the resurrection of the dead did not turn Judaism into a religion of individual salvation.[6] The acceptance of Judaism – I should say its full acceptance, in order to exclude from it the category of pious 'God-fearers' (φοβούμενοι τὸν

$\vartheta\varepsilon\acute{o}\nu$) – continued to mean naturalization and acceptance into the Jewish nation. The ethnic religious character of Judaism was recognized by Gentiles and formalized in Roman law.[7]

This inherent contradiction in Judaism has often been pointed out, and an attempt has been made to resolve it by representing Judaism as a world religion pulled between universalism and particularism, or between universalism and nationalism. It is claimed that in times of persecution or oppression particularism becomes the centre of gravity, while in times of external freedom universalism predominates.

Both universalism and particularism, however, are inextricably interwoven in Judaism, and it is through continuing interpenetration of national and universal elements in it that Judaism asserts its specific idea of God – that the God of Israel is the God of all humanity.

The inner dialectic of the concept of election has been made responsible for the symptoms of one-sidedness and contradiction said to be present in Judaism. The magnificent awareness of God in the Jewish people is rooted in this concept, but the tendency towards isolationism is to be found here too. This isolationism has been described as a Jewish characteristic, and historical explanations have been found for it. It has been argued that a minority, subject to persecution, retreats naturally into a seclusion turned in on itself as a protection against the hostility of its environment, and that pride in itself and contempt for this environment are made the compensation for the external humiliations to which it has to submit. But historical and sociological considerations should not lead us into forgetting that the primary factors in operation here are religious presuppositions. In order to test this, one need only glance at some homiletical statements in the Mekilta which have their origin around the end of the first century and the beginning of the second. In one midrash the meaning of *ve-goy kadosh* 'a sacred nation' is interpreted 'holy and sacred', separated from the nations of the world and from their abominations (Bahodesh 2; Lauterbach II, p. 205), but in another the fact that the Torah was revealed in the desert is explained in the following manner: 'For had the Torah been given in the land of Israel the Israelites could have said to the nations of the world: You have no share in it. But now that it was given in the wilderness publicly and openly in a place that is free for all, everyone wishing to accept it could come and accept it' (Baḥodesh 1;

Lauterbach II, p. 198). Again, in a homily on the war with Amalek, R. Joshua makes Moses say: 'Ruler of the World, this wicked one is coming to destroy Thy children from under Thy wings, who then will read that book of the Law which Thou hast given to them?' This anachronistic reproach of God by Moses is carried even further by R. Eleazar of Modiim, who added to it the following explanation: 'Thy children whom thou wilt in the future scatter to the four winds of the Heaven, as it is said (Zech. 2.10): "For I have spread you abroad to the four winds of the Heaven, etc." ' (Amalek 2; Lauterbach II, p. 158).

We should bear in mind that these reflections are attributed to sages whose external situation in the time and places in which they were living should, according to the isolationist theory, have produced a different reaction on their part. Of course one may argue that the homiletical discussions cannot be conclusive. We shall therefore proceed to an analysis of some halakic sources that deal with these issues, such as the attitude prescribed towards Gentiles, towards foreign nations, and towards different patterns in religion and culture. The question we have to ask here is: can we trace in the halakic sources any more radical trend towards isolationism? Or do they present an affirmation, a response resulting from an internal need to strengthen the ties to tradition and to reinforce and revitalize the inherited concepts and beliefs?

Noachian commandments

The concept that the nations of the world may have a share in the Torah if they wish it, which we encountered in one of the midrashim quoted above, has its halakic expression in the concept of the seven commandments given to all the descendants of Noah. True, the Book of Jubilees (7.20) makes Noah utter a warning that certain commandments must be observed by all. The appearance here of this statement may serve as an indication that the concept already existed at the time Jubilees was written, in the second century BCE, but a precise legal definition of this requirement appears in an anonymous baraita (tAZ 8.4; bSanh 56a). The seven commandments listed concern the administration of justice and the abstention from idolatry, blasphemy, incest, murder, robbery, and eating the limb of a living animal. Not all these are pre-Mosaic injunctions, and not all the pre-Mosaic injunctions are found here. But the list was discussed by the Tannaim of the middle of the second century, and additional prohibitions were then proposed. These include the prohibitions against the drinking of blood of a living animal and against emasculation, sorcery and magical practices, as listed in Deut. 18.10–11. The fact that the list in the baraita was taken as a point of departure proves that this baraita itself had its origin at least in the Yavneh period. I cannot follow the attempt[8] to date the formulation of the seven Noachian commandments to a period during the Hasmonaean era and to view them as regulations governing the behaviour of non-Jewish residents in a sovereign Jewish state. True, the talmudic discussion of the Noachian laws is concerned with the actual enforcement of these laws and the punishment of their transgression by the rabbinical courts, but the rabbis here assume the existence of a non-Jewish jurisdictional authority and define some of the seven laws according to the accepted principles expressed in the term *dineyhem* 'their laws', i.e. the laws customary among the Gentiles. Thus, according to R. Ishmael, Noachians are to be put to death for killing embryos.[9] The prohibitions against incest include some prohibitions according to their laws (viz. the view of the sages who contradict R. Meir; cf. tAZ 8.4; bSanh 57b). Whatever may be the origin of the principle of the Noachian laws, the fact remains that the Tannaim of the second century assumed the existence of a *corpus iuris* common to all nations. The term 'children of Noah' introduced by them also points to the universal character of the concept. Thus we read in mNed 3.11: '[if somebody said] *Qonam!* If I have any benefit from the children of Noah – he is permitted to benefit from Israelites, but not from other nations'; 'children of Noah' is equated with 'Gentiles', אומות העולם. As the Jewish jurisdiction certainly did not extend over Gentiles at the time of the discussion, these halakot dealing with the Noachian laws constitute a valuable document demonstrating the interest taken by those Tannaim in the moral and religious standards of the non-Jewish peoples of their world. I stress the word 'religious', because, in my view, an outstanding feature of the list of the seven Noachian commandments is the inclusion of the requirement to abstain from idolatry. It is worthwhile noting that this prohibition is not included in the six prohibitions enumerated in Jubilees, but the abstention 'from the pollution of idols' is required from Gentiles in Acts 15.20. As I have pointed out elsewhere, the sages of the first half of the second century were aware of an increasing tendency among Gentiles to disregard images and idols, as having no intrinsic worth.[10] The sages, of course, looked upon any symbolical interpretation of images as idolatry, and they took the same view of the emperor cult; but some form of abandonment of idol worship by pagans appeared to them as at least possible and could be included as a commandment given to the descendants of Noah or accepted by them.

Throughout the halakic discussion of the Noachian commandments nothing is said to indicate whether these commandments were observed by Gentiles in reality. The assumption seems to be – as in similar halakic *sugyot* concerning Jews exclusively – that there were followers of the Noachian commandments at the time and also those who transgressed them. We encounter a fundamental change, however, in haggadic midrashim, which have their origin in a different set of problems but which are connected with the issue under review. The Jewish claim to election based upon the willingness of the people of Israel to accept the yoke of the Torah was queried by the nations of the world, who could easily argue: 'Had we been asked we should certainly have accepted it [the Torah]'. Such a contention was refuted by the Tanna R. Simeon b. Eleazar at the end of the second century. This pupil of R. Meir reasons in the following way: If they are not able to keep the seven commandments which were given to the descendants of Noah, and which were accepted by them, how much more would they be unable to keep the commandments if they had been given all the Torah. The reply of R. Simeon b. Eleazar in this passage is prefaced by an imaginative tale which recounts that, before revealing the Torah to Israel, God asked the Gentile nations to receive the Torah, but the sons of Esau, Ammon and Moab, as well as the sons of Ishmael, refused it. The precepts that prompted their refusal are said to be 'Thou shalt not commit adultery', 'Thou shalt not murder', and 'Thou shalt not steal', which are included among the Noachian laws. It is obvious that this story represents a historical interpretation or a repetition of the view of R. Simeon b. Eleazar. But at the same time the story shows that the background, or *Sitz im Leben*, of the dictum of R. Simeon b. Eleazar was uttered in a polemical context and involved the issue of election. His statement is thus an assertion of self-affirmation which has not yet assumed the character of self-isolation. The narrator does not exclude other nations from the possibility of fulfilling their obligations in observing the commandments given to them. We may find support for our interpretation in the well-structured and humorous midrash appearing at the beginning of the treatise *Abodah Zarah* in the Babylonian Talmud concerning the Day of Judgment. The Gentile nations plead not guilty of transgression because they had not been offered the Torah. This plea is refuted by the story of God's visit to all the nations and their refusal to receive the Torah. The story is quoted in the name of R. Johanan, who, incidentally, still recalls R. Simeon b. Eleazar (pMaas 1.2; 48d). The discussion, however, does not end here, for the nations of the world continue to argue; and when challenged that they do not even keep the seven Noachian commandments, they retort, 'and Israel who received the Torah, did they keep it?' The Lord calls upon witnesses from the Gentile nations, beginning with Nimrod, the contemporary of Abraham, down to Nebuchadnezzar and Darius, and they testify that Israel observed the Torah: 'As it is said (Isa. 40.9) "Let them bring forth their witnesses, that they may be justified." ' The beginning of the quoted verse, which is 'Let all nations be gathered', serves as the opening of the midrash. I do not want to dwell now on the paradox this represents, according to which Israel needs the testimony of the Gentile nations in order to justify its claim to election. The allegory belongs to a later period, but it was prompted by the statement of R. Simeon b. Eleazar and is self-affirmative in character. In saying the above, I do not deny that remarks which were not uttered in a deprecatory sense in their original context could, if quoted in isolation, easily become predicamental.

The rabbis and the Gentiles

Perhaps even more significant to our discussion than the treatment of the seven Noachian laws are the halakot dealing with the validity of certain rituals in which a Gentile participated, for these offer evidence from daily life. MShek 7.6 relates in the name of R. Simeon that seven things were ordained by the Court [i.e. the Sanhedrin] 'and one of them was that if a Gentile sent his whole-offering from a region beyond the sea and the drink offerings also, these are offered, but if he did not, they are to be offered at the charges of the congregation'. The Babylonian Talmud discusses whether this mishnah agrees with the view of R. Jose the Galilean, who also permitted acceptance of peace-offerings from a Gentile (bMen 73b). The mishnah certainly predates these Tannaim, for it refers to an ordinance issued by the Supreme Court during the temple period. According to the Tosefta (tShek 3.11), if a Gentile brought peace-offerings and gave them to an Israelite, the latter may eat them, and if he gave them to a priest, the priest may eat them. The participation of a Gentile therefore does not invalidate the worthiness of these offerings. In the same way the heave-offerings or tithes or hallowed things given by a Gentile are all valid (mTer 3.9). There is, however, a divergence of opinions over the acceptance of contributions from Gentiles for temple repairs. According to one baraita they should be accepted, while another states that they should not. R. Johanan found a way to harmonize both sources. The problems raised in the treatment of dedications by Gentiles to the sanctuary, or to a synagogue, are all the result, we may say, of internal facets of the halakah. If there is a difference between the treatment of Jewish and non-Jewish dedications it results rather from a consideration of the Gentiles' lack of familiarity with the principles of the halakah and a desire to avoid giving offence to the donor. R. Johanan taught that the prohibition on exchanging an object dedicated to a synagogue only applies if this is to be done for a secular purpose; if for a religious purpose, it is permitted to exchange the object dedicated. But the same R. Johanan ruled that a candlestick or lamp dedicated by a Gentile to a synagogue may not be exchanged, even for a religious purpose, before the name of its owner is forgotten. The reason given is that a Gentile donor would notice such a change and protest against it (bArak 6a–b).

This consideration is very close to the principle designated in the Mishnah (mGit 5.8) as the 'paths of peace', i.e the laws to be observed for the sake of peace with the Gentiles. For instance, the poor among the Gentiles are not to be prevented from the benefit of gathering gleanings (*leqet*), the forgotten sheaf (*shikhah*) or *pe'ah*. All these constitute impositions for the support of the poor, but are of a purely Jewish nature, having no parallel in the outside world. When, out of halakic reasons, it is stated that the poor tithe may not be given to Gentiles, it is at the same time recommended to give them 'prepared unsanctified grain [i.e., grain from which the various tithes have been separated] for the sake of [their] gratitude (tPeah 3.1). The facets of life in a mixed community are shown clearly in the following baraita: 'In a town where there are Jews and Gentiles, the administrators [of charity funds] collect from the Jews and from the Gentiles, for the sake of peace. One mourns the non-Jewish dead and consoles non-Jewish mourners and buries the non-Jewish dead, for the sake of the paths of peace.'[11] A discussion dating from the second century over the style of funeral orations is very instructive in this respect: 'R. Judah said: "[The eulogy on a Gentile is] alas! O Faithful witness who ate the fruit of his own labour." "If so", the sages objected to him, "what then have you left to be said for men who are virtuous?" He replied, "if he [i.e. the Gentile or slave] was virtuous why not lament him in this manner?" '[12]

We may now turn to another set of halakot which are also concerned with the relationship to Gentiles. Although these halakot derive from the same period and are attributed to the same sages, we are struck by the wide gap separating them from those considered earlier. We need only read the first chapter of Abodah Zarah in the Mishnah and the Tosefta, and the corresponding expositions in the Palestinian and Babylonian Talmud, to see the difference. Two reasons are given for the prohibitions codified in them: the fear of the infiltration of idolatry and abhorrence of Gentile ways. Gentiles are suspected of bestiality, lewdness and bloodshed. The first continues the reasoning of Mosaic law; and the second, while partly based on the warnings of the Torah to keep away from the abominations of other peoples, is also an outcome of more recent experience, the contacts with certain strata in the pagan society of the Hellenistic and Roman world. Of course we have to be aware that lack of contact and continuous separation of one member of society from another helps to foster suspicion and encourages the drawing of general conclusions from individual experiences. The immoral behaviour of 'Gaius of Gadara and Lucius of Susitha',[13] who would sneak into each other's homes and cohabit with each other's wives, became a symbol of Gentile conduct, and even the account of a friendly visit of condolence by R. Meir to the house of a Gentile Avnimos (Oenomaus) of Gadara ends with a biting remark which suggests that Avnimos was not certain of his paternity and was therefore mourning only the death of his mother (RuthR 2.8).

Such suspicions were not without influence in halakic prescriptions concerning the participation of Gentiles in performances of a ritual nature. In this respect the halakah concerning the performance of circumcision of a Jew by a Gentile has great significance. According to the Tosefta (tAZ 3.12), 'A Jew may circumcise a Gentile for the purpose of conversion to Judaism, but a Gentile may not circumcise a Jew, for they [Gentiles] are suspect of bloodshed; [this is] the opinion of R. Meir; the sages say: "A Gentile may circumcise a Jew if others are standing over him [but] if the two are alone it is forbidden, for the [Gentiles] are suspect of bloodshed." '

Another controversy reported in the talmudic discussion of the subject introduces a completely different principle concerning circumcision by Gentiles and Samaritans: 'In a town in which there is no Jewish physician and there is a Gentile and a Samaritan, the Gentile should perform the circumcision and not the Samaritan; these are the dicta of R. Meir. R. Judah says: "Let the Samaritan perform it and not the Gentile." ' The reason for invalidating circumcision by a Gentile is not explicitly stated. Again, in another source, R. Judah states that circumcision by Samaritans is not valid because of their religious beliefs, 'because of their intention, which is directed towards Mount Gerizim'. R. Joseph sharply refutes this argument. 'Where do we find in the Torah that circumcision needs intention? Let him continue to circumcise for the sake of Mount Gerizim for as long as he lives.'[14] According to this view, the prohibition on performing circumcision by a Gentile can only be explained by the suspicion that it will endanger the life of the person undergoing circumcision. R. Judah the Patriarch is the first authority to whom is attributed a deduction from scripture which excludes Gentiles from performing circumcision. Gen. 17.9–10 reads: 'And you shall keep my covenant. . . . This is my covenant, which you shall keep, between me and you and your seed after you: Every manchild among you shall be circumcised.' R. Judah interpreted 'you and your seed after you' to exclude the Samaritan and the Gentile alike.[15] In the Palestinian Talmud this interpretation is ascribed to R. Levi while Rav finds support in Gen. 17.13, *himol yimol*, which he reads *hamal yimol*, 'the circumcised alone shall circumcise'.[16] According to this interpretation, a Samaritan and a circumcised Gentile should not be excluded. We find similar discussions on the validity of ritual objects such as *zizit*, *tefillin*, *mezuzot* and copies of the holy scripture produced by Gentiles. The continuing interest in these problems cannot be described only as 'self-

281

isolation'. A retreat into self-isolation would not require so much reasoned consideration. Rather, on the one hand it seems to be the outcome of theological reasons that the Jewish nation and its specific way of life must remain uncompromised and, on the other, the concern of the halakists with the obligation to respond to the will of God and at the same time to make this response workable. We may consider the various halakot within the limits of these two aims. Their purpose was not isolation and separation *per se*. We therefore do not need to resort to apologetics or quote the disparaging opinions of Greeks and Romans about Jews[17] in order to justify the Jewish suspicions and allegations concerning pagans.[18] As we have noted, these were mainly based upon individual observations and generalizations, in the same way as were the allegations made by pagans concerning Jews. Both had many features in common, not always sympathetic ones. It will suffice to quote the following mishnah: 'If he found an abandoned child in the city and most of the people were Gentiles, it may be deemed a Gentile child; if most of them were Israelites, it may be deemed an Israelite child; if they were equal, it may be deemed an Israelite child. R. Judah says: "It should be determined by which are more wont to abandon children" ' (mMaksh 2.7). Members of both communities are equally suspect of the crime of abandoning children, and according to the opinion of R. Judah in the Mishnah one may even assume a case in which the majority of those guilty of abandoning children were Jews.[19] The proximity of Jews and Gentiles in cities raised many problems, a number of which are dealt with in the same tractate of the Mishnah. We shall concern ourselves with one that leads to the core of an issue designated by Max Weber as that of 'double-faced ethics'. This is an attitude which makes a distinction between the moral code of behaviour towards a fellow citizen or co-religionist and that towards outsiders. The mishnah we are concerned with reads: 'If he found lost property in the city and most of the people were Gentiles, he need not proclaim it; if most of them were Israelites, he must proclaim it; if they were equal, he must proclaim it' (mMaksh 2.8). The restitution of lost objects is based upon the principle of reciprocity, a principle which underlies the biblical law of the prohibition on charging interest on loans, as only applying to Jews. Philo justifies this difference by saying: 'Those who are not of the same nation he [Moses] describes as aliens, reasonably enough, and the condition of the alien excludes any idea of partnership . . .' (*Leg. spec.* II.73). The anonymous comment of the Sifre which states: ' "Unto a stranger thou mayest lend upon usury" is a positive command-ment',[20] was interpreted by the majority of the commentators on the Sifre as adding the transgression of a positive command-ment in a case where a Jew lends money to a fellow Jew upon usury, an interpretation that is in accordance with the wording of the mishnah: 'One may borrow [money] from, or lend it to a Gentile upon usury' (mBM 5.6). The strictness with which the prohibition against usury was treated by the Tannaim, who compare one who trangresses it to an atheist, led to a tendency to include within its scope the lending of money even to Gen-tiles: 'R. Simeon b. Eleazar said: "One who has money and does not lend it upon usury, concerning him Scripture states: He that putteth not out his money to usury . . . shall never be moved." '[21] BMakk 24a states explicitly, 'even the money of a Gentile'. The Babylonian Talmud (bBM 70b) ascribes the pro-hibition against taking usury from a Gentile to R. Ḥuna. His son R. Ḥiya brings his father's opinion into concordance with the above-mentioned mishnah by limiting the permission only to cases in which the lender is in need of sustenance. A later Amora explains that the extension of the prohibition was the outcome of a desire to avoid a transgression of the prohibition concerning fellow Jews.[22] Such a departure from the pentateu-chal law may be explained by the desire to ensure that Jewish moral conduct should be found acceptable by non-Jews. This attitude is reflected in the exemplary story related about Simeon b. Shetah, who had returned a lost object to a Gentile. When approached about why he had troubled to do so, he replied: 'Do you think that Simeon b. Shetah is a barbarian? Simeon b. Shetah prefers the pronouncement "Blessed be the God of the Jews" above all the wealth of this world.'[23]

Sanctification of the name of the Lord, or at least the avoid-ance of the profanation of his name, became a leading principle in deciding problems of relations towards Gentiles. An anony-mous baraita reads: 'He who robs a Gentile must make resti-tution. Robbery from a Gentile is more serious than robbery from a Jew, because of the profanation of the Name' (tBK 10.15). The traditions concerning 'the robbery of a Gentile' are of par-amount importance to the question raised at the beginning of our discussion. Judaism did not become a self-enclosed move-ment at Yavneh. The reverse is true. The halakah just quoted belongs to the Yavneh period, as is clearly stated in the account, reported in several sources, about the Roman officers who visited R. Gamaliel for instruction. They studied mishnah, midrash, halakot and haggadot, and at the hour of parting said to him: 'All the Torah is good and praiseworthy, except for this one thing – that you say: "It is permitted to rob a Gentile and forbidden to rob a Jew." '[24] R. Akiba expounded that robbery of a Gentile is forbidden from the verse Lev. 25.48 (bBK 113a). On the other hand, he also applied the principle of 'infringement of sanctification' to relationships towards non-Jews in a divergent opinion from that of R. Ishmael.

> In a suit arising between an Israelite and a heathen, if you can justify the former according to the laws of Israel, justify him, and say: This is our law. So also, if you can justify him by the laws of the Gentiles, justify him, and say to the other party: This is your law. But if this cannot be done we use subterfuges to circumvent him. This is the view of R. Ishmael, but R. Akiba said that we should not attempt to circumvent him on account of the sanctification of the Name (bBK 113a).

It is obvious from these sources that the authorities quoted are of the opinion that hitherto robbery of a Gentile had not been explicitly forbidden. The Palestinian Talmud states: 'At that time Rabban Gamaliel ordained that robbery of a Gentile is forbidden because of the profanation of the Name.'[25] We do not have precise information on the conditions governing foreigners during the Hasmonaean and Herodian periods, but the sources clearly reflect a tendency towards a more open and equitable attitude to outsiders.

Greek language and literature

An investigation of the prevailing attitude towards the Greek language and its literature leads to similar results. A wide knowledge of the Gentile world is displayed in the talmudic and midrashic literature. We need only refer to the two volumes of Krauss's *Lehnwörter*, especially the classified index of Immanuel Löw (according to the different spheres of life) and to Saul Lieberman's *Greek in Jewish Palestine* and *Hellenism in Jewish Palestine*.[26] These provide ample evidence of the acquaintance of the Tannaim and Amoraim with the languages, institutions, religions, beliefs and superstitions of the Graeco-Roman world. The archaeological discoveries in a centre like Beth Shearim, in which sages were active in the second and third centuries, have also revealed the dimension of art on the cultural scene. It is therefore difficult to understand the existence of a ban against the teaching of the Greek language and studies.[27] One may easily conclude that the ban was not actually applied, and that these studies were not limited to the circles of the Jewish leadership, such as members of the House of Rabban Gamaliel, who were permitted to have their children taught Greek because of their close connection with the government authorities.

On the question of the origin of the ban, I think that it may be assumed that the opposition it represents to Greek ways and culture is an inheritance of the struggle of the *hasidim* against Hellenization. The wording of the ban also points to this origin: 'Execrated be the man who rears pigs and execrated be he who teaches his son Greek' (bSot 49b; bBk 82b; bMen 64b). The abhorrence of swine thus expressed is probably connected with the decree of Antiochus Epiphanes that Jews should build altars and sacrifice pigs upon them (I Macc. 1.47) and with the fact that Jews were martyred because of their defiance of the king's command to eat pig's flesh.[28] That the Hasmonaeans should proclaim such a ban after their victory, or perhaps even during the war against the Greeks, in the form of an execration (*'aror*) is understandable. According to the Babylonian Talmud, the rulings against the breeding of pigs and the teaching of Greek originated from an incident in the course of the fratricidal struggle between the Hasmonaean princes, Hyrcanus II and Aristobulus II, when the people besieged inside the temple received a pig in exchange for their gold which they had lowered from the wall (bBK 82b). The Palestinian Talmud (pBer 4.7b; pTaan 4.68d) reports two incidents with a similar motif, but the time indicated is of a general character only. The opening of the first account states that it happened 'in the days of the kingdom of Greece . . .' and that the people outside the city sent two goats instead of two lambs, which caused a delay in the offering of the *tamid*. The second opens 'in the days of the wicked kingdom', and this time the besieged obtained two pigs in exchange; a tremor shook the wall, the *tamid* ceased, and the temple was destroyed. It seems a futile task to try to reconstruct historical events from these stories. Whatever their origin, the Palestinian Talmud does not mention a ban against the teaching of Greek in this context. This ban is attributed in a short chronological note, without any legendary embellishment, to the time of the *polemos* of Quietus,[29] Trajan's general who subdued the Jewish revolt under that emperor. If our assumption is correct and the ban originated in the times of struggle against Hellenization, we can also understand that this early ruling had to be reiterated from time to time, when the failure to keep it reached too great dimensions, and especially in troubled periods. One such occasion was during the internal strife among the Hasmonaean princes. Their Greek names and other manifestations of acculturation prove how far they had moved from the originators of the ban. That it had to be renewed during the times of Quietus shows that it had not been generally accepted (see Tosafot BK 82b, *ad ve-asur*) and had to be reiterated. When R. Joshua, who lived close to the time of the revolt under Trajan, was asked whether it is permissible for a man to have his son instructed in Greek wisdom, he did not answer the question with an absolute 'no' but gave a more sophisticated answer: 'Let him teach him Greek at a time when it is neither day nor night, for it is written (Josh. 1.8) "Thou shalt meditate therein day and night" ' (tAZ 1.20). The reply of R. Joshua does not declare a ban on the teaching of Greek, but points out the difficulty of doing so without causing neglect to the primary duty of the study of the Torah. The proposal to find a reason for the ban in the reply of R. Joshua is rejected in the Palestinian Talmud (pSot 9.16; 24b) because the consequences could lead to such an extreme situation that a man could not have his son taught a profession. Thus the argument is reduced *ad absurdum*. The reply to R. Joshua is reminiscent of the discussion between R. Ishmael and R. Simeon b. Yohai over the permissibility of performing work of any kind (bBer 35b). In this case the verse Deut. 11.14, 'that thou mayest gather in thy corn', is contrasted with Josh. 1.8, 'This book of the Law shall not depart out of thy mouth'. 'Should we understand the latter verse literally? But we were taught "that thou mayest gather in thy corn" [means] deal with it [the book of the Law] according to the customary way of life – this is the opinion of R. Ishmael. R. Simeon b. Yohai said: "If one ploughs at the proper time and sows at the time for sowing and harvests at harvest-time, what will happen to the study of Torah?" ' Abaye remarks, 'Many have done like R. Ishmael and succeeded, while others who have done like R. Simeon have failed'. R. Ishmael was also the Tanna who deduced that 'therefore choose life' (Deut. 30.19) means 'choose a profession' (pSot 9.16; 24c; pKid 1.7; 61a). Yet it is still reported that, when asked by his nephew, Ben Dama, whether it was permissible for him to study Greek wisdom after he had completed the study of the whole of the Torah, R. Ishmael gave him the same reply as R. Joshua (bMen 99b). This can only mean, in the context, that one is never permitted to discontinue giving his full attention to Torah study.

It is clear that the question of the teaching and study of the Greek language and its literature remained under consideration during the second century, and evidence of a positive attitude towards it in practice is abundant. R. Eleazar Hisma, a pupil of R. Joshua, is the author of the saying (mAboth 3.18) 'Qinnim and Niddah are essentials of the Torah; the canons of Astronomy and Gematria[30] are *parpraiot* of wisdom.' The correct reading[31] is *parpdaiot*: i.e., propaedeutic studies. Similar pronouncements are found in Greek pagan and Christian literature. R. Eleazar's interest in numbers is described in an exaggerated fashion, and we are told that he could count the drops of water in the sea (bHor 10a). It is significant that R. Johanan could find no other reason for the ban on Greek wisdom than the fear of 'informers'.[32] None of the sources indicate that there was any consideration that the knowledge of a foreign language or foreign learning could lead to idolatry and to the adoption of strange customs and ways of life. The prohibition is never explained as having been dictated by the necessity to ward off foreign influences. Certainly, nothing which issued from Yavneh or Usha or Tiberias can be interpreted as intending to increase isolation of the community by restricting the use of the Greek language and the study of its literature. R. Johanan b. Zakai argued against the Sadducees: '[Concerning] the holy scriptures, according to our love for them, so is their uncleanliness; the writings of "Homeros", which are not dear to us, do not defile the hands' (mYad 4.6). In a comment on R. Akiba's prohibition of reading external books we read in the Palestinian Talmud: 'But he who reads the books of "Homeros" and other works, that were written beyond that [i.e. scriptures] is considered as one who reads secular documents.'[33] R. Judah the Patriarch declares that 'in Eres Israel there is no room for the Aramaic language, there is only room for the holy language and for Greek' (bBK 83a).

Tolerance of dissent

The self-affirmative character of the various prohibitions we have mentioned so far will be seen more clearly if we examine the rulings and dicta concerning heretics and their writings and teachings. When we come to explain the term *minim*, which is usually translated as 'sectarians' or 'heretics', we encounter great difficulties. This is because our sources derive from a time in which it was taken for granted that the opposition to dissenters had been successful, and they could be declared 'outsiders'.[34] No clear distinction is made between the different heretical groups, and there has been much guess-work in the attempt to identify the ideas and trends of thought which they represent. The invocation against heresy in the twelfth benediction of the ʿAmidah has been regarded as an addition by R. Gamaliel II and as being directed against converts to Christianity.[35] The main evidence relied upon for this attribution is that the Genizah fragments of the ʿAmidah have this version: 'The apostates [*meshummadim*] shall have no hope if they do not return to your Torah, the Nazarenes (*noṣrim*) and the *minim* shall perish immediately, etc.' That this was the formula recited in the presence of R. Gamaliel II in Yavneh is rather doubtful. The mention of apostates at the beginning of the list points rather to the period after Bar Kokhba. The Nazarenes (*noṣrim*) are distinguished from *minim*. The first allegation that the Jews were in the habit of cursing the Christians in synagogue comes from Justin Martyr, who wrote about 150 CE. We know now, however, that the origin of this invocation was much earlier even than the times of R. Gamaliel and was intended to include all groups who separated themselves from the community.[36]

We are not told who the *minim* were. In the times of R. Gamaliel this term may have denoted various sects. After the Bar Kokhba revolt, when the separation of the Christians of various groups became final, they were included among the *minim*, and to emphasize their inclusion the *noṣrim* are mentioned explicitly.

Obviously, in the process of forming a new community, the transitional period is used for missionary purposes. At the same time the parent body launches a counter-attack and attempts to exclude the new group in order to protect itself from infiltration. Thus an act of self-affirmation hastens the process of final separation. We see here that a prayer, formerly directed against *perušim*, i.e. those leaving the community altogether, was subsequently aimed at excluding those who wanted to stay within the synagogue in order to change it and introduce their own teachings. The tannaitic sources reporting differences between Sadducees, Essenes and Pharisees do not imply a distinction between those who belong to the house of Israel and those who are outside it. Rather they indicate three parties with different views and practices within the same ethnic and religious group. This impression is confirmed by Josephus in his description of the three *haireseis*, schematic though it is (*Ant.* XVIII.11–22). We face a different approach, however, when we look at the sources dealing with *minim*. It does not seem sufficient to state that a change of attitude took place, from the spirit of tolerance that allowed the coexistence of different sects, to one of intolerance, a phenomenon common in late antiquity.[37] We have to ask ourselves the reason for the greater tolerance and for the change. The impression given by the sources is that, in the period which we are discussing, conceptual differences were disregarded as long as a common line of behaviour was accepted in matters of ritual and praxis. The dictum ascribed to a Sadducean priest, 'Although we interpret (differently), we do not act differently' (tYom 1.8), concerns a time when the Pharisees gained a decisive influence in the temple. It may be assumed that when high priests, who were Sadducees, were the ruling authorities, the position was not very different[38] and that outbreaks of internal strife like those reported to have taken place in the time of Alexander Jannaeus, according to Josephus, or during the office of an anonymous priest, according to talmudic evidence, were exceptional. The war against Rome in 70 CE not only destroyed the temple and put an end to the last vestiges of Jewish national and political independence, but also caused a profound change in the whole structure of Jewish society and institutions, and in consequence in their relationships to dissenting groups. With the disappearance of such unifying bonds as the temple, the Sanhedrin and the festival pilgrimages to Jerusalem, the demand for allegiance to a single normative set of doctrines and teachings became stricter. Within the academies of the sages a large measure of freedom was allowed for differences of opinion, not only in the area of doctrine and belief but also in that of halakah. Nevertheless, a dissenting member was obliged to bow to the decision of the majority after it had been taken and could not act in accordance with the rejected opinion. The tradition relating the excommunication of R. Eliezer b. Hyrcanus is a true depiction of this attitude. There is no evidence to show that people were excommunicated on the ground of harbouring non-orthodox beliefs.[39] The term 'ban' does not appear in the narrations concerning the most famous heretic of tannaitic times, Elisha b. Abuyah. He is described as one who had separated from the community and denied himself the possibility of repentance. He is designated *aher*, i.e. an 'outsider',[40] but it is not known whether he formed or joined another group. He is, however, accused of having desecrated the Divine Name and of having caused other people to sin.

Certain usages of a sectarian character are described as *derekh aheret*, 'a path of heterodoxy', and some of them were rejected, not because they were heretical in and of themselves but because they had been adopted by *minim*.[41] The etymology of the word *min* is not clear. It probably denotes a group of pupils who considered themselves a 'species' or 'gens'. None of the sources of the first century, certainly not before the year 70, use this term. The texts in which *minim* are mentioned belong to the second century, mostly after 135, or the third century. In these the term is used to designate various groups. Sometimes they represent dualists, sometimes Gnostics of various sects,[42] sometimes Gentile Christians, sometimes Judaeo-Christians,[43] and often pagans. The themes of the discussions differ accordingly and have been surveyed by many scholars.[44] But none of the sources mentioning *minim* treat them as belonging to the community; instead they are treated as outsiders.

To the list in mSanh 10.1, which enumerates those who have no share in the world to come, R. Akiba adds: 'and also those who read the outside books'. The Palestinian Talmud[45] identifies 'the outside books' as the books of Ben Sirah and of Ben La'anah. The Babylonian Talmud quotes a Tanna who taught that by 'outside books' 'the books of *minim*' are meant, i.e. 'the books of the outsiders'. The Amora R. Joseph adds: 'It is also forbidden to read in the book of Ben Sirah' (bSanh 100b). We are not told who the *minim* are, but the identification indicates that they are not a group within the community, but outside it. Another source in which books of *minim* are mentioned, although in a different sense and context, confirms the suggested identity of the *minim*. Tosefta Shabbat[46] states: 'The *gilionim* and the books of *minim* may not be saved from a fire but they are to be left burning in their place.' The word *gilionim* in this context has been examined by many scholars and a large literature has accumulated around it, as it was thought to be an allusion to the gospels (*evangelia*). Two strong arguments, however, may be adduced against this interpretation. The first is that the same pair of terms appears in a parallel baraita (tYad 2.13): 'The *gilionim* and the books of *minim* do not render the hands unclean.' In this case there can be no doubt that *gilionim* are the blank spaces of the book, as is obvious from mYad 3.4; but while the Mishnah deals with the blank spaces that are part of the book, the Tosefta gives the ruling for the detached ones. The second reason why it is impossible that *gilionim* should mean *evangelia* is that the plural designating the gospels as a Christian corpus of writings appears for the first time in the work of Irenaeus and its use in the Tosefta is very improbable.[47] The books of the *minim* mentioned in this context are their copies of the holy scriptures, to which the Tannaim apply the same rule as to the cut-off blank spaces. They are not holy and should not be saved from a fire on the Sabbath. These *minim* are the same group whose books are identified with the books of outsiders, the reading of which is forbidden. In connection with the ruling on the books of the *minim*, the Tosefta quotes two sayings by contemporaries of R. Akiba. R. Tarfon said:

> May I bury my son if I would not burn them [i.e. the books of the *minim*], together with their Divine Names. For even if some one pursued me [to kill me] I would enter a house of a foreign cult [for protection] but not the houses of these, for the worshippers of other cults do not know Him [the Lord] and deny Him, but these do know Him and yet deny Him.

R. Ishmael said:

> If in order to make peace between husband and wife the Lord ordered that a book written in sanctity should be blotted out in water, [concerning] the books of the *minim*, who are stirring up enmity[48] between Israel and their Father in heaven, how much more so should their books be blotted out, they and their Divine Names. About them the scripture (Ps. 139.20–21) says: 'Do not I hate them, O Lord, that hate thee? And am not I grieved with those that rise up against thee?'

The harsh dictum of R. Ishmael furnishes a clue to understanding the main reason for the radical, embittered attitude adopted towards the *minim*. They are accused of stirring up enmity between Israel and their Father in heaven. The centrality of the concept of Israel's election, founded on the covenant concluded at the revelation on Mount Sinai, was challenged by the tragic events following the destruction of the second temple, and even more so after the Bar Kokhba Revolt. From the end of the first century, sages like R. Gamaliel II and R. Joshua were confronted with assertions that the Lord had turned away his face from Israel, that he had severed his relations with them (bHag 5b; bYeb 102b). Similar assertions, accompanied by ridicule, were made by the *minim* who argued with R. Meir and his wife Bruria in an encounter that took place between 136 and 160 in Tiberias. The same was reported in the time of R. Hanina b. Hama between 220 and 250, and at the end of the century such allegations became a standing topic in the homilies of the Amoraim. The writings of Justin Martyr, as well as of Origen and his opponent Celsus, provide us with ample evidence of this type of confrontation.[49] The arguments against the doctrine of election, and especially the claim to form a new community of elect as put forward by the Judaeo-Christians and Jewish Gnostics, were considered by the sages to constitute a threat to the faith of the members of their own community. It could be understood that pagans were puzzled by the doctrine of election. In addition the sages themselves did not deny the degradation of Judaism inherent in subjection and the imposition of an alien yoke, and they laid down that an intending proselyte coming to be converted should be asked: 'What reason have you for seeking conversion? Do you not know that Israel today is in travail, persecuted, swept [from place to place], harassed and full of suffering?' Only one who acknowledged this fact was to be accepted.[50] Jews who denied the doctrine of election were therefore treated as traitors and renegades. In conformity with the above saying of R. Tarfon, we read in a baraita:[51] 'We do not bring up Gentiles and shepherds of small cattle and we do not cast them in, but we cast in *minim*, informers and apostates and do not bring them up.' While the coupling of 'Gentiles and shepherds of small cattle' is not clear, the grouping of '*minim*, informers and apostates' is significant. They are not condemned because of their teaching, but because of their infidelity towards their community. While to Christians heresy mainly implied doctrinal dissent,[52] in Judaism doctrinal dissent did not make a Jew into a heretic, a *min*. What made a Jew a heretic was not a slackness in observing the precepts, or even alienation from tradition, but the act of denying the election of the Jews; for that act destroys the conceptual basis on which the separate existence of the Jewish people is founded and endangers its survival. The *minim* are treated in the same way as the Samaritans. The differentiation between non-Jews and those suspected of heresy comes to the fore in the following halakah: 'If a Gentile pronounces a blessing using the Name, one responds "Amen"; if a Samaritan pronounces a blessing one does not respond "Amen", unless one has heard the entire blessing.' It is therefore not surprising that the severe attitude adopted by the sages towards the *minim* did not influence their general conception of the human race and Israel's position in it. There is no doubt that R. Akiba is referring to all mankind when he declares, 'Beloved is man in that he was created in the image (of God); still greater was the love, in that it was made known to him that he was created in the image of God' (mAb 3.21 [15]). The claim that only Israelites were thought to be images of God,[53] and that the dictum refers only to the Jewish people, overlooks the continuation of R. Akiba's words: 'Beloved is Israel that they are called children of God, etc.', which proves clearly that the first sentence does not refer to Israel. The acknowledgement of the unity of mankind, and the recognition of the basic principle of the election of man as God's image, does not diminish in any sense the special status of Israel as the people to whom special love was shown by giving them the instrument with which the world was created, the Torah. This is what is new about normative self-definition in this period: the precise balance of the universalism and particularism.

Unity of mankind

The prevailing conception of the unity of mankind, notwithstanding its differences and peculiarities, is conveyed in the following story which also probably belongs to the time of R. Akiba:

> A Gentile inquired of R. Joshua, saying to him: 'You have festivals and we have festivals, when you rejoice we do not rejoice and when we rejoice you do not rejoice. When do we both rejoice?' [R. Joshua said] 'When the rain falls.' 'Why so?' 'Because it is written: 'The meadows are clothed with flocks'' (Ps. 65.14). What follows? "Shout unto God all the earth" (66.1). The Priests, Levites and Israelites are not enumerated, but all the earth.'[54]

Another interpretation in a similar spirit and style is transmitted according to one source by R. Jeremiah and to another source by R. Meir, both from the second half of the second century. The wording of Lev. 18.5: 'You shall therefore keep my statutes and my judgments which a man shall do and live by them' is given the following interpretation: 'Whence do we know that even a Gentile who occupies himself with the Torah is like a high priest? Scripture teaches "which a man shall do and live by them". It does not say the Torah of the Priests, Levites and Israelites but "And this is the Torah of man". And furthermore, it does not say "Open the gates that the Priests, Levites and Israelites may come in", but that the righteous Gentile who keeps faith may come in.'[55] It is still my opinion that the word *goy* here does not apply only to 'semi-proselytes', or even to 'God-fearers', but to Gentiles who have shown an interest in Judaism and its teachings. Nevertheless, the explanation which I have given elsewhere,[56] that a statement like that of R. Jeremiah is the outcome of a personal experience with exceptional individuals, righteous Gentiles who had stood by the Jews in hours of adversity, does not seem to be adequate. Personal experience may have played a certain role, but the tenor of conclusions drawn from such experience is determined by the predilections and mentality of the person who has experienced them. It is not a coincidence that the R. Joshua, who suggested a day of rejoicing common to Jews and Gentiles, is the same sage who argues against the view of his colleague, R. Eliezer b. Hyrcanus, and declares: 'There are righteous men among the nations who have a share in the world to come' (tSanh 13.2). One might also find a connection between the teaching attributed to R. Meir concerning a Gentile studying Torah and the incident reported about his disciple, Judah b. Shamua, who pleaded to the Roman officials on behalf of his people: 'In the name of heaven, are we not your brethren? Are we not the children of our father? Why are we different from all other nations that you impose harsh duress upon us?'[57] It is thus that self-affirmation may base itself on an appeal to common humanity. We should bear in mind, however, that not all the dicta and precepts of the sages are intended to demonstrate fundamental concepts; some of them are immediate reactions to specific circumstances without any practical implication.

We may find such an example in the much-discussed baraita concerning charity as practised by Gentiles, which reports that Rabban Johanan b. Zakkai reversed his teaching concerning

Gentiles (bBB 10b). He had previously stated: 'Just as the sin-offering makes atonement for Israel, so charity makes atonement for the Gentiles', but he subsequently endorsed the interpretation of Prov. 14.34, by one of his pupils, according to which it is affirmed: 'Righteousness exalts a nation – this is Israel; and the kindness of other nations is sin.' I once suggested[58] that there seems to be a connection between the reported change in R. Johanan's appreciation of the charity of Gentiles and his reaction towards the outcry of despair by his pupil R. Joshua. When the latter saw the temple in ruins, he exclaimed: 'Woe unto us that this place, the place where the iniquities of Israel were atoned for, is laid waste.' R. Johanan said to him: 'My son, be not grieved; we have another atonement like this one. And what is it? It is acts of loving kindness, as it is said, "For I desire mercy and not sacrifices"' (Hos. 6.6). R. Johanan b. Zakkai does not deny the atoning force of sacrifice, but in the prevailing circumstances he stresses the atoning quality of compassion and loving kindness. Formerly, when Israel had the temple and the sacrifices as a means of atonement, the practice of charity made atonement possible for the nations of the world; now, however, the destruction of the temple has deprived them of the means of atonement. Just as the answer to R. Joshua does not express the fundamental view of R. Johanan towards sacrifice, so his acceptance of the interpretation of Prov. 10.34 does not constitute a reversal of his attitude towards Gentiles. Both are immediate reactions to the destruction of the temple and to the necessity of self-affirmation.

About two centuries later the namesake of R. Johanan b. Zakkai, the Amora R. Johanan, is credited with the dictum: 'A Gentile who studies the Torah renders himself deserving of death' (bSanh 59a). Can this be thought to demonstrate an isolationist policy? We should first note that the same R. Johanan also states: 'Any affliction in which Israel and the Gentiles are partners is an affliction, but any affliction of Israel by itself is not an affliction' (DeutR 2.22). The common denominator between Israel and the Gentiles is not only limited to times of affliction. This Amora also concerned himself with the problem of atonement for the sins of Gentiles. His school is to be credited with the idea that the seventy bullocks offered during the seven days of the Sukkot festival correspond to the seventy nations of the world. He himself exclaimed: 'Woe to the nations of the world, for they had a loss and do not know what they have lost. When the temple was in existence the altar atoned for them, but now who shall atone for them?'[59] This exclamation reminds us of the attitude towards this question of his great namesake, R. Johanan b. Zakkai. The Amora R. Johanan also interpreted the verse, 'You sit and speak against your brother; you slander your own mother's son?' (Ps. 50.20): 'If you have accustomed your tongue to speak against your brother who is not of your nation, you will eventually slander the son of your own nation' (DeutR 6.9; Tanhuma Pequde 7). This dictum, like the last quoted, does not suggest an approach of exclusiveness. How then are we to explain the dictum (bSanh 59a) concerning a Gentile who studies the Torah? What category of 'Gentile' is meant by R. Johanan? The answer is clearly indicated in the continuation of his sentence in which he explains: 'Because scripture says, "Moses commanded us a Torah, an inheritance (*moraša*) of the congregation of Jacob.' Read not an "inheritance" (*moraša*) but (*meorasa*), a "betrothal".' The testimony adduced only makes sense if it is directed against Gentiles who study the Torah in order to claim that its inheritance is no longer the right of 'Israel of the flesh' but of the 'new Israel', the 'Israel of the spirit'.

By the middle of the third century such a claim was well known from the writings of the founders of Christianity. It is interesting that the redactor of the Babylonian Talmud, who was less conscious of the claims of Christians than the scholars in Eres Israel, confronted the dictum of R. Johanan with that of R. Meir and solved the contradiction by limiting the positive attitude of R. Meir to Gentiles who study the Noachian laws and the condemnation of R. Johanan to those who study the other portions of the Torah. But this differentiation renders the proof adduced by R. Johanan from scripture meaningless. We may find support for our suggestion in the juxtaposition of another dictum of R. Johanan with an earlier teaching. According to this tannaitic midrash, 'Whoever disavows idolatry acknowledges the whole Torah',[60] a dictum which probably belongs to a time of widespread proselytization, when not all would-be converts were expected to embrace full Judaism. R. Johanan said instead (bMeg 13a): 'Everyone who disavows idolatry is called a Jew, as it is written, "There are Jewish men whom you have appointed over the affairs of Babylon. . .who serve not your gods nor worship the golden image which you have set up" ' (Dan. 3.12). The point of departure of the dictum of R. Johanan is the fact that Mordecai is called a *yehudi* while he was actually a descendant of the tribe of Benjamin. Thus true negators of idolatry are Jews. In practice, however, R. Johanan encouraged 'the bringing of people beneath the wings of the Shekinah', i.e. their full acceptance of Judaism. If we are correct in our understanding of the dictum concerning Gentiles who study Torah, we may also be able to uncover the meaning of another enigmatic pronouncement by R. Johanan. He said 'Gentiles outside Ereṣ Israel are not idolaters; they are merely keeping to their ancestral customs' (bHull 13b). Here the Gentiles outside Ereṣ Israel are contrasted with those in Ereṣ Israel who are not keeping to their ancestral customs. By these, R. Johanan could only mean the Christians, whether pagans who had adopted Christianity or Judaeo-Christians of different sorts. These are, no doubt, the same people whom he had excluded from the study of Torah, and whose gospel he calls *ʿavon gilayon*. Although he held that the manifold heresies were responsible for the exile of Israel from its land,[61] at the same time he stated the opinion that whoever says a wise thing, even among the nations of the world, is called a sage (bMeg 16a).

Conclusion

Let us now return to the question we set at the beginning of our discussion. Can the sources of the first three centuries CE be thought to reflect in any way an increasing inclination towards self-isolation? It seems to me that the sources we have analysed do not justify existing assertions that the anxious and zealous fixation on the letter of the Torah, or the hedges which rabbinic Judaism built around the Torah, resulted in manifest opposition by its exponents to a more open attitude towards the outside world.[62] Even those sages who considered the Jewish concepts of religion to be fundamentally different from those of other peoples recognized that certain mental attitudes and predispositions are common to all men. The intense interest evinced by the sages in the outside world was furthered by the contacts existing between Jews in the homeland and those of the Diaspora. The visits undertaken by many of these scholars to Alexandria, Rome and other Mediterranean cities augmented their intimate knowledge of the conditions of their environment. Nevertheless, their consciousness of the distinction between Israel and the other nations is emphatic. It goes together with the distinction between light and darkness, sacred and profane, Sabbath and weekdays, as it is formulated in the Havdalah blessing recited at the termination of the Sabbath and festivals (bPes 103b; pBer 5.2; 9b). Nevertheless, with all the emphasis put upon this distinction, we cannot discern any traces of an idealization of self-segregation. Even sages who expressed particularistic or exclusive views were not opposed to proselytism, but welcomed it. On the other hand, even the most enthusiastic advocates of proselytism were strongly opposed to missionary activities based upon and fulfilled by a conception of Judaism which entailed national self-surrender. In the contemporary conditions, the affirmation of faith could only be guarded against the dangers of syncretism from a standpoint of religious and national unity. The attraction of proselytes was considered to be dependent upon the conduct of Israel. It was to uphold this conduct that the sages erected fences and hedges around the Torah. They did not do so for the purpose of self-isolation, but of self-affirmation. R. Oshaia said in the third century: 'To what may the matter be compared? To a man watching a garden. If he watches it from without, the whole of it is watched; if he watches it from within, the section before him is watched and the section behind him is not watched' (bYeb 21a). The watcher of the garden, however, left the doors open to those who were ready to enter. In their relations with other nations, most of the sages would have satisfied themselves with the declaration of Micah (4.5): 'For all people will walk every one in the name of his God and we will walk in the name of the Lord our God for ever and ever.' Those who cherished a greater attachment to the prophecy of Zephaniah (3.9) – 'thus will I turn to the peoples a pure language, that they may all call upon the name of the Lord, to serve him with one consent' – would have been more inclined to expect its realization in an eschatological future.

Notes

1 Interpretation and the Tendency to Sectarianism: an Aspect of Second Temple History

1. Ezra 2.64 (= Neh. 7.66) has 42,360 for the *aliyah* led by Zerubbabel but this number is too high. Only a small percentage of the population was taken into captivity in the first place – 4,600 according to Jer. 52.30 which, however, may not include women and children – and only a small percentage of the next two generations would have returned.

2. *haggolah* (Ezra 1.11; 9.4; 10.6), *bene haggolah* (Ezra 4.1; 8.35; 10.7,16); *bene galuta'* (Ezra 6.16); *shebi haggolah* (Ezra 2.1; 6.19f.); *haqqahal* or *kol-haqqahal*, a Deuteronomic term, cf. Deut. 23.1 (Ezra 2.64; 10.1, 12, 14; Neh. 5.13; 8.2,17) or *qehal haggolah* (Ezra 10.8); *zera' haqqodesh* (Ezra 9.2; cf. Isa. 6.13, a gloss which probably refers to the post-exilic community, as is clearer in 1QIsa); *zera' yiśra'el* (Neh. 9.2).

3. Ezek. 11.15, 17.

4. Specific stipulations in Deut. forbid intermarriage with the natives (7.3–4) and exclude certain categories from membership in the *qahal* (23.2–7). The Holiness Code (H), however, is probably also involved, especially Lev. 18.24–30 and 20.24–26 where the separation of Israel from the nations is made to correspond to the distinction between clean and unclean. The same stem (*bdl*) is often used in Ezra-Neh. with reference to the separation of the *golah* from the *'amme-ha'ares* (Ezra 6.21; 8.24; 10.8, 11, 16; Neh. 9.2; 10.29; 13.3, 28).

5. *kol hannibdal mittum'at goye-ha'ares* (Ezra 6.21; cf. Neh. 9.2).

6. Taking the view, implied by the text, that the Artaxerxes in question was the first of that name. It should be added that the current tendency is to opt for Artaxerxes II, and therefore for a later date (398 BCE), but the arguments are not decisive.

7. Ezra 10.1–44. It is assumed that title to property was contingent on membership in the cultic community; see Ezek. 11.15, 17; Lev. 25.23.

8. Neh. 9.2; 10.29–31. Chapters 9 and 10 may not, however, have been originally connected.

9. Neh. 13.1–9, 23–30. In general, Nehemiah's reforms follow the Deuteronomic law: Neh. 5.6–13; cf. Deut. 23.20; Neh. 10.30 and 13.25; cf. Deut. 7.3; Neh. 10.31b; cf. Deut. 15.1–3; Neh. 13.10; cf. Deut. 14.27–29.

10. Ezra 9.11f.; 10.11; Neh. 9.2; 10.29–40; 13.1–3.

11. Ezra 10.5; Neh. 10.1, 30. The 'excommunication formula' occurs
at Ezra 10.8 and Neh. 5.13 (*wehu' yibbadel miqqehal haggolah*); cf. the
formula in H and P (*nikretah hannepesh hahi' me'ammeha*), e.g. Lev. 7.20;
17.4. At Isa. 66.5, where the brethren of those who 'tremble at his
word' cast them out, there occurs *niddāh*, common in Mishnaic Hebrew. On excommunication in rabbinic literature see C.-H. Hunzinger,
'Spuren Pharisäischer Institutionen in der frühen rabbinischen Überlieferung', *Tradition und Glaube*, 1971, pp. 147–56.

12. Henri Cazelles, 'La mission d'Esdras', *VT* 4, 1954, pp. 113ff.; E.
Sellin and G. Fohrer, *Introduction to the Old Testament*, ET 1968, p. 192;
G. Fohrer, *History of Israelite Religion*, ET 1972, pp. 358f.; R. J. Coggins,
The Books of Ezra and Nehemiah, 1976, p. 108.

13. 'The law of your God which is in your hand (*bidak*)' (Ezra 7.14;
cf. v. 25) has led to this conclusion, but *bidak* need not be translated so
literally.

14. Deut. 4.6 especially, but also 1.13, 15; 16.19; 34.9.

15. Ezra 9–10; cf. Deut. 7.1–4.

16. Neh. 10.30; cf. Deut. 7.1–4; 10.31a; cf. Deut. 5.12–15; 10.31b; cf.
Deut. 15.1–5, but also Lev. 25.2–7; 10.35–39 (first fruits and tithes); cf.
Deut. 26.1–11; 14.22–29; 18.4. See also n. 9 above.

17. Neh. 7.73b–8.18; cf. Lev. 23.33–43.

18. Deut. 15.1–3 deals with the remission of debts and Lev. 25.2–7
with the release of crops.

19. Ex. 30.11–16 (P) stipulates a half-shekel; II Chron. 24.6 does not
specify the amount, but since both here and in the Nehemiah covenant
it is a question of the Mosaic law (Neh. 10.30), it would be reasonable
to conclude that the law known to the Chronicler specified one-third
of a shekel. The half-shekel does not seem to be attested before the
Roman period (*Ant.* III. 194–6; *Bell.* V. 187; VII. 218; Matt. 17.24; Philo,
Leg. spec. I.77f.). The wood offering (see also Neh. 13.31), at a later
time brought nine times every year (mTaan 4.5), is based on Lev.
6.5f.(P).

20. Chron. refers frequently to 'the law of Yahweh' (I 16.40; 22.12;
II 17.7–9; 31.3f.; 34.14), 'the commandments of Yahweh' (I 28.7f.; II
24.20), 'the statutes and ordinances' (I 22.13; II 7.17), 'the commandment of Moses' (II 8.12), 'the law of Moses (the man of God)' (II 23.12;
30.16), 'the book of Moses' (II 25.4), 'the book of the law' (II 34.15),
'the book of the covenant' (II 34.30f.) and uses 'scriptural' formulae –
'as it is written' (*kakkatub*) (I 16.40; II 23.18; 25.4; 30.5, 18; 31.3) and
others like it (I 6.34; 15.15; 24.19; II 7.17; 8.12; 30.16; 33.8). II Chron.
25.4 (= II Kings 14.6) is interesting since a specific quotation from
Deut. 24.16 is presented as belonging to 'the law, the book of Moses'.
While Chron. follows the Deuteronomic History, and even intensifies
some of its characteristic features (e.g. divine retribution), it takes ritual
laws from P (I 6.34; 16.40; II 2.3; 13.11 [cf. Ezra 3.2–6]; 24.6; 26.17f.;
31.4 [cf. Neh. 10.35–7]) which suggests that it was felt necessary to
supplement D with P.

21. The 'law for the king' (Deut. 17.14–20), for example, could hardly have been part of a law-code sanctioned by the Persian government.

22. During Nehemiah's governorship the great fast and penance was held on the 24th day of the seventh month (Neh. 9.1), no doubt in keeping with the commemorative fast instituted during the exile or shortly after the return (Zech. 7.5; 8.19). According to H (Lev. 23.27–32) and P (Lev. 16.29–34), however, the fast of *yom hakkippurim* falls on the 10th day of the seventh month.

23. Thus, the elaboration of an oral law and the position that later stipulations simply render explicit what is implicitly contained in re-vealed law imply canonicity. We are assuming further that the editorial history of the Pentateuch in the post-exilic period – on which much work still remains to be done (of the kind being done by R. Rendtorff; see his *Das überlieferungsgeschichtliche Problem des Pentateuch*, 1977) – must be seen as a process leading to a canonical law and narrative. In this respect I concur with Brevard S. Childs's statement that 'essential to understanding the growth of the canon is to see this interaction between a developing corpus of authoritative literature and the com-munity which treasured it', *Introduction to the Old Testament as Scripture*, 1979, p. 58.

24. Commemorating different stages in the capture and destruction of Jerusalem and the temple.

25. Divorce is not prohibited in the Pentateuch; in fact Deut. 24.1–4 presupposes that it is licit. Mal. 2.16 does not actually say it is pro-hibited but that it is hateful to Yahweh.

26. According to bTaan 28a prophets returned from exile decided on the wood offering, and the earlier prophets (i.e. Samuel and David) established the twenty-four *mishmarot* each one of which was repre-sented in turn at the temple by its *ma'amad* (bTaan 26a, 27a). Thus both of these had prophetic warranty of sorts, though according to another attestation (bShabb 104a) prophets were not allowed to introduce new ordinances. On the Maccabean innovations see Elias Bickerman, *From Ezra to the Last of the Maccabees*, 1962, first published 1947, pp. 99 (fighting on sabbath), 118–21 (Sukkoth in Kislev), 130f. (Day of Nica-nor). It may be added that Esther was problematic because of Purim; hence the insistence of Tannaitic scholars that it was authored by the Holy Spirit (bMeg 7a). The much discussed absence of Esther fragments at Qumran may be due to the fact that the group did not celebrate this festival; see Sid Z. Leiman, *The Canonization of Hebrew Scripture*, 1976, p. 35. Bickerman, *From Ezra*, p. 62, also notes that Jubilees claims divine warranty for the ritual precepts of greater severity than those in the Pentateuch which it contains.

27. On 11QPs[a] see James A. Sanders, 'Cave 11 Surprises and the Question of Canon', *New Directions in Biblical Archaeology* (ed. Freedman and Greenfield), 1969, pp. 101ff.; 'The Qumran Psalm Scroll (11QPs[a]) Reviewed', *On Language, Culture and Religion* (ed. Black and Smalley), 1974, pp. 79–99; 'Text and Canon: Concepts and Method', *JBL* 98, 1979, pp. 5–29, especially p. 25; M. H. Goshen-Gottstein, 'The Psalms Scroll

(11QPsᵃ) – A Problem of Canon and Text', *Textus* 5, 1966, pp. 22ff.; S. Talmon, 'The Textual Study of the Bible – A New Outlook', *Qumran and the History of the Biblical Text* (ed. Cross and Talmon), 1975, pp. 378ff. On the significance for canon of the Temple Scroll see Yigael Yadin, *Megillat Ha-Miqdash* I, 1978, pp. 298–300.

28. Isa. 56.1–8; cf. Deut. 23.2–9 and Ezek. 44.7f.

29. As against the restrictive practices of the Qumran community (e.g. 1QS 11. 20–22) early Christianity shared with Pharisaism (cf. Matt. 23.15) an openness to proselytes, though the programmatic statement at Gal. 3.28 annulling the distinction between Jew and Greek, slave and free, male and female – with its remarkable correspondence to a well-known prayer in the Siddur – was not necessarily typical of all early Christian churches. There were clearly many points of dispute about conditions for membership: e.g. as reflected in Acts 15.

30. Hag. 1.2; cf. Zech. 1.12; 7.5.

31. Isa. 66.1–4. It goes against the most obvious sense of vv. 3f. to interpret them as a polemic against syncretism, as in Claus Westermann, *Isaiah 40–66*, ET 1975, pp. 413f.

32. Especially Acts 7.2–53, on which see Marcel Simon, *St Stephen and the Hellenists in the Primitive Church*, 1958; *Jewish Sects at the Time of Jesus*, ET 1967, pp. 99–103.

33. One of the accusations levelled at Antiochus IV is that he changed 'the times and the law' (Dan. 7.25). For the importance of the calendar in Jubilees, Enoch and at Qumran see the remarks of D. S. Russell, *The Method and Message of Jewish Apocalyptic*, 1964, pp. 54, 61, 208f. Morton Smith, 'The Dead Sea Sect in Relation to Ancient Judaism', *NTS* 7, 1960–61, pp. 351f., emphasizes the importance of the interpretation of purity laws for the formation of sects.

34. See especially Isa. 57.1f., 20f.; 65.1–16; 66.1–5, 18–24. It is doubtful whether the situation was as clear-cut as Paul D. Hanson, *The Dawn of Apocalyptic*, 1975, suggests. While we reserve evaluation of his thesis until later, we may note his treatment of Isa. 63.16 which is taken to presuppose the rejection of a minority by the community as a whole designated as 'Abraham' and 'Israel' (pp. 92ff.). In this instance the context makes it clear that what is said cannot be construed to refer to a prophetic minority ostracized by the majority, for the writer speaks of the community to which he belongs as Yahweh's people, the tribes of his heritage, his servants, *whose temple and cities have been destroyed*. It would therefore more naturally refer to a sense of alienation from the community's ancient traditions and founding events.

35. Isa. 66.2, 5. On the verb *niddah* used here, see n. 11.

36. E.g. Pss. 12; 37; 86; 116; 142.

37. Apart from these four instances (Isa. 66.2, 5; Ezra 9.4; 10.3) the verbal adjective occurs only twice in the Hebrew Bible (Judg. 7.3; I Sam. 4.13). The specific religious sense, attested in all cases except Judg. 7.3, is associated not so much with awe but fear (Eli's fear for the fate of the ark) and scrupulous dread of violating the law. In three of the four relevant instances the object is the word or words of

Yahweh and in the fourth (Ezra 10.3) his commandment (*miṣwah*). It is precisely this regularity of usage which suggests that this may be a title of a group of strict observants (cf. Ebionites).

38. See especially Isa. 60.1f., 5a, 7; 61.10f. Isa. 66.14 reads like a response to the taunts of the 'brethren'.

39. See J. Blenkinsopp, *Prophecy and Canon*, 1977, pp. 120–3.

40. *she'erit (ha'am)*, Hag. 1.12, 14; 2.2; Zech. 8.6, 11; *peleṭah*, Ezra 9.8, 13–15; Neh. 1.2; Joel 2.3; 3.5 ('as Yahweh has said' perhaps refers to a text such as Isa. 4.2; cf. 10.20; 37.31f.); *'abde YHWH*, Isa. 56.6; 63.17; 65.9, 13–15; 66.14; *matta' YHWH*, Isa. 61.3; cf. *neser matta'i*, 60.21. The same term occurs in the Damascus Document (CD I 5–12) apparently with reference to the early *hasidim*; see also 1QS 8.5 and 11.8; I En. 93.5; *zera' haqqodesh*, Ezra 9.2; cf. Neh. 9.2; Isa. 6.13b (an important gloss; 1QIsa has *zera' haqqodesh* as at Ezra 9.2).

41. E.g. the appointed time at Mark 1.15 and in the eschatological discourse in Matt. 24. On the earlier interpretations of the saying see Peter R. Ackroyd, *Exile and Restoration*, 1968, pp. 90, 153, 175f., 240ff.; 'Two Historical Problems of the Early Persian Period', *JNES* 17, 1958, pp. 23–7; C. F. Whitley, 'The Term "Seventy Years Captivity" ', *VT* 4, 1954, pp. 60–72; also *VT* 7, 1957, pp. 416–418; P. Grelot, 'Soixante-dix semaines d'années', *Bibl* 50, 1959, pp. 169–86; G. R. Driver, 'Sacred Numbers and Round Figures', *Promise and Fulfilment*, 1963, pp. 62–90.

42. *semah* (Jer. 25.3; 33.15) at Zech. 3.8 and 6.12; *hotam* (Jer. 22.24) at Hag. 2.23. Through LXX, which translates *semah* as *anatolē*, with the possibility of a shift of meaning from something rising from the ground to a star rising in the sky, this title entered early Christianity (Matt. 2.2, 9; Luke 1.78).

43. E.g. II Macc. 2.1–8, the tradition that Jeremiah hid the tent, ark and altar of incense in a cave until the last days; 15.12–16, the vision of Jeremiah giving a golden sword to Judas Maccabee seen by Onias III; II Macc. 7 and IV Macc. 8–17 (cf. Assumpt. Mos. 9.1–7), the mother and seven sons which seems to be based on Jer. 15.9; Dan. 9, reinterpretation of the seventy weeks; Matt. 16.14, the belief that Jesus was Jeremiah *redivivus*, etc. Professor James Charlesworth has also drawn my attention to I-IV Bar. and *The Abode of the Rechabites* as part of this 'Jeremiah tradition'.

44. 'His servants the prophets' (Zech. 1.6) is a Deuteronomic expression: I Kings 14.18; 15.28; 18.36; II Kings 9.7, 36; 10.10; 14.25; 17.13, 23; 21.10; 24.2; Jer. 7.25; 25.4; 26.5; 29.19; 35.15; 44.4; Amos 3.7 (a Deuteronomic insertion); 'the former prophets': Zech. 1.4; 7.12.

45. Zech. 1.19 etc. At 1.12 the angel refers to Jer. 25.12 (the seventy years); the smiths (1.20) seem to refer to Isa. 54.16f.; the man with the measuring line (2.5) is reminiscent of Jer. 31.38–40 and Ezek. 47.3. The 'man' whom Ezekiel encounters in vision (8.2; 40.3) has something in common with Zech., but he does not interpret and answer questions. The *angelus interpres* will reappear in Daniel.

46. Hag. 1.13; Mal. 3.1; cf. v. 23.

47. Zech. 1.12; 1.14 (*koh 'amar YHWH*).

48. The pattern appears most clearly in Revelation.

49. The Jonah legend appears to contain a critique of salvation-prophecy, which implied unconditional judgment on hostile nations, on the basis of the more enlightened prophetic teaching of repentance in Ezek. 18.23 and especially Jer. 18.7f.

50. BBB 12a; also the ratification of Pharisaic practices with reference to the *bath qol*, the surrogate for prophecy (bErub 21b; cf. bSan 11a; bYoma 9b).

51. For a discussion of the issues see my *Prophecy and Canon*, pp. 96–138.

52. It will be noted that most of the studies of Old Testament prophecy give little attention to the Second Temple period. The following deal with one aspect or another of that history: A. Jepsen, *NABI. Soziologische Studien zur alttestamentlichen Literatur und Religionsgeschichte*, 1934; Adolphe Lods, *The Prophets and the Rise of Judaism*, ET 1937; A. R. Johnson, *The Cultic Prophet in Ancient Israel*, ²1962; T. Chary, *Les prophètes et le culte à partir de l'exil*, 1955; E. Hammershaimb, *Some Aspects of Old Testament Prophecy from Isaiah to Malachi*, 1966, pp. 91–112; O. Steck, *Israel und das gewaltsame Geschick der Propheten*, 1967, and 'Das Problem theologischer Strömungen in nachexilischer Zeit', *EvTh* 28, 1968, 447f.; P. Grech, 'Interprophetic Re-Interpretation and Old Testament Eschatology', *Augustinianum* 9, 1969, pp. 242f.; Bruce Vawter, 'Apocalyptic: Its Relation to Prophecy', *CBQ* 22, 1960, pp. 33–46; D. L. Petersen, *Late Israelite Prophecy*, 1977; J. Vermeylen, *Du prophète Isaïe à l'apocalyptique*, 1977.

53. Otto Plöger, *Theocracy und Eschatology*, ET 1968.

54. Martin Hengel, *Judaism and Hellenism*, ET 1974, Vol. I, p. 176; also Vol. II, p. 118 n. 462, for some of the principal reviews; see also my *Prophecy and Canon*, pp. 114–6.

55. *Theocracy and Eschatology*, p. 24.

56. Morton Smith, *Parties and Politics that Shaped the Old Testament*, 1971.

57. *Parties and Politics*, p. 111; see also his paper 'The Dead Sea Sect in Relation to Ancient Judaism', *NTS* 7, 1960–61, pp. 351f.

58. He speaks of Nehemiah as founder of a Deuteronomic sect but wonders whether this may not be retrojection of a sect existing at the time of the Chronicler, 'The Dead Sea Sect', pp. 354, 358f.

59. Frank Moore Cross, Jr, 'New Directions in the Study of Apocalyptic', *Journal for Theology and Church. 6: Apocalypticism*, 1969, pp. 157–65; *Canaanite Myth and Hebrew Epic*, 1973, pp. 343–6.

60. E.g. the date of the final edition of the Pentateuch, Job and Chron. On the last named see W. F. Albright, 'The Date and Personality of the Chronicler', *JBL* 40, 1921, pp. 104–24 (the Chronicler is identified with Ezra and the Pentateuch essentially complete by the end of the sixth century); David Noel Freedman, 'The Chronicler's Purpose', *CBQ* 23, 1961, pp. 436–42, and 'Canon of the Old Testament', *IDBSupp*, p. 123; Frank Moore Cross, Jr, 'A Reconstruction of the Judean Restoration', *Interp* 29, 1975, pp. 187–201.

61. Paul D. Hanson, *The Dawn of Apocalyptic*, and earlier papers, 'Old Testament Apocalyptic Re-examined', *Interp* 25, 1971, pp. 454–79; 'Jewish Apocalyptic against its Near Eastern Environment', *RB* 78, 1971, pp. 31–58; 'Zechariah 9 and the Recapitulation of an Ancient Ritual Pattern', *JBL* 92, 1973, pp. 37–59.

62. E.g. to describe the Zadokite or Temple party (allowing for the moment the propriety of these terms) as anti-eschatological leaves one wondering about the visionary and apocalyptic-like elements in Ezek. inclusive of 40–48, and the supportive role of Hag. and Zech. to whom, incidentally, he gives little attention. It may be noted, in passing, that Viktor Aptowitzer, *Parteipolitik der Hasmonäerzeit im rabbinischen und pseudoepigraphischen Schrifttum*, 1927, traced the Sadducees to the Zadokite party represented by the high priest Joshua and the Pharisees to their enemies the (non-Zadokite) Ithamarites, the traditionalist party, represented by Ezra.

63. *Dawn of Apocalyptic*, p. 29.

64. See Hengel, *Judaism and Hellenism* I, pp. 180–96, 88f. on Egyptian and Babylonian apocalyptic texts of the Graeco-Syrian period, especially the Demotic Chronicle, the Potter's Oracle and Berossus.

65. See notes 23, 26 and 27 above. As Sid Z. Leiman has shown, *The Canonization of Hebrew Scripture*, pp. 120ff., the idea that the canon was 'fixed' at Yavneh must now be laid to rest, an idea which seems to go back to H. E. Ryle's *The Canon of the Old Testament*, published in 1892, and to presuppose a 'Council of Jamnia' comparable to those of Nicaea or Chalcedon. Against Leiman, however, I do not believe that anything which can be called canonization took place before Yavneh.

66. Ben Sira 7.29–31; 35.1–11; 45.6–24; 49.11f.; 50.1–21.

67. The function of the eschatological Elijah is described in terms borrowed from Isa. 49.6. Ben Sira 48.10 is the earliest known interpretation of Mal. 3.23f.

68. Using the verb *darash*, cf. the *doresh hattorah* of Qumran.

69. Temple scribes are mentioned in a decree of Antiochus III; Josephus, *Ant*. XII.142; cf. XI.128. For the situation after the exile see Hag. 2.11–13; Zech. 7.2; Mal. 2.6f.; Ezra 7.11f.; Josephus, *Bell*. III.252; *Vita* 8; Test. Levi 13.2–6 etc.

70. Josephus, *Ap*. I.41, on which see my 'Prophecy and Priesthood in Josephus', *JJS* 25, 1974, pp. 250f.

71. See my *Prophecy and Canon*, pp. 116f., and the references given in the notes.

72. Even more clearly if we read *nibba'* at 50.27b ('. . . who out of his heart prophesied wisdom'); see Hengel, *Judaism and Hellenism* II, p. 89, n. 199.

73. We do not know whether this was associated either with the temple or the synagogue; the influence of Greek *paideia* may well have led to schools or academies quite independent of both. We cannot easily imagine Qoheleth lecturing in such explicitly religious and traditional settings.

74. See my *Prophecy and Canon*, pp. 24–9, for a summary and references covering the period prior to Deut.

75. II Sam. 8.17; 20.25; I Kings 4.2f.; II Kings 12.10; 22.3–10.

76. E.g. Deut. 1.13; 4.6; 16.19; 32.6, 29.

77. See also his condemnation of the 'handlers of the Law' (*tośepe-hattorah*) at 2.8, a class which is there distinguished from priests, shepherds (rulers) and prophets.

78. I Chron. 24.6 (under David), II Chron. 34.13 (under Josiah). Levites toured the country giving instruction in the Law under Jehoshaphat (II Chron. 17.7–9).

79. Ezra 7.6, 11; Neh. 8.1 etc. During the great assembly of the seventh month Ezra read the Law and the Levites helped the people understand it (Neh. 8.7). The precise meaning of the next verse is unclear, much depending on the translation of *meporash*. The most likely sense is that of a running commentary or exposition, as implied by NEB.

80. Ezra too enjoyed a kind of prophetic inspiration since the hand of Yahweh (a phrase taken from the old prophetic tradition) was on him (Ezra 7.6, 28; cf. Ezek. 1.3; 3.22 etc.).

81. Elias Bickerman, *Der Gott der Makkabäer*, 1937.

82. *Der Gott der Makkabäer*, pp. 126–33; Hengel, *Judaism and Hellenism* I, pp. 258–60.

83. Jason (Jesus), brother of Onias III, bought the high priesthood from Antiochus IV and intensified efforts already initiated by the 'lawless men' to introduce the Greek way of life (II Macc. 4.7–17). Jason was eventually outbid by Menelaus (Menahem), a Tobiad (II Macc. 4.23–29) who was executed in 162.

84. I Macc. 1.41–50; II Macc. 6.1–11. It is essential to Bickerman's thesis that the edict was in reality the work of the 'Greek party' led by Menelaus (*Der Gott der Makkabäer*, pp. 120–6; Martin Hengel, *Judaism and Hellenism* I, pp. 288f.), a view which seems to be supported by Josephus (especially *Ant.* XII.240).

85. For indications of pre-Maccabean *hasidim* see below, pp. 21f.

86. Language reminiscent of the warlike Nazirites and Levites of early Israel; cf. also II Chron. 17.16, referring to a certain Amasiah during the reign of Jehoshaphat, a volunteer for the service of Yahweh (*hammitnaddeb laYHWH*), accompanied by *gibbore-hayil*. Victor Tcherikover, *Hellenistic Civilization and the Jews*, repr. 1975, p. 199, has correctly emphasized the warlike character of these *hasidim*.

87. II Macc. is an abridged edition of a five-volume history by Jason of Cyrene covering the years 176–160. It was probably composed around the beginning of the first century BCE. The author had a high regard for the Zadokite priesthood, passed over in silence the assumption of the high priesthood by the successors of Judas, praised the strict observance of the laws and the willingness to die rather than transgress them (e.g. the scribe Eleazar, 6.18–31), believed in the resurrection of the just (7.9ff.; 14.46), intercession for the dead (12.39–45),

and the intervention of angels (e.g. in the legend of Heliodorus, 3.22–30).

88. I Macc. 3.13 speaks of ἐκκλησία πιστῶν which accompanied Judas into battle. Parallelism between *hasidim* and *'emunim* in certain psalms (12.2; 31.24) suggests that this term (= πιστοί) may also refer to Asidaeans.

89. As argued by Plöger, *Theocracy and Eschatology*, passim, and *Das Buch Daniel*, 1965, p. 30.

90. The crisis will not be overcome by human means (8.25); when the *maśkilim* fall they shall receive 'a little help' (11.34), doubtless referring to the Maccabees whose intervention dates from a mature point in the struggle against the 'reform party'.

91. It was his successor Jason who took the initiative in introducing Greek ways (II Macc. 4.7–17). The death of Onias III is probably referred to at Dan. 9.26 and 11.22, as also at I En. 90.8. The Damascus Document (CD 6.2f.) speaks of *mebonim* and *hakamim*, interpreters of the Law, who were raised up by God during the troubles preceding the foundation of the community for which the rule was written, in all likelihood the Qumran community. H. H. Rowley, *The Zadokite Fragments and the Dead Sea Scrolls*, 1952, pp. 67ff., identified Onias with the *moreh hassedeq*.

92. Dan. 12.3; the *maśkilim* will turn many to righteousness (*masdiqe ha-rabbim*) cf. Isa. 53.11 (*yasdiq saddiq 'abdi la-rabbim*).

93. Dan. 7.18, 22, 27. That 'the saints' may refer primarily to the heavenly hosts led by Michael, with whom the faithful on earth are associated in their struggle, seems plausible, and is confirmed by Qumran beliefs, especially in the War Scroll (1QM). See J. J. Collins, 'The Son of Man and the Saints of the Most High in the Book of Daniel', *JBL* 93, 1974, pp. 50–66.

94. As argued by Hengel, *Judaism and Hellenism* I, pp. 29f., following Aage Bentzen, *Daniel*, ²1952, pp. 29ff. On the ethos and setting of the stories see W. L. Humphreys, 'A Life-style for Diaspora: A Study of the Tales of Esther and Daniel', *JBL* 92, 1973, pp. 211ff.; J. J. Collins, *The Apocalyptic Vision of the Book of Daniel*, 1977, pp. 36ff.

95. See also Dan. 11.33f.; I Macc. 1.60–64; II Macc. 6.7–7.41.

96. E.g. Dan. 4.10, 'the watcher, the holy one' who came down from heaven in Nebuchadnezzar's dream; 6.22, the angel who saved Daniel in the lions' den; the angel-interpreter of the visions: 7.16; 8.13f.,16–26 (Gabriel); 9.21; 10.5–14; 10.18–11.1; 12.1 (Michael); 12.5–7. Angelic activity is also in evidence in II Macc., e.g. 3.22–30; III Macc. 6.18; IV Macc. 4.10 and especially in En. and several Qumran texts.

97. Dan. 4.21; cf. 2.36; 5.26. Vocabulary and structure may be taken to reflect exegetical practice among the early *hasidim*.

98. Especially the 'formula quotations' in Matt., on which see Krister Stendahl, *The School of Saint Matthew*, ²1968, pp. 181–202.

99. 1QS 1. 22-2. 1. Note the similarity in form: *na'awinu* [*pasha'nu, hata*]'*nu, hirsha'nu* (1QS 1. 24f.); *hata'nu, 'awinu, hirsha'nu, maradnu* (Dan. 9.5).

100. For Wellhausen see my *Prophecy and Canon*, pp. 17–23. While Walther Eichrodt, *Theology of the Old Testament*, ET, 2 vols, 1961, 1967, does not follow the developmental model of Wellhausen, he consistently portrays the later biblical and post-biblical period as dominated by legalism and in a state of decline and dissolution (e.g. I, pp. 63f., 169, 258; II, pp. 299, 313, 315, 464).

101. Martin Noth, *The Laws in the Pentateuch and Other Essays*, ET 1966, pp. 85–107, especially 106f. On this issue see most recently A. H. J. Gunneweg, *Understanding the Old Testament*, ET 1978, pp. 125–8.

102. E.g. II Chron. 15.12–15, Asa's covenant and oath; 29.10, Hezekiah; 34.31f., Josiah; Neh. 10.1.

103. Dan. 11.28,30; I Macc. 1.15; 2.20 etc.; Jub. 23.19. The Qumran covenanters refer to themselves frequently as *berit, berit hadashah, berit ʿolam, yahad berit ʿolam*.

104. There are some interesting but perhaps inconclusive indications of connections of some kind between the *hasidim* and Levites. The adjective *maśkil(im)* is used of Levites at II Chron. 30.22 and some psalms which have been suspected of deriving from early hasidic circles (see n. 108) are ascribed to levitical authorship (i.e. Pss. 50; 79; 85). The description of the *asidaioi* at I Macc. 2.42–44 as 'mighty men of Israel' is reminiscent of the warlike Levites of early Israelite tradition, and Levites play a role in the holy war in Chron. and the Qumran War Scroll (1QM). Geza Vermès, *The Dead Sea Scrolls in English*, 1968, pp. 22–25, has argued that the Qumran *maśkil* was a Levite.

105. The so-called Book of Noah (especially 1 En. 6–11) and the Apocalypse of Weeks (91.12–17; 93) are widely thought to be pre-Maccabean. For an up-to-date assessment see Michael Stone, 'The Book of Enoch and Judaism in the Third Century BCE', *CBQ* 40, 1978, pp. 479ff. The extremely speculative and esoteric nature of this material suggests that it does not come from the same circles as Daniel.

106. I Macc. 1.24b–28, 36–40; 2.6–13; 3.3–9, 45, 50–53; 7.17, 37f.; 9.21; 14.4–15; Dan. 2.20–23; 3.33; 4.34f.; 6.26f.

107. E.g. Ps.16, in which the poet speaks of himself as *hasid* (v.10), refers to those who choose another god (v.4), speaks of prayerful watch and vigil at night (v.7); Ps. 37, which runs through the whole nomenclature of piety, speaks of the wisdom of the *saddiq* and devotion to the law; in Ps. 50, of Asaphite origin, we hear of the covenant of the *hasidim*; Ps. 116.5 speaks of the death of the *hasid* and Ps. 149 is a hymn of praise performed in the *qehal hasidim*. One of the psalms from Qumran Cave 11 also speaks of the *qehal hasidim* and Ps. Sol.16 of the *synagōgai hosiōn*. James A. Sanders, *Discoveries in the Judaean Desert of Jordan IV. The Psalms Scroll of Qumran Cave 11*, 1965, pp. 64ff., thinks that the former may be proto-Essene or Hasidic.

108. See Stone, 'The Book of Enoch and Judaism in the Third Century BCE.'

109. Blenkinsopp, *Prophecy and Canon*, pp. 103-9.

110. E.g. sayings against Egypt in verse (Isa. 18.1-19.15) have been amplified by five *bayyom hahu'* prose passages introducing the theme

of eschatological reversal (curse to blessing) by referring to circumstances and events of the Jewish Diaspora in Egypt. The great judgment-poem in Isa. 2.6–22 is a particularly interesting case exhibiting a high level of exegetical activity including a *bayyom hahu'* prose addition (v. 20) and a manifestly apocalyptic *excipit* (v. 22). My study of the editorial history of this text is to appear in a future issue of *ZAW*.

111. ' . . . es ist der Versuch, jenes Moment der prophetischen Verkündigung zu verwirklichen, das über die deuteronomische Bewegung, die babylonische Gola in die Gemeinde Esras und Nehemias eingegangen ist, den heiligen Rest, das wahre Israel, darzustellen.' O. Plöger, 'Prophetisches Erbe in den Sekten des frühen Judentums', *ThLZ* 79, 1954, col. 293.

112. On the two historians see Hengel, *Judaism and Hellenism* I, pp. 88ff.

113. 1QS 5. 1,6; 6. 13; cf. II Chron. 17.16 (n. 87 above).

114. See Hengel, *Judaism and Hellenism* I, pp. 243f., on *yahad* = *to koinon*, with reference to the work of Bardtke, Schneider and Dombrowski; also Frank Moore Cross, Jr, *The Ancient Library of Qumran*, 1961, pp. 79f.

115. *Ant.* XIII. 171–3; XVIII. 12–15; a certain Judas described as *mantis* (not *prophētēs*) is mentioned at *Bell.* I. 78–80; *Ant.* XIII. 311–313; Menahem at *Ant.* XV. 371–9; Simon at *Bell* II. 111-113; *Ant.* XVII. 345–8.

116. The Deuteronomic prophet (Deut. 18.15–18) is referred to at 1QS 9.11 and in 4QTest. The same text was important for the Samaritans, Ebionites and other early Christian groups; see, e.g., John 1.21; 6.14; 7.40; Acts 3.22.

117. *perushim* may derive from *parash*, meaning 'withdraw' or 'secede', but other suggestions have been made. If Paul, himself a Pharisee, was making a pun at Rom. 1.1 when he speaks of being 'set aside for the gospel' (*aphōrismenos*), he may have understood it in the way suggested.

118. *Ant.* XIII. 288–98; cf. bKidd 66a where the ruler is Alexander Jannaeus. It should be added that Josephus had mentioned them earlier when dealing with the reign of Jonathan (*Ant.* XIII. 172f.) but without inferring that they were active then.

119. On Pharisee *prognōsis* see *Ant.* XV. 3,370; XVII. 41–3,172–6; on their veneration for the prophets, *Bell.* II.411; cf. Matt. 23.29ff.

120. See E. Schürer, *The History of the Jewish People in the Age of Jesus Christ* § 17.3 (2), ET, rev. ed., I, 1973, pp. 381f. with bibliography.

121. In general, early Christianity and Pharisaism had more in common than appears at first sight; friendly contacts receive special emphasis in Luke (7.36; 11.37; 13.31; 14.1).

122. Rudolph Meyer, *TDNT* VI, pp. 825f.

123. References in Christian sources are summarized in Marcel Simon, *Jewish Sects at the Time of Jesus*, 1967.

124. The point of view of the Qumran community is discussed in E. P. Sanders, *Paul and Palestinian Judaism*, 1977, pp. 244–55.

2 Christian and Jewish Self-Definition in Light of the Christian Additions to the Apocryphal Writings

1. For the sake of convenience, I am using the Christian terms 'Old Testament', 'Old Testament' Apocrypha, and 'Old Testament' Pseudepigrapha.

2. For a definition of Pseudepigrapha, see Charlesworth, *The Pseudepigrapha and Modern Research* 1976, pp. 17–25.

3. R. A. Kraft, 'Christian Transmission of Greek Jewish Scriptures: A Methodological Probe', *Paganisme, Judaïsme, Christianisme*, 1978, pp. 207–26.

4. See S. Pines, *An Arabic Version of the Testimonium Flavianum and its Implications*, 1971. The *testimonium flavianum* occurs in Josephus, *Ant.* XVIII. 63f. The parallel passage in the work of the tenth-century chronologist Agapius, *Kitāb al-'Unwān*, can be found in Pines' book; for the English see pp. 8–11, for the Arabic (and Josephus' Greek) see p. 14, for a juxtaposition of a literal English translation of the Arabic and Greek see pp. 16f. The only section of the Arabic text that looks suspiciously 'Christian', or not from Josephus, is the end: 'he was *perhaps* the Messiah. . . ' (Pines' italics).

5. See Turdeanu's publications in *Oxford Slavonic Papers*, ns 10, 1977, pp. 1–38; *Revue des Études Romaines* 13-14, 1974, pp. 163–94; 15, 1975, pp. 145–79, 180–86; and *Revue des Études Slaves* 47, 1968, pp. 53f. Recent books are the following: M. Loos, *Dualist Heresy in the Middle Ages*, 1974; B. Primov, *Les Bougres: Histoire du pope Bogomile et de ses adeptes*, 1975.

6. J. H. Charlesworth, 'The SNTS Pseudepigrapha Seminars at Tübingen and Paris on the Books of Enoch', *NTS* 25, 1979, pp. 315–23.

7. For discussions on the problems involved in discerning interpolations and distinguishing them from redactions, see Charlesworth, 'Reflections on the SNTS Pseudepigrapha Seminar at Duke on the Testaments of the Twelve Patriarchs', *NTS* 23, 1977, pp. 296–304.

8. K. Kohler, 'Über die Ursprünge und Grundformen der synagogalen Liturgie: Eine Studie', *MGWJ*, nf. 1, 1893, pp. 441–51, 489–97; idem, 'Didascalia', *JE* IV, pp. 588–94; idem, 'The Essene Version of the Seven Benedictions as Preserved in the VII Book of the Apostolic Constitutions', *HUCA* 1, 1924, pp. 410–25.

9. W. Bousset, 'Eine jüdische Gebetssammlung im siebenten Buch der apostolischen Konstitutionen', *Nachrichten von der Königlichen Gesellschaft der Wissenschaften zu Göttingen*, Philologisch-historische Klasse 1916, pp. 435–89.

10. E. R. Goodenough, 'The Mystic Liturgy', *By Light, Light: The Mystic Gospel of Hellenistic Judaism*, 1935, pp. 306–58. The translation of the Hellenistic Synagogal Prayers used herein is by Dr David Darnell and will be included in the new edition of the Pseudepigrapha to be published by Doubleday. I am grateful to Doubleday and the translators for permission to use the new translations. Italics denote Christian

interpolations. For further information on these prayers, especially the original language, date, and provenance, see the introduction in that volume. The Greek is from F. X. Funk, *Didascalia et Constitutiones Apostolorum*, 1905.

11. The poetic structure, unlike the Davidic Psalter, is not conveniently arranged into near parallel lines according to *parallelismus membrorum*; it is more similar to the poetic structure in the *Hodayot*, hence it is impossible to use poetic structure as a criterion to decide whether these prepositional phrases have been added. It would have been ideal, of course, if the length of parallel lines in poetic structure had been similar to the pre-Pauline Christological hymn in Phil. 2.6–11, in which Paul's addition at the end of v. 8, θανάτου δὲ σταυροῦ, can be discerned.

12. For the Hebrew text, English translation, and significant comments, see W. D. Davies, *The Setting of the Sermon on the Mount*, 1966, pp. 272–77. The *birkat ha-minim* was added perhaps by Samuel the Small around 85 CE, although it is also possible (and probable if E. E. Urbach is correct, see his discussion in ch. 12 below) that *minim* did not denote 'Christians' and that this specification was demanded and added much later. Scholars have tended to see the relations between Jews and Christians coming to a halt either around 85, the date frequently given to the *birkat ha-minim*, or after 131(2)–35, the dates of the Bar Kokhba revolt. It is clear, however, that both anti-Jewish feelings and philo-Judaism were strong among different Christian groups up until at least the fourth century. Polemical attacks against Judaizing Christians by John Chrysostom (esp. *Hom. adv. Jud.* 1.1; 1.3; 1.6 [PG 48, cols. 844, 847f., 852]) and prohibitions against entering the synagogues in the *Apostolic Constitutions* (2.61; 4.17; 6.27) demonstrate that Christians were frequenting the synagogues in the fourth century. See W. A. Meeks and R. L. Wilken, *Jews and Christians in Antioch in the First Four Centuries of the Common Era*, 1978, pp. 30–36.

13. See the discussions by M. de Jonge, 'Christian Influence in the Testaments of the Twelve Patriarchs', *Studies on the Testaments of the Twelve Patriarchs: Text and Interpretation*, ed. M. de Jonge, 1975, pp. 193–246. M. de Jonge accurately assesses the situation when he states of Test. Levi 18 that 'the redactor has done his work so thoroughly that it is very difficult to find the pre-Christian and possibly Essene elements' (p. 219). It is interesting to observe that de Jonge, who thinks that 'the Testaments are a Christian document written by a Christian author who used much Jewish material in composing it' (p. 195), here speaks not about an author but about a redactor. My own research convinces me that we should talk only about a Christian redactor or Christian redactors of the Testament.

14. For a judicious review of the contributions by scholars towards understanding that the Testaments are a Jewish document with Christian interpolations, see G. B. Coleman, *The Phenomenon of Christian Interpolations into Jewish Apocalyptic Texts* (Vanderbilt University, Ph.D.), 1976. For a discussion of recent research on the Testaments, see G.

Delling, 'Testamente der zwölf Patriarchen', *Bibliographie zur jüdisch-hellenistischen und intertestamentarischen Literatur 1900–1970*, ²1975, pp. 167–71; Charlesworth, 'Testaments of the Twelve Patriarchs', *The Pseudepigrapha and Modern Research*, pp. 211–20; and M. de Jonge (ed.), *Studies on the Testaments, passim.* For H. C. Kee's introduction and translation see the forthcoming Doubleday edition of the Pseudepigrapha. Kee's translation is used herein; italics denote (what I think are) Christian interpolations.

15. Against Schnapp and Bousset, both of whom argue that there was a single Christian interpolator, Charles argued that the evidence reveals 'a succession of interpolators'. See his important discussion of Christian interpolations and their character in 'Testaments of the XII Patriarchs', *HDB* IV, 1902, pp. 721–75. The selections of the interpolations to the Testaments discussed herein are those which may be by one scribe. Interpolations probably by different (and later) scribes are purposely excluded because of our present focus.

16. For recent discussions on these issues see Charlesworth, *NTS* 23, 1977, pp. 296–304.

17. This emphasis has appeared in many recent publications, see for example Charlesworth, 'Jewish Astrology in the Talmud, Pseudepigrapha, the Dead Sea Scrolls, and Early Palestinian Synagogues', *HTR* 70, 1977, pp. 183–200.

18. Charles, *HDB* IV, p. 722.

19. Ibid., p. 723; see J. Becker, *Untersuchungen zur Entstehungsgeschichte der Testamente der zwölf Patriarchen*, 1970, pp. 375f. H. D. Slingerland, after evaluating the fruits of research on the Testaments, states 'that the real value of the Testaments of the Twelve Patriarchs is its use as a primary source for the way of life of some ancient community or communities' (p. 113), and perceives his own monograph as 'a prolegomenon to the quest for the ancient Christian community which redacted or composed the Testaments' (p. 113). See his *The Testaments of the Twelve Patriarchs: A Critical History of Research*, 1977.

20. W. Bousset, 'Die Testamente der zwölf Patriarchen', *ZNW* 1, 1900, pp. 141–75, 187–209.

21. Charles, *HDB IV*, p. 722.

22. Unless otherwise noted the Greek is taken from M. de Jonge, *Testamenta XII Patriarcharum*, ²1970.

23. Kee in *The Pseudepigrapha of the Old Testament*, in press.

24. The Greek is from Charles's *The Greek Versions of the Testaments of the Twelve Patriarchs*, 1908, p. 48. A. Hultgård also claims that Test. Levi 10.2 has been redacted by a Christian. He believes, however, that only 'Saviour of the World' (de Jonge's text) constitutes the interpolation. He sees this interpolation to be Christian because of the influence from John 4.42 and I John 4.14 and the observation that in intertestamental Judaism God was not the Saviour of the World but the σωτὴρ τοῦ Ἰσραήλ (cf. I Macc. 4.30, III Macc. 7.16). These and many other very important observations are found in Hultgård's *L' eschatologie des Testaments des Douze Patriarches*, 1977, pp. 93f.

25. Here, I believe, we have a portion of a Jewish polemic against the priests who control the Jerusalem Temple. The date usually assigned to the Testaments, 100 BCE (see Charlesworth, *The Pseudepigrapha and Modern Research*, p. 212), would indicate that it shares these traditions with CD and 11QTemple.

26. Charles's text; my translation.

27. Charles's text; my translation.

28. Translation of the Armenian is by J. Issaverdens and can be found in his *The Uncanonical Writings of the Old Testament Found in the Armenian MSS of the Library of St Lazarus*, 1907, p. 319. Italics denote the words which I think were added by a Christian. Issaverdens' italics are removed.

29. See Charles in R. H. Charles (ed.), *The Apocrypha and Pseudepigrapha of the Old Testament* II, 1913, p. 359. His brackets are removed; my italics incorporated. The Greek excerpts of Test. Benj. 10 are from Charles's text.

30. Charles, *Pseudepigrapha*. His brackets deleted; my italics added.

31. If this argument is correct, then 'for their unrighteousness', is also part of the Christian redaction. The Jewish core – that is left before and after the redaction – would then have read, 'And the Lord shall judge Israel first [redaction]. And then shall He judge all the Gentiles [redaction].' Charles's translation; bracketed insertions mine.

32. Charles, *Pseudepigrapha*; his brackets omitted, my italics supplied.

33. Ibid.

34. See esp. S. van Tilborg, *The Jewish Leaders in Matthew*, 1972.

35. Charles, who is here followed by many commentators including Kee, argued that many of the christological additions are heretical. He claimed that some of the passages are docetic and others are patripassian. Even if some passages could be read as docetic, however, it is also obvious that the same applies to the Gospel of John. Some of the verses, such as Test. Sim. 6.10f., which have been considered to be patripassian, may in fact reflect Monarchianism, which in its early form was not necessarily heretical and simply maintained that Jesus was to be identified with God, because a power from the Father had rested upon him. It is wise to heed the well-recognized caution that we must not define as heretical ideas that were only much later considered to be heretical; triumphant orthodoxy must not be read back into earlier historical periods.

36. For bibliography and further discussion see Charlesworth, *The Pseudepigrapha and Modern Research*, pp. 125–30. The Greek and Latin excerpts are taken from R. H. Charles, *The Ascension of Isaiah*, 1900.

37. Translations from the Ascens. Isa. are by Michael Knibb; they will be published in the new edition of the Pseudepigrapha being prepared by Doubleday.

38. 'After two months of days' Mary, alone with Joseph, and a pregnant virgin, sees 'a small infant' and then observes, 'after her astonishment had worn off', that her womb was the same as before she had conceived (11.5–10). Joseph then also sees the infant. As with

Isaiah later (11.39), Joseph and Mary are commanded, 'Do not tell this vision to anyone' (11.11). Mary obviously did not need a midwife (11.14; cf. Odes of Solomon 19.9).

39. Perhaps we can see evidence of doctrinal dispute between the various Christian communities in at least two passages. In 9.13, there is an idea which might be seen as docetic; after Christ has descended there will be some who 'will think that he is flesh and a man'. The doctrine that Christ is to descend into Hades, the *descensus ad inferos*, is apparently denied in 10.8; according to this verse, the Father instructs the Son that he shall descend through the firmament and through the world 'as far as the angel who (is) in Sheol, but you shall not go as far as Perdition'.

40. E. P. Sanders even argues that the view of the principal author is '*that of the angel* in the dialogues'. The covenant no longer brings 'the benefits of God's protection from torment and even destruction. . . only the perfectly righteous, who are few, will be saved by God, and that only after suffering and pain', *Paul and Palestinian Judaism*, 1977, esp. p. 418, italics his.

41. All translations from IV Ezra are by B. M. Metzger and will appear in the Doubleday edition of the Pseudepigrapha. The source of the above Latin excerpts is R. L. Bensly, *The Fourth Book of Ezra: The Latin Version Edited from the MSS*, 1895.

42. Heraclitus's quotation is preserved in Plutarch, *De Pythiae oraculis* 6 (397A). The translation is by F. C. Babbit and taken from the Loeb edition. The Greek text and English translation are conveniently collected by J. J. Collins in his *The Sibylline Oracles of Egyptian Judaism*, 1974, pp. 1, 119. Translations of the Sibylline Oracles are by J. J. Collins and will appear in the Doubleday edition of the Pseudepigrapha.

43. The two Books that would have been numbered 9 and 10 are not lost; the confusion is caused by two distinct collections of the Sibylline Oracles in the manuscripts. The second collection contains Books '9' and 10', but these are identical with material found in Books 1–8 and, therefore, are omitted in editions.

44. The Greek is from J. Geffcken, *Die Oracula Sibyllina*, 1902.

45. A. Kurfess dates these Christian expansions 'to the period shortly after Hadrian; the date of composition is thus about 150. . .'. See his 'Christian Sibyllines' in *NT Apoc* II, p. 708. In his introduction to the Sibylline Oracles in the Doubleday edition of the Pseudepigrapha, Collins dates the Christian expansions to Books 1 and 2 'no later than AD 150'.

46. Kurfess argued that Book 7, which dates from the end of the second century, used Book 6: *NTApoc* II, p. 708. Collins, however, is not persuaded by Kurfess's argument and cautions that all that is certain is that Book 6 antedates Lactantius, who quotes from it.

47. Kurfess characterizes Book 7 as a form of 'gnosticizing' and dates it near the end of the second century: *NTApoc* II, p. 708. Collins cautions that the data will not permit us to assign a date to Book 7; the best that can be said is that it predates Lactantius, who used it.

48. J. Geffcken, *Komposition und Entstehungszeit der Oracula Sibyllina*, 1902, esp. pp. 34–37.

49. Kurfess, *NTApoc* II, p. 708.

50. J. G. Gager, 'Some Attempts to Label the *Oracula Sibyllina*, Book 7', *HTR* 65, 1972, pp. 91–7.

51. Collins in the Doubleday edition of the Pseudepigrapha.

52. S. Pines demonstrates that in a tenth-century treatise of ʿAbd al-Jabbār, which contains interpolations from Jewish Christian traditions, there is abundant evidence of major rifts within Christianity. Reminiscent of some passages in Ascens. Isa. is the claim by Jewish Christians that 'the Christians' have abandoned 'the religion of Christ'. Pines astutely observes that Jewish Christians may have found 'coexistence with Jews' easier than with 'Christians' (p. 44). Pines is arguing for the possibility that Jewish Christians 'may have intermingled with and exercised a certain influence on Jewish sects' (p. 44). We have seen evidence of a reverse influence, and that could increase the possibilities Pines has perceived. See Pines, *The Jewish Christians of the Early Centuries of Christianity According to a New Source*, 1966. Also see R. A. Kraft's judicious review of this booklet in *JBL* 86, 1967, pp. 329f., and R. McL. Wilson's cautions about the importance of the document in 'The New Passion of Jesus in the Light of the New Testament and Apocrypha', *Neotestamentica et Semitica* (ed. Ellis and Wilcox), 1969, pp. 264–71. Research on Jewish Christianity is greatly facilitated by A. F. J. Klijn and G. J. Reinink's *Patristic Evidence for Jewish-Christian Sects*, 1973.

53. At the same time, the 'Jewish community, overwhelmingly, continued to recognize the basically legal character of Judaism, as is evident from the creation of the Talmud, both the Palestinian and Babylonian versions': H. M. Orlinsky, *The Bible as Law: God and Israel under Contract*, 1978, p. 19.

54. Morton Smith, 'Early Christianity and Judaism', *Great Confrontations in Jewish History* (ed. Wagner and Breck), 1977, p. 41, demonstrates how 'the emergence of Christianity and rabbinic Judaism as distinct entities' was 'a gradual process of distinction and definition'. With Smith we have seen that Christianity evolved during the first two centuries in and through 'conflicts with other Jewish groups'. After this period, as Smith states, 'two practically independent religions' 'live side by side' evolving 'principally by the needs of their own internal developments, not by their relation to each other' (p. 61).

3 Inspiration and Canonicity: Reflections on the Formation of the Biblical Canon

1. S. Z. Leiman, *The Canonization of Hebrew Scripture*, pp. 9f.

2. See bMeg 7a and the discussion in Leiman, *Canonization*, pp. 102–20.

3. See bMeg 14a: 'Many prophets arose in Israel, even double the

number of Israelites who came out of Egypt. But only prophecies required for all generations were written down.'

It may be that by 'written down' the rabbis intended 'included in the biblical canon'. Cf. the usage of *ktb* at bYom 29a. Thus, the rabbis may have recognized that much of what the biblical authors had to say was reduced to writing without being accorded biblical status – precisely because it was not required for all generations. See especially tYad 2.14.

4. Leiman, *Canonization*, pp. 132–5 and notes.

5. Cf. M. Smith, *Palestinian Parties and Politics that Shaped the Old Testament*, 1971, pp. 148–50.

6. For purposes of this presentation, I have excluded the talmudic justifications for the ban against reading Ben Sira. These talmudic justifications are probably later than Jerome; they are ambiguous; and in the case of the Babylonian Talmud, the justification relates to a late, faulty, and otherwise unknown version of Ben Sira. See Leiman, *Canonization*, pp. 86–102 and notes.

7. Jerome, *Comm. in Hier.* V.67 (CCSL 74, pp. 284f.).

8. Origen, *Ep. ad Africanum* 8 (PG 11, cols. 64f.).

9. For related Jewish traditions see L. Ginzberg, *Legends of the Jews* VI, 1928, p. 426 n. 106. Add R. Kasher, 'Ha-Toseftot ha-Targumiyot le-Haftarat Shabbat Ḥanukkah', *Tarbiz* 45, 1975–6, pp. 41–2, and correct J. Braverman, *Jerome's Commentary on Daniel*, 1978, p. 129 n. 16, accordingly.

10. For the translation, see J. Braverman, *Jerome's Commentary*, p. 128. The original Latin (see above, n. 7) reads as follows: 'Aiunt Hebraei hos esse presbyteros, qui fecerint stultitiam in Israhel et moechati sunt uxores ciuium suorum, quorum uni loquitur Danihel: inueterate dierum malorum et alteri: semen Chanaam et non Iuda, species decepit te et concupiscentia peruertit cor tuum! Sic faciebatis filiabus Israhel et illae metuentes loquebantur uobiscum; sed non filia Iudae sustinuit iniquitatem uestram. Quodque propheta nunc loquitur: et locuti sunt uerbum in nomine meo mendaciter, quod non mandaui eis, illud significari putant, quod miseras mulierculas, quae circumferuntur omni uento doctrinae, sic deceperint, quo dicerent eis, quia de tribu erant Iuda, Christum de suo semine esse generandum; quae inlectae cupidine praebebant corpora sua quasi matres futurae Christi. Sed illud, quod in praesentiarum dicitur: quos frixit rex Babylonis in igne, uidetur Danihelis historiae contraire. Ille enim asserit eos ad sententiam Danihelis a populo esse lapidatos; hic uero scriptum est, quod frixerit eos rex Babylonis in igne. Unde et a plerisque ac paene omnibus Hebraeis ipsa quasi fabula non recipitur nec legitur in synagogis eorum. "Qui enim", inquit, "fieri poterat, ut captiui lapidandi principes et prophetas suos haberent potestatem?" Magisque hoc esse uerum affirmant, quod scribit Hieremias, conuictos quidem esse presbyteros a Danihele, sed latam in eos sententiam a rege Babylonis, qui in captiuos ut uictor et dominus habebat imperium.'

11. Z. H. Chajes, *Kol Sifre MaHaRaTS Ḥayot* I, 1958, pp. 94–5.

12. See bSanh 52b and Rashi's comments ad loc.

13. See mSanh 5.2; cf. mMakk 1.4.

14. S. Zeitlin, 'An Historical Study of the Canonization of the Hebrew Scriptures', *PAAJR* 3, 1930–31, pp. 121–58. Cf. his 'Jewish Apocryphal Literature', *JQR* 40, 1949–50, pp. 223–50.

15. Zeitlin, 'An Historical Study', p. 149. Cf. Zeitlin's views on Susanna, ibid., pp. 149–51, which echo those of Chajes. Zeitlin's disciple, S. B. Hoenig, repeats his mentor's views in the entry 'Susanna', *IDB* IV, pp. 467f. See also H. M. Orlinsky, 'The Canonization of the Bible and the Exclusion of the Apocrypha', in his *Essays in Biblical Culture and Bible Translation*, 1974, especially pp. 277–86; and his 'The Septuagint as Holy Writ and the Philosophy of the Translators', *HUCA* 46, 1975, p. 100 n. 14. Cf. C. A. Moore, *Daniel, Esther, and Jeremiah: The Additions*, 1977, pp. 80f.

16. Rudolf Meyer, *TDNT* III, p. 982.

17. For an early rabbinic adumbration of modern scholarly discussion of the problem, see D. Hoffmann (ed.), *Midrasch Tanna'im* II, Berlin 1909, p. 159, bottom. For the definitive modern treatment, see M. Greenberg, 'Some Postulates of Biblical Criminal Law', in *The Jewish Expression* (ed. Goldin), 1976, pp. 18–37.

18. Especially instructive is the fact that Jerome's informant was unaware of the discrepancy between the book of Susanna and talmudic teaching regarding conflict of testimony. Apparently, what was obvious and decisive for Chajes and Zeitlin was of no consequence for Jerome's informant.

19. A similar phenomenon occurred in the medieval period when the Zohar assumed canonical status among the Kabbalists. The fact that its teaching conflicted at times with talmudic teaching and with the received halakah was noticed, but did not prevent it from assuming canonical status even among such ranking talmudists as Joseph Karo and Elijah Gaon of Vilna.

20. By 'sacred texts', religious (*sifre qodesh*) rather than secular (*sifre hol*) or profane writings are intended. Such religious writings are studied (by some) and venerated (by all) but are not accorded biblical status.

21. Leiman, *Canonization*, pp. 16–204.

22. It was precisely the inspired status of these biblical books that was at stake in the rabbinic discussions. As to why their inspired status was suspect, see Leiman, *Canonization*, p. 132.

23. So already Zeitlin, 'Jewish Apocryphal Literature', p. 233.

24. For possible evidence that some rabbinic authorities accorded Ben Sira biblical status, see Leiman, *Canonization*, p. 81 and notes 343 and 345; p. 99 and notes 470 and 471. If indeed some rabbinic authorities accorded Ben Sira biblical status, it is likely that those authorities dated Ben Sira to Simon I, who in rabbinic sources was viewed as a contemporary of the last of the prophets and of Alexander the Great. For the rabbinic sources on Simon I, see J. M. Grintz, מבואי מקרא, Tel Aviv 1972, pp. 36–7. For an early dating of Ben Sira, see R. H. Charles

(ed.), *The Apocrypha and Pseudepigrapha of the Old Testament* I, pp. 293–4, and cf. E. Rivkin, 'Ben Sira and the Nonexistence of the Synagogue', in *In the Time of Harvest*, 1963, pp. 348–50 (Appendix A).

25. Leiman, *Canonization*, pp. 92–102.

26. For the historian, these two enterprises (the history of the formation of the biblical canon *vis-à-vis* the role played by the biblical canon in history) must not be confused. Such confusion appears to be the trademark of many who engage in so-called canon criticism, about which I shall have more to say elsewhere. Suffice to say here that while both enterprises merit the careful attention of modern scholarship, they are hardly interchangeable parts.

4 Jewish Acceptance and Rejection of Hellenism

1. J. G. Droysen, *Geschichte des Hellenismus*, 1836–43; ²1877–78.

2. See Arnaldo Momigliano, 'Hellenism', *EJ* VIII, 1972, col. 291, and *Essays in Ancient and Modern Historiography*, Middletown, Connecticut 1977, pp. 307–12.

3. Walter Bauer, *Wörterbuch zum Neuen Testament*, ⁵1958, col. 499; ET, *A Greek-English Lexicon of the New Testament*, ²1979, pp. 251f.; G. W. H. Lampe, *A Patristic Greek Lexicon*, 1961–68, p. 451b; cf. H. Windisch, *'Hellēn'*, *TDNT* II, pp. 507–16.

4. II Macc. 2.21.

5. II Macc. 4.13; much later, Tacitus (*Hist.* V.8.2) recorded the false tradition that Antiochus IV had tried to impose Greek ways upon the Jews; see Jonathan A. Goldstein, *I Maccabees*, 1976, pp. 131–59, 250f.

6. M. Hengel, *Judaism and Hellenism*, ET, 2 vols., 1974.

7. Ibid. I, p. 252.

8. See, e.g., Hecataeus of Abdera apud Josephus, *Ap.* I.190–93. On the authenticity of the passage, see below, n. 62.

9. See Werner Jaeger, *Paideia*, ET, 3 vols., 1939–45.

10. II Macc. 12.19, 24.

11. II Macc. 7; the author finds it necessary to mention the fact that on occasion the martyrs speak, not Greek, but 'the ancestral language' (vv. 8, 21, 27).

12. The greater part of the protest literature of the conquered peoples was indeed directed against the Greek-speaking rulers. See the perceptive remarks of Samuel K. Eddy, *The King Is Dead*, 1961, pp. 333f.

13. See David Lelyveld, *Aligarh's First Generation*, 1978.

14. Greeks resented the fact that *Hellenized* Jews would not worship Greek gods; see, e.g., Josephus, *Ant.* XII.125.

15. See below, pp. 73–84.

16. See Martin P. Nilsson, *Die hellenistische Schule*, 1955; Henri I. Marrou, *A History of Education in Antiquity*, ET 1964, pp. 147–86 (to be corrected by Nilsson, pp. 34–42), 256–60; Jean Delorme, *Gymnasion*, 1960.

17. M. I. Rostovtzeff, *The Social and Economic History of the Hellenistic World*, 2 vols., ²1957.

18. Ex. 23.31–33; 34.15f.; Deut. 20.15–19; cf. Ex. 23.23f. Ideally, the Promised Land should be defined by the borders given in Num. 32.33–42; 34.1–15; and Josh. 15–19, including the holdings of the Transjordanian tribes, who surely were bound by the laws against idolatry. If the Jews could not hold all of the promised territory, they were still bound to enforce the Torah in whatever part of it they controlled.

19. Josh. 9.3–27; cf. Deut. 20.10–15.

20. Ezra 9.1f.; Neh. 9.2.

21. Neh. 13.24.

22. Mek. Pisha 5 (Lauterbach, I, pp. 34, 36).

23. Ex. 22.23–24; Lev. 18.3–30; cf. Deut. 20.19; II Kings 17.8–12.

24. See below, n. 113.

25. I shall discuss the origins and date of Dan. 1–6 in my commentary on Daniel. Though there are some later interpolations, the basic stuff of the chapters was written well before the time of Alexander the Great. For argument placing Jewish acceptance of Dan. 1–6 as early as the second half of the third century BCE, see Elias Bickerman, *Four Strange Books of the Bible*, 1967, pp. 92, 100.

26. For a general treatment of the confrontation in the second century BCE, see Gaston Colin, *Rome et la Grèce de 200 à 146 avant Jésus-Christ*, 1905, pp. 348–72.

27. Plautus, *Bacchides* IV.4.101–2 (742–43); *Mostellaria* I.1.21 (22) and I.1.61 (64); Titinius apud Paulus Diaconus (ed. Müller), p. 215, line 5. Cf. Horace, *Satires* II.2.11.

28. Cicero, *Pro Flacco* 11–12, 23; *Post reditum in Senatu* 6.14; *In Pisonem* 29.70; *De oratore* 1.47 and 102; *Epistulae ad Quintum fratrem* I.1.

29. Polybius XXXIX.1; Plutarch, *Cato Major* 3.7.

30. See Jacques Heurgon, *The Rise of Rome to 264 B.C.*, 1973, pp. 75–94, 239–44.

31. Pliny, *Historia naturalis* VII.30.113.

32. Valerius Maximus, *Factorum et dictorum memorabilium libri* II.2.2; Cicero, *In Verrem* II.4.66, §147.

33. Cicero, *Academica priora* II.2.5; Plutarch, *Cato Major* 22.1–23.3; Gellius XV.11.1; Valerius Maximus, *Factorum* IV.3.6; Plutarch, *Pyrrhus* 20.3–4; Suetonius, *De rhetoribus* 1; Athenaeus XII.547a. Plautus, *Curculio* II.3.9–19 (288–98) may be a blast against philosophers, but it could also be a mere attack on Greek parasites.

34. *Post reditum in Senatu* 6.14.

35. Cato, *Oratio* apud Gellius I.15.8, and *Carmen de moribus* apud Gellius XI.2; *M. Catonis praeter librum de re rustica quae extant* (ed. Henricus Jordan), Lipsiae 1860, pp. 58, 83. Cf. Cicero, *De re publica* IV.9.

36. Cato, quoted by Pliny, *Historia naturalis* XXIX.7.14. Cf. Livy XXIX.19, where Scipio is condemned for reading Greek books, and Cicero, *Academica priora* II.2.5.

37. Livy XXIX.19; Plutarch, *Cato Major* 3.7; cf. Cicero, *De re publica* IV.4.

38. Cicero, *Epistulae ad Atticum* II.4.7; Delorme, *Gymnasion*, pp. 223–432.

39. Livy, *Periocha* XLVIII; Velleius Paterculus I.15; Valerius Maximus II.4.2; Augustine, *De civitate Dei* I.31; Tertullian, *Apol.* 6; *De spectaculis* 10; Colin, *Rome et la Grèce*, pp. 370f. Cf. Cicero, *De re publica* IV.10.

40. Plautus, *Asinaria* I.3.47–49 (199–201); Colin, *Rome et la Grèce*, p. 364; Fritz Pringsheim, *The Greek Law of Sale*, 1950, pp. 87–92.

41. Cicero, *Epistulae ad Quintum fratrem* I.1.

42. The confrontation continued, long beyond the fall of the Roman republic. See Juvenal III.60–125.

43. Lampe, *Lexicon*, p. 451b.

44. Cf. Windisch, '*Hellēn*', *TDNT* II, pp. 507–8. One of the most frequent meanings of *yavan* in Jewish texts is 'the Seleucid empire', and *yevani* then correspondingly means 'of the Seleucid empire'. See Goldstein, *I Maccabees*, p. 192. Mere Jewish opposition to rule by a foreign empire, even if that empire bears the name 'Greece', is not to be viewed as Jewish opposition to Hellenism. On the references in Jewish literature to the real confrontation with the Seleucid Antiochus IV, see below, pp. 75–81.

45. Windisch, *TDNT* II, pp. 509–16; Lampe, *Lexicon*, p. 451b. Pagan writers seem to have followed the same practice as Paul and the church Fathers, in opposing 'Jew' to 'Greek'. See Menahem Stern, *Greek and Latin Authors on Jews and Judaism* I, 1974, pp. 96 (Hermippus of Smyrna apud Origen, *Contra Celsum* I.15 [GCS I, p. 67]), 145–7, 152–54 and 410–12 (Poseidonius, Apollonius Molon, and Apion apud Josephus, *Ap.* II.89–96), 218 (Nicolaus of Damascus, *Historiae*, apud Josephus, *Ant.* XII.125–26), and 252 and 254 (Nicolaus of Damascus, *De vita sua*, apud Constantinus Porphyrogenitus, *Excerpta de insidiis* [ed. de Boor], pp. 2f.); cf. Julian, *Adv. Gal.* 229c–230a and *Fragmenta breviora* 6, and the pagan spokesman (Porphyry?) quoted apud Eusebius, *Praep. evang.* I.2.1–4. Hellenized Jews, it would appear, usually did not wish to give the impression that they were not Greeks, whereas pagan Greeks, especially those who were anti-Jewish, found the antithesis natural. Thus, Paul and the church Fathers may be reflecting pagan Greek, rather than Jewish usage.

46. Windisch, *TDNT* II, pp. 507f.

47. I shall treat the document at II Macc. 11.23–26 in my commentary to II Maccabees. For the present, see Christian Habicht, 'Royal Documents in Maccabees II', *Harvard Studies in Classical Philology* 80, 1976, pp. 7–10, 15–17.

48. *Judaism and Hellenism* I, pp. 6–266.

49. Clearchus apud Josephus, *Ap.* I.176–83; Hecataeus of Abdera apud Diodorus XI.3 and apud Josephus, *Ap.* I.183–204 (see below, n. 62); Victor A. Tcherikover and Alexander Fuks, *CPJ* I. A brief survey of the archaeological evidence can be found in the notes to Morton Smith, *Palestinian Parties and Politics that Shaped the Old Testament*, 1971, pp. 57–81.

50. See Elias Bickerman, *Studies in Jewish and Christian History* I, 1976, pp. 167–200.

51. See George W. E. Nickelsburg, 'Apocalyptic and Myth in 1 Enoch 6–11', *JBL* 96, 1977, pp. 383–405; cf. *Sib. Or.* 3.105–57 (but there the author pretends to be a pagan Greek).

52. Noteworthy are the following, though we lack clear evidence for dating them in the first of our four periods: (i) The Orphic Hymn apud Pseudo-Justin, *Cohortatio ad gentiles* 15 and Eusebius, *Praep. evang.* XIII.12. See Nikolaus Walter, *Der Thoraausleger Aristobulos*, 1964, pp. 184–86, 202–61; Yehoshua Gutman, *The Beginnings of Jewish-Hellenistic Literature* I, 1958, pp. 148–70 (in Hebrew). (ii) The epic *On Jerusalem* of Philo the poet apud Eusebius, op. cit., IX.20, 24, and 37. See Y. Gutman, 'Philo the Epic Poet', *SH* 1, 1954, pp. 36–63. (iii) The Tragedy *Exagogē* by Ezekiel apud Eusebius, op. cit. IX.28.4; 29.16. See Gutman, *Beginnings* II, pp. 9–65 [in Hebrew]. (iv) *Sib. Or.*, especially Book 3. See John J. Collins, *The Sibylline Oracles of Egyptian Judaism*, 1974.

53. Hecataeus of Abdera (see above, n. 49, and below, n. 62); Megasthenes apud Clement of Alexandria, *Stromateis* I.15.72.5 (GCS 2, p. 46); see Gutman, *Beginnings* I, pp. 39–107.

54. Aristobulus apud Eusebius, *Praep. evang.* XIII.12.1.

55. Hengel, *Judaism and Hellenism* I, pp. 115–52.

56. Hengel (ibid. II, p. 105 n. 372) does not accept Morton Smith's confident assertion ('The Image of God', *BJRL* 40, 1958, p. 474), that ὁ ὤν at Greek Ex. 3.14 reflects Platonic vocabulary. Plato, however, on a few occasions may have used τὸ ὄν (not ὁ ὤν) to mean 'God'; see *Phaedo* 65c, *Republic* VI.501d, VII.518c and 537d, and IX.582c; hence, Smith may be right.

57. Hengel, *Judaism and Hellenism* I, pp. 131–53.

58. Ben Sira 36.9–17 is an exceedingly bold prayer asking God to overthrow the foreign rulers, even if the enemy is not named. We have taken care to exclude from our study expressions of mere opposition to foreign rule. Otherwise, in Ben Sira's book, the only attacks on non-Jews are in 50.25–26. Mentioned there are the inhabitants of Seir (i.e., the Idumaeans) and of Philistia, as well as that foolish nation that dwells in Shechem (i.e., the Samaritans). Of these, only the inhabitants of Philistia could at all be called Greeks, and even they were probably still regarded as non-Greek; see Goldstein, *I Maccabees*, pp. 260, 420–21. The Greek manuscripts of Ben Sira, instead of 'Seir' have 'the mountain of Samaria'. If correct, that reading might refer to the Graeco-Macedonian military colony in the city of Samaria; see Goldstein, *I Maccabees*, pp. 245f. Even then, Ben Sira does not attack them as Greeks or even as pagans, but only as vexatious neighbours. He does not bother to praise Nehemiah or the high priest Simeon II for seeing to the separation of Jews from Gentiles.

59. See Gutman, *Beginnings* I, pp. 129–31.

60. Cf. *Aristeas* 121.

61. Hecataeus apud Diodorus XL.3.4; cf. Diodorus XXXIV–XXXV.1.2–3 (from Poseidonius?).

62. Hecataeus apud Josephus, *Ap.* I.193. On the authenticity of the passage, see Hans Lewy, 'Hekataios von Abdera', *ZNW* 31, 1932, pp. 117–32; Gutman, *Beginnings* I, pp. 66–71. Menahem Stern (*Greek and Latin Authors on Jews and Judaism* I, pp. 21–24) still has doubts about the passage of interest to us, because Josephus quotes Hecataeus as *admiring* the Jews for destroying pagan shrines and altars. Hecataeus, however, is known to have shared Plato's admiration for peoples who adhered tenaciously to their own laws. It is not inconceivable that Hecataeus and Plato could have admired even Jewish abhorrence of idolatry. No one has shown why Hecataeus could not have admired the Jews for adhering to their own laws. Even as a Jewish forgery, the passage would be important testimony for our purposes: it would attest that long before the time of Josephus it was believed that Jews in the days of Hecataeus did not tolerate pagan worship on their own soil. In this case, the evidence of the lack of pagan settlement in Judaea proper, which we are about to consider, would confirm the veracity of the hypothetical forger's testimony.

Ruinous punishment for tolerating idolatry even of pagans on the holy soil: Ex. 34.13f.; Deut. 7.25f.; I Kings 11.1–13; 18.18f. (many of the prophets of Baal probably came with Jezebel from Tyre). Cf. Philo, *Legat.* 200–2; Josephus, *Ant.* XVIII.120–22.

63. I Kings 8.41–43.

64. II Macc. 2.12; 3.2; Josephus, *Ant.* XII.138–41.

65. Victor Tcherikover, *Hellenistic Civilization and the Jews*, 1959, pp. 431f. n. 73.

66. Tcherikover and Fuks, *CPJ* I, Nos. 2a and 2b. For the archaeological finds, see above, n. 49.

67. II Macc. 4.28f. The garrison was so small it did not even attempt to restore order during the riot against Lysimachus (vv. 40–42).

68. II Macc. 14.14; I Macc. 1.34; 3.36; Dan. 11.39.

69. See Joseph A. Fitzmyer, 'The Languages of Palestine in the First Century A.D.', *CBQ* 32, 1970, pp. 502f., 507–12.

70. Contrast Babylon, where a theatre was built early in the Hellenistic age. Even if the theatre was built by Greek settlers, not by Hellenized Babylonians, the contrast with Judaea remains. The gymnasium at Babylon seems to have been founded later than the theatre. See Erich Schmidt, 'Die Griechen in Babylon und das Weiterleben ihrer Kultur', *Archäologischer Anzeiger*, 1941, pp. 834–44; Delorme, *Gymnasion*, pp. 431f., 475, 483f.; A. Mallwitz, 'Das Theater von Babylon', in F. Wetzel, E. Schmidt and A. Mallwitz, *Das Babylon der Spätzeit*, 1957, pp. 17–27.

71. E.g., the Jews of Alexandria; see Josephus, *Bell.* II.488 and Salo W. Baron, *A Social and Religious History of the Jews*, ²1952, I, pp. 188, 380f. (n. 29).

72. I Macc. 1.11–14; II Macc. 4.7–9.

73. On all this, see Goldstein, *I Maccabees*, pp. 162, 173 n. 4.

74. II Macc. 4.7–10; Goldstein, *I Maccabees*, pp. 104–21.

75. II Macc. 4.11: Josephus, *Ant.* XII.138–46; see E. Bickerman, 'La

charte séleucide de Jérusalem', *REJ* 100, 1935, pp. 4–35; Élie Bikerman [*sic*], 'Une proclamation séleucide relative au temple de Jérusalem', *Syria* 25, 1946–48, pp. 67–85.

76. See n. 47.

77. The document cannot refer to the decrees of Antiochus IV which imposed a 'pagan' cult upon the Jews. As I have shown, the imposed cult was not Greek (Goldstein, *I Maccabees*, pp. 131–58). Thus, 'the changeover to Greek practices' must be an expression referring to the decrees on behalf of Jason the high priest. The secretaries of the royal government must have had good reason so to refer to those decrees. Something must have been said in them about permitting Jews to follow Greek patterns of living.

78. I shall treat the document at Josephus, *Ant*. XII.258–64 in an appendix to my forthcoming *II Maccabees*. For the present, see Goldstein, *I Maccabees*, pp. 136f.

79. II Macc. 4.13; in the wide sense of 'Greek culture', 'Greek behaviour', the term appears here for the first time in the surviving Greek literature.

80. II Macc. 4.12.

81. II Macc. 4.13–15.

82. II Macc. 4.27. The writer's indignation, far from being shared by many contemporaries of the events, could at that time have been only a sectarian view. The Essenes similarly were scandalized that Jerusalem's privies lay beneath the temple mount. See *Jerusalem Revealed* (ed. Yigael Yadin), 1976, pp. 90f.

83. Emil Schürer, *Geschichte des jüdischen Volkes im Zeitalter Jesu Christi*, § 24.I, ⁴1901–11, vol. II, pp. 286–90; ET, *The History of the Jewish People in the Age of Jesus Christ*, rev. ed., vol. II, 1979, pp. 245–50.

84. Dan. 8.12f.; 11.31; 12.11; I Macc. 1.45, 54–59.

85. II Macc. 4.18–20. Just as the mention of Antiochene citizenship for Jews implied increased association of Jews with Greek pagans, so did participation of Jews in the games at Tyre. Yet the writer does nothing to call attention to the fact. We may guess that Jason of Cyrene, a Jewish Greek, did not regard Jewish association with Greeks, even on the holy soil, as a sin in itself.

86. II Macc. 4.16f.

87. In II Macc. 6 the non-Greek traits of the imposed cult are not visible. The gods to be worshipped seem to be Greek Zeus and Dionysus.

88. See Goldstein, *I Maccabees*, p. 67.

89. I Macc. 1.11.

90. I Macc. 1.14f.

91. I Macc. 1.15.

92. See Goldstein, *I Maccabees*, pp. 200f. At Jub. 15.1–14, the author condemns only the omission of circumcision, not the operation to disguise it.

93. *Ant*. XII.241.

94. J. A. Goldstein, 'The Tales of the Tobiads', in *Christianity, Judaism*,

and Other Greco-Roman Cults III (ed. Neusner), 1975, pp. 85–123, esp. pp. 121–23.

95. I Macc. 1.11–15, 64; II Macc. 4.16f.; 5.17–20; 6.12–17; 7.18, 32f., 38.

96. Hecataeus apud Josephus, *Ap.* I.191f. See above, n. 62.

97. Proof for this dating was given in an appendix to this paper as presented at the McMaster Symposium, but will be published separately in an article.

98. The sect was ancestral to the Essenes of Qumran.

99. See especially Jub. 22.16–22.

100. Jub. 23.16–24.

101. Jub. 23.20.

102. II Macc. 4.32–50; 13.8.

103. Menelaus is never accused in II Maccabees of aping the Greeks.

104. Goldstein, *I Maccabees*, pp. 40–42, especially n. 12.

105. Ibid., pp. 42–44.

106. For the chronology and the interpretation of the texts, see Goldstein, *I Maccabees*, pp. 41f., 162–64, 212f. As George Nickelsburg will show, I Enoch 92–104 also may be early and antedate the persecution. He informs me that the Ethiopic at I Enoch 99.2, 14 accurately reflects the Greek and was wrongly translated by Charles. Nothing is left in those chapters to suggest that the author refers to Jews who participated in the gymnasium. Though idol-worship is mentioned, nothing shows that the cults are Greek. The author is offended, not by their Greekness, but by the fact that they are pagan.

107. Goldstein, *I Maccabees*, p. 40.

108. Test. Mos. 5.1–6.

109. Test. Mos. 5.3 speaks in general terms of 'whoring after strange gods'. The words, however, are strangely joined to their context by *et quia*: '*deuitabunt iustitiam et accedent ad iniquitatem et contaminabunt inquinationibus domum seruitutis suae et quia fornicabunt post deos alienos.*' The strange syntax suggests that the words are an interpolation by a later writer who was convinced that the Hellenizers were idolaters. Moreover, the author goes on in 5.4–6 to give a long series of explanatory details (expressed in Latin by clauses beginning with *enim*), and not once there does he speak of idol worship.

110. Goldstein, *I Maccabees*, pp. 4–26, 62–89.

111. For the present, see Elias Bickerman, 'Ein jüdischer Festbrief vom Jahre 124 v. Chr.', ZNW 32, 1933, pp. 233–54.

112. The Hasmonaeans either expelled non-Jews from the reconquered Promised Land or required them to become Jews (I Macc. 13.11; 14.46, 50; II Macc. 14.14; Josephus, *Ant.* XIII. 257f., 318, 397; *Megillat Ta'anit* 15 Sivan; see also Michael Avi-Yonah, *The Holy Land*, 1966, pp. 74–6, and cf. Josephus, *Vita* 112f.).

Hengel (*Judaism and Hellenism*, I, pp. 304–9) misreads the minds of ancient pious Jews in thinking their fear that *Hellenizers* might again bring apostasy upon them made them 'repudiate' Hellenism. Not Hellenizers, but the wrath of God was what they feared, and they knew from experience that the wrath of God had been directed only against a few aspects of Hellenism.

113. Gymnasia were so obviously abominable to God that the rabbis did not need to mention them. Concerning the other structures, we have the tradition preserved in Sifra Ahare Mot pereq 13 (to Lev. 18.3; ed. Weiss, p. 86a). I translate from *Sifra or Torat Kohanim according to Codex Assemani LXV* (ed. Louis Finkelstein), 1956, p. 372: 'What is the meaning of the text (Lev. 18:3), "Nor shall you follow their customs"? That you should not adopt their established usages, such as theatres, circuses, and stadia.' On the origins of the passage, see J. N. Epstein, *Mebo'ot le-sifrut ha-tannaim*, 1957, p. 640. For *haquqin* as 'established', cf. *Sifra*, p. 85d top (ed. Weiss), and p. 370, lines 4f. (ed. Finkelstein).

114. Josephus, *Ant.* XV. 268, XVII. 161, 175, 194, 255; *Bell.* I. 659, 666; II. 44; Schürer, *Geschichte*, §22.II.2, vol. II, p. 61; ET, *History*, vol. II, p. 55. Cf. Josephus, *Ant.* XV. 328–33, 341.

115. Josephus, *Bell.* I. 422.

116. Cf. Josephus, *Ant.* XV. 328–30. On the supposed Herodian gymnasium at Jericho, see Ehud Netzer, 'Jericho from the Persian to the Byzantine Periods', *Encyclopedia of Archaeological Excavations in the Holy Land* II, 1976, pp. 568–70.

117. See for the present Bickerman, *Studies* I, pp. 109–36.

118. I shall argue these points in a future study of *Aristeas*.

119. *Aristeas* 284.

120. *Aristeas* 128–42, 180–84. Cf. bAZ 8a (bottom).

121. Cf. Hengel, *Judaism and Hellenism* I, pp. 67–9.

122. See *Greece* ('Hachette World Guides'), 1955, p. 532, and Philippe Bruneau, *Recherches sur les cultes de Délos à l'époque hellénistique et à l'époque impériale*, 1970, pp. 480–93.

123. See D. G. Mitten, 'A New Look at Ancient Sardis', *BA* 29, 1966, pp. 61–5.

124. Josephus, *Ant.* XII. 120.

125. Philo, *Quod omnis probus* 141; *Ebriet.* 177; see also Baron, *Social and Religious History* II, p. 9.

126. Philo, *Quod omnis probus* 26.

127. Philo, *Opif. mund.* 17.

128. Philo, *Spec. leg.* II. 230.

129. E.g. Philo, *Mut. nom.* 172; *Somn.* I. 69.

130. Tcherikover and Fuks, *CPJ* II, no. 153, lines 92–93; cf. Josephus, *Ant.* XII. 120.

131. BAZ 8a (bottom).

132. Josephus, *Ant.* XIII. 318.

133. Josephus, *Ant.* XVI. 150–59, 400–3; XVII. 191, 304–14.

134. See the interpolation at Test. Mos. 7.2–6; bBB 3b; Abraham Schalit, *König Herodes*, 1969, pp. 646–49. Josephus (*Ant.* XV. 328–30) tells how Herod excused himself to Jews for having erected Hellenizing and even idolatrous structures and sculptures *outside Judaea proper*, but Josephus himself does not there censure Herod. For demonstration

that Test. Mos. 6–7 contains interpolations, see *Studies on the Testament of Moses*, ed. G. W. E. Nickelsburg, Jr, 1973, pp. 5–58.

135. See Bickerman, *Studies* I, pp. 225–74.

136. See Saul Lieberman, *Greek in Jewish Palestine*, 1942, esp. pp. 15–28.

137. See Saul Lieberman, *Hellenism in Jewish Palestine*, 1950, pp. 100–4. In an article to be published soon, 'Rabbinic Bans on Aspects of Hellenistic Culture', I deal with the prohibition on teaching Greek recorded at mSot 9.14 and related matters.

138. Fragments in Eusebius, *Hist. eccl.* VII.32.16–18; *Praep. evang.* VIII.9.38–10.17; XIII.12.1–16. See the work of Walter cited above, n. 52.

139. See my forthcoming *II Maccabees*, on II Macc. 6.18–31.

140. BBK 83a, Sot 49b; Lieberman, *Greek*, pp. 1 and 20, and *Hellenism*, pp. 104f. I treat the rabbinic texts on *hokmat yevanit* in the article mentioned in n. 137.

The rabbinic term *epikuros* (mSanh 10.1 and Ab 2.4) is derived from colloquial anti-Epicurean Greek usage ('an undisciplined person'). Cf. Joseph Geiger, 'To the History of the Term *Apikoros*', *Tarbiz* 42, 1972–73, pp. 499–500 (in Hebrew, with English summary on p. xiv). The rabbis mostly use the word to refer to Jews and never to refer to a member of a philosophical sect or even to an imitator of Greeks; see bSanh 99b–100a, pSanh 10.1 (27d–28a). The word is used of a Gentile at bSanh 38b.

There is no evidence that rabbinic authorities after the time of Gamaliel II so actively fostered the study of *hokmat yevanit*. The abstention of the rabbis from forbidding the study of philosophy does not mean that they themselves studied it or valued it highly. See Saul Lieberman, 'How Much Greek in Jewish Palestine?', *Biblical and Other Studies* (ed. Altmann), 1963, pp. 123–31.

141. Plato, *Republic* X. 595–607.

142. *Sib.Or.* 3. 419–31.

143. BSanh 100b; pSanh 10.1 (28a); Lieberman, *Hellenism*, pp. 105–14.

144. BHag 15b.

145. Josephus, *Bell.* I. 155–56; *Ant.* XIV. 74–76.

146. See, e.g., Philo, *Legat. ad Gaium* 200–2.

147. mAZ 1.8; Maimonides, *Mishneh torah, Madda᾿, Hilkot ῾abodah zarah* 7.1 (*Abot de Rabbi Nathan* 31; ed. Schechter, p. 33b), translated in Anthony J. Saldarini, *The Fathers According to Rabbi Nathan (Abot de Rabbi Nathan), Version B*, 1975, pp. 181f.; pAZ 4.4 (43d end). On the passage in *Abot de-Rabbi Nathan*, see also Jacob Neusner, *A Life of Rabban Yohanan ben Zakkai*, 1962, p. 106 n. 1.

148. Cf. Isa. 10.5–19.

5 Limits of Tolerance in Judaism: The Samaritan Example

1. Cf. bKidd 75b. For the differentiated view of the problem by the rabbis cf. G. Alon, *Mehqarim be-Toledot Yisra'el* II, repr. 1970, pp. 1–14.

2. Cf. I. M. Jost, *Geschichte des Judenthums und seiner Secten*, I, 1857, p. 44; A. Brüll, *Zur Geschichte und Literatur der Samaritaner nebst Varianten zum Buche Genesis*, 1876, p. 8; P. Antoine, 'Garizin', *DBS* 3, 1938, p. 543; E. König, 'Samaritan Pentateuch' in *HDB* V, 1904, p. 68; Chr. Cellarius, *Collectanea historiae Samaritanae*, 1688, p. 29; Y. Kaufmann, *Toledot ha-'Emunah ha-Yisra'elit mime qedem 'ad sof Bayit ha-Sheni* II, 1960, p. 201. J. Macdonald laments with good reason in *The Theology of the Samaritans*, 1964, p. 14: 'Almost every chapter in books which include a history of the Samaritans assumes that their beginning is to be sought in the events described in II Kings 17.'

3. Cf. O. Eissfeldt, *Einleitung in das Alte Testament*, ³1964, pp. 403f.; ET, *The Old Testament: An Introduction*, 1965, p. 301.

4. R. J. Coggins, *Samaritans and Jews*, 1975, pp. 13ff.

5. S. Talmon, 'Biblical Tradition on the Early History of the Samaritans' (in Hebrew), *Eretz Shomron*, 1973, pp. 19–33.

6. For Talmon, 'Tradition', p. 27, it is the *de iure* formula for a *de facto* renunciation.

7. Cf. R. J. Coggins, 'The Old Testament and Samaritan Origins', *ASTI* 6, 1968, p. 41: 'The first source is concerned with a tradition centred upon Bethel.'

8. Cf. Coggins, 'Origins', p. 39: 'It appears that this section was originally aimed against the alien intruders in the service . . .'

9. Cf. Eissfeldt, *Einleitung*, p. 748: *Introduction*, p. 551.

10. Coggins ('Origins', p. 41) correctly undertook this delimitation. It does not go far enough, however, to take these verses as 'editorial harmonisation'. The Chronicler uses here what is for him a typical formula. Cf. B. S. Childs, 'A Study of the Formula "Until this Day" ', *JBL* 82, 1963, pp. 279–92.

11. R. Stiehl, 'Erwägungen zur Samaritanerfrage' in *Die Araber in der Alten Welt* IV, 1967, pp. 204–24.

12. This is also clear from Assyrian sources independent of this biblical reference. Cf. Macdonald, *Theology*, p. 22; Talmon, 'Tradition', p. 28; Coggins, *Samaritans*, pp. 17ff.; T. H. Gaster, 'Samaritans', *IDB* IV, 1962, pp. 190–97. The procedure followed by King Josiah agrees fully with the deuteronomic pericope II Kings 17.25–28 and its anti-Bethel bias. This does not mean that one should derive the later Samaritan teachings from traditions in the northern kingdom as Talmon does in 'Tradition', p. 33.

13. J. A. Montgomery (*The Samaritans*, 1907, p. 50) had described this situation correctly by referring to Sargon's own deportation report. Also Jer. 41.4 proves the positive attitude towards Jerusalem. W. J.

Notes to pages 91–93

Moulton ('Samaritans', *Encyclopaedia of Religion and Ethics* XI, 1920, p. 162), refers also to this passage.

14. Coggins, *Samaritans*, p. 15.

15. Already Jost, *Geschichte*, p. 51, had recognized this. From this followed also a *terminus a quo* of the middle of the fourth century BCE for the building of the temple on Mount Gerizim.

16. W. O. E. Oesterley (*A History of Israel* II, 1932, p. 146), says: '. . . it looks as though it owed its position here to later Jewish hatred of the Samaritans.'

17. Opposed by U. Kellermann ('Erwägungen zum Problem der Esradatierung', ZAW 80, 1968, p. 86), who gives the time of the Megabyzos upheaval (448-446 BCE) as the anchor point for the dating. Cf. Kaufmann, *Toledot*, p. 195. E. Meyer too favours an early dating, *Die Entstehung des Judentums*, 1896, p. 125 (around 458 BCE).

18. Cf. Montgomery, *Samaritans*, p. 59. M. Smith (*Palestinian Parties and Politics that Shaped the Old Testament*, 1971, pp. 196f.) rejected the view of A. Alt ('Die Rolle Samarias bei der Entstehung des Judentums', *Kleine Schriften* II, 1953, p. 329), according to which Jerusalem stood under the hegemony of Samaria.

19. This judgment is shared by Moulton, 'Samaritans', p. 163; B. Z. Lurie, 'Reshit ha-Perud ben Shabe ha-Golah la-Shomronim', in *Le-Zeker Dr J. P. Korngreen*, 1964, p. 160, and E. Bickerman, *From Ezra to the Last of the Maccabees*, 1962, p. 42. Only I. H. Eybers ('Relations between Jews and Samaritans in the Persian Period', *Biblical Essays* 1966, p. 79) rejects this view, but for unconvincing reasons.

20. It is not necessary to assume, as E. Bickerman does ('The Historical Foundations of post-Biblical Judaism' in L. Finkelstein [ed.], *The Jews* I, 1949, p. 88) that the 'conversion of the heathen immigrants to the service of the God of Israel was complete . . .'. Such a conversion was not even necessary!

21. To this extent the assumption of P. Ḥurgin ('Hitbadlut ha-Shomronim', *Horeb* 1, 1936–37, p. 142) is interesting. He considers it striking that the Samaritans do not say anything about the destruction of their temple, the existence of which is, apart from this text, only witnessed by Josephus. Therefore, he assumes that the Samaritans never had a temple on Mount Gerizim, but only an altar. In this connection the supposition of J. Bowman ('Pilgrimage to Mount Gerizim', *Eretz Israel* 7, 1964, p. 24) is important: 'However the pilgrimage service antedates the fourth century CE and is at least as old as the fifth century BCE if not older.' J. Bowman ('The Samaritans and the Book of Deuteronomy', *Transactions of the Glasgow University Oriental Society* 17, 1957–58, p. 11) correctly points out that there might be a continuity here with an old Canaanite cultic high place. However, Ḥurgin ('Hitbadlut', p. 129) opposes the assumption that the 'Samaritans' could have had a cult of their own at the time of Ezra.

22. For the different possible datings of the beginning of the activity of Ezra see Kellermann, 'Esradatierung', p. 62.

23. K. Koch, 'Ezra and the Origins of Judaism', *JSS* 19, 1974, p. 184.

Cf. also H. H. Rowley, 'The Samaritan Schism in Legend and History' in *Israel's Prophetic Heritage*, 1962, p. 218: 'Ezra was primarily concerned with the religious purity of the Jews.' The 'messianic' character of the task of Ezra is also stressed by Kaufmann, *Toledot*, p. 205.

24. Koch, 'Ezra', p. 190. Also M. Noth, *Geschichte Israels*, ⁵1963, p. 304; ET, *History of Israel*, ²1960, p. 337; H. Cazelles, 'La mission d'Esdras', p. 131.

25. See Smith, *Parties*, p. 197.

26. Kaufmann (*Toledot*, p. 194) is certainly right that Ezra, at least in the representation of the Chronicler, could not see them as Jews.

27. K. Koch, 'Haggais unreines Volk', *ZAW* 79, 1967, p. 65; Meyer (*Entstehung*, p. 125) refers to Ezra 5.6, which lacks any allusion to these events.

28. According to Meyer (*Entstehung*, p. 127) the Chronicler means here the 'Samaritans'. So also Cazelles, 'Esdras', p. 131, n. 1.

29. Bickerman, 'Judaism', p. 88. Also Bickerman, *Maccabees*, p. 44.

30. Cf. Moulton, 'Samaritans', p. 162. Similarly Rowley, 'Schism', pp. 215ff., and Talmon, 'Tradition', pp. 26f.

31. Coggins, *Samaritans*, p. 67.

32. The absence of such a distinction by Rowley is also criticized by Coggins, *Samaritans*, p. 63. Rowley ('Schism', p. 216) in essence takes a political conflict for granted, yet fails to make a clear distinction between the two groups.

33. The same observation is made by Talmon, 'Tradition', p. 30, and M. Z. Segal, 'Niss'uey ben Kohen Gadol 'im Bat Sanballaṭ u-binyan Miqdash Gerizim', *Sefer Asaf*, 1953, p. 412.

34. Koch, 'Ezra', p. 194.

35. Koch, 'Ezra', p. 193. One should compare here the Samaritan Ezra traditions. K. Haacker ('Die Schriftzitate in der samaritanischen Chronik II', in *Das Institutum Judaicum der Universität Tübingen in den Jahren 1968–1970*, p. 43) remarks concerning Chronicle II that 'the importance of Ezra for the origin of the Jewish-Samaritan schism is not a point of contention'.

36. Thus Coggins, *Samaritans*, p. 71. In this connection one should refer to the thoroughly negative image of Ezra put forward by the Samaritans. Here one can agree with Coggins (*Samaritans*, p. 73) when he says: ' . . . Ezra represents an exclusiveness based on Jerusalem and its claims to a unique status. It was this traditional picture of Ezra which made him so unacceptable a figure to the later Samaritans.'

37. That this is the intention of the Chronicler was pointed out by M. Delcor, 'Hinweise auf das Samaritanische Schisma im AT', *ZAW* 74, 1962, p. 282, and Noth, *Geschichte*, p. 320; *History*, p. 353; O. Plöger, *Theokratie und Eschatologie*, Neukirchen² 1962, p. 54, ET, *Theocracy and Eschatology*, 1968, pp. 40f.

38. Thus Delcor, 'Hinweise', p. 284; G. Gerleman, 'Samaritaner', in *Biblisch-Historisches Handwörterbuch* III, 1966, p. 1661; Plöger (*Theokratie*, p. 54, ET, pp. 40f.,) remarks that an anti-eschatological tendency is consistent with this intention of the Chronicler.

39. Cf. Kaufmann, *Toledot*, p. 190.

40. This leads to the view that in Ezra 4.1–4 the opposite is reported of what really happened. Thus Meyer (*Entstehung*, p. 124) thinks that in reality the returning exiles requested that the inhabitants of the north would co-operate in the rebuilding of the temple. They, however, declined, since Judah had always been foreign to them. Cf. S. J. Rubinstein, *Zur Geschichte der Entstehung der samaritanischen Gemeinde*, 1906, pp. 17–20. Also Oesterley (*History*, p. 151) does not see evidence in Ezra 4.1–5 for a Samaritan involvement in the building of the temple. Cf. on this point Smith, *Parties*, p. 197.

41. Cf. Delcor, 'Hinweise', p. 285. W. E. Barton (*The Samaritan Pentateuch*, 1903, p. 611) connects it with Neh. 13.28 and sees the origin of the Samaritan schism 'in the opposition that arose against Nehemiah's attempt to divorce the priests who had married foreign women'.

42. Cf. Talmon, 'Tradition', p. 26. K. Galling ('Serubbabel und der Wiederaufbau des Tempels in Jerusalem' in *Verbannung und Heimkehr*, 1961, p. 76), draws attention to the economic circumstance that the Samarians in the year 538 had to pay for the building of the temple in Jerusalem. Furthermore, there was the threat that Samaria would lose taxes because of the reorganization of Jerusalem.

43. Against J. Hamburger, 'Samaritaner' in *Real-Encyclopädie des Judentums* II, 1901, p. 1067, and Eybers, 'Relations', p. 73. Ḥurgin ('Hitbadlut', p. 138), correctly recognized the situation.

44. This view of the situation is gaining ground. The distinction between the original tension and the final split is drawn with increasing clarity. This is shown by the observations of J. Morgenstern (*Die Verleumdungen gegen die Juden und die der Juden gegen die Samaritaner*, 1878, p. 23) and Noth (*Geschichte*, p. 318; *History*, p. 352), who suspects a renewal of the north-south conflict. Y. Herschkowits ('Ha-Kutim be-Dibre ha-Tanna'im', *Sefer Asaf*, 1940, p. 78) stresses the basic equality of the northern and southern Israelites in the area of religion. The political causes of the conflict are pointed out by Coggins, 'Origins', p. 43, and also J. Purvis, ''Or hadash 'al ha-Historiyah ha-Qedumah shel ha-Shomronim', in *Hebrew Studies in America* III, 1974, p. 26. Untenable is the position of Kaufmann, *Toledot*, p. 206, according to whom at the time of Ezra there was no possibility of assimilation to Judaism.

45. There is an extensive treatment of the passage in A. Büchler, 'La relation de Josèphe concernant Alexandre le Grand', *REJ* 36, 1898, pp. 1–26.

46. Cf. also Segal, 'Miqdash Gerizim' and V. Tcherikover, *Hellenistic Civilisation and the Jews*, 1959, p. 44.

47. Ḥ. Shmueli, 'Sanballat ha-Ḥorani Ḥatno ve-Yessud Miqdash Gerizim', *Le-Zeker Shemu'el Dim*, 1958, p. 22.

48. Segal, 'Miqdash Gerizim'.

49. This view of the situation is stressed by Segal, 'Miqdash Gerizim', pp. 409f., against Büchler, 'Relation', p. 4. Büchler had not recognized that the Manasseh source has an anti-Samaritan bias. This fact is stressed even more by Shmueli, 'Sanballat', p. 22. H. G. Kippenberg

(*Garizim und Synagoge*, 1971, pp. 52–57), makes a more precise analysis in his characteristically careful way. He does not distinguish, however, two sources and thus against Büchler takes the report to be of Jewish origin. M. Delcor ('Vom Sichem der hellenistischen Epoche zum Sychar des Neuen Testamentes', *Zeitschrift des deutschen Palästina-Vereins* 78, 1962, p. 36), agrees with Büchler.

50. This seam was recognized in all literary critical studies. Cf., in addition to Büchler, Segal, 'Miqdash Gerizim', p. 408 and Tcherikover, *Civilization*, p. 44.

51. Moulton, 'Samaritans', pp. 162f. He means, however, that Neh. 13.28f. contains such a tradition about the beginning of the schism. Oesterley, *History*, p. 143; J. Jeremias, 'Samareia', *TDNT* VII, p. 89, n. 2; K. Schubert, 'Die Kultur der Juden I' in E. Thurnher (ed.) *Handbuch der Kulturgeschichte*, 1970; Segal ('Miqdash Gerizim', p. 413) refers only to an increasing alienation and disregards that there were no Samaritans at that time.

52. The first expression of doubt comes from Ḥurgin, 'Hitbadlut', p. 136. Only Purvis (''Or', p. 38) expresses it clearly and stresses that Josephus in fact does not say anything about the origin of the Samaritans.

53. Delcor ('Sichem', p. 36) noted a contradiction between *Ant.* XI. 324 and *Ant.* XI.342. Also Z. Ben-Ḥayyim ('Gerizim, Har Gerizim', *Entsiklopediah Mikra'it* II, 1954, p. 558), takes the existence of a previous cult for granted. One could add the observation that *Ant.* XI.311, which belongs to the Manasseh source, leaves the impression that Sanballat was himself priest of the temple. For it is specifically mentioned that he was already old when Manasseh came to him to be installed as high priest by Darius. According to the Samaritan book Joshua (ch. 45) Sanballat was a Levite.

54. This fact is mentioned time and again in the literature; Montgomery, *Samaritans*, p. 67; Noth, *Geschichte*, p. 319 (*History*, p. 354); J. D. Purvis, 'Ben Sira and the Foolish People of Shechem', *JNES* 24, 1965, p. 88.

55. Cf. F. M. Cross, Jr, 'The Discovery of the Samaria Papyri', *BA* 26, 1963, pp. 110–21 and P. W. Lapp, 'The Samaria Papyri', *Archaeology* 16, 1963, p. 205: 'It became clear that the documents had been taken to the cave by refugees fleeing from Samaria when the forces of Alexander the Great destroyed it in 331 B.C.' Bickerman (*Ezra*, p. 41) goes as far as seeing this event as the cause of the definitive break between 'Judah and Ephraim'.

56. Neither Segal ('Miqdash Gerizim', p. 410), nor Tcherikover (*Civilization*, p. 44) has paid any attention to this circumstance. Similarly, however, Montgomery, *Samaritans*, p. 68, and especially H. H. Rowley, 'Sanballat and the Samaritan Temple', *BJRL* 38, 1955–56, pp. 166–98 (= *Men of God*, London 1963, pp. 246–76).

57. This happens only in *Ant.* XI. 302.

58. There is hardly any need to share Rowley's pessimistic view in

'Sanballat', p. 187, when he says: 'We have therefore no means of knowing when the Samaritan Temple was built.'

59. The actual attitude of Alexander the Great to the Samaritans, i.e. proto-Samaritans, would have been negative; cf. Tcherikover, *Civilization*, pp. 45ff. He also refers to the fact that in the Talmud Alexander the Great is mentioned favourably in an anecdotal context.

60. Segal ('Miqdash Gerizim', p. 410), sees nothing more in it than an expression of the Samaritan evaluation of Sanballat as a national hero.

61. Today such a date is widely accepted; cf. Ben-Ḥayyim, 'Gerizim', p. 558; Kippenberg, *Garizim*, p. 56; Segal, 'Miqdash Gerizim', p. 411; J. Jeremias, *Die Passahfeier der Samaritaner*, 1932, p. 57. Cf. also Eybers, 'Relations', p. 81; L. E. Browne, *Ezekiel and Alexander*, 1952, p. 3. A few authors have arrived at a similar date by a completely different route. A. Spiro ('Samaritans, Tobiads, and Judahites in Pseudo-Philo', *PAAJR* 20, 1951, p. 312) assumes that the 260 years' duration of the Rahuta mentioned in the Samaritan sources means nothing other than the duration of the Samaritan temple. If one adds 128 years to the 260 – 128 BCE as the date of the destruction of the temple – then one arrives at 388 BCE as the date of the building. The same argumentation with an appeal to the Malef (Codex Gaster 1169, fol. 88a) is found in Gaster, 'Samaritans', *IDB* IV, p. 193. Browne (*Ezekiel*, p. 23) takes the 390 days in Ezek. 4.5 as the 390 years' duration of the exile of the northern kingdom. By subtracting these 390 years from 722 BCE, the date of the destruction of the northern kingdom, one arrives exactly at the year 332 BCE.

62. Thus Segal, 'Miqdash Gerizim', p. 411. Cf. Meyer, *Entstehung*, p. 124f.

63. To that extent the pessimistic judgment of Rowley, 'Schism', p. 217, has been superseded.

64. G. E. Wright and E. F. Campbell, Jr, 'Sichem', *RB* 72, 1965, p. 420; W. G. Dever, 'Excavations at Shechem and Mount Gerizim' (in Hebrew), *Eretz Shomron*, 1973, p. 9; cf. also Purvis, ''Or', p. 28 and E. F. Campbell, Jr and J. F. Ross, 'The Excavations of Shechem and the Biblical Tradition', *BA* 26, 1963, pp. 25f. Spiro ('Samaritans', p. 312) and following him Gaster ('Samaritans', p. 193) want to establish the precise date of the building as 388 BCE on the basis of certain Samaritan number indications.

65. Alt, 'Rolle Samarias'. Cf. Bickerman, *Ezra*, p. 45. Especially clearly Bickerman, 'Judaism', p. 88: ' . . . only the pride of the former Assyrian aristocrats, loath to acknowledge the supremacy of the southern rival, was responsible for the foundation of the Samaritan temple.'

66. C. Colpe, 'Samaria', *RGG* ³, 5, 1961, col. 1352: 'Through this a basis had been created for a separation also in the cultic area.' Smith (*Parties*, p. 200) opposes this thesis.

67. Talmon, 'Tradition', pp. 32f.

68. Archaeological evidence has shown that Shechem after a long

interval was settled again from the fourth century BCE on. Cf. G. E. Wright, *Shechem. The Biography of a Biblical City*, 1965.

69. The idea of H. M. Miklin ('Sel'a ha-Shomronim be-Har Gerizim', *Jerusalem* 11–12, 1916, p. 177) is interesting. He suggests that the Samaritans had looked for a rock, similar to the one in Jerusalem, and found it on Mount Gerizim.

70. A. Cowley, 'Samaritans' in *EB* IV, 1903, col. 4259: '. . . rendered re-union impossible'; J. W. Nutt, *A Sketch of Samaritan History, Dogma, and Literature*, 1874; G. Beer, 'Samariter, Samaritaner' in *PW*, 2nd series, 1A2, 1920, col. 2107; Colpe, 'Samaria', p. 1354; H. Haag, 'Samaria', *LTK* 9, 1964, col. 294; Gaster, 'Samaritans', *IDB* IV, p. 192. Finally, C. Thoma (*Christliche Theologie des Judentums*, 1978, p. 63) implicitly represented this viewpoint. His position is very much dependent on A. Mikolášek, 'Les Samaritains gardiens de la Loi contre les Prophètes', *Communio Viatorum* 12, 1969, pp. 139–48. It is more than questionable, however, whether the later Samaritan views can be attributed to so early a period on the basis of the sources.

71. So especially Coggins, 'Origins', *ASTI* 6, p. 45: '. . . the "orthodox" view of *one* sanctuary was far from universally accepted.'

72. Treated extensively by Kippenberg, *Garizim*, pp. 54f.

73. Rowley, 'Sanballat', pp. 187ff. So also Kippenberg, *Garizim*, p. 59; F. M. Cross, Jr, 'Aspects of Samaritan and Jewish History in Late Persian and Hellenistic Times', *HTR* 59, 1966, p. 207; Coggins, *Samaritans*, p. 101.

74. Thus Ben-Ḥayyim, 'Gerizim', p. 558; Kippenberg (*Garizim*, p. 55), calls it an 'elaboration of Neh 13.28'. Cf. also Herschkowits, 'Ha-Kutim', p. 82.

75. Cf. Tcherikover, *Civilization*, p. 42: 'Legend filled the vacuum. . .'. Furthermore, he refers to the negative attitude of Alexander the Great towards the Samaritans. The aetiological character of this account is mentioned time and again in the literature. Cf. Bickerman, 'Judaism', p. 88. Gaster ('Samaritans', p. 192) notes here a Samaritan tendency. A counterbalance had to be created over against the Judaic appeal to Cyrus.

76. Thus Coggins, 'Origins', p. 43; Coggins (*Samaritans*, p. 58) correctly insists on the important distinction between Samarians and Samaritans.

77. Cf. Rowley, 'Schism', in *Israel's Prophetic Heritage*, p. 217. To be sure, he stresses that the political differences between Sanballat I and Nehemiah threatened to poison their relationship.

78. This is stressed mainly by Ḥurgin, 'Hitbadlut', pp. 133–5.

79. A. Schalit, 'Pereq be-Toledot Milhemet ha-Miflagot be-Yerushalayim be-Sof ha-Me'ah ha-Ḥamishit u-be-Tehilat ha-Me'ah ha-Rebi'it lifne ha-Sefirah', in *Sefer Yohanan Levy*, 1949, pp. 252–72.

80. For this thesis to be of any importance here, this formation of parties would have had to continue into the last third of the fourth century BCE.

81. J. Bowman, 'The Importance of Samaritan Researches', *Annual*

of Leeds University Oriental Society I, 1958–59, p. 43. Cf. Cowley, 'Samaritans', col. 4261: '. . . the Samaritans acquired their law and their priestly system about 430 B.C.'

82. Cf. Rowley, 'Schism', p. 214: 'The Zadokite priesthood of the Temple was not disposed to share its privileges with others.'

83. For the role of Ezekiel in the solution of this problem, see Rowley, 'Schism', p. 213, and Gaster, 'Samaritans', p. 192.

84. Thus E. Auerbach, 'Der Aufstieg der Priesterschaft zur Macht im alten Israel', *SupplVT* 9, 1963, p. 247.

85. Thus J. Bowman (*Samaritanische Probleme*, 1967, p. 40) can say with justification: 'An essential trait, if not the decisive moment of Samaritan self-understanding, lies in the concept of a priestly religion.'

86. Especially important in this connection are the elaborations of J. C. Lebram, 'Nachbiblische Weisheitstraditionen', *VT* 15, 1965, pp. 230–36. He distinguishes between two currents in post-exilic Judaism, namely an 'exclusively theocratic' and a 'hokmatic' one. He counts the Samaritans in the latter group. 'By describing the Samaritans as an intransigent group within the Wisdom schools it is understood that there were also hokmatic circles (e.g. Sirach, Proverbs, Kohelet) which did not separate from Jerusalem.' He also refers to a joining of 'hokmatic and priestly traditions'.

87. J. Bowman, 'Researches', p. 54. Cf. also J. Bowman, 'Is the Samaritan Calendar the Old Zadokite One?', *PEQ* 91, 1959, pp. 23–37. This view is questioned by Coggins, *Samaritans*, p. 143, although he does not minimize the role of the priests in any way. Interesting is the observation made by J. T. Milik, *The Books of Enoch*, 1976, pp. 65f., in connection with 4Q260B. He compares this text with the Samaritan book Asatir and comes to the conclusion: 'Hence the Samaritans, just like the Judaeans, must have had, since the Persian era, a service of twenty-four families of priests in their temple on Mount Gerizim.' The evaluation of the Samaritan Chronicles involves a difficult methodological problem. From the extremely important contributions on this issue by A. D. Crown we should mention: 'New Light on the Inter-Relationships of Samaritan Chronicles from Some Manuscripts in the John Rylands Library', *BJRL* 54, 1971–72, pp. 282–313, and 55, 1972–73, pp. 86–111.

88. It is not possible to treat the overall relationship of Qumran to the Samaritans. On this point, see especially the critical and constructive description of the state of research by R. Pummer, 'The Present State of Samaritan Studies: I and II', *JSS* 21, 1976, pp. 39–61; 22, 1977, pp. 27–47; J. Bowman, 'Contact between Samaritan Sects and Qumran?', *VT* 7, 1957, pp. 184–89; J. M. Ford, 'Can We Exclude Samaritan Influence from Qumran?', *RQ* 6, 1967, pp. 109–29. On the question of the role of Deut. 18.18 in Qumran and by the Samaritans, cf. F. Dexinger, *Der Taheb. Die 'messianische' Gestalt bei den Samaritanern* (typescript), 1978, pp. 340–53.

89. Thus Montgomery, *Samaritans*, p. 69, says: '. . . that the crystallization of the dissenters into an independent sect was due rather to

their excommunication by the Jewish church than to their own will.'
For the development of the apocalyptic groups, cf. F. Dexinger, *Henochs
Zehnwochenapokalypse und offene Probleme der Apokalyptikforschung*, 1977.
   90. Rowley ('Sanballat', p. 185) doubts that such a shrine was founded for Manasseh.
   91. Kippenberg, *Garizim*, p. 76.
   92. Coggins, *Samaritans*, pp. 83ff.; Montgomery, *Samaritans*, p. 154;
Ḥurgin, 'Hitbadlut', p. 141; Bowman, *Probleme*, p. 33; Purvis, 'Foolish
People', p. 89. The results of the work of R. Pummer should be mentioned here: 'The Book of Jubilees and the Samaritans', *Église et Théologie* 10, 1979, pp. 147–78. According to him there is no evidence for
a 'possible connection between Jubilees and the Samaritans'.
   93. Purvis ('Foolish People', p. 89), is of this opinion; Coggins (*Samaritans*) does not choose sides.
   94. Cf. Coggins, *Samaritans*, p. 83.
   95. Coggins, *Samaritans*, p. 85.
   96. For the text see H. Lichtenstein, 'Die Fastenrolle. Eine Untersuchung zur Jüdisch-Hellenistischen Geschichte', *HUCA* 8/9, 1931–1932,
p. 339. Cf. Coggins, *Samaritans*, pp. 83f., and Kippenberg, *Garizim*,
pp. 74ff. For the passage, however, see especially Purvis, 'Foolish
People'.
   97. Purvis, 'Foolish People', pp. 92ff. Cf. Smith, *Parties*, and Tcherikover, *Civilization*, pp. 46f.
   98. Tcherikover, *Civilization*, p. 47.
   99. Coggins, *Samaritans*, pp. 84f.
   100. Cf. Kippenberg, *Garizim*, p. 76.
   101. Delcor ('Sichem', p. 37) argues against the view in which the
'Sidonians of Shechem' are Samaritans. His own proposal solves the
problem satisfactorily.
   102. Kippenberg, *Garizim*, p. 79. J. Goldstein (above, pp. 76f.) unfortunately makes no distinction between both groups and attributes
everything to the Samaritans.
   103. Kippenberg, *Garizim*, p. 85.
   104. Against the view of A. Van den Born and W. Baier, 'Samaritaner', *Bibel-Lexikon* (ed. H. Haag), ²1968, col. 1515.
   105. There is no evidence that the proto-Samaritans were more open
to the Hellenizing politics of Antiochus than the Jews as, for example,
Gaster ('Samaritans', *IDB* IV, p. 193), and Colpe ('Samaria', *RGG*³ 5,
col. 1352), assume.
   106. Kaufmann, *Toledot*, wants to reduce the whole development to
the point that there was at that time no longer a possibility for a *formal*
acceptance into Judaism.
   107. Ḥurgin, 'Hitbadlut', p. 127.
   108. Already Ḥurgin ('Hitbadlut', p. 127), noted the contradiction
with everything we know today about the Samaritans. Cf. especially
Coggins, 'Origins', p. 42: '. . . for the more that is discovered about
the Samaritans' own customs and beliefs, as in many ways a particularly conservative group within Judaism, the less such a description as

that in II Kings 17 seems relevant, even as a caricature.' Cf. also Gaster, 'Samaritans', p. 192: 'Nothing in subsequent Samaritan doctrine . . . betrays any indebtedness to Assyrian ideas.'

109. Thus H. Reland, *Dissertatio des Samaritanis*, 1707, p. 5: 'Omni illo tempore quin idola coluerunt Samaritani, dubitari nequit, . . .'. Cellarius, *Collectanea*, p. 30: 'Tunc enim exspiravit idolatria praesertim cum Manasses pontifex . . . religionem instituerit. . .'.

110. For the same treatment of Samaritans and Minim in the later tradition see Urbach (below, p. 293).

111. The ethnic argument is viewed by J. Jeremias (*Jerusalem zur Zeit Jesu*, Göttingen 1962, p. 392; ET, *Jerusalem in the Time of Jesus*, 1969, pp. 355f.) as the real basis for the definitive separation.

112. It is generally assumed today that this involves an *ad hoc* hypothesis. Cf. Montgomery, *Samaritans*, p. 27: '. . . Hebrews of Hebrews. . .'; Oesterley, *History*, p. 142; Rowley, 'Schism', p. 222: 'There is more reason to question the racial purity of the people of Jerusalem than those of Samaria.' Gaster (*Samaritans*, p. 192), mentions both groups of inhabitants of the north: '(*a*) the remnant of the native Israelites; and (*b*) the foreign colonists. For tendentious reasons, however, the Jewish version ignores the former, the Samaritan version, the latter.' It is incomprehensible how Tcherikover (*Civilization*, p. 40) can still hold the opinion: '. . . the Samaritans, who were the offspring of intermarriage between Israelites and other peoples settled there by Sargon of Assyria'.

113. This tendency is noted by Coggins, *Samaritans*, p. 87.

114. Present-day research only touches on the problem. Montgomery, *Samaritans*, p. 156: 'But unfortunately he (i.e. Josephus) no more than reflects the current Jewish prejudices of his day.' Coggins, *Samaritans*, p. 16: 'We cannot tell how much earlier than Josephus . . . this tradition of interpretation went; it may well be that it was comparatively recent in his time.' More precise is the conclusion of Kippenberg, *Garizim*, pp. 33f. n. 1: 'The name Kûtîm-Samareitai thus arose between the end of the second century BC and the first century AD.'

115. This had already been established by Jost, *Geschichte*, p. 49, and he concluded 'that from that point on they formed a real religious sect'. This view was then expressed time and again and clarified especially by Purvis in his studies on the Samaritans. J. Purvis, 'The Origin of the Samaritan Sect', *HTR* 56, 1963, p. 329. Cf. already Montgomery, *Samaritans*, p. 77: 'The Samaritan sect at last comes forth into the clear light of day in the Maccabaean period. . .'. Cf. also Talmon, 'Tradition', p. 33; Koch, 'Ezra', p. 197.

116. Cf. Noth, *Geschichte*, p. 338; *History*, pp. 376f.

117. In the literature it is stressed frequently how much the final break was determined by the destruction of the temple. J. Taglicht (*Die Kuthäer als Beobachter des Gesetzes nach talmudischen Quellen nebst Berücksichtigung der samaritanischen Correspondenz und Liturgie*, 1888, p. 17) speaks of 'hate . . . carried to extremes'. Smith, *Parties*, p. 185. Cf. also

Wright, *Biography*, p. 262 n. 26. Bowman ('Researches', p. 46) correctly stresses that the destruction of the temple may also have caused an internal Samaritan crisis. Thoma, *Theologie*, is completely right when he points out that the Samaritan schism 'was not experienced by the early Jews as a shattering of the religious and national unity'. Thoma's statement is supported by the history of interpretation of II Kings 17, according to which the Samaritans did not belong to this unity to begin with.

118. Thus Büchler, 'Relation', *REJ* 36, p. 23. He also considers it possible, however, that the proto-Samaritan Sanballat source originated at this time.

119. Cf. F. Dexinger, 'Das Garizimgebot im Dekalog der Samaritaner', *Studien zum Pentateuch*, 1977, pp. 111–33.

120. Cf. for the motivation S. Kohn, *De pentateucho samaritano eiusque cum versionibus antiquis nexu*, 1865, p. 10. With this we have a clear witness of Samaritan thinking from the pre-Christian period. As L. Schiffman (*The Halakhah at Qumran*, 1975) has stressed correctly, the status of the sources with respect to their purposes in terms of religious law is completely different: 'There is no way of knowing what the Samaritan law was like in the pre-Christian period.' For the state of research on Samaritan halakhah, cf. Pummer, 'Present State', *JSS* 21, pp. 58–60.

121. M. F. Collins ('The Hidden Vessels in Samaritan Traditions', *JSJ* 3, 1972, p. 100) thinks that the aim was to elevate these 'deuteronomic northern worship traditions' to a Mosaic commandment. It would be more precise to say that they wanted to give it the central place.

122. Thus Jost, *Geschichte*, p. 48: 'Very ancient memories were attached to Mount Gerizim.' Segal ('Miqdash Gerizim', p. 414), calls this relationship 'artificial'. Rowley, 'Schism', p. 212, however, thinks 'that from the start the Samaritan community was aware of all in the book of Deuteronomy that pointed to Shechem'.

123. Cf. Spiro, 'Samaritans', *PAAJR* 20, pp. 311ff. Segal ('Miqdash Gerizim', p. 411) recognized correctly that the theologizing did not precede but was the result of the building of the temple.

124. Bickerman, *Maccabees*, p. 45. See on this point also Urbach (below, p. 281).

125. N. J. McEleney, 'Orthodoxy in Judaism of the First Christian Century', *JSJ* 4, 1973, p. 25. Cf. for this 'catalogue' the treatment by Urbach (below, pp. 273f.).

126. McEleney, 'Orthodoxy', p. 21. The difference from the situation in Christianity is described by Urbach (below, p. 292).

127. Cf. D. E. Aune, 'Orthodoxy in First Century Judaism? A Response to N. J. McEleney', *JSJ* 7, 1976, pp. 1–10; L. L. Grabbe, 'Orthodoxy in First Century Judaism?', *JSJ* 8, 1977, pp. 149–53; in answer to both, N. J. McEleney, 'Orthodoxy in Judaism of the First Christian Century. Replies to David E. Aune and Lester L. Grabbe', *JSJ* 9, 1978, pp. 83–88.

128. Aune, 'Orthodoxy', p. 2.

129. Aune, 'Orthodoxy', p. 3.
130. L. Baeck, 'Hat das überlieferte Judentum Dogmen?', *Aus drei Jahrtausenden*, 1958, p. 24.
131. M. Simon (*Les sectes Juives au temps de Jésus*, 1960, p. 8) says: 'In their case (i.e. the Samaritans) one can truly speak of a sect in the modern sense of the word.' Cowley ('Samaritans', *EB* IV, col. 4260), represents the opposite viewpoint: 'The Samaritans are by no means a Jewish sect.'
132. Cf. Montgomery, *Samaritans*, p. 176: '. . . the fault of the Samaritan sects was not that of heresy but rather of schism.'
133. Stiehl, 'Samaritanerfrage', p. 206.
134. Already Montgomery, *Samaritans*, p. 176, hesitated: '. . . if we may use the term of Christian theology. . .'. Basic aspects of the sectarian problematic of that time are treated by E. P. Sanders, *Paul and Palestinian Judaism*, 1977, p. 267.
135. Grabbe, 'Orthodoxy', pp. 152f.
136. Hamburger's formulation in 'Samaritaner', *Real-Encyclopädie* II, p. 1063, is interesting: 'The renunciation of these three dogmas [i.e. holiness of Mount Gerizim, unholiness of Jerusalem, denial of the resurrection] was put up by rabbinic Judaism as the essential condition for Samaritans who entered Judaism.'
137. Urbach points out the structural differences (below, pp. 272–4).

6 At the Crossroads: Tannaitic Perspectives on the Jewish-Christian Schism

*The author is exceedingly grateful to Professor David Weiss Halivni for his careful reading of the paper and the suggestions he made regarding the rabbinic sources.
1. See my 'Jewish Sectarianism in Second Temple Times', to appear in *Great Schisms in Jewish History* (ed. Jospe and Wagner), 1981, pp. 1–46.
2. For the views of Philo of Alexandria see S. Belkin, *Philo and the Oral Law*, 1940, pp. 44–8. While the evidence is not entirely conclusive, there is no reason to believe that Philo's full-fledged proselyte was any different from that of the Palestinian sages of his time.
3. Much of the material pertaining to the Qumran sect has been collected in C. Rabin, *Qumran Studies*, 1957, pp. 53–70.
4. On the Samaritan schism, see R. J. Coggins, *Samaritans and Jews*, 1975, and the study of F. Dexinger above.
5. A similar conclusion is reached from the Christian sources by M. Smith, 'Early Christianity and Judaism', *Great Confrontations in Jewish History* (ed. Wagner and Breck), 1977, pp. 47–9. Smith writes, p. 48, '. . . the dispute between the Pharisees and the followers of Jesus. . . did not primarily or principally concern the question whether or not Jesus was the Messiah. On the contrary, the matter in dispute was the Christians' non-observance of the law.'
6. I here translate MS Kaufmann. Significant variants from manu-

scripts and early editions will be noted throughout this study, although no effort will be made to present a complete critical apparatus for each text cited. All punctuation and translation are mine.

7. לא is omitted in MS Paris and in *ed. princ.*

8. Natronai Gaon (719–730) explained that this refers to a bondwoman belonging to someone else. For if he married his own bondwoman, it would be assumed that he freed her and, therefore, the children would be Jewish. Other geonim, however, disagreed. See B. M. Lewin, *'Otsar Ha-Ge'onim* VII, 1936, to bYeb 23a. This geonic controversy was not merely theoretical but involved the status of actual children.

9. The reading נכרית in *ed. princ.* (without the copulative *waw*) is clearly an error. Cf. mYeb 2.5.

10. For a detailed discussion, see immediately below.

11. J. N. Epstein, *Mebo'ot le-Sifrut ha-Tanna'im*, 1957, pp. 414f.

12. *Masseket 'Arayot ve-Yuhasin.*

13. For scriptural derivation see bKidd 68a-b and pKidd 3.12 (ed. Krot. 3.14; 64d). Cf. also D. Weiss Halivni, *Mekorot u-Mesorot, Nashim,* 1968, to bKidd 68a, pp. 703f.

14. I here translate MS Vienna (ed. S. Lieberman, *Tosefta*, 1955-73).

15. MS Erfurt: והולידו.

16. MS Erfurt: אלע', abbreviation for אלעזר.

17. MS Erfurt omits 'in the name of R. Simeon'.

18. Lev. 18.6–19; 20.11f., 14, 17, 19–21. Cf. Deut. 27.22f.

19. There is great debate on the meaning of *karet* in the Bible. See S. Loewenstamm, 'Karet, Hikkaret', *'Entsiqlopediah Miqra'it* IV, 1962, pp. 330-32. To the rabbis it was either early death or childlessness. The mention of *karet* in this passage excludes two other groups of forbidden marriages: those imposed by the rabbis (*sheniyyot*) and those mentioned in the Torah but for which execution by the court is prescribed. See Maimonides, H. 'Issure Bi'ah 1.1–8.

20. For the derivation of *mamzer*, see S. Loewenstamm, 'Mamzer', *'Entsiqlopediah Miqra'it* V, 1968, pp. 1-3. The *mamzer* is mentioned in Deut. 23.3.

21. MKidd 3.12, 4.1, tKidd 5.1–2.

22. For other sources taking the same view, see S. Lieberman, *Tosefta ki-Fshutah* [abbreviated henceforth as *TK*], 1955-73, ad loc. Note especially Sifra Emor pereq 5.4; ibid., parasha 14.1 (ed. Weiss 97c, 104c).

23. For Rabbi Simeon's view, see Lieberman, *TK*, ad loc. Cf. especially tYeb 1.10 where the same view is expressed by R. Eleazar (ben Shammua), a disciple of R. Akiba who lived at about the time of the Bar Kokhba revolt.

24. S. M. Passamaneck, 'Some Medieval Problems in Mamzeruth', *HUCA* 37, 1966, pp. 124, 126.

25. So D. Pardo, *Ḥasde David*, 1776, to tKidd 4.16. Cf. D. Weiss Halivni, *Mekorot u-Mesorot, Nashim* to bYeb 49a and Sifre Deut 248 (ed. Finkelstein, pp. 276f.).

26. Maimonides, *Perush ha-Mishnayot*, ad loc. It is very likely that originally the halakah considered the offspring of Gentile fathers and

Jewish women to be *mamzerim*. Later on, it was ruled that they were not.

27. There was no question to the rabbis that mixed marriages were forbidden. All the halakic rulings regarding the status of the children fall into the halakic category of *be-di-ʿavad*, after the fact.

28. Or the grandchildren, so Rashi ad loc.

29. It is interesting to note that Ex. 34.15 singles out the threat of apostasy of Jewish girls through intermarriage while Deut. 7.1-4 concentrates on the apostasy of sons.

30. Y. Kaufmann, *Toledot ha–ʾEmunah ha-Yisraʾelit* IV, 1966–67, pp. 296–301. C. Tchernowitz (*Toledot ha-Halakah* III, 1953, p. 108) suggests that men could convert by circumcision but that no method was available for women.

31. For the rabbis, Ruth was the archetype of the convert. See B. Bamberger, *Proselytism in the Talmudic Period*, 1968, pp. 195–9. We do not mean to enter the dispute regarding the date of the book of Ruth. We are speaking here of the story as told in the Bible in its historical setting.

32. This midrash is discussed in an unpublished section of my Brandeis University dissertation, *The Halakhah at Qumran*, 1974, pp. 160–4.

33. See V. Aptowitzer, 'Spuren des Matriarchats im jüdischen Schrifttum (Schluss)', *HUCA* 5, 1928, pp. 261–77.

34. The view of the rabbis that the prohibition of Ammon and Moab applied only to males of these nations is certainly assumed in the book of Ruth. Otherwise, we should have expected the book to conceal the nationality of Ruth, especially in light of her being an ancestress of King David.

35. We shall return below to the problem of God-fearers and semi-proselytes in the Hellenistic world.

36. Cf. Mek RSh b. Yohai to Ex. 12.48 (p. 37); bKer 9a; Gerim 2.4.

37. See the amoraic explanation in bKer 9a (and *Tosafot* ad loc.).

38. The text translated is the Vilna ed. The Venice edition offers no differences of consequence. MS variants are noted where they occur.

39. MS Munich omits בזמן הזה.

40. MS Munich omits שבאת.

41. MS Munich omits בזמן הזה but writes בזמן before שישראל. This is probably an error, the scribe's *Vorlage* containing a reading similar to that of the printed editions.

42. MS Munich reads ומסוחפים and omits the copulative *waw* on the next word.

43. MS Vat. Ebr. 111 adds מיד, probably under the influence of the continuation of the passage in which it occurs.

44. Cf. mAbot 2.1, 4.2 and *Mahazor Vitry* to mAbot 2.1. Probably the terms lighter and heavier refer to the ease or difficulty of performance of the commandment.

45. For *ʿawon* as punishment for iniquity, see *BDB*, p. 731.

46. Lev. 19.9; 23.22.

47. Deut. 24.19.

48. Lev. 19.9; 23.22.

49. Deut. 26.12–13 (cf. Rashi).

50. The reading שכרו in MS Vat. Ebr. 111 is clearly an error.

51. Presumably he indicates his acceptance in a formal declaration.

52. BYeb 47b indicates that the Palestinian Amora R. Yohanan required three and even directed the Tanna (memorizer) in his academy to emend the text of the baraita to say three. Cf. also bYeb 46b. It is most likely that the tannaitic halakah required only two while the Amoraim required three. The Tannaim saw the function of these scholars as witnesses and so required two while the Amoraim saw it as that of a court, the minimum size of which was three.

53. MS Munich: עומדין לו על גבו:

54. Note that the text says כישראל, and not simply ישראל. This is probably because there are certain small differences between the legal status of an Israelite and a convert, most important of which was that the convert may marry certain classes prohibited to Israelites.

55. MS Munich omits נשים.

56. For reasons of modesty.

57. Cf. E. Urbach, *Ḥazal*, 1971, pp. 480–94 (ET, *The Sages* I, pp. 541–54).

58. The text translated is that reconstructed by Lieberman in his edition. This reconstruction is supported by parallels (see Lieberman, ad loc.), especially Sifra Qedoshim pereq 8.2 (ed. Weiss, 91a).

59. This entire first clause is accidentally omitted in MS Vienna (Lieberman).

60. This is the reading of MS Vienna. MS Erfurt: אחד.

61. Rashi (bBekh 30b) explains *diqduq soferim* as a stringency of the rabbis.

62. BShab 31a. Cf. Bamberger, *Proselytism*, pp. 223–5.

63. While it is difficult to date this narrative, we should note that it indicates that the Tannaim dated the dual-Torah concept as far back as the time of Hillel and Shammai.

64. J. Neusner ('Rabbinic Traditions about the Pharisees before AD 70: The Problem of Oral Transmission', *JJS* 22, 1971, pp. 1–18) argues for a Yavnean date. He is certainly correct that it is unattested before Yavneh. We would view it as the result of a long and complex prehistory and would see it developing into its present form in the second half of the first century CE.

65. Cf. Bamberger, *Proselytism*, pp. 225–8.

66. Herodotus, II. 104.

67. J. Licht, 'Milah', *ʾEntsiqlopediah Miqraʾit* IV, pp. 896–8. It is uncertain whether circumcision in Egypt was practised by all classes or only by certain groups. If it were limited to those of certain status, we could understand why the Israelite slaves were uncircumcised in Egypt.

68. M. Stern, *Greek and Latin Authors on Jews and Judaism* I, 1974, pp. 169f., 225, 300, 312, 315 (although the Jews never practised female circumcision), 325, 356, 415, 436, 442–4, 525f., 528. The second most

prominent sign was Sabbath observance. Sabbath observance, moreover, was much more widespread among non-Jews in the Graeco-Roman period than was circumcision.

69. E. M. Smallwood, 'The Legislation of Hadrian and Antoninus Pius against Circumcision', *Latomus* 18, 1959, pp. 334–47.

70. See Lieberman, *TK*, ad loc. and Smallwood, 'The Legislation of Hadrian and Antoninus Pius against Circumcision: Addendum', *Latomus* 20, 1961, pp. 93-96.

71. Bamberger, *Proselytism*, pp. 21f. Cf. Gen. 34.14–24.

72. For full discussion, see Licht, 'Milah', pp. 898–900.

73. E.g. K. Kohler, 'Circumcision', *JE* IV, p. 94, based on the interpretation of the view of Ananias as expressed to Izates of Adiabene (*Ant.* XX.38–42).

74. See above, n. 68. On Philo, see Belkin, p. 47.

75. H. H. Rowley, 'Jewish Proselyte Baptism and the Baptism of John', *From Moses to Qumran*, 1963, pp. 225f. (originally in *HUCA* 15, 1940, p. 327). Cf. I. Abrahams, *Studies in Pharisaism and the Gospels*, First Series, (1917) 1967, pp. 36–46.

76. See the exhaustive study of A. Büchler, 'The Levitical Impurity of the Gentile in Palestine before the Year 70', *JQR* NS 17, 1926–27, pp. 1–81. He argues that the origin of these laws is in the period immediately preceding the outbreak of the revolt in 66 CE (pp. 1–3, 80).

77. Bamberger, *Proselytism*, pp. 43f., Rowley, 'Jewish Proselyte Baptism', pp. 227–30.

78. Rowley, pp. 211–35. Contrast D. Flusser, 'Tevilat Yohanan ve-Khat Midbar Yehudah', *Yahadut u-Meqorot ha-Natserut*, 1979, pp. 81–112.

79. So Bamberger, *Proselytism*, p. 44.

80. For the number, see above, n. 52.

81. I here translate MS Kaufmann. MS Munich preserves only orthographic variants. This mishnah also appears in Eduy 5.2. The reading פסח for פסחים seems to have originated in *ed. princ.* It probably is a misinterpretation of an abbreviation. Cf. G. Alon, 'Tum'at Nokhrim', *Mehqarim be-Toledot Yisra'el* I, pp. 121–47, translated in G. Alon, *Jews, Judaism and the Classical World*, 1977, pp. 146–89. Alon argues for an early dating of proselyte immersion, which he understands to be based on the general concept of the impurity of the Gentiles, a concept which, he says, can be shown to predate the Herodian period. Alon sees proselyte immersion as predating Christian baptism, although to him the character of each is markedly different.

82. While this is the view of most commentators, contrast Meiri, who assumes he could simply immerse in the morning and eat of the sacrifices that evening. Purification from the impurity of the dead involved sprinkling of the water (in which the ashes of the burnt red heifer were mixed) on the third and seventh days. Maimonides (H. Qorban Pesah 6.7) clarifies the view of the Hillelites. He asks how it is possible to stop the new proselyte from eating the paschal sacrifice

(a commandment of the Torah punishable by excision) in order to prevent an error in later years (a rabbinic ordinance). He answers that the Hillelites did not allow one circumcised so close to Passover to immerse for purposes of conversion, so that he would not attain Jewish status until after the paschal sacrifices were eaten. In other words, they made sure that the conflict between the Torah's law and their ordinance would never actually occur.

83. Translating MS Vienna (ed. Lieberman).

84. MS Erfurt: יוסה בר' יהודה, MS London: יוסי.

85. MS Erfurt: לא נחלקו. D. Weiss Halivni (*Mekorot u-Mesorot Mo'ed*, 1975, pp. 284 and 302) shows that the phrase *lo' neḥelequ* can be taken to mean that according to either the Tanna or the redactor of the statement there was another view to the effect that 'they did argue'. In our case, this may mean that there was an opposing view which stated that there was a dispute between the houses of Hillel and Shammai as to whether a Jew circumcised on the day before Passover might eat of the paschal lamb that year.

86. MSS Erfurt and London and *ed. princ.*; זר but Lieberman, *TK*, ad loc., shows conclusively that the reading of MS Vienna is to be preferred.

87. *Ed. princ.*: בר' צדוק, clearly an error which simply repeated the name of the last Tanna cited.

88. *Stratiōtai* (Lieberman, *TK*, ad loc.).

89. See Lieberman, *TK*, ad loc.

90. The specific mention of the handmaiden is, according to Lieberman, indication that our tosefta is based on a specific midrash halakah. See *TK*, ad loc.

91. *Ṭebilah*, from the root *ṭbl*.

92. *Hazzayah* or *hazza'ah* from the root *nzh*.

93. See n. 84 and Lieberman, *TK*, ad loc.

94. S. Zeitlin ('The Halaka in the Gospels and its Relation to the Jewish Law in the Time of Jesus', *HUCA* 1, 1924, pp. 357–63, and 'A Note on Baptism for Proselytes', *JBL* 52, 1933, pp. 78f.) has dated immersion to a very late date. Cf. the response of L. Finkelstein, 'The Institution of Baptism for Proselytes', *JBL* 52, 1933, pp. 203–11.

95. Translating the text of MS Kaufmann.

96. See J. Preuss, *Biblical and Talmudic Medicine*, ET 1978, pp. 354–7.

97. Ibid., pp. 375f.

98. Because of the difficulties in identifying the disease *ṣara'at*, so often explained as leprosy, we leave this word untranslated. See Y. Tass, 'Ṣara'at', (*d*), *'Entsiqlopediah Miqra'it* VI, 1971, pp. 776–8 and Preuss, *Biblical and Talmudic Medicine*, pp. 323–39. Preuss's discussion of this disease is somewhat outdated and the view of Tass is to be preferred.

99. So I. Lipshitz, *Tiferet Yisra'el*, repr. 1952–53, ad loc. Cf. Maimonides, H. Mehussere Kapparah 1.1.

100. Cf. B. Levine, 'Kippurim', *Eretz Israel* 9, 1969, pp. 88–95.

101. Aaron Hyman, *Toledot Tanna'im ve-Amoraim* I, 1964, pp. 181–4.

102. So Lieberman, *TK* to tPes 7.14.

103. Translating MS Munich. The baraita is also found in bRSh 31b. This baraita is in agreement with the anonymous first clause of mKer 2.1, for it is precisely because this proselyte is not in the category of one lacking atonement that the Tannaim strove at first to preserve some means of making the offering. After all, the offering was essential to the conversion process. In the view of R. Eliezer b. Jacob, that the convert is simply 'lacking in atonement', the offering would have no purpose after the destruction of the temple. Gerim 2.4 seems to have misunderstood this. It construes R. Eliezer b. Jacob as stating that the convert must still set aside the money for the offering. But to R. Eliezer there is absolutely no reason to do so since the purpose of the offering no longer existed after the destruction. On the contrary, R. Eliezer b. Jacob in mKer is in accord with the view which Gerim 2.4 ascribes to R. Simeon, that one simply need not bring the offering.

104. *Ba-zeman ha-zeh* is a technical term for the period after the destruction of the temple. It is almost always used in reference to problems of adapting halakah to fit the new circumstances in which there were no temple and sacrifices. The impact of the destruction on numerous areas of ritual cannot be overstated. The entire subject of how the halakah was adjusted to the new reality requires a thorough study.

105. So Rashi to bKer 9a in accordance with bKer 10b. But Rashi to bRSh 31b says it is a quarter *sheqel*, which would be twice as much, basing himself on bYom 55b. Tosafot to bRSh 31b suggests that the value rose as a result of inflation.

106. BRSh 31b: שמעון בן אלעז׳ (ed. Venice). Cf. *Diqduqe Soferim*, ad loc.

107. Hebrew עליה. So also MS Vat. Ebr. 119 and bRSh 31b, although ed. Vilna reads עליו. If this pronoun refers to the baraita or halakah as understood object, a feminine form would be more correct.

108. See above, n. 106.

109. Such baraitot were often formulated or taught by the Amoraim in whose names they are handed down. The Amoraim viewed such baraitot as having less authority than those transmitted in the name of Tannaim but as being more authoritative than Amoraic material. See Ch. Albeck, *Mehqarim be-Baraita ve-Tosefta ve-Yahasan la-Talmud*, 1969, pp. 15–43. In the case of Bar Kappara we should also remember that he was one of those transitional individuals who bridged the period of the Tannaim and the Amoraim and can be regarded simultaneously as both a Tanna and an Amora. See Y. D. Gilat, 'Bar Kappara', *EJ* IV, cols. 227f.

110. Translating the Venice ed. No significant variants were found in MS Munich or MS Vatican Ebr. 111.

111. Regarding the 'fathers' and 'mothers' who left Egypt, see above, p. 122.

112. Translating the Venice ed.

113. Gerim 1.2 (*Sheva' Massekhtot Qetanot* [ed. M. Higger], 1970–71) reads Akiba.

114. Translating the Venice ed.

115. MS Leiden adds: טבל ולא מל, which has been erased by another hand. (See J. N. Epstein, *Mebo'ot Le-Sifrut Ha-'Amora'im*, 1962, p. 589.) Indeed, the deletion of these words is necessary according to the context.

116. A *genizah* fragment in L. Ginzberg, *Seride Ha-Yerushalmi*, 1909, reads: שאינו טובל.

117. This translation is to be preferred to 'nocturnal emission' or 'nocturnal pollution', as it is more in keeping with the halakic definition. See 'Ba'al Qeri', *'Entsiqlopediah Talmudit* IV, Jerusalem 1952, pp. 130–48.

118. Cf. the treatment of R. Eliezer's view by Y. D. Gilat, *Mishnato shel R. 'Eli'ezer ben Hyrcanus*, 1968, p. 163. In this context Gilat's general remarks about the history of circumcision and proselytes are also of interest.

119. See the survey of views in Bamberger, *Proselytism*, pp. 48f.

120. The gemara (bYeb 46b) interprets the controversy differently in order to explain the reasons given by the baraita for the views of R. Eliezer and R. Joshua. The gemara claims that both of them agreed (*kuleh 'alma* here includes both of them but cannot include the view of the sages) that one who immersed but was not circumcised was a valid proselyte. The disagreement was only regarding one who was circumcised but did not immerse. R. Eliezer considers him a valid proselyte while R. Joshua does not. *Tosafot Yeshanim*, ad loc. (cf. *Tosafot* as well), perceived that this interpretation does not fit the language of the baraita at all. *Tosafot Yeshanim* explains this problem by saying that the view of R. Joshua was phrased as it is only because of the need to accommodate the phraseology of the entire baraita to the view of the sages that both circumcision and immersion are required. Since we see the reasons as a secondary addition to the baraita, we cannot accept the gemara's casuistic reinterpretation of the baraita to suit the reasons. As to the explanation of the Tosafists, probably the view of the sages was also a later addition since it is not given a reason. It would have followed the addition of the reasons to the views of R. Eliezer and R. Joshua in the Babylonian recension. If so, it is impossible to believe that the entire baraita was phrased to accord with the view of the sages. In fact, the reverse is the case. The view of the sages was phrased as a response to the views of Rabbis Eliezer and Joshua. For all these reasons the amoraic explanation of this baraita in the Babylonian gemara cannot be accepted. We should note that this explanation is absent from the Palestinian gemara, where the reasons and the view of the sages are also absent.

121. The Babylonian gemara quotes a second baraita (bYeb 46b) according to which the view of the sages is accepted by R. Jose and that of R. Eliezer by R. Judah. (Cf. Halivni, ad loc.) R. Judah is Judah bar Ilai, and R. Jose is Jose bar Halafta. Both of these were third

generation Tannaim. It is, therefore, easy to understand why they would echo the views of their second generation predecessors.

122. Halivni, *Mekorot u-Mesorot, Nashim*, p. 55 n. 6. Halivni prefaces the explanation with 'perhaps'.

123. הטבילה מעכבת.

124. אף. Cf. Halivni, *Mekorot u-Mesorot, Mo'ed*, p. 263 and J. N. Epstein, *Mabo le-Nusaḥ ha-Mishnah* II, ²1964, pp. 1007–32.

125. For similar amoraic statements regarding both men and women, see bYeb 45b and Bamberger, *Proselytism*, pp. 47f.

126. BYeb 46a-b.

127. Cf. Halivni, *Nashim*, p. 55 n. 6 and Bamberger, *Proselytism*, p. 52.

128. Bamberger, *Proselytism*, pp. 51f.

129. On slavery in Second Temple and rabbinic times, see E. E. Urbach, 'Hilkot 'Abadim ke-Maqor la-Historiyah ha-Ḥebratit bi-Yeme ha-Bayit ha-Sheni u-vi-Tequfat ha-Mishnah ve-ha-Talmud', *Zion* 25, 1960, pp. 141–89.

130. For a detailed account see Bamberger, *Proselytism*, pp. 124–31. Cf. also Gilat, pp. 162f.

131. See e.g. Maimonides, H. Ïssure Bi'ah 13.12.

132. John Hyrcanus forcibly converted the Edomites to Judaism (*Ant.* XIII. 257f.). There is an account that his son Aristobulus I forcibly converted the Itureans, although A. Schalit sees this as referring to his father's conquest of the Golan ('Aristobulus I [Judah]', *EJ* III, col. 440).

133. E. Schürer, *A History of the Jewish People in the Age of Jesus Christ*, § 31.5, ET II, ii, 1898, pp. 291–327; Bamberger, *Proselytism*, pp. 133–8; S. Lieberman, *Greek in Jewish Palestine*, ²1965, pp. 68–90. I was especially helped by a seminar paper by Stuart Miller of New York University entitled 'Proselytes and God-fearers in Non-Rabbinic Sources of the First Century CE' (January 1975).

134. By using the term 'community' I intend to indicate that the Tannaim had a large group of followers within the population of Palestine after 70 CE, perhaps including almost the entire Jewish community. The work of the rabbis was not limited to the four cubits of the schoolhouse but extended to areas of daily life in which the Tannaim functioned as judges, teachers, and religious leaders.

135. Translating MS Kaufmann. While some Mishnah texts begin with the clause stating that all Israel have a share in the world to come, it is clear from the omission of this clause in most manuscripts that it is secondary. We have therefore omitted it from discussion. See Urbach, *Ḥazal*, p. 588 n. 11 (ET, *The Sages* II, pp. 991–2). Finkelstein (*Mabo le-Massektot 'Abot ve-'Abot de-Rabbi Natan*, 1950, pp. 104–7) takes the view that the original context of this clause and the entire mSanh 10.1 was the introduction to mAbot in its early form as a Pharisaic document. There is, however, simply no way of proving this ingenious theory.

136. Other texts read אלו. It might be objected that the *waw* of ואלו might indicate that it was preceded by the clause concerning the por-

tion of all Israel (above, n. 135), the *vav* serving as the *vav* of contrast meaning 'but'. On the other hand, all the previous chapters begin with *ve-elu*. Rather, we should see the *vav* here as functioning much like Arabic *fa*. Cf. Halivni, *Mekorot u-Mesorot, Mo'ed*, p. 526 n. 2**.

137. On *heleq*, see Finkelstein, p. 221, who sees the usage here in a temporal rather than a spatial sense. He understands the word to mean 'future', or 'lot'.

138. On the world to come and its various definitions in rabbinic and medieval Judaism, see Finkelstein, pp. 213–21.

139. The words מן התורה are added in many texts. Nonetheless, they must be seen as a late addition (Finkelstein, p. 229). The addition was probably made under the influence of the many midrashim attempting to establish the basis of this concept in the Bible. The quotation of this mishnah in pPeah 1.1; 16b shows that this clause was not part of the original text.

140. Transliterated in accord with the vocalization of MS Kaufmann. Cf. E. Ben-Yehudah, *Millon Ha-Lashon Ha-'Ivrit* I, 1959, p. 349 n. 1.

141. See A. Hyman, 'Maimonides' "Thirteen Principles" ', *Jewish Medieval and Renaissance Studies* (ed. Altmann), 1967, pp. 119–44. For a general bibliography on dogma and creed in Judaism, see Hyman, p. 120 n. 7. [See further Dexinger's discussion above, pp. 109ff. (ed)].

142. The view expressed here is effectively a compromise between the two possibilities discussed in Hyman, 'Maimonides' "Thirteen Principles" ', pp. 122f. On the one hand, it is difficult to accept the view of Maimonides and Joseph Albo that one must affirm these beliefs to have a share in the world to come. On the other hand, Hyman's assumption that on the surface there is no relation between this mishnah and required belief is overstated, especially when one takes into consideration the tenuous relationship of the statement 'All Israel has a share in the world to come' to the rest of the mishnah. See above n. 135.

143. Translating the Venice ed.

144. MS Munich here reads 'the world to come', but MS Florence accords with ed. Venice. R. N. Rabbinovicz, *Diqduqe Soferim*, ad loc., prefers the reading of the printed editions. Indeed, it seems that the version of MS Munich has substituted the interpretation for the text itself. Cf. *Hiddushe Rabbenu David Bonfil* (ed. Y. Lipshitz), 1966–67, p. 79, and (pseudo-)Ran, ad loc.

145. On the principle of 'measure for measure', see E. E. Urbach, *Hazal*, pp. 325f., 386f. (ET, *The Sages*, I, pp. 371f. and pp. 436ff.).

146. Josephus, *Bell.* II.165. Cf. *Ant.* XVIII.16 and E. Schürer, *History*, § 26.1, ET II.ii, 1898, pp. 13f.; rev. ed., II, 1979, p. 391.

147. Finkelstein, *Mabo'*, p. 228.

148. See J. Neusner, 'Rabbinic Traditions', pp. 1–18.

149. But cf. E. E. Urbach, *Hazal*, pp. 254–8 (ET, *The Sages* I, pp. 286–90). If the wider use of Torah could be proven for Palestine before 70 CE, we could say that the 'Torah' in our mishnah and mAbot 1.1 is meant to include the 'traditions of the elders' ascribed by Josephus to

the Pharisees. These traditions were a forerunner of the tannaitic oral Law.

150. A. J. Heschel, *Torah min ha-Shamayim ba-'Aspaqlaryah shel ha-Dorot* II, 1965, pp. 100–45.

151. Cf. V. Tcherikover, *Hellenistic Civilization and the Jews*, 1959, pp. 152–74.

152. S. Krauss, *Griechische und Lateinische Lehnwörter im Talmud, Midrasch und Targum* II, 1964, repr. p. 107.

153. BSanh 99b-100a, pSanh 10.1; 27d. Cf. ''Apiqoros', *'Entsiqlopediah Talmudit* II, pp. 136f. which also contains an excellent survey of the medieval halakic discussion.

154. Cf. Maimonides, *Perush ha-Mishnayot*, ad loc. (ed. Vilna, p. 124a) who derives the word from Aramaic פקר.

155. Josephus, *Ant.* X.277–80, Cf. G. Deutsch, 'Apikoros', *JE* I, pp. 665f., and S. Lieberman, 'How Much Greek in Jewish Palestine?', *Biblical and Other Studies* (ed. Altmann), 1963, p. 130.

156. On these beliefs of Epicurus, see J. M. Rist, *Epicurus*, 1972, pp. 146–8, and G. Strodach, *The Philosophy of Epicurus*, 1963, pp. 52–5.

157. Josephus, *Bell.* II. 164f.; *Ant.* XIII.173.

158. Schürer, *History* § 26.1, II, ii, p. 15; rev. ed., II, p. 393.

159. L. Finkelstein sees our mishnah as part of an ancient Pharisaic document going back as far as the 'men of the great assembly', a view which we find difficult to accept. He sees the specific passage under discussion here, however, as being a later addition. At the same time he suggests that it must have been added at a time when Epicureanism was making inroads into the Jewish people. Unfortunately, however, it is not possible to determine precisely the status of Epicurean beliefs among Jews at this time so as to pinpoint the time in which our mishnah was formulated.

160. Accordingly, the word 'even' (Hebrew *'af*) in our passage should be understood as part of the words of the Tannaim, R. Akiba and Abba Saul, rather than as an addition of some redactor, as was the case in the passage discussed above, p. 135. Further, it is extremely unlikely in light of the nature of the doctrinal offences described here that the anonymous clause was formulated in the Yavnean period and was then, at the same time, glossed by R. Akiba and Abba Saul.

161. Translating Zuckermandel's ed. Cf. bRSh 17a, ed. Venice and *Diqduqe Soferim*, ad loc., as well as the discussion in R. T. Herford, *Christianity in Talmud and Midrash*, 1903, pp. 118–25.

162. According to Rashi ad bRSh 17a, in the version of *Diqduqe Soferim* the *minim* here are the *talmide yeshu*, the disciples of Jesus, in other words, the early Jewish Christians.

163. ושפורשין מדרכי ציבור is too general a classification to belong to this list. Delete it with Rashi and *Diqduqe Soferim*, ad loc.

164. The text here mentions Jeroboam and Ahab and then adds two classes of transgressors extremely difficult to explain precisely and not relevant to our study.

165. See B. Kedar, 'Netherworld, In the Aggadah', *EJ* XII, cols. 997f. for a treatment of Gehenna in rabbinic texts.

166. Contrast, however, the view of Rashi to bRSh 17a, who sees the offence of the informer as causing financial loss to fellow Jews.

167. The printed edition of rabbinic texts usually read *mumar*, lit. one who was changed or converted, for the Hebrew *meshummad*, lit. 'one who was destroyed'. Christian censors replaced *meshummad* with *mumar*, which they deemed less offensive. Indeed, the word *mumar* itself is most probably an invention of the Christian censors.

168. *TK* III, p. 402 n. 45.

169. Translating the Venice ed. The version in tHor 1.5, ed. Zuckermandel, seems corrupt and hence we rely on the baraita as preserved by the gemara.

170. MS Munich reads: אוכל... והשותה (*Diqduqe Soferim*, ad loc.).

171. I.e., an animal that would have died of itself if not slaughtered ritually. Such animals are termed *terefot*, literally 'torn animals', and are forbidden according to halakah.

172. Translating with Jastrow, s.v. שקף.

173. The reading 'R. Judah' found in some late printed texts is clearly an error. See *Diqduqe Soferim*, ad. loc.

174. Generally termed *sha'atnez* and prohibited according to Lev. 19.19 and Deut. 22.11.

175. The redactor of the baraita in its present form added the *vav* before *'ezehu* which stood in the material before him in order to ease the transition. Nevertheless, the awkwardness as well as the apparent redundancy of the formulation give evidence of its building blocks. Indeed, this redundancy was felt by the Amoraim, who interpreted the first clause to refer to the *meshummad* and the second to the *min*.

176. Sifra Vayyiqra' parashah 2.3 (ed. Weiss, p. 40). On this passage cf. E. P. Sanders, *Paul and Palestinian Judaism*, 1977, pp. 83f. Cf. pShek 1.4 (ed. Krot. 1.5, 46b).

177. Reading מקבלי ברית with Weiss and MS Rome, Assemani 66 (ed. Finkelstein), New York 1956.

178. Translating the Venice ed.

179. MSS Hamburg and Rome (*a*) add 'of you' a second time (*Diqduqe Soferim*. ad loc.).

180. All MSS read הדרומין (*Diqduqe Soferim*, ad loc.).

181. See D. Weiss Halivni, 'Yesh Mevi'im Bikkurim', *Bar-Ilan* 7–8, 1969–70, p. 79.

182. Two more passages show that the Tannaim did not consider the *meshummadim*, or for that matter any other transgressors, as non-Jews. Instead they are listed separately from the *goyim*, the non-Jews. See bAZ 26a–b; bGitt 45b. On apostates in the writings of Philo, see H. Wolfson, *Philo* I, 1968, pp. 73–85.

183. Maimonides, H. Melakhim 11.3 states that R. Akiba and his contemporaries erred in thinking Bar Kokhba (Bar Kosiba) to be the Messiah. Needless to say, no accusation of heresy was lodged against these scholars.

184. Baron, *A Social and Religious History of the Jews*, 1952, II, p. 129. The divisions during the revolt are well documented in D. Rhoads, *Israel in Revolution, 6–74 C.E.*, 1976, pp. 94–149.

185. According to Acts 6.7 the 'number of disciples multiplied greatly in Jerusalem' (RSV). Nevertheless, the picture one gets from Acts is of a small, close-knit group.

186. See F. F. Bruce, *New Testament History*, 1972, pp. 279–90.

187. Cf. Bruce, *New Testament History*, pp. 265–78.

188. D. Sperber, 'Min', *EJ* XII, cols. 1–3.

189. R. T. Herford, *Christianity in Talmud and Midrash*, pp. 361–97; G. Alon, *Toledot ha-Yehudim be-Erets Yisra'el bi-tequfat ha-Mishnah veha-Talmud* I, repr. 1967, pp. 179–92.

190. Cf. Y. M. Elbogen, *Ha-Tefillah be-Yisra'el*, 1972, pp. 27–9, 31, 40; G. Forkman, *The Limits of the Religious Community*, 1972, pp. 90–2.

191. Translated from ed. Venice 30a. Cf. bMeg 17b and Herford, *Christianity in Talmud and Midrash*, pp. 125–35.

192. MS Munich סדר.

193. 'Benedictions' is omitted in MS Munich.

194. This is in accord with the view that the men of the Great Assembly composed, but did not place in order the Eighteen Benedictions (L. Ginzberg, *Perushim ve-Ḥiddushim bi-Yerushalmi* I, 1941, p. 322; Halivni, *Mekorot u-Mesorot, Mo'ed*, p. 489.

195. Contrast M. Ydit ('Birkhat Ha-Minim', *EJ* IV, col. 1035), who says that Samuel Ha-Qatan 'revised its text after it had fallen into oblivion'. This is impossible in light of the use of the verb *tqn* which refers to composition or formulation of a text.

196. MS Florence and some *rishonim* read ירד (*Diqduqe Soferim*, ad loc.). This reading seems to be influenced by the continuation of the baraita, which is set in a liturgical context, for *yrd* is a technical term for serving as precentor (*yrd* followed by *lifne ha-tevah*, 'to go down before the ark'). Indeed, the precentors in early synagogues stood at a level below that of the worshippers. We, however, prefer the reading *'md*. The first part of the baraita takes place in the setting of the academy of Yavneh where Rabban Gamaliel sought a Tanna to compose a benediction against the *minim*. The following year, Samuel Ha-Qatan's 'amnesia' occurred in a liturgical context as he was serving as precentor. This view is supported by pBer 5.3 (ed. Krot. 5.4, 9c).

197. While it seems from the context that he forgot the text of this blessing, an amoraic passage in pBer 5.3 (ed. Krot. 5.4, 9c) suggests that he skipped the entire blessing.

198. PBer 5.3 (ed. Krot. 5.4, 9c) in its Aramaic version of our baraita reads: משקיף עליהון, 'he looked at them'. Ginzberg, *Perushim* IV, 1961, p. 276 takes this as indicating that the correct reading is Hebrew עליהם. More probably, the Amoraim were confused by this strange use of the hif'il of *šqf* and so modified the object pronoun. The word *bah* clearly refers to the benediction.

199. MS Munich: 'more than two'.

200. Literally, 'bring him up'. Cf. n. 196.

201. Hyman, *Toledot Tanna'im ve-'Amoraim* III, p. 1148. Hyman failed to realize that the stories about Samuel Ha-Qatan and Hillel are apocryphal.

202. Joseph Heinemann, *Ha-Tefillah bi-Tequfat ha-Tanna'im ve-ha-'Amoraim*, 1966, p. 142 (ET, *Prayer in the Talmud: Forms and Patterns*, pp. 225f.), and Lieberman, *TK* I, pp. 53f.

203. Cf. Midrash Tanhuma' (ed. Buber), Lev., p. 2a.

204. למשומדים אל [ת]הי [תקוה] אם לא ישובו לתורתיך. הנוצרים והמינים כרגע יאבדו.[מהרה] ימחו מסיפר החיים ועם צדיקים אל יכתיבו. בא"י [מכניע] זידים.
(J. Mann, 'Genizah Fragments of the Palestinian Order of Service', *HUCA* 2, 1925, p. 306, restored in accord with S. Schechter, 'Genizah Specimens', pp. 657, 659).

205. See also Luke 6.22, Forkman, *The Limits of the Religious Community*, pp. 105f., and S. Krauss, 'The Jews in the Works of the Church Fathers', *JQR*, os 5, 1892–93, pp. 130–4.

206. Krauss, ibid.

207. The famous statement, 'An Israelite, though he sins, is (still) an Israelite', although based on bSanh 44a, was not seen as a halakah until much later. See J. Katz, ''Af 'al pi she-Ḥata ' Yisra'el Hu' ', *Tarbiz* 27, 1957–58, pp. 203–17. Katz takes the view that the use of this statement as a halakic dictum originated with Rashi. On the other hand, halakic use of the statement appears in Midrash Aggadah (ed. S. Buber) to Num., p. 162, to indicate that impurity could be contracted by killing a Jewish apostate, since he still retained his Jewish identity despite his transgressions. (This reference is noted in Halivni, *Mekorot u-Mesorot, Nashim*, p. 67 n. 3.) This tradition is without parallel. Since much of the material in this text comes from the school of Moses Ha-Darshan, it seems that Rashi was only reflecting a usage already prominent in the French exegetical tradition. Rashi did not originate the halakic use of this sentence. Cf. also J. Katz, *Exclusiveness and Tolerance*, 1962, pp. 67–81 and the many medieval responsa he cites; L. Ginzberg, *An Unknown Jewish Sect*, ET 1970, p. 105; and G. Blidstein, 'Who is Not a Jew? – The Medieval Discussion', *ILR* 11, 1976, pp. 369–90.

208. The use of bans in talmudic times was intended as a means of discipline. Under no circumstance did they imply any effect on the personal status of the person banned, only on the way he and his neighbours related to one another. Cf. Forkman, *The Limits of the Religious Community*, pp. 92–105.

209. See G. F. Moore, 'The Definition of the Jewish Canon and the Repudiation of Christian Scriptures', reprinted in *The Canon and Masorah of the Hebrew Bible* (ed. S. Leiman), 1974, pp. 115–41.

210. Translating MS Vienna (ed. Lieberman).

211. MSS Erfurt and London omit מפני הדליקה.

212. So Lieberman, *TK*, ad loc. and S. Leiman, *The Canonization of Hebrew Scripture*, 1976, pp. 190f. n. 511.

213. This is an oath formula. MS Erfurt: בניי.

214. MSS Erfurt and London: שאני שורפן (London omits the א).

215. The talmudic *rodef*, 'pursuer', is chasing his victim in order to kill him.

216. *Bayit*, 'house', is probably used here to refer to a temple or house of worship.

217. Ed. princ. and MS Erfurt: בו. London omits.

218. Erfurt and London: לעשות(abbreviated in London).

219. Num. 5.23.

220. MS Erfurt: שמי.

221. MS Erfurt adds: וקנאה ותחרות.

222. MSS Erfurt and London: שישרפו.

223. MS Erfurt: מפני המפלות.

224. MS Erfurt: מפני.

225. It should be mentioned in passing that R. Tarfon is not to be identified with the Tryphon with whom Justin Martyr conducted his dialogue.

226. Translating MS Erfurt (ed. Zuckermandel). Cf. Leiman, *Canonization*, p. 109 and notes, and Herford, *Christianity in Talmud and Midrash*, pp. 160f.

227. Leiman, *Canonization*, pp. 102–20.

228. We refer here to the formal legitimization of Gentile Christianity by the church in Jerusalem (Bruce, *New Testament History*, pp. 269f.). From the point of view of Rome, the Emperor Nerva (ruled 97–98) exempted the Christians from the *fiscus judaicus*, thereby declaring Christianity a separate religion (Bruce, *New Testament History*, p. 390).

229. Moore, 'Jewish Canon', pp. 123f.

230. Many of the later Jewish Christians in Palestine were in reality Judaizing Christians – not Christians of Jewish halakic status. We speak here, however, of the halakically Jewish Christians.

231. Schürer, *History* § 21.iii. rev. ed., I, 1973, pp. 553–5.

232. Bruce, *New Testament History*, pp. 390–2.

233. For the rabbinic attitude to Christians after Bar Kokhba, see Urbach, *Ḥazal*, p. 485 (ET, *The Sages* I, pp. 543f.).

7 On the Problem of Roman Influence on the Halakah and Normative Self-Definition in Judaism

*I am indebted to those who have given me the benefit of their comments on various drafts of this study, both at the symposium and later. Particular thanks are due to Mr Martin Goodman, Dott. Daniela Piattelli, and Professors E. P. Sanders, E. E. Urbach, H. J. Wolff, and R. Yaron. The usual caveats against guilt by association apply; on various points I have remained obdurate.

1. For an historical survey, see Boaz Cohen, *Jewish and Roman Law* I, 1966, pp. 3–12. For a bibliography of work published in Hebrew, see Nahum Rakover, *Otsar ha-Mishpat*, 1975, pp. 138–40 (nos. 3443–79).

2. See also Bernard S. Jackson, 'Evolution and Foreign Influence in Ancient Law', *The American Journal of Comparative Law* 16, 1968, pp. 372–

90, esp. 373f.; idem, *Essays in Jewish and Comparative Legal History*, 1975, p. 249.

3. E.g. Vinogradoff, Seebohm, Laveleye, Letourneau, Dareste. Maine himself was willing to combine his evolutionism with a poetic diffusionism: 'Except the blind forces of Nature, nothing moves in this world which is not Greek in its origin' ('The Effects of Observation of India on Modern European Thought', in *Village-Communities in the East*, ⁷1895, p. 238). Compare in anthropology Morgan, McLennan and Tylor.

4. E.g. David Heinrich Müller, *Die Gesetze Hammurabis und ihr Verhältnis zur mosäischen Gesetzgebung sowie zu den XII Tafeln*, 1903. Compare in anthropology the school of Boas; in 1920 R. H. Lowie went so far as to assert that 'cultures develop mainly through borrowings due to chance contact' (*Primitive Society*, 1920, p. 441).

5. E.g. Martin David, 'The Codex Hammurabi and its Relation to the Provisions of Law in Exodus', *Oudtestamentische Studien* 7, 1950, pp. 149–78, and literature cited in Jackson, *Essays*, p. 249 n. 90. Compare in anthropology the approaches of Malinowski and Radcliffe-Brown.

6. Alan Watson, *Legal Transplants*, 1974; idem, *Society and Legal Change*, 1977.

7. Some of them are discussed in my *Essays*, pp. 134–39; see also my 'History, Dogmatics and *Halakhah*', *Jewish Law in Legal History and the Modern World*, 1980, pp. 1–25.

8. On (1) and (5) see also the recent remarks of Keith Hopkins, *JRS* 68, 1978, pp. 178–86, esp. 180, 182f., in his review of Fergus Millar, *The Emperor in the Roman World*. Cf. in a different context, Ken Foster's review of Michael Zander, *Legal Services for the Community*, in *Journal of the Society of Public Teachers of Law* 14/4, 1979, p. 302.

9. 'History, Dogmatics and *Halakhah*'; *Essays*, pp. 22–4, on the question of significance as regards the identity of the Jewish legal system.

10. Civil as opposed to criminal. But that distinction is not easy to apply to Jewish law, where the category of *dine qenasot* includes both multiple restitution and corporal punishment. For the purposes of this inquiry, the most significant boundary is between capital and non-capital cases, and 'civil' is used in the sense of the latter.

11. I concur with those who doubt the historicity of pSanh 1.1 etc. (which claim the removal of capital jurisdiction 40 years earlier), although it must be said that there is no necessary inconsistency between this and the rival tradition of removal in 70 (bSanh 37b, etc.). Indeed, the impression of flux which this brief survey of civil jurisdiction presents may be thought to strengthen the possibility that capital jurisdiction was removed c. 30 CE, only to be restored at some time before its (at least *de iure*) final removal in 70. However, the likely motivation of the tradition antedating the removal to c. 30 is so clear that its historicity must still, on balance, be doubtful. The problem has been discussed most recently by Ernst Bammel, 'Die Blutgerichtsbarkeit in der römischen Provinz Judäa', *JJS* 25, 1974, pp. 35–49, esp. 43–7;

S. Safrai, 'Jewish Self-Government', *The Jewish People in the First Cen-tury*, 1974, pp. 398–400. See also E. E. Urbach, 'The Sanhedrin of 23 and Capital Punishment', *Proceedings of the Fifth World Congress of Jewish Studies* II, 1973, pp. 38ff., esp. 47.

12. I refer here to the theory of Mary Douglas, *Implicit Meanings*, 1975, pp. 217f., who writes: 'The more coherent and all-embracing the classification, the more the pressure needed to sustain its general credibility against rival schemes.'

13. Literally, cases involving money, but including much of that which corresponds to our laws of contract, tort, property (real and personal) and succession. The principal areas normally excluded from the term are capital cases, cases involving fines (*dine qenasot*, above, n. 10), and cases involving marriage and divorce. But the ambit of the term can vary according to the context, and the latter two areas are not always excluded.

14. PSanh 1.1 (18a).

15. E.g. R. Leszynsky, 'Simon ben Schétah', *REJ* 63, 1912, p. 216, following Hertzfeld; see also Bammel, 'Blutgerichtsbarkeit', p. 43 n. 52.

16. For which see Emil Schürer, *The History of the Jewish People*, § 10, ET, rev. ed., Vol. I, 1973, pp. 221–3.

17. Arnaldo Momigliano, *Ricerche sull'Organizzazione della Giudea sotto il Dominio Romano*, 1967, pp. 4f. On Judaea at this period see also A. Schalit, *Roman Administration in Palestine*, (in Hebrew), 1937, pp. 55ff.; Daniela Piattelli, 'Ricerche Intorno alle Relazioni Politiche tra Roma e L' *EΘΝΟΣ ΤΩΝ 'ΙΟΥΔΑΙΩΝ* dal 161 A.C. al 4 A.C.', *Bullettino dell' Istituto di Diritto Romano* 3, Series 13, 1972, pp. 219–347, at 290–302; shortened English version in *ILR* 14, 1979, pp. 195–236, at 215–19.

18. E. Mary Smallwood, *The Jews under Roman Rule*, 1976, p. 39; see also Michel S. Ginsburg, *Rome et la Judée*, 1928, pp. 86ff.; Schalit, *Roman Administration*, p. 17; Piattelli, 'Ricerche Intorno', pp. 303–6 (ET, *ILR* 14, pp. 219–20).

19. J. Juster, *Les Juifs dans l'Empire Romain* II, 1914, p. 116; cf. Gins-burg, *Rome et la Judée*, pp. 130f. I am not aware of any subsequent evidence that has invalidated this observation. Josephus has Titus give as an instance of Roman humanity the fact that 'we maintained the laws of your forefathers and permitted you, not only among yourselves but also in your dealings with others, to live as you willed', *Bell.* VI. 333–34. While Josephus's apologetics must be taken into account, it would hardly have served his purpose to put into the mouth of the Roman general any manifest falsity.

20. Cicero, *Ad Atticum* VI. 1.15; *In Verrem* II.3.6, § 15. See W. W. Buckland, 'L'edictum provinciale', *Revue historique de droit français et étranger* 13, 1934, pp. 81, 85ff.; Giovanni Pugliese, 'Riflessioni sull' editto di Cicerone in Cilicia', *Synteleia Vincenzo Arangio-Ruiz* II, 1964, pp. 972–86. Frequently, the constitution of the province was settled by a *lex data* sponsored by the conquering general, and this sometimes included guarantees of jurisdictional autonomy. See Cicero, *In Verrem* II.2.15, § 39, on the *lex Rupilia* for Sicily (the confirmation of which by

Verres in his edict was merely declaratory). Elsewhere we find autonomy promised by imperial edict, as in the (significantly qualified) fourth edict of Augustus to Cyrene (7–4 BCE): see for the text and Latin translation *Fontes Iuris Romani Antejustiniani* I (ed. S. Riccobono), ²1941, p. 409; Fernand de Visscher, *Les édits d'Auguste découverts à Cyrène*, 1940, pp. 20–3 for text and French translation, 132–4 for discussion. There could also be treaties of cession which might seek to guarantee local institutions, as in the case of Bithynia in 74 BCE; see Jean Gaudemet, 'La Juridiction provinciale d'après la correspondance entre Pline et Trajan', *RIDA* 11, 1964, pp. 335–53. But in some provinces, these matters seem to have been left to the (fluctuating – at least until Hadrian's consolidation of the edicts) discretion of the governor, as apparently in Cicero's Cilicia. See A. J. Marshall, 'The Structure of Cicero's Edict', *American Journal of Philology* 85, 1964, p. 190. Judaea appears to fall into this last category. Certainly, we hear of no *lex data*; see Schalit, *Roman Administration*, p. 19.

21. Schürer, *History*, § 17.3(2), Vol. I, pp. 357f.

22. On the relationship between the two, see Schürer, *History*, ibid., pp. 360, 367f.; M. Stern, 'The Province of Judaea', *The Jewish People in the First Century*, pp. 309–15. The sceptical attitude of Theodor Mommsen (*The Provinces of the Roman Empire* II, ET 1909, p. 185 n. 1) to the statement of Josephus on which the alleged dependence of the governor of Judaea is based still commands respect.

23. Notably, testamentary and marital capacity. But just as Roman law tolerated, and in some cases gave limited recognition to, less formal arrangements entered into by those who had lost full private law rights, one may assume that the *peregrinus dediticius* was not forbidden to enter into comparable *de facto* arrangements. However, it has been argued with some plausibility that loss of these rights was suffered only by special classes of freedmen who also enjoyed the status of *dediticius*: A. H. M. Jones, *Studies in Roman Government and Law*, 1960, pp. 131f. See also W. W. Buckland, *A Text-book of Roman Law*, ³1963, pp. 97f.; Momigliano, *Ricerche*, pp. 86f.

24. *Tituli ex corpore Ulpiani* XX.14 (*Fontes* II, ²1940, p. 284) explains the testamentary incapacity of the *dediticius* on the grounds that he is neither a Roman citizen nor a *peregrinus 'quoniam nullius certae civitatis est, ut secundum leges civitatis suae testetur'*. But Jones, *Studies*, p. 132, argues that this does not refer to *peregrini dediticii*.

25. Mommsen thought they did; Juster stoutly denied it. On their views, see Alfredo M. Rabello, 'A Tribute to Jean Juster', *ILR* 11, 1976, pp. 231f. In more recent times, Mommsen's view was followed by Gedalyahu Alon, *Toledot ha-Yehudim be-Erets Yisra'el be-Tequfat ha-Mishnah veha-Talmud* I, 1954, p. 43, while Urbach, reviewing Alon in *Behinot* 4, 1953, pp. 66f., aligned himself with Juster. Mommsen's view extended to all Jews throughout the empire, in so far as they were not reduced to slavery. As regards the Jews of Palestine, Safrai, 'Jewish Self-Government', p. 405, still asserts without qualification that the Jews of the land of Israel were considered *dediticii* and lost their rights.

But this is contradicted by Josephus, *Ap.* II.4, who states that Egypt was the *only* province where all the native inhabitants were forbidden participation in Roman citizenship.

26. Momigliano, *Ricerche*, pp. 85–7; cf. Rabello, 'Tribute', p. 232, for further literature.

27. Josephus, *Bell.* III.29–32, 59. See also E. Volterra, 'Nuovi documenti per la conoscenza del diritto vigente nelle provincie romane', *IURA* 14, 1963, p. 55, citing also Josephus, *Vita* 394, 411.

28. *Bell.* IV. 444–7, on Betabris and Caphartoba; *Bell.* VI. 352 on the inhabitants of Jerusalem. But note also VI. 130, where Vespasian, having reduced Jamnia and Azotus, is said to have returned 'with a large multitude who had surrendered under treaty'.

29. E.g. the Idumeans and 40,000 of the Jews of Jerusalem, according to *Bell.* VI. 379, 386. In VI. 384–6 both citizenship and personal desert are taken into account in deciding the fate of each individual.

30. Cf. Salo Baron, *A Social and Religious History of the Jews* II, ²1952, p. 109, although it is not quite clear whether Baron here intends to refer back to this period.

31. Buckland, *Text-book*, p. 97, describes *dediticii* (so far as affects our problems) as 'primarily members of nations which had submitted to Rome, but had, as yet, no constitution conferred on them'. See also Juster, *Les Juifs*, p. 22; Jones, *Studies*, pp. 130f.; A. N. Sherwin-White, *The Roman Citizenship*, 1939, pp. 224f. It is not clear how this might apply to a *section* of the population of a city (as the 40,000 from Jerusalem) who were so designated; it is easier to envisage its application to a whole city, e.g. Jamnia; and some of the traditions regarding R. Johanan b. Zakkai's new settlement there may reflect the regularization of the city's status under his leadership.

32. Above, n. 29; cf. Volterra, 'Nuovi documenti', p. 55 n.46.

33. Cf. Baron, *Social and Religious History* II, p. 108, on the deliberate failure of successive emperors to clarify the legal position of the Jews, both inside and outside Palestine.

34. J. Neusner, *A Life of Yohanan ben Zakkai*, pp. 167–71.

35. Indications of this are seen, e.g., by David Daube ('Jewish Law in the Hellenistic World', *Jewish Law in Legal History and the Modern World* [ed. Jackson], 1980, p. 55) in bShab 116a-b (the story of Imma Shalom, Raban Gamaliel, and the Judaeo-Christian judge – though Daube notes that such a jurisdiction might have been regarded by the Romans as no more than arbitration), and by Rabello ('Tribute', p. 232) in the Murabba'at documents.

36. Safrai, 'Jewish Self-Government', p. 407, expresses some doubt. This is not incompatible with his view (below, n. 47) that R. Gamaliel II received official recognition from the governor of Syria. The latter incident, if historical and if rightly so understood, could well have involved recognition of an already assumed jurisdictional practice.

37. For a more detailed study of these traditions, see M. D. Herr, 'The Historical Significance of the Dialogues between Jewish Sages and Roman Dignitaries', *SH* 22, 1971, pp. 123–50.

38. Had they been designed with this purpose, one might expect them to be more explicit on the point. It is, however, possible that they have been reshaped to reflect later concerns, after the question of jurisdictional recognition ceased to be a live issue.

39. PSanh 1.2 (19b), pSanh 1.4 (19c, 19d), etc. See further Herr, 'Dialogues', pp. 128–32.

40. Jacob Neusner, *Development of a Legend*, 1970, pp. 138f., takes the first of these questions (19b) to be why the homicidal ox was stoned. In fact, the immediate response makes it reasonably clear that the question was really directed to why, additionally, its owner should be put to death.

41. See Schürer, *History*, § 21.I, Vol. I, p. 519 n. 29.

42. 'Dialogues', pp. 128f.

43. Note the common concern with aspects of the law of the goring ox. Both may have been inspired by the conflicts of law rule in mBK 4.3, which also prompted the comparative observation on the law of damage by animals to tBK 4.2, considered below, n. 99.

44. See below, pp. 162f.

45. See Neusner, *Yohanan ben Zakkai*, pp. 218–25; idem, *Development of a Legend*, pp. 139–41, 253–6, concluding: 'I suppose that the dispute-with-gentiles stories do not begin to take shape much before the late Amoraic period and did not circulate widely even then.'

46. On which see Safrai, 'Jewish Self-Government', pp. 404f.

47. Safrai, 'The Status of Provincia Judaea after the Destruction of the Second Temple', *Zion* 27, 1962, pp. 216–22 (Hebrew with English Summary at 7); accepted by Schürer, *History* § 21.I, Vol. I, p. 514 n. 2, although this must be seen in the light of the restricted dependence to which the governor of Judaea was subject. See also Alon, *Toledot* I, pp. 50–2. Alon, too (p. 72), views the Mishnah as recording the granting of permission to exercise powers of leadership.

48. On the nature of the governor of Judaea's subservience, see n. 22 above.

49. E. E. Urbach, 'Class-Status and Leadership in the World of the Palestinian Sages', *Proceedings of the Israel Academy of Sciences and Humanities* 2, 1966, pp. 56f.; *Behinot* 4, 1953, p. 72.

50. *Qar'u*. It may be noted that the argument which follows presupposes that it was the *oral* law that was *read* to them. There are significant variants in the other two versions. While both stress the comprehensive nature of the material which the Romans studied, the Palestinian Talmud contents itself with saying that the Romans 'learned' it, while Sifre Deut shows the greatest sensitivity to the Babylonian Talmud's apparent admission that the 'Sages of Israel' possessed and used a written version of the oral law, contrary to the disapproval voiced by some third-century Palestinian teachers of committing the oral law to writing: in Sifre Deut the officers are told to read the written law and repeat the Mishnah, Midrash, Halakot and Aggadot'.

51. BBK 38a. The translation here quoted is that of Kirzner in the Soncino Talmud. Other versions are found at pBK 4.3 (4b) and Sifre

Deut 344 (Finkelstein, p. 401). For a variety of reasons, I regard the version in the Babylonian Talmud as the oldest extant form of the tradition and Sifre Deut as the youngest. Yerushalmi adds to the specification of what the officers came to learn and adds further examples of discriminatory rules. It appends to its own particular response to the problem the very different approach of the Babylonian Talmud (*eyn anu modi'in*). Sifre Deut includes features of both Yerushalmi and the Babylonian Talmud, and adds a further narrative element of its own in the form of the officers' pretence of being Jewish students. Such a view of the literary history does not, of course, determine the question of the historical priority among the distinct responses (below, n. 52). But we have here a notable example of redactors making use of the literary features of versions which present a different, perhaps rival, *Tendenz* to their own.

52. This is not stated in Sifre Deut, where *gezelo shel goy* is the one example, or in the Babylonian Talmud, where *shor shel kena'ani* (prefer *nokhr:*) is the one example. The different responses of the three sources to the problem of discriminatory laws may be summarized thus: the Babylonian Talmud admits that such a law is wrong, but invokes the Roman story to show that it represents such a minor blemish in the context of the Torah as a whole as not to be significant; Yerushalmi admits that they are wrong and has R. Gamaliel repeal at least one example. The function of the Roman story is to support R. Gamaliel's reasoning: the reform *is* required *mipne hillul hashem*, since Gentiles have actually criticized God's Torah because of it. (The ruling and the rationale are also found anonymously in tBK 10.15; see further Urbach in this volume, below, pp. 283f.). But it then adds the Babylonian Talmud response, which in the context is clearly inappropriate; Sifre Deut, on the other hand, seeks to justify the discriminatory rule, in illustration of the theology of Deut 33.3 (on which it here comments). The function of the Roman story is to suggest that even the Gentiles were not *significantly* offended by it (perhaps an implied rejection of *mipne hillul hashem*). By the time of the redaction of the Babylonian Talmud *sugya* the alternative responses, or at least that represented by R. Gamaliel's *gezerah*, must have been known. At the very least, it appears that the Babylonian redactors did not wish to extend the *gezerah* beyond the particular discriminatory rule in terms of which it was formulated.

53. Earlier commentators took a straightforward view of the reason for Roman interest in the content of Jewish law. See Kirzner in the Soncino translation of bBK, 1935, p. 215 n. 4, for the views of Graetz and Halevy.

54. Alon, *Toledot* I, p. 72; Herr, 'Dialogues', pp. 132f.; Safrai, 'Jewish Self-Government', p. 406.

55. Cf. Cohen, *Jewish and Roman Law* I, pp. 24f.

56. An absurd notion. And if it were true, the rabbis would have had every reason to keep quiet about it.

57. With the different roots, cf. *vehu'ad* (Ex. 21.29) and *noda'* (Ex. 21.36)

in the biblical *fons* of the tannaitic discriminatory law, and the comment of Mekhilta (Nezikin 12; Lauterbach III.96) on the latter.

58. See Y. Yadin, 'Expedition D – The Cave of Letters', *IEJ* 12, 1962, pp. 227–57; idem, *Bar-Kokhba*, 1971, pp. 222–53; H. J. Polotsky, 'The Greek Papyri from the Cave of Letters', *IEJ* 12, 1962, pp. 258–62; Maxime Lemosse, 'Le procès de Babatha', *The Irish Jurist* 3, 1968, pp. 363–76.

59. But see Lemosse, 'Le procès de Babatha', p. 366 n. 3, identifying the site with Zoara.

60. In 106 CE. See further Schürer, *History*, Appendix II, Vol. 1, pp. 585f.

61. Yadin, *Bar-Kokhba*, p. 236.

62. Or, if not, Christian: E. Seidl, 'Juristische Papyruskunde', *Studia et Documenta Historiae et Juris* 33, 1967, p. 551.

63. Seidl, ibid.

64. Below, pp. 167f. and nn. 99–101.

65. The summons to the guardian to appear before the governor's court in Petra is dated 12 October 125. See Yadin, *Bar-Kokhba*, pp. 240f.

66. Lemosse, 'Le procès de Babatha', p. 369, thinks that Babatha had a definite choice of forum.

67. Alon, 'Those Appointed for Money', in *Jews, Judaism and the Classical World*, 1977, pp. 374–432 (ET of *Meḥqarim be-Toledot Yisra'el* II, pp. 15–57). See also Safrai, 'Jewish Self-Government', pp. 412–17.

68. It should be remembered that those living outside recognized *civitates* fell under direct Roman rule. See Jones, *Studies*, p. 133.

69. See below, p. 169, on disapproval of recourse to Gentile courts; mGitt 9.8 on a bill of divorce given under compulsion of a Gentile court.

70. The very history of which is supplemented by the archive. The name of the governor at the time of Babatha's suit was previously unknown: Yadin, *Bar-Kokhba*, p. 241; see also Schürer, *History*, Appendix II, n. 60, Vol. I, p. 585; Lemosse, 'Le procès de Babatha', p. 367 n. 6.

71. Seidl, 'Juristische Papyruskunde', p. 551; H. J. Wolff, 'Le droit provincial dans la province romaine d'Arabie', *RIDA* 23, 1976, pp. 271–90; Arnaldo Biscardi, 'Nuove testimonianze di un papiro arabo-giudaico per la storia del processo provinciale romano', *Studi in onore di Gaetano Scherillo* I, 1972, pp. 111–52, esp. 138. On Romanization of local law in Egypt in the second century, see Modrzejewski, 'La Règle de Droit dans l'Egypte Romaine', *Proceedings of the Twelfth International Congress of Papyrology*, 1970, pp. 344–47.

72. See below, p. 169.

73. See e.g. Mommsen, *The Provinces of the Roman Empire* II, pp. 223ff.; M. Avi-Yonah, 'Palaestina', *PW*, Suppl. XIII, 1973, col. 405.

74. PSanh 7.2 (24b). Cf. Juster, *Les Juifs* II, p. 106; Smallwood, *The Jews under Roman Rule*, p. 475 n. 33. And see M. D. Herr, 'Persecution and Martyrdom in Hadrian's Days', *SH* 23, 1972, pp. 94f. H.-P. Chajes ('Les Juges juifs en Palestine de l'an 70 à l'an 400', *REJ* 39, 1899, p. 43)

saw the tradition as reflecting the effects of the revolt under Antoninus Pius (following Graetz).

75. The ban on Jews from entering Jerusalem (*Aelia Capitolina*) perhaps evokes the rule of Roman law that *dediticii* were forbidden to reside within one hundred miles of Rome. But, in fact, the population of Jerusalem itself appears on this occasion to have been enslaved: Mommsen, *The Provinces of the Roman Empire* II, p. 218.

76. Origen, *Ad Africanum* 14 (PL 11, cols. 81–84). Cf. Schürer, *History*, § 21.I, Vol. I, p. 526; Safrai, 'Jewish Self-Government', p. 410; Urbach, 'Class Status', pp. 70ff. On Roman jurisdiction in cases of theft, see my *Theft in Early Jewish Law*, 1972, pp. 251–60.

77. On the question of dating, see H. F. Jolowicz and B. Nicholas, *An Historical Introduction to the Study of Roman Law*, [3]1972, pp. 345f. n. 5.

78. The literature is vast, and the problems complex, in part because the text of the decree has been preserved only in a fragmentary Greek version (PGiess. 40; for Meyer's text and an important early discussion, see M.-J. Bry, 'L'Édit de Caracalla', *Études d'histoire juridique offertes à P. F. Girard par ses élèves* I, 1912, pp. 1–42) which has a lengthy gap. For further literature, see Baron, *Social and Religious History* II, pp. 374f. n. 25; Jones, *Studies*, pp. 129–40; Sherwin-White, *Roman Citizenship*, pp. 220–7; Jolowicz and Nicholas, *Historical Introduction*, pp. 345–7; C. Sasse, *Die Constitutio Antoniniana*, 1958, pp. 134–43. The recent study of Hartmut Wolff, *Die Constitutio Antoniniana und Papyrus Gissensis 40 1*, 2 vols., 1976, came to my attention too late to be taken into account.

79. Jones, *Studies*, p. 135. But some have seen the motive for the decree as primarily fiscal. See J. Gaudemet, *Institutions de l'Antiquité*, 1967, pp. 530f.

80. The whole matter is controversial. An admirable discussion has been provided by Joseph Modrzejewski, 'La Règle de Droit', pp. 347–9. The alternative view is that the effect of the *c.Antonin.* was to bestow double citizenship, so that the former provincial *peregrini* had a choice of laws (Schönbauer). This, however, is too radical. More appealing is Modrzejewski's suggestion (p. 354), that 'les coutumes locales pérégrines sont devenues des coutumes provinciales romaines' – a solution which both avoids the need to resort to any of the solutions at nn. 82–83, 85–86, below, and which adds a further element of uncertainty to the situation, in the form of the problems of conflict between the 'Roman' and the 'customary' elements in this new, integrated legal order. According to Modrzejewski, the newly-acquired Roman citizenship imposed no obligation to employ Roman law, but rather conferred the privilege of using juristic acts reserved for Roman citizens (i.e. under the *ius civile*).

81. *Codex Theodosianus* 2.1.10; see now Rabello, 'Tribute', pp. 236–8.

82. Unlikely not only on the grounds that such a status was essentially temporary (above, n. 31) and was revoked by conferment of any civic status or local autonomy (see Sherwin-White, *Roman Citizenship*, p. 225), but also in view of the fact that the phrase *chōris tōn dedeitikiōn*

in PGiess. 40 (*if* that phrase does qualify the grant of citizenship rather than some subsidiary provision [Jones] and *if* PGiess. does provide a version of the *c.Antonin.* at all [Sherwin-White]) was probably not intended to refer to the generality of *peregrini dediticii* but rather to special classes of freedmen and surrendered *barbarians* (viz. enemy populations living *outside* the boundaries of the Empire), as plausibly argued by Jones, *Studies*, p. 134. See also Sherwin-White, *Roman Citizenship*, p. 224.

83. See Buckland, *Text-book*, p. 98. The view was held by Meyer and Marquadt that the Jews fell under this exception: see Bry, 'L'Édit de Caracalla', p. 31 n. 3. But the exception is of doubtful status. There is evidence that the native Egyptian peasants, who did pay the poll tax, nevertheless became citizens. See Sherwin-White, *Roman Citizenship*, pp. 220f.; Jolowicz and Nicholas, *Historical Introduction*, pp. 346f.; Jones, *Studies*, pp. 132f.

84. See Baron, *Social and Religious History* II, p. 109.

85. The view of Rabello, 'Tribute', pp. 234f. If this is correct, one must understand *Cod. Theod.* 2.1.10 as merely declaratory of the existing *de iure* position (which is by no means impossible).

86. A theory noted and given some qualified support by Jones, *Studies*, p. 135.

87. Daube, 'Jewish Law', pp. 57f. For the change as immediately apparent in Egypt, see Jolowicz and Nicholas, *Historical Introduction*, p. 470.

88. *Cod. Justin.* 1.9.1.

89. There is no indication that the parties did possess Roman citizenship, nor is it likely that both sides consented to submit the case to Roman law in view of the differences between Roman and Jewish law and their likely impact on the interests of the parties. A third explanation, in terms of the lack of an alternative forum in Antioch (cf., perhaps, the situation of Babatha, considered above), is also unlikely. Another possibility is that the Roman administration may have decided to intervene because of the special interests of the fisc.

90. See also Daube's treatment of the story of Bana'ah ('Jewish Law', pp. 50–52) in terms of the rules of arbitration.

91. See Jolowicz and Nicholas, *Historical Introduction*, p. 74. Clear evidence of the availability of a choice of law to those granted Roman citizenship is provided by a Greek inscription from Rhodes, where the effects of a grant of citizenship to a Syrian are recorded. See Pierre Roussel, 'Un Syrien au service de Rome et d'Octave', *Syria* 15, 1934, pp. 33–74 (para. 8); Fernand de Visscher, 'Le statut juridique des nouveaux citoyens romains et l'inscription de Rhosos', *L'Antiquité Classique* 13, 1944, pp. 11–35; 14, 1945, pp. 29–59. See also B. Lifschitz, 'Études sur l'Histoire de la Province Romaine de Syrie', *ANRW* II.8, 1977, pp. 4f.

92. Jolowicz and Nicholas, *Historical Introduction*, pp. 73f.

93. Baron, *Social and Religious History* I, p. 240. On the juridical

problems of double citizenship in Egypt, see Modrzejewski, 'La Règle de Droit', pp. 349–52.

94. Acts 6.9. See Stern, 'The Province of Judaea', pp. 338f.; Rabello, 'Tribute', p. 231.

95. Jones, *Studies*, pp. 135ff. Both suggestions, however, are simply attempts to fill the long gap in PGiess. 40, and must be regarded as conjectural, despite their plausibility.

96. Baron, *Social and Religious History* I, p. 241.

97. Cicero, *Ad Atticum* VI.1.15.

98. Not strictly a formula. It has been noted that even under the *cognitio extra ordinem*, a provincial governor might delegate the hearing of the case to a *iudex*, whether from inside or outside the bureaucracy, and his instructions to such a delegate might well resemble a formula. Thus the differences between the two systems might in practice be slight. See Lemosse, 'Le procès de Babatha', pp. 375f.; Jolowicz and Nicholas, *Historical Introduction*, p. 398; Biscardi, 'Nuove testimonianze', pp. 134f. For the blank formulae of the Babatha archive, see H. J. Polotsky, 'Three Greek Documents from the Family Archive of Babatha', *Eretz Israel* 8, 1967, pp. 46–51, esp. 51; Erwin Seidl, 'Ein Papyrusfund zum klassischen Zivilprozessrecht', *Studi in onore di Giuseppe Grosso* II, 1968, pp. 345–61, esp. 360f., and 348, 350–3 on the procedure.

99. See Seidl, 'Juristische Papyruskunde', p. 551; idem, 'Papyrusfund', p. 348; Lemosse, 'Le procès de Babatha', p. 370; Volterra, Review of P. J. Parsons, *The Oxyrhynchus Papyri* XLII, IURA 26, 1975, pp. 191f.; A. Biscardi, 'Sulla Identificazione degli "Xenokritai" e sulla loro Attività in P. Oxy. 3016', *Festschrift für Erwin Seidl zum 70. Geburtstag*, 1975, pp. 15–24, for discussion; further literature and discussion in Biscardi, 'Xenokritai', *Novissimo Digesto Italiano* 20, 1975, pp. 1087–90. The recently discovered example in POxy. 3016 appears to support this meaning, and many take Cicero's *peregrini iudices* in the same sense, though the argument for the latter does not appear to me to be compelling. The term also occurs elsewhere, and in some contexts must mean 'foreign judges'.

100. I take this to mean 'non-Roman'. In the context of Arabia at this period, the *xenokritai* are unlikely to represent a reflection of the institution found earlier among Greek city states of using *metapempta dikasteria* – judges from other Greek cities. For the latter, see David Magie, *Roman Rule in Asia Minor*, 1950, vol. I, pp. 113, 525, 648; vol. II, pp. 963f. n. 8., 1382f. n. 36, 1517f. n. 49; de Visscher, *Édits d'Auguste*, pp. 130–2.

101. Unlike Cicero's Cilicia, where the implication of the passage appears to be that the autonomy granted by Cicero encompassed the use of local law.

102. Alon, 'Those Appointed for Money', p. 384 n. 35 (English), II, p. 22 n. 35 (Hebrew). The difficulty raised by Alon in terms of Roman procedure is now removed in the light of the considerations discussed in n. 98 above.

[It should be noted that the translation in the English edition is seriously misleading, the result of the difficulties of translating technical Roman procedure into Hebrew and then retranslating into English. For 'The formulary proceedings, with their inherent division between judgment *in iure* by the ruler and *in judaico* (*sic*) by the civil magistrate, were replaced by . . .' read: 'The formulary proceedings, with their inherent division between judgment *in iure* by the magistrate [i.e. the praetor or provincial governor – B. S. J.] and *in judicio* by the lay judge, were replaced . . .'.]

103. TBK 4.2; pBK 4.3 (4b). In the latter it is attributed to R. Ḥiyya.

104. Associating the ruling with Yerushalmi's response to the criticism of discriminatory rules, above, n. 52. The text appears immediately before the story of the Roman inquiry and occurs in the Gemara which comments on the discriminatory rule of the Mishnah.

105. Safrai, 'Jewish Self-Government', p. 408 (the reference there to Gittin 78b should read 88b); cf. Falk, 'Jewish Private Law', in the same volume, at p. 505.

106. POxy. 3015, in the volume cited above, n. 99.

107. Mek. Nez. 1 (Lauterbach III, pp. 1–2; to Ex. 21.1) on the basis of the Munich MS.

108. Preferred by Horovitz and Rabin, p. 246.

109. Babatha herself, it may be noted, had not acquired the ability to write. See Yadin, *Bar-Kochba*, p. 241.

110. As, indeed, appears from rabbinic sources. See Saul Lieberman, 'Roman Legal Institutions in Early Rabbinics and the Acta Martyrum', *JQR* 35, 1944–5, pp. 1–57.

111. See Z. W. Falk, 'Zum fremden Einfluss auf das jüdische Recht', *RIDA* 18, 1971, pp. 11–23; idem, *Introduction to Jewish Law of the Second Commonwealth* II, 1978, pp. 326f., stressing the Greek origins of Jewish guardianship practices, and commenting with further literature on this aspect of the Babatha archive.

112. Lifschitz, 'Études'. For *peregrini*, on the other hand, it was precisely in the areas of property and commercial law that access to Roman law was, in principle, most available, through the recognized *fictiones* of the *ius honorarium*. In this manner, it has been argued, the *ius gentium* was available also to provincial *peregrini*, since the provincial edict extended those of Rome to the province. See Buckland, 'L'Edictum Provinciale', p. 94.

113. Above, p. 168. Neither distinguished between '*tam*' and '*mu'ad*' in the manner of Jewish law. A possible indication that the reference is to Roman law may be derived from the fact that the parallel Gemara commentary to the Mishnah here includes the baraita of the Roman inquiry (bBK 38a, discussed above, pp. 162f.).

114. Safrai, 'Jewish Self-Government', p. 417; on a Jewish *agoranomos* in Caesarea in the time of Trajan, see B. Lifschitz, 'Césarée de Palestine, son histoire et ses institutions', *ANRW* II. 8, 1977, p. 505. On the office, see Magie, *Roman Rule in Asia Minor* I, pp. 645f.; D. Sperber, 'On the Office of Agoranomos in Roman Palestine', *Zeitschrift der deutschen Morgenländischen Gesellschaft* 127, 1977, pp. 227–43.

115. Above, n. 12.

116. E.g. the UK Sale of Goods Act, 1893, despite its self-description as 'An Act codifying the Law relating to the Sale of Goods'.

117. See the Egyptian evidence cited below, p. 177 and n. 133.

118. The lack of the full range of technical legal sources is reflected, e.g., in some of the straightforward requests for technical advice sent by Pliny, when governor of Bithynia, to the Emperor Trajan. See A. N. Sherwin-White, 'Trajan's Replies to Pliny: Authorship and Necessity', *JRS* 52, 1962, p. 122, on *Epist.* 49 and 68.

119. Livy, III.34.

120. B. Cohen, *Jewish and Roman Law* I, pp. 17–21.

121. Cohen's first example, noxal surrender in the Roman *actio de pauperie* and mBK 3.8, well illustrates the point. A broad general remedy in Roman law (hand over the offending animal or pay damages) is here suggested as a parallel to a specific issue which forms but a tiny aspect of the application of a quite different and more sophisticated remedy (*ḥaṣi nezeq migufo*) in rabbinic law. The only point in favour of influence is that the Jewish problem (dead ox when alive worth *exactly* half the price of the live ox, the carcase of the dead ox being *absolutely* worthless) sounds highly theoretical, and thus might be thought to have been prompted by speculation of some kind – but speculation on when the Twelve Tables remedy might correspond to *ḥaṣi nezeq migufo* is only one possible form.

122. See Fritz Schulz, *History of Roman Legal Science*, 1946, pp. 91 (on the beginnings of edictal commentary in the late Republic) and 189–203 (on its great development from the beginning of the Principate).

123. Cicero, *Ad Atticum* VI.1.15. For a review of the literature on the problem, see Gérard Chalon, *L'Édit de Tiberius Julius Alexander*, Olten and Lausanne 1964, pp. 73–5; see also Giovanni Pugliese, 'Riflessioni sull' editto di Cicerone in Cilicia', pp. 972–86; A. J. Marshall, 'The Structure of Cicero's Edict', pp. 185–91; Modrzejewski, 'La Règle de Droit', pp. 341–4.

124. Listed and summarized in Chalon, *L'Édit*, pp. 251–6.

125. Marshall, 'The Structure of Cicero's Edict', p. 188; D. R. Shackleton Bailey, *Cicero's Letters to Atticus* III, 1968, p. 248. This view is maintained also for the later period (against Buckland, 'L'edictum provinciale', pp. 86, 91f., and others) by Chalon, *L'Édit*, p. 73 n. 30. But such reproduction would be far more understandable in Cicero's day than a century later, in the light of the stabilization of the edicts resulting from both bureaucratic and political factors.

It has been persuasively argued that at Rome a single edict was put out by the *praetor urbanus* and the *praetor peregrinus* contrary to the previous assumption of two quite independent documents: Alan Watson, *Law Making in the Later Roman Republic*, 1974, pp. 67ff.

126. Bailey's translation: *Cicero's Letters to Atticus* III, pp. 92f. See further Buckland, 'L'edictum provinciale', pp. 83f., approved by Marshall, 'The Structure of Cicero's Edict', p. 190, for the technical reason for the inclusion of these matters.

127. On which see Schulz, *History of Roman Legal Science*, pp. 191–2; O. Lenel, *Palingenesia Iuris Civilis* I, 1889, pp. 189–237; Antonio Guarino, 'Gaio e l' "edictum provinciale" ', *IURA* 20, 1969, pp. 154–71, esp. 168ff., contesting the view of Remo Martini (*Ricerche in tema di editto provinciale*, 1969) that the text of the edict on which Gaius commented was that of the urban praetor.

128. Buckland, 'L'edictum provinciale', pp. 87f. on von Velsen; Ranon Katzoff, 'The Provincial Edict in Egypt', *Tijdschrift voor Rechtsgeschiedenis* 37, 1969, p. 428, suggests that the commentary was written on the particular edict of the province where Gaius resided.

129. Notably the best preserved (below, n. 135), which Chalon (*L'Édit*, pp. 69ff.) distinguishes from the Ciceronian model, suggesting that such purely administrative edicts were issued as special edicts when political conditions required, rather than as regular promulgations at the beginning of the term of office. The edict of Tiberius Julius Alexander was not typical of all the Egyptian edicts (Chalon, pp. 79ff.), but the others do not fall into Cicero's pattern either.

130. For the view that the *edictum provinciale* was issued only in the senatorial provinces, see Katzoff, 'The Provincial Edict in Egypt', p. 419; Chalon, *L'Édit*, pp. 70f. Moreover, the formulary system was not used in Egypt, so that the technical function of Cicero's edict would there have been inapplicable: see Modrzejewski, 'La Règle de Droit', pp. 341ff.

131. Buckland, *Text-book*, p. 11. But even this does not require the conclusion that the edict included private law material. Hadrian himself referred to a permanent edict on the *jurisdiction* of the Roman governor – *Const. Tanta*, 18.

132. It appears that a formal act of publication by each provincial governor was still required. See also Raphael Taubenschlag, *The Law of Greco-Roman Egypt in the Light of the Papyri*, ²1955, pp. 33f. The inclusion of supplementary material peculiar to that province was not excluded: Buckland, loc. cit. It may plausibly be argued that the lack of juristic commentaries on the *edictum provinciale* before Gaius reflects the greater variability of the text (as compared with the edict[s] at Rome) before the stabilizing effect of the Julianic consolidation was felt.

133. See Taubenschlag, *The Law of Greco-Roman Egypt*, p. 28; Chalon, *L'Édit*, pp. 251ff.

134. Jolowicz and Nicholas, *Historical Introduction*, p. 98; R. W. Lee, *The Elements of Roman Law*, London ⁴1956, p. 11.

135. That of Tiberius Julius Alexander, of 68 CE, edited by Chalon, *L'Édit*.

136. Not, at least, for the first two centuries. Lieberman, *Hellenism in Jewish Palestine*, ²1962, pp. 6ff., has considered the later rabbinic evidence bearing on the matter.

137. Seidl, 'Papyrusfund', p. 348, suggests that the bad Greek of Babatha's 'formulae' shows that they are translations from a Latin edict, *Sed quaere*.

138. For an account of the problem and a brief history of the role of the jurists, see J. A. C. Thomas, *Textbook of Roman Law*, 1976, pp. 40–54.

139. Above, n. 122.

140. See the statistics in Jacob Neusner, *The Rabbinic Traditions about the Pharisees before 70*, 1971.

141. Schulz, *History of Roman Legal Science*, pp. 40f., 89f., 138.

142. Taubenschlag, *The Law of Greco-Roman Egypt*, p. 36.

143. Cohen, *Jewish and Roman Law* I, p. 157 n. 152.

144. Paul Collinet, *Histoire de l'École de Droit de Beyrouth*, 1925, pp. 16–20, is sure that the school existed by the turn of the century, and is inclined to date it at some undefined period of the second century.

145. *Audivimus etiam in Alexandrina splendidissima civitate et in Caesarensium et in aliis quosdam imperitos homines devagare et doctrinam discipulis adulterinam tradere* – Const. *Omnem*, s. 7. See Schulz, *History of Roman Legal Science*, pp. 123, 273.

146. For an example, see below, pp. 189f.

147. Nor is direct evidence of such channels always a necessary condition, since their existence may sometimes rightly be inferred from the other factors in the situation, as argued above, p. 180, in relation to the commentary of Gaius *ad edictum provinciale* and more generally below.

148. I refer not only to the fact that ancient sources rarely make explicit acknowledgment of foreign influence, but also to the general necessity for an interpretative framework, implicit or (preferably) explicit, in order to attach any meaning to the words of the ancient source.

149. The typology follows that set out in my 'History, Dogmatics and *Halakhah*'. The question of Roman influence on the halakah is so immense and complicated that it may be more profitable at this stage to seek clarification of the problem rather than attempt either a superficial review of all the evidence (if that were possible) or conclusions from a limited number of examples. It may be noted that despite the mass of material which he accumulated, Boaz Cohen was always very reluctant to draw general conclusions from it – a measure, perhaps, of the theoretical difficulties involved.

150. I concede, of course, that judgments as to what are 'extremely close' parallels or 'clearly attested' channels of transmission themselves involve a theoretical stance.

151. The traditional approach is often expressed in terms of a denial that such a development occurred: the complete range of halakot was given at Sinai in the form of the *torah shebe'al peh*. There have, however, been significant variations on the scope and meaning of *torah shebe'al peh* in the views held by orthodox scholars.

152. For its scope by the end of the Republic, see the volumes of W. A. J. Watson: *The Law of Obligations in the Later Roman Republic*, 1965; *The Law of Persons in the Later Roman Republic*, 1967; *The Law of Property*

in the Later Roman Republic, 1968; *The Law of Succession in the Later Roman Republic*, 1971.

153. For the documentation for the Ptolemaic period, much of it reaching back to the third and second centuries BCE, see Taubenschlag, *The Law of Greco-Roman Egypt*; E. Seidl, *Ptolemäische Rechtsgeschichte*, ²1962; H. J. Wolff, *Das Recht der griechischen Papyri Ägyptens in der Zeit der Ptolemäer und des Prinzipats*, 1978. A useful introduction, 'Hellenistic Private Law', is provided by Wolff in *The Jewish People in the First Century* I, 1974, pp. 534–60.

154. I assume that the significant increase in the scope of the halakah occurred later, despite the views of many who would push much of this development much further back. Such questions of dating are crucial to any conclusions regarding foreign influence, but the argument cannot be pursued here. Suffice it to say that datings earlier than the earliest authority to whom a saying is attributed require to be proved; and that such attributions must be critically viewed in proportion to their temporal separation from the document in which they occur and the availability of contemporary or near-contemporary attestations. I agree with Halivni's remarks elsewhere in this volume (ch. 8, n. 16, pp. 381f.) – if he does not understate the position – and with the general approach of Jacob Neusner.

155. E.g., the Jewish community in Alexandria, in respect of both Roman and Hellenistic law; the Jewish community at Rome; the Jewish community at Sparta (see Baron, *Social and Religious History* I, p. 185); apart from experience of Roman legal administration in Judaea itself. For this purpose, we need not seek literary channels, though no doubt some of these were indirectly available. It would be particularly interesting to know whether the rabbis were aware of the work of non-sacerdotal Republican jurists who concerned themselves with religious law (above. pp. 178f.).

156. I refer here to forms of diachronic structuralism based upon theories of cognitive development. See my 'Towards a Structuralist Theory of Law', *The Liverpool Law Review* 2, 1980, pp. 29f.; *Structuralism and Legal Theory*, 1979, pp. 45–47.

157. These are taken up below, under the rubric 'Reduction to Writing'.

158. Cf. the form of mBK 1.1, which I do *not* regard as ancient on this score. (Some writers exhibit a tendency to regard as 'ancient halakah' – second century BCE and earlier – anything which may have been influenced by Greek thought. This should be a self-evident *non sequitur*.) In fact, there is reason to believe that mBK 1.1 represents a very late stage in the compilatorial process (see my remarks in 'Maimonides' Definitions of *Tam* and *Mu'ad*', *JLA* 1, 1978, pp. 168f.); indeed it well fits into Halivni's account, below, pp. 206–9, of controversial contributions of R. Judah himself.

Arguments from consistency are often associated with the development of respect for precedent and may have their historical origin in the tactics of persuasion of large popular juries in classical Athens, an institution which was quite foreign to Jewish law as regards both the role of representation and the nature of the tribunal's composition.

The διαίρεσις/*divisio* into *genera* and *species* is not the only Graeco-Roman organizing technique adopted by the rabbis. There are also plenty of examples of the μερισμός/*partitio*. On these techniques, see Dieter Nörr, *Divisio und Partitio*, 1972. Similar to but distinguishable from the *partitio* is the 'enumeration pattern', studied by W. Sibley Towner, *The Enumeration of Scriptural Examples*, 1971: whereas the *partitio* lists parts of a single whole or category, the enumeration pattern lists phenomena which are similar. Towner, pp. 2ff., relates the enumeration pattern to ancient Near Eastern 'list-science'. But this does not exclude the possibility that its adoption by rabbinic literature in the tannaitic period was prompted by awareness of the Graeco-Roman technique.

159. For Roman indebtedness to Greece in these respects, see esp. Schulz, *History of Roman Legal Science*, who went so far as to describe the period from the end of the Second Punic War to the fall of the Republic as the 'Hellenistic period of Roman Jurisprudence'. A more sceptical view has recently been taken by Alan Watson, *Law Making*, ch. 16.

160. Chomsky and Lyons, within the context of linguistic structuralism, appear prepared to claim the existence of some substantive universals in the human mind. If this were applied to our context, it is possible that the distinction between *karka* and *metaltelin* (cf. *immobilia/mobilia*) could be a candidate for such status.

161. Laws concerning fines; cf. the Roman *actio ad poenam persequendam*.

162. The written and the oral Torah. The Greek distinction, famous from the *Antigone*, was taken over by the Romans, but even then its Greek origin was stressed. Ulpian quotes it in Greek (*Dig.* 1.1.6.1, *Ulp. lib. 1 Institutionum*, though Schulz, *History of Roman Legal Science*, pp. 171f., has doubted the attribution), as does Justinian, *Inst.* I.II.3.

It may be noted that the value claims of the unwritten law, *nomos agraphos*, may not be irrelevant to the use made of the distinction in Jewish law: see also I. F. Baer, *Yisra'el be-Amim* 1955, pp. 99, 141 n. 1; *aliter*, Urbach, *The Sages*, 1975, I, pp. 290f.; but see Lieberman's denial that the term is used in this sense when quoted in pRSh 1.3 (57b); 'How Much Greek in Jewish Palestine?', *Biblical and Other Studies* (ed. Altmann), 1963, pp. 128f.

163. The public institutions and the criminal law (cf. the Roman *ius publicum*) were dealt with in Sanhedrin-Makkot, separately from the *ius privatum*, found in Baba Kamma-Baba Batra. Daube suggests that the alternative title for the latter, *yeshu'ot*, may likewise reflect the Roman concern with remedies: 'The Civil Law of the Mishnah: The Arrangement of the Three Gates', *Tulane Law Review* 18, 1944, p. 358.

164. Both the first and the last, in so far as they concern the separation of criminal law, may have been especially important as regards

the *de facto* limits of Roman jurisdictional interference. See Daube, 'The Civil Law of the Mishnah', pp. 364f.

165. The distinction between written and unwritten law appears to have been a commonplace. Cf. the modern observation, however ill-founded, that the British constitution is unwritten.

166. Alan Watson, above, n. 6, is such a one.

167. The alternative here refers, *inter alia*, to such internal systematic factors as are mentioned in section 5, including the needs of deep structural systems of transformation identified by structuralists.

168. Exemplified by Mary Douglas's own later critique of her interpretation of biblical dietary laws (*Purity and Danger*, 1966, ch. 3) in *Implicit Meanings*, p. 144.

169. Douglas, *Purity and Danger*, p. 49. In this context, analysis of the debate concerning the prohibition of seething a kid in its mother's milk (discussed in my 'History, Dogmatics and *Halakhah*', pp. 16f.) is instructive.

170. 'Pure' in the sense that it does not fulfil systemic needs such as those mentioned in n. 167 above. It is, however, doubtful whether any form of intellectual attraction may be regarded as really 'pure'. We should not forget that foreign influence operates through the minds of individuals involved (whether as ordinary subjects or leadership élites) in the system. Even pure scholasticism satisfies psychological needs of an aesthetic nature, and to that extent may be regarded as 'functional'. Moreover, it may be hasty to insist on too rigid a distinction between intellectual (as in n. 167) and aesthetic systems.

171. Above, n. 156.

172. David Daube, 'Methods of Interpretation and Hellenistic Rhetoric', *HUCA* 22, 1949, pp. 239–64; idem, 'Alexandrian Methods of Interpretation and the Rabbis', *Festschrift Hans Lewald*, 1953, pp. 27–44; Saul Lieberman, *Hellenism in Jewish Palestine*, pp. 47–82. Daube (1953) and Lieberman (1962) are reprinted in Henry A. Fischel (ed.), *Essays in Greco-Roman and Related Talmudic Literature*, 1977, where a descriptive bibliography (pp. xxxi–lxxvi) including further items relevant to the present question will be found. I do not enter here into the dispute whether the *gezerah shavah* reflects Hellenistic influence only as regards its terminology.

173. I use this term to denote both forms of argument (e.g. *gezerah shavah*) *proprio sensu*, and particular arguments. For the Roman connection as regards the latter, see e.g. David Daube, 'Derelictio, Occupatio and Traditio: Romans and Rabbis', *LQR* 77, 1961, pp. 382–9, where the Jewish sources may contain a negative reflection of a particular Roman or rhetorical argument.

174. Such a reserve is not accepted by Daube (reviewing my *Essays* in *JJS* 28, 1977, pp. 79f.), who infers from R. Simeon b. Yohai's father's connections with Rome, and his own leadership of a mission to Rome to plead for the annulment of anti-Jewish decrees (plus his contacts there with the head of the rabbinical academy at Rome), a familiarity with Roman juristic work sufficient to base a theory that R. Simeon

was influenced by juristic traits and arguments especially associated with the (late first century BCE) jurist Labeo. Thus R. Simeon's interest in the reason for a rule is associated with Labeo's concern for *ratio*; R. Simeon's concern for the *kelal* with Labeo's introduction of the notion of *regula*; and R. Simeon's approval of someone else's ruling but for a different reason with Labeo's approval *nova ratione*. These parallels are suggestive and invite a systematic investigation. If these traits are indeed peculiar to R. Simeon in Jewish law and Labeo in Roman, and there are no better attested channels of transmission, the parallels might afford the basis of an inference that access to Roman juristic literature was in fact greater than the direct evidence suggests. On *mipneh mah*, however, see Lieberman, *Hellenism in Jewish Palestine*, ²1962, p. 48. As for the historical data (assuming it to be reliable) regarding R. Simeon and his father adduced by Daube, I am not convinced that it can bear the inference which Daube seeks to draw.

175. This suggestion should not be taken to imply a complete separation of these two settings. Some of those features of Roman *juristic* argument (e.g. the classification by *genera* and *species*, and the drawing of conclusions therefrom) appear to have been taken from the rhetoricians, who in this respect transmitted the Greek philosophical position. The argument *a minori ad maius* may be deployed in juristic writing, although characteristic of the orator. But fundamentally there does appear to be a distinction between arguments directed at analysis and arguments directed at persuasion, and it may be profitable to review both the Jewish and the Graeco-Roman techniques in this light. Schulz, *History of Roman Legal Science*, provides much useful material. See also P. Stein, *Regulae Iuris*, 1966, pp. 33–48.

For the analysis of legal argument, see Ch. Perelman and L. Olbrechts-Tyteca, *The New Rhetoric: A Treatise on Argumentation*, ET 1969, with considerable attention to the Greek and Hellenistic material; Julius Stone, *Legal Systems and Lawyers' Reasonings*, 1964; Ch. Perelman, *Logique juridique: nouvelle rhétorique*, 1976; Neil MacCormick, *Legal Reasoning and Legal Theory*, 1978. The distinction made in the text between 'forensic' and 'scholastic' argument relates to what, in the terms of Perelman and Olbrechts-Tyteca, are different forms of rhetoric.

176. E.g. David Daube, 'Some Forms of Old Testament Legislation', *Proceedings of the Oxford Society of Historical Theology*, 1944–45, pp. 36–46, and elsewhere; cf. applications to Roman law in his *Forms of Roman Legislation*, 1956; Reuven Yaron, *The Laws of Eshnunna*, 1969, pp. 60–71; Jackson, *Essays*, pp. 161–6. For a bibliographical survey of form-critical work on biblical law, see W. Malcolm Clark, 'Law', *Old Testament Form Criticism* (ed. Hayes), 1974, pp. 99–139.

177. Cf. p. 184 above.

178. Cf. more generally Daube, 'The Civil Law of the Mishnah', p. 365.

179. That, too, has been the subject of debate, although the differences are restricted to a relatively narrow time-span, between 212 and

214 CE. See Jolowicz and Nicholas, *Historical Introduction*, pp. 345f. n. 5, for the literature.

180. Here as often the comparison with Egypt is tantalizing but problematic. There are papyrological references to ὁ τῶν Αἰγυπτίων νόμος which Taubenschlag, *The Law of Greco-Roman Egypt*, p. 6 (and n. 14 for further material), concluded referred to a second-century codification of Egyptian law. If so, this could reflect Egyptian response to the Roman edicts. But the evidence for such a code is slight, and its existence disputed. See H. J. Wolff, 'Faktoren der Rechtsbildung im hellenistisch-römischen Ägypten', *Zeitschrift der Savigny-Stiftung für Rechtsgeschichte* (Romanistische Abteilung 70), 1953, pp. 20–57, at 42–44, who identifies it with νόμος τῆς χώρας; J. R. Rea, *The Oxyrhynchus Papyri* XLVI, 1978, p. 30 on POxy. 3285.

181. Above, p. 183 and p. 398 n. 163.

182. 'The Civil Law of the Mishnah', pp. 359–66.

183. Roman private law included the law of persons, whereas family law was kept apart from the rest of the civil law found in Nezikin, Baba Kamma-Baba Batra.

184. Within the ordinances of Ex. 21–22. See especially the sequence from Ex. 21.18–22.17.

185. Discussions include J. Rogerson, 'Structural Anthropology and the Old Testament', *Bulletin of the School of Oriental and African Studies* 33, 1970, pp. 490–500; Daniel Patte, *What is Structural Exegesis?*, Philadelphia 1976; Jean Calloud, *Structural Analysis of Narrative*, ET 1976; J. A. Emerton, 'An Examination of a Recent Structural Interpretation of Genesis xxxviii', *VT* 26, 1976, pp. 79–98; Alan W. Miller, 'Claude Lévi-Strauss and Genesis 37–Exodus 20', *Shiv'im: Essays and Studies in Honor of Ira Eisenstein*, 1977, pp. 21–52; David Jobling, *The Sense of Biblical Narrative*, 1978.

186. The question is allied to that of the extension of the innate to substantive universals; see above, n. 160.

187. *History of Roman Legal Science*, p. 183.

188. Though not necessary the *edictum provinciale*, even if that followed the pattern of Cicero's edict.

189. Even assuming that they were known in rabbinic circles (a question to which curiously little attention appears to have been paid). This argument, it should be noted, assumes that rabbinic Judaism did not define the sect out of Judaism.

190. For some of the other aspects of legal science here treated, we can make some progress without the *ipsissima verba* of the period. A notable example is the reconstruction of the 'agenda' of the pre-70 Pharisees by Jacob Neusner, *Rabbinic Traditions* – which bears upon the scope of the legal system as understood by at least one major antecedent of the rabbinic halakah.

191. Based upon 'synchronic structuralism', as argued in the work cited above, n. 156.

192. This does not exclude the role of environmental factors in shaping and modifying the structure of the internal logical system itself.

But it is suggested that the latter, once established, will play a creative role in the further development of the system. The problem is akin to that of the natural status of substantive universals, mentioned above, n. 160.

193. For a partial bibliography, see R. W. M. Dias, *A Bibliography of Jurisprudence*, London ³1979, pp. 254–6, with short digests of the articles.

194. Following the definition of 'structure' in Jean Piaget, *Structuralism*, ET 1971, pp. 3–16. The logical relation of which each rule should be seen as a part need not entail a relationship wherein the rule is a concretization of a more abstract principle or value, according to Lévi-Strauss: see further Jackson, *Structuralism and Legal Theory*, p. 6; 'Structuralist Theory of Law', pp. 8f.

195. MBK 7.4. See further Jackson, 'Foreign Influence in the Early Jewish Law of Theft', RIDA 18, 1971, pp. 25–42, reprinted in *Essays*, pp. 235–49, esp. pp. 244–6; for the contrary view, which does see the parallel as reflecting Roman influence, see David Daube, in his review of *Essays*, n. 174 above.

196. *Dig.* 48.13.11.2.

197. Cohen, *Jewish and Roman Law* II, p. 579, on bBekh 13a.

198. See my 'Liability for Animals in Roman Law: An Historical Sketch', *The Cambridge Law Journal* 37, 1978, pp. 122–43, esp. pp. 138–40.

199. Viz., had not been officially notified as vicious, in accordance with the procedure understood by the rabbis as required by Ex. 21.29 and 36.

200. The extension still appears to be controversial in the period of R. Akiba. A full analysis of the evidence for the tannaitic development must await another occasion.

201. Ex. 21.28, *'naqi'*. The term, of course, could be variously interpreted. See my *Essays*, pp. 127f.

202. Particularly of *hasi nezeq migufo*, the rabbinic understanding of the remedy of Ex. 21.36, which was adopted also for injuries to free men. In fact, it is by no means certain that the owner was completely free of civil liability even in the biblical period.

203. It was not inevitable that the remedy chosen should be that based on Ex. 21.36 (the rule for an ox which killed another ox). It would have been possible to restrict *naqi* in v. 28 to the case of fatal injuries, or to the (rabbinic understanding of the) capital liability of v. 29 (cf. R. Judah b. Bathyra, Mek. Nez. 10; Lauterbach III, pp. 80f.; to 21.36), and thus to conclude that the remedy for non-fatal injuries to a free man was *full* damages. The choice of *hasi nezeq migufo* is parallel to the remedy of the Roman *actio de pauperie* in that both represented a lesser quantum of damages than that available where greater fault was shown (in Jewish law, the case of *mu'ad*, in Roman law the *actio legis Aquiliae* [with no trace here of the availability of noxal surrender] where *culpa* was shown). Thus there is also a structural parallel between the two systems, of which, however, the rabbis are unlikely to

have been aware. But they may well have realized that the *actio de pauperie* often produced less than full compensation.

204. Without having to resort to an inference of their existence on the basis of the apparent influence itself.

205. *Dig* 9.1.3.; Lenel, *Palingenesia* I, p. 205 no. 182.

206. E.g. D. Sperber, 'Flight and the Talmudic Law of Usucaption: A Study in the Social History of Third Century Palestine', *RIDA* 19, 1972, pp. 29–42, esp. 33f., where he argues that the liberalization of *hazaqah* under R. Johanan reflects the interests of owners forced to flee from their property because of the burden of taxation.

207. Notably, Moshe Greenberg, 'Some Postulates of Biblical Criminal Law', *Yehezkel Kaufmann Jubilee Volume*, 1960, pp. 5–28.

208. There are exceptions, such as Lev. 24.22, as seen by the rabbinic use made of it.

209. See my critique of Greenberg in 'Reflections on Biblical Criminal Law', *JJS* 24, 1973, pp. 8–38, esp. 12f., reprinted in *Essays* pp. 25–63, esp. 31f. Some progress towards solving the difficulty may be made by comparing relational structures rather than abstract principles inferred from single concrete norms, but much work remains to be done in this area.

210. E.g. Daube, above, n. 174. Lieberman (*Hellenism in Jewish Palestine*, pp. 78f.) notes that the name Mekilta is an exact terminological equivalent to *kanōn*. On the Greek and Roman technique, see Peter Stein, *Regulae Iuris*.

211. On the Roman collections, see Schulz, *History of Roman Legal Science*, pp. 173–83; Bruno Schmidlin, *Die Römischen Rechtsregeln: Versuch einer Typologie*, 1970.

212. Above, p. 188.

213. See D. N. MacCormick, 'Law as Institutional Fact', *LQR* 90, 1974, pp. 102–29.

214. See Cohen, *Jewish and Roman Law* I, pp. 179–278, on the adoption of *peculium* as a translation of *segullah*, and the equivalent institutions in Jewish law.

215. Reuven Yaron, *Gifts in Contemplation of Death in Jewish and Roman Law*, 1960, pp. 18f. et pass., on this and other institutions of the law of succession. See also I. F. Baer, 'The Historical Foundations of the Halakha' (in Hebrew), *Zion* 27, 1962, pp. 132–7.

216. E.g. Moshe Gil, 'Land Ownership in Palestine under Roman Rule', *RIDA* 17, 1970, pp. 11–54, esp. p. 16, on *hazaqah*; Cohen, *Jewish and Roman Law* II, pp. 558–60, on usufruct (= *akhilat perot*), and pp. 433–56 on *antichresis* (influence here occurring for the most part in the amoraic period); I. F. Baer, 'The Historical Foundations of the Halakha' (in Hebrew), *Zion* 17, 1952, pp. 24–8, on mBB I–II (including the remarkable claim at p. 27: *berov* (!) *hilkhot hamishnah shel seder nezikin venashim ata motze simanim lehashpaʿat hamishpat hayevani*).

217. See esp. Elias Bickerman, 'Two Legal Interpretations of the Septuagint', *RIDA* 3, 1956, pp. 81–97, reprinted in his *Studies in Jewish*

and Christian History I, pp. 201–15. *Aliter*, Falk, Review of E. Koffmann, *Doppelurkunden . . .*, in *Bibl* 50, 1969, p. 416.

218. For examples, see Emil Schürer, *History*, § 22.II, Vol. II, 1979, p. 54.

219. Against such an argument advanced in respect of *diathēkē* by Solomon Zeitlin ('Testamentary Succession: A Study in Tannaitic Jurisprudence', *The Seventy-Fifth Anniversary Volume of the JQR*, 1970, p. 575, reprinted in his *Studies in the Early History of Judaism* IV, 1978, p. 194) see my *Essays*, pp. 235f. n. 2.

220. See Jolowicz and Nicholas, *Historical Introduction*, pp. 103f.

221. So Jolowicz and Nicholas, ibid., p. 103. But others consider the *ius gentium* to be purely Roman, but lacking the strict forms of the *ius civile*.

222. See David Daube, 'Negligence in the Early Talmudic Law of Contract (Peshi'ah)', *Festschrift Fritz Schulz* I, 1951, pp. 124–47, esp. 130f.

223. Daube, 'Negligence', pp. 139–42, developed in one context by Jackson, 'Maimonides' Definitions', *JLA* 1, pp. 172–5. This provides a good example of interaction between a foreign concept and the internal logic of the system, here its doubts about the admissibility of a prescriptive notion of nature.

224. For the comparison, see Leopold Auerbach, *Das jüdische Obligationenrecht*, 1870 (repr. 1976), pp. 159–67; for further literature see Fuss's introduction to the 1976 reprint, at pp. 11f., and *The Principles of Jewish Law* (ed. Menachem Elon), Jerusalem 1975, col. 246 (reprinted from *EJ* XII, cols. 1315f., s.v. 'Obligations, Law of'). M. Silberg, *Talmudic Law and the Modern State*, 1973, pp. 66–70, stresses the special features of the Jewish concept of obligation.

225. An *obligatio civilis* could be enforced through the normal procedures of the civil law; an *obligatio naturalis* could not be directly enforced, though its existence was recognized in various ways, and it could often be used as a defence. See Buckland, *Text-book*, pp. 552–6; more recently, Alberto Burdese, 'Dubbi in tema di "naturalis obligatio" ', *Studi. . .Scherillo* II, 1972, pp. 485–513; P. Didier, 'Les obligations naturelles chez les derniers Sabiniens', *RIDA* 19, 1972, pp. 239–74.

226. The distinctions relate to the effects attached to acts prohibited by statute: in a *lex perfecta* the act, if committed, is invalid; in a *lex minus quam perfecta* the act is valid, but a penalty is imposed; in a *lex imperfecta* the act is valid and no penalty is imposed. The classification is later than the second century, though examples of its effects are early. See Buckland, *Text-book*, pp. 6f. n. 5; Jolowicz and Nicholas, *Historical Introduction*, pp. 87f.

227. Asher Gulak, *History of Jewish Law I: Law of Obligation and its Guaranties* (in Hebrew), 1939, pp. 111–16. The cases so classified tend to be tortious, and distinct from those where the court will not enforce an (often contractual) obligation but will allow a measure of self-help and afford the beneficiary of the obligation a defence. Indeed, Jewish law is more complex than Roman law as regards the modes of incom-

plete obligation. Here too any influence has to be considered in the context of the internal logic of the system. I have argued elsewhere that *dine 'adam/dina shamayim* implies a concern with the limits of human cognition: 'The Concept of Religious Law in Judaism', *ANRW* II.19.1, 1979, pp. 33–52.

228. Cf. Elon on the relationship of conflicts of law to the problem of foreign influence: *Principles of Jewish Law*, col. 32. However, the scribe may resist the challenge and opt for double documentation, as suggested by Reuven Yaron, 'C.P. Jud 144 et alia', *IURA* 13, 1962, pp. 170–5, esp. 170f., in respect of *CPJ* 144.

229. For the most part, they consist of applications of rules of the system. But it should be noted that the drafting of legal deeds may be subjected to analysis in terms of the N + E scale (see 'Legal Drafting', above, p. 185) in the same way as legislative provisions.

230. The leading study is still A. Gulak, *Das Urkundenwesen im Talmud im Lichte der griechisch-aegyptischen Papyri und des griechischen und römischen Rechts*, 1935. See also Ludwig Blau, *Papyri und Talmud in gegenseitiger Beleuchtung*, 1913; Ze'ev W. Falk, *Introduction to Jewish Law of the Second Commonwealth* I, 1972, pp. 135–43; II, 1978, p. 239. On the interpenetration of Greek and Roman elements in the Egyptian deeds, see Taubenschlag, *The Law of Greco-Roman Egypt*, pp. 41, 43ff.

231. See E. E. Urbach, 'The Laws Regarding Slavery as a Source for Social History of the Period of the Second Temple, the Mishnah and Talmud', *Papers of the Institute of Jewish Studies London* I, 1964, pp. 58ff. The importance of notarial practice as a source of transmission of foreign ideas, extending sometimes to whole institutions, is rightly stressed by Bickerman, 'Two Legal Interpretations'.

232. As in the last example, where the Greek practice may lie behind the Roman 'informal' method of *manumissio per epistulam*. Such methods were particularly appropriate in the provinces. But the Greek model is the more likely source of the Jewish development in this case. Much here depends upon the dating of the Jewish development. For any consideration of influence in notarial form must also take seriously the continuing importance of the ancient Near Eastern scribal tradition, as observed at Elephantine (below n. 234).

233. In the post-classical period of Roman law, there is a fascinating mixture of Greek and Oriental influences at work on Roman law.

234. Reuven Yaron, *Introduction to the Law of the Aramaic Papyri*, 1961, esp. ch. X.

235. Texts in *Discoveries in the Judaean Desert* II (eds. P. Benoit, J. T. Milik and R. de Vaux), 1961; Elisabeth Koffmann, *Die Doppelurkunden aus der Wüste Juda*, 1968. Studies include Volterra, 'Nuovi documenti', *IURA* 14, pp. 29–70; Reuven Yaron, 'The Murabba'at Documents', *JJS* 11, 1960, pp. 157–71; M. R. Lehmann, 'Studies in the Murabba'at and Nahal Hever Documents', *RQ* 4, 1963, pp. 53–81; see also the review of Koffmann by Z. W. Falk, pp. 261–3. Although the documents show considerable compliance with rabbinic law, there are also notable foreign elements. Yaron, 'The Murabba'at Documents', p. 169, remarks

upon the syncretistic tendencies revealed by the legal formulae (cf. Modrzejewski, 'Les Juifs et le droit hellenistique: Divorce et égalité des époux', *IURA* 12, 1961, pp. 162–93, esp. 192), but rejects any 'wholesale assertions of influence' in favour of a point-by-point approach. Of particular interest is the Roman style wife's *repudium* in PMur. 19. These documents, of course, must be assessed along with Yadin's texts from the Cave of Letters ('Expedition D') regrettably still unpublished.

236. But see also the Greek deeds written by Egyptian Jews, published in *CPJ*, as rightly stressed by Falk, *Jewish Law* I, p. 136. PEnt. 23, studied by E. Volterra ('Intorno a P. Ent. 23', *Journal of Juristic Papyrology* 15, 1965, pp. 21–8) is a third century BCE petition to the Egyptian king on a matter of private law. Particular interest has focused upon *CPJ* 144, an instrument of divorce by mutual consent of 13 BCE, despite some doubts as to whether the parties were in fact Jewish. See Volterra, 'Nuovi documenti', pp. 44ff.; Joseph Modrzejewski, 'Les Juifs', pp. 162–93 (whose views provide a good example of foreign influence as providing a spur to some particular aspect of the internal logic of the legal system); Reuven Yaron, 'C.P. Jud 144 et alia', pp. 170–2; Daniela Piattelli, 'Alcune osservazioni su C.P.J. 144', *IURA* 18, 1967, pp. 121–4.

237. Particularly, norm and *ma'aseh*.

238. Saul Lieberman, 'Roman Legal Institutions in Early Rabbinics and the Acta Martyrum', *JQR* 35, 1944–45, pp. 1–57; further comparative material in Jonah Ostrow, 'Tannaitic and Roman Procedure in Homicide', *JQR* 48, 1958, pp. 352–70. Of course, visibility does not entail acceptance, as in the case of bail pending the physical consequences of an assault: see Cohen, *Jewish and Roman Law* II, pp. 578f., on Mek. ad Ex. 21.19 (the reference to the Lauterbach edition at 578 n. 3 should read III, p. 54).

239. See my *Essays*, pp. 248f., and further literature there cited, on the use of judicial oaths. See, however, A. Ehrman, 'Law and Equity in the Talmudic Concept of Sale', *JJS* 18, 1957, pp. 177–86, at 183, for a suggestion that Roman law influenced the attempt to enforce the consensual contract (i.e. in the absence of *kinyan*) by means of *mi shepara* etc.

240. The dating of this development to the first three centuries should not, perhaps, be too categorical, particularly if taken to imply that there were no significant developments in Jewish self-definition thereafter. It is enough, for present purposes, to accept that Jewish self-definition underwent significant development in this period.

241. Quoted from the press publicity for Volume 1 of this series.

242. George P. Fletcher, *Rethinking Criminal Law*, 1978, p. 102 etc.; see also his 'The Metamorphosis of Larceny', *Harvard Law Review* 89, 1976, pp. 469–530 at 476, 485. Fletcher's relationship to the theory underlying the present paper is discussed in Jackson, *Structuralism and Legal Theory*, pp. 39–41, and 'Structuralist Theory of Law', pp. 23–5.

243. No necessary correlation between these two distinctions is in-

tended: there may be a conscious decision to communicate something at the level of implication, a phenomenon taken into account in the development of this argument below.

244. Of course, such sources have to be evaluated critically for the information they provide on this issue: but so do the Jewish sources.

245. For the purposes of normative self-definition, it would hardly suffice to prove that the Jews were aware of their possession of a large corpus of extra-biblical laws. Many cultures, particularly in the Graeco-Roman culture area, had significant corpora of customary laws. The claim that such law was Sinaitic, however, entailed in addition a view of the distinctiveness and special normative status of these laws.

246. *Rabbinic Traditions* III, p. 304.

247. This caveat is intended to take account of the extent to which issues not raised by the priestly writers arise in the post-biblical development, as stressed by Neusner, 'Ritual Without Myth: The Use of Legal Materials for the Study of Religions', *Religion* 5, 1975, p. 93, and elsewhere.

248. This suggestion is a variant on that of Daube ('The Civil Law of the Mishnah', pp. 360f.), who assumes the civil law to have been equally developed by that time (while noting that the attack of Paul and his followers was directed chiefly against the ritual law, pp. 366f.), and who sees the Jewish reaction as taking the form of sticking 'more firmly to the old customs, to insist more emphatically on the Torah as the sole guide even in affairs of everyday life'.

249. See my 'Legalism', *JJS* 30, 1979, pp. 1–22, at 7f., 15f.

250. See p. 198 below, on the baraita of R. Ishmael.

251. As shown, for example, by the capacity of the extended *gezerah shavah* to imply an analogy from one law to another from the mere common occurrence of a term, even though the analogy is not substantively related to the common term itself.

On the intimate interrelationship between methods of interpretation and the nature of the text to be interpreted, see David Daube, 'The Influence of Interpretation on Writing', *Buffalo Law Review* 20, 1970, pp. 41–59.

252. Jacob Neusner, *A History of the Mishnaic Law of Purities* XXI, 1977, pp. 166–90, and in his earlier work on the rabbinic traditions regarding the Pharisees and Eliezer. This does not, however, imply a decreasing level of coherence in the halakah, despite the saying of R. Jose in bSanh 88a–b, and the extravagant conclusion drawn by J. Newman, *Halachic Sources*, 1969, pp. 15f.

253. Here used in its primary meaning within the Roman legal system – the law applicable to citizens and *peregrini* alike – rather than its 'speculative' meaning – the law common to all mankind, viewed by some as a product of *naturalis ratio*. See Francis de Zulueta, *The Institutes of Gaius* II, 1953, pp. 12f.

254. Above, p. 197 and n. 251.

255. Attached to the beginning of Sifra.

256. In the sense that its rules would thereby become more accessible

and perhaps more authoritative. Whether this was the object of the compilation of the Mishnah is, of course, disputed. As to its effect, see Halivni elsewhere in this volume.

257. E.g. Neusner, 'Form and Meaning in Mishnah', *JAAR* 45, 1977, pp. 27–54; and in *Purities* XXI, ch. V.

258. A partial exception is the rabbinic understanding of the *kelal*.

259. In the senses described above, pp. 189–94.

260. A useful catalogue, classified according to subject-matter, of talmudic sources which explicitly refer to foreign law, and thereby provide evidence of the knowledge which is a necessary condition of foreign influence, may be found in Isidor Jeiteles, 'Fremdes Recht im Talmud', *Jahrbuch der Jüdisch-Literarischen Gesellschaft* 21, 1930, pp. 109–28.

261. See especially Aquinas, *Summa Theologiae* 1a2ae, qu. 101.2, 102.2, for the argument that the ceremonial law was primarily figurative.

262. Izhak Englard, 'Research in Jewish Law – Its Nature and Function', *Modern Research in Jewish Law* (ed. Jackson), 1979, pp. 24f., 57.

263. The questions of distinctiveness and normativity are quite separate here. The argument in the text relates to distinctiveness. But even if the content of the civil law was regarded by Judaism (thus begging the question: by which Jews?) as distinctively Jewish, it does not follow that it was accepted as legally normative. My colleague Martin Goodman, of the University of Birmingham (UK), argues that there is little evidence of popular acceptance of the binding character of rabbinic institutions and law before the mid-third century, and intends to present his evidence for such claims in the near future.

264. According to the theory proposed above, such foreign influence may be inherently less likely, though not excluded in principle.

265. The degree to which such assumptions underlie many traditionalist arguments is, however, a matter for legitimate speculation. One suspects, for example, that S. Albeck ('Law and History in Halakhic Research', *Modern Research in Jewish Law*, pp. 1–20) would subscribe to them, were he to address questions of this nature.

266. 'Law and History', pp. 9ff.

267. This is my interpretation of the implications of Albeck's theory. He does not address himself to precisely these issues.

268. See my 'Modern Research in Jewish Law: Some Theoretical Issues', *Modern Research in Jewish Law*, pp. 145ff., 152ff.

269. In the sense defined above, pp. 192f.

270. In addition to the articles by Neusner cited above, nn. 247 and 257, and the relevant sections of *Purities*, reference may be made to 'The History of Earlier Rabbinic Judaism: Some New Approaches', *HR* 16, 1977, pp. 233–6; 'History and Structure: The Case of Mishnah', *JAAR* 45, 1977, pp. 161–92; 'The Tasks of Theology in Judaism: A Humanistic Program', *JR* 59, 1979, pp. 71–86.

271. Jackson, 'The Concept of Religious Law in Judaism', *ANRW* II. 19.1, pp. 33–52.

272. For the distinction, see above, p. 199. There is, of course, no

necessary correlation between the type of inner logic ('metaphysical' or 'theological') and its location in either the conscious or the subconscious spheres. Some of Neusner's conclusions relate to a logic which is 'theological' but which is still claimed to exist on the conscious (though implied) level, and we should certainly expect the halakah to possess such a dimension; equally, we may expect some of the metaphysical beliefs to exist only at the subconscious level.

273. In considering the extent to which the content of the halakah is relevant to the growth of normative self-definition, I have not concerned myself with the realm of the explicit. But clearly, the same kinds of question, as to whether and what elements of the content were regarded as distinctive, and whether such a view became normative, may be asked here as are posed in relation to the formal features of the system. It would be surprising if some elements of the explicit level of content did not prove relevant. The same applies to beliefs explicitly treated in the tannaitic sources, for which see F. P. Sanders, *Paul and Palestinian Judaism*, 1977.

274. This, it may be noted, is a significantly different understanding of normative self-definition from that which is adopted by Schiffman in this volume. According to the formulation in the text, a rule or belief may be normative even if failure to adhere to or embrace it does not result in juridical exclusion from the community; it looks (again) to social psychology rather than to law. I have no doubt that both tests are important: that of Schiffman may define the outer limits of identity while that in my text alludes to some kind of inner community. The difference points to an important conclusion, which does not depend upon the accuracy or usability of either Schiffman's test or mine: that there may exist different grades or types of normative self-definition, each of which may be of importance, though for different purposes.

8 The Reception Accorded to Rabbi Judah's Mishnah

1. Cf. G. A. Kohut, *Aruch Completum*, 1878–1892, s.v. משנה.

2. Rav Sherira Gaon, ed. B. M. Lewin, Haifa 1921, p. 30.

3. For a very erudite treatise on the subject see Malakhi b. Jacob Ha-Kohen, *Yad Malakhi*, 1767, ch. 661. The question has arisen in scholarly debate as to whether or not R. Judah intended his Mishnah to be a code. Some have found in the very nature of R. Judah's classificatory decisions an indication that this was his intention. This may stand for the present purpose. It is beyond the scope of this paper to show through a detailed analysis of the whole Mishnah that the evidence favours the position that R. Judah intended his Mishnah to be a code (albeit a limited code, for many common laws such as, for instance, pertaining to the donning of phylacteries and wearing the prayer shawl are omitted from R. Judah's Mishnah). A key passage is R. Johanan's statement in bHull 85a: ראה רבי דבריו של ר' מאיר באותו ואת בנו ושנאה בלשון חכמים ודר' שמעון בכיסוי הדם ושנאה בלשון חכמים

'Rabbi approved of R. Meir's view in connection with the law of "It and its young" and stated it (in the Mishnah) as the view of the Sages, and he (Rabbi) approved of R. Simeon's view in connection with the law of covering up the blood and stated it (in the Mishnah) as the view of the Sages.' It is extremely difficult to accept the argument of those who do not view the Mishnah as a code ('non-codists') that R. Johanan is not referring to R. Judah, who is commonly called Rabbi and who was his teacher, but to an obscure, unknown earlier Tanna.

On the other hand, the fact that there are contradictions in R. Judah's Mishnah affecting the classification of some laws does not necessarily lead to the conclusion – and this is the non-codist's strongest argument – that R. Judah did not intend his Mishnah to be used for practical purposes. Later codists adopted a rule *vis-à-vis* the Talmud that wherever there is a contradiction, the law found in the tractate that deals primarily with laws similar in content to the law about which there is a contradiction (like a law pertaining to the Sabbath found in Tractate Shabbath) is the law which commands greater authority. A similar rule may also have existed in the time of the Mishnah, so that even when there was a contradiction the student knew which law to follow (contradictions in the same tractate are not that numerous and therefore constitute no serious problem to the codist); that such a rule existed at the time of the Mishnah was assumed, as a fact, by Tosafot, ad bKidd 66b and by Ḥavot Yair, Ch. 94, p. 50a. When the contradiction is between a law included in a series and a law stated by itself, bSanh 34b says that we should follow the law stated by itself.

4. Cf. Z. Frankel, *Darkhe ha-Mishnah*, repr. 1959, ch. 5; J. N. Epstein, *Mebo'ot le-Sifrut ha-Tanna'im*, 1957, p. 242. Later scribes often added to the Tosefta from the Mishnah or omitted from the Tosefta parts already found in the Mishnah.

5. See Ch. Albeck, *Meḥqarim be-Baraita ve-Tosefta*, Jerusalem 1946, pp. 66–89.

6. BErub 92a; bYeb 43a; bNid 62b.

7. In bNid 62b this retort is attributed to R. Johanan as an answer to an איתיביה question by R. Simon b. Lakish (Resh Lakish). These exchanges between R. Johanan and Resh Lakish have been noted to be fictitious. See Tosafot, bBB 154b ad ברם, and parallels.

8. See also Ch. Albeck's comment in his edition of GenR, p. 1259.

9. BTaan 21a; bKet 69b; pKet 6.7 (31a); pKidd 1.1(58d).

10. R. Johanan once told Ilfa: 'If you had not engaged in business, you might have become head of the Academy.' This tells us a great deal about Ilfa's scholarly stature, but not why he turned to business and lost his chance of becoming head of the Academy. Could it be that his strong defence of R. Judah's Mishnah had something to do with it?

Also bKet 103b and parallel relate that when R. Hanina and R. Ḥiyya were engaged in a dispute (more accurately, were quarrelling or contending with each other), כי הוו מינצי רבי חנינא ור' חייא,'R. Ḥanina said to R. Ḥiyya: Do you venture to dispute with me? Were the Torah, God forbid, to be forgotten in Israel, I would return it by means of my dialectical arguments.'

There is hardly a dispute between R. Ḥanina and R. Ḥiyya in the Talmud. In a few instances R. Ḥanina quotes R. Ḥiyya approvingly. Could it be that R. Ḥanina – whom R. Judah designated as his successor to be head of the academy – and R. Ḥiyya were disputing (quarrelling or contending with each other) about the relative merits of R. Judah's Mishnah? Even so, one is at a loss to explain Resh Lakish's statement in bSukk 20a: 'When the Torah was forgotten from Israel, Ezra came up from Babylon and established it; when it was forgotten again, Hillel the Babylonian came up and established it; and when it was again forgotten, R. Ḥiyya and his sons came up and established it.' Even the most partisan R. Hiyyaite cannot deny that there was Torah in Israel during the time of R. Judah.

11. Cf. bBK 69b and Rashbam, bBB 79b ad מתני. See also Jacob Brüll, *Mabo la-Mishnah* II, 1885, reprinted 1970, p. 56.

12. I took this as a general rule concerning the anonymous mishnah whether the disagreement is in the Mishnah (in an earlier place) or in a baraita. See, however, Ramban (Rashba and Ritba), bYeb 42b ad סתם. Cf. bSanh 34b, סתמא דרבים עדיף, 'an anonymous mishnah which expresses the opinion of the majority is preferable'. When R. Johanan asked R. Yanai in bShab 140a why he decided against an anonymous mishnah of R. Judah, R. Yanai retorted: 'If so (that I can't decide against R. Judah's anonymous mishnah) what is the difference between you and me? The mishnah follows a minority view.' Cf. also bHull 137b. It is not clear wherein lies R. Yanai's superiority, in knowing that originally the mishnah followed a minority view or in daring to override a classificatory decision of R. Judah, something that R. Johanan presumably did not do. See Tosafot, bHull 77a, ad בלשון.

13. BSanh 86a.

14. MPeah 3.6; mShebi 9.5; mYeb 4.13.

15. Cf. Rashi, bSot 22a ad שמורין:

תנאים מבלים עולם... בהוראות טעות... יש משניות הרבה במשניות דאמרינן הא מני ר' פלוני היא ויחידאה היא ולית הלכתא כותיה. 'Those who recite Mishnah (without Gemara) destroy the world because of their erroneous decisions. For there are many mishnayot (of which the Gemara says) they were taught by an individual rabbi; they represent a minority view; and the law does not follow them.'

16. For the classical literature on the subject see R. Samson of Chinon, *Sefer Keritut* (ed. S. B. Sofer), Jerusalem 1965, pp. 261–63 and the notes therein; also Epstein, *Mebo'ot le-Sifrut ha-Tanna'im*, pp. 188ff.; and our little note in *Mekorot u-Mesorot, Mo'ed*, p. 589 n. 4. Some rabbis in the Babylonian Talmud (some, not all, for there is no consistency on that) apparently viewed Rabbi's role (and the role of the editor of the baraita) merely as a juxtaposer of earlier sources in their respective languages, to the extent that when a pericope agrees with a certain Tanna in one respect and disagrees in another respect, so that the language of the pericope cannot be the Tanna's, these rabbis preferred

either to emend the text (e.g. bBer 15b: חסורי מחסרא והכי קתני) or posit a divergent tradition of that Tanna (e.g. bPes 95b: תרי תנאי ואליבא דר"פ) and make the pericope agree with the language of the Tanna, rather than saying that Rabbi (and the editor of the baraita) eclectically and in his own language partially agreed and partially disagreed with the opinions of that Tanna: סבר לה כוותיה בחדא ופליג עליה בחדא. Nevertheless, Ludwig Blau overstates the case when he admonishes in *Magyar Zsido Szemle* 25, 1908, pp. 153ff. (quoted also in *Sinai* 83, 1978, p. 116) that 'it is a mistake to think that since the Mishnah was composed in the second century, anything in the Mishnah that does not bear the stamp of antiquity is to be assigned to the second century. The opposite is the truth. Anything in the Mishnah that cannot be shown to be of second-century origin ought to be considered much older.' Cf. J. Neusner, *A History of the Mishnaic Law of Purities* XXI, 1977, pp. xxiii–xv.

17. Not without an occasional protest. Cf. pErub 1.4; 19a: א"ר מנא מכיון דאיתמר' הלכה כרבנן שבקין ליחיד ועבדין כרבנן. R. Manna, a fourth century Palestinian scholar, protests that a view which Rabbi codified as anonymous, should have the status of a majority opinion (see the Penei Moshe, ad loc.) and as such it should be followed. Dissenting views are to be considered minority views, and are to be rejected.

18. A similar attempt was made by Maimonides in his *Mishnah Torah* and he did not succeed either.

19. Throughout this essay we mentioned only those instances where the Amoraim explicitly state that they are abandoning R. Judah's classificatory decision in favour of another view in a baraita. There are, however, numerous instances where the Amoraim interpret a mishnah in compliance with a baraita. When that interpretation is a forced one, one may assume that the Amoraim knew that they were not faithfully reflecting R. Judah's opinion as much as they were imposing the baraita's authority on the mishnah. Twice the Babylonian Talmud (BK 96b; Arak 29a [see also RSh 28b]) expresses amazement at Rav for having abandoned a mishnah in favour of a baraita: ורב שביק מתניתין ועביד כברייתא? One cannot fail to see in this an erosion of R. Judah's authority.

9 The Politics of Reconciliation: The Education of R. Judah the Prince

When MSS readings are cited, I have utilized either facsimile editions or microfilms, the latter at either the Jewish National and University Library, Jerusalem, or the Jewish Theological Seminary, New York. I would like to thank Rabbi David Freedman for allowing me to consult the microfilm of MS Göttingen 3.

1. Daniel is omitted in MSS Oxford 366, London 400 and Göttingen 3. He is added between the lines in MS Munich 140. The version in MS Munich 95 is garbled. I quote acording to MS Vat. 134 and the first printed edition.

2. I follow the reading in MS Göttingen 3, שמעון הצדיק ומתתיה בן

יוחנן כהן גדול חשמונאי ובניו which agrees with the emendation proposed by Alon, *Meḥqarim be-Toledot Yisra'el I*, 1957, p. 24. The text thus agrees with our conceptions of Maccabean history. See further Goldstein, *I Maccabees*, 1976, pp. 17-19. The readings in the other MSS seem to suggest that the Hasmonaean was someone other than Mattathias. See R. N. Rabbinovicz, *Diqduqe Soferim*, 1867–97, ad loc.

3. I follow MS Munich 95 and the Halberstam manuscript cited by Rabbinovicz, ad loc. בית רבינו וחכמי דורו . Other MSS read וחכמי הדורות or וחכמי ישראל שבדורות . I have adopted the reading in MSS Munich 95 and Halberstam in order to keep the text more specific – R. Judah and his contemporaries are seen as saviours in their day, as were Daniel, Mordechai and Esther, and the Hasmonaeans in their times. The reading חכמי הדורות is too open-ended. I suspect it was produced when the 'Roman' exile continued longer and longer. The process ultimately yielded חכמי ישראל שבדורות, the most open-ended of all.

4. BMeg 11a. This text should be compared with the Genizah fragment published by L. Ginzberg, *Ginzei Shechter I*, 1928, pp. 92f. Ginzberg argues, ibid., p. 91, that the Genizah fragment comes from a work compiled prior to the abolition of the Patriarchate, but the point is beyond proof. Cf. further the version in LevR 36.2, pp. 841f., according to MS כ . In that version each of the world empires honours Israel and her leaders, except for the Roman kingdom.

5. The Patriarchs are called Hillelites throughout this article in spite of Neusner's argument that the Patriarchal claim to be descended from Hillel was a fabrication. See e.g. Neusner, *Rabbinic Traditions about the Pharisees* III, 1971, pp. 202f., 218f. and 258. I retain the usage Hillelite both because it is conventional and because I find Neusner's case appealing but not completely persuasive.

6. See tSanh 11.8; pShab 16.1; 15c and parallels; bGitt 59a. The date of the baraita in bMeg 11a is hard to determine, thus we do not know whether it reflects the judgment of R. Judah's contemporaries, near contemporaries, or later generations. Two questions cannot be adequately answered: (1) the significance of introducing this baraita with the phrase במתניתא תנא (on which see Ch. Albeck, *Meḥqarim be-Baraita*, 1946, pp. 48–53); (2) the literary comparison between our text, EsthR Proem 4, and the Genizah fragment discussed above n. 4. In the light of the argument in n. 3 above I think it probable that the judgment of contemporaries or near contemporaries is reflected in our passage.

7. Velleius II.127.2.

8. I owe these insights to the work of Sir Ronald Syme, especially to his *The Roman Revolution*, Oxford 1939.

9. Alon, *Meḥqarim I*, pp. 259–73; Alon, *Toledot ha-Yehudim be-Erets Yisra'el be-Tequfat ha-Mishnah veha-Talmud I*, 1954, pp. 193–201; II, 1958, pp. 69–78, 129–148. E. E. Urbach, 'Class Status and Leadership in the World of the Palestinian Sages', *Proceedings of the Israel Academy of Sciences and Humanities* 2, 1966, pp. 38–74; Urbach, 'Mi-Yehuda la-Galil', *Memorial Volume for Jacob Friedman*, 1974, pp. 63–75.

10. A. I. Baumgarten, 'The Akiban Opposition', *HUCA* 50, 1979,

pp. 192 ff.;in that article I analyse pHag 3.1; 78d. Finkelstein has argued for Hillelite versus Akiban competition in very different terms from mine, and on the basis of other sources. His arguments require careful critical scrutiny. He has further proposed that Hillelite-Akiban friction is the cause of the intrusion of the Hillelite Patriarchs in the Pharisaic chain of tradition, mAb 1.16–2.3. See L. Finkelstein, 'Introductory Study to Pirke Abot', *JBL* 57, 1938, pp. 24–29.

11. Alon, *Toledot* II, pp. 72–75, 144; Urbach, 'Mi-Yehuda la-Galil', p. 71. R. Ammi b. Qarha reported in the name of Rav that R. Simeon b. Gamaliel II announced legal decisions in the name of his court (pBB 10.14; 17d). As noted by Urbach ('Mi-Yehuda la-Galil', p. 71), this represented a concession to conciliate opponents. R. Ammi b. Qarha is otherwise unknown. See W. Bacher, *Tradition und Tradenten,* repr. 1966, p. 478 n. 13.

12. Analysis of these sources will help fill the gap noted (but over-stated) by L. Levine, 'The Jewish Patriarch in Third Century Palestine', *ANRW* II. 19.2, 1979, p. 655.

13. He is missing in the other two principal Palestinian lists, pHag 3.1; 78d and CantR 2.5. Cf. bYeb 62b.

14. Many sources report that Meir was Akiba's student. See e.g. pBer 2.1; 4b and parallels; pSanh 1.2; 19a. He is on the three Palestinian lists of Akiba's students: GenR 61.3, p. 660; CantR 2.5; pHag 3.1 (78d). See also bSanh 86a. Even the stories in pHag 2.1; 77b–c and parallels that make him a student of Elisha b. Abuya are built on the notion that he was Akiba's student. It should be noted that the latter set of sources is highly tendentious: R. Meir performs miracles, and can even alter divine judgments. The stories in pHag 2.1; 77b–c and parallels should be carefully analysed and the points for which the stories are arguing identified. I plan to devote a future article to these texts.

15. Sifre Zutta, p. 305 (Horovitz).

16. TGitt 1.5, on which see S. Lieberman, *TK Nashim*, p. 791.

17. See further A. I. Baumgarten, 'R. Judah I and his Opponents', *JSJ* (forthcoming).

18. On the circles around R. Meir and Akiban circles in general as anti-Patriarchal see Baumgarten, 'The Akiban Opposition', pp. 189 ff.

19. On the meaning of the phrase see Amos 8.12 and Sifre Deut 305 (Horovitz/Finkelstein, p. 325). Compare Z. W. Rabinovitz, *Shaarei Torat Erets Israel* (=*STEI*), 1940, p. 353, who emends unnecessarily.

20. Rabinovitz, *STEI*, p. 353. Throughout this section of the article I treat all details of the stories as if they were factual. Only on that assumption can they be properly understood. That is not to say that I accept the historicity of the various accounts; see below, pp. 222-4.

21. Rabinovitz, *STEI*, p. 353.

22. Sifre Zutta, p. 277. Translation from S. Lieberman, *Hellenism in Jewish Palestine*, ²1962, p. 32. E. Z. Melamed, 'Lishna Maᶜaliah ve-Kin-uyye Soferim be-Sifrut ha-Talmud', *Benjamin DeVries Memorial Volume*, 1968, pp. 119–48, has collected many passages which illustrate R. Eleazar's aphorism. Aristotle (*Rhetoric* III.17; 1418b) offers similar advice

to the orator who wants to win the favour of his audience.

23. It is difficult if not impossible to know who is responsible for salvaging Patriarchal honour. Did R. Judah tell the story with the change himself, or should the change be attributed to some later narrator or scribe? How did the MSS which read עלי derive that reading? Is it the original version without the pro-Patriarchal correction or is it a correction of the pro-Patriarchal version for the sake of clarity? See further below n. 24. However the changes be understood and in whichever direction they went, it is important to note that many of the examples cited by Melamed are similar. That is, a version of one of his examples may contain the euphemism while another version will not; the euphemism may be in one manuscript and not in others.

24. Following the first edition and the *Vorlage* of MS Vat. 111. The reading in that MS is particularly significant. The original reading was עליו, but as that seemed unclear to the scribe he crossed out the final letter, leaving עלי. Compare the reading עלי in MSS Munich 95 and 141.

25. The word mishnah is ambiguous and can have many meanings, as was shown by J. N. Epstein, *Mabo le-Nusaḥ ha-Mishnah* (=*Mabo*), ²1964, pp. 806f.

26. Should one read Eleazar or Eliezer? This difficulty is encountered almost every time R. Eleazar or Eliezer is cited. For a discussion of this case see Epstein, *Mabo*, pp. 1163f. and Lieberman, *TK Nashim*, pp. 94ff.

27. On מאברין versus מעברין see Epstein, *Mabo*, pp. 8, 43 and 183.

28. Rejecting the emendation proposed by Rabinovitz, *STEI*, p. 199 and following the reading in the first printed edition.

29. On staring as a sign of anger see S. Lieberman, *Ha-Yerushalmi ki-Fshuto*, 1934, p. 289.

30. This is a proverb, as suggested by Lieberman, ibid. Cf. Rabinovitz, *STEI*, p. 199.

31. PErub 5.1; 22b. The end of the text is notably apologetic. The good intentions and actions of the great rabbis are stressed.

32. On R. Johanan as a student of R. Hoshaya see e.g. pTer 10.3; 47a.

33. TBM 2.30; tHor 2.5; pBM 2.13 (8d); pHor 3.4(48b). The reading in pHor is confirmed by the Genizah fragment published by L. Ginzberg, *Yerushalmi Fragments from the Genizah*, 1909, p. 282. One further question: in whose mishnah is the student enlightened, his own or the teacher's? I presume the ambiguity is deliberate. In either case, proper respect must be shown.

34. BBM 33a.

35. MAb 6.3.

36. BMen 18a, according to the first printed edition. MS Vatican 120 has only very minor disagreements from the readings of the first printed edition.

37. MS Munich 95 has only the first of the internal variants; MS Vatican 118 has only the second. These two manuscripts are presum-

ably shortening the original which already contained the double version.

38. TYom Tob 3.8. See further, Lieberman, *TK Mo'ed*, pp. 972f.

39. I follow the *Tosafot* on bMen 18a and J. N. Epstein, *Mebo'ot le-Sifrut ha-Tannaim* [henceforth cited as *Tannaim*], 1957, p. 158. Cf. M. Jastrow, *A Dictionary of the Targumim, the Talmud Babli and Yerushalmi and the Midrashic Literature*, repr. 1950, p. 825.

40. *Aruch ha-Shalem* (ed. G. A. Kohut), 1878–92, II, p. 328.

41. See e.g. MTann Deut, p. 220 and Sifre Deut 355 (Horovitz/Finkelstein, p. 420).

42. ואמרי לה is usually employed to introduce a variant version of the authorities associated with a given opinion. See W. Bacher, *Tradition und Tradenten*, pp. 524–33. At other times, there is a substantial difference between the content of the versions preserved, as in the representative examples collected by Epstein, *Mabo*, p. 691. I have found a few examples in which the internal variants hardly differ from each other and mean virtually the same thing, as in our case in bMen 18a. See bBer 2b; ר' אחאי ואמרי לה ר' אחא אומר. These are two versions of the same name, as is clear from information assembled by Ch. Albeck, *Mabo la-Talmudim*, 1969, pp. 443–44. See also bErub 13b: נמנו וגמרו נוח לו לאדם שלא נברא יותר משנברא. עכשיו שנברא יפשפש במעשיו ואמרי לה ימשמש במעשיו. Distinction between the two idioms for paying careful attention to one's deeds (see tNeg 6.7) is forced as shown in *Aruch ha-Shalem* VI, pp. 458f. Note the comparison between bKet 12a and pKet 1.1; 25a. See also bYeb 25b: אני הרגתי את בעלה בכניסתי ללוד ואמרי לה בכניסתו ללוד. Whether the husband was killed while the husband or the murderer was entering Lud is irrelevant to the legal question under discussion, hence there is little difference between the alternatives. For a further discussion of the significance of evidence of this sort see D. Weiss Halivni, *Mekorot u-Mesorot, Mo'ed*, p. 389 n. 3. Professor Halivni has kindly informed me that he plans to discuss the question further in his forthcoming volume, in the comments on bPes 38a.

43. Cf. tZeb 2.17 and the comments of S. Lieberman, *Tosefeth Rishonim* II, 1939, p. 205.

44. Following MSS Munich 6 and Oxford 366 and reading לו, as against the reading לפנינו in the first printed edition, MSS Munich 95 and London 400. The story makes best sense if the food was first brought to the master and eaten with his approval. On the other hand, since R. Judah is the narrator and the one who ate the food, it is easy to understand how the reading לפנינו arose.

45. The text as a whole should be compared with tSukk 2.2 and pSanh 7.2; 24b. See the discussion in Lieberman, *TK Mo'ed*, pp. 850f. and compare Rabinovitz, *STEI*, p. 521.

46. The saying is attributed to R. Johanan in MS Oxford 366, but this is a common error, of the same type as discussed by Epstein, *Mabo*, pp. 1204f.

47. *Tosafot* on bMen 18a, followed by Epstein, *Tannaim*, p. 180.

48. See W. S. Green, 'The Talmudic Historians', *The Modern Study of the Mishnah* (ed. Neusner), 1973, p. 115.

49. I. H. Weiss, *Dor Dor ve-Dorshav* II, ⁴1904, pp. 147f.

50. R. Judah was definitely young when he studied with R. Judah b. Ilai, tMeg 2.8 and parallels. He was also young when he studied with R. Johanan b. Nuri in Beth Shearim, tSukk 2.2 and pSanh 7.2; 24b. See further Lieberman, *TK Mo'ed*, pp. 850f. In general, stories about student days in rabbinic sources are stories about the youth of the principals. See tSukk 2.3 and tEduy 2.2; mAb 5.21; tBekh 6.11; Sifra, Emor, Parasha 1.6 (Weiss, p. 94a).

51. Epstein, *Tannaim*, pp. 158f. Was there a Mishnah of R. Eleazar used by R. Judah, or only a mishnah (cf. n. 25)? Neusner's research on the order of Purities leads him to conclusion that Mishnahs of the various Akibans were not employed by R. Judah. See J. Neusner, *A History of the Mishnaic Law of Purities* XXI, 1977, pp. 112, 125 and 300f.

52. Baumgarten, 'R. Judah I'. See especially the analysis there of pDem 2.1; 22c.

53. Baumgarten, 'The Akiban Opposition', pp. 194f.

54. Ibid., pp. 189f.

55. Herod took great care in matters relating to the education of his heirs, Josephus, *Ant.* XV.342f.; XVI.86 and 203; XVII.12. Numerous examples for Graeco-Roman dynasties could also be cited.

56. This point emerges clearly from the study of the Patriarch as a Scholarch now being prepared by my friend Shaye J. D. Cohen of the Jewish Theological Seminary.

57. See bHor 14a and pBetz 5.2; 63a. See also the discussion in Baumgarten, 'R. Judah I', and 'The Akiban Opposition', pp. 189f.

58. See pDem 2.1; 22c and the discussion in Baumgarten, 'R. Judah I'.

59. Augustus married his stepson Tiberius to his daughter Julia, making Tiberius the adopted father and protector of Augustus's heirs designate, Lucius and Gaius (Julia's sons by her late husband, Agrippa). This scheme failed when Tiberius realized that it was working as intended – too much to the advantage of his wards and too little to his own – hence he went into exile. See R. Syme, *Roman Revolution*, pp. 416–18; idem, *Tacitus* I, 1958, p. 425. Dynastic marriages are regularly concluded with similar objectives; they too sometimes fail, and for similar reasons. Herod's alliances can stand as ready examples: Josephus, *Ant.* XIV.300 and 325; XVII.15.

60. It is impossible to know how sincere R. Simeon b. Gamaliel II was when he sent his son to R. Eleazar. That is, did he intend to effect some sort of true reconciliation or did he mean to exploit the situation to his advantage? Each of these explanations may be partially true. Furthermore, judgments of sincerity are notoriously hard; when attempted they have been a source of debate. See e.g. M. Hammond, *The Augustan Principate*, ²1968, pp. 384–86.

61. Tiberius perceived the intention behind Augustus's plans and acted accordingly. But for the chance of the untimely death of both Lucius and Gaius, Tiberius would have permanently left the active scene of Roman politics. See Syme, *Roman Revolution*, p. 418. The

stakes in the case of R. Eleazar b. Shammua and his students were lower.

62. Had there been no negative reaction one would have to conclude that R. Simeon b. Gamaliel's intentions were so sincere and thoroughly convincing that all suspicions of exploitation were quelled. While it is true that we are told of R. Simeon's great modesty and amicability, such extreme virtues seem unlikely for an effective political leader. Moreover, similar assertions are made for R. Judah (e.g. mSot 9.15). In R. Judah's case these assertions come from a source which was produced in the circle of his ardent admirers; see Epstein, *Mabo*, p. 977. In addition, the assertion contradicts almost everything we know about R. Judah's character. The sources concerning R. Judah are therefore to be regarded with some suspicion. See Alon, *Toledot* II, pp. 130f.; see also Baumgarten, 'R. Judah I'. The sources concerning R. Simeon b. Gamaliel II should be similarly viewed and the extent of his modesty not exaggerated. See further Baumgarten, 'The Akiban Opposition', p. 193 n. 53. R. Simeon b. Gamaliel II knew how to insist on Patriarchal prerogative: bHor 14a and pBikk 3.3; 65c. Cf. Urbach, 'Mi-Yehuda la-Galil', p. 72.

63. Baumgarten, 'R. Judah I'. In addition to the evidence cited there, the following example deserves attention. Josephus's dislike for the various fanatical anti-Roman groups is well known (e.g. *Bell.* VII. 252–274). He calls them criminals and madmen, insisting that in the end they received the punishment they deserved at the hands of God. In Eleazar b. Yair's last speech to the defenders of Masada, Josephus makes Eleazar say the following: 'For it was not of their own accord that those flames which were driving against the enemy turned back on the wall constructed by us; no, all this betokens *wrath at the many wrongs which we madly dared to inflict upon our countrymen*' (*Bell.* VII.332).

64. Four of the five sources analysed in this article are baraitot in the Babylonian Talmud. Other evidence for competition between Akibans and the Patriarchate is decisively (and unambiguously) Palestinian. See the sources discussed in my 'The Akiban Opposition', pp. 179-97.

It is possible that the pro-Patriarchal stories in Babylonian sources do not go back to Patriarchal circles but are the product of the well known tendency in the Babylonian Talmud to present political events in Palestine in a light favourable to the Patriarchate. Even if this explanation be preferred, it would not change the basic interpretation presented, which concentrates on the meaning of the sources explained as coming from the Akiban camp.

On Babylonian versions of events in Palestine see S. Safrai, 'Tales of the Sages in the Palestinian Tradition and the Babylonian Talmud', *SH* 22, 1971, pp. 214-20. See further Baumgarten, 'The Akiban Opposition', p. 181 n. 7. See also Goldenberg's analysis of the Gamaliel deposition stories: R. Goldenberg, 'The Deposition of Rabban Gamaliel II: an Examination of the Sources', *JJS* 23, 1972, pp. 175, 185–87. A point apparently overlooked by Goldenberg deserves mention. In the Palestinian version, pBer 4.1; 7c-d, the statement of Gamaliel's superior lineage ('The sprinkler son of a sprinkler should sprinkle. Should he who is neither a sprinkler nor a son of a sprinkler say to the sprinkler son of a sprinkler: Your water comes from a cave and your ashes from roasting?') is made to R. Eleazar b. Azariah by a messenger (either a washerman or R. Akiba). In the Babylonian version, bBer 27b-28a, it is put in the mouth of R. Joshua, the originator of the controversy. In the Babylonian version, even the controversial R. Joshua (mRSh 2.8–9) recognizes R. Gamaliel's *prima facie* claim to the Patriarchate. On the attitude of Babylonian sources to the Hillelites see also Halivni's comments above, p. 208.

65. R. Eleazar b. Shammua may have been the father of R. Simeon b. Eleazar. This conclusion was proposed by several nineteenth-century scholars: Z. Frankel, *Darke ha-Mishnah*, 1959, pp. 184 and 211; J. Brüll, *Mabo la-Mishnah* I, 1876, p. 236; W. Bacher, *Die Agada der Tannaiten* II, 1903, p. 275. The idea was opposed by other scholars: Weiss, *Dor Dor ve-Dorshav* II, p. 165; Aaron Hyman, *Toledot Tannaim ve-Amoraim*, p. 1157; I. Burgansky, 'Simeon ben Eleazar', *EJ* XIV, col. 1454. If R. Eleazar b. Shammua was his father, son and father shared the same politics. R. Simeon b. Eleazar is known as a devoted student of R. Meir and as a bitter critic of the Patriarchate. See Baumgarten, 'R. Judah I', and 'Akiban Opposition', p. 190.

66. R. Simeon b. Yohai is on all the Palestinian lists of Akiba's students: GenR 61.3, p. 660, CantR 2.5 and pHag 3.1; 78d, in which he plays a very prominent part. See also bYeb 62b. On R. Judah as his student see tErub 5.24; pErub 9.1; 25c and pShab 10.5; 12c. The anonymous comment in pShab 10.5; 12c would deny that R. Judah studied with R. Simeon b. Yohai, insisting that R. Jacob b. Korshai was R. Judah's teacher. This, however, is the usual (but incorrect) view of the Palestinian Talmud; the other sources cited above make it clear that R. Judah studied with R. Simeon b. Yohai. See further Epstein, *Tannaim*, p. 180, and below n. 73.

67. Epstein, *Tannaim*, pp. 148–58.

68. PShab 10.5; 12c. See further my discussion of R. Johanan ha-Sandlar's use of this phrase (pHag 3.1; 78d) in 'The Akiban Opposition', pp. 184f. See also I. Gafni, 'Yeshivah u-Metivtah', *Zion* 43, 1978, p. 8 n. 33.

69. TMeg 2.8; pMeg 2.4(73b); pPes 4.1(30d); pShab 8.1(11b). Epstein, *Tannaim*, pp. 106–25. R. Judah b. Ilai was an Akiban. He is on all the lists of Akiba's students, and he often quotes Akiba. See e.g. tKel BM 6.7 and tOhal 4.2.

70. Judah b. Ilai was called מוריינה (דבי) נשיאה in pShab 8.1;11b and parallels and in bMen 104a. He was also called ראש המדברים בכל מקום (bBer 63b and parallels). The exact meaning of these various titles is unclear; see H. Mantel, *Studies in the History of the Sanhedrin*, 1965, pp. 147–50; Urbach, 'Mi-Yehuda la-Galil', pp. 70–71. However these titles be understood, R. Judah b. Ilai had a prominent place in the Patriarchal court. See Epstein, *Tannaim*, p. 107.

71. TBer. 4.15 (according to the Erfurt MS and first printed edition);

Notes to page 225

tPes 1.4; tYomTob 2.12; tBK 9.30; tZeb 8.17; tHull 6.8. R. Judah also reports incidents which occurred at the court of R. Gamaliel II: tTer 2.13; tKet 8.1 and tGitt 1.4.

72. Thus we cannot say whether he took a stance more favourable to the Patriarchate because he was already well disposed towards the Hillelites (as indicated by his already holding some sort of office), or whether he received the office as a reward for having moved closer to the Patriarchate. Other sources concerning R. Judah b. Ilai confirm my interpretation of his political position. In contrast to the anti-Patriarchal Akibans who are consistently portrayed as being on good terms with R. Meir (above, p. 214), R. Judah b. Ilai is represented as having disapproved of R. Meir. See the sources and discussion in Epstein, *Tannaim*, p. 107, to which should be added R. Judah's pointed remarks in CantR 2.4.

It is worth noting that both his father and son, R. Ilai and R. Jose b. Judah, figure in stories concerning the Patriarch: tPes 2.15; Sifre Deut 335 (Horovitz/Finkelstein, p. 385) (but compare the MSS variants and the version in M. Tann. Deut p. 205); GenR 76.8, p. 906; pDem 1.1 (21c); 7.1(26a); pShebi 6.4(37a). For comments on the R. Ilai story see Urbach, 'Mi-Yehuda la-Galil', pp. 65f. To my knowledge there has been no real discussion of the R. Jose b. Judah stories.

73. The evidence concerning R. Meir requires further extended consideration. For a preliminary discussion see Baumgarten, 'R. Judah I'. The case of R. Jacob b. Korshai, the principal teacher of R. Judah according to the Palestinian Talmud (see pShab 10.5(12c); pPes 4.1(30d) and pPes 10.1(37b) would properly belong to the full discussion of the evidence concerning R. Meir (R. Jacob's teacher). See further S. Safrai, 'Jacob b. Korshai', *EJ* IX, col. 1221 and Epstein, *Tannaim*, p. 193.

74. The nature of the evidence is, of course, to blame. See the discussions above, pp. 222-4. The question of the reliability of rabbinic evidence has received much attention in recent years. See e.g. W. S. Green, 'What's in a Name – the Problematic of Rabbinic Biography', *Approaches to Ancient Judaism*, 1978, pp. 85ff.

75. We can only speculate on R. Judah's reasons for giving Akiban teaching the place he did in his Mishnah. To some extent our speculations depend on the answer given to a much debated larger question: R. Judah's intentions and goals in compiling the Mishnah. See the sharp disagreement between Epstein (*Tannaim*, pp. 205–11, 225–26), who sees the Mishnah as a law code, and Albeck (*Mabo la-Mishnah*, 1959, pp. 270–83), who sees the Mishnah as a compendium of Oral Law intended for students. Between these extremes, but closer to Epstein, is the view of Urbach, 'Mishnah', *EJ* XII, col. 104; for a fuller statement of Urbach's position see his Hebrew review article of Albeck's *Mabo* published in *Molad* 17, 1959, pp. 422–40. Urbach sees R. Judah as intending to compile an authoritative canon of mishnayot; the very fact of the existence of an authoritative canon helped decide the law. See further Halivni's comments above, pp.379f.n. 3.

76. On the Akiban coloration of the Mishnah see Halivni's remarks, above, p. 210. Cf. Urbach, 'Mishnah', col. 104.

10 Birkat Ha-Minim *and the Lack of Evidence for an Anti-Christian Jewish Prayer in Late Antiquity*

*I am grateful to Professors David Goodblatt, Wayne Meeks and John Townsend for their reading of the MS and for their helpful suggestions.

1. S. Schechter published two medieval Egyptian liturgical fragments in 1898 in 'Genizah Specimens', *JQR*, os 10, 1898, pp. 657, 659. For an updated bibliography on the issues generated by the text, see P. Schäfer, *Studien zur Geschichte und Theologie des rabbinischen Judentums*, 1978, p. 53 n. 3.

2. See J. Heinemann, *Prayer in the Talmud: Forms and Patterns*, 1977, p. 225 and literature cited (n. 20) (Hebrew original, p. 142 n. 20).

3. A similar development seems to have taken place in Christianity in the same period. Compare Paul (I Cor. 6.9) with Ignatius (*Philadelphians* 3.3) for the development from social disrupters to theological dissidents who in the case of Ignatius are probably Jewish Christians. See P. J. Donahue, 'Jewish Christianity in the Letters of Ignatius of Antioch', *VC* 32, 1978, pp. 81–93.

4. This is how it apparently functions in the Talmudim, see pBer 5.4; 9c and bBer 28b–29a. The texts, however, are somewhat problematic, see Sh. Goren, *Ha-Yerushalmi ha-Meforash*, 1961, pp. 210f.

5. See Y. M. Elbogen, *Ha-Tefillah be-Yisrael be-Hitpathutah ha-Historit*, 1972, pp. 28f., who based himself on Midrash Tanhumah (ed. Buber) *Vayyiqra'* 3 (Leviticus, p. 3). For a possible scenario, see J. L. Martyn, *History and Theology in the Fourth Gospel*, ²1979, pp. 59–61.

6. N. Perrin (*The New Testament: An Introduction*, 1974), who accepts Martyn's analysis, tries to wriggle out of this difficulty by saying, 'its presence in the synagogue liturgy would force out of the synagogue community those *who knew themselves to be designated Nazarenes or Minim'* (p. 230, my italics).

7. See next section entitled '*Minim*'.

8. See G. Alon, *Mehqarim be-Toledot Yisra'el* I, 1957, p. 192.

9. See, for example, two widely-read treatments from different perspectives: W. H. C. Frend, *Martyrdom and Persecution in the Early Church*, 1965, p. 179; and S. W. Baron, *A Social and Religious History of the Jews* II, ²1952, p. 135. It is difficult to find studies which question this assumption.

10. See M. Goldstein, *Jesus in the Jewish Tradition*, 1950, p. 45, and literature cited.

11. TBM 2.33.

12. TSanh 13.5.

13. Midrash Tanhuma (ed. Buber) *Vayyiqra'* 3. L. Ginzberg, without citing this source, came to the same conclusion. He, however, adds that 'benediction' may be used euphemistically (see Job 1.5; 2.5, 9 et

Notes to page 228

al.), *A Commentary on the Palestinian Talmud* III, 1941, p. 280. The 'curse theory' for *birkat ha-minim* is supported by Y. Cohen, *Peraqim be-Toledot Tequfat ha-Tannaim*, 1978, p. 117.

14. Goldstein, *Jesus in the Jewish Tradition*.

15. Ibid., pp. 46f. For a sophisticated comprehensive treatment of the issues involved, see A. F. Segal, *Two Powers in Heaven: Early Rabbinic Reports About Christianity and Gnosticism*, 1977.

16. A. Büchler, 'The Minim of Sepphoris and Tiberias in the Second and Third Centuries', *Studies in Jewish History*, 1956, p. 271; S. Lieberman, 'The Martyrs of Caesarea', *Annuaire de l'institut de philologie et d'histoire orientales et slaves* 7, 1944, p. 398; M. Simon, *Verus Israel*, ²1964, p. 238; H. Hirschberg, 'Allusions to the Apostle Paul in the Talmud', *JBL* 62, 1943, pp. 73–87.

17. Büchler, 'The Minim of Sepphoris', p. 252; S. Lieberman, *Greek in Jewish Palestine*, ²1965, p. 141 n. 196. K. G. Kuhn tries to solve the problem by positing a temporal distinction: Minim in older texts were Jews while in later texts (from 180–200) they refer 'no longer to heretics within Judaism, but to those of other beliefs mostly Christian', 'Giljonim und Sifre Minim', *Judentum – Urchristentum – Kirche* (ed. Eltester), 1960, p. 39.

18. An apparent exception to the thesis that *min* in early Palestinian rabbinic literature denotes Jew is the statement at the end of mSot (9.15) that 'the kingdom will revert to *minut*'. This statement is problematic all around. It is not clear where it belongs, who said it, or what it means.

Although the statement appears in the Mishnah of the printed editions, recent research has shown that it is a later appendage based on the bSanh 97a (see Epstein, *Mabo le-Nusah ha-Mishnah* II, 1948, p. 976; and Ch. Albeck, *Mishnah, Seder Nashim*, 1959, p. 394). Thus it is missing in the Leningrad MS published by A. Katsch, *Ginze Mishnah*, 1970, p. 77; the Pisaro or Constantinople edition of the Mishnah (Jerusalem 1970) p. 200; and the Parma MS (Jerusalem 1970) p. 162. Only the Kaufman MS (Jerusalem 1968) approximates it, reading והמלכות תהא מינות (p. 245).

Is the statement then tannaitic or amoraic? In bSanh 97a it is cited in the name of R. Nehemiah as a baraita, indicating that it is tannaitic. Elsewhere in later documents (CantR 2.13.4; *Seder Eliyahu Zutta* 15, ed. Friedman, p. 12 and n. 46) it is also cited in the name of R. Nehemiah. If this is the tanna of that name and the statement accurately reflects the original terminology, then the statement is truly problematic. Scholars have discerned in the expression 'the kingdom will revert to *minut*' an allusion to the Christian takeover of the Roman Empire. It is hard to believe that about 175 CE a rabbi would have noticed anything to make that suggestion credible. An alternative which is not wholly satisfying is to interpret the 'kingdom' as referring to the internal Jewish administration, since the Patriarchate had the aura of royalty. The statement thus reflects the menace of Jewish heresies, which we know was a constant problem.

392

On the other hand, R. Nehemiah may be the amora of that name (see *Entsiklopediah le-Ḥokme ha-Talmud*, ed. M. Margoliot, 1964, p. 666; and A. Hyman, *Toledot Tanna'im ve-'Amoraim*, 1964, p. 926a). This supposition is reinforced by the fact that the statement does not appear originally in any tannaitic document and that the statement is always cited with other amoraic statements about the coming of the son of David (even the cited R. Nehorai could be the Amora). The difficulty is that the statement is introduced by *TNY'* – the sign of a tannaitic citation. This, however, may be the work of a scribe who, knowing the Mishnah Sotah and the fact that generally 'R. Nehemiah' refers to the tanna (indeed, it is claimed that anonymous sections of the Tosefta are the work of R. Nehemiah just a little before in the same tractate – bSanh 86a), just assumed that this was a citation from the Mishnah and therefore inserted the term *TNY'*. If this be so, then the expression 'the kingdom will revert to *minut'* is a Babylonian amoraic statement from about 325 CE! In the text of the paper, we show that the Babylonian Talmud used *min* indiscriminately and frequently of Gentiles. Accordingly, this expression does not contradict the thesis that in early Palestinian rabbinic literature *minim* are Jews.

19. H. Hirschberg's interpretation ('Once Again – The Minim', *JBL* 67, 1948, pp. 305–18, 309ff.) is ingenious but unconvincing.

20. This is also the reading of the parallel in bAZ 26a according to the Spanish MS (ed. Abramson), New York 1957.

21. Justin, *Dial.* 19 and 92; Tertullian, *Adv. Marc.* 5.9 and *Adv. Jud.* 4, cf. *The Gospel of Thomas* 53 (I owe this reference to the kindness of Professor Wayne Meeks). See GRabb 11.6 (ed. Theodor-Albeck), p. 94, and notes, esp. end of n. 6, and parallels.

22. *Midrash ha-Gadol Leviticus* (ed. Steinsaltz), p. 735. The parallel in the Babylonian Talmud (Yeb 102b) reads *min*. See below for the discussion of *min* in that Talmud.

23. E. E. Urbach, 'The Homiletical Interpretations of the Sages and the Exposition of Origen on Canticles, and the Jewish-Christian Disputation', *SH* 22, 1971, pp. 248–75, originally in Hebrew, *Tarbiz* 30, 1960, pp. 148–70; R. Kimelman, 'R. Yohanan and Origen on the Song of Songs: A Third Century Jewish-Christian Disputation', *HTR* 72, (forthcoming). See also the statement of 'the nations of the world' in Midrash Tanhuma (ed. Buber) Ba Shellaḥ 24 (Exodus, p. 67) and N. R. M. de Lange, *Origen and the Jews*, Cambridge 1976, pp. 93f.

24. See works cited in n. 23.

25. Lieberman, *Greek in Jewish Palestine*, p. 141 n. 196.

26. Lieberman, 'The Martyrs of Caesarea', p. 440.

27. BAZ 65a according to the Spanish MS. The similar expression in bHull 13b is by a Babylonian.

28. PYeb 8.1; 8d. See S. Lieberman, *Midreshe Teman*, 1970, p. 8, *contra* G. F. Moore, 'The Definition of the Jewish Canon and the Repudiation of Christian Scriptures', *The Canon and Masorah of the Hebrew Bible* (ed. Leiman), 1974, p. 124.

The thesis that Palestinian material was subject to linguistic alteration in the hands of Babylonian amoraim is demonstrated by the various studies of M. Moreshet in the *Henoch Yalon Memorial Volume*, 1974, and in the *Archive of the New Dictionary of Rabbinic Literature*, 2 vols., 1972–74.

29. Büchler, 'The Minim of Sepphoris'.

30. J. Jocz, *The Jewish People and Jesus Christ*, 1949, p. 180.

31. R. Payne-Smith, *Thesaurus Syriacus*, 1897–1901, p. 2094; F. Schwally, *Idioticon des christlich-palästinischen Aramäisch*, 1893, p. 50. My point is that the usage is attested to in the above, not that Christian Palestinian Aramaic was used in Babylonia.

32. As do L. Finkelstein, *Ha-Perushim ve-Anshe Keneset ha-Gedolah*, 1950, p. 34 n. 119; and Hirschberg, 'Once Again – The Minim', p. 318 n. 78.

33. For the text, parallels, and comments, see J. Neusner, *Eliezer Ben Hyrcanus*, 1973, I, pp. 400–3, cf. II, pp. 366f.

34. For an updated comprehensive discussion of this cognomen for Jesus, see J. Maier, *Jesus von Nazareth in der talmudischen Überlieferung*, 1978, pp. 260–67.

35. BAZ 16b–17a. On 'the Nazarene' see n. 91 below.

36. See p. 241 below.

37. KohR 7.26.3, see ibid. 1.8.4. It is possible that only the first interpretation is R. Issi's while the rest was added. For our purposes it makes no difference.

38. See K. G. Kuhn, *Achtzehngebet und Vaterunser und der Reim*, 1950, pp. 18ff.

39. Advocates of this position are legion. Among recent authors, see Martyn, *History and Theology in the Fourth Gospel*, p. 58 n. 78; W. D. Davies, *The Setting of the Sermon on the Mount*, 1966, pp. 278f.; and J. T. Townsend, 'The Gospel of John and the Jews; The Story of a Religious Divorce', *Antisemitism and the Foundations of Christianity* (ed. Davies), 1979, pp. 72–97, esp. 86. This position goes back at least as far back as S. Krauss, 'The Jews in the Works of the Church Fathers', *JQR* os 5, 1892–93, pp. 130ff.

40. See Townsend, 'The Gospel of John and the Jews'.

41. See Jocz, *The Jewish People and Jesus Christ*, pp. 56f., for several suggestions. Even the updated note in Elbogen, *Ha-Tefillah*, p. 31, has to equivocate by saying, 'The explicit mention of the *minim* who repudiate Judaism in general; and that of the *nosrim* in particular.' This gives the erroneous impression that the text reads first *minim* and then *nosrim* rather than the reverse. R. Wilde, *The Treatment of the Jews in the Greek Christian Writers*, 1949, p. 119 n. 126, says: 'In Acts 24:5 we read τῆς τῶν Ναζωραίων αἱρέσεως, which may safely be said to represent the Hebrew expression, *nosrim* and *minim*. Such equivalence is both a sign of the great antiquity of such expressions and a further reason for their probable inclusion in the original curse formula.' This clever, but far-fetched, suggestion ignores the construction of the Greek.

42. In French: Simon, *Verus Israel*, p. 236; in English: Martyn, *History and Theology in the Fourth Gospel*, p. 58; in German: P. Riessler, *Altjüdisches Schrifttum ausserhalb der Bibel*, 1928, p. 9, cited from S.

Krauss, 'Zur Literatur der Siddurim', *Festschrift für Aron Freimann*, 1935, p. 138 n. 10. See also Baron, *Social and Religious History*.

43. E.g. Davies, *Sermon on the Mount*, p. 276, who goes on to argue for a major interaction between Judaism and Christianity in the Yavnean period. See also E. Lerle, 'Liturgische Reformen des Synagogengottesdienstes als Antwort auf die judenchristliche Mission des ersten Jahrhunderts', *NovT* 10, 1968, pp. 31–42. An exception is Jocz, *The Jewish People and Jesus Christ*, pp. 51–7, who excludes *nosrim* from the original formulation, but perceives a major interaction between the two.

44. E.g., M. Avi-Yonah, *The Jews of Palestine: A Political History from the Bar Kokhba War to the Arab Conquest*, ET 1976, p. 142 (Hebrew original, p. 122). Cf. Cohen's critique (*Peraqim*, p. 138 n. 328) precisely on this point.

45. A. Marmorstein, 'The Amidah of the Public Fast Days', *JQR* 15, 1924, pp. 409–18, 415–17. See also the Oxford MS of *Seder R. Amram Gaon* (ed. Goldschmidt), p. 25, n. to line 9.

46. Jesus is called *ha-nosri* (see n. 91 below) only in Babylonian literature. (References have been censored from the standard printed editions, see S. M. Haberman's edition of R. Rabbinovicz, *Ma'amar al Hadpasat ha-Talmud*, Jerusalem 1965, p. 28 nn. 25f.) Each body of literature is consistent in its use of terminology. Not only is Jesus referred to as *ha-nosri* in Babylonian amoraic sources (bSanh 103a; bBer 17b), but even alleged tannaitic material (such as bSanh 43a; 107b; bSot 47a) contained therein employs the identifying *ha-nosri*. This tendency is so strong that the same episode when found in a tannaitic document (tHull 2.24) reads 'Jesus ben Pantiri' while the parallel in the Babylonian Talmud (bAZ 16b–17a, Spanish MS, p. 28 line 21) reads 'Jesus *ha-nosri*'. This phenomenon renders unnecessary the analysis of J. Klausner, *Jesus of Nazareth*, ET repr. 1953, p. 38.

47. The Hebrew term will be discussed in n. 91 below. Still, it should be noted that the Hebrew is no more clear than the Greek. For the different theories, see R. E. Brown, *The Birth of the Messiah*, 1977, pp. 207–13; and H. H. Schaeder in *TDNT* IV, pp. 874–9.

48. BAZ 6a, 7b, see *Diqduqe Soferim* and Spanish MS ad loc.

49. This fallacy is well-nigh universal. An exception may be M. Liber, 'Structure and History of the *Tefilah*', *JQR* 40, 1949, p. 350 n. 43. He, however, never seems to have worked out the implications of his insight.

50. Among recent commentators, see R. E. Brown, *The Gospel According to St John*, Garden City 1966, pp. LXXXV, 380; Martyn, *History and Theology in the Fourth Gospel*, pp. 51–62; R. Kysar, *The Fourth Evangelist and His Gospel – An Examination of Contemporary Scholarship*, 1975, pp. 149–54; and S. Pancaro, *The Law in the Fourth Gospel*, 1975, pp. 245–50.

51. See W. A. Meeks, ' "Am I a Jew?" – Johannine Christianity and Judaism', *Christianity, Judaism and Other Greco-Roman Cults* I (ed. Neus-

ner), 1975, pp. 163–86; and Townsend, 'The Gospel of John and the Jews'.

52. See D. Hare, *The Theme of Jewish Persecution of Christians in the Gospel according to St Matthew*, 1967, p. 55.

53. Even Martyn (*History and Theology in the Fourth Gospel*, p. 55 n. 69 point 1) considers this a serious possibility. His arguments for rejecting it are unconvincing. His first point is based on Justin, which as will be shown below does not support his contention that John is responding to a situation that emerged by virtue of *birkat ha-minim*. His second point, concerning rabbinic tradition on the nature of the charges that led to Jesus' death, is based on evidence much later than John and, in any case, is irrelevant to *birkat ha-minim*. The mere fact that the benediction is not mentioned in any tannaitic document may tend to support Wayne A. Meeks's position, cited there, that the talmudic 'scenes portray as punctiliar events in Gamaliel's time what was actually a linear development stretching over a lengthy period and culminating in the pertinent formulation of the Birkath ha Minim, perhaps quite a bit later than Gamaliel'. The talmudic evidence (above, n. 4) is also insufficiently precise to enable the historian to trace the introduction of the benediction back to Samuel the Small under the auspices of Rabban Gamaliel.

In general, historians should be careful of the use of Jewish leadership groups in the gospels. Frequently, their presence serves as a foil to Jesus (i.e. to show current Christians how to respond to Jewish charges). The precise name of the group was rather unimportant to the aim of the authors, who generally did not know the differences between them anyhow. For the synoptics, see M. J. Cook, *Mark's Treatment of the Jewish Leaders*, 1978. For John, see Meeks, ' "Am I a Jew?" ', pp. 172 and 182 n. 72; and U. Wahlde, 'The Terms for Religious Authorities in the Fourth Gospel. A Key to Literary Strata', *JBL* 98, 1979, pp. 231–53.

54. Luke 6.22 is something quite different. The answer of K. L. Carroll ('The Fourth Gospel and the Exclusion of Christians from the Synagogues', *BJRL* 40, 1957–58, pp. 19–32, esp. 19f.) is not to the point.

55. So W. Schrage, *TDNT* VII, p. 848.

56. Pancaro (*The Law in the Fourth Gospel*, p. 249) entertains this possibility but rejects it because of his understanding of the relationship between *birkat ha-minim* and ἀποσυνάγωγος. Once serious doubt is cast on that relationship, he would presumably consider the fabrication suggestion seriously. Hare (*Jewish Persecution*, p. 55) in a similar vein says, 'John's peculiar hostility toward the Jews makes it difficult for us to know whether these passages represent historical facts or unfulfilled predictions on the part of the author.' Also P. Winter (*On the Trial of Jesus*, ²1974, p. 128) emphasized that a statement's veracity is to be seen in the light of an author's aim. Thus an assertion may be aimed at guaranteeing the fulfilment of a saying of Jesus rather than reflecting a contemporary reality (thus the relationship of John 9.22 and 12.42 to 16.2). As Perrin (*The New Testament*) says, 'The gospel and letters of

John give the impression of carefully composed wholes, of being a response to the internal dynamics of the genius and vision of the author rather than to the external dynamics of a concrete historical situation and need' (p. 222).

57. See T. L. Schram, *The Use of Ioudaios in the Fourth Gospel*, 1974.

58. See Townsend, 'The Gospel of John and the Jews', p. 8; and Meeks, ' "Am I a Jew?" ', p. 180 nn. 63f., for literature on these issues. This orientation accounts for the peculiarity that the closely related Johannine epistles are devoid of any significant reference to Judaism, including the Law, the Jews, Israel, the scriptures, Abraham, Moses, the prophets (even Isaiah!), the Sabbath, circumcision, and even the idea of the 'fulfilment of scripture'. Indeed, not a single verse of scripture is cited; see Pancaro, *The Law in the Fourth Gospel*, pp. 250f.

59. The assumption here that rabbinic enactments were immediately enforceable everywhere points to an effectiveness and power which can only be documented, and even then with difficulty, a century or two later. See R. Kimelman, 'Third-Century Tiberias: The Alliance between the Rabbinate, the Patriarchate, and the Urban Aristocracy', Supplement Volume to *ANRW* II.8, forthcoming.

If a Palestinian milieu is necessary to explain John's use of terms, then a more likely candidate is Qumran, which seems to have had a parallel in the expulsion from the community (cf. 1QS 6.24–7.25; 8.16f., 22f.). This parallel becomes more cogent in the light of the views of numerous scholars who have correlated Qumran material with the background of an early edition of John. (See e.g. J. H. Charlesworth (ed.), *John and Qumran*, 1972.) Besides the alleged connection between John and *birkat ha-minim* there is no explicit connection between John and rabbinic Judaism. Thus the suggestion of a connection has little historical support. In the light of the various connections between John and Qumran it is simpler to extend the connection to cover the practice of exclusion, if there were such a practice, rather than to create a new one with rabbinic Judaism. Indeed, the connection with the Samaritans seems, at least, as strong and would cover what Martyn, *History and Theology in the Fourth Gospel*, p. 55 n. 69, point 2, perceives as a 're-markable degree of correspondence between the *two* elements mentioned in John . . . and the two measures referred to by Justin'. This is a correspondence which I do not find striking. On the Samaritan connection, see Meeks, ' "Am I a Jew?" ', pp. 176f.; and J. D. Purvis, 'The Fourth Gospel and the Samaritans', *NovT* 17, 1975, p. 11 n. 1, for bibliography.

60. For the need of this practice, see S. Lieberman, 'Roman Legal Institutions in Early Rabbinics and in the Acta Martyrum', *JQR* 35, 1944–45, p. 23 n. 150.

61. Justin, *Dial.* 38, cf. 17, 108. Similarly, for John, see Pancaro, *The Law in the Fourth Gospel*, p. 502.

62. This analysis vitiates Strecker's objections ('On the Problem of Jewish Christianity', Appendix I to W. Bauer, *Orthodoxy and Heresy in Earliest Christianity*, ET 1971, p. 274), to the suggestion that the struc-

ture of *Dial.* 47 (which mentions Jews cursing Christ in the synagogue) is a 'logical arrangement . . . attributed to mere abstraction'.

63. 'Cum . . . Christus usque in hodiernum diem a Iudaeis anathema fiat', Origen, *Hom.* II.8 *in Ps.* xxxvii (xxxvi) (PG 12, 1387); cf. *Comm. in Matt.* XVI.3 (on Matt. 20.17–19; GCS X, p. 469).

64. Thus Origen was so willing to curse and damn those who converted to Judaism (*Comm. Ser. in Matt.* 16 [on 23.16; GCS XI, p. 30], cited by Krauss, *JQR* 5, p. 146).

65. Origène, *Homélies sur Jérémie*, ed. P. Nautin (SC 232), 1976, p. 164.

66. See de Lange, *Origen and the Jews*, 1976, esp. pp. 39–47.

67. For the sources in Origen dealing with the converts, the tribunals, and those who attended at his sermons, see de Lange, *Origen and the Jews*, pp. 165 n. 79, 161 n. 48, 188 nn. 79f. respectively. On the dating of the two Homilies, see Nautin (ed.), *Homélies*, p. 19 n. 1.

68. de Lange, *Origen and the Jews*, pp. 85f.

69. As J. Parkes wrote, '. . . the Church of the second century was no more the Church of the fourth than was the Judaism of the second century the complete Judaism of the Talmud. Neither had yet absorbed or rejected various intermediate groups which existed at the earlier period' (*The Conflict of the Church and the Synagogue*, repr. 1969, p. 94).

70. Jerome, *Comm. in Amos* I, on 1.11f. (CCSL 76, p. 227): they blaspheme (*blasphemant*) the Christian people. *Comm. in Isa.* II, on 5.19 (CCSL 73, p. 76): they anathematize (*anathematizent*) the Christian name. Ibid., XIII, on 49.7 (p. 538): they curse (*maledicunt*) Christ. Ibid., XIV, on 52.4–6 (p. 578): they utter curses (*congerunt maledicta*) against the Christians. Incidentally, we should not exclude the possibility that Jerome heard that the prayer mentioned *nosrim* and read into it what he knew from Origen and Justin.

71. Krauss, 'The Jews in the Works of the Church Fathers', *JQR* 5, 1892–93, p. 132; see also his 'Zur Literatur der Siddurim', p. 126.

72. See D. S. Wiesen, *St Jerome as a Satirist*, 1964, pp. 188–94.

73. Translated in Klijn and Reinink, *Patristic Evidence for Jewish-Christian Sects*, 1973, p. 201.

74. *Pan.* 29.9.1, cited in Klijn, *Patristic Evidence*, pp. 173f.

75. See Klijn and Reinink, *Patristic Evidence*, p. 50. Klijn and Reinink cast doubt on Jerome's personal acquaintance with the Nazoraeans. Their major argument is that Jerome gives allegedly conflicting reports about their belief regarding the birth of Jesus. In one place, Jerome writes that the Nazoraeans believed Jesus was 'the son of the carpenter' (*Comm. in Matt.* II, on 13.53f. [ed. E. Bonnard, SC 242, 1977, p. 294]), while elsewhere (*Epistle* 112.13, CSEL 55, p. 381) he writes of their belief in the Virgin birth. Although this appears to be contradictory, any group which read Matt. 1.18–25 and especially Luke 1.26–39; 2.5; and 3.23 could easily have made both above statements as Christian literature had previously done, see Brown, *The Birth of the Messiah*, pp. 521ff., esp. n. 12.

76. On the other hand, there may be no difference between them.

Epiphanius may be just being judgmental while Jerome is presenting their own self-understanding. Epiphanius says elsewhere about them that they 'did not keep the name Jews; they did not call themselves Christians, but Nazoraeans. . . . But actually they remained wholly Jewish and nothing else' (*Panarion* 29.7.1, trans. Klijn, *Patristic Evidence*, p. 173).

77. See E. P. Sanders, 'The Covenant as a Soteriological Category and the Nature of Salvation in Palestinian and Hellenistic Judaism', *Jews, Greeks and Christians: Religious Culture in Late Antiquity* (ed. Hamerton-Kelly and Scroggs), 1976, pp. 11–14.

78. Jerome, *Comm. in Isa.* XVI, on 59.15 (CCSL 73, p. 686): 'expulerint de synagogis', cited by Krauss, 'The Jews in the Works of the Church Fathers', *JQR* 6, 1894, p. 237 n. 5.

79. It will not do to say that Christians came mostly on the Sabbath when *birkat ha-minim* is not recited. Attitudinally, that is, from the point of view of synagogal receptivity, it makes no difference. For the considerable attraction of Judaism for Christians, at least through the fourth century, see R. L. Wilken, *Judaism and the Early Christian Mind*, 1971, esp. 'Jewish-Christian Relations in the Roman Empire', pp. 9–38.

80. See S. Gero, 'Jewish Polemic in the Martyrium Pionii and a "Jesus" Passage from the Talmud', *JJS* 29, 1978, pp. 164–68, esp. 164.

81. *The Acts of the Christian Martyrs* 13.1; 14.1 (ed. H. Musurillo), 1972.

82. See Krauss, 'The Jews in the Works of the Church Fathers', *JQR* 5, 1892–93, p. 147 n. 2; and above, n. 67.

83. See Krauss, 'The Jews in the Works of the Church Fathers', *JQR* 6, 1893–94, p. 238 nn. 2 and 9.

84. *Epistle 52 to Nepotion.*

85. Chrysostom, *Homilies against the Jews* 1.3.3–4; 1.4.6; 1.5.2; 1.5.7; 1.6.2; 1.8.1; 2.3.5; 4.7.3–4; 4.7.7; 5.12.12; 6.6.6; 6.7.3–4; 6.7.7.; 7.6.10; 8.8.7–9.

86. *Apostolic Constitutions* 2.61.1; 8.47.65; Council of Laodicea, Canon 29.

87. Chrysostom, *Homily* 8.8.8.

88. Ibid., 8.8.9 (PG 48, col. 941); ET P. Harkins, *The Fathers of the Church* LXVIII, Washington 1979, p. 238.

89. See Meeks and Wilken, *Jews and Christians in Antioch*, 1978. This receptivity continued through the Middle Ages. See Isidore Loeb, 'La controverse religieuse entre les juifs au moyen âge en France et en Espagne', *RHR* 17, 1888, pp. 324ff.

90. Nothing is being implied, positively or negatively, about the controversy whether this group was directly related to the Jerusalem church or not.

91. Originally the rabbinic term was נצרים (*naṣrim*), not נוצרים (*noṣrim*). Rabbinic Hebrew tends to write *plene* as opposed to biblical Hebrew, which tends to write *defectivi* (see W. Weinberg, 'The History of Hebrew *Plene* Spelling: From Antiquity to Haskalah', *HUCA* 46, 1975, pp. 457–87, esp. 473 n. 49). Thus נצרים in the Bible is pronounced

nosrim (see Jer. 4.16; 31.6[5]). A term which appears in both *plene* and *defectivi* in rabbinic sources was probably written *defectivi* originally but later changed by a scribe to a form which he thought would facilitate pronunciation. נצרים without the *plene vav* is the equivalent of Nazoraeans. Once knowledge of the Nazoraeans disappeared, the pronunciation was forgotten and the *plene vav* was inserted to conform to biblical pronunciation. This often happened to no longer understood rabbinic terms. (Thus much of the speculation on the origin of *nosrim* is unnecessary, see C. Rabin, 'Noṣerim', *Textus* 5, 1966, pp. 44–52, 49–51.)

There is widespread evidence that נצרים is the original reading. Of the six versions of *birkat ha-minim* that reflect the Genizah formulation published by Marmorstein (n. 45) three read נצרים. In addition, Professor Shimon Sharvit informs me that one Genizah fragment (T-S K 27.33) is vocalized וְהַנְצְרִים, and that the fifteenth century *Siddur*

'Aram Ṣob'a (Cincinnati 407) reads:וְהַנְּצָרִים precluding the reading והנוצרים.

In talmudic literature the term appears unambiguously once (bTaan 27a). The fragment MS from the Genizah of that source reads הנצרים (ed. Malter, New York 1930, p. 128, line 15). A version cited by the *Aruch* (ed. Kohut), V, p. 375 n. 2 reads הנצרים. A variant in *Masket Soferim*, ed. Higger, p. 301 ad line 22 reads הנצרים. Also the Meiri (ed. A. Sofer, Vienna 1934, p. 81) reads הנצרים (note that the Maharsha reads הגלילים – the Galileans!).

The same applies to the use of נוצרי for Jesus in the standard printed texts. Thus the Spanish MS of bAZ (6a) reads נצרי, as do medieval commentators. So e.g. Rabad (ed. A. Sofer, New York 1961, p. 10 to bAZ 6a) and Nimuke Yosef in *Shitat ha-Kadmonim* (ed. M. Y. Blau, New York 1969, p. 191 to bAZ 17a) read נצרי. Even in *Sefer Ha-Qabbalah* (ed. G. Cohen, Philadelphia 1967, p. 15, lines 65, 74; p. 30, line 94; p. 230 n. 28) the text or a variant reads נצרי after 'Jesus'. Finally, an early post-talmudic work *Teshubot ha-Geonim* (ed. A. E. Harkavy, Berlin 1887, repr. Jerusalem 1966) in sections 11 and 431 reads נצרי and נצריים respectively.

92. Some see another allusion in bShabb 116a. This has not gained acceptance; see J. Lauterbach, *Rabbinic Essays*, 1951, pp. 569f.; and the edition of Steinsaltz, Jerusalem 1969, p. 511.

93. BGitt 57a.

94. Epstein, p. 1255.

95. So S. Klein (cited in ET of bGitt [Soncino Press], p. 263 n. 40) and G. F. Moore (*Judaism in the First Centuries of the Christian Era* II, repr. 1962, p. 67 n. 1).

96. See the discussion on pp. 231f. above.

97. BTaan 27b.

98. Lauterbach, *Rabbinic Essays*, p. 567.

99. Baron, *Social and Religious History* II, p. 134.

100. *Maseket Soferim* 17.4, ed. Higger, p. 301. (R. T. Herford, *Christianity in Talmud and Midrash*, 1903, p. 172, notes the reference as 17.5.)

101. Herford, loc. cit.

102. H. J. Schoeps, *Jewish Christianity*, ET 1969, p. 114.

103. Davies, *The Setting of the Sermon on the Mount*, p. 283.

104. Neither I Cor. 16.2, Acts 20.7, nor Rev. 1.10 (which is clearly later than 70 CE) constitute evidence that Sunday was already the Christian 'Sabbath'. See S. Bacchiocchi, *From Sabbath to Sunday: A Historical Investigation of the Rise of Sunday Observance in Early Christianity*, 1977, pp. 90–131.

105. With regard to the minimal impact of Christianity on Judaism before 70, see E. E. Urbach, 'Yerushalayim shel Matta ve-Yerushalayim shel Ma'alah', *Yerushalayim le-Doroteha* (Israel Exploration Society), 1968, pp. 156–71, esp. 156–60.

106. See Kimelman, 'Third Century Tiberias', n. 139.

107. Eusebius (*Hist. eccl.* III.27.5) mentions that a second group of Ebionites observed the Sabbath as did the Jews and Sunday as did the Christians. Epiphanius (*Panarion* 29.7) describes a group whose characteristics overlap those of Eusebius's Ebionites and calls them Nazoraeans.

108. As e.g. the aforementioned Kefar Saknin and Kefar Semai. The other major locations were in nearby Transjordan and Coele-Syria: see Schoeps, *Jewish Christianity*, pp. 28ff.; Klijn, *Patristic Evidence*, pp. 47, 50; and G. Strecker, *Das Judenchristentum in den Pseudoklementinen*, 1958, p. 253. R. Johanan had extensive contact with these areas; see Kimelman, 'Third Century Tiberias', n. 197. One of these communities, Bos(t)ra in Auranitis, was not only a Jewish Christian centre in the third century (J. Daniélou, 'That the Scripture Might be Fulfilled, Christianity as a Jewish Sect', *The Crucible of Christianity* [ed. Toynbee], 1969, p. 281) but maintained contact with R. Johanan, his colleagues and students. Indeed, two of those, Resh Laqish and R. Abbahu, exercised rabbinic authority there (see *Sefer ha-Yishub* [ed. S. Klein], 1939, pp. 23f.). The Midrash even records a story about a convert to Judaism from there (Tanhuma Shoftim 10; see Lieberman, *Greek in Jewish Palestine*, pp. 144f. n. 25). Despite the distance from Bostra to Tiberias extensive contact could be maintained between the two by virtue of the Roman road which connected them (see M. Avi-Yonah, *The Holy Land: From the Persian to the Arab Conquest*, 1966, p. 187). Bostra was probably also the first stop after the desert for Babylonians coming to Palestine (pBer 3.1; 6a).

109. Baron, *Social and Religious History* II, p. 134, cf. ibid., p. 380 n. 6, referring to Aptowitzer, 'Bemerkungen zur Liturgie und Geschichte der Liturgie', *MGWJ* 74, 1930, pp. 104–27, esp. 110–12.

110. The *Didache* 14 regards Sunday as a day of communion, confession, and reconciliation. Ignatius (*Magnesians* 9) emphasizes its joyful character which precluded any fasting. This emphasis on joy is also reflected in the *Epistle of Barnabas* 15.10. The last two sources were directed against Jewish Christians or Judaizing Christians; see Bacchiocchi, *From Sabbath to Sunday*, pp. 213–23.

111. In fact, according to R. L. Odom, the admonition of Tertullian (d. 220) 'that Sunday keepers should defer their business until the next

day is the *first known instance* of any suggestion or directive to make the common labor taboo on Sundays' (*Sabbath and Sunday in Early Christianity*, 1977, p. 299). Even the Sunday laws of Constantine in 321 did not create a Sabbath rest (ibid., p. 265). Indeed, as late as the Council of Laodicea (c. 360) abstention from work on Sunday was only a recommendation (Canon 29); and according to Bacchiocchi, *From Sabbath to Sunday*, 'the complete application of the Sabbath commandment to a bodily rest to Sunday was not accomplished before the fifth and sixth centuries' (p. 310). Whatever be the case in the West, Saturday remained the Sabbath in the East for hundreds of years to come (see Odom, ibid., p. 250). Thus R. Johanan of third-century Palestine was unlikely to have conceived of Sunday as the Christian 'Sabbath'. This is all the more unlikely if the subject is Christians before 70, as already noticed by Yosef David Sinzheim, *Yad David*, 1799, p. 256a.

112. Similar logic lies behind the promotion of Saturday fasting by R. Johanan's younger contemporary, Bishop Victorinus (fl. 275–304). He contended that the sadness and hunger resulting from the fast would enable Christians to avoid 'appearing to observe the Sabbath with the Jews' (*De fabrica mundi*, CSEL 49.5; ANF VII, pp. 341f.). For a discussion of the text, see Odom, *Sabbath and Sunday*, p. 225 n. 7.

113. *NTApoc* I, p. 458. On the provenance of the document, see ibid., p. 442.

114. *Didascalia Apostolorum*, ET R. Hugh Connolly, Oxford 1929, p. 183. Pagination follows this edition.

115. See ibid., lxxxvii–xci; and A. F. J. Klijn, *The Acts of Thomas*, 1962, p. 221.

116. A. Marmorstein, 'Judaism and Christianity in the Middle of the Third Century', *HUCA* 10, 1935, pp. 223–63, esp. 231f.

117. G. Strecker, 'On the Problem of Jewish Christianity', pp. 254–7, 271.

118. H. J. Schoeps, *Theologie und Geschichte des Judenchristentums*, 1949, pp. 61f. Cf. A. F. J. Klijn, 'The Study of Jewish Christianity', *NTS* 20, 1973–74, pp. 419–31, esp. 430 n. 4.

119. *Die Syrische Didaskalia* (ed. J. Flemming), 1904, pp. 257–387, esp. 366 n. 1; G. Kretschmar, 'Origenes und die Araber', *ZTK* 50, 1953, pp. 260–4.

120. See n. 108 above.

121. *Constitutiones Apostolorum* 4.3.15 and 5.3.20. Sunday fasting is also evidenced by Bar Hebraeus, *Book of the Dove*, ET 1919, p. 28.

122. Victorinus (see n. 112) had a similar concern, *mutatis mutandi*.

123. See R. Murray, 'The Exhortation to Candidates for Ascetical Vows at Baptism in the Ancient Syriac Church', *NTS* 21, 1974–75: '*nazîr* is a title of Christ in the Syriac *Acts of Judas Thomas* 48 . . . and *nazîrûtâ* remained a word for ascetical self-denial' (p. 63 n. 2).

124. See Schäfer, *Studien zur Geschichte und Theologie des rabbinischen Judentums*, pp. 48ff.; and Marmorstein, 'The Amidah'. It is possible that there was no fixed original formulation. In general, the benedictions of the *ʿamidah* had the subject matter fixed but not the formulation.

This situation would help explain why the Talmud thinks it credible that Samuel the Small could have forgotten the text even though he was the one who originally emended it (bBer 28b–29a).

125. See S. Lieberman, 'Tiqune Yerushalmi', *Tarbiz* 4, 1932, 6, p. 377; Epstein, *Mabo*, pp. 1076, 1080; and M. Lehman, 'Iyunim BeVav Ha-Perush (Explicativum)' , *Sinai* 85, 1979, pp. 200–15.

126. *Tosefta ki-Fshutah* III, p. 206 n. 16: גליונים וספרי מינים means גליונים של ספרי המינים (my emphasis).

11 Ruler of this World:
Attitudes about Mediator Figures and the Importance of Sociology for Self-Definition

1. It would go too far afield now to summarize the many relationships which scholars have posited between Judaism, Christianity and Gnosticism. Perhaps since Gnosticism was first described by church Fathers, Christian scholars have been the most interested in the problem. Although there is agreement among them in correlating Christianity with Gnosticism, there is hardly any agreement on a theory which would explain that correlation. Particularly thorny has been the problem of whether Gnosticism or Christianity is the chronological predecessor. Did Christianity grow out of a gnostic environment or did Gnosticism grow out of a Christian one? The early church Fathers saw Gnosticism as a Christian heresy, and they first reported the term 'gnostic' as a description of it. But from Graetz's time forward it became clear that the question of priority could not be addressed without careful study of Jewish texts. See A. F. Segal, *Two Powers in Heaven; Early Rabbinic Reports about Christianity and Gnosticism*, 1977, pp. 1–30 and esp. pp. 14–18. Also see Carsten Colpe, *Die religionsgeschichtliche Schule*, 1961; W. Meeks, *The Prophet-King*, 1967, pp. 6–17; E. Yamauchi, *Pre-Christian Gnosticism*, 1973, pp. 13–28; L. Ginzberg, *Die Haggada bei den Kirchenvätern*, 1899; I. Heinemann, *Darkhe ha-Agadah*, Jerusalem ²1954; S. Lieberman, *Greek in Jewish Palestine*, ²1965, and *Hellenism in Jewish Palestine*, ²1962; E. E. Urbach, *The Sages*, ET 1975, and 'Teshubat Anshe Ninevah ve-Havikuah ha-Yehudi-Notsri', *Tarbiz* 20, 1950, pp. 118–22.

2. For a summary of research on the gnostic problem, see R. Haardt, 'Zur Methodologie der Gnosisforschung', *Gnosis und Neues Testament* (ed. Troeger), 1973, pp. 77–88.

3. See E. M. Mendelson, 'Some Notes on a Sociological Approach to Gnosticism', *Le origini dello gnosticismo*, 1967, pp. 668–76; Hans Kippenberg, 'Versuch einer soziologischen Verortung des antiken Gnostizismus', *Numen* 17, 1950; Kurt Rudolph, 'Das Problem einer Soziologie und sozialen Verortung der Gnosis', *Kairos* 19, 1977, pp. 35–54; Petr Pokorný, 'Der soziale Hintergrund der Gnosis', *Gnosis und Neues Testament* (ed. Troeger), 1973, pp. 77–88; Peter Munz, 'The Problem of "Die soziologische Verortung des antiken Gnostizismus" ', *Numen* 19,

1972, pp. 41–51; Henry Green, 'Gnosis and Gnosticism: A Study in Methodology', *Numen* 24, 1977, pp. 95–134; and 'Suggested Sociological Themes in the Study of Gnosticism', *VC* 31, 1977, pp. 169–80; Elaine Pagels, 'The Demiurge and His Archons', *HTR* 69, 1976, pp. 301f.

4. The phrase ὁ ἄρχων τοῦ κόσμου τούτου appears in John 12.31; 14.30 (with κόσμος in the attributive position but no change in meaning); and 16.11, but nowhere else in the New Testament.

5. ὁ Θεὸς τοῦ αἰῶνος τούτου appears in II Cor. 4.4. 'The rulers of the darkness of the world', (lit: κοσμοκράτορας τοῦ σκότους τούτου) appears in Eph. 6.12, and 'prince of the power of the air' appears in Eph. 2.2. The title 'ruler of the world' is applied to Beliar in the earlier part of the Ascension of Isaiah (1.3; 2.4; 10.29). Ignatius has ὁ ἄρχων τοῦ κόσμου τούτου several times (*Eph.* 17.1; 19.1). No terminological exactitude is maintained but the reference to supernatural opposition is unmistakable.

6. See John 16.11.

7. See the recent article by A. W. Carr, 'The Rulers of This Age – Corinthians ii.6–8', *NTS* 23, 1976, pp. 20–35. Carr deals primarily with the Pauline corpus, while assuming that the Ruler of this World in the FG is Satan. He mounts an argument that the 'rulers of this age' in Paul are the earthly rulers who crucified Jesus (which may or may not be correct). He is far too cavalier in dismissing Cullmann's theory of a double – divine and human – referent for the Pauline term. Nevertheless, his review of research on the subject is very useful, and so I have not reproduced his bibliographical entries. I do not think it is necessary to distinguish Pauline from other usages as carefully as he must to come to his conclusions. One can expect a certain residual parallel between rulers on earth and in heaven in most Hellenistic writing even if it is taken ironically. In a different way we both agree that the terms should be linked to human opponents. See below.

8. John 9.22; 12.42; 16.2

9. See especially John 16.2.

10. See Wayne Meeks, ' "Am I a Jew?" Johannine Christianity and Judaism', *Christianity, Judaism and Other Greco-Roman Cults* (ed. Neusner), 1975, p. 172.

11. See Ignatius, *Eph.* 17.1; 19.1.

12. J. T. Milik, 'Milki-sedeq et Milki-rasha dans les anciens écrits Juifs et Chrétiens', *JJS* 4, 1972, pp. 95–144, and *RB* 79, 1972, pp. 77–97.

13. It is amazing how often this fact is ignored; J.H. Bernard, for instance (*The Gospel According to St John*, 1928, II, p. 441), relies on Lightfoot to claim that the Prince of the World is a standard title for Satan in Jewish literature, without mentioning the significant rabbinic exception. Of course, it would be remarkable for an angel to be called the 'God' of this world in rabbinic literature, although Moses is so called by the biblical Exodus account. *Archōn* is a standard translation for the Hebrew s–r; s–r (Prince) and *archōn* (ruler) are normal epithets for angelic beings in Hebrew and Greek literature respectively. For more information on the concept of mediator, see A. Oepke, *TDNT*

IV, s.v. *Mesitēs*, pp. 602, 615, and J. Fossum, Dissertation, Utrecht. Herb Basser reminds me that many of the functions of the negative 'Lord of this World' can be seen in rabbinic portrayals of Satan, Sar Gehinnom and the *yetzer ha-ra*. See KohR 4.15; NumR 11.5; MPs 9.5, p. 82; Tanhuma Noah 19; Eqev 11; ExodR 41; bShab 104a, 105b; bBB 16b; bSukk 52a-b.

14. R. Jonathan infers that the psalm must have been said by the Prince of this World because David was not old enough to see that the statement was true. Obviously R. Jonathan is aware that it is not easy to verify that righteousness is always rewarded in this world. He must then understand the psalm to describe the final retribution of souls in the next life, or else the comment about David makes no sense at all. One notes a rather similar argument in Acts 2.24–31 where Luke concludes that Ps. 16.8–11 must refer to a future Messiah, not David himself, since David died.

15. See *III Enoch* (ed. H. Odeberg), repr. 1973, esp. pp. 47 and 53 in the Hebrew section. In 30.2 the Prince of the World pleads in favour of the world before the Holy One. In 38.1, he is the ruler of the heavenly bodies. See also 10.3; 48.9(c); 46.2 and 14.1–3 where Metatron takes over these functions. In bHull 60a, the Tosafot (s.v. *pasuk*) deny an identification between the two figures. But what is important is the existence of a primary angelic mediator with charge over the world, not whether tradition invariably called him Metatron or distinguished between him and the Lord of the World.

16. See Gershom Scholem, *Major Trends in Jewish Mysticism*, repr. 1961, pp. 40–79, and especially *Jewish Gnosticism, Merkabah Mysticism, and Talmudic Tradition*, 1965, pp. 43f., 48–51 and notes.

17. See H. Odeberg, *III Enoch*.

18. Odeberg and Scholem disagree about the relationship between the Prince of this World and Michael. Scholem notes that one of the Tosafot rejects the identification between the two and that they are never brought into relation by the talmudic or midrashic passages. In Pirqe de R. Eliezer, ch. 27, however, Michael is given the title Prince of this World, while a magic bowl inscription calls Metatron the Great Prince of All the World. (See C.D. Isbell, *Corpus of the Aramaic Incantation Bowls*, 1975, nos. 34.4; 49.1; 56.12). Scholem suggests that a previous linking of Metatron to Michael may account for the identification with the Prince of this World. The use of Ps. 37.25 Scholem finds secondary, because the root idea of *n'r* is 'servant' at the divine throne rather than 'youth'. However, Scholem may not have taken adequate account of the Psalm passage taken together with Daniel traditions where God, as the Ancient of Days, is helped through the Son of Man, who is viewed as a young warrior in rabbinic tradition. These speculations about God's human appearance are quite old. Scholem was forced to admit that one manuscript of Shiur Koma does mention the 'Lord of the World' and that Metatron and he are described with the same language. In general Scholem's caution is to be taken over Odeberg's enthusiasm. But in this one case, Tosafot to bYeb 16b

explain the title *na'ar* as a reference to Ps. 37.25 and I am inclined to agree, once the importance of Dan 7.13f. is seen. See Mek Shirta 4, Bahodesh 5 for an example of this tradition and the rabbinic condemnation of it by means of the designation 'two powers'. For a discussion of its antiquity see my book *Two Powers in Heaven*, ch. 2. For relevance to the Name of God traditions, see the work of G. Quispel, especially 'Qumran, John and Jewish Christianity', *John and Qumran*, ed. J. H. Charlesworth, London 1972, esp. pp. 149f.

19. See 'Lord of all the earth' in Josh. 3.11, 13; Micah 4.13; Zech. 4.11; 6.5; Ps. 97.5. In Judith 2.5 the title is applied to Nebuchadnezzar (ὁ κύριος πάσης τῆς γῆς). See W. Hallo, *Early Mesopotamian Royal Titles*, 1957, pp. 21–9, 49–56; A. Petitjean, *Les oracles du Proto-Zacharie: Un programme de restauration pour la communauté juive après l'exil*, Paris 1969.

There are a series of problems concerning the title *'El 'Olam*, its cognates and equivalents in Ugaritic. It is difficult to say whether or not the title designates an independent divinity or is a standard epithet. Then too the meaning of the term is not so clear as it should be. Does it signify eternal Lord, or Lord of the World? Apparently the original term was the former while the latter meaning is derivative. Also it is possible that the original term connoted the lord of the underworld; therefore, the Hebrew appropriation may have been a deliberate epithet favouring monotheism in that *Yhwh* (not Mot or Shamash, etc.) was Lord of the Dead as well as the Living. See Alan Cooper, 'Divine Names and Epithets', *Ras Shamra Parallels* III (ed. Fisher), 1979.

20. See W. H. Waddington, *Inscriptions grecques et latins de la Syrie*, 1870, 2631; *CIS* II, 3912; A. J. Jaussen and R. Savignac, *Mission archéologique en Arabie* I, 1909, pp. 172f., 177. J. Teixidor (*The Pagan God, Popular Religion in the Greco-Roman Near East*, 1977) concludes that by the mid-third century *mry 'lm'* is no longer an epithet of Ba'al Shamin but a divine name to which a devotee might offer a separate invocation.

21. G. A. Cooke, *A Text-Book of North-Semitic Inscriptions*, 1903, p. 295 no. 133. At Efca, however, 'Lord of the World' probably refers to Bel and not to Ba'al Shamin. See M. Gawlikowski, *Recueil d'inscriptions palmyréniennes provenant des fouilles syriennes et polonaises récentes à Palmyre*, 1974, pp. 60f. nn. 125f.

22. The classic work on rabbinic titles for God was A. Marmorstein, *The Old Rabbinic Doctrine of God* I: *The Names and Attributes of God*, 1927. However, this has been supplemented by Urbach, *The Sages*, see esp. chs. 4, 7, 8, 9. See also J. G. Weiss, *JJS* 10, 1959, pp. 169–71; E. J. Weisenberg, 'The Liturgical term Melekh Ha-'Olam', *JJS* 15, 1964, pp. 1–56; J. Heinemann, 'Once More Melekh Ha-'Olam', *JJS* 15, 1964, pp. 149–54.

23. Derekh Eretz 4.

24. See e.g. Ex. 24.10 and Deut. 32.8.

25. BBer 7b.

26. See GenR 17.4, pp. 155–6; MPs 8.26, p. 74; PRK, Parah, p. 61; KohR 7.23.

27. GenR 39.1, p. 365.

28. ExR 5.19. This is substantiated as a Hellenistic polemic against tyranny in Philo's *Legatio ad Gaium* 8, where Gaius is described as having succeeded to τὴν ἡγεμονίαν πάσης γῆς καὶ θαλάσσης (rule over all the land and sea). See below, p. 261.

29. See my *Two Powers in Heaven*, pp. 35–37, and below, n. 60.

30. NT Apoc II, p. 370.

31. PGM III, pp. 211f.

32. That is, the title 'Lord of the World' and closely similar titles, many of which are listed in the preceding discussion.

33. See Mary Douglas, *Natural Symbols: Explorations in Cosmology*, 1973, pp. 91, 122, 144–5, 153, 199. See also Sheldon Isenberg and Dennis F. Owen, 'Bodies, Natural and Contrived: The Work of Mary Douglas', *Religious Studies Review* 3, 1977, pp. 1–17.

34. Of course, Douglas is also interested in the relationship between social structure and religion and she is not the only scholar with these interests. One might just as easily mention Durkheim, Topitsch or Fromm, all of whom posit a relationship between social and political structures and conceptual thinking about divinity. Douglas is representative of the position not only because she asks the question clearly but because she suggests that concepts of the human body might provide the link between the two. As we have already seen, the 'Lord of the World' is clearly a human figure projected into heaven and hence grist for her mill. See Peter Munz, 'The Problem of "Die soziologische Verortung des antiken Gnostizismus" '.

35. Douglas, *Natural Symbols*, p. 137.

36. In the case of witchcraft accusations, the society's ideology has not developed the ability to comprehend the hostility from within, so that it posits an outside danger. This also seems partially true of the Johannine community. But the analogy is not complete. See below, p. 267 for a more complete discussion. I have not entered into Douglas's specific theoretical constructions, not because she concentrates on African witchcraft belief, but because I do not want us to be needlessly distracted from our major inquiry. But I do want to maintain that, no matter how much one would want to object to the analogy between African witchcraft and the early Christian community, her model does offer some important perspectives on our problem. Basically, she, like other social scientists, is pointing to a congruence between social structure on the one hand and theology on the other. This observation has been profitably used to study Qumran. See Sheldon Isenberg, 'Mary Douglas and Hellenistic Religions: The Case of Qumran', SBL 1975 Seminar Papers, pp. 179–85.

37. See, for instance, J. H. Charlesworth, 'A Critical Comparison of the Dualism in 1QS 3:13–4:26 and the "Dualism" Contained in the Gospel of John', *NTS* 15, 1968–69, pp. 389–418. It is clear from Charlesworth's article that the dualisms of the two communities have unique aspects and affinities and that it would be wrong to underes-

timate the this-worldly/other-worldly, above/below, good/evil dichotomies of John.

38. See Rudolf Bultmann, *The Gospel of John*, ET 1971, p. 86.

39. See John 9.22; 12.42; 16.2. While the report may be exaggerated by the evangelist or even refer to non-rabbinic synagogues, we certainly know some of the mechanisms by which rabbinic leaders sought to silence heresy. They standardized prayer and ritual, seeking to censor any leader of the congregation who inserted suspicious clauses in prayer. (See mMeg 4.5 and parallels.) The penalty was probably neither death, as the gospel implies (16.2), nor *herem* nor *nidui*, which seem to be later and were primarily used within the rabbinic community, not as weapons against heretics. Instead, we should probably assume that this kind of opposition to the Christian heresy was restricted to special uses of already existent instruments such as exclusion from the synagogue service, the prayer against the *minim*, charges of magic, 'leading astray', etc. See J. Louis Martyn, *History and Theology in the Fourth Gospel*, ²1979, pp. 12–45; Goeran Forkman, *The Limits of the Religious Community*, 1972; C.–H. Hunzinger, *Die jüdische Bannpraxis im neutestamentlichen Zeitalter*, 1954; and J. E. Mignard, *Jewish and Christian Cultic Discipline to the Middle of the Second Century*, 1966; J. Heinemann, *Prayer in the Talmud: Forms and Patterns*, ET 1977, and the essays of Urbach, Schiffman, and Kimelman in this volume for various opinions on this vexing issue.

40. See John 5.9–18; 7.21–24; 9.13–16.

41. On this issue see the ground-breaking work of N. A. Dahl, 'The Johannine Church and History', *Current Issues in New Testament Interpretation* (ed. Klassen and Snyder), 1962, pp. 129f.

42. John 6.15; 11.4–6; 19.12.

43. See Meeks, 'The Man from Heaven in Johannine Sectarianism', *JBL* 9, 1972, pp. 44–72.

44. See Martyn, *History and Theology in the Fourth Gospel*, esp. pp. 17–45. One need not assume, however, that the opposition of the Jews involved the killing of Christians. The statements that the Jews sought to kill Jesus can be derived from the events of Jesus' life, the traditions of the church, and the fears of the Johannine community. They need not reflect the actual policy of the rabbis. See below.

45. See Judah Goldin, 'Not by means of an Angel and not by means of a Messenger', *Religions in Antiquity* (ed. Neusner), 1968, pp. 412–24. See also David Flusser, 'Not by means of an angel. . .' (Hebrew), *Toray Yeshurun* 29, 1971–72, pp. 18–20.

46. See my *Two Powers in Heaven*.

47. See e.g. the Mek Bahodesh 5 and Shirta 4, to Ex. 15.3 and 20.2. Compare with the Mekilta of R. Simeon, at the same place.

48. See Philo, *Somn.* I. 227–9; *Quaest. in Gen.* II.62. It is clear from Philo's discussion that the terminology of 'second God' or divinity is carefully chosen. The assertion of divinity seems to be a way of avoiding making any intermediary equal with God. The Creator and all angels and other forms of mediation are not separate creatures, rather

part of God himself. Ironically the term 'second God' is used by Philo to avoid the charge of dualism. One can perhaps see a similar strategy in the Johannine community. Asserting Jesus' divinity through identity with the *Logos* has the effect of denying the possibility of any other mediation, or more exactly of tying up all mediations – exceptional, incarnate and eschatological – in one figure. Of course, it opens the Johannine church to the charge of 'two powers in heaven', a charge which the rabbis probably would also have levied against Philo or anyone of similar disposition, had they been familiar with their writings.

49. See the use of Isa. 14 in bSanh 43a.

50. See, for example, the article by Jonathan Z. Smith, 'The Prayer of Joseph', *Religions in Antiquity*, p. 254, where ascent traditions about Enoch, Moses and especially Jacob are discussed.

51. See my article on ascension in *ANRW* II 23.2 (forthcoming).

52. For a summary of the various possibilities see R. Brown, *The Gospel according to St John*, 1966, pp. lxxiiif. See also Martyn, *History and Theology in the Fourth Gospel*; Quispel, 'Qumran, John and Jewish Christianity'.

53. In these paragraphs, I am relying on the consensus of Bultmann, Brown and Martyn without forgetting that they differ greatly in detail in characterizing the various groups.

54. See n. 39.

55. See bBer 28b.

56. See Kimelman, above, pp. 234 ff, and Urbach, below, pp. 290 ff. The consensus among scholars of Jewish liturgy (see Heinemann, n. 39 above) is that there was no single authoritative version.

57. It would be too much to say (*pace* Kimelman) that the rise of Christianity had no effect on Judaism. The seriousness of the challenge of the '*minim*' (of whom the Christians are the principal and most important members if not the only component) and the special enactments necessary to defeat them are surely everywhere reflected in rabbinic literature. It is impossible to say how much of rabbinic thought received encouragement from the Christian menace, since it evolves according to its own logic. But this does not mean that no effect was felt. Hence, though Kimelman is using sound judgment in warning against over-interpreting the *birkat ha-minim* as the equivalent to formal excommunication, one must also be on guard against undervaluing the evidence. Kimelman has emphasized the fact that the rabbis did not explicitly curse the Christians by name in the service. He has not shown that the *birkat ha-minim* was not taken by the Christians and Jews alike to have included Christians. One only has to allow for slight exaggeration (and the church Fathers like Tertullian went far beyond slight exaggeration in their polemical zeal) to see that the church Fathers' claims are in agreement with rabbinic evidence. One must posit only that *min* referred to 'sectarian' or 'heretic' in general, not a specific sect, to clarify this position. (Kimelman grants this as a possibility, pp. 231f. but does not exploit the implications of his observations at

this point.) Whether or not the Christians liked the idea of being called sectarians or heretics (i.e. *minim*), they appear to know that they are meant by the phrase. The reports of the church Fathers are yet more puzzling if they do not apply to the *birkat ha-minim*.

58. Martyn, *History and Theology*, p. 160.

59. Justin (*Dial.* 16f., 47f., 93f., 108, 123, 133f.) says that Jews curse Jesus in synagogues. See above and R. Kimelman's essay. A word must be said about L. Schiffman's argument that it is halakically impossible to cease being Jewish. It is possible to exaggerate the importance of this conclusion since ideological crimes like 'denying the root' had the effect of exclusion from the reconstructed Israel of the world to come (mSanh 10 and the talmudic comments). Then too, extrapolations from rabbinic law may not describe the entire social situation. What is more important in cases of self-definition is to see the perspective of each side. In the Johannine situation, the Christian community clearly considers itself distinct from the Jews, though it may be closer to the Jewish community than Luke and may contain members who were Jews at birth. The effect of considering Jewish Christians as Jews in rabbinic law may have been to obligate them to rabbinic law, but there is no evidence that Christians were treated in this way or that they desired to be obligated by rabbinic rulings. Furthermore, I see no certain evidence that synagogues opposing the Christian community in John were yet fully rabbinic. The archaeological evidence of Tcherikover and Fuks, *CPJ*, to take a single example, would suggest that rabbinic hegemony came to Egypt only after the native community had been severely damaged by antisemitism. On the other hand, edicts like the silencing of *minim* in synagogues are likely to reflect more general Jewish practice which the rabbis only standardized when they took over the control of synagogue life.

60. This is speculative, of course, and so I shall not suggest that the positive view of the angel *must* have antedated the negative one. It is also possible that the gospel community (or another community like it) understood the phrase polemically against the God of the Jews but not the Lord of Deliverance who was not 'of this world'. See Sifre Deut 329, pp. 379–80, Mek Shirta 4, Bahodesh 5 for the rabbinic answer that the God of Israel is God both of this world and the world to come Evidence that the name of God was associated with the Lord of the World comes to us from the magical papyri (*PGM* III.211f.) where Adonai is praised as 'Lord of the World'. Though it is impossible to be sure whether the figure is meant to be negative or positive because magicians prayed to both demons and gods, one could surmise that he is meant to be positive because he is in good company (Zeus, Iao, Raphael, and Sabaoth). Furthermore, it is clear that ancient Jewish tradition ascribed to God the title 'Lord of all worlds'. See 1QGenAp 2.4.

61. For instance, on the Spirit of Truth, see Test. Jud. 20.1–5. Compare with 1QS 4.23–24. Also see R. Brown, 'The Paraclete', Appendix v, *The Gospel According to St John*, pp. 1135–44. Also Windisch, *The Spirit Paraclete in the Fourth Gospel*, ET 1968; N. Johanson, *Parakletoi*, 1940

Otto Betz, *Der Paraklet: Fürsprecher im häretischen Spätjudentum, im Johannes-Evangelium und in neu gefundenen gnostischen Schriften*, 1963; George Johnston, *The Spirit-Paraclete in the Gospel of John*, 1970; A. R. C. Leaney, 'The Johannine Paraclete and the Qumran Scrolls', *John and Qumran* (ed. Charlesworth), 1972, pp. 38–61.

62. Even in Pauline writings, e.g. I Cor. 12.11 and Rom. 8.16, the Holy Spirit performs voluntary actions.

63. This phenomenon is somewhat analogous to the use of the phrase 'first-born of Satan' as used in orthodox and heretical Christianity. See N. A. Dahl, 'Der Erstgeborene Satans und der Vater des Teufels (Polyk 7:1 und Joh 8:44)', *Apophoreta*, 1964.

64. II Thess. 2.4; Rev. 13.5f.; also Rev. 13.4, 8, 12.

65. J. H. Charlesworth, 'Christian and Jewish Self-Definition in Light of the Christian Additions to the Apocryphal Writings', above, p. 43.

66. Douglas's model allows for some further distinctions. She plots two variables – group pressure (which she calls 'group') against level of symbolic classification (which she calls 'grid') and proposes that societies can be described by the patterns which their individuals evince on the graph (see *Natural Symbols*, pp. 49f., 83f.). It seems to me that the Jewish community should be defined as high grid/high group – or, at least, they are heading in that direction as they grow more and more rabbinized. With respect to the Roman Empire, of course, they should be classified as a small group, but they respond to that challenge in a specific way and in a way different from typical small groups. The rabbis see the only enemy as the outsider; within, all is governed to an extraordinary degree by social piety, purity rules and sacralized institutions. The Johannine community, on the other hand, is still a small group with a dualist cosmology – that is, it has a high group, but a lower grid. (See Douglas, *Natural Symbols*, p. 91.)

67. J. Fossum has found the angel of the Lord as demiurge in Samaritan traditions. See his contribution on 'The Samaritan Origin of the Concept of the Demiurge', Yale International Conference on Gnosticism, April 1978.

68. This may be compared with Origen who, in his commentary on John 2.34, criticizes Gnostics for believing that the demiurge is God of the Jews. See Elaine Pagels, 'Origen and the Prophets of Israel', *JANES* 5, 1973, pp. 235f.

69. See Meeks, *The Prophet-King*, pp. 76–8. Also 'The Divine Agent and his Counterfeit in Philo and the Fourth Gospel' in *Aspects of Religious Propaganda in Judaism and Early Christianity* (ed. Fiorenza), 1976.

70. Here it seems to me fair to note that this predominantly mythological use of the term 'Jew' contributes to antisemitism within the church. While the statements are antisemitic and have been used by antisemites within the church for generations, in its own context, the Johannine church was a minority group, not the persecutor.

71. Normally one speaks of myth in a constitutive sense, e.g., see B. Malinowski, *Myth in Primitive Psychology*, 1926. One study of the polemical role of myth may be found in Edmund Leach, 'Myth as a

Justification for Faction and Social Change', *Political Systems of Highland Burma*, 1954, pp. 264–78. See also R. Wilson, *Genealogy and History in the Biblical World*, 1976; L. Laeyendecker, *Religie en Conflict*, 1968; for the ancient Near East: P. Machinist, 'Literature as Politics: The Tikultu-Ninurta Epic and the Bible', *CBQ* 28, 1976, pp. 455–82; T. Jacobsen, *The Treasures of Darkness*, 1976, pp. 167–91, esp. 183–91; C. Loew, *Myth, Sacred History and Philosophy*, 1969, pp. 21–32; A. Leo Oppenheim, *Ancient Mesopotamia*, 1977, pp. 171–83.

72. Segal, *Two Powers in Heaven*. The ignorant gnostic demiurge is to a great degree a characterization of the monotheistic god of the rabbis. He it is who claims, ignorantly, to be unique (Deut. 6.4; 32.39; Isa. 44–47, etc.) when every Gnostic would know that there is a higher god of salvation.

73. See above nn. 3 and 67, and Pagels, 'The Demiurge and his Archons'. She argues that the same epithets characterize the demiurge and the orthodox bishops in gnostic exegesis. After our study of the Johannine community, all these tactics ought to look familiar. See also Klaus Koschorke, *Die Polemik der Gnostiker gegen das kirchliche Christentum*, 1978.

74. Throughout history men as disparate as Heracleides, Machiavelli, Marx and Adam Smith have noted the importance of conflict in group definition. See Georg Simmel, *Conflict*, ET 1955; Lewis Cozer, *The Functions of Social Conflict*, 1956; Raymond Marb and Richard Snyder, 'The Analysis of Social Conflict Toward an Overview and Synthesis', *Journal of Conflict Resolution* I, 1957, pp. 217–48; J. Himes, 'The Function of Racial Conflict', *Social Forces* 45, 1966, pp. 1–10; Pierre van den Berghe, 'Dialectic and Functionalism: Toward a Theoretical Synthesis', *American Sociological Review* 28, 1963, pp. 695–705; J. Horton, 'Order and Conflict: Theories of Social Problems as Competing Ideologies', *American Journal of Sociology* 71, 1966, pp. 701–13.

75. See Meeks, ' "Am I a Jew?" ', especially pp. 120–1.

76. See the works of Mary Douglas listed above, p. 407, as well as her introduction to *Witchcraft, Confessions and Accusations*, 1970, pp. xiii–xxxvi: 'Thirty Years after *Witchcraft, Oracles, and Magic*'.

77. See pp. 259f. above.

78. My deepest thanks to W. A. Meeks, N. A. Dahl, J. Gager, A. Cooper, E. Pagels, I. Gruenwald, H. Green, J. Fossum, to my colleagues at Yale, Princeton and Toronto, to J. Charlesworth, R. Kimelman, E. P. Sanders, E. E. Urbach and the other members of the group for their many helpful suggestions both through correspondence and seminar for improving this essay (and to M. Salloum for her patience in typing it). I regret that the following works reached my attention too late to affect substantially the writing of this paper: Urban C. von Wahlde, 'The Terms for Religious Authorities in the Fourth Gospel: A Key to Literary Strata?', *JBL* 98.2, 1979, pp. 231–53; R. Brown, *The Community of the Beloved Disciple*, 1978; John T. Townsend, 'The Gospel of John and the Jews: The Story of a Religious Divorce' in *Antisemitism and the Foundations of Christianity* (ed. Davies), 1979. It should be evident

that the last writer is in striking disagreement with me over fundamental issues.

12 Self-Isolation or Self-Affirmation in Judaism in the First Three Centuries: Theory and Practice

1. My translation of *Entschränkung*, a term coined by Adolf Harnack
for the title of the first chapter of his *Mission und Ausbreitung des
Christentums*, ²1924. [The ET, *The Expansion of Christianity in the First
Three Centuries*, 1904, has 'Diffusion and Limits'.]

2. L. Baeck, *The Essence of Judaism*, ET repr. 1970, pp. 71–3.

3. J. Guttmann, *Die Idee der religiösen Gesellschaft im Judentum*, 1922,
p. 55.

4. See the articles of H. Bergman, 'Israel and the *Oikumene*', R.
Loewe, 'Potentialities and Limitations of Universalism in the *Halakhah*',
and K. Wilhelm, 'The Idea of Humanity in Judaism', in *Studies in
Rationalism, Judaism and Universalism, in Memory of Leon Roth* (ed. R.
Loewe), 1966. See also M. R. Konwitz, 'Judaism and the Democratic
Ideal', *The Jews, Their Role in Civilization* (ed. Finkelstein), ⁴1971, pp.
366ff.

5. G. F. Moore, *Judaism* I, 1927, p. 19ff. See also M. Smith, *Palestinian
Parties and Politics that Shaped the Old Testament*, 1971, pp. 142ff.

6. E. E. Urbach, *The Sages, Their Concepts and Beliefs*, 1975, I, pp.
439ff., 652ff.; II, pp. 991ff.

7. J. Juster, *Les Juifs dans l'empire Romain* II, 1914, p. 20.

8. L. Finkelstein, 'Some Examples of the Maccabean Halaka', *JBL* 49,
1930, pp. 21–5.

9. See Urbach, *The Sages*, p. 243.

10. See Urbach, 'The Rabbinical Laws of Idolatry in the Second and
Third Centuries in the Light of Archaeological and Historical Facts',
IEJ 9, 1959, pp. 149ff.

11. TGit 5(3).4f.; pGit 5.4(47c); bGit 61a; and see S. Lieberman, *TK,
Nashim*, p. 850.

12. Semahot I.9. *The Tractate of Mourning*, ET D. E. Zlotnik, New
Haven 1966, p. 32, and notes, p. 99.

13. *Pesikta rabbati*, 21.18, ET W. G. Braude, New Haven 1968, p. 443;
and see S. Lieberman, *Greek in Jewish Palestine*, ²1965, p. 89.

14. pShab 19.1 (17a); pYeb 8.1 (9a); bAZ 27a.

15. BAZ 27a, and the commentaries of R. Hananel, ad אתה; and
Rashi, ibid. See, however, Rashi, *Menahot* 42a, ad אתה.

16. In the Babylonian Talmud and in GenR 46.9, p. 467, it is the
deduction of R. Johanan.

17. See I. Heinemann, 'Judaism in the Eyes of the Ancient World'
(in Hebrew), *Zion* 4, 1939, pp. 28ff.; M. Stern (ed.), *Greek and Latin
Authors on Jews and Judaism* I, 1974.

18. Many examples of this sort may be found in the otherwise
learned book of M. Guttmann, *Das Judentum und seine Umwelt*, 1927,

but not all comparisons are to be blamed as apologetic. See, for example, E. Bickerman, 'The Historical Foundations of Post-Biblical Judaism', *The Jews, Their History* (ed. Finkelstein), ⁴1970, p. 96. Comparing Ben Sira with Cato the censor, he writes: 'But Cato surpassed the Jewish moralists in his anti-alien feelings', and he adduces evidence to prove this statement.

19. TMaksh 1.8 has a different version. On the religious status of the abandoned child, see bYom 84b; bKet 15a; bKid 73a.

20. Sifre Deut 263 (Finkelstein/Horovitz, p. 285; on 23.21).

21. PBM 5.11 (10d); tBM 6.18, in the name of R. Simeon.

22. Robert P. Maloney has not paid attention to this development in his otherwise well documented article, 'Usury in Greek, Roman and Rabbinic Thought', *Traditio* 27, 1971, pp. 79ff.

23. PBM 2.5 (8c), the exact date of the story is unknown; it does not quote mMaksh 2.8, but it mentions anachronistically an opinion of Rav transmitted by his pupil R. Ḥuna.

24. Sifre Deut 344 (Finkelstein/Horovitz, p. 401); pBK 4.3 (4b); bBK 38a. The note in the Soncino translation, p. 644 n. 6, is apologetic in character and is unfounded, even if based upon the authority of Graetz. See also M. D. Herr, 'The Historical Significance of the Dialogues between Jewish Sages and Roman Dignitaries', *SH* 22, 1971, p. 132.

25. It appears to me, however, that the authentic source relating the visit of the Roman officers is contained in the Sifre. It points only to the discrimination regarding robbery of a Gentile. It does not report any change in the ruling and concludes with the promise of the emissaries not to report back their objection. What we may certainly learn from the story is that the anonymous halakah quoted from tBK does not belong to the time before R. Gamaliel and R. Akiba. The two other sources are of later origin. In bBK the story was adapted to the discrimination in the Mishnah with regard to the rulings about an ox of an Israelite which gores the ox of an alien and vice versa. But this discrimination was dealt with before in the *sugya* by R. Johanan and R. Abahu. They justify the discrimination by asserting that the Gentiles have not observed the seven commandments of the 'Children of Noah'. They do not refer to the baraita in which the Roman commissioners use the argument of the *sugya*. In the Palestinian Talmud the story has a further expansion. The emissaries assert that they found everything in the Torah praiseworthy with the exception of two things. But besides *gezelo shel nokri* and the goring ox, we find two additional items listed. The finale of the story has a humorous feature: the two Romans forget everything before reaching their destination. See B. S. Jackson in this volume, p. 163.

26. See also S. Lieberman, 'How much Greek in Jewish Palestine?', *Biblical and Other Studies* (ed. Altmann), 1963, pp. 123–41; M. Smith, *Tannaitic Parallels to the Gospels*, 1951, pp. 9ff.

27. See lately R. J. Zvi Werblowsky, 'Greek Wisdom and Proficiency', *Paganisme, Judaïsme, Christianisme*, 1978, pp. 55ff.

28. II Macc. 6.22; 7.42. See E. Wiesenberg, 'Related Prohibitions,

Swine Breeding and the Study of Greek', *HUCA* 27, 1956, p. 213. Wiesenberg noted the connection; he has not, however, drawn the right conclusion and his propositions are unfounded.

29. MSot 8.14. Our texts have 'Titus', but the right reading is to be found in the Kaufman and Cambridge Manuscripts and in the Antonin fragment of the Genizah, published by A. I. Katsch, *Ginze Mishnah*, 1970, p. 77. Wiesenberg, ibid., adopted the vulgar reading and built upon it. (See also tSot 15.8; and S. Lieberman, *TK Nashim*, p. 767.)

30. See S. Sambursky, 'The Term Gematria', *Tarbiz* 45, 1976, p. 268.

31. As proposed by A. Wasserstein, 'Astronomy and Geometry as Propaedeutic Studies in Rabbinic Literature', *Tarbiz* 43, 1974, p. 53.

32. PSot 9.16 (24c); see E. E. Urbach, 'The Secret of the Ein Gedi Inscription and its Formula', *Tarbiz* 40, 1970, p. 29.

33. PSanh 10.1 (28a); and see S. Lieberman, *Hellenism in Jewish Palestine*, ²1962, p. 108.

34. See E. E. Urbach, 'Class Status and Leadership in the World of the Palestinian Sages', *Proceedings of the Israel Academy of Sciences and Humanities* 2, 1966, p. 39.

35. PBer 4 (8a); bBer 28b. See I. Elbogen, *Der jüdische Gottesdienst in seiner geschichtlichen Entwicklung*, repr. 1967, pp. 36, 252; G. Alon, *Toledot ha-Yehudim be-Erets Yisra'el be-Tequfat ha-Mishnah veha-Talmud I*, 1954, pp. 180ff. L. Finkelstein, 'Development of the Amidah', *JQR* ns 16, 1925–6, p. 19 (=*Pharisaism in the Making*, 1972, p. 263).

36. The correct reading in tBer 3.25 is 'one should include the *minim* among the פרושים - separatists', see S. Lieberman, *TK Zeraim*, p. 58.

37. See A. Momigliano, 'Empieta ed eresia nel mondo antico', *Rivista Storica Italiana* 83, 1971, pp. 771–91.

38. See my 'Class Status and Leadership', p. 46 n. 8.

39. V. Eppstein, 'When and how the Sadducees were excommunicated', *JBL* 85, 1966, pp. 213–24, is not convincing. The use of the word 'excommunication' is not justified. See also the criticism of J. Neusner, *A Life of Yohanan ben Zakkai*, ²1970, p. 92, n. 1. The story about the excommunication of R. Eliezer b. Hyrcanus as told in bBM 59a–b bears a legendary character, but the reason given for the excommunication, his refusal to subordinate to the view of the majority, is certainly historical. I could not find any proof for Neusner's conjecture (*Eliezer Ben Hyrcanus I*, 1973, p. 255) according to which there is a connection between the excommunication and the political differences between R. Eliezer as representative of the peace-party and R. Joshua, who belonged to the war-party, a conjecture which also contradicts Neusner's views in his *Life of Yohanan*, p. 232.

40. See the sources listed in Urbach, *The Sages* II, p. 892 n. 75. For the different etymologies of the word *aher*, see Ch. Yalon, *Studies in the Hebrew Language* (in Hebrew), Jerusalem 1971, p. 293.

41. See S. Lieberman, 'Light on the Cave Scrolls from Rabbinic Sources', *PAAJR* 20, 1951, p. 404 (=*Texts and Studies*, 1974, p. 199).

42. See G. Vermès, 'The Decalogue and the Minim', *In Memoriam Paul Kahle*, 1968, pp. 232ff.; Urbach, *The Sages* I, p. 30.

43. See A. D. Nock, 'Gnosticism', *HTR* 57, 1964, pp. 255ff.; H. J. W. Drijvers, 'Edessa und das jüdische Christentum', *VC* 24, 1970, pp. 27ff.

44. See W. Bacher, 'La science de la vieille tradition juive', *REJ* 38, 1899, pp. 211–19; M. Friedlaender, 'Minim, Minouet et Guilionim dans le Talmud', *REJ* 38, 1899, pp. 194–203. A. Büchler, 'The Minim of Sepphoris and Tiberias in the Second and Third Centuries', *Studies in Jewish History,* 1956, pp. 245–74.

45. PSanh 10.1 (28a). The passage beginning with בגון starts an interpretation which is not part of the addition of R. Akiba. S. Z. Leiman (*The Canonization of the Hebrew Scripture*, p. 100) seems to differ.

46. TShab 13(14).5, ed. S. Lieberman, p. 58; see *TK Moed*, p. 206 n. 16 and the following note.

47. This fact was pointed out by K. G. Kuhn in his article: 'Giljonim und sifre minim', *Judentum—Urchristentum—Kirche* (ed. Eltester), ²1964, pp. 24–61. The word play *'avon gilayon* (און גליון) in bShab 116b is attributed to the school of R. Meir and to R. Johanan; see R. N. Rabbinovicz, *Diqduqe Soferim*, p. 260.

48. The parallel in Babylonian Talmud 'jealousy, enmity and wrath'; see also Sifre Num 16 (Horovitz, p. 21).

49. See A. Büchler, 'The Minim of Sepphoris and Tiberias', pp. 253–57. E. E. Urbach, 'The Homiletical Interpretations . . . on Canticles', *SH* 22, 1971, p. 273; *The Sages* I, p. 527; S. T. Lachs, 'R. Abbahu and the Minim', *JQR* 40, 1970, pp. 197–212.

50. BYeb 47a; and see Urbach, *The Sages* I, p. 547.

51. TBM 2.33; see also bAZ 26a.

52. See A. Momigliano, 'Empietà', p. 787.

53. See J. Jervell, *Imago Dei. Gen. 1, 26f. im Spätjudentum*, 1960. This author bases himself upon a talmudic sentence (bYeb 61a; bKer 6b), 'Cattle and heathen are not *'adam* .'As Morton Smith ('On the Shape of God and the Humanity of Gentiles', *Religions in Antiquity* [ed. Neusner], 1968, pp. 315–26), rightly pointed out, the usage of *'adam* is determined by the contexts in which it occurs. Since the law was accepted only by Israelites' most of its provisions concern them alone. The primary meaning of *'adam* was well established in rabbinic usage. M. Guttmann (*Das Judentum und seine Umwelt*, pp. 180ff.) already pointed to this obvious fact, but he treated the subject apologetically and so he quoted deprecatory pronouncements made by others, e.g. that in the NT the heathen are compared with dogs or that King Baldwin I wrote from Constantinople to Pope Innocent III of the Greek Christians; 'Haec est gens quae Latinos non hominum nomine sed canum dignabatur, quorum sanguinem effundere paene inter merita reputabant.'

54. GenR 13.6, p. 116. According to some MSS it was R. Joshua b. Karha who gave this answer. Midrash to Ps. 111.7 reads R. Joshua b. Hananiah, and DeutR 7.1 has R. Johanan b. Zakkai. J. Neusner (*Development of a Legend*, 1970, p. 78) quoted it from there and comments, 'This defender of the faith story occurs nowhere else'.

55. Sifra Ahare Mot pereq 13.13; see Urbach, *The Sages* II, p. 932 n. 71.

56. See ibid., pp. 543ff.

57. BRSh 19a; bTaan 17b.

58. In my article 'Religious and Social Tendencies in the Talmudical Teachings on Charity' (in Hebrew), *Zion* 16, 1951, pp. 1–9. See J. Neusner, *A Life of Yohanan ben Zakkai*, p. 184, where this article is quoted in n. 1 as 'Rabbinic Theodicy', and the Appendix pp. 246ff. See also Neusner, *Development of a Legend*, p. 103; E. P. Sanders, *Paul and Palestinian Judaism*, 1977, pp. 207ff.

59. BSukk 55b. I could not find any tannaitic source for the idea of correspondence between the seventy bullocks and the seventy nations. The reading 'R. Eliezer' in the Venice edition is a clear mistake, and all MSS have 'R. Elazar'; see *Diqduqe Soferim*, ad loc., p. 182.

60. Sifre Deut 28 (Horovitz/Finkelstein, p. 123); see also Sifre Num 111 (Horovitz, p. 116).

61. PSanh 10.6 (29c).

62. See, for example, M. Hengel, *Judaism and Hellenism*, ET 1974, I, p. 313, or R. A. Kraft, 'The Multiform Jewish Heritage of Early Christianity', *Christianity, Judaism and Other Greco-Roman Cults* III (ed. Neusner), 1975, p. 178.

Bibliography

Abrahams, I., *Studies in Pharisaism and the Gospels*, First Series, Cambridge 1917, repr. New York 1967.

Ackroyd, Peter R., *Exile and Restoration* (OTL), 1968.

—'Two Historical Problems of the Early Persian Period', *JNES* 17, 1958, pp. 23–7.

Albeck, Ch., *Mabo la-Mishnah* (*Introduction to the Mishnah*), Jerusalem 1959.

— *Mabo la-Talmudim* (*Introduction to the Talmuds*), Tel Aviv 1968.

— *Mehqarim be-Baraita ve-Tosefta* (*Studies in the Baraita and Tosefta*), Jerusalem 1946, repr. 1969.

— *Mishnah, Seder Nashim*, Tel Aviv 1959.

Albeck, S., *Dine ha-Mamonot ba-Talmud* (*The Law of Property and Contract in the Talmud*), Tel Aviv 1976.

— 'Law and History in Halakhic Research' [ET of *Dine ha-Mamonot*, pp. 13–31], *Modern Research in Jewish Law* (ed. B. S. Jackson; *JLA* Suppl. 1), 1979, pp. 1–20.

Albright, W. F., 'The Date and Personality of the Chronicler', *JBL* 40, 1921, pp. 104–24.

Alon, G., *Jews, Judaism and the Classical World* (ET of *Mehqarim be-Toledot Yisra'el*), Jerusalem 1977.

— *Mehqarim be-Toledot Yisra'el* (*Studies in Jewish History*), 2 vols., Tel Aviv 1957, repr. Jerusalem 1970.

— 'Those Appointed for Money', in *Jews, Judaism and the Classical World*, Jerusalem 1977, pp. 374–432 (ET of *Mehqarim be-Toledot Yisra'el* II, pp. 15–57).

— *Toledot ha-Yehudim be-Erets Yisra'el be-Tequfat ha-Mishnah veha-Talmud* (*History of the Jews in the Land of Israel in the Period of the Mishnah and the Talmud*), 2 vols., Tel Aviv 1954–55, repr. 1967

Alt, A., 'Die Rolle Samarias bei der Entstehung des Judentums', *Kleine Schriften* II, Munich 1953, pp. 316–37.

Ambrière, F., ed., *Greece* ('Hachette World Guides'), Paris 1955.

Antoine, P., 'Garizin', *DBS* 3, 1938, pp. 535–61.

Aptowitzer, V., 'Bemerkungen zur Liturgie und Geschichte der Liturgie', *MGWJ* 74, 1930, pp. 104–27.

Bibliography

— *Parteipolitik der Hasmonäerzeit im rabbinischen und pseudoepigraphischen Schrifttum*, Vienna 1927.

— 'Spuren des Matriarchats im jüdischen Schriftum (Schluss)', *HUCA* 5, 1928, pp. 261–77.

Auerbach, E., 'Der Aufstieg der Priesterschaft zur Macht im alten Israel', *VTSupp* 9, 1963, pp. 236–49.

Auerbach, Leopold, *Das jüdische Obligationenrecht*, Berlin 1870, repr. Gedera 1976.

Aune, D. E., 'Orthodoxy in First Century Judaism? A Response to N. J. McEleney', *JSJ* 7, 1976, pp. 1–10.

Avi-Yonah, Michael, *The Holy Land: From the Persian to the Arab Conquest*, Grand Rapids 1966.

— *The Jews of Palestine: A Political History from the Bar Kokhba War to the Arab Conquest*, ET New York 1976.

— 'Palaestina', *PW*, Suppl. XIII, 1973, cols. 321–454.

Bacchiocchi, S., *From Sabbath to Sunday: A Historical Investigation of the Rise of Sunday Observance in Early Christianity*, Rome 1977.

Bacher, W., *Die Agada der Tannaiten* II, Strasbourg 1903.

— 'La science de la vieille tradition juive', *REJ* 28, 1899, pp. 211–19.

— *Tradition und Tradenten*, Leipzig 1914, repr. Berlin 1966.

Baeck, L., *The Essence of Judaism*, ET New York 1961, repr. 1970.

— 'Hat das überlieferte Judentum Dogmen?', *Aus drei Jahrtausenden*, Tübingen 1958, pp. 12–27.

Baer, I. F., 'The Historical Foundations of the Halakha' (in Hebrew), *Zion* 17, Jerusalem 1952, pp. 1–55; ibid., 27, 1962, pp. 117–55.

— *Yisra'el be-Amim* (*Israel among the Nations*), Jerusalem 1955.

Bailey, D. R. Shackleton, *Cicero's Letters to Atticus* III, Cambridge 1968.

Bamberger, B., *Proselytism in the Talmudic Period*, New York 1968.

Bammel, Ernst, 'Die Blutgerichtsbarkeit in der römischen Provinz Judäa', *JJS* 25 (*Studies in Jewish Legal History in Honour of David Daube*), 1974, pp. 35–49.

Bar Hebraeus, *Book of the Dove*, ET A. J. Wensinek, Leden 1919.

Baron, Salo W., *A Social and Religious History of the Jews*, 2 vols., New York, ²1952.

Barton, W. E., *The Samaritan Pentateuch*, Oberlin, Ohio 1903.

Bauer, W., *Orthodoxy and Heresy in Earliest Christianity*, ET Philadelphia 1971, London 1972.

— *Wörterbuch zum Neuen Testament*, Berlin ⁵1958; ET W. F. Arndt and F. W. Gingrich, *A Greek-English Lexicon of the New Testament*, Chicago and Cambridge 1957, ²1979.

Baumgarten, A. I., 'The Akiban Opposition', *HUCA* 50, 1979, pp. 179–97.

— 'R. Judah and his Opponents', *JSJ* (forthcoming).

Becker, J., *Untersuchungen zur Entstehungsgeschichte der Testamente der zwölf Patriarchen* (AGAJU 8), 1970.

Beer, G., 'Samariter, Samaritaner', *PW*, 2nd series 2A2, 1920, cols. 2105–10.

Belkin, S., *Philo and the Oral Law*, Cambridge, Mass. 1940.

419

Bibliography

Ben-Ḥayyim, Z., 'Gerizim, Har Gerizim', *Entsiqlopediah Mikra'it* II, Jerusalem 1954, pp. 554–8.

Benoit, P., J. T. Milik and R. de Vaux, eds., *Discoveries in the Judaean Desert* II, Oxford 1961.

Bensly, R. L., *The Fourth Book of Ezra: The Latin Version Edited from the MSS* (with introd. by M. R. James; Texts and Studies 3.2), Cambridge 1895.

Bentzen, Aage, *Daniel* (Handbuch zum Alten Testament 19), Tübingen ²1952.

Ben-Yehudah, E., *Millon Ha-Lashon Ha–'Ivrit* I, New York and London 1959.

Bergman, H., 'Israel and the "*Oikumene*" ', *Studies in Rationalism, Judaism and Universalism, in Memory of Leon Roth* (ed. R. Loewe), London and New York 1966, pp. 747–65.

Bernard, J. H., *The Gospel according to St John* (International Critical Commentary), 2 vols., Edinburgh and New York 1928.

Betz, Otto, *Der Paraklet: Fürsprecher im häretischen Spätjudentum, im Johannes-evangelium und neugefundenen gnostischen Schriften*, Leiden 1963.

Bickerman, E., 'La charte séleucide de Jérusalem', *REJ* 100, 1935, pp. 4–35.

— *Four Strange Books of the Bible*, New York 1967.

— *From Ezra to the Last of the Maccabees*, 1947, repr. New York 1962.

— *Der Gott der Makkabäer*, Berlin 1937.

— 'The Historical Foundations of Post-Biblical Judaism', *The Jews, Their History* (ed. L. Finkelstein), New York ⁴1970, pp. 72–118.

— 'Ein jüdischer Festbrief vom Jahre 124 v. Chr.', *ZNW* 32, 1933, pp. 233–54.

— 'Une proclamation séleucide relative au temple de Jérusalem', *Syria* 25, 1946–48, pp. 67–85.

— 'Two Legal Interpretations of the Septuagint', *RIDA* 3, 1956, pp. 81–97; repr. in his *Studies in Jewish and Christian History* (AGAJU 9) I, 1976, pp. 201–15.

Biscardi, Arnaldo, 'Nuove testimonianze di un papiro arabo-giudaico per la storia del processo provinciale romano', *Studi in onore di Gaetano Scherillo* I, Milan 1972, pp. 111–52.

— 'Sulla Identificazione degli "Xenokritai" e sulla loro Attività in P. Oxy. 3016', *Festschrift für Erwin Seidl zum 70. Geburtstag* (ed. H. Hübner), Cologne 1975, pp. 15–24.

— 'Xenokritai', *Novissimo Digesto Italiano* 20, 1975, pp. 1087–90.

Blau, Ludwig, 'A prófétai lekziók behozatalának kora és oka', *Magyar Zsido Szemle* 25, Budapest 1908, pp. 150f.

— *Papyri und Talmud in gegenseitiger Beleuchtung* (Schriften herausgegeben von der Gesellschaft zur Förderung der Wissenschaft des Judentums), Leipzig 1913.

Blenkinsopp, J., *Prophecy and Canon*, Notre Dame and London 1977.

— 'Prophecy and Priesthood in Josephus', *JJS* 25, 1974, pp. 239–62.

Bibliography

Blidstein, G., 'Who is Not a Jew? – The Medieval Discussion', *ILR* 11, 1976, pp. 369–90.

Bousset, W., 'Eine jüdische Gebetssammlung im siebenten Buch der apostolischen Konstitutionen', *Nachrichten von der Königlichen Gesellschaft der Wissenschaften zu Göttingen*, Philologisch-historische Klasse 1916, pp. 435–89.

— 'Die Testamente der zwölf Patriarchen', *ZNW* 1, 1900, pp. 141–75, 187–209.

Bowman, J., 'Contact between Samaritan Sects and Qumran?', *VT* 7, 1957, pp. 184–89.

— 'The Importance of Samaritan Researches', *Annual of Leeds University Oriental Society* I, 1958–59, pp. 43–54.

— 'Is the Samaritan Calendar the Old Zadokite One?', *PEQ* 91, 1959, pp. 73–8.

— 'Pilgrimage to Mount Gerizim', *Eretz Israel* 7, Jerusalem 1964, pp. 17–28.

— *Samaritanische Probleme*, Stuttgart 1967.

— 'The Samaritans and the Book of Deuteronomy', *Transactions of the Glasgow University Oriental Society* 17, 1957–58, pp. 9–18.

Braverman, J., *Jerome's Commentary on Daniel*, Washington, D.C. 1978.

Brown, R. E., *The Birth of the Messiah*, New York 1977.

— *The Community of the Beloved Disciple*, New York 1978.

— *The Gospel According to St John I–XII* (AB 29), 1966.

Browne, L. E., *Ezekiel and Alexander*, London 1952.

Bruce, F. F., *New Testament History*, London and Garden City, New York 1972.

Brüll, A., *Zur Geschichte und Literatur der Samaritaner nebst Varianten zum Buche Genesis*, Frankfurt 1876.

Brüll, J., *Mabo la-Mishnah* (*Introduction to the Mishnah*) I–II, Frankfurt 1876, 1885, repr. Jerusalem 1970.

Bruneau, Philippe, *Recherches sur les cultes de Délos à l'époque hellénistique et à l'époque impériale*, Paris 1970.

Bry, M.-J., 'L'Édit de Caracalla', *Études d'histoire juridique offertes à P. F. Girard par ses élèves* I, Paris 1912, pp. 1–42.

Buckland, W. W., 'L'edictum provinciale', *Revue historique de droit français et étranger* 13, 1964, pp. 81–96.

— *A Text-book of Roman Law* (ed. P. Stein), Cambridge ³1963.

Büchler, A., 'The Levitical Impurity of the Gentile in Palestine before the Year 70', *JQR* n.s. 17, 1926–27, pp. 1–81.

— 'The Minim of Sepphoris and Tiberias in the Second and Third Centuries', *Studies in Jewish History* (ed. I. Brodie and J. Rabbinowitz), London 1956, pp. 245–74.

— 'La relation de Josèphe concernant Alexandre le Grand', *REJ* 36, 1898, pp. 1–26.

Bultmann, Rudolf, *The Gospel of John: A Commentary*, ET G. R. Beasley-Murray (from German ed. of 1964), Oxford and Philadelphia 1971.

Bibliography

Burdese, A., 'Dubbi in tema di "naturalis obligatio" ', *Studi in onore di Gaetano Scherillo* II, Milan 1972, pp. 485–513.

Burgansky, I., 'Simeon ben Eleazar', *EJ* XIV, Jerusalem 1972, cols. 1554f.

Calloud, Jean, *L'analyse structurale du récit*, Lyons 1973; ET D. Patte, *Structural Analysis of Narrative*, Philadelphia and Missoula 1976.

Campbell, E. F., Jr and J. F. Ross, 'The Excavations of Shechem and the Biblical Tradition', *BA* 26, 1963, pp. 2–27.

Carr, A. W., 'The Rulers of This Age – I Corinthians ii.6–8', *NTS* 23, 1976, pp. 20–35.

Carroll, K. L., 'The Fourth Gospel and the Exclusion of Christians from the Synagogues', *BJRL* 40, 1957–58, pp. 19–32.

Cazelles, Henri, 'La mission d'Esdras', *VT* 4, 1954, pp. 113–40.

Cellarius, Chr., *Collectanea historiae Samaritanae*, Zeitz 1688.

Chajes, H.-P., 'Les Juges juifs en Palestine de l'an 70 à l'an 500', *REJ* 39, 1899, pp. 39–52.

Chajes, Z. H., *Kol Sifre MaHaRaTS Hayot* I, Jerusalem 1958.

Chalon, Gérard, *L'Édit de Tiberius Julius Alexander*, Olten/Lausanne 1964.

Charles, R. H., ed., *The Apocrypha and Pseudepigrapha of the Old Testament*, 2 vols., Oxford 1913.

— *The Ascension of Isaiah*, London 1900.

— *The Greek Versions of the Testaments of the Twelve Patriarchs*, Oxford 1908.

— 'Testaments of the XII Patriarchs', *HDB* IV, 1902, pp. 721–75.

Charlesworth, J. H., 'A Critical Comparison of the Dualism in 1QS 3:13–4:26 and the "dualism" Contained in the Gospel of John', *NTS* 15, 1968–69, pp. 389–418.

— 'Jewish Astrology in the Talmud, Pseudepigrapha, the Dead Sea Scrolls, and Early Palestinian Synagogues', *HTR* 70, 1977, pp. 183–200.

— ed., *John and Qumran*, London 1972.

— *The Pseudepigrapha and Modern Research* (SCS 7), 1976.

— ed., *The Pseudepigrapha of the Old Testament*, New York (forthcoming, 1982).

— 'Reflections on the SNTS Pseudepigrapha Seminar at Duke on the Testaments of the Twelve Patriarchs', *NTS* 23, 1977, pp. 296–304.

— 'The SNTS Pseudepigrapha Seminars at Tübingen and Paris on the Books of Enoch', *NTS* 25, 1979, pp. 315–23.

Chary, T., *Les prophètes et le culte à partir de l'exil*, Tournai 1955.

Childs, Brevard S., *Introduction to the Old Testament as Scripture*, London and Philadelphia 1979.

— 'A Study of the Formula "Until this Day" ', *JBL* 82, 1963, pp. 279–92.

Clark, W. Malcolm, 'Law', *Old Testament Form Criticism* (ed. John H. Hayes), San Antonio 1974, pp. 99–139.

Coggins, R. J., *The Books of Ezra and Nehemiah* (Cambridge Bible Commentaries), 1976.

Bibliography

— 'The Old Testament and Samaritan Origins', *ASTI* 6, 1968, pp. 35–48.

— *Samaritans and Jews*, London 1975.

Cohen, Boaz, *Jewish and Roman Law*, 2 vols., New York 1966.

Cohen, Y., *Peraqim be-Toledot Tequfat ha-Tannaim*, Jerusalem 1978.

Coleman, G. B., *The Phenomenon of Christian Interpolations into Jewish Apocalyptic Texts: A Bibliographical Survey and Methodological Analysis* (Vanderbilt University, Ph.D.), 1976.

Colin, Gaston, *Rome et la Grèce de 200 à 146 avant Jesus-Christ*, Paris 1905.

Collinet, Paul, *Histoire de l'École de Droit de Beyrouth*, Paris 1925.

Collins, J. J., *The Apocalyptic Vision of the Book of Daniel* (Harvard Semitic Monographs 16), Missoula 1977.

— *The Sibylline Oracles of Egyptian Judaism* (SBLDS 13), 1974.

— 'The Son of Man and the Saints of the Most High in the Book of Daniel', *JBL* 93, 1974, pp. 50–66.

Collins, M. F., 'The Hidden Vessels in Samaritan Traditions', *JSJ* 3, 1972, pp. 97–116.

Colpe, Carsten, *Die Religionsgeschichtliche Schule*, Göttingen 1961.

— 'Samaria', *RGG*[3] 5, 1961, cols. 1350–55.

Cook, M. J., *Mark's Treatment of the Jewish Leaders* (SupplNovT 51), 1978.

Cooke, G. A., *A Text-Book of North-Semitic Inscriptions*, Oxford 1903.

Cooper, Alan, 'Divine Names and Epithets', *Ras Shamra Parallels* III (ed. L. R. Fisher), Rome 1979.

Cowley, A., 'Samaritans', *EB* IV, 1903, cols. 4256–65.

Cozer, Lewis, *The Functions of Social Conflict*, Glencoe, Ill. 1956.

Cross, Frank Moore, Jr, *The Ancient Library of Qumran*, Garden City, New York 1961.

— 'Aspects of Samaritan and Jewish History in Late Persian and Hellenistic Times', *HTR* 59, 1966, pp. 201–11.

— *Canaanite Myth and Hebrew Epic*, Cambridge, Mass. 1973.

— 'The Discovery of the Samaria Papyri', *BA* 26, 1963, pp. 110–21.

— 'New Directions in the Study of Apocalyptic', *Journal for Theology and Church. 6: Apocalypticism*, New York 1969, pp. 157–65.

— 'A Reconstruction of the Judean Restoration', *Interp* 29, 1975, pp. 187–201.

Crown, A. D., 'New Light on the Inter-Relationships of Samaritan Chronicles from Some Manuscripts in the John Rylands Library', *BJRL* 54, 1971–72, pp. 282–313; ibid., 55, 1972–73, pp. 86–111.

Dahl, N. A., 'Der Erstgeborene Satans und der Vater des Teufels (Polyk 7:1 und Joh 8:44)', *Apophoreta. Festschrift für E. Haenchen*, Berlin 1964, pp. 70–84.

— 'The Johannine Church and History', *Current Issues in New Testament Interpretation* (ed. W. Klassen and G. F. Snyder), New York and London 1962, pp. 124–42.

Daniélou, J., 'That the Scripture Might Be Fulfilled, Christianity as a Jewish Sect', *The Crucible of Christianity* (ed. A. Toynbee), London 1969, pp. 261–82.

Bibliography

Daube, David, 'Alexandrian Methods of Interpretation and the Rabbis', *Festschrift Hans Lewald*, Basel 1953, pp. 27–44.

— 'The Civil Law of the Mishnah: The Arrangement of the Three Gates', *Tulane Law Review* 18, 1944, pp. 351–407.

— 'Derelictio, Occupatio and Traditio: Romans and Rabbis', *LQR* 77, 1961, pp. 382–89.

— *Forms of Roman Legislation*, Oxford 1956.

— 'The Influence of Interpretation on Writing', *Buffalo Law Review* 20, 1970, pp. 41–59.

— 'Jewish Law in the Hellenistic World', *Jewish Law in Legal History and the Modern World* (ed. B. S. Jackson; *JLA* Suppl. 2), 1980, pp. 45-60.

— 'Methods of Interpretation and Hellenistic Rhetoric', *HUCA* 22, 1949, pp. 239–64.

— 'Negligence in the Early Talmudic Law of Contract (Peshi'ah)', *Festschrift Fritz Schulz* I, Weimar 1951, pp. 124–47.

— Review of Jackson, *Essays*, *JJS* 28, 1977, pp. 79–80.

— 'Some Forms of Old Testament Legislation', *Proceedings of the Oxford Society of Historical Theology*, 1944–45, pp. 36–46.

David, Martin, 'The Codex Hammurabi and Its Relation to the Provisions of Law in Exodus', *Oudtestamentische Studien* 7, Leiden 1950, pp. 149–78.

Davies, W. D., *The Setting of the Sermon on the Mount*, Cambridge 1966.

de Jonge, M., 'Christian Influence in the Testaments of the Twelve Patriarchs', *Studies on the Testaments of the Twelve Patriarchs: Text and Interpretation* (ed. M. de Jonge; Studia in Veteris Testamenti Pseudepigrapha 3), Leiden 1975, pp. 193–246.

— *Testamenta XII Patriarcharum* (Pseudepigrapha Veteris Testamenti Graece 1), Leiden ²1970.

de Lange, N. R. M., *Origen and the Jews*, Cambridge 1976.

Delcor, M., 'Hinweise auf das Samaritanische Schisma im AT', *ZAW* 74, 1962, pp. 281–91.

— 'Vom Sichem der hellenistischen Epoche zum Sychar des Neuen Testamentes', *Zeitschrift des deutschen Palästina-Vereins* 78, Wiesbaden 1962, pp. 34–48.

Delling, G., 'Testamente der zwölf Patriarchen', *Bibliographie zur jüdisch-hellenistischen und intertestamentarischen Literatur 1900–1970* (TU 106), 1975, pp. 167–71.

Delorme, Jean, *Gymnasion*, Paris 1960.

Deutsch, G., '*Apikoros*', *JE* I, pp. 665f.

Dever, W. G., 'Excavations at Shechem and Mount Gerizim' (in Hebrew), *Eretz Shomron. The Thirtieth Archaeological Convention*, Jerusalem 1973, pp. 8f.

de Visscher, Fernand, *Les édits d'Auguste découverts à Cyrène*, Paris and Louvain 1940.

— 'Le statut juridique des nouveaux citoyens romains et l'inscription de Rhosos', *L'Antiquité Classique* 13, Brussels 1944, pp. 11–35.

— 'Le statut juridique des nouveaux citoyens romains et l'inscription de Rhosos', *L'Antiquité Classique* 14, 1945, pp. 29–59.

Bibliography

Dexinger, F., 'Das Garizimgebot im Dekalog der Samaritaner', *Studien zum Pentateuch. Walter Kornfeld zum 60. Geburtstag* (ed. G. Braulik), Vienna 1977, pp. 111–33.
— *Henochs Zehnwochenapokalypse und offene Probleme der Apokalyptikforschung* (SPB 29), 1977.
— *Der Taheb. Die 'messianische' Gestalt bei den Samaritanern* (typescript), Vienna 1978.
de Zulueta, Francis, *The Institutes of Gaius*, 2 vols., Oxford 1946, 1953.
Dias, R. W. M., *A Bibliography of Jurisprudence*, London ³1979.
Didier, P., 'Les obligations naturelles chez les derniers Sabiniens', *RIDA* 19, 1972, pp. 239–74.
Donahue, P. J., 'Jewish Christianity in the Letters of Ignatius of Antioch', *VC* 32, 1978, pp. 81–93.
Douglas, M., *Implicit Meanings*, London 1975.
— *Natural Symbols: Explorations in Cosmology*, London 1970, New York 1973.
— *Purity and Danger*, London and New York 1966.
— , ed., *Witchcraft, Confessions and Accusations* (Association of Social Anthropologists Monograph 9), London 1970.
Drijvers, H. J. W., 'Edessa und das jüdische Christentum', *VC* 24, 1970, pp. 4–33.
Driver, G. R., 'Sacred Numbers and Round Figures', *Promise and Fulfilment. Essays Presented to S. H. Hooke* (ed. F. F. Bruce), Edinburgh 1963, pp. 62–90.
Droysen, Johann Gustav, *Geschichte des Hellenismus*, 2 vols., Hamburg 1836–43; 2nd ed., 6 vols. in 3, Gotha 1877–78.
Eddy, Samuel K., *The King Is Dead*, Lincoln, Nebraska 1961.
Ehrman, A., 'Law and Equity in the Talmudic Concept of Sale', *JJS* 18, 1957, pp. 177–86.
Eichrodt, Walther, *Theology of the Old Testament*, 2 vols., ET (OTL) 1961–67.
Eissfeldt, O., *Einleitung in das Alte Testament*, Tübingen ³1964; ET, *The Old Testament: An Introduction*, Oxford and New York 1965.
Elbogen, Ismar, *Der jüdische Gottesdienst in seiner geschichtlichen Entwicklung*, ³1931, repr. Hildesheim 1967.
Elbogen, Y. M., *Ha-Tefillah be-Yisrael be-Hitpathutah ha-Historit*, Tel Aviv 1972.
Elon, Menachem, ed., *The Principles of Jewish Law*, Jerusalem 1975.
Emerton, J. A., 'An Examination of a Recent Structural Interpretation of Genesis xxxviii', *VT* 26, 1976, pp. 79–98.
Englard, Izhak, 'Research in Jewish Law – Its Nature and Function', *Modern Research in Jewish Law* (ed. B. S. Jackson; JLA Suppl. 1), 1979 pp. 21–65. ET of *Mishpatim* 7, 1975–76, pp. 34–65).
Eppstein, V., 'When and How the Sadducees Were Excommunicated', *JBL* 85, 1966, pp. 213–24.
Epstein, J. N., *Mabo le-Nusah ha-Mishnah (Introduction to the Text of the Mishnah)*, 2 vols., Jerusalem 1948, ²1964.

Bibliography

— *Mebo'ot le-Sifrut ha-Tannaim (Introductions to Tannaitic Literature*; ed. E. Z. Melamed), Jerusalem 1957.

— *Mebo'ot Le-Sifrut Ha-'Amora'im*, Jerusalem 1962.

Eybers, I. H., 'Relations between Jews and Samaritans in the Persian Period', *Biblical Essays*, Potchefstroom 1966, pp. 72–89.

Falk, Z. W., *Introduction to Jewish Law of the Second Commonwealth* (AGAJU 11), 2 vols., Leiden 1972–78.

— 'Jewish Private Law', *The Jewish People in the First Century* (ed. S. Safrai and M. Stern), Assen 1974, pp. 504–34.

— Review of E. Koffmahn, *Die Doppelurkunden aus der Wüste Juda, Bibl* 50, 1969, pp. 414–18; also in *Tijdschrift voor Rechtsgeschiedenis* 37, Groningen 1969, pp. 261–63.

— 'Zum fremden Einfluss auf das jüdische Recht', *RIDA* 18, 1971, pp. 11–23.

Finkelstein, L., 'Development of the Amidah', *JQR* ns 16, 1925–26, pp. 1–43, 127–70 (=*Pharisaism in the Making*, New York 1972).

— *Ha-Perushim ve-Anshe Keneset ha-Gedolah*, New York 1950.

— 'The Institution of Baptism for Proselytes', *JBL* 52, 1933, pp. 302–11.

— 'Introductory Study to Pirke Abot', *JBL* 57, 1938, pp. 13–50.

— *Mabo le-Massektot 'Abot ve-'Abot de-Rabbi Natan*, New York 1950.

— , ed., *Sifra or Torat Kohanim according to Codex Assemani LXV*, New York 1956.

— 'Some examples of the Maccabean Halaka', *JBL* 49, 1930, pp. 20–42.

Fischel, Henry A., ed., *Essays in Greco-Roman and Related Talmudic Literature*, New York 1977.

Fitzmyer, Joseph A., 'The Languages of Palestine in the First Century A.D.,', *CBQ* 32, 1970, pp. 501–31.

Flemming, Johannes, ed., *Die Syrische Didaskalia* (TU 25.2), 1904.

Fletcher, George P., 'The Metamorphosis of Larceny', *Harvard Law Review* 89, 1976, pp. 469–530.

— *Rethinking Criminal Law*, Boston and Toronto 1978.

Flusser, David, 'Not by Means of an Angel . . .' (in Hebrew), *Toray Yeshurun* 29, 1971–72, pp. 18–20.

— 'Tevilat Yohanan ve-Kat Midbar Yehudah', *Yahadut u-Meqorot ha-Natserut*, Tel Aviv 1979, pp. 81–112.

Fohrer, G., *History of Israelite Religion*, ET, Nashville 1972, London 1973.

Ford, J. M., 'Can We Exclude Samaritan Influence from Qumran?', *RQ* 6, 1967, pp. 109–29.

Forkman, G., *The Limits of the Religious Community*, Lund 1972.

Fossum, J., 'The Samaritan Origin of the Concept of the Demiurge', Yale International Conference on Gnosticism, April 1978.

Foster, Ken, Review of Michael Zander, *Legal Services for the Community, Journal of the Society of Public Teachers of Law* 14/4, 1979, pp. 301–3.

Frankel, Z., *Darke ha-Mishnah (The Paths of the Mishnah)*, 1859, repr. Tel Aviv 1959.

Freedman, David Noel, 'Canon of the Old Testament', *IDBSuppl*, pp. 130–36.

— 'The Chronicler's Purpose', *CBQ* 23, 1961, pp. 436–42.

Bibliography

Frend, W. H. C., *Martyrdom and Persecution in the Early Church*, Oxford 1965.

Friedlaender, M., 'Minim, Minouet et Guilionim dans le Talmud', *REJ* 38, 1899, pp. 194–203.

Funk, F. X., *Didascalia et Constitutiones Apostolorum*, Paderborn 1905.

Gafni, I., 'Yeshivah u-Metivtah', *Zion* 43, Jerusalem 1978, pp. 12–37.

Gager, J. G., 'Some Attempts to Label the *Oracula Sibyllina*, Book 7', *HTR* 65, 1972, pp. 91–7.

Galling, K., 'Serubbabel und der Wiederaufbau des Tempels in Jerusalem', *Verbannung und Heimkehr. Festschrift für K. Rudolph*, Tübingen 1961, pp. 67–96.

Gaster, T. H., 'Samaritans', *IDB* IV, 1962, pp. 190–97.

Gaudemet, J., *Institutions de l'Antiquité*, Paris 1967.

— 'La Juridiction provinciale d'après la correspondance entre Pline et Trajan', *RIDA* 11, 1964, pp. 335–53.

Gawlikowski, M., *Recueil d'inscriptions palmyréniennes provenant des fouilles syriennes et polonaises récentes à Palmyre*, Paris 1974.

Geffcken, J., ed., *Die Oracula Sibyllina* (GCS 8), 1902.

— *Komposition und Entstehungszeit der Oracula Sibyllina* (TU 23.1), 1902.

Geiger, Joseph, 'To the History of the Term *Apikoros*' (in Hebrew), *Tarbiz* 42, Jerusalem 1972–73, pp. 499f.

Gerleman, G., 'Samaritaner', *Biblisch-Historisches Handwörterbuch* III (ed. B. Reicke and L. Rost), Göttingen 1966, pp. 1660f.

Gero, S., 'Jewish Polemic in the Martyrium Pionii and a "Jesus" Passage from the Talmud', *JJS* 29, 1978, pp. 164–68.

Gil, Moshe, 'Land Ownership in Palestine under Roman Rule', *RIDA* 17, 1970, pp. 11–54.

Gilat, Y. D., 'Bar Kappara', *EJ* IV, cols. 227f.

— *Mishnato shel R. 'Eli'ezer ben Hyrkanus*, Tel Aviv 1968.

Ginsburg, Michel S., *Rome et la Judée*, Paris 1928.

Ginzberg, L., *Die Haggada bei den Kirchenvätern*, Amsterdam 1899.

— *Ginzei Shechter, Genizah Studies in Memory of Dr S. Shechter* I, New York 1928.

— *Legends of the Jews* VI, Philadelphia 1928.

— *Perushim ve-Ḥiddushim be-Yerushalmi (A Commentary on the Palestinian Talmud)*, 4 vols., New York 1941–61.

— *Seride Ha-Yerushalmi (Yerushalmi Fragments from the Genizah)*, New York 1909.

— *An Unknown Jewish Sect* (ET of *Eine unbekannte jüdische Sekte*, 1922), New York 1970.

Goldenberg, R., 'The Deposition of Rabban Gamaliel II: an Examination of the Sources', *JJS* 23, 1972, pp. 167–90.

Goldin, Judah, 'Not by Means of an Angel and Not by Means of a Messenger', *Religions in Antiquity: Essays in Memory of E. R. Goodenough* (ed. J. Neusner; Supplements to *Numen* 14), Leiden 1968, pp. 412–24.

Goldschmidt, D., ed., *Seder R. Amram Gaon*, Jerusalem 1971.

Goldstein, Jonathan A., *I Maccabees* (AB 41), Garden City 1976.

— 'Rabbinic Bans on Aspects of Hellenistic Culture' (forthcoming).
— 'The Tales of the Tobiads', *Christianity, Judaism, and Other Greco-Roman Cults: Studies for Morton Smith* (ed. J. Neusner; SJLA 12) III, 1975, pp. 85–123.
Goldstein, M., *Jesus in the Jewish Tradition*, New York 1950.
Goodenough, E. R., *By Light, Light: The Mystic Gospel of Hellenistic Judaism*, New Haven 1935.
Goren, Sh., *Ha-Yerushalmi ha-Meforash*, Jerusalem 1961.
Goshen-Gottstein, M. H., 'The Psalms Scroll (11QPsᵃ) – A Problem of Canon and Text', *Textus* 5, Jerusalem 1966, pp. 22–33.
Grabbe, L. L., 'Orthodoxy in First Century Judaism?', *JSJ* 8, 1977, pp. 149–53.
Grech, P., 'Interprophetic Re-Interpretation and Old Testament Eschatology', *Augustinianum* 9, Rome 1969, pp. 235–65.
Green, Henry, 'Gnosis and Gnosticism: A Study in Methodology', *Numen* 24, Leiden 1977, pp. 95–134.
— 'Suggested Sociological Themes in the Study of Gnosticism', *VC* 31, 1977, pp. 169–80.
Green, W. S., 'The Talmudic Historians', *The Modern Study of the Mishnah* (ed. J. Neusner; SPB 23), 1973, pp. 107–21.
— 'What's in a Name – The Problematic of Rabbinic Biography', *Approaches to Ancient Judaism* (ed. W. S. Green), Missoula 1978, pp. 77–96.
Greenberg, Moshe, 'Some Postulates of Biblical Criminal Law', *Yehezkel Kaufmann Jubilee Volume* (ed. M. Haran), Jerusalem 1960, pp. 5–28, repr. in *The Jewish Expression* (ed. J. Goldin), New Haven 1976, pp. 18–37.
Grelot, P., 'Soixante-dix semaines d'années', *Bibl* 50, 1959, pp. 169–86.
Grintz, J. M., *Mabo'ey Miqra*, Tel Aviv 1972.
Guarino, Antonio, 'Gaio e l' "edictum provinciale" ', *IURA* 20, 1969, pp. 154–71.
Gulak, A., *Das Urkundenwesen im Talmud im Lichte der griechisch-aegyptischen Papyri und des griechischen und römischen Rechts*, Jerusalem 1935.
— *History of Jewish Law I: Law of Obligation and Its Guaranties* (in Hebrew), Jerusalem 1939.
Gunneweg, A. H. J., *Understanding the Old Testament*, ET (OTL), 1978.
Gutman, Yehoshua, *The Beginnings of Jewish-Hellenistic Literature* I (in Hebrew), Jerusalem 1958.
Guttmann, Julius, *Die Idee der religiösen Gesellschaft im Judentum* (Bericht der Hochschule für die Wissenschaft des Judentums), Berlin 1922.
— 'Philo the Epic Poet', *SH* 1, 1954, pp. 36–63.
Guttmann, Michael, *Das Judentum und seine Umwelt*, Berlin 1927.
Haacker, K., 'Die Schriftzitate in der samaritanischen Chronik II', *Das Institutum Judaicum der Universität Tübingen in den Jahren 1968–1970*, pp. 38–47.
Haag, H., 'Samaria', *LTK²* 9, 1964, cols. 292–95.

Bibliography

Haardt, R., 'Zur Methodologie der Gnosisforschung', *Gnosis und Neues Testament* (ed. Karl-Wolfgang Troeger), Berlin 1973, pp. 77–88.

Habicht, Christian, 'Royal Documents in Maccabees II', *Harvard Studies in Classical Philosophy* 80, 1976, pp. 1–18.

Halivni, David Weiss, *Mekorot u-Mesorot (Sources and Traditions), Moʿed*, Jerusalem 1975.

— *Mekorot u-Mesorot, Nashim*, Tel Aviv 1968.

— 'Yesh Meviʾim Bikkurim,' *Bar-Ilan* 7-8, Ramat Gan 1969–70, p. 79.

Hallo, W., *Early Mesopotamian Royal Titles*, New Haven 1957.

Hamburger, J., 'Samaritaner', *Real-Encyclopädie des Judentums* II, Leipzig 1901, pp. 1062–71.

Hammershaimb, E., *Some Aspects of Old Testament Prophecy from Isaiah to Malachi*, Copenhagen 1966.

Hammond, M., *The Augustan Principate*, New York, ²1968.

Hanson, Paul D., *The Dawn of Apocalyptic*, Philadelphia 1975.

— 'Jewish Apocalyptic against Its Near Eastern Environment', *RB* 78, 1971, pp. 31–58.

— 'Old Testament Apocalyptic Re-examined', *Interp* 25, 1971, pp. 454–79.

— 'Zechariah 9 and the Recapitulation of an Ancient Ritual Pattern', *JBL* 92, 1973, pp. 37–59.

Hare, D., *The Theme of Jewish Persecution of Christians in the Gospel according to St Matthew*, Cambridge 1967.

Harnack, Adolf, *Das Wesen des Christentums*, Leipzig ²1908, ET of 1st ed., *What is Christianity?*, London and New York 1901.

— *Die Mission und Ausbreitung des Christentums in den ersten drei Jahrhunderten*, 2 vols., Leipzig ⁴1924; ET of 1st ed., *The Expansion of Christianity in the First Three Centuries*, 2 vols., London and New York 1904–05.

Heinemann, I., *Darkhe ha-Agadah*, Jerusalem² 1954.

— 'Judaism in the Eyes of the Ancient World' (in Hebrew), *Zion* 4, 1939, pp. 269–93.

Heinemann, J., *Ha-Tefillah bi-Tequfat ha-Tannaʾim ve-ha-ʾAmoraim*, Jerusalem 1964, ²1966; revised ET, *Prayer in the Talmud: Forms and Patterns* (SJ 9), 1977.

— 'Once More Melekh HaʿOlam', *JJS* 15, 1964, pp. 149–54.

Hengel, Martin, *Judaism and Hellenism*, ET, 2 vols., London and Philadelphia 1974.

Hennecke, E. and W. Schneemelcher, eds., *New Testament Apocrypha* (= *NTApoc*), ET (ed. R. McL. Wilson), 2 vols., London and Philadelphia 1963–65, repr. 1973–74.

Herford, R. T., *Christianity in Talmud and Midrash*, London 1903, repr. New York 1975.

Herr, M. D., 'The Historical Significance of the Dialogues between Jewish Sages and Roman Dignitaries', *SH* 22, 1971, pp. 123–50.

— 'Persecution and Martyrdom in Hadrian's Days', *SH* 23, 1972, pp. 85–125.

Bibliography

Herschkowits, Y., 'Ha-Kutim be-Dibre ha-Tanna'im', *Sefer Asaf*, Jerusalem 1940, pp. 71–105.

Heschel, A. J., *Torah min ha-Shamayim ba–'Aspaqlaryah shel ha-Dorot* II, London and New York 1965.

Heurgon, Jacques, *The Rise of Rome to 264 BC.*, Berkeley and Los Angeles 1973.

Higger, M., ed., *Maseket Soferim*, New York 1937, repr. Jerusalem 1970.

— ed., *Sheva Massektot Qetanot*, Jerusalem 1970–71.

Himes, J., 'The Function of Racial Conflict', *Social Forces* 45, Chapel Hill, N.C. 1966, pp. 1–10.

Hirschberg, H., 'Allusions to the Apostle Paul in the Talmud', *JBL* 62, 1943, pp. 73–87.

— 'Once Again – The Minim', *JBL* 67, 1948, pp. 304–18.

Hoenig, S.B., 'Susanna', *IDB* IV, pp. 467ff.

Hopkins, Keith, Review of Fergus Millar, *The Emperor in the Roman World*, *JRS* 68, 1978, pp. 178–86.

Horton, J., 'Order and Conflict: Theories of Social Problems as Competing Ideologies', *American Journal of Sociology* 71, Chicago 1966, pp. 701–13.

Hultgård, A., *L'eschatologie des Testaments des Douze Patriarches* (Acta Universitatis Upsaliensis, Historia Religionum 6), Stockholm 1977.

Humphreys, W. L., 'A Life-Style for Diaspora; A Study of the Tales of Esther and Daniel', *JBL* 92, 1973, pp. 211–23.

Hunzinger, C.-H., *Die jüdische Bannpraxis im neutestamentlichen Zeitalter*, Göttingen 1954.

— 'Spuren Pharisäischer Institutionen in der frühen rabbinischen Überlieferung', *Tradition und Glaube. Festgabe für Karl Georg Kuhn* (ed. G. Jeremias, H.-W. Kuhn, and H. Stegemann), Göttingen 1971, pp. 147–56.

Ḥurgin, P., 'Hitbadlut ha-Shomronim', *Horeb* 1, Jerusalem 1936/37, pp. 127–50.

Hyman, A., 'Maimonides' "Thirteen Principles" ', *Jewish Medieval and Renaissance Studies* (ed. A. Altmann), Cambridge, Mass. 1967, pp. 119–44.

Hyman, Aaron, *Toledot Tanna'im ve-'Amoraim (History of the Tannaim and Amoraim)* I and III, repr. Jerusalem 1964.

Isbell, C. D., *Corpus of the Aramaic Incantation Bowls* (SBLDS 17), 1975.

Isenberg, Sheldon, 'Mary Douglas and Hellenistic Religions: The Case of Qumran', SBL 1975 Seminar Papers, pp. 179–85.

Isenberg, Sheldon, and Dennis F. Owen, 'Bodies, Natural and Contrived: The Work of Mary Douglas', *Religious Studies Review* 3, Waterloo, Ontario 1977, pp. 1–17.

Issaverdens, J., *The Uncanonical Writings of the Old Testament Found in the Armenian MSS of the Library of St Lazarus*, Venice 1907.

Jackson, B. S., 'The Concept of Religious Law in Judaism', *ANRW* II: *Principat*, 19.1, *Religion (Judentum: Allgemeines)*, 1979, pp. 33–52.

— *Essays in Jewish and Comparative Legal History* (SJLA 10), 1975.

Bibliography

— 'Evolution and Foreign Influence in Ancient Law', *The American Journal of Comparative Law* 16, Baltimore 1968, pp. 372–90.

— 'Foreign Influence in the Early Jewish Law of Theft', *RIDA* 18, 1971, pp. 25–42.

— 'History, Dogmatics and *Halakhah*', *Jewish Law in Legal History and the Modern World* (ed. B. S. Jackson: *JLA* Suppl 2), 1980, pp. 1–25.

— 'Legalism', *JJS* 30, 1979, pp. 1–22.

— 'Liability for Animals in Roman Law: An Historical Sketch', *The Cambridge Law Journal* 37, 1978, pp. 122–43.

— 'Maimonides' Definitions of *Tam* and *Mu'ad*', *JLA* 1, 1978, pp. 168–76.

— ed., *Modern Research in Jewish Law (JLA* Suppl 1), 1979.

— 'Modern Research in Jewish Law: Some Theoretical Issues', *Modern Research in Jewish Law*, pp. 136–57.

— 'Reflections on Biblical Criminal Law', *JJS* 24, 1973, pp. 8–38.

— *Structuralism and Legal Theory*, Liverpool 1979 [an Occasional Paper obtainable from the Department of Law, Liverpool Polytechnic, Hamilton House, 24 Pall Mall, Liverpool L3 6HR].

— *Theft in Early Jewish Law*, Oxford 1972.

— 'Towards a Structuralist Theory of Law', *The Liverpool Law Review* 2, 1980, pp. 5–30.

Jacobsen, T., *The Treasures of Darkness: A History of Mesopotamian Religion*, New Haven 1976.

Jaeger, Werner, *Paideia*, ET, 3 vols., Oxford, England and Cambridge, Mass. 1939–45.

Jastrow, M., *A Dictionary of the Targumim, the Talmud Babli and Yerushalmi and the Midrashic Literature*, 1926, repr. New York 1950.

Jaussen, A. J., and R. Savignac, *Mission archéologique en Arabie* I, Paris 1909.

Jeiteles, Isidor, 'Fremdes Recht im Talmud', *Jahrbuch der Jüdisch-Literarischen Gesellschaft* 21, Frankfurt-am-Main 1930, pp. 109–28.

Jepsen, A., *NABI. Soziologische Studien zur alttestamentlichen Literatur und Religionsgeschichte*, Munich 1934.

Jeremias, J., *Jerusalem zur Zeit Jesu*, Göttingen [3]1962; ET, *Jerusalem in the Time of Jesus*, London and Philadelphia 1969.

— *Die Passahfeier der Samaritaner* (BZAW 59), 1932.

— 'Samareia', *TDNT* VII, pp. 88–94.

Jervell, J., *Imago Dei, Gen. 1, 26f. im Spätjudentum, in der Gnosis und in den paulinischen Briefen* (Forschungen zur Religion und Literatur des Alten und Neuen Testaments 76), 1960.

Jobling, David, *The Sense of Biblical Narrative (Journal for the Study of the Old Testament*, Supplement Series 7), Sheffield 1978.

Jocz, J., *The Jewish People and Jesus Christ*, London 1949.

Johanson, N., *Parakletoi*, Lund 1940.

Johnson, A. R., *The Cultic Prophet in Ancient Israel*, Cardiff [2]1962.

Johnston, George, *The Spirit-Paraclete in the Gospel of John*, Cambridge 1970.

Bibliography

Jolowicz, H. F., and B. Nicholas, *An Historical Introduction to the Study of Roman Law*, Cambridge ³1972.

Jones, A. H. M., *Studies in Roman Government and Law*, London 1960.

Jost, I. M., *Geschichte des Judenthums und seiner Secten* I, Leipzig 1857.

Juster, J., *Les Juifs dans l'Empire Romain*, 2 vols., Paris 1914.

Kasher, R., 'Ha-Toseftot ha-Targumiyot le-Haftarat Shabbat Hanukkah', *Tarbiz* 45, Jerusalem 1975–76, pp. 27–45.

Katsch, A. I., ed., *Ginze Mishnah*, Jerusalem 1970.

Katz, J., ''Af 'al pi she-Hata' Yisra'el Hu*'', *Tarbiz* 27, 1957–58, pp. 203–17.

— *Exclusiveness and Tolerance*, New York 1962.

Katzoff, Ranon, 'The Provincial Edict in Egypt', *Tijdschrift voor Rechtsgeschiedenis* 37, Groningen 1969, pp. 415–37.

Kaufmann, Y., *Toledot ha-'Emunah ha-Yisra'elit mime qedem 'ad sof Bayit ha-Sheni (The History of the Religion of Israel)* II, Jerusalem 1960; IV, Tel Aviv 1966/67.

Kedar, B., 'Netherworld, In the Aggadah', *EJ* XII, cols. 997f.

Kellermann, U., 'Erwägungen zum Problem der Esradatierung', *ZAW* 80, 1968, pp. 55–87.

Kimelman, R., 'R. Yohanan and Origen on the Song of Songs: A Third Century Jewish-Christian Disputation', *HTR* (forthcoming).

— 'Third Century Tiberias: The Alliance between the Rabbinate, the Patriarchate, and the Urban Aristocracy', *ANRW* II: *Principat*, 8, *Politische Geschichte*, Supplement vol. (forthcoming).

Kippenberg, H. G., *Garizim und Synagoge*, Berlin 1971.

— 'Versuch einer soziologischen Verortung des antiken Gnostizismus', *Numen* 17, Leiden 1950, pp. 211–31.

Klausner, J., *Jesus of Nazareth*, ET London 1925, repr. New York 1953.

Klein, S., ed., *Sefer ha-Yishub*, Jerusalem 1939.

Klijn, A. F. J., *The Acts of Thomas* (SupplNovT 5), 1962.

— and G. J. Reinink, *Patristic Evidence for Jewish-Christian Sects* (SupplNovT 36), 1973.

— 'The Study of Jewish Christianity', *NTS* 20, 1973–74, pp. 419–31.

Koch, K., 'Ezra and the Origins of Judaism', *JSS* 19, 1974, pp. 173–97.

— 'Haggais unreines Volk', *ZAW* 79, 1967, pp. 52–66.

König, E., 'Samaritan Pentateuch', *HDB* V, 1904, pp. 68–72.

Koffmahn, Elisabeth, *Die Doppelurkunden aus der Wüste Juda*, Leiden 1968.

Kohler, K., 'Circumcision', *JE* IV, p. 94.

— 'Didascalia', *JE* IV, pp. 588–94.

— 'The Essene Version of the Seven Benedictions as Preserved in the VII Book of the Apostolic Constitutions', *HUCA* 1, 1924, pp. 410–25.

— 'Ueber die Ursprünge und Grundformen der synagogalen Liturgie: Eine Studie', *MGWJ*, nF 1, 1893, pp. 441–51, 489–97.

Kohn, S., *De pentateucho samaritano eiusque cum versionibus antiquis nexu*, Leipzig 1865.

Kohut, G. A., *Aruch Completum*, Vienna and Berlin 1878–1892 = *Aruch ha-Shalem*, 8 vols., New York 1878–92.

Bibliography

Konwitz, M. R., 'Judaism and the Democratic Idea', *The Jews, Their Role in Civilization* (ed. L. Finkelstein), New York ⁴1971.

Koschorke, Klaus, *Die Polemik der Gnostiker gegen das kirchliche Christentum*, Leiden 1978.

Kraft, R. A., 'Christian Transmission of Greek Jewish Scriptures: A Methodological Problem', *Paganisme, Judaïsme, Christianisme: Influences et affrontements dans le monde antique. Mélanges offerts à M. Simon*, Paris 1978, pp. 207–26.

— 'The Multiform Jewish Heritage of Early Christianity', *Christianity, Judaism and Other Greco-Roman Cults: Studies for Morton Smith* (ed. J. Neusner; SJLA 12) III, 1975, pp. 175–99.

— Review of S. Pines, *The Jewish Christians of the Early Centuries of Christianity, JBL* 86, 1967, pp. 329f.

Krauss, S., *Griechische und lateinische Lehnwörter im Talmud, Midrasch und Targum*, 2 vols., 1898–99, repr. Hildesheim 1964.

— 'The Jews in the Works of the Church Fathers', *JQR* os 5, 1892–93, pp. 122–57; ibid., os 6, 1893–94, pp. 82–99, 225–61.

— 'Zur Literatur der Siddurim', *Festschrift für Aron Freimann* (ed. Alexander Marx and Hermann Meyer), Berlin 1935, pp. 125–40.

Kretschmar, G., 'Origenes und die Araber', *ZTK* 50, 1953, pp. 260–4.

Kuhn, K. G., *Achtzehngebet und Vaterunser und der Reim*, Tübingen 1950.

— 'Giljonim und sifre minim', *Judentum – Urchristentum – Kirche: Festschrift für J. Jeremias* (ed. W. Eltester; Beiheft zur ZNW, 26), 1960, ²1964, pp. 24–61.

Kurfess, A., 'Christian Sibyllines', *NTApoc* II, pp. 703–45.

Kysar, R., *The Fourth Evangelist and His Gospel – An Examination of Contemporary Scholarship*, Minneapolis 1975.

Lachs, S. T., 'R. Abbahu and the Minim', *JQR* 40, 1970, pp. 197–212.

Laeyendecker, L., *Religie en Conflict*, Meppel 1968.

Lampe, G. W. H., *A Patristic Greek Lexicon*, Oxford 1961–68.

Lapp, P. W., 'The Samaria Papyri', *Archaeology* 16, New York, 1963, pp. 204–6.

Lauterbach, J., *Rabbinic Essays*, Cincinnati 1951.

Leach, Edmund, 'Myth as a Justification for Faction and Social Change', *Political Systems of Highland Burma*, Boston 1954, pp. 264–78.

Leaney, A. R. C., 'The Johannine Paraclete and the Qumran Scrolls', *John and Qumran* (ed. J. H. Charlesworth), London 1972, pp. 38–61.

Lebram, J. C., 'Nachbiblische Weisheitstraditionen', *VT* 15, 1965, pp. 167–237.

Lee, R. W., *The Elements of Roman Law*, London ⁴1956.

Lehman, M., 'Iyunim BeVav HaPerush (Explicativum)', *Sinai* 85, Jerusalem 1979, pp. 200–15.

Lehmann, M. R., 'Studies in the Manuscripts of the Murabbaʿat and Nahal Ḥever Documents', *RQ* 4, 1963, pp. 53–81.

Leiman, Sid Z., *The Canonization of Hebrew Scripture: The Talmudic and Midrashic Evidence*, Hamden, Conn. 1976.

Lelyveld, David, *Aligarh's First Generation*, Princeton 1978.

Bibliography

Lemosse, Maxime, 'Le procès de Babatha', *The Irish Jurist* 3, Dublin 1968, pp. 363–76.

Lenel, O., *Palingenesia Iuris Civilis* I, Leipzig 1889, repr. Graz 1960.

Lerle, E., 'Liturgische Reformen des Synagogengottesdienstes als Antwort auf die judenchristliche Mission des ersten Jahrhunderts', *NovT* 10, 1968, pp. 31–42.

Leszynsky, R., 'Simon ben Schetah', *REJ* 63, 1912, pp. 216–31.

Levine, B., 'Kippurim', *Eretz Israel* 9, Jerusalem 1969, pp. 88–95.

Levine, L., 'The Jewish Patriarch in Third Century Palestine', *ANRW* II: *Principat*, 19.2 *Religion (Judentum: Palästinisches Judentum)*, 1979, pp. 649–88.

Lewin, B. M., *Otsar Ha-Ge'onim* VII, Jerusalem 1936.

Lewy, Hans, 'Hekataios von Abdera', *ZNW* 31, 1932, pp. 117–32.

Liber, M., 'Structure and History of the *Tefilah*', *JQR* 40, 1949, pp. 331–57.

Licht, J., 'Milah', *'Entsiqlopediah Miqra'it* IV, Jerusalem 1962, pp. 896–98.

Lichtenstein, H., 'Die Fastenrolle. Eine Untersuchung zur Jüdisch-Hellenistischen Geschichte', *HUCA* 8/9, 1931, pp. 257–351.

Lieberman, Saul, *Greek in Jewish Palestine*, New York 1942, ²1965.

— *Ha-Yerushalmi ki-Fshuto*, Jerusalem 1934.

— *Hellenism in Jewish Palestine*, New York 1950, ²1962.

— 'How Much Greek in Jewish Palestine?', *Biblical and Other Studies* (ed. Alexander Altmann), Cambridge, Mass. 1963, pp. 123–41; repr. in his *Texts and Studies*, New York 1974, pp. 216–34.

— 'Light on the Cave Scrolls from Rabbinic Sources', *PAAJR* 20, 1951, pp. 395–404; repr. in his *Texts and Studies*, pp. 190–99.

— 'The Martyrs of Caesarea', *Annuaire de l'institut de philologie et d'histoire orientales et slaves* 7, 1944, pp. 365–446.

— *Midreshe Teman*, Jerusalem 1970.

— 'Roman Legal Institutions in Early Rabbinics and the Acta Martyrum', *JQR* 35, 1944–45, pp. 1–57; repr. in his *Texts and Studies*, pp. 57–111.

— 'Tiqune Yerushalmi', *Tarbiz* 4, Jerusalem 1932, pp. 377–79.

— *Tosefeth Rishonim* II, Jerusalem 1939.

— , ed., *Tosefta*, New York 1955–73.

— *Tosefta ki-Fshutah*, 9 vols., New York 1955–73 (=*TK*).

Lifschitz, B., 'Césarée de Palestine, son histoire et ses institutions', *ANRW* II: *Principat*, 8, *Politische Geschichte*, 1977, pp. 490–518.

— 'Etudes sur l'histoire de la province romaine de Syrie', ibid., pp. 3–30.

Lipshitz, I., *Mishnayot Tiferet Yisra'el*, repr. New York 1952–53.

Lipshitz, Y., ed., *Ḥiddushe Rabbenu David Bonfil* (Sanhedrei Gedolah 1), Jerusalem 1966–67.

Lods, Adolphe, *The Prophets and the Rise of Judaism*, ET London 1937.

Loeb, Isidore, 'La controverse religieuse entre les chrétiens et les juifs au moyen âge en France et en Espagne', *RHR* 17, 1888, pp. 133–56.

Loew, I., *Myth, Sacred History and Philosophy*, New York 1969.

Loewe, R., 'Potentialities and Limitations of Universalism in the Halakha', *Studies in Rationalism, Judaism and Universalism, in Memory of Leon Roth* (ed. R. Loewe), London and New York 1966, pp. 115–50.

Loewenstamm, S., 'Karet, Hikkaret', *'Entsiqlopediah Miqra'it* IV, Jerusalem 1962, pp. 330–32.

— 'Mamzer', *'Entsiqlopediah Miqra'it* V, 1968, pp. 1–3.

Loos, M., *Dualist Heresy in the Middle Ages*, Prague 1974.

Lowie, R. H., *Primitive Society*, New York 1920.

Lurie, B. Z., 'Reshit ha-Perud ben Shabe ha-Golah la-Shomronim', *Le-Zeker Dr J. P. Korngreen* (ed. A. Weiser *et al.*), Tel Aviv 1964, pp. 159–68.

MacCormick, D. Neil, 'Law as Institutional Fact', *LQR* 90, 1974, pp. 102–29,

— *Legal Reasoning and Legal Theory*, Oxford 1978.

Macdonald, J., *The Theology of the Samaritans*, London and Philadelphia 1964.

Machinist, P., 'Literature as Politics: The Tikultu-Ninurta Epic and the Bible', *CBQ* 28, 1976, pp. 455–82.

Magie, David, *Roman Rule in Asia Minor*, 2 vols., Princeton 1950.

Maier, J., *Jesus von Nazareth in der talmudischen Überlieferung*, Darmstadt 1978.

Maine, H. J. S., 'The Effects of Observation of India on Modern European Thought', *Village-Communities in the East and West*, London ⁷1895.

Malakhi b. Jacob Ha-Kohen, *Yad Malakhi*, Leghorn 1767.

Malinowski, B., *Myth in Primitive Psychology*, London 1926.

Maloney, Robert P., 'Usury in Greek, Roman and Rabbinic Thought', *Traditio* 27, New York 1971, pp. 79–109.

Mann, J., 'Genizah Fragments of the Palestinian Order of Service', *HUCA* 2, 1925, pp. 269–338.

Mantel, H., *Studies in the History of the Sanhedrin*, Cambridge 1965.

Marb, Raymond and Richard Snyder, 'The Analysis of Social Conflict: Toward an Overview and Synthesis', *Journal of Conflict Resolution* 1, Ann Arbor 1957, pp. 217–48.

Margoliot, M., ed., *Entsyklopediah le-Ḥokme ha-Talmud*, Tel Aviv 1964.

Marmorstein, A., 'The Amidah of the Public Fast Days', *JQR* 15, 1924, pp. 409–18.

— 'Judaism and Christianity in the Middle of the Third Century', *HUCA* 10, 1935, pp. 223–63.

— *The Old Rabbinic Doctrine of God I: The Names and Attributes of God*, London 1927.

Marrou, Henri I., *A History of Education in Antiquity*, ET New York 1964.

Marshall, A. J., 'The Structure of Cicero's Edict', *American Journal of Philology* 85, Baltimore 1964, pp. 185–91.

Martini, Remo, *Ricerche in tema di editto provinciale*, Milan 1969.

Martyn, J. L., *History and Theology in the Fourth Gospel*, New York ²1979.

McEleney, N. J., 'Orthodoxy in Judaism of the First Christian Century', *JSJ* 4, 1973, pp. 19–42.

Bibliography

— 'Orthodoxy in Judaism of the First Christian Century. Replies to David E. Aune and Lester L. Grabbe', *JSJ* 9, 1978, pp. 83–8.

Meeks, W. A., ' "Am I a Jew?" – Johannine Christianity and Judaism', *Christianity, Judaism and Other Greco-Roman Cults: Studies for Morton Smith* (ed. J. Neusner: SJLA 12) I, 1975, pp. 163–86.

— 'The Divine Agent and His Counterfeit in Philo and the Fourth Gospel' in *Aspects of Religious Propaganda in Judaism and Early Christianity* (ed. E. S. Fiorenza), South Bend, Ind. 1976.

— 'The Man from Heaven in Johannine Sectarianism', *JBL* 9, 1972, pp. 44–72.

— *The Prophet-King, Moses Traditions and Johannine Christology* (SupplNovT 14), 1967.

— and R. L. Wilken, *Jews and Christians in Antioch in the First Four Centuries of the Common Era* (SBL Sources for Biblical Study 13), 1978.

Melamed, E. Z., 'Lishna Maᶜaliah ve-Kinuyye Soferim be-Sifrut ha-Talmud' ('Polite Language and Euphemisms in Talmudic Literature'), *Benjamin De Vries Memorial Volume* (ed. E. Z. Melamed), Jerusalem 1968, pp. 119–48.

Mendelson, E. M., 'Some Notes on a Sociological Approach to Gnosticism', *Le origini dello gnosticismo* (ed. U. Bianchi; Supplements to *Numen* 12), Leiden 1967, pp. 668–76.

Meyer, E., *Die Entstehung des Judentums*, Halle 1896.

Meyer, Rudolph, 'Prophecy and Prophets in the Judaism of the Hellenistic-Roman Period', s.v. 'Prophētēs', *TDNT* VI, pp. 812–28.

— 'The Canon and the Apocrypha in Judaism', s.v. 'Kruptō', *TDNT* III, pp. 978–87.

Mignard, J. E., *Jewish and Christian Cultic Discipline to the Middle of the Second Century*, Boston 1966.

Miklin, H. M., 'Selᶜa ha-Shomronim be-Har Gerizim', *Jerusalem* 11–12, Jerusalem 1916, pp. 176f.

Mikoláŝek, A., 'Les Samaritains gardiens de la Loi centre les Prophètes', *Communio Viatorum* 12, Prague, 1969, pp. 139–48.

Milik, J. T., ed., *The Books of Enoch. Aramaic Fragments of Qumran Cave 4*, Oxford 1976.

— 'Milki-sedeq et Milki-rasha dans les anciens écrits Juifs et Chrétiens', *JJS* 4, 1972, pp. 95–144, and *RB* 79, 1972, pp. 77–97.

— (See also under Benoit.)

Miller, Alan W., 'Claude Lévi-Strauss and Genesis 37–Exodus 20', *Shivᶜim: Essays and Studies in Honor of Ira Eisenstein* (ed. Ronald A. Brauner: for Reconstructionist Rabbinical College), New York 1977, pp. 21–52.

Miller, Stuart, 'Proselytes and God-fearers in Non-Rabbinic Sources of the First Century C.E.', unpublished seminar paper 1975.

Mitten, David Gordon, 'A New Look at Ancient Sardis', *BA* 29, 1966, pp. 61–5.

Modrzejewski, J., 'Les Juifs et le droit hellénistique: Divorce et égalité des époux', *IURA* 12, 1961, pp. 162–93.

— 'La Règle de Droit dans l'Egypte Romaine', *Proceedings of the Twelfth*

Bibliography

International Congress of Papyrology (ed. Deborah H. Samuel), Toronto 1970, pp. 317–77.

Momigliano, A., 'Empieta ed eresia nel mondo antico', *Rivista Storica Italiana* 83, Turin 1971, pp. 771–91.

— *Essays in Ancient and Modern Historiography*, Middletown, Conn. 1977.

— 'Hellenism', *EJ* VIII, 1972, cols. 290–95.

— *Ricerche sull'Organizzazione della Giudea sotto il Dominio Romano*, Bologna: Annali della R. Scuola Normale Superiore di Pisa, Ser. 2, Vol. III, 1934; repr. Amsterdam 1967.

Mommsen, Theodor, *The Provinces of the Roman Empire* II, ET W. P. Dickson, London 1909.

Montgomery, J. A., *The Samaritans*, Philadelphia 1907, repr. New York 1968.

Moore, C. A., *Daniel, Esther and Jeremiah: The Additions* (AB 44), 1977.

Moore, G. F., 'The Definition of the Jewish Canon and the Repudiation of Christian Scriptures', repr. in *The Canon and Masorah of the Hebrew Bible: An Introductory Reader* (ed. S. Z. Leiman), New York 1974, pp. 115–41.

— *Judaism in the First Centuries of the Christian Era: The Age of the Tannaim*, 3 vols., Cambridge, Mass. 1927–30, repr. 1962.

Moreshet, M., *Archive of the New Dictionary of Rabbinic Literature*, 2 vols., Ramat Gan 1972–74.

— *Henoch Yalon Memorial Volume* (ed. E. Kutscher et al.), Ramat Gan 1974.

Morgenstern, J., *Die Verleumdungen gegen die Juden und die der Juden gegen die Samaritaner*, Berlin 1878.

Moulton, W. J., 'Samaritans', *Encyclopaedia of Religion and Ethics* XI, Edinburgh and New York 1920, pp. 161–67.

Müller, David Heinrich, *Die Gesetze Hammurabis und ihr Verhältnis zur mosäischen Gesetzgebung sowie zu den XII Tafeln*, Vienna 1903.

Munz, Peter, 'The Problem of "Die soziologische Verortung des antiken Gnostizismus" ', *Numen* 19, Leiden 1972, pp. 41–51.

Murray, R., 'The Exhortation to Candidates for Ascetical Vows at Baptism in the Ancient Syriac Church', *NTS* 21, 1974–75, pp. 59–80.

Musurillo, H., ed., *The Acts of the Christian Martyrs*, Oxford 1972.

Netzer, Ehud, 'Jericho from the Persian to the Byzantine Periods', *Encyclopedia of Archaeological Excavations in the Holy Land* II (ed. Michael Avi-Yonah), Englewood Cliffs, N.J. 1976, pp. 568–70.

Neusner, Jacob, *Development of a Legend* (SPB 16), 1970.

— *Eliezer Ben Hyrcanus: The Tradition and the Man*, 2 vols. (SJLA 3–4), 1973.

— 'Form and Meaning in Mishnah', *JAAR* 45, 1977, pp. 27–54.

— 'The History of Earlier Rabbinic Judaism: Some New Approaches', *HR* 16, 1977, pp. 216–36.

— *A History of the Mishnaic Law of Purities* (SJLA 6), 22 vols., 1973–77.

— 'History and Structure: The Case of Mishnah', *JAAR* 45, 1977, pp. 161–92.

Bibliography

— *A Life of Rabban Yohanan ben Zakkai* (SPB 6), 1962, ²1970.
— 'Rabbinic Traditions about the Pharisees before AD 70: The Problem of Oral Transmission', *JJS* 22, 1971, pp. 1–18.
— *The Rabbinic Traditions about the Pharisees before 70*, 3 vols., Leiden 1971.
— 'Ritual Without Myth: The Use of Legal Materials for the Study of Religions', *Religion. A Journal of Religion and Religions* 5, London 1975, pp. 91–100.
— 'The Tasks of Theology in Judaism: A Humanistic Program', *JR* 59, 1979, pp. 71–86.
Newman, J., *Halachic Sources*, Leiden 1969.
Nickelsburg, George W. E., 'Apocalyptic and Myth in 1 Enoch 6–11', *JBL* 96, 1977, pp. 383–405.
— ed., *Studies on the Testament of Moses* (SCS 4), 1973.
Nilsson, Martin P., *Die hellenistische Schule*, Munich 1955.
Nock, A. D., 'Gnosticism', *HTR* 57, 1964, pp. 255–79.
Nörr, Dieter, *Divisio und Partitio*, Berlin 1972.
Noth, M., *Geschichte Israels*, Göttingen ⁵1963; ET, *The History of Israel*, London and New York ²1960.
— *The Laws in the Pentateuch and Other Essays*, ET Edinburgh and Philadelphia 1966.
Nutt, J. W., *A Sketch of Samaritan History, Dogma, and Literature*, London 1874.
Odeberg, H., ed., *III Enoch*, Cambridge 1928, repr. New York 1973.
Odom, R. L., *Sabbath and Sunday in Early Christianity*, Washington 1977.
Oepke, A., 'Mesitēs', *TDNT* IV, pp. 598–624.
Oesterley, W. O. E., *A History of Israel*, 2 vols., Oxford 1932.
Oppenheim, A. Leo, *Ancient Mesopotamia*, Chicago 1977.
Orlinsky, H. M., *The Bible as Law: God and Israel under Contract* (Annual Horace M. Kallen Lecture, 1976), New York 1978.
— *Essays in Biblical Culture and Bible Translation*, New York 1974.
— 'The Septuagint as Holy Writ and the Philosophy of the Translators', *HUCA* 46, 1975, pp. 89–114.
Ostrow, Jonah, 'Tannaitic and Roman Procedure in Homicide', *JQR* 48, 1958, pp. 352–70.
Pagels, Elaine, 'The Demiurge and His Archons', *HTR* 69, 1976, pp. 301–24.
— 'Origen and the Prophets of Israel', *JANES* 5, 1973, pp. 335–44.
Pancaro, S., *The Law in the Fourth Gospel* (Suppl *NovT* 42), 1975.
Pardo, D., *Ḥasde David*, Livorno 1776.
Parkes, J., *The Conflict of the Church and the Synagogue*, London 1934, repr. New York 1969.
Passamaneck, S. M., 'Some Medieval Problems in *Mamzeruth*', *HUCA* 37, 1966, pp. 121–45.
Patte, Daniel, *What is Structural Exegesis?*, Philadelphia 1976.
Payne-Smith, R., *Thesaurus Syriacus*, Oxford 1897–1901.
Perelman, Ch., *Logique juridique: nouvelle rhétorique*, Paris 1976.
— and L. Olbrechts-Tyteca, *La nouvelle rhétorique: traité de l'argumen-*

Bibliography

tation, Paris 1958; ET J. Wilkinson and P. Weaver, *The New Rhetoric: A Treatise of Argumentation*, Notre Dame 1969.

Perrin, N., *The New Testament: An Introduction*, New York 1974.

Petersen, D. L., *Late Israelite Prophecy* (SBLMS 23), 1977.

Petitjean, Albert, *Les oracles du Proto-Zacharie: Un programme de restauration pour la communauté juive après l'exil*, Paris 1969.

Piaget, Jean, *Structuralism*, ET London 1971.

Piattelli, Daniela, 'Alcune osservazioni su C.P.J. 144', *IURA* 18, 1967, pp. 121–4.

— 'Ricerche Intorno alle Relazioni Politiche tra Rome e L'*EΘΝΟΣ ΤΩΝ ΙΟΥΔΑΙΩΝ* dal 161 A.C. al 4 A.C.', *Bullettino dell' Istituto di Diritto Romano* 3, Series 13, 1972, pp. 219–347; shortened ET in *ILR* 14, 1979, pp. 195–236.

Pines, S., *An Arabic Version of the Testimonium Flavianum and Its Implications*, Jerusalem 1971.

— *The Jewish Christians of the Early Centuries of Christianity according to a New Source* (Proceedings of the Israel Academy of Sciences and Humanities 2.13), Jerusalem 1966.

Plöger, O., *Das Buch Daniel* (Kommentar zum Alten Testament 18), Gütersloh 1965.

— 'Prophetisches Erbe in den Sekten des frühen Judentums', *TLZ* 79, 1954, cols. 291–6.

— *Theokratie und Eschatologie*, Neukirchen ²1962; ET, *Theocracy and Eschatology*, Oxford and Philadelphia 1968.

Pokorný, Petr, 'Der soziale Hintergrund der Gnosis', *Gnosis und Neues Testament* (ed. K.-W. Troeger), Berlin 1973, pp. 77–88.

Polotsky, H. J., 'The Greek Papyri from the Cave of Letters', *IEJ* 12, 1962, pp. 258–62.

— 'Three Greek Documents from the Family Archive of Babatha', *Eretz Israel* 8, Jerusalem 1967, pp. 46–51.

Preisendanz, K., *Papyri Graecae Magicae*, 3 vols., Dresden 1928–42 (=*PGM*).

Preuss, J., *Biblical and Talmudic Medicine*, ET New York and London 1978.

Primov, B., *Les Bougres: Histoire du pope Bogomile et de ses adeptes*, trans. M. Ribeyrol, Paris 1975.

Pringsheim, Fritz, *The Greek Law of Sale*, Weimar 1950.

Pugliese, Giovanni, 'Riflessioni sull' editto di Cicerone in Cilicia', *Synteleia Arangio-Ruiz* II, Naples 1964, pp. 972–86.

Pummer, R., 'The Book of Jubilees and the Samaritans', *Eglise et Théologie* 10, Ottawa 1979, pp. 147–78.

— 'The Present State of Samaritan Studies: I and II', *JSS* 21, 1976, pp. 39–61; ibid., 22, 1977, pp. 27–47.

Purvis, J. D., 'Ben Sira and the Foolish People of Shechem', *JNES* 24, 1965, pp. 88–94.

— 'The Origin of the Samaritan Sect', *HTR* 56, 1963, p. 329.

— 'The Fourth Gospel and the Samaritans', *NovT* 17, 1975, pp. 161–98.

Bibliography

— ' 'Or hadash 'al ha-Historiyah ha-Qedumah shel ha-Shomronim', Hagut Ivrit be-Amerika III (Hebrew Studies in America, ed. M. Zohari), Tel Aviv 1974, pp. 23–31.

Quispel, G., 'Qumran, John and Jewish Christianity', John and Qumran (ed. J. H. Charlesworth), London 1972, pp. 137–55.

Rabbinovicz, R. N., Diqduqe Soferim, Munich 1867–97.

— Ma'amar al Hadpasat ha-Talmud (ed. S. M. Haberman), Jerusalem 1965.

Rabello, Alfredo M., 'A Tribute to Jean Juster', ILR 11, 1976, pp. 216–87.

Rabin, C., 'Noserim', Textus 5, Jerusalem 1966, pp. 44–52.

— Qumran Studies, Oxford 1957.

Rabinovitz, Z. W., Shaarei Torat Erets Israel, Jerusalem 1940 (= STEI).

Rakover, Nahum, Otsar ha-Mishpat (A Bibliography of Jewish Law), Jerusalem 1975.

Rea, J. R., The Oxyrhynchus Papyri LXVI, London 1978.

Reland, H., Dissertatio de Samaritanis, Rhenus 1707.

Rendtorff, R., Das überlieferungsgeschichtliche Problem des Pentateuch (BZAW 147), 1977.

Rhoads, D., Israel in Revolution, 6–74 C.E., Philadelphia 1976.

Riccobono, S., ed., Fontes Iuris Romani Antejustiniani, 3 vols., Florence ²1940–43.

Riessler, P., Altjüdisches Schrifttum ausserhalb der Bibel, Augsburg 1928.

Rist, J. M., Epicurus, Cambridge 1972.

Rivkin, E., 'Ben Sira and the Nonexistence of the Synagogue', in In the Time of Harvest (ed. D. J. Silver), New York 1963, pp. 348–50.

Rogerson, J., 'Structural Anthropology and the Old Testament', Bulletin of the School of Oriental and African Studies 33, 1970, pp. 490–500.

Rostovtzeff, M. I., The Social and Economic History of the Hellenistic World, 2 vols., Oxford ²1957.

Roussel, Pierre, 'Un Syrien au service de Rome et d'Octave', Syria 15, 1934, pp. 33–74.

Rowley, H. H., 'Jewish Proselyte Baptism and the Baptism of John', From Moses to Qumran, London and New York 1963, pp. 211–35 (originally in HUCA 25, 1940, pp. 313–34).

— 'The Samaritan Schism in Legend and History', Israel's Prophetic Heritage. Essays in Honour of J. Muilenburg (ed. B. W. Anderson and W. Harrelson), London and New York 1962, pp. 208–22.

— 'Sanballat and the Samaritan Temple', BJRL 38, 1955/56, pp. 166–98 (= Men of God, London 1963, pp. 346–76).

— The Zadokite Fragments and the Dead Sea Scrolls, London and New York 1952.

Rubinstein, S. J., Zur Geschichte der Entstehung der samaritanischen Gemeinde, Libau 1906.

Rudolph, Kurt, 'Das Problem einer Soziologie und sozialen Verortung der Gnosis', Kairos 19, Salzburg 1977, pp. 34–54.

Russell, D. S., The Method and Message of Jewish Apocalyptic (OTL), 1964.

Ryle, H. E., The Canon of the Old Testament, London 1892.

Safrai, S., 'Jacob b. Korshai', EJ IX, 1972, cols. 1220f.

Bibliography

— 'Jewish Self-Government', *The Jewish People in the First Century* (ed. S. Safrai and M. Stern), Assen 1974, pp. 377–419.

— 'The Status of Provincia Judaea after the Destruction of the Second Temple', *Zion* 27, Jerusalem 1962, pp. 216–22.

— 'Tales of the Sages in the Palestinian Tradition and the Babylonian Talmud', *SH* 22, 1971, pp. 214–20.

Saldarini, Anthony J., *The Fathers According to Rabbi Nathan (Abot de Rabbi Nathan), Version B* (SJLA 11), 1975.

Sambursky, S., 'The Term Gematria', *Tarbiz* 45, Jerusalem 1976, pp. 268–71.

Samson of Chinon, *Sefer Keritut* (ed. S. B. Sofer), Jerusalem 1965.

Sanders, E. P., 'The Covenant as a Soteriological Category and the Nature of Salvation in Palestinian and Hellenistic Judaism', *Jews, Greeks and Christians: Religious Culture in Late Antiquity: Essays in honor of W. D. Davies* (ed. R. Hamerton-Kelly and R. Scroggs; SJLA 21), 1976, pp. 11–44.

— *Paul and Palestinian Judaism: A Comparison of Patterns of Religion*, London and Philadelphia 1977.

Sanders, James A., 'Cave 11 Surprises and the Question of Canon', *New Directions in Biblical Archaeology* (ed. David Noel Freedman and Jonas C. Greenfield), New York 1969, pp. 113–30.

— *Discoveries in the Judaean Desert of Jordan IV. The Psalms Scroll of Qumran Cave 11 (11QPsª)*, Oxford 1965.

— 'The Qumran Psalm Scroll (11QPsª) Reviewed', *On Language, Culture and Religion in Honour of Eugene Nida* (ed. Matthew Black and W. Smalley), The Hague/Paris 1974, pp. 79–99.

— 'Text and Canon: Concepts and Method', *JBL* 98, 1979, pp. 5–29.

Sasse, C., *Constitutio Antoniniana*, Wiesbaden 1958.

Schaeder, H. H., 'Nazarēnos, Nazōraios', *TDNT* IV, pp. 874–9.

Schäfer, P., *Studien zur Geschichte und Theologie des rabbinischen Judentums* (AGAJU 15), 1978.

Schalit, A., 'Aristobulus I (Judah)', *EJ* III, col. 440.

— *König Herodes*, Berlin 1969.

— 'Pereq be-Toledot Milhemet ha-Miflagot be-Yerushalayim be-Sof ha-Me'ah ha-Hamishit u-be-Tehilat ha-Me'ah ha-Rebi'it lifne ha-Sefirah', *Sefer Yohanan Levy* (ed. I. Guttmann and M. Schwabe), Jerusalem 1949, pp. 252–72.

— *Roman Administration in Palestine* (in Hebrew), Jerusalem 1937.

Schechter, S., 'Genizah Specimens', *JQR* os 10, 1898, pp. 197–206, 654–9.

Schiffman, L., *The Halakhah at Qumran*, unpublished PhD dissertation, Brandeis University 1974.

— *The Halakhah at Qumran* (SJLA 16), 1975.

— 'Jewish Sectarianism in Second Temple Times', *Great Schisms in Jewish History* (ed. R. Jospe and S. Wagner), New York 1981, pp. 1–46.

Schmidlin, Bruno, *Die Römischen Rechtsregeln: Versuch einer Typologie*, Cologne and Vienna 1970.

Bibliography

Schmidt, Erich, 'Die Griechen in Babylon und das Weiterleben ihrer Kultur', *Archäologischer Anzeiger* (Beiblatt zum Jahrbuch des Deutschen archäologischen Instituts 56), Berlin 1971, pp. 834–44.

Schoeps, H. J., *Jewish Christianity*, ET Philadelphia 1969.

— *Theologie und Geschichte des Judenchristentums*, Tübingen 1949.

Scholem, Gershom, *Jewish Gnosticism, Merkabah Mysticism and Talmudic Tradition*, New York ²1965.

— *Major Trends in Jewish Mysticism*, New York ³1954, repr. 1961.

Schrage, W., 'Aposynagōgos', *TDNT* VII, pp. 848–52.

Schram, T. L., *The Use of Ioudaios in the Fourth Gospel*, Utrecht 1974.

Schubert, K., 'Die Kultur der Juden I', *Handbuch der Kulturgeschichte* (ed. E. Thurnher), Frankfurt 1970.

Schürer, Emil, *Geschichte des jüdischen Volkes im Zeitalter Jesu Christi*, 4 vols., Leipzig ⁴1901–11; ET, *The History of the Jewish People in the Age of Jesus Christ*, 6 vols., Edinburgh and New York 1885–91, repr. 1898–1900; new ed., completely revised by G. Vermès, F. Millar and M. Black, Edinburgh and Naperville, I, 1973, II, 1979, III forthcoming.

Schulz, Fritz, *History of Roman Legal Science*, Oxford 1946.

Schwally, Friedrich, *Idioticon des christlich-palästinischen Aramäisch*, Giessen 1893.

Segal, A. F., *Two Powers in Heaven: Early Rabbinic Reports about Christianity and Gnosticism* (SJLA 25), 1977.

Segal, M. Z., 'Niss'uey ben Kohen Gadol 'im Bat Sanballat u-binyan Miqdash Gerizim', *Sefer Asaf*, Jerusalem 1953, pp. 404–14.

Seidl, E., 'Juristische Papyruskunde', *Studia et Documenta Historiae et Juris* 33, Rome 1967, pp. 503–80.

— 'Ein Papyrusfund zum klassischen Zivilprozessrecht', *Studi in onore di Giuseppe Grosso* II, Turin 1968, pp. 345–61.

— *Ptolemäische Rechtsgeschichte*, Glückstadt and New York ²1962.

Sellin, E., and G. Fohrer, *Introduction to the Old Testament*, ET Nashville 1968, London 1970.

Rav Sherira Gaon, *Iggeret* (ed. B. M. Lewin), Haifa 1921.

Sherwin-White, A. N., *The Roman Citizenship*, Oxford 1939.

— 'Trajan's Replies to Pliny: Authorship and Necessity', *JRS* 52, 1962, pp. 114–25.

Shmueli, H., 'Sanballat ha-Horani Hatno ve-Yessud Miqdash Gerizim', *Le-Zeker Shemu'el Dim*, Jerusalem 1958, pp.'313–41.

Silberg, M., *Talmudic Law and the Modern State*, New York 1973.

Simmel, G., *Conflict*, ET Kurt H. Wolff, Glencoe, Ill. 1955.

Simon, Marcel, *Les sectes juives au temps de Jésus*, Paris 1960; ET, *Jewish Sects at the Time of Jesus*, Philadelphia 1967.

— *St Stephen and the Hellenists in the Primitive Church*, London 1958.

— *Verus Israel*, Paris ²1964.

Sinzheim, Yosef David, *Yad David*, Offenbach 1799.

Slingerland, H. D., *The Testaments of the Twelve Patriarchs: A Critical History of Research* (SBLMS 21), 1977.

Smallwood, E. Mary, *The Jews under Roman Rule* (SJLA 20), 1976.

Bibliography

— 'The Legislation of Hadrian and Antoninus Pius against Circumcision', *Latomus* 18, Brussels 1959, pp. 334–47.

— 'The Legislation of Hadrian and Antoninus Pius against Circumcision: Addendum', *Latomus* 20, 1961, pp. 93–6.

Smith, Jonathan Z., 'The Prayer of Joseph', *Religions in Antiquity. Essays in Memory of E. R. Goodenough* (ed. J. Neusner; Supplements to *Numen* 14), Leiden 1968, pp. 253–94.

Smith, Morton, 'The Dead Sea Sect in Relation to Ancient Judaism', *NTS* 7, 1960/61, pp. 347–60.

— 'Early Christianity and Judaism', *Great Confrontations in Jewish History* (ed. S. Wagner and A. Breck), Denver 1977.

— 'The Image of God', *BJRL* 40, 1958, pp. 473–512.

— *Palestinian Parties and Politics that Shaped the Old Testament*, New York and London 1971.

— 'On the Shape of God and the Humanity of Gentiles', *Religions in Antiquity, Essays in Memory of E. R. Goodenough* (ed. J. Neusner; Supplements to *Numen* 14), Leiden 1968, pp 315–26.

— *Tannaitic Parallels to the Gospels*, Philadelphia 1951.

Sperber, D., 'Flight and the Talmudic Law of Usucaption: A Study in the Social History of Third Century Palestine', *RIDA* 19, 1972, pp. 29–42.

— 'Min', *EJ* XII, cols. 1–3.

— 'On the Office of Agoranomos in Roman Palestine', *Zeitschrift der deutschen morgenländischen Gesellschaft* 127, Wiesbaden 1977, pp. 227–43.

Spiro, A., 'Samaritans, Tobiads, and Judahites in Pseudo-Philo', *PAAJR* 20, 1951, pp. 279–355.

Steck, O., *Israel und das gewaltsame Geschick der Propheten* (Wissenschaftliche Monographien zum Alten und Neuen Testament 23), Neukirchen-Vluyn 1967.

— 'Das Problem theologischer Strömungen in nachexilischer Zeit', *EvTh* 28, 1968, pp. 445–58.

Stein, P., *Regulae Iuris*, Edinburgh 1966.

Steinsaltz, A., ed., *Midrash ha-Gadol Leviticus*, Jerusalem 1969.

Stendahl, Krister, *The School of Saint Matthew*, Philadelphia ²1968.

Stern, M., ed., *Greek and Latin Authors on Jews and Judaism* I, Jerusalem 1974.

— 'The Province of Judaea', *The Jewish People in the First Century* (ed. S. Safrai and M. Stern), Assen 1974, pp. 308–76.

Stiehl, R., 'Erwägungen zur Samaritanerfrage', *Die Araber in der alten Welt* IV (ed. F. Altheim and R. Stiehl), Berlin 1967, pp. 204–24.

Stone, Julius, *Legal Systems and Lawyers' Reasonings*, London 1964.

Stone, Michael, 'The Book of Enoch and Judaism in the Third Century BCE', *CBQ* 40, 1978, pp. 479–92.

Strecker, G., *Das Judenchristentum in den Pseudoklementinen*, Berlin 1958.

— 'On the Problem of Jewish Christianity', Appendix 1 to W. Bauer, *Orthodoxy and Heresy in Earliest Christianity*, ET Philadelphia 1971, London 1972, pp. 241–85.

Bibliography

Strodach, G., *The Philosophy of Epicurus*, Evanston 1963.

Syme, Ronald, *The Roman Revolution*, Oxford 1939.

— *Tacitus*, 2 vols., Oxford 1958.

Taglicht, J., *Die Kuthäer als Beobachter des Gesetzes nach talmudischen Quellen nebst Berücksichtigung der samaritanischen Correspondenz und Liturgie*, Berlin 1888.

Talmon, S., 'Biblical Tradition on the Early History of the Samaritans' [in Hebrew], *Eretz Shomron*. The Thirtieth Archaeological Convention, Jerusalem 1973, pp. 19–33.

— 'The Textual Study of the Bible – A New Outlook', *Qumran and the History of the Biblical Text* (ed. Frank M. Cross and Shemariyahu Talmon), Cambridge, Mass. 1975, pp. 321–400.

Tass, Y., 'Ṣara'at', *'Entsiqlopediah Miqra'it* VI, Jerusalem 1971, pp. 776–78.

Taubenschlag, Raphael, *The Law of Greco-Roman Egypt in the Light of the Papyri*, Warsaw ²1955.

Tcherikover, Victor, *Hellenistic Civilization and the Jews*, Philadelphia 1959, repr. 1975.

Tcherikover, Victor A. and Alexander Fuks, *Corpus Papyrorum Judaicarum* (= *CPJ*), 3 vols., Cambridge, Mass. 1957–64.

Tchernowitz, C., *Toledot ha-Halakah* III, New York 1953.

Teixidor, J., *The Pagan God, Popular Religion in the Greco-Roman Near East*, Princeton 1977.

Thoma, C., *Christliche Theologie des Judentums*, Aschaffenburg 1978.

Thomas, J. A. C., *Textbook of Roman Law*, Amsterdam 1976.

Tilborg, S. van, *The Jewish Leaders in Matthew*, Leiden 1972.

Towner, W. Sibley, *The Enumeration of Scriptural Examples* (SPB 22), 1971.

Townsend, J. T., 'The Gospel of John and the Jews; The Story of a Religious Divorce', *Antisemitism and the Foundations of Christianity* (ed. Alan Davies), New York 1979, pp. 72–97.

Turdeanu, E., 'Une curiosité de l'Hénoch slave: Les phénix du sixième ciel', *Revue des Études Slaves* 47, 1968, pp. 53–54.

— 'Dieu créa l'homme de huit éléments et tira son nom des quatre coins du monde', *Revue des Études Romaines* 13/14, 1974, pp. 163–94.

— 'La légende du prophète Jérémie en Roumain', *Revue des Études Romaines* 15, 1975, pp. 145–86.

— 'Le Testament d'Abraham en slave et en roumain', *Oxford Slavonic Papers* ns 10, 1977, pp. 1–38.

Urbach, E. E., 'Class Status and Leadership in the World of the Palestinian Sages', *Proceedings of the Israel Academy of Sciences and Humanities* 2, 1966, pp. 38–74.

— *Ḥazal*, Jerusalem 1971; ET, *The Sages* (see below).

— 'Hilkot 'Abadim ke-Maqor le-Historiyah ha-Ḥevratit bi-Yeme ha-Bayit ha-Sheni u-vi-Tequfat ha-Mishnah ve-ha-Talmud', *Zion* 25, Jerusalem 1960, pp. 141–89; ET, 'The Laws Regarding Slavery as a Source for Social History of the Period of the Second Temple, the Mishnah

Bibliography

and Talmud', *Papers of the Institute of Jewish Studies London* I (ed. J. G. Weiss), Jerusalem 1964, pp. 1–94.

— 'Mishnah', *EJ* XII, 1972, cols. 93–109.

— 'Mi-Yehuda la-Galil' ('From Judah to Galilee'), *Memorial Volume for Jacob Friedman* (ed. S. Pines), Jerusalem 1974, pp. 63–75.

— 'The Rabbinical Laws of Idolatry in the Second and Third Centuries in the Light of Archaeological and Historical Facts', *IEJ* 9, 1959, pp. 149–65, 229–45.

— 'Religious and Social Tendencies in the Talmudical Teachings on Charity' (in Hebrew), *Zion* 16, 1951, pp. 1–27.

— Review of Ch. Albeck, *Mabo la-Mishnah*, *Molad* 17, 1959, pp. 422–40.

— Review of G. Alon (Hayehudim be'artsam bitekufat hatana'im), *Behinot* 4, 1953, pp. 61–72.

— *The Sages, Their Concepts and Beliefs*, 2 vols., Jerusalem 1975 (ET of Hazal, Jerusalem 1971).

— 'The Sanhedrin of 23 and Capital Punishment', *Proceedings of the Fifth World Congress of Jewish Studies* II, Jerusalem 1973, pp. 37–48.

— 'The Secret of the Ein Gedi Inscription and its Formula', *Tarbiz* 40, Jerusalem 1970, pp. 27–30.

— 'Teshubat Anshe Ninevah ve-Havikuah ha-Yehudi-Notsri', *Tarbiz* 20, 1950, pp. 118–22.

— 'Yerushalayim shel Matta ve-Yerushalayim shel Ma'alah', *Yerushalayim le-Doroteha* (Israel Exploration Society), Jerusalem 1968, pp. 156–71.

Van den Berghe, Pierre, 'Dialectic and Functionalism: Toward a Theoretical Synthesis', *American Sociological Review* 28, Chicago 1963, pp. 695–705.

Van den Born, A., and W. Baier, 'Samaritaner', *Bibel-Lexikon* (ed. H. Haag), Einsiedeln ²1968, cols. 1513–15.

Vawter, Bruce, 'Apocalyptic: Its Relation to Prophecy', *CBQ* 22, 1960, pp. 33–46.

Vermès, Geza, *The Dead Sea Scrolls in English*, Harmondsworth 1968.

— 'The Decalogue and the Minim', *In Memoriam Paul Kahle* (ed. M. Black and G. Fohrer; BZAW 103), 1968, pp. 232–40.

Vermeylen, J., *Du prophète Isaïe à l'apocalyptique*, Paris 1977.

Volterra, E., 'Intorno a P. Ent. 23', *Journal of Juristic Papyrology* 15, New York 1965, pp. 21–8.

— 'Nuovi documenti per la conoscenza del diritto vigente nelle provincie romane', *IURA* 14, 1963, pp. 29–70.

— Review of P. J. Parsons, *The Oxyrhynchus Papyri* XLII, *IURA* 26, 1974, pp. 182–94.

Waddington, W. H., *Inscriptions grecques et latines de la Syrie*, Paris 1870.

Wahlde, Urban C. von, 'The Terms for Religious Authorities in the Fourth Gospel: A Key to Literary Strata?', *JBL* 98, 1979, pp. 231–53.

Walter, Nikolaus, *Der Thoraausleger Aristobulos* (TU 86), 1964.

Wasserstein, A., 'Astronomy and Geometry as Propaedeutic Studies in Rabbinic Literature', *Tarbiz* 43, 1974, pp. 53–7.

Watson, Alan, *Law Making in the Later Roman Republic*, Oxford 1974.

Bibliography

— *Legal Transplants*, Edinburgh 1974.

— *Society and Legal Change*, Edinburgh 1977.

Watson, W. A. J., *The Law of Obligations in the Later Roman Republic*, Oxford 1965.

— *The Law of Persons in the Later Roman Republic*, Oxford 1967.

— *The Law of Property in the Later Roman Republic*, Oxford 1968.

— *The Law of Succession in the Later Roman Republic*, Oxford 1971.

Weinberg, W., 'The History of Hebrew *Plene* Spelling: From Antiquity to Haskalah', *HUCA* 46, 1975, pp. 457–87.

Weingarten, S., 'Reshitan shel ha-Haftarot' ('The Origins of the Haftarah'), *Sinai* 83, 1978, pp. 105–36.

Weisenberg, E. J., 'The Liturgical Term Melekh Ha ʿOlam', *JJS* 15, 1964, pp. 1–56.

Weiss, I. H., *Dor Dor ve-Dorshav* II, Wilna ⁴1904.

Weiss, J. G., 'On the formula melekh ha-ʿolam as anti-Gnostic protest', *JJS* 10, 1959, pp. 169–71.

Werblowsky, R. J. Z., 'Greek Wisdom and Proficiency in Greek', *Paganisme, Judaïsme, Christianisme. Mélanges offerts à Marcel Simon*, Paris 1978, pp. 55–60.

Westermann, Claus, *Isaiah 40–66*, ET (OTL) 1975.

Wetzel, F., E. Schmidt and A. Mallwitz, *Das Babylon der Spätzeit* (Wissenschaftliche Veröffentlichungen der Deutschen Orient-Gesellschaft 62), Berlin 1957.

Whitley, C. F., 'The Term "Seventy Years Captivity" ', *VT* 4, 1954, pp. 60–72.

— 'The Seventy Years Desolation – A Rejoinder', *VT* 7, 1957, pp. 416–18.

Wiesen, D. S., *St Jerome as a Satirist*, Ithaca 1964.

Wiesenberg, E., 'Related Prohibitions, Swine Breeding and the Study of Greek', *HUCA* 27, 1956, pp. 213–33.

Wilde, R., *The Treatment of the Jews in the Greek Christian Writers*, Washington 1949.

Wilhelm, K., 'The Idea of Humanity in Judaism', in *The Studies in Rationalism, Judaism and Universalism, in Memory of Leon Roth* (ed. R. Loewe), London and New York 1966.

Wilken, R. L., *Judaism and the Early Christian Mind*, New Haven 1971. (See also under Meeks).

Wilson, R., *Genealogy and History in the Biblical World*, New Haven 1976.

Wilson, R. McL., 'The New *Passion* of *Jesus* in the Light of the New Testament and Apocrypha', *Neotestamentica et Semitica: Studies in Honour of Matthew Black* (ed. E. E. Ellis and M. Wilcox), Edinburgh 1969, pp. 264–71.

Windisch, H., 'Hellēn', *TDNT* II, pp. 504–16.

— *The Spirit-Paraclete in the Fourth Gospel*, ET Philadelphia 1968.

Winter, P., *On the Trial of Jesus* (SJ 1), ²1974.

Wolff, Hans Julius, *Das Recht der griechischen Papyri Ägyptens in der Zeit der Ptolemäer und des Prinzipats* (Handbuch der Altertumswissenschaft 10.5.2), Munich 1978.

— 'Le droit provincial dans la province romaine d'Arabie', *RIDA* 23, 1976, pp. 271–90.
— 'Hellenistic Private Law', *The Jewish People in the First Century* (ed. S. Safrai and M. Stern), Assen 1974, pp. 534–60.
— 'Faktoren der Rechtsbildung im hellenistisch-römischen Ägypten', *Zeitschrift der Savigny-Stiftung für Rechtsgeschichte* (Romanistische Abteilung 70), Weimar 1953, pp. 20–57.
Wolff, Hartmut, *Die Constitutio Antoniniana und Papyrus Gissensis 40 1*, 2 vols., Bonn 1976.
Wolfson, H., *Philo* I, Cambridge, Mass. 1968 (= 1947).
Wright, G. E., *Shechem. The Biography of a Biblical City*, New York 1965.
— and E. F. Campbell, Jr, 'Sichem', *RB* 72, 1965, pp. 415–22.
Yadin, Y., *Bar-Kokhba*, London and New York 1971.
— 'Expedition D – The Cave of Letters', *IEJ* 12, 1962, pp. 227–57.
— ed., *Jerusalem Revealed*, New Haven and London 1976.
— *Megillat Ha-Miqdash* I, Jerusalem 1978.
Yalon, Ch., *Studies in the Hebrew Language* (in Hebrew), Jerusalem 1971.
Yamauchi, E., *Pre-Christian Gnosticism*, London 1973.
Yaron, Reuven, 'C. P. Jud 144 et alia', *IURA* 13, 1962, pp. 170–5.
— *Gifts in Contemplation of Death in Jewish and Roman Law*, Oxford 1960.
— *Introduction to the Law of the Aramaic Papyri*, Oxford 1961.
— *The Laws of Eshnunna*, Jerusalem 1969.
— 'The Murabba'at Documents', *JJS* 11, 1960, pp. 157–71.
Ydit, M., 'Birkat Ha-Minim', *EJ* IV, col. 1035.
Zeitlin, S., 'The Halaka in the Gospels and Its Relation to the Jewish Law in the Time of Jesus', *HUCA* 1, 1924, pp. 357–63.
— 'An Historical Study of the Canonization of the Hebrew Scriptures', *PAAJR* 3, 1930–31, pp. 121–58.
— 'Jewish Apocryphal Literature', *JQR* 40, 1949–50, pp. 223–50.
— 'A Note on Baptism for Proselytes', *JBL* 52, 1933, pp. 78–9.
— 'Testamentary Succession: A Study in Tannaitic Jurisprudence', *The Seventy-Fifth Anniversary Volume of the JQR*, 1970, pp. 574–81, repr. in his *Studies in the Early History of Judaism* IV, New York 1978, pp. 193–8.

Index of Names

For classical and Christian authors see also Index of Passages

Index of Passages

BIBLE

463

RABBINIC LITERATURE

Mishnah

Tosefta

Index of Passages: Rabbinic

Mekilta

Index of Passages: Rabbinic

APOCRYPHA AND PSEUDEPIGRAPHA

Index of Passages: Christian Authors and Works

CHRISTIAN AUTHORS AND WORKS

CLASSICAL AUTHORS